Four Creations

The Civilization of the American Indian Series

FOUR CREATIONS

An Epic Story of the Chiapas Mayas

EDITED AND TRANSLATED BY
GARY H. GOSSEN

ILLUSTRATIONS BY Marián López Calixto

FOREWORD BY Miguel León-Portilla

AFTERWORD BY Jan Rus

WITH CONTRIBUTIONS BY
Manuel López Calixto, Marián López Calixto,
Xalik López Castellanos, Xalik López Setjol,
Mateo Méndez Tzotzek, and Xun Méndez Tzotzek

UNIVERSITY OF
OKLAHOMA PRESS
NORMAN

Also by Gary H. Gossen

Chamulas in the World of the Sun: Time and Space in a Maya Oral Tradition (Cambridge, 1974)

(ed., with Miguel León-Portilla) *South and Mesoamerican Native Spirituality: From the Cult of the Feathered Serpent to the Theology of Liberation* (New York, 1993)

(ed., with Robert Carmack and Janine Gasco) *The Legacy of Mesoamerica: History and Culture of a Native American Civilization* (Englewood Cliffs, N.J., 1996)

Telling Maya Tales: Tzotzil Identities in Modern Mexico (New York, 1999)

This book is published with the generous assistance of the Foundation for the Advancement of Mesoamerican Studies.

Library of Congress Cataloging-in-Publication Data

Four creations: an epic story of the Chiapas Mayas / edited and translated by Gary H. Gossen with contributions by Manual López Calixto . . . [et al.]; foreword by Miguel León-Portilla; afterword by Jan Rus.

p. cm. – (The civilization of the American Indian series; v. 245)

Includes bibliograhical references and index.

ISBN 0-8061-3331-7 (hardcover : alk. paper)

1. Tzotzil Indians–Folklore. 2. Tzotzil mythology–Mexico–Chamula. 3. Legends–Mexico–Chamula. 4. Creation–Mythology–Mexico–Chamula. I. Gossen, Gary H. II. Series.

F1221.T9 F68 2002

398.2'089'9745–dc21

2001055690

Four Creations: An Epic Story of the Chiapas Mayas is Volume 245 in The Civilization of the American Indian Series.

The paper in this book meets the guidelines for permanence and durability of the Committee on Production Guidelines for Book Longevity of the Council on Library Resources, Inc. ∞

1 2 3 4 5 6 7 8 9 10

For Eleanor,

WHO HAS LOVINGLY SHARED WITH ME THE CREATION OF THIS BOOK

Contents

Maps

Foreword

Since at least the period of their classic splendor—from the third to the eighth centuries A.D.—up to the present time, the Mayas have given expression to their thoughts and feelings in a great variety of forms. The result is a treasure trove of works created first in the oral tradition and later in the written word as well.

When the Maya Classic horizon lit up, and perhaps years before, the Mayas preserved their sacred words and other messages by means of carved or painted images accompanied by glyphic inscriptions. Epigraphers today are reading hundreds of those texts, which are carved on monuments—stele, altars, lintels, painted on polychrome vases and ceramics, and written in the few extant Maya books, or codices.

One can read genealogical and other historical records, stories of the deeds of the lords and warriors, their relations to the universe of the gods, the cycles of time, eclipses and other celestial happenings, prophecies, prayers, hymns, and other written utterances, religious or profane. And when Maya Classic splendor grew dim and the carved inscriptions became scarce, probably due to social turmoil or other incidents, the oral tradition and the painted books kept alive the ancient wisdom, worldview, ancestral beliefs, and memory of a past conceived as forever cyclical and recurrent.

The arrival of the Spaniards and the invasion and conquest perpetrated by them profoundly affected their written literature. Most of their books, seen as bearers of idolatrous beliefs, were burned. The native priests, custodians of both the books and the traditions, were persecuted, although—in the long run—they were not totally silenced.

From the Mayas of Yucatan we have valuable testimonies proving that some of their native priests managed to preserve expressions of their ancient beliefs and the memory of their past in written form. The Yucatec priests, who learned alphabetic writing from the friars, transferred old traditions and the contents of some of their books into this written form. The resulting texts in Maya, known today as the *Books of Chilam Balam,* contain the records of events along a series of *katuns,* or twenty-year periods—including years of Spanish presence—as well as prophecies, prayers, songs, and numerous other texts describing the ancient worldview, beliefs, and rituals.

Parallel processes occurred in other Maya regions, mainly in what is today Guatemala. The result there was also the transfer into the alphabet of what otherwise would inevitably have been lost. Among the K'iche' Mayas the celebrated *Popol Vuh,* Book of Counsel, is no doubt the best-known example. Its writer succinctly described his process. He saved from oblivion "the root of the former word . . . , the mysteries, the illuminations." Thus, he said, writing already within the word of God (that is to say, when the Christians were already there), he transcribed what was in a book that had been written long ago and whose face was by then hidden. By so doing, one could have "a sight of the Book of Counsel, a bright sight of things to come."

Other ancient texts were rescued in a similar manner during the colonial centuries in the Yucatan peninsula and among the K'iche's, Cakchiquels, and other speakers of Maya languages. The production of such a corpus of texts was indeed a great achievement, although, with the passage of time, some of them were in danger of being lost. We know that not a few disappeared.

Already in the nineteenth century, scholars had "rediscovered" several of those writings and begun to study them as ethnohistorical records, making them available to a learned elite. Few people outside the scholars' circle—and much less the Mayas themselves—had access to those old texts. However, no one thought that the Mayas—including those who rebelled at various times in Yucatan, Guatemala, and Chiapas—had continued to produce any kind of literature. Letters written by some Indian leaders in the rebellions were an exception worthy of attention.

We now know that in many Maya communities the elders remained deeply concerned about the preservation of their old memories, sacred accounts, worldview, songs, and prayers. Those elders, along with others, not only preserved such recollections but also transmitted them to as many members of their communities as possible. In this manner something of the ancient word was kept and cherished at the innermost of the people's hearts.

And now, in our own time, something unexpected has happened: a Maya literature, at once ancient and modern, has begun to blossom. On the one hand, with the help of ethnologists and linguists, a new generation of Maya writers came into existence. Like those who rescued the *Books of Chilam Balam,* the *Songs of Dztibalché,* the *Book of the Bacabs,* the *Popol Vuh,* the *Annals of the Cakchiquels,* and other Maya texts, these new native writers took advantage of the alphabet to express themselves. At first they wrote with a pencil or a pen, then with an ordinary typewriter, and now some of them use a computer. Thus poems and narratives in several Maya languages, inspired by the ancient traditions or the contemporary concerns of the people, are being produced and sometimes published. In addition some researchers who have been in close contact with Maya elders and other custodians of the ancestral tradition, after long conversations with them, have applied themselves to eliciting the words conveying the ancient wisdom, which could reveal the thoughts and feelings that for centuries had provided roots for the Mayas.

I will not mention here the names and works either of the modern Maya writers or of the Maya elders and sages whose words have been elicited by the Mayanist ethnologists. It is more pertinent to refer to the work we presently have in our hands—the conveyor of testimonies that was given by several Maya Tzotzil persons to a man who has lived several years among them, speaks their language very well, and cherishes and admires them. Gary Gossen, with his Harvard Ph.D. and, above all, with his unusual sensitivity and open-mindedness, is responsible for eliciting one of the larger—if not the largest—known corpuses of Maya texts. If I wanted to refer to a parallel enterprise, I would compare the results of his research to the gigantic contribution achieved by Friar Bernardino de Sahagún (1499–1590), who spent part of his long life working among the Nahuas of Central Mexico.

Both Sahagún and Gossen, in order to delve into the worldview, history, beliefs, and rituals of the native peoples with whom they worked, had long dialogues with knowledgeable persons about their culture. In both cases the dialogues were carried out in the indigenous language and the names of the participants were duly recorded. Also, both researchers left precise descriptions of the way in which they obtained their testimonies—that is to say, in what contexts and following what procedures they did so. Furthermore, as a result of the work of both researchers, numerous carefully transcribed texts, together with drawings and paintings, have been saved for posterity. For us, and obviously also for the Nahuas and Tzotzils, they are invaluable historical testimonies as well as, in many cases, genuine literary jewels.

In the case of Gossen's research, six storytellers provided testimonies during "many hundreds of hours" between 1965 and 1980. These six Tzotzils are duly introduced in the preface to the book, and their names reappear at the heads of the seventy-four texts, indicating one of them as the teller of each text. The close relationship that Gossen established with his storytellers was crucial for his understanding of their testimonies. As he says, "the source of the ethnographic notes that accompany each narrative" is to be found in the long conversations he had with them.

Gossen tells us that the seventy-four texts he presents here in both Tzotzil and English are but a part of the tremendously large number of testimonies he collected, which total five thousand manuscript pages. He faced the problem of how to organize his materials without giving offense to those materials in the process. He found the solution to the problem, he says, in "Chamula Tzotzil cosmology and history which, like those of many Indian communities in Mesoamerica and elsewere in the New World, are laid out a priori in a dramatic story line—a sequence of creations, destructions, and restorations—which yields time present." Following such a "story line," Gossen distributed his testimonies among the four cosmic epochs identified in Maya—including Tzotzil Maya—cosmology. This coincides with what he presented in his book, *Chamulas in the World of the Sun: Time and Space in a Maya Oral Tradition*, which is recognized by many as a classic of Maya ethnohistory.

The testimonies are thus offered following the sequence of the four cosmic epochs, from the first creation of the earth, the heavens, the underworld, man and woman, maize, animals, and so forth; continuing with the happenings of the other three epochs; and ending with texts related to our own times. In contrast with the accounts of the cosmic epochs provided by the *Popul Vuh*, in which the primeval happenings that are recorded are all related to the successive creations of man, the epochs in the texts collected by Gossen are organized in relation to historical occurrences recalled by the Tzotzil people and identified by Gossen. This allows us to perceive substantial changes in the Maya Tzotzil mentality and worldview vis à vis that of the ancient K'iche' Mayas. The changes, a consequence of the passage of time and the unavoidable exposure to new influences that have affected those living in Chiapas, give testimony on the one hand to the authenticity of the texts and, on the other, to the manner in which the modern Mayas have established their own cosmic and historic periodization.

Much could be said regarding the contents of the texts. I think it is important to draw attention to the great variety of their subjects and forms of expression. Some of the texts convey a solemn, sacred tone, as can be seen in the first five as well as others scattered through the collection that narrate the way in which everything was created at the beginning of the first epoch. Their solemn tone becomes humorous at times, however, as when Our Father, the creator, asks man if he wants a mate and he answers, "Not really." The narration goes on to tell how man is given a mate, but he and she "did not know anything about sex." It is the Demon Pukuj who shows them how to proceed. When the demon afterward asks them, "How was it? Did it feel good when you did it?" the man—who later on, with the woman, feels ashamed about it in front of Our Father—answers, "Oh! It felt great to do it!"

In many of the texts the identification of the Sun with Christ is either implicitly or explicitly asserted. He, the Sun/Christ, Our Father, along with Our Mother in Heaven, integrate the supreme divine duality, as in several other sacred expressions of the ancient Mayas, Nahuas, and other Mesoamericans. The Tzotzils, as Gossen says, have developed a syncretic interpretation of the doctrines taught to them by the missionary friars within their own religious context. Thus, to the Tzotzils, Christ, the Sun, and the celestial Mother, the Virgin, have taken the place of the primordial divine couple.

Gossen rightly notes that, like the *Popol Vuh* and several Nahuatl narratives, the Tzotzil texts speak of the destruction of the various epochs. People living in the first epoch perished in a boiling rain. And, as in other Mesoamerican accounts of the time of destruction in that epoch, the Tzotzil texts describe how people became monkeys and remained in the woods. The creations of people in the other epochs and descriptions of what subsequently happened to humans, various animals, and the earth mingle with biblical accounts identified by Gossen as related to Our Father, the Virgin Mary, and saints such as Saint John, patron of the town of Chamula. Other texts, as those dealing with the man who went to the underworld, war and peace with the Guatemala chief, and the origin and nature of the Ladinos, deserve particular attention.

In his notes Gossen points to historical or semihistorical accounts as relevant to the separation of the various epochs. Such is the case with the text that closes the third epoch, in which the figure of the father of Mexican independence, Miguel Hidalgo, is highly praised. He is described there as "he who began to show and tell us" important lessons, among them, "how to pray to Our Father Sun, how to work, how to read and write." In a word, "he began to show us everything." Similar cases are those of the "Account of Those Who Followed Pajarito" (the Tzotzil leader in a bloody rebellion that took place in 1910 and 1911) and the text, "About How the Carranza Soldiers Came to Live with Us Forever as Rats," considered by Gossen to be "a mythological account of the Mexican Revolution." According to him, these stories and others from earlier time periods reflect "a contemporary variant of Maya cyclical time-reckoning, in which heroes emerge when they are needed to resolve conflicts and then disappear, sometimes leaving instructions to people to call on them again in a future time of need." The last text, which, as Gossen remarks, "provides important information on the Protestant movement in Chamula," is entitled by his storyteller, "An Account of the Protestant Prayer Makers Who Perished by Fire." The storyteller, Xalik López Castellanos, did not like the Protestants at all; he describes them, among other things, as people who "by night were thieving."

Gossen has brought us the words of the Tzotzil sages—a treasure trove of stories both sacred and mundane. It is a literature that has many links with the glorious past of the Mayas and also illuminates a variety of ocurrences in the everyday lives of the people today. In the texts one can hear both the voice of an ancient oral tradition and, at other times, a storyteller's spontaneous recollections of a gamut of happenings. The dramatis personae include Our Father and Our Mother, men and women, and animals and plants that have existed in different epochs. The humans in the texts have tasted the recurrent experience of suffering; they know about the Spanish conquest, servitude, and discrimination. Cataclysms and wars have torn them down. But there are also stories about fateful events such as the acquisition of maize and the ludicrous lesson on how to have sex. The present corpus of Tzotzil texts—which at times recall the contents of the *Popol Vuh*, the ancient Maya Bible—becomes for us a magical mirror in which many wonder-causing things can be contemplated. In addition to the testimony of the word, Gossen has obtained numerous images for us. Sometimes of an innocent simplicity but always deeply expressive, they are drawn by a modern Tzotzil *ah dz'ibob,* painter-scribe, who vividly depicts what the narrative conveys.

In these drawings and in his integral approach to the native word, which unveils the core of the culture, Gossen's work resembles that of Friar Bernardino de Sahagún. Gossen, like Sahagún, has been intensely concerned with the stylistic and linguistic aspects of his enterprise. In his introduction he describes some of the most noticeable features of the language in which the texts were delivered, including its frequent parallel expressions and its abundant metaphors and puns. He has rightly perceived and appreciated the elegance and precision in the statements of his friends, the storytellers. Like Sahagún, he knows that these men possess an innate capacity as rhetoricians. Like their forefathers, they are true masters of the word, which is reflected in the manner in which they transmit their thoughts and feelings.

We owe great thanks to Gary Gossen for his magnificent gift. He has enriched us and the Tzotzil nation with this corpus of Maya literature, which is both a chapter of Mesoamerican expression and a chapter of a truly universal literature. A word of thanks must also be addressed to the staff of the University of Oklahoma Press, who have believed in the value of this rich collection of testimonies. The texts convey the word—and the breath—of a Maya people who for thousands of years have lived, suffered, and created culture in the luminous highlands of Chiapas.

MIGUEL LEÓN-PORTILLA

Preface

With one hundred million people, Mexico is by far the most important and influential Spanish-speaking nation in the world. When one also considers that the more than forty Spanish-speaking nations constitute the third-ranking block of human populations speaking a single language (after English and Chinese), the importance of Mexico looms large in current human affairs. However, Mexico's people include about fifteen million who do not speak Spanish as their native language. This large minority speaks one of the more than fifty Indian languages that survive in Mexico today. Among these languages, Tzotzil Maya ranks about seventh in number of speakers, with more than two hundred thousand. San Juan Chamula, among the Tzotzil-speaking peoples, is by far the most important community, with a population of more than one hundred thousand native speakers. Furthermore, the Maya people of the state of Chiapas, including many Tzotzil speakers, are at the epicenter of the Maya Zapatista insurrection, one of the current hot spots of New World ethnic politics. Since its inception in 1994, this armed and highly articulate movement, mingling "guns and poetry," has convulsed the public life of the entire state and confounded local and national political officials, even as it has gained an enormous international cartel as a postmodern plea for social justice.

Although this book is about a local, minority understanding of history and identity, in a narrative form that is somewhat distant from Western documentary history, it is important to consider the place of Tzotzil Mayas in modern Mexico. The turmoil in the state of Chiapas, with an Indian demographic presence that constitutes almost half of the population, presents a substantial challenge to Mexico. Chiapas is very large, extremely rich in natural resources, and possessed of an extensive arable land base that remains—as it was in the colonial period—mainly in the hands of a small percentage of the Ladino (Spanish-speaking white and mestizo Mexican) population. The Maya Zapatistas' demands that the Mexican state deal substantively and comprehensively with the reality of the nation's cultural pluralism have not, as of this writing, been fully addressed.

For centuries, Mexico—like many other nations, including the United States—has assumed that marginalized native people would "rationally" choose to assimilate to the majority Western culture that dominates the state apparatus if only they had the material means and the cultural and linguistic skills to do so. That model, however, belongs to another era. The native voices that speak from Chiapas today, like those in other parts of the world, seek something else altogether. Although the

Zapatistas and other Maya cultural and literary groups have issued many statements outlining their general goals—including respect for Indian traditions and languages in administrative policies and school curricular materials and access to the print and broadcast media—comprehensive articulations of what constitutes an "Indian outlook" on Maya history and identity are only now appearing. During the last twenty years, the Maya Writers' Cooperative (The House of the Writer), in San Cristóbal de las Casas, has published literary works in a dual-language (Indian and Spanish) format and has produced community outreach activities, including plays and puppet shows performed in Indian languages. There is also an important publication series, Letras Mayas Contemporáneas, supported by the National Indigenous Institute (Instituto Nacional Indigenista), that lists some seventy titles in and out of print.

This book also contributes to the record of what modern Maya people have said about who they are and where they come from. Together, its seventy-four native texts tell an epic history of the Tzotzil-speaking people of San Juan Chamula, one of the most conservative of all modern Maya communities in Mexico and Guatemala today. The native testimonies, presented in the original Tzotzil with English verse translations, are organized according to four chronological sections that follow their attribution by the narrators to one of four cyclical creations, destructions, and restorations that lead to the present era, the Fourth Creation. This system of native historical reckoning represents a modern survival of the intellectual universe of ancient Mesoamerica that is evident in ancient glyph texts and contact-period documents such as the *Popol Vuh* and the *Florentine Codex*. Besides providing a view of the way in which the contemporary native people of Chiapas understand their past, present, and future, this book, by extension, suggests ways in which they are inclined to respond to the challenges and opportunities of the present time.

San Juan Chamula, like tens of thousands of communities around the world, is relatively marginal and poor, but it is also vital and resilient in its political, social, artistic, and intellectual presence. Over the past 450 years Chamulas have not stood by passively and pathetically in order to be acted upon by successive generations of Western exploitation. As the texts in this book show, Chamulas have been astute observers—indeed, very often, clever manipulators—of the instruments of colonial domination used to subjugate them physically, materially, and spiritually. Their self-awareness, cultural imagination, and creativity are readily apparent when we eschew Western political hegemony, methods of analysis, and models for understanding the past and the Western macroview of global historical processes that we believe somehow privilege us to understand what "really happened." What really happened, of course, amounts to a story among many stories. This book records some of those many other stories.

The main section of the book constitutes a native history of a modern Maya community as it was remembered, understood, and passed on to me by six Chamula

Tzotzils themselves. I would like to emphasize the status of this work as a native history in order to highlight from the very beginning that it does not pretend to be a documentary history or an ethnography of San Juan Chamula. Although I have provided supplementary ethnographic and historical information in the notes, my intention at all times has been to contextualize and clarify the Chamula Tzotzil narrators' point of view. The world portrayed in the texts is a local interpretation of life as it was lived and understood by a few individuals between the years 1960 and 1980 who lived in a few hamlets contiguous to the ceremonial center of the home *municipio* of San Juan Chamula.

In using home *municipio* I refer to the local administrative unit, analogous to the county or township in Anglo American countries, that was set up by colonial Spain and continues into the modern era. In predominantly Indian regions of Spain's New World colonies, the *municipio* was deliberately designed to segregate indigenous communities from criollo (Spanish) and mestizo (mixed indigenous and Spanish) communities and also from one another. San Juan Chamula (hereafter sometimes referred to simply as Chamula) is typical of such *municipios* in that its separate indigenous identity is marked by the use of a distinct dialect of the Maya Tzotzil language, distinctive traditional dress (both male and female), and a particular variant of Maya Christian belief and practice. Out-migration of Chamulas to other parts of Chiapas and Mexico has radically accelerated in the late twentieth century, and the resulting diaspora communities exhibit many variants of continuity and change in traditional Chamula ethnic identity as it exists in the parent *municipio*. However, the narrators whose texts appear in this book were conservative traditionalists in that they lived in the parent *municipio* and participated in what was, in the decades of the 1970s and 1980s, the core of traditional Chamula custom.

By *traditional* I do not mean to say that what is recorded here portrays a traditional Maya social universe, curiously preserved in the twentieth century so that we can view a preconquest Maya lifestyle and worldview. The reader will quickly see, after reading several texts, that the Chamulas have received and processed many ideas and motifs from European and other sources. All of these have been rendered their own, so that the historical origins of particular parts are irrelevant to them. Once appropriated, these imported ideas and truths become as canonically true and completely local as the older Maya ideas that can also be identified in the stories. Whatever the diverse origins of the texts, however, the sacred order and social world that are remembered and set down here belong to a premodern era in the sense that all of the testimonies assume that San Juan Chamula—its people, its language, and its customs—lies, both literally and figuratively, at the center of the universe. Many tens of thousands of Chamulas still live in this circumscribed universe.

A BRIEF HISTORY OF THE PROJECT

When I began my ethnographic fieldwork in San Juan Chamula in the summer of 1965, I dreamed of one day compiling a comprehensive narrative history of this Maya community in Highland Chiapas, based primarily on its own storytellers' accounts. The product of that dream, this project has come to fruition over a period of more than thirty years. It is but one of hundreds of such histories that might have been set down, for San Juan Chamula is still a primarily monolingual Maya Indian township, where oral tradition remains alive and vital in virtually all public and domestic settings. This project is therefore far from being salvage ethnography. The challenge lay not so much in finding able narrators and live traditions but, rather, in finding the time, the setting, the tranquility, the resources to compensate narrators for time lost to other productive activities, and, most of all, the will (my own and that of others) to undertake the project.

All of these contingencies came together, thanks to a tranquil moment in history and to many individuals and granting agencies. This window of opportunity for the genesis and primary collection of data for the project came during the period 1965–80. The 1980s saw a radical decline in economic opportunities for Indians in Chiapas, resulting in political destabilization throughout the state and large-scale out-migration of highland Indians in search of land and other economic openings. There followed a period of civil unrest, exacerbated by the influx of political refugees from then-ongoing violence in Guatemala. Needless to say, the conditions of fieldwork became more difficult. The 1990s brought economic and political panic with revised state and national policies of neoliberalism and the Mexican government's retreat from providing protective umbrellas such as land reform and subsidies of basic commodities for the rural poor. The year 1994 brought NAFTA (the North American Free Trade Agreement) and the Zapatista rebellion, both of which have convulsed life in Chiapas in such a way that few Indian townships are now without the internecine dispute of progovernment and pro-Zapatista factions. Everyone—including the Mexican Army and its Indian surrogates or paramilitaries—watches everyone else come and go, and notices with whom they do so. These days it is not easy to be a "local," much less a stranger. In short, the social tranquility necessary for further elaboration of this project as an ongoing collaborative effort of transcription and translation in the company of native storytellers has disappeared, at least for the present and near future.

RATIONALE FOR THE PROJECT

My impetus to undertake the project was personal and romantic as well as academic. I liked the idea of helping to add to the archive of the world's traditional literature the voice of the Tzotzil Mayas, who, prior to 1960, had few published materials on their language or verbal art forms. As of approximately 1960, published works and unpublished manuscripts pertaining to Tzotzil language and literature numbered fewer than a dozen, most of them long out of print, unpublished, or otherwise inaccessible. Unlike many other Mesoamerican peoples—particularly the Yucatec, Kaqchikel, and K'iche' Mayas; the Chols; the Zapotecs and Mixtecs of the Valley of Oaxaca; and the Nahuas of Central Mexico—the Tzotzil-speaking people were a low-profile presence in a cosmopolitan region that produced many extraordinary cultural expressions in the Precolumbian period. Highland Chiapas produced no influential city-states nor any major texts of hieroglyphic inscriptions, and even the colonial period in Highland Chiapas produced remarkably few documents written in Indian languages.

This silence on the written record seems odd and unfortunate, for a close look at colonial and modern history reveals dramatic moments of instrumental action on the part of the Tzotzils. They and the closely related Tzeltal peoples have been actively engaged in forging the colonial and modern history of the region, even though written testimony in native languages is sparse to nonexistent. Several stunning examples testify to this, including the so-called Tzeltal Revolt of 1712, the nineteenth-century War of Santa Rosa (or, as Indians remember it, Cuxcat's War), the early twentieth-century Pajarito Rebellion, and the rise of Protestantism in the last few decades of the twentieth century. The emergence of Protestantism as a serious contender for Indian converts has been accompanied by exceeding violence in Highland Chiapas, and, as in the other struggles, Chamulas have been major participants. Most recently, the Maya Zapatista movement, which has a strong constituency in Tzotzil-speaking communities in Highland Chiapas, has placed the once-marginal communities of the region in a high-profile position in both the Mexican nation and the world. In summary, the Tzotzil Maya story is indispensable for an understanding of Chiapas history and for an understanding of the place of Maya people in modern Mexico and Central America, and I saw an opportunity to contribute to that understanding.

RATIONALE FOR THE BOOK

This collection of texts does not have the great sweep of historical purpose that epics possess. No state or unified people emerges at the end of this book. There is no appeal for political sovereignty or any latent desire for it, nor is there any semblance of a culture hero such as El Cid Campeador, who sacrificed all for the sake of his people, his religion, and his country. The protagonist of this long story is not an individual but the Tzotzil Indian community itself, with its cultural separateness and self-assigned moral superiority. There is no epic ending to the story. The final text in the book, which describes the rise of the Protestant movement and associated violence, is not heroic or particularly upbeat; it is open-ended, uncertain, and full of violence and fission, as life is in almost all Tzotzil communities today. However, the book—in its totality and in its parts—speaks eloquently of the trials and troubles and some of the rewards of being Indian in a Mexican mestizo state. If there is a subtext that binds all the texts of the Four Creations together, it is that of Chamula Tzotzil autonomy in a pluralistic Mexican nation.

For the native people of Mesoamerica, particularly the Mayas, cultural autonomy has become a major issue in our time. This movement is now well advanced in Guatemala, and Mexico does not lag far behind. One of the resounding statements that appeared as a preamble to Roundtable One at the National Indigenous Forum, held January 3–8, 1996, in San Cristóbal de las Casas, concerned the subject of cultural autonomy:

> We are the people who were the original inhabitants of Mexico. We have exercised, and will continue to determine who we are according to our own premises. We are the bearers of our own culture and of our own agenda.
>
> In a profound sense, we consider ourselves to be Mexicans. This is so even though the founders of the Mexican state and all governments that have followed in their footsteps have ignored our existence. This is so even though many Mexican men and women regard us with condescension and ignorance, virtually denying our existence. Because of this, we affirm once again on this occasion our existence as a people . . .
>
> We are not asking anybody to grant us autonomy. We have always had it and we have it today. No one can "give" us the capacity to be ourselves, to think and act in ways that are governed by our own way of looking at the world. However, we have not been free, either during the Spanish colonial regime or under the post-Independence Mexican state, to exercise freely our separate identity as a people. Throughout our long struggle of resistance, we have always been obliged to express our identity against a repressive backdrop of Mexican state representatives and Mexican state institutions.
>
> ¡Basta! [Enough!] We have had enough of this. . . . We wish to enjoy the full freedom to continue being who we are. We wish to create conditions that will make this possible. We believe that Mexico itself will be truly free only when all of us are free. (Foro Nacional Indígena 1996, my translation)

The general cultural and political scenario of Chiapas is similar in some respects to that of other Mesoamerican ethnic affirmation movements that are currently in progress. Rapid cultural change, great political flux, diminished economic opportunities for Indians, rapid emergence of new media and high-tech communication, new pressures to acculturate combined with new counterforces in the hands of sophisticated Indian leaders, to promote cultural affirmation—all are converging in our time to make the knowledge and wisdom of the past harder to find just as this information is deemed by some younger members of these communities to be critically important as a reference point for forging their future. I hope that these texts will be of help in providing a reservoir of knowledge.

THE STORYTELLERS AND THEIR CHANGING WORLD

Chamula Tzotzil life and thought—like other Maya cultural expressions, both ancient and modern—move forward by reassessing the past in much the same manner that a weaver moves forward on the frame of a loom, building new fabric by returning time and again to the pattern of the warp while also adding new material, perhaps also new patterns and designs. It is evident that this mode of remembering and acting in history does not vanish in times of rapid social change, even with radical departures from traditionalism such as those expressed in the rise of Protestantism and the Maya Zapatista movement in the 1990s.

In this book I yield the floor to the Chamula Tzotzil narrators themselves. I have spent many hundreds of hours with each of the six men whose narratives make up this book, in their homes and cornfields and in my office and home. We have shared countless dirty jokes, drinks, and gossip. Virtually all that I know of Chamula life and thought has come from them directly or through them indirectly, as they patiently answered countless questions. They accompanied me here and there, and each became, in his own way, my mentor and teacher.

All six of the men were neighbors in three small hamlets—Nab ta Petej, Milpoleta, and Jteklum (the municipal center)—of the one hundred or so that make up the *municipio.* Four of the six were related by lineage and marriage. Their collective knowledge of the culture was thus truly "local knowledge." I cannot claim any systematic sampling strategy for my ethnographic reporting, because that option was not politically feasible. Between 1965 and 1980 these men, my close friends, helped me in innumerable ways when other sources of information would not and could not work. This small group of consultants and friends, however, represents a broad spectrum of men in Chamula society. They are, in the present time, typical. There are winners and losers. Although I had not planned it this way, the book has become a kind of memorial project, for four of the six narrators are now deceased.

✠ ✠ ✠

Mateo Méndez Tzotzek, of Nab ta Peteh hamlet, was sixty years of age in 1979. He reminded me of Santa Claus. Joyous and forthcoming, he never failed to find something pleasant with which to embellish each day, each working session, and every social encounter. A part-time shaman and corn farmer, he was one of the few

Chamula men I knew who had never worked as a migrant laborer. Because of his limited financial resources, he was never able to pursue a career in the civil and religious cargo system of public service. He was monolingual in Tzotzil, as close to a "traditional" Chamula as I ever met. Mateo dictated all of his stories as tape recordings, which other narrators and I transcribed. However, he participated in all translation sessions, providing details and interpretations that were not explicit in the text. He is now deceased.

Xun Méndez Tzotzek, aged about thirty-five when I first worked with him in 1969, was Mateo's nephew. Like Mateo's, his life in Nab ta Petej was a hard one; he lacked land and other resources and had spent the better part of his life, from the age of fifteen, as a migrant laborer on the coffee plantations and large-scale corn-farming operations of the Pacific Lowlands. Although he was able to support his family minimally with this income, he never accumulated sufficient savings to enable him to assume a position in the civil-religious hierarchy of the town center. This disappointment notwithstanding, he nevertheless sought local prestige and modest income through the practice of traditional curing. His career as a shaman failed when he became an alcoholic and could not manage to get through the long prayer recitations that were required for the curing rituals.

Xun had enjoyed a brief interlude of economic success in the late 1950s and 1960s, when he worked as a paid assistant for U.S. anthropologists with the University of Chicago Man-in-Nature Project. In this context he learned to write Tzotzil. However, alcoholism also compromised this employment, and he resumed his usual pattern of migrant labor on the coffee plantations that he had begun as a young man. Xun worked with me as an assistant for many months in 1968 and 1969, and during this time I came to respect him a great deal for his keen and poetic intelligence. He was particularly patient and adept at explaining during our translation sessions what was obvious to him but not explicitly stated in his written texts. He had the natural gifts of an intellectual and a wonderful ability to synthesize large subjects, searching for complexity and multiple meanings beneath surface simplicity. (The best example of his art is found in text 3, which is a long and beautiful account of the origins of the human condition and the moral order.) Xun died in the mid-1970s of complications related to alcoholism.

Xalik López Setjol, about twenty-five years of age in 1965, began a promising adult life as a late teenager when he was given the prestigious job of *escribano* (scribe) for the cargo officials in the municipal center. One of a dozen promising bilingual young men who also served in this position, he had a bright future as an heir apparent to important political and religious positions in the community. He was literate in Spanish and Tzotzil, a skill that had been finely honed in his many months of association with the University of Chicago Man-in-Nature Project in the late 1950s. He also had intimate knowledge of traditional Chamula lore, for his father was a renowned shaman.

Xalik befriended me during my first field season in the summer of 1965, and I stayed for several days in his father's home before being asked to leave because of domestic conflict over my presence. I later roomed with him for several weeks at his store in the municipal center. He subsequently spent almost two months working with me on the first phases of my text collection project. A brilliant young man, he gave me early assurance that a large repository of traditional narrative knowledge abounded in San Juan Chamula.

When I returned to Chamula for a long field stay in 1968, I was shocked to learn that Xalik had "disappeared." I learned this meant he had been assassinated and disposed of, with no subsequent investigation, over allegations that he had taken a bribe from Mexican government officials to inform them about the location of clandestine, illegal Chamula stills (used for making rum). Whether or not the allegations were true, the dark cloud of this incident hung over his family, so that they were forced into exile in San Cristóbal, where I became reacquainted with his father. Through Xalik's tragic demise, I learned that rising stars may fall quickly in Chamula. I have always wondered whether his association with me and the University of Chicago crew had emboldened him to challenge the pragmatics of local politics. I have never found out, for my every inquiry about him was answered with "he disappeared."

Manuel López Calixto is the brother of Marián López Calixto, whom I will introduce below. Manuel and Marian's mother was a Méndez Tzotzek, the sister of Xun, whom I introduce above. Thus, Manuel and Marián López Calixto, Xun Méndez Tzotzek—their maternal uncle, and Mateo Méndez Tzotzek—their great-uncle, were closely related, making for an interesting case of traditional knowledge that may have had some common sources.

Manuel had the gentle manner of Saint Francis. Sweet and unassuming, he took a great interest in our children, animals, vegetable garden, and flowers. As he was ever soft-spoken and prone to slow, contemplative, extremely polite interaction, I often thought he would have made a good monk or poet. I had good evidence for the latter proclivity, as the reader will see. However, like most Chamulas of his age and modest resources, he had followed the routine of migrant labor on the coffee plantations since the age of twelve. Manuel did not imagine that he had the skills of a writer. He came to me looking for work as a gardener, but I was struck by his almost mystical feeling for the natural and social world. I taught him to read and write in Tzotzil, and so he came into my close circle of friends and assistants. Manuel's health, always frail, failed in the early 1980s, and he died of tuberculosis.

Marián López Calixto, Manuel's younger brother, cannot be thoroughly introduced, for that would require details of recent political history that I do not know. He rose to the position of highest status—that of *presidente municipal*—in the years after our close working relationship. Marián came to me as an ambitious young man in search of a career as an artist and writer. Although he had received minimal primary education (six years) in San Juan Chamula, he appeared to be a young man on fire with visions of a future as a leader and chronicler of his community. He has effectively achieved both these goals, and we will undoubtedly see more of him in the future. Not only has he served with distinction in the highest elective office in his community, but he has also worked as a collaborator in the highly successful Maya Writers' Cooperative (Sna Jtz'ibajom), which, in the 1980s and 1990s, has labored successfully to produce dramatic productions, puppet shows, and publications in native languages of Chiapas that have won international recognition. Marián López Calixto is a superstar in the Maya cultural renaissance that is now in progress in Chiapas. I remember him as a wildly colorful young man, with a penchant for highlighting lurid and funny themes—often in the same package—in his narratives. Marián is the artist responsible for all the line drawings in this book; he is also responsible for tuning me in to the latent themes of sex, violence, and family intrigue in Tzotzil narrative that are not always obvious on the surface.

Xalik López Castellanos (one of his many pseudonyms) is a man of many identities and talents. For reasons of his and my choice, I will not tell too much of his life history. He is an amazing ethnographic observer and dear friend who has led many lives—most of them sad—in relation to his own community. He now lives as a divorced and politically disgraced exile in a modest house in a new settlement on the outskirts of San Cristóbal. Xalik has transcended all these personal tragedies to become a master storyteller and chronicler of his life and times. He came to my attention as a potential assistant for my research through his work as a highly respected employee for the University of Chicago Man-in-Nature Project. Thoroughly literate in both Tzotzil and Spanish, he has helped me as a faithful friend for over twenty-five years. The distinguishing features of Xalik's narration are its historical precision, ethnographic detail, and sometimes darkly humorous editorial commentary. In another phase of his life, which has now begun, he will be a great ethnographer and chronicler, so accurate is his attention to detail. Needless to say, I have learned much from him.

These six men and their families were the anchors of the social networks my family and I built in Chamula. Over a period of almost five years between 1965 and 1985, I returned again and again to these friends, and they never failed me.

I should explain why no female narrators are represented in this collection. I tried to expand my social networks to include women who had both the personal freedom and the discretionary time to devote to my collection project. However, at the time of my fieldwork, women were (and to some extent they still are) constrained by the custom of avoiding contact with unrelated men except in the limited and ephemeral interaction of buying and selling at the marketplace and participation, in gender-segregated groups, in formal ritual events. Despite this limitation in the collection, I am pleased to refer the reader to a superb account of the role of women in Chamula society, including excellent accounts of their narrative traditions and other oral testimonies. This work, *With Our Heads Bowed: The Dynamics of Gender in a Maya Community* (1993) by my student Brenda Rosenbaum, may, to some extent, serve to balance the overtly male bias of my collection. I have not in any way attempted to edit out of my narrators' testimonies the gender bias and gender-linked asymmetries and related violence that, however we may judge them, are characteristic of traditional Tzotzil society.

FROM FIELD TO TEXT

CIRCUMSTANCES OF COLLECTION

It is relevant to mention that none of the texts were recorded from an on-site performance. All were written or transcribed from oral recitation in my office at the Harvard Ranch. The texts are neither oral performances nor products solely of the written word; rather, they lie somewhere in between. Three of the storytellers learned as adults to write Tzotzil in the International Phonetic Alphabet (I.P.A.) thanks to the University of Chicago Man-in-Nature Project, which preceded my field study in Chiapas. I also taught two others literacy in Tzotzil. One storyteller, who was nonliterate, dictated his stories into the tape recorder, and others subsequently transcribed the tapes. After the texts were written in Tzotzil, I translated each into Spanish with its author or narrator at my side; this close working relationship is the source of the ethnographic notes that accompany the narratives. The stories that make up this book, then, belong to what might be called a transitional period in Tzotzil literature. The styles remain oral in their composition, and my conversations about the subject matter, as recorded in the ethnographic notes, are dialogical in a way that is not unnatural to oral/aural means of transmission. Comment and conversation typically accompany oral performances in Chamula and elsewhere. However, the means and the circumstances of recording and transcription in my collection project have created texts that are modern in the sense that they are the product of the first generation of literate Tzotzil speakers. Nevertheless, these storytellers wrote and performed in a style that was closely linked to the conventions of oral performance, for all—with the exception of Marián López Calixto—had reached adolescence and early adulthood as monolingual Tzotzil speakers. They knew only the oral style. With the exception of Marián, none had been exposed to any formal education, with its fairly rigid standards of written exposition. All, of course, were exposed to the peculiar forms of scriptorial assistance requested by anthropologists.

FROM ONE VERSION TO ANOTHER

The texts all began as excellent Tzotzil transcriptions, for the six storytellers were native speakers and were all highly professional in their approach to the work. Nevertheless, the translations began as unpolished, provisional creations, for all parties involved had Spanish as a lingua franca, not a native language. The editing and honing that led to the verse translations in English that are presented here was a lengthy process, lasting from 1965 until 1980. The whole corpus of five thousand manuscript pages was collected and corrected in Tzotzil and translated into Spanish. This entailed adding more texts, correcting old transcriptions and preparing new ones, conducting many new interviews, preparing the notes, and supervising the preparation of the drawings. However, even as I was adding new material, I realized early in my Chiapas field season of 1977–79 that publishing the entire corpus was not a realistic goal. As I was finishing the whole, I saw that I should begin editing, concentrating my attention on the present collection of seventy-four texts. I spent much of my 1977–79 field season getting this edited collection into workable shape. I spent major parts of the following decade (1980–90) moving the project from a dream to a possibility.

ORTHOGRAPHY

Another factor that affected the history of the project was an unexpected crisis in orthography. Actually, this amounted to a crisis only for me; it was a positive and revolutionary moment for the Highland Chiapas Indian community. The years 1980 to the present have witnessed nothing less than a Highland Chiapas literary renaissance. Among other results of this movement, standardization of the orthography of Indian languages became a critically important issue. We all had to find and use a common, easily accessible, publishable, and understandable notation. Whether one used a standard typewriter or an electronic word processor, the old I.P.A. notation had to go; nobody wanted to deal with its ambiguity and strangeness. Why should they write *¢eb* (girl) when they could easily write *tzeb* or *tseb* and have the certainty that, with Spanish phonology, the Tzotzil sounds could be understood by all interested parties? For better or worse, the Spanish language—with its phonology and orthography, as the lingua franca of Chiapas—had the last word. The transcribed collection was typed in I.P.A. conventions in a generation prior to word-processing. Therefore, the orthography had to be converted manually, and the entire corpus of texts was reentered so that it could be electronically manipulated for editorial purposes. The orthographical note in the introduction gives a set of notational equivalents in I.P.A. and the current standard system.

GENRES, TRUTH, AND THE FOUR CREATIONS

All of the texts that make up this book belong to two closely related speech genres: true ancient narrative (*batz'i ʔantivo k'op*) and true recent narrative (*batz'i ach' k'op*). These two narrative forms are distinguished from each other only with reference to historical associations. *Ancient* denotes the first three cyclical creations and *recent* denotes the fourth—that is, the present era—that Tzotzils recognize in their cosmology. Both ancient and recent narratives relate events that are regarded as *true*, as distinct from *false*. Indeed, there are at least two separate genres—*jut k'op* (lies) and *ixtol k'op* (jokes) that specifically include *invented* material, often rendered in narrative style. The stories that make up this book, however, are regarded by their tellers as true. It may prove somewhat unsettling to the Western reader to contemplate a world in which anthropomorphic sun and moon deities, talking rabbits, coyotes, snakes, and earth lords that trap whole busloads of people in their caves along the Pan American Highway (circa 1950) have the same reality status as the Mexican Revolution and the current conflicts related to Chamula Protestant converts. However, the grand chronicle of memory that is recorded here assumes just such a merging of the plausible and thoroughly remarkable in the fabric of events leading to and constituting the present era. The magical realism that is associated with Gabriel García Márquez and other Latin American writers in the twentieth century comes far closer to capturing the nature of Chamula historical reckoning than does any form of Western historical epistemology.

While all of my storytellers—indeed, all the Chamulas I knew—generally agreed that the history of time was laid out in a sequence of four cyclical creations, destructions, and restorations, there was absolutely no agreement regarding the antiquity of these periods as translated into years. Opinions as to the beginning of the modern era, the Fourth Creation, varied from seventy years ago (1900, the approximate date of birth of a consultant's grandparents) to tens of thousands of years ago. Similar differences of opinion prevailed regarding the antiquity of the other three creations. What was constant, however, was a sense of the kinds of events that occurred in each period. The First Creation emerges as a period of primordial creation and experimentation with life-forms and the construction of the cosmos itself. The Second and Third Creations together constitute a kind of heroic period, a time of remarkable events of great importance (such as the founding of San Juan Chamula) and creative genius (such as the genesis of different kinds of animals, plant species, and human communities with their respective customs) but no longer inbued with the theatrical "first time" wonder of life becoming. This heroic period might be characterized as a time of routinization and colonization of the earth. The Fourth Creation deals with events of the present era, a time when people are fully modern and ethnic groups are as we would recognize them today.

Many of the events attributed to the Fourth Creation correspond with events that we, as Westerners, might recognize in our own reckoning of nineteenth- and twentieth-century Chiapas and Mexican history, such as the Mexican Revolution and the construction of the Pan American Highway. Other events attributed to the Fourth Creation show that contemporary Chamulas live in an everyday world that is sometimes radically different from our own.

These four creations, or epochs, or earths (from the Tzotzil *banamil*) constitute the organizational scheme of the book. This scheme belongs to the Tzotzils, and each story is faithfully placed in the epoch to which its narrator attributed it. This book, therefore, is their history.

CHAMULA TZOTZILS AS OTHERS

Of all the challenges that I had to overcome in this project, the greatest of all lay in my own psyche and predispositions. Many years ago, I wanted to find in the project a romanticized Other, a mystical, New Age, spiritual world that was not my own—something divested of the ordinariness of shopping malls, video games, and American pop culture. I was initially predisposed to edit out anything that compromised the Chamula Tzotzils as my own idealized, romantic Others, bearers of "ancient traditions." This notion is long gone, however. I now know that the Chamula Tzotzils, like myself, carry the burden and the joy of what they have been and what they aspire to be, and that their lives and ours have been in strained communication for many hundreds of years. They are as aware of us, of our culture's invasive presence in their world, as we are of them. What has this epiphany taught me? These stories express not only an ancient Maya world of perpetual change but also a modern Maya world that lives as much in a global culture as we do. At the same time narrators throughout this book express a determination to live and think in their own way. Therefore, I have sought a tone in the translations that casts the Chamula Tzotzils neither as archaic curiosities nor as romantic Others nor as the people who live in my community in Deep Springs, California. To borrow from Alan Riding, who wrote so perceptively of Mexico as a whole, I have tried to represent the Chamula Tzotzils and give voice to them as our "distant neighbors."

Acknowledgments

I conceived the idea of writing a book such as this thirty-six years ago last summer (July 2001), when I first went to Chiapas as a graduate student. This long period, spanning all my professional life thus far, has involved the support of many institutions and foundations as well as countless acts of generosity and friendship from individuals in the United States and Mexico: my teachers, colleagues, students, friends, and family.

Because the project has been so long in coming to fruition, I would like to express my particular gratitude to those foundations and institutional entities that invested in me and the idea for this book without seeing immediate results. To the National Institutes of Health, the Woodrow Wilson Fellowship Fund, and the National Science Foundation go my gratitude for funding my graduate education and initial field research (1964–70), done when I was affiliated with Harvard University. In the years 1977–79, I was supported by a Guggenheim Fellowship, a National Endowment for the Humanities summer grant, and another National Institutes of Health field research grant. These grants supported my research in one of the Chamula diaspora communities, Rincón Chamula. Between 1984 and 1986, with Robert M. Carmack as coprincipal investigator, I received another field research grant from the National Institutes of Health for further research in the Chamula diaspora communities. Of crucial significance for the realization of the present book was a 1989–91 translation grant from the National Endowment for the Humanities, for moving the original Tzotzil transcriptions and Spanish and English translations to the verse translations in electronic format that were used to produce this book. Throughout the project, from 1971 to 1999, I received periodic faculty research grants from the University of California at Santa Cruz and the State University of New York at Albany. The Office of Academic Affairs at the University at Albany also contributed a subvention that facilitated the publication of earlier versions of some of the texts that appear in this book. All this support is gratefully acknowledged.

Portions of the English translation of the Tzotzil texts have appeared in different versions in previous publications as follows: *Telling Maya Tales: Tzotzil Identities in Modern Mexico* (Routledge Press, © 1999), by Gary H. Gossen, chaps. 2–5, reproduced by permission of Routledge, Inc. part of the Taylor & Francis Group. *The Legacy of Mesoamerica: History and Culture of a Native American Civilization*, edited by R. M. Carmack, J. Gasco, and G. H. Gossen (Prentice-hall, 1996), chap. 13, reprinted by permission of Pearson Education, Inc., Upper Saddle River, N.J.,

07458; *Chamulas in the World of Sun: Time and Space in a Maya Oral Tradition,* by Gary H. Gossen (Harvard University Press, 1974); *In the Language of Kings: An Anthology of Mesoamerican Literature—Pre-Columbian to the Present,* edited by Miguel León-Portilla and Earl Shorris (W. W. Norton, 2001), book 2, section 7 (1–5); *South and Mesoamerican Native Spirituality: From the Cult of the Featherbed Serpent to the Theology of Liberation,* edited by Miguel León-Portilla and Gary H. Gossen (Crossroad press, 1993), pp. 413–35, used with permission of the Crossroad Publishing Company; *Supplement to the Handbook of Middle American Indians,* vol. 3 of *Literatures,* edited by Munro S. Edmonson and Victoria Bricker (University of Texas Press, 1985), pp. 64–106; *Man: Journal of the Royal Anthropological Institute,* n.s. 10: 448–61 (19750; *Tlalocan* 8: 131–65 (1980); *Estudios de Cultura Maya* 11: 267–83 (1978); *Journal of Latin American Lore* 3 (2): 249–78 (1977), reproduced with permission of The Regents of the University of California.

When the expense of publishing the book in a dual-language format, with full notation and native drawings, became an issue, a generous subvention grant from the Foundation for the Advancement of Mesoamerican Research (FAMSI) came to the rescue in February 2000, making the present publication possible. I am particularly grateful to Sandra Noble, director of FAMSI, and to David Freidel, who suggested FAMSI as a possible source of support. Through the entire process, Jeff Burnham, then acquisitions editor at the University of Oklahoma Press, was a steadfast supporter of the project, and I thank him and his excellent editorial staff for seeing it through to completion.

Foremost among the personal debts I accumulated over a period of thirty-six years is the one I owe to my Harvard graduate adviser and long-term professional colleague, Evon Z. Vogt, who introduced me to Maya studies long ago and had everything to do with making my fieldwork possible. Vogtie, to those who know him, is a legendary mentor. Founder and sustaining force of the Harvard Chiapas Project, of which I was a part, he facilitated everything—financial, intellectual, and logistical—in the initial phases of my fieldwork in Chiapas, demanding nothing in return but my fidelity to the ideal of doing fieldwork in native languages and sharing data that might be relevant to others. In addition to my long personal and professional ties to Vogtie himself, the Harvard Chiapas Project produced a loyal cadre of fellow graduate students and peers who have helped me as colleagues and friends at various stages of this project over the last three decades.

I am deeply indebted to Robert M. Laughlin, whose interest in Tzotzil language and literature preceded my own by a few years. His monumental work, *The Great Tzotzil Dictionary of San Lorenzo Zinacantán* (1975), has been my constant companion for the last three decades—even between 1965 and 1975, when it existed only as thousands of file slips in two shoe boxes. Bob's appreciation of Tzotzil verbal art, his many publications in Tzotzil literature, and his activities in the facilitation of the Maya literary renaissance currently underway in Chiapas have been an inspiration to me. He has also answered hundreds of queries about the nuances of Tzotzil word use and verbal play.

To Victoria R. Bricker go my special thanks for many decades of friendship and shared interest in Maya studies. She has generously shared her field notes and profound knowledge of Maya cultural history with me and, most recently, has provided excellent advice on the preparation of this volume. In particular I appreciate her understanding—greater than my own—of the linguistic markers that define ancient and contemporary Maya verse structure.

Jan Rus, whom I first knew as a Harvard undergraduate and later as a fellow fieldworker in Chiapas, has contributed heavily to this book as a good friend and collaborator. I am deeply honored that he agreed to write the afterword, and I want to thank him for the meticulous care with which he read the entire manuscript, including all the notes, for ethnographic and historical accuracy. Jan and his wife, Diane, have also generously made their photographic archive of contemporary Chiapas available to me.

I owe a particular debt of thanks to Thor Anderson, another Chiapas Project associate and fellow fieldworker, for his deep understanding of the meaning of Chamula material culture and its symbolic significance. Thor has provided encouragement for this project throughout its long genesis and has also sensitized me to the importance of providing minute details on everyday material culture in the form of ethnographic notes.

Among the Harvard Chiapas Project people, George and Jane Collier and Frank Cancian have provided valuable insights into the ecological and economic forces and related patterns of domestic life that have created the modern Chiapas Maya world. Priscilla Rachun Linn and Patrick Menget left their voluminous field notes in the Harvard Chiapas Project archive; their view of Chamula religious and supernatural life have been useful to me in my interpretations of Chamula life-crisis rituals and public religious observance.

The late Michelle Zimbalist Rosaldo was the first colleague to call my attention to the fact that Tzotzil Mayas speak formally in "pairs," the intensity of this poetic phenomenon increasing with the emotional intensity of the message. Michelle was a person of many insights, with a gift for sensitive reading of the poetics of oral literature. The stylistic conventions of this book are inspired by her insight.

I would like to thank a number of extraordinary teachers who played a part in my choosing anthropology as a career and helped me understand the nature of academic life and scholarship. These include María Eugenia Bozzoli de Willie, to whom I owe my calling to the field of anthropology; Alan Dundes, my first teacher of folklore and mythology, who assured me that what I was doing was important to the world archive of oral literature; and Munro S. Edmonson, who introduced me to Mesoamerican verbal art and literature and helped me realize that one of the world's great ancient civilizations and many of its native languages and literatures were still thriving in modern Mexico and Guatemala.

I was also privileged, while at Harvard, to become acquainted with the late Alfonso Villa Rojas, who became a solid friend, facilitating my successful crossing of a number of bureaucratic hurdles with the Mexican government in order to gain permission to conduct fieldwork in Chiapas.

In almost five years of fieldwork in Chiapas, my family and I were befriended by countless individuals. In Chamula itself, I will never forget the kindnesses extended to us by a number of families for whom our presence in their homes as guests was, initially at least, often awkward and embarrassing. I remember with special fondness the extended families of Xalik López Calixto and Xalik López Castellanos. Five of the storytellers in the book came from these families. I also appreciate the warm hospitality of Xalik Gómez Oso and and his brother Xun Gómez Oso. They and their families welcomed us into a broad range of activities in their everyday lives, from corn farming to funerals, from field-rat trapping to curing rituals and sweatbaths.

In San Cristóbal de las Casas, we enjoyed the unconditional friendship and generosity of Leopoldo y Carmen Velasco, Alejandro and Polita García, Vicente Reyes, and Prudencio Moscoso, even though, on occasion, they found our association with the Indian community of San Juan Chamula hard to understand. In San Cristóbal we also enjoyed the friendship and support of the late Gertrude (Trudi) Duby de Blom, who in the 1960s and 1970s was the undisputed grande dame of Chiapas Maya studies.

My wife, Eleanor, and I also became acquainted with a number of American citizens who chose to make Mexico and San Cristóbal their home. These friends, all of whom were sympathetic to the Indian community and its needs and causes, helped us in many ways. The late Nancy Modiano helped me immeasurably, bringing my work to the attention of Mexican officials and facilitating the translation of several of my works into Spanish. To Janet Maren and Marcey Jacobson, retired Americans who live in San Cristóbal, go my deep thanks and appreciation for their company, friendship, and astute understanding of local affairs. Marcey kindly made her extraordinary photographic archive of Chiapas Indian communities available to me.

I would like to thank Miguel León-Portilla, Mexico's foremost living historian of Nahuatl culture and literature, for his encouragement over many years. His kind agreement to write the foreword to this book is a great honor for me.

I would also like to thank my Spanish colleague Manuel Gutiérrez Estévez, of the Universidad Complutense de Madrid, for his substantial contribution to my knowledge and understanding of Spain's profound contribution to the formation of modern Maya art and thought. His insights have helped me in the preparation of historical notes on religious themes that appear in the book's texts. I extend my deep thanks to him for not permitting me to be a New World provincial.

Over many years I have been inspired by Barbara and Dennis Tedlock's work on the contemporary Mayas of Highland Guatemala as well as grateful for their friendship. They offered helpful comments to me during the review process of this manuscript at the University of Oklahoma Press.

Particular assistance and encouragement on the preparation of this volume have also come from Victor Montejo, a Jacaltec Maya who is a major voice in the Maya literary renaissance of Guatemala. I am also indebted to the late Linda Schele and her coauthor and collaborator, David Freidel, who urged me to finish this project in the interest of providing modern Maya data that might illuminate the meaning of ancient Maya epigraphy and art. David also played a significant role in helping me obtain the support of the Foundation for the Advancement of Mesoamerican Studies in the form of a subvention for this publication. I would also like to express my appreciation for the assistance of June Nash as a consultant in my recent publication and grant applications in relation to the Maya Zapatista Movement.

My debts to students, friends, and colleagues at the University of New York at Albany are substantial. Above all, I want to express my deep gratitude to my students Brenda Rosenbaum and Thomas Van Alstyne for the thousands of hours they have invested in the transformation of the Tzotzil texts and translations into modern orthography and electronically manageable formats. Brenda, a native Guatemalan and also a fieldworker in Chamula, brought many useful critical insights to bear on minute matters of translation and ethnographic detail. I was particularly appreciative of her perspective on all matters having to do with the translation because she had, in the context of her fieldwork, access to female perspectives on Chamula lives and times; my own contacts with women were limited by Chamula custom. She corrected many errors in the Tzotzil transcription and called my attention to a number of problems in my translation. I greatly appreciate her substantial contribution to this project.

I am extremely grateful to Tom Van Alstyne for his tireless labor in manually entering thousands of changes in the Tzotzil orthography from the International Phonetic Alphabet to the common spelling conventions that are now the norm for writing Chiapas Indian languages. He also formatted the working electronic file for the dual-language parallel text that appears in this book. His working knowledge of Tzotzil and fluent mastery of Spanish gave him an expert editorial eye for errors in transcription and translation.

Duncan Earle, who worked with Robert M. Carmack and me as field director of the Chiapas Project in the 1980s, has also contributed valuable insights regarding the selection of texts as well as the contents of the notes and bibliography for this book.

Other graduate students, all of them now on their way to productive careers, have contributed substantially to this project over the past decade. These include Gwynne Jenkins, Brent Metz, Antonella Fabri, Quetzil Castaneda, Timothy Smith, and Miguel Aguilera.

At the University of New York at Albany, I would like to thank a number of faculty colleagues who have given generously of their time and knowledge to assist me in the final stages of the project. Over the past few years, I have given particular attention to testing the sound of translations in informal performance settings. In spring 2000 Nahuatl scholar Louise Burkhart provided me with the opportunity to present and discuss one of the texts in the course of a three-hour seminar on Native American literature. Her comments were particularly useful, as she has had a great deal of experience with similar kinds of Mesoamerican oral texts.

During the year 2000 I had the singular good fortune to spend a good bit of time in consultation about this project with Albany colleagues Judith Johnson, a nationally acclaimed poet and performance artist, and Barbara Chepaitis, a successful fiction writer and professional storyteller. Their advice on my translations was particularly valuable because they are both creative writers who regard interactive, live performance as central to their artistic mission. I am grateful to my friend and colleague Richard Wilkinson, a physical anthropologist who is at heart a creative writer, for his critical eye for stylistic clarity and simplicity in parts of the manuscript that he kindly agreed to read. During the summer of 2001, while I was involved with the final editing of the manuscript, I enjoyed the generous and cheerful support of my new community at Deep Springs College, California. I am particularly grateful to Alex Blasdel, a student at Deep Springs, for his capable editorial assistance.

Above all, I should thank the members of my family, who have steadfastly helped and encouraged me through the several decades of this project. I appreciate the expert and cheerful secretarial assistance of my sister-in-law, Elizabeth Frischman, who spent many months in Chiapas typing Tzotzil transcriptions and provisional Spanish translations from the original longhand texts. She was ever cheerful and upbeat. I also thank my son Nicholas for giving up an entire month of his summer vacation to help me with proofreading and correction of the copyedited manuscript. I have followed a number of his suggestions for more appropriate word choice in the final translations.

Finally, to my wife, Eleanor, to whom this book is dedicated, I owe the greatest debt of gratitude. She has been with me and has helped me immeasurably in every stage of the project. I recall that the idea for the book was the subject of my letters to her from the field in the summer of 1965. She played a key role in helping me select the stories from the larger corpus that would eventually become this book. As recently as April 2002, she was the steady hand, editorial adviser, and faithful friend who helped me prepare the final version of this book for submission to the University of Oklahoma Press.

Editorial Methods

CHALLENGES, OPPORTUNITIES, AND PROVISOS

Many problems had to be resolved and criteria established before I could move ahead with the Chamula project. First, there was the problem of sheer magnitude. The 184 narratives that comprise my general collection—all of which appear as short abstracts in an appendix to my book, *Chamulas in the World of the Sun: Time and Space in a Maya Oral Tradition* (1974: 253–346)—amount in manuscript form to approximately five thousand pages, including English translations and ethnographic notes. I chose to reduce the manuscript by 60 percent, from five thousand to two thousand pages, without omitting major story types or sacrificing the interesting variations from one storyteller to another as each of them related versions of the same story. I retained the over-all story line of the corpus as a whole, which is chronological, and I tried to retain a rough parity of space devoted to each of the four creations, or epochs, that make up the sum total of human history in the Tzotzil worldview. It was also important that each of my principal storytellers be well represented in the final product. In the end 74 of 184 narratives were retained.

I have also chosen to retain whole narratives. No part of any text was edited for style. All introductory material, all concluding material, and all (often tedious) redundancy has been retained. However, in order to make the cut in the present collection, a story had to have the capacity to stand alone as an account with a beginning, middle, and end. For example, if an account were merely an explanation of why we have such-and-such a custom, I did not include it, judging it to be a footnote to something else rather than a story on its own. I consequently favored what I considered to be the better narratives. The entire collection can be consulted in abstract form (Gossen 1974).

The second challenge concerned the fact that the texts alone speak rather poorly for themselves; they need interpretive help. The world does not need one more compendium of freestanding folklore texts, of which hundreds of tomes were compiled in the nineteenth and twentieth centuries, most of them without contextualizing essays, comparative notes, or any effort to render their poetics and meaning accessible to the reader. I could not, without editing and ethnographic framing, expect the scholarly or lay public to enjoy just another collection of stories. There had to be a story line.

Fortunately, Chamula Tzotzil cosmology and history, like those of many Indian communities in Mesoamerica and elsewhere in the New World, are laid out in a dramatic story line—a sequence of creations, destructions, and restorations that yields time present. These epochs are usually four in number (as they are for the Tzotzils), although the Aztec cycle and modern Nahuatl accounts identify the present creation as the fifth. In all cases the present amounts to a fragile holding pattern that may come to a precipitous end if people fall into sin and error. Because this sequential order is such a dependable organizing principle, it was possible to use it throughout my fieldwork, text collection, and translation sessions as an easily understood organizating principle. All narrators for this book, at my request, could explicitly identify the creation to which each of their narratives belonged. I have adhered faithfully to their classification, even when it yielded some interesting variations in historical attribution (for example, the "Tar Baby" story is attributed to both the First [text 6] and Third [text 37] Creations).

While I have faithfully retained the historical place of each story according to its narrator's attribution (First Creation, Second Creation, and so forth), I am responsible for the order of the narratives within each of the four sections, or creations. I have sought to place all the texts attributed to a given epoch in juxtapostion with one another so as to tell a plausible story of an epoch. I am forced to acknowledge, however, that Tzotzils do not tell the entire story of creation *as a whole cycle, ever,* except in a highly cryptic, symbolically opaque, and radically edited form on the occasion of their performance of The Festival of Games, their ritual of solar renewal, which occurs annually in February (see Gossen 1999: 105–58). At this greatest of all their many public spectacles, the stories that are told in this book profoundly and fundamentally inform what is going on. However, not one of these texts actually appears in the spoken script of the festival. The book contains the "text" of the festival: the history of humankind. The Chamulas ignore the full texts of the stories in the festival's "script," referring to them only in the highly distilled language of symbolic words and ritual action. They clearly prefer the more sensory pleasures of food, drink, tobacco, fireworks, song, dance, and ritual drama. Why? More fun, perhaps. Also, they take for granted the basic information contained in the stories and do not feel obliged to recite publicly that which is common knowledge.

While this book can be seen as a register of Chamula Tzotzil common knowledge, I am aware that its content is a historical contrivance. Using the written word, in Chamulas' own combined words, the book is a totality that no individual Chamula Tzotzil—even one of its most committed intellectuals—would ever articulate or set down. It would be regarded as unnecessary to do so, as for there would always be an elder who would know the totality more fully. Even the notes are clarifications made by narrators of truths they took to be self-evident, though they were not obvious to me. But times are changing. Where will the elders be a generation hence?

Third, I have chosen to present the collection in this book with the critical commentary limited to historical and ethnographic clarification and comparative commentary in the notes, which I prepared in close consultation with the texts' authors (see Gossen 1974, 1985, 1999). Following the introduction, the stories themselves take center stage. The line drawings that appear throughout the book are intended to serve as native critical commentary as well as illustrations of the texts. The artist, Marián López Calixto (himself one of the narrators in the book), chose the subjects that he deemed worthy of illustration. Many details of setting and character that escaped my exegetical effort in the notes appear illuminated, often with wonderful humor, in the drawings.

EDITORIAL AND ETHNOGRAPHIC NOTES

STORY TITLES

Chamula Tzotzil narrators do not assign particular titles to stories. The closest they come to this is some vague statement such as "the one about rabbit and coyote." Almost all the text titles that appear in this book derive from extracts from the texts themselves. For example, the title of the first story—"Of Our Father Sun in Heaven"—comes directly from the first line of the story: "Here is a story of Our Father Sun in Heaven."

NOTES

The notes, for the most part, constitute exegetical information that came from the narrators during translation sessions. Some of these notes also refer the reader to other sources and to cross-references in the book itself.

For selected comparative Mesoamerican literature that is relevant to particular texts, I refer the reader to the following concordance of the present text numbers with the corresponding text numbers, page numbers, and story titles that appear as plot abstracts of the same texts in my earlier work, *Chamulas in the World of the Sun: Time and Space in a Maya Oral Tradition* (1974). Each of these abstracts carries a comparative literature note. These notes are not reproduced here, although all of the titles as well as new titles that may be of comparative interest appear in the bibliography at the end of the book.

Present Text Number	Gossen 1974 Text Number	Gossen 1974 Page Number
Text 1	Text 152	330
Text 2	Text 145	328
Text 3	Text 182	345–46
Text 4	Text 156	332
Text 5	Text 168	338
Text 6	Text 176	342–43
Text 7	Text 149	329
Text 8	Text 17	343–44
Text 9	Text 161	334
Text 10	Text 144	327–28
Text 11	Text 137	324
Text 12	Text 133	322
Text 13	Text 169	338–39
Text 14	Text 164	336
Text 15	Text 153	331
Text 16	Text 163	335
Text 17	Text 183	346
Text 18	Text 175	342
Text 19	Text 136	323–24
Text 20	Text 165	336
Text 21	Text 114	312
Text 22	Text 167	338
Text 23	Text 131	320–21
Text 24	Text 116	313–14
Text 25	Text 123	317
Text 26	Text 115	312–13
Text 27	Text 129	319–20
Text 28	Text 112	311
Text 29	Text 113	311–12
Text 30	Text 120	315–16
Text 31	Text 118	314–15
Text 32	Text 115	262
Text 33	Text 128	319
Text 34	Text 109	309–10
Text 35	Text 106	308
Text 36	Text 105	307
Text 37	Text 96	302–303

Text 38	Text 94	301–302
PRESENT TEXT NUMBER	GOSSEN 1974 TEXT NUMBER	GOSSEN 1974 PAGE NUMBER
Text 39	Text 89	298–99
Text 40	Text 74	291
Text 41	Text 98	303–304
Text 42	Text 97	303
Text 43	Text 103	306
Text 44	Text 25	267
Text 45	Text 80	293–94
Text 46	Text 75	291–92
Text 47	Text 76	294
Text 48	Text 81	294–95
Text 49	Text 39	274–75
Text 50	Text 54	282
Text 51	Text 47	279
Text 52	Text 63	286
Text 53	Text 29	269
Text 54	Text 52	281
Text 55	Text 35	272–73
Text 56	Text 3	255–56
Text 57	Text 73	291
Text 58	Text 49	279
Text 59	Text 48	278–79
Text 60	Text 61	285–86
Text 61	Text 79	87–88, 293
Text 62	Text 27	269
Text 63	Text 55	282
Text 64	Text 41	275–76
Text 65	Text 53	281–82
Text 66	Text 45	27
Text 67	Text 51	280
Text 68	Text 56	283
Text 69	Text 36	273
Text 70	Text 33	271
Text 71	Text 34	271–72
Text 72	Text 30	269
Text 73	Text 31	270
Text 74	Text 9	259

ILLUSTRATIONS

The line drawings are intended as a form of native exegesis or textual criticism, as one of the narrators, Marián López Calixto, produced them in a setting that allowed him total freedom—that is, complete independence from my supervision—to illustrate what he found interesting in the complete set of texts available to him. These drawings, which helped me with particular details in the translations, also supply the reader with a native visual text that complements the verbal text.

LEGENDS TO ILLUSTRATIONS

All of the legends that accompany the illustrations come directly from the corresponding text. Illustrations are placed near these parts of the text, with their legends numbered sequentially.

ORTHOGRAPHICAL NOTE

Aside from a very few colonial sources (Gossen 1985), the modern history of Tzotzil as a written language and literature is very recent, dating from about 1960. Therefore, orthography has not yet been standardized. There are two common modern notions: column 1 is closer to the conventions of the International Phonetic Alphabet; column 2 acquiesces to the realities of available typeface and broader intelligibility to both English and Spanish speakers, and is also closer to the orthography used in older Tzotzil/Spanish–Spanish/Tzotzil manuscripts. Equivalences of consonant notations are generally as follows. Some manuscripts and published texts use a combination of both orthographies, as I shall in this book. All Tzotzil texts in this book have been standardized to use the symbols in **boldface** below.

I am using a combination of both notations for these consonants (boldface characters in columns 1 and 2) so as to represent the correct Tzotzil sound value together with simplicity of notation. Other Tzotzil consonants in my orthography are pronounced with their I.P.A. sound values.

(1)		(2)
ʔ (glottal stop) as in	=	7 or ' or ʔ as in
ʔon 'avocado'	=	*7on* or *'on* or *ʔon*
h as in *hmeʔ* 'my mother'	=	***j*** as in ***jmeʔ***

š as in *ši* 'he or she said'	=	***x*** as in ***xi***
s as in ***sik*** 'cold'	=	*z* as in *zik*
č as in *čiʔ* 'sweet'	=	***ch*** as in ***chiʔ***
č' as in *ʔič'* 'chile'	=	***ch'*** as in ***ʔich'***
¢ as in *¢eb* 'girl'	=	***tz*** or ***ts*** as in ***tzeb*** or ***tseb***
¢ as in *¢'iʔ* 'dog'	=	***tz'*** or ***ts'*** as in ***tz'iʔ*** or ***ts'iʔ***
k as in ***kom*** 'to remain'	=	*c* as in *com*
k' as in ***k'an*** 'to want'	=	*c'* and in *c'an*
b (glottalized) as in ***nab*** 'lake'	=	*m* as in *nam*

Tzotzil vowels have these sound values:

a [a] as in f*a*ther
e [ɛ] as in b*e*t
i [i] as in b*ee*t
o [o] as in b*oa*t
u [u] as in L*u*ke

A brief note is in order regarding the use of <b> in my transcriptions. Phonologically, the phoneme /b/ in Tzotzil has three regular and predictable phonetic allophones. It is realized as a preglottalized [b] intervocalically, as a preglottalized [m] when it occurs syllable finally, and as a plain [b] elsewhere. In Tzotzil dictionaries all three instances of the realization of /b/ are transcribed simply as <b>. For the sake of consistency and uniformity I have followed this practice, though my consultants transcribed the intervocalic instances of /b/ as <'b> and the syllable-final instances as <m>, reflecting the phonetic manifestations in those contexts.

PUNCTUATION

I have tried to provide exact correspondence of punctuation between the Tzotzil transcription and the corresponding English at the ends of verse lines. However, in the Tzotzil text I have left out any punctuation, including quotation marks, within lines in order to avoid the possible confusion of punctuation and phonological symbols. I have also eliminated question marks at the ends of Tzotzil lines in order avoid confusion between the question mark (?) and the glottal stop (ʔ), which bear a close resemblance to each other. By leaving the Tzotzil text relatively uncluttered with the conventions of English punctuation, quotation marks, and capitalization, I hope that the archival value of the native text will be preserved for any future use.

Translation Methods

THE RATIONALE FOR VERSE TRANSLATION

A basic issue that had to be resolved concerned the format of the English translation. To this day there is no consensus among scholars or Native Americans themselves regarding the way in which Maya oral narratives are best translated into English or any other language. This problem in relation to Tzotzil oral literature is discussed at length elsewhere (Gossen 1985). Suffice it to say that our generation's preeminent scholars of Mesoamerican and North American Native literatures disagree on the subject. Miguel León-Portilla (1969: 76–78), Munro S. Edmonson (1971), and Victoria R. Bricker (1981) have tended to favor couplets and verse rendering of Maya and other Native American literature. Robert Laughlin, a leading scholar of contemporary Tzotzil narrative, steadfastly embraces literal, pithy, funny prose translations (1977). Dennis Tedlock, the most recent translator of the *Popol Vuh* (1985), has convincingly demonstrated that this great text has the voices of many genres, from songs of praise to highly stylized magical formulas to ordinary narratives. He argues for a mixed format, with much of the text rendered as straight prose and other parts, when appropriate, rendered as couplets and other more formal verse structures. Dell Hymes (1981) has argued convincingly that North American native literature is a free-flowing art form with discernible verse and prose structures intermingled.

I find myself ambivalent on this issue. My decision to use verse in the book has ultimately to do with personal taste and preference. I believe the form I have chosen makes it possible to translate the oral nature of the material faithfully. The verse format follows the stylistic conventions of Tzotzil formal style, the foundation of which (as is the case in so many oral traditions of the world) consists of dyadic structures of ideas, sound, and syntax. Stylistic patterns of Tzotzil and details of my translation strategy are discussed at length in two studies (Gossen 1974, 1985). The dyadic structures (and multiples thereof) that characterize Tzotzil narrative style are marked linguistically; therefore, my decisions regarding the way in which to render the verse structure of narrative texts in translation are for the most part suggested by the original Tzotzil. The verse-structure format is also intimately linked to Tzotzil cosmology and religion.

Tzotzil poetics depend heavily on the metaphor of heat, which in turn is related to the centrality of solar devotion in Tzotzil religion and cosmology. Heat is divine and primordial; its primary referent is the Sun creator—giver of temporal, spatial, and social order. Heat, like its primary Sun referent, is cyclical. Each day finished is both a cycle of heat completed and an affirmation of the holy integrity of the Sun deity. The same can be said of each year, each agricultural season, each festival, each human life, and the cycle of creation. In all, cycles of heat express the most basic principles of everyday and sacred order. Furthermore, the essential sacraments of Chamula religious practice—incense, candles, fireworks, tobacco, rum, aromatic plant materials—are perceived as cycles of heat that begin with a "cold" substance such as resin, wax, gunpowder, leaves, or cane juice. In ritual practice these "cold" substances, when used as sacraments, become the essence of heat—smoke, aroma, noise, drunkenness—that is used to communicate, like to like, with the Sun deity and the saints. It is said, for example, that incense is the only food of Our Lord Sun/Christ (see text 10).

For the Tzotzils language—particularly stylized forms of it as expressed in narrative, ritual language, prayer, and song—is also a sacred substance, a sacrament. Narratives of the type that make up this book are placed by Tzotzil speakers on the "hot" end of a classificatory spectrum that contrasts with ordinary speech, which is "cold." Those genres that are used to refer and render homage to deities and to refer to one another in ritual contexts are therefore classified as "hot" in the sense that the heart is heated with the heightened rituality of the occasions when these genres are used. Tzotzil storytelling occurs in a behavioral setting—sitting around the fire, walking on the path, resting with fellow workers on the coffee plantations—that elicits the formality of "extra-conversational" performer/audience interaction. Ordinary conversational language is "cold" in the sense of being secular and without predictability of form or content, whereas storytelling has a predictable content and a predictable setting—usually leisure time—and, therefore, a semiformal style. The couplet is the elementary structure of this style (see Gossen 1974, 1985).

COUPLETS

The formal couplet—a paired and parallel linguistic structure—is the universal, quintessential building block of all Chamula formal language (that is, ritual speech, prayer, and song). Narrative composition does not permit such a sweeping and easy generalization. In the case of narrative, the couplet is far from universal: there are single lines, multiples of three and four lines, and—in highly emotional and thematically important moments of some narratives (see text 3)—repetition in parallel structures that is extended to units of eight and ten. I believe, however, that clear couplet format lies at the center of gravity of narrative exposition. Edmonson has described this form for classic K'iche' Maya, as it appears in the *Popol Vuh:*

> A close rendering of the Quiché [*sic*] inevitably gives rise to semantic couplets, whether they are printed as poetry or as prose. In no case, so far as I can determine, does the Quiché text embellish this relatively primitive poetic device with rhyme, syllabification, or meter, not even when it is quoting songs. The form itself, however, tends to produce a kind of "keying," in which two successive lines may be quite diverse but must share key words which are closely linked in meaning. (1971: xii)

I have noted the disagreements that exist regarding this stylistic matter. The argument will perhaps never be resolved, as it concerns oral exposition, for which the only canon is the production of convincing re-creation in performance. The conventions that make a good performance are not random or completely idiosyncratic. There is a way to do it well. I am convinced that the couplet—however imperfect, erratic, or expandable—remains the dominant form when formal discourse occurs. Whatever the variants of the theme may be, pairing of ideas and phrases—semantic and syntactic couplets—is as common to Tzotzil language use as corn is to the Tzotzil diet. In a recent publishing project, the *Norton Anthology of Mesoamerican Literature,* in which about a dozen of my texts appear (León-Portilla and Shorris 2001), space constraints forced the editors to make the decision to elide the semantic couplet structure that appears in this book, turning some of the texts into prose narrative. I was not at all disappointed with the result, for the couplet is an artistic structure that makes for good mnemonics for both tellers and listeners whether it is rendered as verse or prose. I was impressed by the fact that the couplet structure as a reinforcing and reiterative device worked well as prose narrative. It came across simply as good storytelling, which it was and is. As Edmonson notes above, whether the couplet is written as prose or verse, the structure is discernible.

The couplet as a unit of narrative composition has a number of variants. The types are as follows.

SEMANTIC COUPLETS

The semantic couplet is characterized by repeating ideas without necessarily repeating exact syntax. I have elsewhere called this *nonparallel repetition* (1974b: 408). Analogous to Edmonson's K'iche' semantic couplet, it occurs frequently in Tzotzil narrative and conversation. An example can be seen in the second and third verses of text 1 in this book (see boldface below). This set of couplets follows a single *title line* (1), which has no companion line or reiteration. The semantic couplets and variations below typify the stylistic structure of the entire book:

1. Here is an account of Our Father Sun in Heaven.

2. **So, now. It was Our Father Sun in Heaven,**
   It was he who made the sky.
   He was still living on earth when he made the sky, the stars,
   and the earth.

3. **"Let the heavens be!" said Our Father in Heaven.**
   Quickly, the heavens appeared.

PARALLEL SYNTAX

A second basic form of the couplet follows parallel syntax, or *parallel repetition* (Gossen 1974: 407–409), in addition to explicit semantic redundancy. The couplet based on parallel syntax can be freely constructed and idiosyncratic (see "Free Construction" below) or can behave as a fixed formula (Lord 1958) that enters as a whole two-part unit into the composition of prayers, ritual speech, and song as well as narrative (see "Fixed Formulas" below).

Free Construction

There are hundreds of examples of parallel syntax that occur in this book as a poetic device for building new couplets and other multiples of the narrator's choice. The following example (also taken from text 1 of this book) begins with a semantic couplet (verse 5) and moves on to utilize a three-part parallel construction (verse 6, in boldface below):

5. "Let the earth be," declared Our Father Sun in Heaven.
   Quickly, the earth came forth.

6. **But first the heavens appeared.**
   He made the stars second.
   He made the earth third.

The narrative couplet based on parallel syntax, more than the semantic couplet, tends to serve as a narrative emphatic marker; a way of stylistically communicating information that—in the view of the narrator—is of relatively great thematic importance. Here, for example, is a passage (text 3, verse 71) taken from the point at which

Our Father Sun/Christ has just presented woman to man. The narrator highlights this moment in the elevated speech that he attributes to the Sun/Christ. The creator deity declares, in greatly expanded parallel syntax (this time multiplied by a factor of seven), the "purpose of woman":

71. **"Here you have the one who will make tortillas for you to eat.**
Here you have the one who will dwell in your house.
Here you have the one who will make your clothes.
Here you have the one who will make your food.
Here you have the one who will sleep with you.
Here you have the one who will share your food.
Here you have her," said Our Father.
"Very well," said the man.

Fixed Formulas

Although relatively rare in the narrative tradition, there are numerous examples in this book of formulaic couplets and phrases that are utilized as poetic devices. I use *formula* in the sense that Albert Lord (1958) and others have discussed, meaning that a whole couplet (or other narrative unit) moves freely about as a "bound" entity, never changing as it migrates from one narrative to another, even from one genre to another. A simple example comes from two syntactically linked formulaic couplets from Anglo American folk music. The following farewell freely migrates, intact, through hundreds of different song texts:

Oh, Father [Mother], dig my grave,
Dig it both deep and narrow.
Sweet William [or other], died for me today,
I'll die for him tomorrow.
(From a version of "Barbara Allen" that I learned as a child from my grandparents.)

Exactly the same kinds of fixed formulas exist by the hundreds in Tzotzil ritual poetry, prayer, and song and sometimes find their way into narrative performance. A good example from verses 3 and 5, text 3, follows (boldface below); I shall then give an example of the way in which this same couplet structure is expressed in a prayer text:

1. Here is an account of how the world began long ago.
How, in ancient times, the world was not at all like it is today.

2. Long ago, there were only seas.
There were no people.

3. Well, Our Father began to consider this:
"**My children, my offspring**, could never thrive here on top of the sea,"
reflected Our Father.

4. It would be better for me to sweep away the sea, said Our Father.
"If I don't, nothing will thrive,

5. "**Neither my children,**
Nor my offspring," declared Our Father.

Embedded in the following prayer text from the induction ceremony of the steward (*mayol* [Tz.] or *mayordomo* [Sp.]) for San Juan, composed entirely of fixed formulas, is the very same formula used in the narrative cited above. In this ritual, held on December 22, the inductee includes the following lines in his prayer of petition to San Juan:

May your flowery countenance shine in white radiance,
May your flowery face shine in soft brilliance.
That you may watch over us,
That you may care for us,
And your musicians
And your canoneers
And your cook.
May nothing befall us,
May nothing harm us.
Great San Juan,
Great patron.
Now you are to be delivered at my feet,
Now you are to be delivered into my hands,
And those of my spouse, my companion;
And those of my father and my mother;
And those of your children, your offspring.
(Full text appears in Gossen 1996: 463.)

INTERROGATIVE COUPLETS

Another type of couplet structure depends on the question-and-answer format. It obviously includes semantic redundancy and continuity, but the coupling strategy involves the didactic mode of teaching, via interrogation. Although this poetic device appears sporadically throughout the book, the single best sustained example of it appears in text 18, concerning the destruction of the first people:

1. Monkeys were still people long ago.
The people became monkeys because they were evil.

2. **And what were the deeds of these people long ago?**
They used to eat their own children long ago.

3. **What size were their children when they ate them?**
They were already nearly grown up when they ate them,
For it is said that they were at the age of seeking wives when they killed them to eat.

4. **How did they slay their children to eat them?**
The monkeys clubbed their children to death with sticks.
That's how they did it when monkeys were still people long ago. . . .
(Interrogative pattern continues through verse 10.)

SCANSION AND TRANSLATION

While fixed formal couplets, parallel and expanded narrative couplets, and interrogative couplets are all neatly marked by syntax, nonparallel semantic couplets—which, as I have noted, constitute the principal poetic device in Chamula Tzotzil narrative art—are sometimes not so clearly marked linguistically. The way in which the components of semantic couplets are marked, the way in which they work, and the manner in which they provide a guide to translation in verse format are as follows.

Because Tzotzil written literature has existed for only one generation, it does not have a canonic form of representation, either that of the native-language transcription or of translation into Spanish, English, or other modern languages. All of this is presently in flux. Therefore, the best that any of us who care about this emergent literature can muster is our best effort to present good transcriptions and translations. The transcription issue seems to be on the road to resolution via a standardized orthography (see general discussion above and the orthographical note that appears in the Editorial Methods section). The translation problem presents more challenges.

A promising key to the problem lies in a single letter *e*. This tiny particle behaves as a final phrase marker that linguists call an enclitic. Typically occurring at the end of noun and verb phrases, it may be suffixed to any final consonant or vowel, including another *e*. It seems that this *e* has no lexical or semantic function. It occurs alike in the narrative present and past tenses. Native speakers repeatedly say that its effect on the meaning is nil; one simply uses it because it "sounds right" to do so. This *e*, however, does seem to carry information about the reality status of the event, indicating that it has happened and that someone might plausibly think it to be true. Furthermore, the enclitic *e* invariably precedes a slight pause in the flow of speech. The *e* thus becomes a kind of oral phrase marker or punctuation mark.

After I spent a number of years reflecting on the function of this small enclitic particle, its importance became clearer to me when I realized that its relative presence or absence depended on the speech genre that was being used. In other words, the enclitic *e* appears to have a discourse function. I mounted a detective project in order to explore this theory, doing a comparative study of four hundred lines each of three genres: ordinary speech (*loˀil k'op*), prayer (*resal*), and narrative (*batz'i antivo k'op,* true ancient narrative, and *batz'i ach' k'op,* true recent narrative). I counted the absolute and relative frequency of recourse to the use of the enclitic *e* in phrases, finding that it appears in everyday speech about 25 percent of the time, while in formal genres such as prayer, the average is considerably less—about 10 to 12 percent of the time. In the narrative mode, however, the frequency averages well over 60 percent, in particular texts often reaching 80 to 90 percent. The enclitic *e* is thus far more likely to appear in the narrative mode of speaking than in everyday dialogue or formal speech.

I shall illustrate the stylistic place of the enclitic *e* by reference once again to the first lines of text 1 of this book; they are typical of many thousands that follow. Words with the attached enclitic *e* appear in boldface:

1. loˀil yuˀun jtotik ta vinajel.
   Here is a story of Our Father Sun in Heaven.

2. veno, ti jtotik ta **vinajele**.
   So, now. It was Our Father in Heaven.
   ˀaˀ la la spas li **vinajele**.
   It was he who made the sky.
   nakal toˀox la ta banumil ti k'alal la smeltzan ti **vinajele**, ti **k'anale**, ti **banumile.**
   He was still living on the earth when he made the sky, the stars, and the earth.

3. "meltzajan vinajel," xi la ti **jtotike.**
   Let the heavens be," said Our Father Sun in Heaven.
   jlikel la meltzaj ti **vinajele.**
   Quickly, the heavens appeared.

In this case, which is not unusual, both couplet 2 and couplet 3 are fully marked by the terminal enclitic *e* at the ends of all five lines that constitute them. Line 1, the title line, is unmarked, for the narrative is not yet launched; the rhythm has not yet begun. Two other alternatives are plausible as translation options; indeed, I have been encouraged by a number of colleagues to move in these directions in order to offer good translations. Here are alternative renderings, in two modes, of the example just cited:

1. *Prose:*

   Well, now, it was Our Father Sun in Heaven who made the sky. He was still living on the earth when he made the sky, the stars, and the earth.

2. *Verse, strictly following terminal phrase markers:*

   Well, now, it was Our Father in Heaven,
     It was he who made the sky.
   He was still living on the earth when he made
     The sky,
     The stars,
     The earth.

The first—the prose version—denatures the passage, however, because it ignores the narrative phrase marker (the enclitic *e*) that typifies oral narrative style. It also ignores the fact that key lines are followed by one or more reiterations of the first; that is to say, it ignores the essential structure of Tzotzil verse style. The second alternative, the strictly rendered verse translation, rigidly follows the mandate of recognizing all terminal phrase markers. This strikes my eye and ear as precious and overworked—entirely overdone; it ignores the fact that telling a story is not as formal an occasion as praying, engaging in ritual speech, or singing. The prose rendering sounds not formal enough, while the second, verse version sounds like ethnopoetic overkill, introducing a baroque complexity where it is not indicated. My choice—verse translation to free-form semantic couplets—follows the pattern suggested by the original Tzotzil and Tzotzil views of language and performance as well as the canons of my personal taste.

VOICE

In this translation I have sought a voice in Standard American English that is my own, tempered by over thirty-five years of hearing, speaking, writing, transcribing, and translating Tzotzil. I have also been influenced by almost two generations of Western and Native American scholars and artists who have sought to bring the voices of Native American verbal art to the attention of the scholarly and lay public. Moreover, I have enjoyed the counsel of many friends and colleagues—among them professional storytellers, novelists, poets, and translators from Western and non-Western languages. All of them agree on one essential thing: that translation does not—indeed, cannot—reproduce the reality of another language, another culture, another time, or another aesthetic. Rather, translation recreates for the present a subjective semblance of the spirit and intention of the original text, using whatever means are available—including a range of speech dialects known to the translator—in order to achieve this at a given time for a given audience.

This translation project involves the voies of six very different people, all of whom address subjects ranging from the sublime and cosmic to the banal and obscene, from the bureaucratic and formal to the illicit and intimate. It also involves the diverse voices that I use in the various aspects of my own life, including the middle-class dialect of Wichita, Kansas; the farm-country dialect of southeastern Kansas; and the variant of Standard American English that I use in East and West Coast academic communities. Like everyone, I have various voices that I use in different settings, and I have tried to utilize all of these to express the variety of tones used by the narrators in this book. The book's translations have also been influenced by the King James translation of the Psalms of David. Like the storytelling style of the Chamulas, that of the Psalms (which derive from oral sources in Hebrew and Greek) has come down to us as antiphonal couplets. I have found these great poems to be a source of inspiration in the preparation of the translations. With all of these voices and styles at my disposal, I came to the realization that homogenizing the voices in the book so that they would sound the same—like some omniscient meta-narrator—would probably be a mistake. Therefore, this book speaks in a number of voices, matching not only the particular qualities of an individual narrator's style but also the type of subject matter that is being addressed, influenced by my own voice as well.

FURTHER STYLISTIC MATTERS

LITERALITY

Since the native text is provided in its entirety, I have felt free to avoid any attempt at literal or interlinear translation. Linguists and Tzotzil speakers themselves could undoubtedly achieve such precision, but I am convinced that any attempt at literal translation usually fails as an entertaining work to be read. Absolute fidelity to the word often amounts to loss of intelligibility. As an example, I would like to cite a passage of text 51, "Bitten to Death by the Backwards Wailing Man." This story is from the Fourth Creation, an event of the modern era. It is a modern horror story, rather like a Grade B movie in the United States from the 1930s. The monster strikes:

2. A certain man had gone for a walk in the woods.
Now, when he was well within the forest, it all began.
It was then that he heard a monster crying out from the forest.
"Uuuuuuu!" cried the Backwards Wailing Man.

3. This is what the man did:
He mocked the Backwards Wailing Man defiantly.
"Uuuuuuu!" answered the man.

4. As for this man,
He had his trusty gun.

5. As for his gun,
He had it right there with him. . . .

The story marches on to tragedy as the victim tries to kill the monster and fails; he is slain, his friend goes to get the army, and they, too, fail and are slaughtered by the monster.

I highlight this passage to call attention to the liberty I have taken in translation, for this is a wild, wonderful, tragic story, yet it emerges in truncated pieces if it is faithfully and literally translated. Literally rendered, the lines would read:

2. There was a man who went for a walk in the woods.
Well, the man arrived in the woods.
Then he heard a demon crying out in the woods.
"Uuuuuuu!" said the Backwards Wailing Man.

3. Such [or thus] the man:
He answered the Backwards Wailing Man.
"Uuuuuuu!" said the man.

4. Such [or thus] with the man:
He had his small gun.

5. Such [or thus] with his gun:
He carried it with him.

The original Tzotzil works nicely. It is a great story by a virtuoso storyteller. Literally rendered, however, as shown above, it is boring and stilted in English. I have obviously embellished the final version considerably to capture the spirit of what is a fast-moving action adventure story. To this end I have taken many liberties with the literality of the Tzotzil text while also taking seriously the smallest nuances of the narrator's word choice; for example, the *small* of *small gun* in the literal translation does not carry the diminutive intimacy of the Tzotzil adjective *ʔuni,* which means "cherished and small"; hence it becomes a *trusty gun* in the final translation.

If one multiplies such liberties by the thousands, the total result is very different from a literal translation. I have sought, rather, a recreation of each narrative in English, paying special attention to the idiosyncrasies of each storyteller, his subject, and also to the supplementary information that frequently came to light during translation sessions with the storyteller. These supplementary data are found in the notes for each text. I also found that Marián López Calixto's illustrations helped me immeasurably during the final translations, particularly when I was attempting to recreate verbally certain anatomical characteristics of monsters such as the Backwards Wailing Man and the Demon Pukuj.

TRANSITIONAL AND INTRODUCTORY CLAUSES

The issue of transitional clauses matters a great deal, as more than half of all lines begin with some "launching platform" in the form of *well, then, but,* and so forth. However, there are only a limited number of them, so they occur with relentless frequency. Many are Tzotzil narrative war-horses: *vaʔi ʔun* or *vaʔun* (so), *jech* (such, thus), and *ti k'alal* (when). There are other transition and "starter" clauses that are Spanish loan words, most notably *pero* (but), *veno* (from *bueno,* fine; good; well, then; okay), and *entonse* (from *entonces,* then).

I have taken great liberty with these phrases—often totally ignoring their literal meaning, sometimes ignoring them altogether, sometimes making complete sentences where only fragments occurred in the original—for such license proved to be the only salvation from absolute tedium in the translations. Sometimes, a broad interpretation of these transitional clauses provided the opportunity to give dignity and elegance to particularly beautiful passages. In text 1, for example, the content of the first passage is stunning and lovely:

1. Here is a story of Our Father Sun in Heaven.

2. So, now. It was Our Father Sun in Heaven,
   It was he who made the sky.
   He was still living on the earth when he made the sky, the stars,
      and the earth.

The clause that introduces verse 2 in Tzotzil is *veno,* from Spanish *bueno,* which translates as "good," and in colloquial Mexican speech, as "okay, then," or "now, then." *Bueno* is also the preferred way of saying "hello" when answering the telephone in Mexico. None of these literal or colloquial uses of *bueno* in Spanish express the considerable seriousness of the cosmogonic moment that is being addressed in the Tzotzil text, utilizing *veno* as a loan word, so I felt that something more was required. I found inspiration for an alternative in Seamus Heaney's introduction to his recent translation of *Beowulf* (2000). Writing of the first word in the Anglo-Saxon poem, *hwaet,* which launches the narrative (not unlike *veno* in the Tzotzil text), he states:

> And when I came to ask myself how I wanted *Beowulf* to sound in my version, I realized I wanted it to be speakable by one of those relatives [of my own]. I therefore tried to frame the famous opening lines in cadences that would have suited their voices, but that still echoed with the sound and sense of the Anglo-Saxon:
>
> *Hwaet wē Gār-Dena in geār-dagum*
> *þēod-cyninga þrym gefrūnon,*
> *hū ða æþelingas ellen fremedon.*
>
> Conventional renderings of *hwaet* . . . tend toward the archaic literary: *lo, hark, behold, attend,* and—more colloquially—*listen* . . . . But in Hiberno-English Scullion-speak the particle *so* came naturally to the rescue, because in that idiom *so* operates as an expression that obliterates all previous discourse and narrative and at the same time functions as an exclamation calling for immediate attention. So, *so* it was:
>
> *So. The Spear-Danes in the days gone by*
> *and the kings who ruled them had courage and greatness.*
> *We have heard of those princes' heroic campaigns.*
> (Heaney 2000: xxvii–xxviii)

Inspired by Heaney's account, I found the confidence to try something different in order to make a limited number of Tzotzil transitional phrases and "launcher clauses" sound right in my voice, according to tone of the situation. That is why the narrator of the first text says, as he introduces his magnificent story:

> *So, now. It was Our Father in Heaven,*
> *It was he who made the sky. . . .*

It is also why such introductory and transitional phrases are rendered in many different ways throughout this book.

VERBS AND ADJECTIVES

Although Tzotzil dictionaries give a positively breathtaking range of verbs and adjectives that relate to human affairs and human nature, animal nature and utterances, and supernaturals' character qualities and voices, I was faced with the dilemma of a very limited range of these words that actually appeared in the narratives. On the thousands of occasions in which people and other beings are quoted as saying something in the texts, a tiny range of verbs is used, most of them based on *-al* (to say), *-ut* (to tell, to say to, to scold, to criticize, to rebuke, to reproach, to reprimand, to bawl out, to harm), or *tak'* (to answer, to reply). The range of translation options for this small number of verbs of utterance had to be either small or large; I opted for large. Therefore, if the setting requires *declared* or *pronounced,* I render forms of *-al* in translation with such words. Similarly, if the circumstances are stressful, forms of *-al* become *cried, yelled,* or *shrieked.* Ironically, *-avan* (to shout) occurs only occasionally but often seems called for in other contexts. But it is not there. In short, I have taken great liberty with the translation of common, frequently used verbs of utterance in order to avoid a tedious, unrelieved redundancy that does not reflect the nuances of the verbal art or of that which is actually being done and said.

Similar problems occur in connection with adjectives. Although many hundreds of adjectives exist in Tzotzil, few are used in narrative with reference to qualities of individuals and other living beings who appear as actors in narratives. For example, a vast gamut of *badness* is almost invariably rendered with one of two adjectives: *chopol* (evil, ugly) or *mu* (bad, wicked), even though the nuance may actually require *jealous, spiteful, poor* (pitiful), *miserable* (impoverished), *loathesome, ungrateful, damned, or fucking* (as a derogatory). The paucity of adjectival descriptors does not correspond to the nuances of negativity that are actually present, given the contextual background of individual instances and surrounding narrative situations.

ENGLISH USAGE

A few Tzotzil terms—mostly common and proper nouns that have both American and British or English and Spanish equivalents—required an aesthetic judgment as to the term most suitable in the translations. A word choice—for example, *maize* or *corn* and *maize field* or *cornfield;* San José or Saint Joseph; *compadre* or *coparent*—had to sound "right" and make sense to an average, educated speaker of American English. Therefore, *corn* is used in the translation, although *maize* appears in some of the notes. If Spanish saints' names are commonly understood in their Spanish form in American English, the Spanish form is retained. Therefore, Santa Rosa is used in preference to Saint Rose, San José in preference to Saint Joseph, San Juan in preference to Saint John. If a Spanish term such as *compadre* is generally understood, it is used in preference to *coparent,* which exists in English but is never used in any context other than anthropology textbooks. In summary, my constant guide in word choice has been common American English usage.

Although translation and English usage issues related to particular passages are often discussed in their corresponding notes, one of these problems is so pervasive that it requires general comment. I refer to the names of the central divine protagonists of the book: the sun deity and his mother, the moon deity. In the traditional Maya Christian world of belief and practice that is shared by all the narrators whose texts appear in the book, the sun deity (*jtotik,* Our Lord or Our Father; sometimes rendered as *jtotik ta vinajel,* Our Lord in Heaven or Our Father in Heaven; also *jch'ultotik,* Our Holy Father) is one and the same as Jesus Christ. Although, to a Western observer, the modern conception of this deity reflects both Maya and Christian roots, these diverse origins are utterly irrelevant to and unrecognized by traditional (that is to say, non-Protestant) native people. I have therefore chosen to use the terms Sun/Christ, Our Father, and Our Lord as root translations to which other qualifiers (such as *holy, in heaven*) are added as appropriate.

The problems connected with rendering the name of the moon deity in translation are similar. She is known in Tzotzil as *jme'tik* (Our Holy Mother). Like the sun deity, Our Holy Mother Moon, for non-Chamula observers, has an apparent dual origin in ancient Maya belief and Spanish Catholicism, for she is one and the same as the Virgin Mary, the mother of Christ. However, as in the case of the Sun/Christ, traditional Chamula Maya Christians (non-Protestants) do not recognize distinct layers of meaning in the person of the moon deity; she is the unitary moon deity and the Virgin Mary. I have chosen to use the basic terms Our Holy Mother and Our Mother Moon, qualified as appropriate in different contexts.

Four Creations

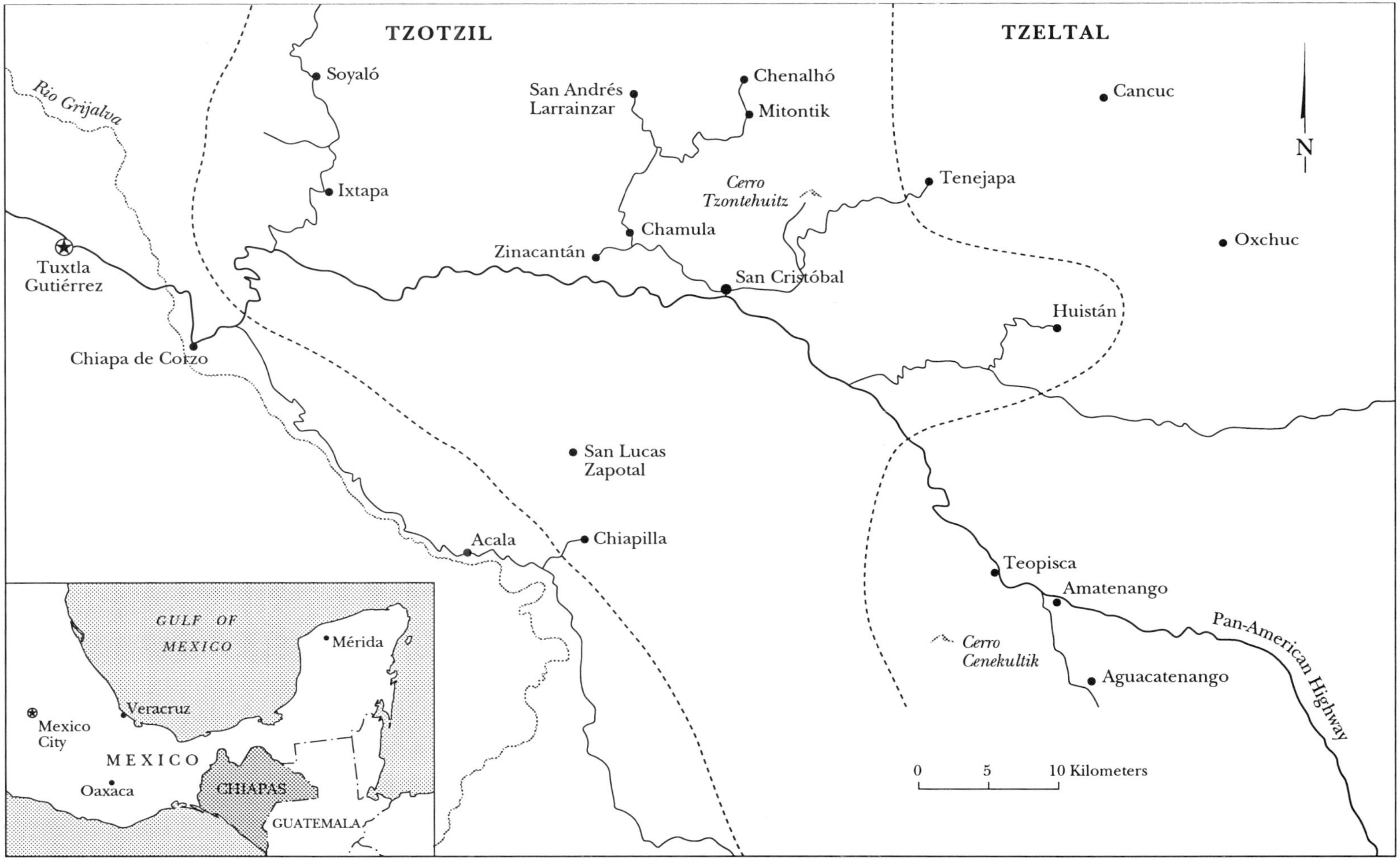

MAP I

Central Chiapas, Mexico, by Evon Z. Vogt

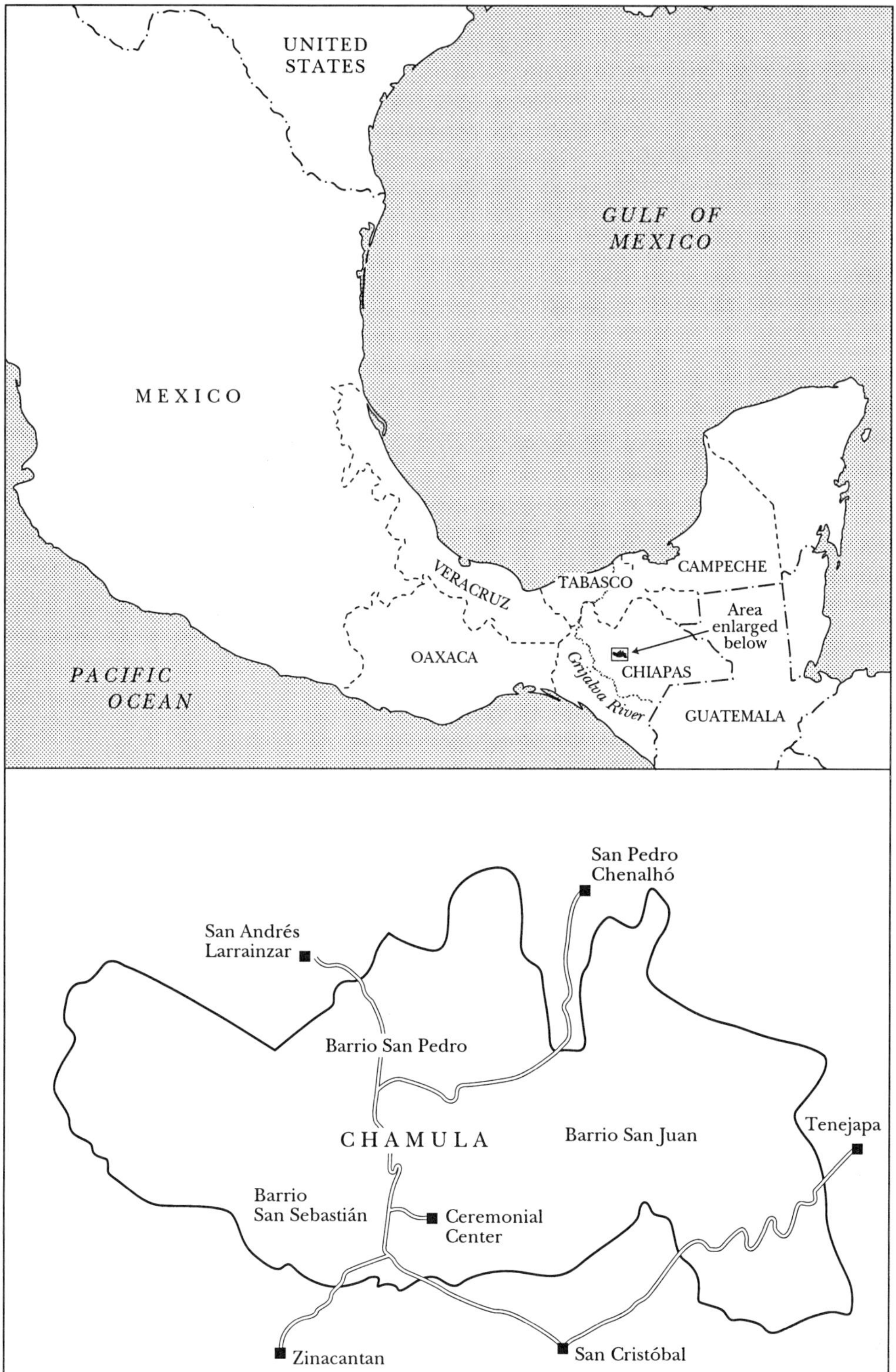

MAP 2

Chamula in Chiapas and Mexico, by Gary H. Gossen

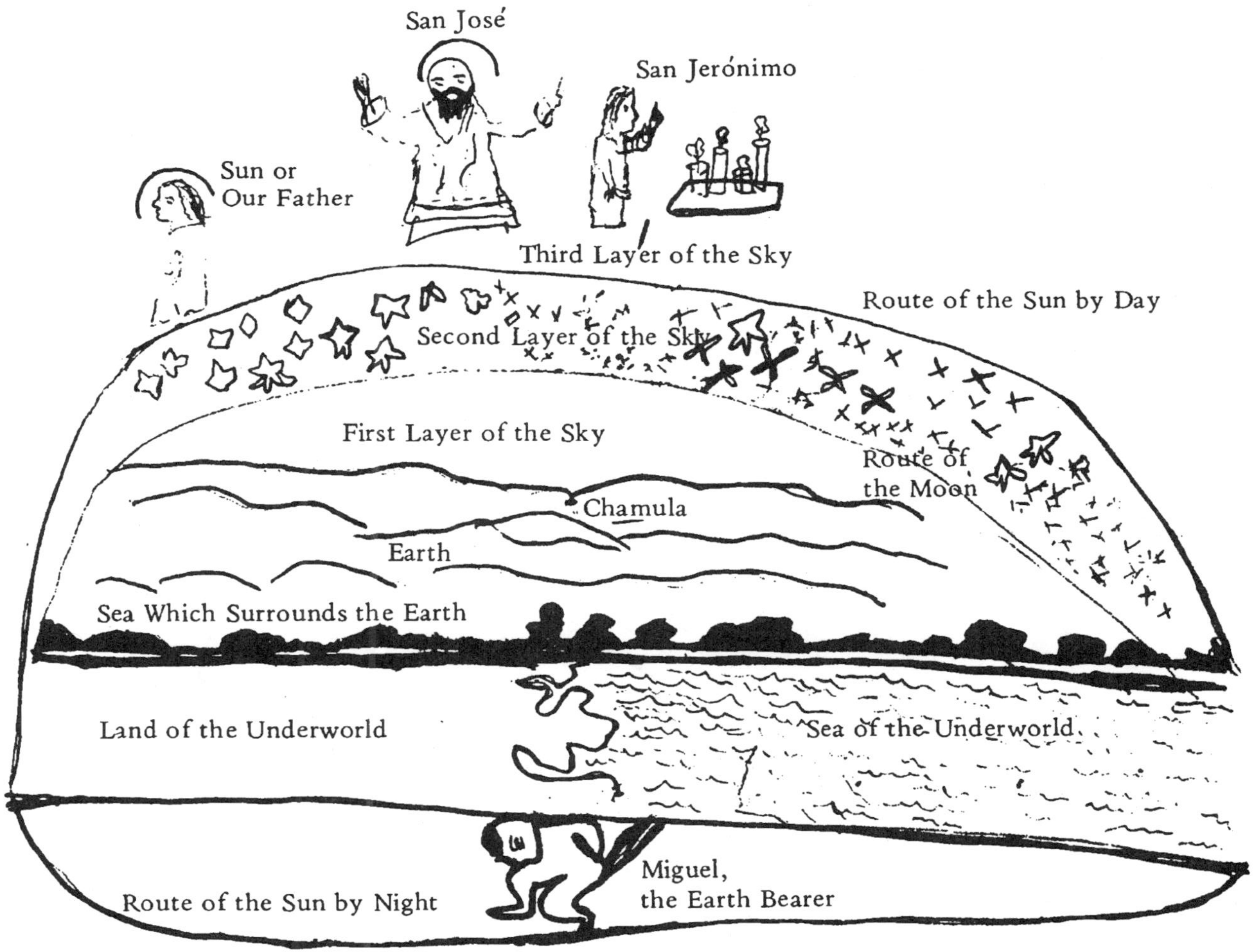

MAP 3
A Chamula chart of the universe, by Marián López Calixto

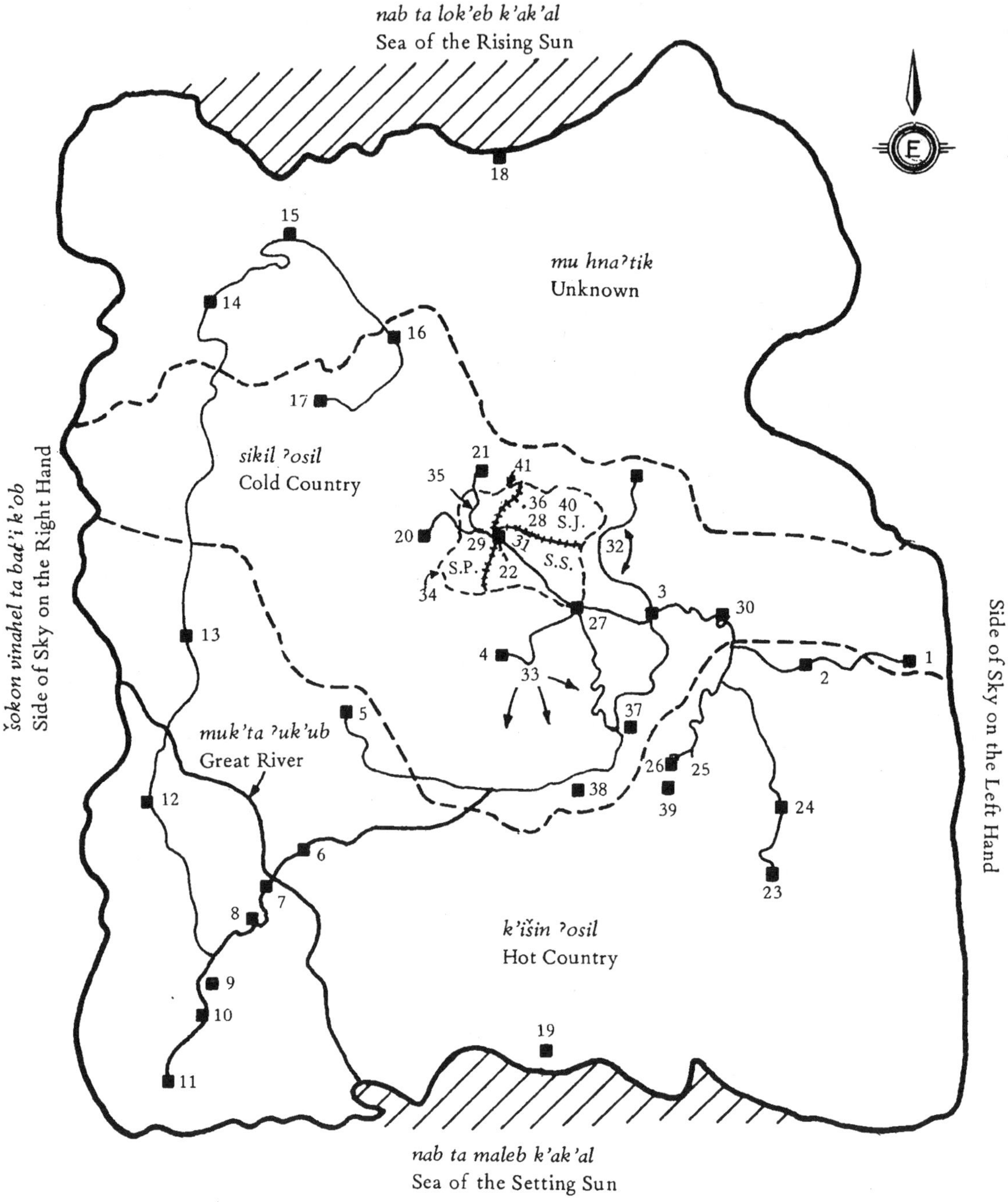

MAP 4

A Chamula chart of the world, by Marián López Calixto. Orientation, east up, follows the original.

Key to map 4

— Major roads
-- Major regional boundary
----- Chamula municipal boundary
+++ Internal Chamula barrio boundary

1. Guatemala
2. Comitán, Ladino town south of San Cristóbal and near Guatemalan border
3. San Cristóbal, Ladino town and principal trading center of the highland area
4. Zinacantán, Tzotzil-speaking *municipio* adjacent to Chamula. Many Chamulas work in the lowland maize fields rented by Zinacantecos and thus have greater contact with them than with other indigenous groups.
5. Simojovel
6. Chiapa de Corzo, lowland Ladino town on Pan-American Highway, west of highlands and just east of Grijalva River
7. Grijalva River bridge on Pan-American Highway near Tuxtla Gutiérrez
8. Tuxtla Gutiérrez, capital of state of Chiapas
9. Arriaga, lowland Ladino town on the way to coffee plantations
10. Huixtla, lowland Ladino town in region of coffee plantations
11. Tapachula, the principal Ladino town in southwestern Chiapas, also near coffee plantations
12. Puebla
13. Mexico City
14. England
15. United States
16. Campeche, capital of Mexican state of the same name
17. Mérida, capital of Mexican state of the same name
18. Place where the sun comes up from the Sea of the Rising Sun
19. Place where the sun sinks into the Sea of the Setting Sun
20. Larrainzar, Tzotzil-speaking *municipio* northwest of Chamula
21. Chenalhó, Tzotzil-speaking *municipio* north of Chamula
22. Chamula Ceremonial Center
23. Pujiltik, a Ladino town in Hot Country
24. Suyitán, Ladino town in Hot Country
25. Venustiano Carranza, lowland Ladino and Indian town, important source of shamans and witches. Nearby is a sacred mountain.
26. Lansavitz, sacred mountain used for Chamula rainmaking ritual
27. Oshyoket, sacred mountain overlooking valley of Zinacantan
28. Calvario San Juan, sacred mountain near Chamula Ceremonial Center
29. Calvario San Pedro, sacred mountain near Chamula Ceremonial Center
30. Teopisca, Ladino town on Pan-American Highway toward Comitán
31. Calvario San Sebastián, sacred mountain near Chamula Ceremonial Center
32. San Cristóbal Mountains, separating *municipios* of San Cristóbal and Chamula
33. Zinacantán Mountains, separating Zinacantán Ceremonial Center from Pan-American Highway
34. Chamula Boundary
35. Sacred waterhole for Chamula barrios of San Pedro and San Sebastián
36. Sacred waterhole for Chamula barrio of San Juan
37. Na Chih, hamlet of Zinacantán located on Pan-American Highway
38. Nabenchauk, hamlet of Zinacantán located on Pan-American Highway
39. Mispia, sacred mountain used for Chamula and dwelling place of patron saint San Juan, Earth Gods, and Chamula soul animals
40. Tzontevitz, sacred mountain in Chamula and dwelling place of patron saint San Juan, Earth Gods, and Chamula soul animals
41. Ojovitz, sacred mountain in Chamula and home of Earth Gods

Introduction

GLOBALIZATION AND THE "END OF HISTORY"

The opening of the twenty-first century has produced a flood of commentaries from around the world that attempt to place contemporary humanity in the flow of history. Some of this commentary is positive, focusing on new technology in aerospace, communication, transportation, and medicine that has contributed to the globalization of humankind. With the exception of current self-assigned outliers such as Afghanistan, modern nations generally agree that applied science has improved the lot of most people—or at least has that potential—so that one can perhaps actually speak of *progress,* both achieved and achievable.

The recent end of the Cold War between 1988 and 1992 provided an intense—albeit brief—moment of euphoria that contributed to a sense of universal progress. Some were led to believe at that time that not only material and physical well-being but also political, social, and economic forms might follow a pattern of increasing, progressive homogenization and globalization. Perhaps the Enlightenment program of universal human progress through liberal democratic institutions, individualism, and philosophical rationalism would truly win the day. Western ideas would cover the globe, facilitating what Francis Fukuyama calls the "end of history."

Things have not turned out that way. As Stanley Tambiah (1996), John Comaroff (1996), Samuel Huntington (1996), and others have noted, what appears to be going on today is more complex. We are witnessing not only the terminal phase of empires but also the accelerated demise of the very idea of the modern nation-state. However, the virtual disappearance of empires and the weakening of the idea of the nation-state in our time have not erased boundaries within and between human communities, nor, in any sense, have the forces of globalization homogenized the collective memories of diverse communities. Indeed, ethnic and religious identities and pragmatic geopolitical alliances that further ethnic interests seem to be the contemporary units of belonging. Old ethnic affirmations and religious affiliations that were suppressed by the colonial era—and, more recently, by the Cold War hegemonies of East and West—have found a window of opportunity for free expression. Furthermore, the fading of the rigid ideologies of the Cold War has provided an opening for the creation of many new ethnic identities and religious expressions, including recombinations of older forms. Some of these ethnic groups and coreligionists have sought forms of judicial and institutional autonomy from the states under whose sovereignty they happen to live; some have chosen to find new homes; some seek for themselves the same land and resources that others also claim as their own—a scenario that has the potential to produce prolonged civil conflict, spanning many generations.

The many variations on these themes include the following general patterns, among others: large-scale voluntary emigration the Soviet Jews; large-scale forced emigration (Kosovo Muslims, and—months later, in the same place—Serbian Eastern Orthodox Christians); wholesale extermination (the Central African states of Burundi and Rwanda); balkanization and segmentation (the former Yugoslavia and the former Soviet Union); ongoing civil war (Sri Lanka, East Timor, and Chechnya); formation of binational and transnational legal identities (Mexican, Dominican, and Puerto Rican links to the United States); new pan-national ethnic alliances (ethnic groups whose members live under different national sovereignties but share common roots, related languages, and common goals, as the Mayas of Guatemala and Mexico and the Kurds of Turkey, Iraq, and Iran); and the emerging model of states as federations of ethnic nations (Canada and South Africa). The United States is the biggest and most influential immigrant nation on earth, yet it faces the dilemma of becoming a pluralistic society while offering a national idea with which its many demographic and ethnic components can identify.

Globalization has gone and will go only so far. Culture, language, ethnic identity, and religion matter a great deal today, just as they always have. Boundaries are part of the human condition. As Clifford Geertz has noted, to be human is not to be a generic "everyman" (1963). With the exception of those who are truly multilingual and multicultural, we become fully functioning adult members of our species only by fulfilling the expectations of a particular culture. Our humanity is dependent on being in a particular place, at a particular time, using the medium of a particular language. All of us bear this burden and partake of its pleasure and pain.

With the convergence in our time of the opposing forces of globalization on the one hand and cultural boundaries on the other, both conflicts and new opportunities are inevitable. Modern Mexico, under whose sovereignty the Chamula Tzotzils—the modern Maya people who are the subject of this book—live, is a case in point.

SAN JUAN CHAMULA

San Juan Chamula is a contemporary Maya community, one of hundreds that thrive today in the Mexican states of Yucatan, Quintana Roo, and Chiapas and in Guatemala and Belize (see maps 1 and 2).

Contemporary Chamula lifestyles span an enormous spectrum that defies easy generalization. Thousands of Chamulas still live in San Juan Chamula, the home *municipio*, as isolated subsistence farmers whose daily round bears some resemblance to older native customs of Maya origin. Other thousands live in emigrant agrarian colonies of various types that are scattered all over the state of Chiapas; these communities find themselves in various states of social change, from conservative ones like Chamula to pragmatic settlements trying to find tolerable modes of coexistence with ethnically diverse new neighbors. Still others live as impoverished suburban dwellers and Protestant exiles in burgeoning colonies around the Mexican trade center of San Cristóbal de las Casas. A few have become wealthy entrepreneurs, specializing in the orange and potato trade. Other hundreds of Chamulas have found their way to the United States as both legal and illegal immigrants.[1]

For a casual modern visitor, Mexican or foreign, the town center of San Juan Chamula has all the trappings of an isolated Indian village that has suddenly met the modern world. There are video-game parlors, banks, stores, schools, clinics, electric lights, potable water sources, two-story homes, many blocks of paved streets, souvenir shops, and so forth. Only twenty-five years ago, the town center had but two gravel-topped access roads, dirt paths, illumination by oil lamps, and a permanent population of perhaps four hundred; it is now a modern Mexican town of three thousand. However, looks are deceiving. San Juan Chamula remains an ethnically homogeneous place with an aggressive and, so far, successful strategy for staying that way. Tourists are charged admission fees and are carefully monitored with regard to photographic privileges and freedom of movement. Mexican mestizos and tourists abound by the thousands on feast days; they are conspicuously absent at other times. San Juan Chamula remains a profoundly Indian place.

How and why is this the case? Although the issues of ethnic continuity and change in indigenous communities in Mesoamerica are a favorite topic in anthropological literature (Chambers and Young 1979), storytelling is seldom mentioned as either an expression or a cause of identity formation and affirmation. Notable exceptions to this generalization do exist—such as Victoria R. Bricker (1981), Allan F. Burns (1983), James M. Taggart (1983), and Dennis Tedlock (1993)—but storytelling is often assigned a supporting role in explaining something else, or the stories are left to speak for themselves as freestanding texts. This is a naive omission, for narrative is fundamental to the creation and re-creation of the Chamula Tzotzil universe(s) in our time. Countless place-names, things, beings, events, and individual people have, according to Tzotil premises, their "secret" (*smelol*)—that is, some formative attribute that is not apparent on the surface of things. This hidden attribute almost always implies a story that lies behind the apparent reality. Dennis Tedlock has identified this opaqueness of reality—"breath on the mirror"—as a centrally important epistemological principle, for both the ancient and contemporary K'iche'

Mayas, as their lives are expressed in the *Popol Vuh* and in modern storytelling (1993). This principle of the opaqueness of reality also has almost countless expressions in contemporary Tzotzil Maya life. The stories-behind-stories range from the seldom spoken, yet often dreamed, accounts of the wanderings of people's individual animal soul companions to the great mysteries of the bodies and deeds of deities, whose presence is revealed to us only through their radiance, our images of them, and physical evidence of their good or ill will. For all of this spectrum, from the individual to the cosmos, stories amplify and deepen apparent reality, even as they inevitably distort and reinvent it.

The narrative chain—stories within stories—has its maximum density in the sacred space of the Chamula Ceremonial Center. Everything started there. From this point of orientation, the center of the universe, the "true people" (*batz'i viniketik*), speaking the "true language" (*batz'i k'op,* as their dialect of Tzotzil is called), trace their deepest genealogical roots and reckon the origins of time and space (see maps 3 and 4). This is also the original—if perhaps no longer the central—source of cultural identity in the diaspora communities that are now found all over the state of Chiapas. The latent forces (and hence, the narratives) that have underwritten these many expressions of Tzotzil identity today have multiplied to include many new outside players and identities—new Others. The new "secrets" (latent, causal forces that lie beneath the apparent reality) now include Protestant missionaries, the Mexican State, NAFTA, the Zapatistas, and numerous expressions of pan-Indian consciousness. However, the narratives that bring these new realities to life and practice are woven on the warp of very old and local ideas. The words—"true ancient words" and "true recent words," as ancient and modern history are rendered in Tzotzil—allow us to approach an understanding of how Chamula Tzotzils think and act in contemporary history.

THE FORMATION OF TZOTZIL LITERATURE IN OUR TIME

Thanks to the efforts of many, including the Tzotzils themselves, their sacred narratives, oral literature, and oral history rank today as one of the best-documented Native American testimonies in the Americas. This emergence is extraordinary in that it has occurred in a single generation. In particular, the Harvard Chiapas Project (1957–1990), founded by Evon Z. Vogt, was responsible for recruiting and supporting a large staff of fieldworkers deeply interested in language and literature. Among this group were Nicholas Colby, Robert Laughlin, John Haviland, Victoria R. Bricker, Jan Rus, and I.[2] Laughlin and several collaborators have published several major collections of Tzotzil narrative and other verbal art forms from Zinacantán (Laughlin 1977, 1980; Karasik 1988; Blaffer 1992). Haviland (1977) and Bricker (1973) have also made major contributions to the documentation of Tzotzil verbal art as it is found in Zinacantán. The present collection of narratives from the Zinacantecos' next-door neighbors, the Chamulas, is an addition to the permanent archive of the Chiapas Highland Maya people's observations and chronicles of their lives and imaginations.

Beyond my personal reasons, larger ethical and political motives for bringing this project to fruition have become ever more important to me over the years, particularly because the decade of the 1990s has produced, in Chiapas, the first known florescence of Maya literary art in 450 years, created by Maya writers themselves (see Laughlin 1994; Breslin 1992; Craig and Everton 1993). A comparable and vigorous florescence in modern Maya literature is also occurring in Guatemala (see Gossen 1996; Warren 1998). Obviously, if literacy in Indian languages is stated as a goal by the Tzotzil and other Maya communities, there must be something to read. Equally important is the demonstration effect. Existing models of Maya literature may serve to inspire future literary creation by native people. Prior to the present generation of literary activity, the only reading materials widely available in Tzotzil were biblical translations, religious tracts, and elementary pedagogical materials. The goals of these texts were, of course, pragmatic ones, aimed at programed social change—evangelical on the one hand and acculturative on the other, as teaching of literacy with Indian-language syllabaries always gave way to the teaching of literacy in Spanish. Native-language literature as an expression and celebration of Indian identity was not part of the state or church agenda (Gossen 1999: 77–104).

However, times are changing. I have borne in mind over the years that major published collections of folklore from peasant societies of Europe in the nineteenth and twentieth centuries eventually came to be regarded as centrally important documents for the legitimation and promotion of nations and national goals. The brothers Jacob and Wilhelm Grimm, folklorists and philologists, labored in the early 1800s to present German fairytales as important testimonies to the particular native roots of that nation's soul, as in *Household Tales* (Grimm 1962) and *Teutonic Mythology* (Grimm 1999). Artists such as Richard Wagner and a number of unsavory politicians, including Adolf Hitler, exploited these themes throughout the last and present centuries in their quest to exalt Teutonic identity and superiority. Elias Lönnrot, a Swedish folklorist, was commissioned by Finland in the 1830s to collect and synthesize stories of that nation's ancient history from diverse oral testimonies that still lived vigorously among the country people at that time. Lönnrot's synthetic work, *The Kalevala* (1963) became nothing less than Finland's national epic.

The turn of the twentieth century has seen no abatement of this pattern. Major folklore collections continue to serve nationalistic purposes. Although sometimes conceived and presented as little more than collections of antiquities, published compendia of national oral traditions have often come to serve as charters for the sovereignty and autonomy of nations and ethnic groups—particularly those whose destinies are being asserted, reasserted, or threatened or are otherwise in flux. Three cases that are fairly close to home illustrate this point. Mexico has virtually reinvented itself in the twentieth century as Revolutionary Mexico on the foundation of revitalized and vigorously celebrated popular art forms, both Indian and mestizo, including verbal and plastic arts as well as music and dance (see Gossen 1996). Ireland is another case in point. The turn of the twentieth century was a particularly turbulent time for the soon-to-be Republic of Ireland. Its claim to independence from Great Britain, granted in 1922 after a terribly violent decade, was underwritten by both aesthetic documents and dramatic political action. William Butler Yeats, the giant of the twentieth-century Irish Renaissance in the arts, championed the Irish independence movement using Irish traditional folklore as the principal source of his aesthetic creation and as an inspiration for his nationalistic cause.[3] In Spain the great ballad scholar Ramón Menéndez Pidal labored through the discouraging decades of the twentieth century—a period that saw the total demise as Spain as a colonial power after 1898, the abortive Republican era of the 1930s, and three decades of Franco's authoritarian rule in the 1930s to 1960s—to produce, for the first time ever, a full synthesis, from a myriad of oral sources, of the national epic, *El Poema del Mio Cid* (1963). Some of the same circumstances—particularly, the short-lived optimism of Republican Spain—saw the rise and short, brilliant career of Spain's greatest twentieth-century literary giant, Federico García Lorca, whose poetry and drama depended heavily on themes and styles drawn from Spanish folklore.

Thus, it is no exaggeration to state that periods of rapid social change and political flux at the national level, combined with nostalgic and utopian desires for ethnic affirmation, have been closely associated with the appearance of major collections of folklore. Some of these collections, in their time or later on, have assumed considerable ideological and political importance. The great K'iche' epic, the *Popol Vuh*, originally a hieroglyphic book, was set down for posterity in a bilingual K'iche' and Spanish manuscript in Latin characters in the 1550s, at a time in which it was clear that the world it represented—the precontact K'iche' kingdom—was doomed. For many contemporary Native Americans, however, this book has become a kind of New World Bible, of as much importance today—bearing memory and desire—as it possessed in sixteenth-century Guatemala. The great Native American scholar Vine Deloria, Jr., author of the disconcerting but influential *Custer Died for Your Sins* (1969), stated on the back cover of Dennis Tedlock's 1985 translation of the *Popol Vuh* that "it will help the *Popol Vuh* to achieve its rightful place as a masterpiece of religious writing, familiar to all those who seek a message that transcends ordinary concerns."

It is not irrelevant to remember that the book of Genesis is believed to have been set down as a written text in the centuries that followed the fall of the First Temple and the reign of King David. As Stephen Mitchell has pointed out (1996:

xxvii–xxix), the Hebrew state was striving to salvage and reinvent itself, and the compendium of texts of diverse origin that comprise Genesis was part of this enterprise of ethnic affirmation in a time of political and social uncertainty.

☩ ☩ ☩

Here, then, is a glorious account—often reverent, sometimes obscene, wildly funny, or contemplative, at times redundant, but always colorful—of the history of the human experience as related by a group of storytellers in San Juan Chamula, Chiapas, Mexico. What follows amounts to more than just a collection of stories. It is a contemporary Maya account of the many and varied wonders of humankind in the course of the four sequential creations, destructions, and restorations, including the present era, in which all of us—for better or worse—find ourselves today.

FIGURE I

"Let the heavens be," said Our Father Sun in Heaven.

Quickly, the heavens appeared.

The First Creation

1

1 loˀil yuˀun jtotik ta vinajel.

2 veno ti jtotik ta vinajele,
ˀaˀ la la spas li vinajele.
nakal toˀox la ta banumil ti k'alal la smeltzan ti vinajele, ti k'anale,
ti banumile.

3 meltzajan vinajel xi la ti jtotike.
jlikel la meltzaj ti vinajele.

4 veno meltzajan ˀestreya xi la ti jtotike.
jlikel la meltzaj ti k'anale.
chijil xa la ta ˀora.

5 meltzajan banumil xi la ti jtotike.
jlikel la meltzaj ti banumile.

6 pera ˀaˀ la baˀyel meltzaj ti vinajele.
ta xchibal la smeltzan k'anal.
ta yoxibal la smeltzan banumile.

7 pero nakal toˀox la ta banumil ti jtotik xchiˀuk smeˀe.
ta k'un to muy k'alal meltzaj ti vinajele.

8 veno li jtotik ta xlok' talel jujun k'ak'ale.
maˀuk jxalik,
riox totik sbi.

TEXT I

Of Our Father Sun in Heaven

Mateo Méndez Tzotzek

Here is a story of Our Father Sun in Heaven. 1

So, now. It was Our Father Sun in Heaven, 2
It was he who made the sky.
He was still living on the earth when he made the sky, the stars,
and the earth.

"Let the heavens be," said Our Father Sun in Heaven. 3
Quickly, the heavens appeared.

"Good, then, let there be stars," said Our Father Sun in Heaven. 4
Quickly, the stars appeared.
In no time at all, they shone brightly.

"Let the earth be," declared Our Father Sun in Heaven. 5
Quickly, the earth came forth.

But first the heavens appeared. 6
He made the stars second.
He made the earth third.

But at that time Our Father still lived on earth with his mother. 7
Afterward, he rose to live there himself, once the heavens were in place.

So it is that Our Father in Heaven comes out every day. 8
However, Our Father, the sun whom we see, is not really Salvador, that is,
the Savior,
The one who is also known as God the Father.[1]

9 ti mero jxalike te nakal ta yoxkajal vinajel.
mu xkiltik ta mas ʔak'ol ʔoy.

10 ʔaʔ li ta xlok' talel jujun k'ak'ale,
riʔox totil sbi.

11 te nakal ta sba kajal vinajel.
ʔaʔ chisk'elotik jujun k'ak'al xchiʔuk smeʔ
ta xchaʔkajal te nakal k'analetik.
ta yoxkajale ʔaʔ te nakal ti jtotik san salvarole.
pero mu xkiltik.

12 pero ti jtotik ta vinajele jun noʔox.
xchiʔuk jun jch'ulmeʔtik.
ʔaʔ noʔox.

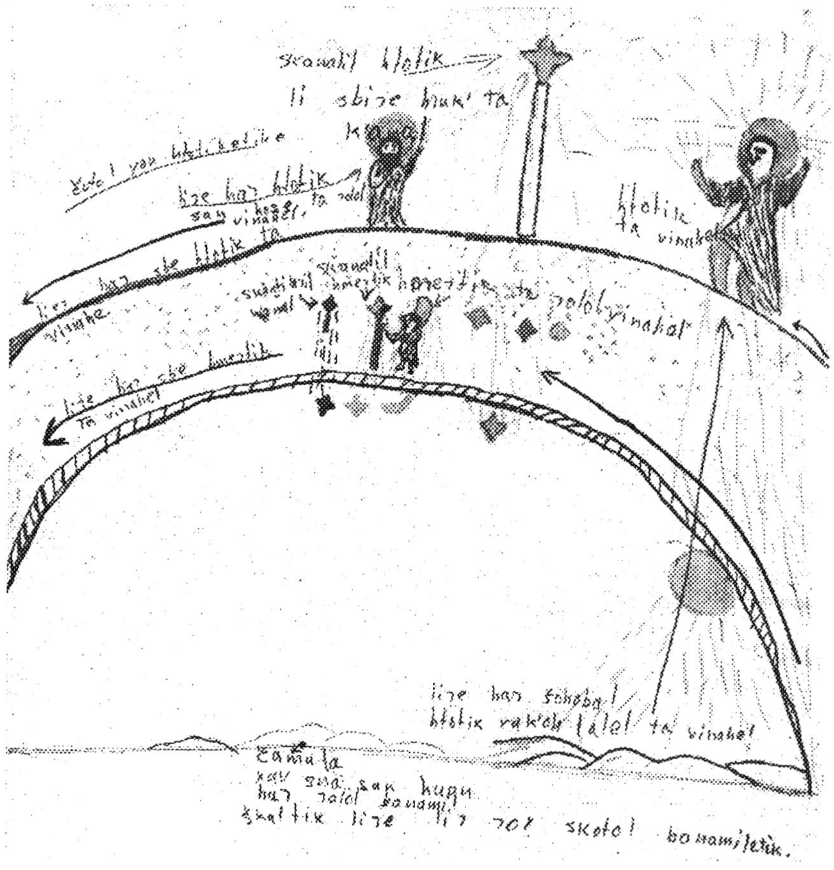

The true Salvador, that is, the Savior, lives there on the third layer of the sky. 9
We are not able to see his true image, for he is above and beyond our
perception.[2]

His image appears every day as the sun. 10
He is called God the Father.

He lives there on the first layer of the heavens. 11
He watches over us every day in the company of his mother.
On the second layer of the heavens live the stars.
On the third layer of the heavens lives Our Father San Salvador,
the Savior, whom we see as the sun.
But what we are able to see of him is not a full image.

For there is but one Holy Father in the heavens, 12
With but one Holy Mother.
They alone, none other.

FIGURE 2

The true Salvador, that is, the Savior, lives there on the third layer
of the sky.
We are not able to see his true image, for he is above and
beyond our perception.

1 jun kuento ta voʔne . . .
ʔoy jun mol ta xloʔilaj.

2 ʔa ti k'alal lik sloʔil ti mole,
yuʔun ʔo te muk'ta ʔuk'um ta stz'el na.

3 ti yoʔ lik yal sloʔile,
yuʔun noj tal ti ʔuk'ume.

4 jech ti mole xiʔ tajmek ti mole k'alal la ti noj ti ʔuk'ume.
ʔentonse jech'o la xal ti yoʔ lik yal sloʔile ti mole.

5 ʔay ta xnoj ti ʔuk'ume jlikel chijnojutik ta ʔora ta ʔuk'um xi.
jaʔ la jech toʔox voʔnee xi ti mole ta sloʔilaj ta k'ixin ʔosil ti mole.
jaʔ jech la jyalbun kaʔi ti ʔanima jmuk'tote xi ti mole.

6. ʔa ti voʔnee ch'abal toʔox la sbe ti ʔuk'umetike.
jech noʔox la tanijem ta banamil ti ʔuk'umetike.

7 jech la ti kirsanoetike ta la xnojik ta nab,
ti jnaklej ti voʔnee.

8 ʔentonse la la snop ti jtotik ta vinajele.
yuʔun puru la nab ti banamil chile.

9 ʔa pere k'usi ta xkut li nabe xi la ti jtotike.
ʔentonse la la sjak'be sbaik xchiʔuk ti ʔanjeletike.

10 pere mi xak'ane ta jpastik sbe li ʔuk'ume.
xut la sbaik xchiʔuk ti anjeletike.

TEXT 2

Let Us Make Pathways for the Rivers

Manuel López Calixto

Here is a story of long ago . . . 1
Here speaks an old man.

When the old man started to talk, 2
It was because there was a large river near his house.

That is why he started to tell his tale, 3
For the river was beginning to flood.

It seems that the old man was scared when he saw the river rising. 4
That is why the old man started to tell his story.

"Ay, if the river rises, we'll drown in the river in no time," he said. 5
"Things were just like this long ago," said the old man when he was talking in Hot Country.
"So my late grandfather told me," said the old man.

"Long ago there were still no pathways for the rivers. 6
The rivers were just spread out over the earth.

The people were just drowning in the great lake, 7
Those who lived long ago.

Then Our Holy Father Sun in Heaven thought about things. 8
For he saw that the earth was nothing but a great lake.

'Ay, but what shall I do with this great lake?' asked Our Holy Father. 9
Then he consulted with the Earth Lords.[1]

'Perhaps you want us to make pathways for the rivers?' suggested the Earth Lords. 10
So they discussed it together, Our Holy Father and the Earth Lords.

11 veno lek ˀoy xi la ti ˀanjele.
la la skomon nopik ti k'u la xi ta xkom sbe ti ˀuk'ume.
entonse koˀol la la snopik xchiˀuk ti jtotik ta vinajele ti anjele.

12 pere mi xak'ane jaˀ chajom be yok ˀanae xi la ti jtotik ta vinajele.
jech la ti ˀanjeletike jlikel ta xch'unbik smantal ti jtotik ta vinajele.

13 ˀentonse jlikel la sjombik sbe ti ˀuk'ume.
k'alal la meltzaj sbe ti ˀuk'ume jlikel la ˀul ti nabe.

14 ˀentonse k'ot la ti jtotik ta vinajele ta yok'omale.
mi meltzaj xa ˀavuˀunik xi la k'otel ti jtotik ta vinajele.

15 k'ot la sk'opon sbaik xchiˀuk ti anjeletike.
veno lek xa ˀoy ˀun xut la sbaik.

16 veno jech xa me ta xkom ˀo kuˀuntik li sbe ˀoˀetike,
xi la komel ti jtotik ta vinajele.

17 veno xi la ti ˀanjeletike.
veno jechun ˀek ˀun.

18 ta xˀech' kules li nab ˀeke xi la ti jtotik ta vinajele.
k'alal mi lilok' talele ta xˀech' kules ti nabe xi la.
k'alal mi liyal ˀele ta xˀech' kules li nab ta maleb k'ak'ale xi la ti jch'ultotike.
ˀentonse mu xa snoj ti nab ti banamile.

19 jaˀ mas lek jaˀ jech ta jnoptik.
xut la sbaik xchiˀuk la ti ˀanjele ti jtotik la ta vinajele.

20 ˀentonse jaˀ la me jech kom sbe ti ˀuk'um voˀnee xi ti mole.
jech'o me la xal ti yoˀ la ˀoy li yochobe.
yuˀun sbe la me ˀuk'um xi.

'It's a good plan,' said the Earth Lords. 11
Together they agreed on where to put the pathways of the rivers.
So it was that Our Father Sun in Heaven and the Earth Lords
were of one mind.

'Do you want to open the way at the foot of your houses? 12
asked Our Father Sun in Heaven.[2]
And with that, the Earth Lords did the bidding of
Our Father Sun in Heaven.

Quickly they scooped out the pathways of the rivers. 13
When the riverbeds were set in order the great lake
quickly began to shrink.

Then Our Father Sun in Heaven arrived on the following day. 14
'Have you done your part?' asked Our Father in Heaven when he arrived.

He came to talk to the Earth Lords. 15
'It looks as though things are in good shape,' he declared
as they spoke together.

'We shall have the riverbeds just like this,' 16
So Our Father Sun in Heaven spoke.

'All right,' said the Earth Lords. 17
'That's fine with us, too.'

'For my part, I shall move to dry up the seas,' said Our Father Sun in Heaven 18
'When I rise, I shall cause the Sea of the Rising Sun to dry up,' he said.
'When I set, I shall cause the Sea of Setting Sun to dry up,'
said Our Holy Father.
'Then the earth will no longer be covered by the sea.[3]

It is a good thing that we are thinking along these lines.' 19
So they discussed it, Our Father Sun in Heaven and the Earth Lords.

So it was that the riverbeds were left that way long ago," said the old man. 20
"'That's why there are sinkholes.
They, too, are the pathways of the rivers," he said.[4]

21 ti yoˀ la mu xnoj ta ˀoˀ ti banamile xi ti mole.
jech'o la xal ti mu la bu ta xnoj ti nabe.

22 yuˀun ta la xˀul jujun k'ak'al li nabe xi ti mole.
k'alal la mi lik' talel ti jtotike ta xˀech' yules ti nabe.
k'alal la mi bat ti jtotike ta la xˀech' yules ti bu la ta xyal ti jtotike.

23 yuˀun ˀoy la nab ta slok'eb k'ak'al.
yuˀun ˀoy la nab ta maleb k'ak'al xi ti mole.

24 pere mu jnaˀtik sjayibal xa ˀavil xi ti mole.
jech'o la me xal ti yoˀ la ˀoy sbe ˀuk'umetike.
pere yuˀun ta la xˀul ti bu ta xk'ote xi ti mole.

25 jtotik lae xchiˀuk la ˀanjeletik la snopik.
ˀentonse ˀak'o la mi xnoj ti ˀuk'ume pere yuˀun ta la xˀul
ti bu ta xk'ote xi ti mole.

26 ˀentonse ˀak'o la mi xnoj ti nabe pero mu xa la xnoj.
mu xavil yuˀun ta la xˀul ti bu la ta xk'ot ta muk'ta nabe.

27 jech ti nabe jaˀ la ti bu la ta xch'ay ti jtotike.
pere jaˀ la ti ta nome xi ti mole.
mu jnaˀtik bu ˀoy ti nabe xi.

28 ˀa pere ˀoˀon xkale mu ta yok vinajel xa xi ti mole.
jaˀ ti bu ta xyal ti jtotike.

29 jech'o xal ti yoˀ la ta xˀul ti nabe.
naˀ mu ta xlajeb xa banamil xi ti mol voˀnee.

"That is why the earth is not covered with water," said the old man. 21
"That is why the sea does not flood.

It is because the sea dries up every day," said the old man. 22
"When Our Father Sun rises, he dries up the sea.
"When Our Father Sun sets, he dries up the other sea
there where he goes down.

For there is a Sea of the Rising Sun. 23
There is also a Sea of the Setting Sun," said the old man.

"Who knows how many years ago all of this happened?" 24
exclaimed the old man.
"But this was the reason why the rivers came to have their pathways;
Only to dry up once they reach the sea," said the old man.

"Our Father planned this with the Earth Lords. 25
So it is that although the rivers become flooded, they are destined to
dry up once they reach their appointed place," said the old man.

"So, therefore, although the seas fill up, they do not flood. 26
Don't you see that it is because water dries up when it reaches
the great sea?

This is what it's like, this sea where Our Father Sun in Heaven goes down. 27
But it's very far away," said the old man.
"We don't really know where it is," he said.

"But I think it is at the foot of the sky," said the old man. 28
"That is where Our Father Sun goes down into the underworld.

So much for why the sea dries up. 29
Perhaps these things happen at the very place where the earth
ceases to be," said the old man.[5]

1 jun kuento k'uxi lik ti banomil ti voˀnee.
veno ˀa ti voˀne lae ch'abal toˀox la jech ˀoy banamil chak k'uchaˀal ta ˀora.

2 puru toˀox la nab ti voˀnee.
muˀyuk la kirsano.

3 veno lik la snop ti jtotike
pero liˀe mu xch'i kalab jnich'nab ma ta ba nabe xi la ti jtotike.

4 jaˀ lek ta jbek' ˀech'el ma nabe xi la ti jtotike.
moˀoje muˀyuk k'usi xch'i.

5 kalab,
jnich'nab xi la ti jtotike.

6 lik la sbek' batel ti nabe.
k'alal la ti la sbek' batel ti nab ta jujot xokon banomile.

7 puru xa la banomil kom ta ˀora,
pero puru la stenlej.

8 muˀyuk la vitzetik,
muˀyuk la kirsano,
muˀyuk la ton,
muˀyuk ta teˀetik.
puru la batz'i banomil.

TEXT 3

Of How the World Began Long Ago

Xum Méndez Tzotzek

Here is a story of how the world began long ago. 1
How, in olden times, the world was not at all like it is today.

Long ago, there were only seas. 2
There were no people.

Well, Our Father started to think about it: 3
"My children, my offspring, could never thrive here on top of the sea,"
reflected Our Father.

"It would be better for me to sweep away the sea," said Our Father. 4
"If I don't, nothing will thrive,

Neither my children, 5
Nor my offspring," declared Our Father.

He proceeded to sweep away the sea. 6
When he had swept away the sea, there remained empty land
on all sides of the earth.

There remained nothing but land 7
But it was very flat.

There were no mountains, 8
No people,
No rocks,
No trees.
Only the earth itself, nothing more.

9 pero bu ta jtabe tal stz'unobal ti kalab jnich'nabe si la ti jtotike.
pero k'usi ma xkut xi la ti jtotike.

10 lik la sjoc' ˀach'el.
k'alal la ti la sjoc' ti ˀach'ele lik la spat ti ˀach'ele.

11 lik la spasbe shol,
lik la yak'be sat.

12 lik la yak'be sk'ob,
lik la yak'be yok.

13 veno k'alal la ti la slok'ta,
chak munyeka ti ˀach'ele.

✠ ✠ ✠

14 lik la smeltzan ta banomil.
k'alal la ti la smeltzan ta banomil ti munyeka ˀach'ele sk'el la yil mi ta xbak'.

15 jaˀ to la yil mu la xbak'.
staoj ˀo la yav ta metzel ti munyeca ˀach'ele.

16 lik la svaˀan ta la sk'el yil mi ta xanav.
jaˀ to la yil staoj ˀo la yav te vaˀal.
mu la xanav.

17 pero k'usi xkut tajmekˀ xi la ti jtotike.
veno lik la snop.

18 jaˀ lek ta jpetkik xi la ti jtotike.
veno lik la spet ti munyeka ˀach'ele.

19 k'alal la ti te spetoj ti munyeka ˀach'ele lik la sjuch' taˀox.
juch' taˀel.

20 k'alal la ti la sjuch' taˀox juch' taˀele.
lik la k'opojuk.

"But where shall I find the seed for my children, my offspring?" 9
wondered Our Father.
"Whatever shall I do?" said Our Father.

He began to dig up some clay. 10
When he had dug up the clay, he started to mold the clay.

He started to make its head, 11
He started to give it a face.

He started to give it hands, 12
He started to put on its feet.

Well, when he had fashioned it, 13
This clay was in the form of a doll.

☩ ☩ ☩

Our Father started to make the earth ready. 14
As he was preparing the land, he watched the doll to see if it moved.

When he saw that it did not move, 15
He went there to the place where the clay doll was lying.

He stood it upright and watched to see if it could walk. 16
Finally, he saw that it remained standing there where he found it.
It was not walking at all.

"But whatever am I going to do about this?" asked Our Father. 17
So he started to think about it.

"I had better take it in my arms," said Our Father. 18
So he proceeded to lift the clay doll into his arms.

When he had taken the clay doll into his arms, he started to rub it. 19
He kept on kneading it.

Once he had kneaded it, he did it again and again. 20
Then it started to speak.

21 lik la pasuk ta bek'et ti ʔach'el toʔoxe.
lik la ʔayanuk xch'ich'el.
lik la ʔayanuk sbakik.

22 k'alal la ti yil ta xk'opoje,
lik la chaʔvaʔan ta la sk'el yil mi ta xanav.

23 yil mu la xanav.
staoj ʔo la yav te vaʔal ʔo.

24 lik la xchaʔmeltzan.
ta la sk'el yil mi ta la xlik.

25 jaʔ to la yil mu la xlik.
staoj ʔo la yav te metzel ʔo ta lumtik.

26 pero k'usi van chkut tajmek xlik xanavuk xlik bak'ukʔ xi la ti jtotike.
jaʔ lek ta jbojkik ta ʔek'el xi la ti jtotike.

27 lik la sbojta ta ʔek'el.
lik la sbasolan ta ʔek'el.
sjunul sbek'tal ti ʔach'el toʔox pas ta viniketike.

28 k'alal la ti la sbasolanbe ta ʔek'el sjunul sbek'tal ti vinike,
jaʔ to la lik bak'uk,
jaʔ to la lik xanavuk,
jaʔ to la lik ʔayanuk stzakalul sbakil.

29 k'alal la ti ʔayan stzakalul ti sbakile,
k'alal la ti pas ta vinike.
k'alal la pas ta kirsano ti ʔach'el toʔoxe.

30 veno lik la snop ti jtotike.
pero k'usi van xkak'be xveʔ xi la ti jtotike.

31 ta la xviʔnah ti vinike.
ta la xveʔ yaʔi.

That which had been clay turned into flesh. 21
Its blood started to form.
Its bones started to form.

When he saw that it could speak, 22
He proceeded to stand it up again to see if it could walk.

Then he saw that it did not walk. 23
He found it standing there in the same place.

He began to remake it. 24
He watched to see if it got up.

Then he saw that it did not get up. 25
He found it in the same place, lying there on the ground.

"But how can I get it to start walking, to start moving?" asked Our Father. 26
"I had better shape it with an axe," said Our Father.

He began to shape it with an axe. 27
He began to hew its fine details with an axe.
And its whole body, which had still been of clay, turned into a man.

Then, when he had sculpted its fine details with an axe, 28
It then began to move,
It then started to walk,
Its whole skeleton started to take shape.

When all the bones came together, 29
Then it turned into a human being.
It was then that that which had been clay turned into a man.

Well, Our Father began to consider things. 30
"Whatever shall I give him to eat?" asked Our Father.

He was hungry. 31
He wanted to eat.

32 pero k'usi van ta skak'beˀ
yipan tajmek xi la ti jtotike.

33 nop la tajmek.
lik la yak'be lum.
spak'be la ta stiˀil ye ti vinike.

34 jaˀ to la yil mu la sk'an slek' ˀochel ta yok' ti lume.
te la pak'al ˀo ta stiˀil ye ti vinike.

35 pero k'usi ta xkak'beˀ
yipan xi la ti jtotike.

36 st'olbe la lok'el ti lum ta stiˀil ye ti vinike.
lik la stul vomol.

37 spak'be la ta stiˀil ye ti vinike.
mu la sk'an slek' ˀochel ta yok'.

38 pero k'usi van ta xkak'be xveˀ tajmek xi la ti jtotike.
te la vaˀal ta snop.

39 pero k'usi ta xkak'be tajmek xveˀ xi la ti jtotike.
lik la snop.

40 lik la st'ol lok'el juteb sbek'tal.
spak'be la ta stiˀil ye ti vinike.

41 k'alal la ti la spak'be sbek'tal ta stiˀil ye ti vinike,
jlikel la ˀi slek' ˀochel ta yok sbek'tal ti jtotike.

42 k'alal la yil ti jtotik jlikel slek' ochel yok' sbek'tal ti jtotike:
ˀa . . . pero mi jaˀ chak'an chaveˀ li jbek'tale.
pero jaˀ to xaveˀ ti mi tzotz la ˀabteje.

43 mi xanaˀ spasbel yav ti jbek'taleˀ xi la ti jtotike.
mi xanaˀ xachaˀbahe.
mi xanaˀ xapas ˀasoke.

"But whatever shall I give him? 32
He's getting very sick," said Our Father.

He thought very hard. 33
He began by offering him dirt to eat.
He patted it on at the side of the man's mouth.

Then he saw that he didn't want to lick the dirt with his tongue. 34
There it remained, stuck by the side of the man's mouth.

"But what shall I give him? 35
He is getting sick," said Our Father.

He peeled off the dirt from the side of the man's mouth. 36
Then he began to gather grass.

He pressed it firmly onto the edges of the man's mouth. 37
But the man did not want to take it up with his tongue.

"But what on earth shall I give him to eat?" wondered Our Father. 38
He stood there, pondering this problem.

But whatever can I give him to eat?" asked Our Father. 39
He entered into deep thought.

He then started to peel off a little bit of his own body. 40
He pressed it beside the man's mouth.

When Our Father put his own body next to the man's mouth, 41
The man quickly took Our Father's body with his tongue.

When Our Father saw that he quickly took his body with his tongue, he said: 42
"Ah! Can it be that it is my body that you crave as food?
But be assured that you will not eat more of it if you do not work hard.

Do you know how to prepare a place for my body?" asked Our Father.[1] 43
"Do you know how to break the ground?
Do you know how to cut weeds?

44 jaˀ to xaveˀik xchiˀuk ˀavajnil xchiˀuk ˀanich'nab.
xuˀuk ta xiabtej xi la ti vinike.

45 veno ta jk'eltikik mi xanaˀ xˀabtej,
mi xanaˀ xavich' ta kux ti jbek'tale xi la ti jtotike.

46 tana ta xkich' ta kux xi la ti vinike.
veno ta xabat ta ˀabtel.

47 ta xkak'bot hun ˀavasarona.
ta xbat kak'tik ˀavil k'uxi chapasbe yav ti jbek'tale xi la ti jtotike.

48 k'uxi ta xachaˀbaj,
k'uxi ta xatz'un ti jbek'tale xi la ti jtotike.

49 ˀilo ˀavasarona.
chijbat kak'tik ˀavil k'uxi chapas k'alal chachaˀbahe xi la ti jtotike.

50 veno bat la yak'be yil ˀabtel ti vinik,
k'usi ta pasel yav ti sbek'tal ti jtotike.

51 k'alal la k'otik ti bu ta xich' pasbel yav ti sbek'tale,
k'ot la yak' ˀiluk k'uxi ta pasel ti yav chobtike.

52 xi xapase.
xi xavute.
xi xaloke xi la ti jtotike.
yak'be la yil chob ti vinike.

53 k'alal la xchan ti chobe:
ˀa . . . jech k'a xal ta chan ti ˀabtele xi la ti jtotike.

54 k'alal la xchan ti ˀabtele k'uxi ta pasel ti yav chobtike,
lik la yak'be yil k'uxi ta tz'unel ti chobtik ti vinike.

You will not eat until you learn this, you and your wife and children." 44
"Very well, I am willing to work," said the man.

"Well, let's see if you know how to work, 45
If you know how to honor my body," said Our Father.

"Very well. I will honor it," said the man. 46
"Good. You are going to work.

I will give you a hoe. 47
Let's go out so I can show you how you are to prepare the place for
my body," said Our Father.

"I will show you how to break the ground, 48
How to plant my body," said Our Father.

"Take a good look at your hoe. 49
I will show you how to use it when you break the ground,"
said Our Father.

With this, he proceeded to show the man how to work, 50
How to prepare the place for Our Father's body.

When they came to the place where they would prepare the place 51
or his body,
Our Father came to show him how to make the cornfield.

"This is how you do it. 52
This is how you proceed.
This is how you clear the field," said Our Father.
He showed the man all about the cornfield.

And so, when the man had learned about the cornfield, Our Father spoke: 53
"Ah, he really has learned to work," said Our Father approvingly.

And when he saw that the man had seen how to prepare the place 54
for the maizefield,
He started to show the man about sowing.

55 xi xavute,
xi xatz'une xi la ti jtotike.

56 k'alal la xchan ti tz'un chobtike,
lik la ˀak'batuk stz'unob ˀixim.

57 k'alal chatz'une,
jaˀ chatz'un ˀo liˀe xi la ti jtotike.

58 ik la ˀak'batuk hun yaventeˀ sventa la ta stz'un ˀo ti chobtike.
k'alal chatz'un ti chobtike,
jaˀ chahom ˀo li banomil liˀe xi la ti jtotike.

59 veno xi la ti vinike.
veno lik la stz'un chobtik ti vinike.

60 k'alal la ti ta xk'ot ta tz'un chobtik ti vinike:
mi lek ˀavoˀntonˀ
mi kontentotˀ xi la ti jtotike.
lek kontentoun xi la ti vinike.

61 mi chak'an ˀachiˀil xi la ti jtotike.
moˀoj xi la ti vinike.

62 veno pero k'usi xkut ta saˀbe xchiˀil xi la ti jtotike.
pero mi moˀoje muˀyuk k'usi sbol ma kalab jnich'nabe xi la ti jtotike.

63 jaˀ lek ta jsaˀbe xchiˀil.
pero mi moˀoje muˀyuk k'usi xveˀ,
muˀyuk buch'u spasbat vah xveˀ xi la ti jtotike.

64 jaˀ lek ta jsaˀtik ˀachiˀil.
moˀoje chavat ˀavoˀnton xi la ti jtotike.

65 pero bu ta jtatik xanaˀ ˀun xi la ti vinike.
moˀoj jnaˀoj xa bu xtal ma ta ˀachiˀile xi la ti jtotike.

"This is how you do it, 55
This is how you plant it," said Our Father.

And so, when he had learned about the sowing of the cornfield, 56
The seed corn was given to him.

"When you sow it, 57
You are to sow it like this," said Our Father.

And so he was given a planting stick for sowing the cornfield. 58
"When you sow the cornfield,
You are to open a hole in the ground," said Our Father.

"All right," said the man. 59
And so it was that the man started to sow his cornfield.

And when Our Father came to where the man was sowing his cornfield, 60
he asked:
"Is your heart pleased?
Are you happy?"
"I am quite happy," said the man.

"Do you want a mate?" asked Our Father. 61
"Not really," said the man.

"Well, now, how am I going to get him to look for a wife?" 62
wondered Our Father.
"If he doesn't, there will be no way for them to multiply, my children,
my offspring," said Our Father.

"It would be better for me to find a mate for him. 63
If I don't do this, he will have nothing to eat,
No one to make him his tortillas," said Our Father.

"We had better look for a wife for you. 64
If we don't, you are going to be sad," said Our Father.

"But where shall we find her? Do you know?" asked the man. 65
"Perhaps I know where your spouse will come from," said Our Father.

66 pero bu xtal xanaˀ ˀunˀ xi la ti vinike.
laˀ xi la ti jtotike.

67 xuˀuk xi la ti vinike.
ˀixtal ˀach'ilteˀ xi la ti jtotike.

68 lik la lok'esbatuk jun xch'ilteˀ ti vinike.
k'alal la ti lok'esbat ti xch'ilteˀ ti vinike,
lik la sjuch'.
ta ˀox juch' tael ti jtotike.

69 k'alal la ti la sjuch' ta ˀox.
juch' taele.

70 toj pasel la ta ˀantz ti xch'ilteˀ toˀox la vinike.
veno liˀ ne jaˀ me ˀachiˀil ˀun.

71 liˀ ne jaˀ me ta spas vaj ˀaveˀ ˀun.
liˀ ne jaˀ me ta xkom ta ˀana ˀun.
liˀ ne jaˀ me ta spas ˀak'uˀ ˀun.
liˀ ne jaˀ me ta spas ˀaveˀel ˀun.
liˀ ne jaˀ me ˀachiˀil ta vayel ˀun.
liˀ ˀune jaˀ me ˀachiˀil ta veˀel ˀun.
liˀ ne xi la ti jtotike.
veno xi la ti vinik.

72 ˀoˀot ˀune chabat ta ˀabtel.
chabat ta pasbe yav chobtik.
ta xabat ta saˀ talel siˀ sventa k'alal ta slakan ˀo panin,
sventa k'alal ta lakan o veˀlil ti ˀantze xi la ti jtotike.

73 veno ˀoˀote chabat ta ˀabtel.
xˀutat la ti vinike.

74 ˀoˀote chabat ta lup talel ˀoˀ.
xˀutat la ti ˀantze.
xi la ti jtotike.

"But where will she come from? Do you have any ideas?" asked the man. 66
"Come," said Our Father.

"All right," said the man. 67
"She is to come from your rib," said Our Father.

With this, he began to take a rib out of the man. 68
When he had taken the rib out of the man,
He started to stroke it.
Our Father kept on stroking it.

Then he stroked and stroked it. 69
Our Father kept on stroking it.

And, surely, that which had been the man's rib turned into a woman. 70
"Good, here is your mate," said Our Father.

"Here you have the one who will make tortillas for you to eat. 71
Here you have the one who will dwell in your house.
Here you have the one who will make your clothes.
Here you have the one who will make your food.
Here you have the one who will sleep with you.
Here you have the one who will share your food with you.
Here you have her," said Our Father.
"Very well," said the man.

"As for you, you will go to work," said Our Father. 72
"You are going to prepare the cornfield for sowing.
You are going to bring wood for boiling the corn,
So that your woman can cook the food," said Our Father.

"You, then, you are to go to work." 73
So it was said to the man.

"You, then, you are going to carry water." 74
So it was said to the woman.
So Our Father said.

75 xuˀuk chibat xi la ti ˀantzee.
ˀilo ˀak'ib chabat ta lup ˀo talel ti ˀoˀe xi la ti jtotike.

76. jech mi ˀo bu la sk'opon jun pukuje,
mu me xatzakbe mi ˀoy k'usi,
sayak'be ˀaloˀ ti pukuje.

77 mi moˀoje ta stub ˀalusalik.
mi moˀoje mu xa xil xˀabteh li vinike xi la ti jtotike.

78 veno mu me xach'unik k'usi xayalbik ti pukuje xi la ti jtotike.
veno xuˀuk xi la xchiˀuk vinik ti ˀantze.

79 mu la naˀik k'usi spasik xchiˀuk ti ˀantze.
mi ˀoy k'usi chapasik xi la ti jtotike.
muˀyuk k'usi ta jpaskutik xi la xchiˀuk ˀantz ti vinike.

80 veno te la ˀoyik ta xˀabtejik.
muˀyuk la mu la snaˀik k'usi ta spasik xchiˀuk ˀantz ti vinike.

81 k'usi van chkut sbolik xi la ti jtotike.
k'alal la ti te xchiˀinoh sbaik ta svayik xchiˀuk ˀantz ti vinike mu la snaˀik k'usi ta spasik.

82 k'ot la ti pukuje.
k'ot la k'oponatikuk ta pukuj xchiˀuk ˀantz ti vinike.

83 lik la sjak' ti pukuje:
ˀa leˀe mi muˀyuk k'usi chapasik xchiˀuk li ˀantze
xˀutat ti vinike.

84 muˀyuk k'usi ta jpaskutik xi la xchiˀuk ˀantz ti vinike.
ˀa . . . pero moˀoj ˀunbi.
mi moˀoj mu xabolik xi la ti pukuje.

85 pero k'usi ta jpaskutik ˀun xi la ti vinik xchiˀuk ti ˀantze.
moˀoj mi xak'ane ta xkak' ˀavil k'usi ta pasel xi la ti pukuje.

"Very well, I am willing," said the woman. 75
"Take care of your jug when you go to carry water," said Our Father.

"Also, by the way, if the Demon Pukuj should talk to you when you are out, 76
Don't take that which he has,
That which the demon offers you to eat.

Otherwise, your radiance will be put out.[2] 77
Otherwise your husband will no longer be able to see to do his work," said Our Father.

"So ignore what the Demon Pukuj tells you," said Our Father. 78
"Very well, then," replied the man and the woman.

The man and the woman did not know anything about sex. 79
"Do you know how to do anything?" asked Our Father.
"No, we have no knowledge," said the man and the woman together.[3]

Well, there they were working and trying to accomplish something. 80
But the man had no knowledge of the woman.

"Well, now. How am I going to get them to multiply?" wondered Our Father. 81
For when the man and the woman were sleeping together, they did not know what to do.

Then the demon appeared. 82
The Demon Pukuj came up to talk to the man and the woman.

The Demon Pukuj began by asking: 83
"You there, don't you and the woman know how to do anything together?"
So it was said to the man.

"We don't seem to be accomplishing anything," said the man and the woman. 84
"Oh, but that will never do.
If you don't do anything, you will not multiply," said the demon.

"But what should we do?" asked the man and the woman. 85
"If you want, I will show you what you should do," said the demon.

86 veno ˀak'bun kil k'usi ta pasel chaˀe xi la ti vinike.
veno ta xkak' ˀavil xi la ti Pukuhe.

87 puch'lan ta ˀora.
ta jpastik ˀavil k'uxi ta pasel xi la ti pukuje.

88 puch'il la ti ˀantze.
k'alal la ti puch'i ti ˀantze jlikel la muy ta ˀora ta sba ˀantz ti pukuje.

89 k'alal la ti te kajal ti pukuj ta sba ti ˀantze,
te la vaˀal sk'eloj ti vinik k'usi ta spas ti pukuje.

90 k'alal la ti laj yak' ˀat ti pukuje,
mi la ˀavil k'usi la jpase xi la ti pukuje.
laj xi la ti vinike.

91 ˀora pasoˀ ˀek ˀun.
jec xapas k'usi la jpas ˀavile xi la ti pukuje.

92 veno lik la spas ti vinike.
jech la lik spas ti k'usi la spas jech ti pukuje.

93 k'alal la ti laj spas jech ti vinik k'usi la spas ti pukuje,
lik la sjak' ti pukuje.

94 k'uxi mi lek ˀavaˀi ta paselˀ xi la ti pukuje.
ˀu . . . toj lek ta pasel tajmek xi la ti vinike.

95 veno jech chapasik ˀo ˀun jaˀ to te xabolik.
mi la chan lek spasel ti ˀantzeˀ xi la ti pukuje.
veno xi la ti vinike.

96 veno k'alal la ti la jyak' ˀiluk komel ti pukuje sut la batel.
k'alal la ti stukik xa la komik xchiˀuk ˀantz ti vinike k'ot la ti jtotike.

97 k'usi la pasik,
ta xanak' ˀabaik xi la ti jtotike.

"Fine. Show us what to do, then," said the man. 86
"Good, I am going to show you," said the demon.

"Lie down, now. 87
Let's have you see what to do," said the demon.

The woman was lying down. 88
Then, when the woman was lying down, the demon lost no time
in climbing on top of the woman.

When the Demon Pukuj topped the woman, 89
The man stood there and watched what the demon did.

Then, when the demon had finished poking in his cock, 90
The Demon Pukuj asked, "Did you see what I did?"
"I did," said the man.

"Now you do it also. 91
Do it just like I showed you," said the demon.

So, the man started to do it. 92
He proceeded to do what the demon had done.

When the man finished doing what the demon had done, 93
The demon started to ask him questions.

"How was it? Did it feel good when you did it?" asked the demon. 94
"Oh! It felt great to do it!" replied the man.

"Well, you have to keep on doing it like that until you have children. 95
Did you learn well what to do with the woman?" asked the demon.
"Yes," said the man.

Well, when the Demon Pukuj had finished giving the lesson, he went away. 96
And when the man and woman were alone, Our Father arrived.

"What were you doing? 97
Why are you hiding?" demanded Our Father.

98 ta la snak' sbaik xchiˀuk ˀantz ti vinike.
ta la xk'exavik tajmek yuˀun ti jtotike.

99 k'uchaˀal chak'exavik xi la ti jtotike.
ch'abal yuˀun ˀay jun vinik.
liˀ ˀay yalbunkutik mantal sob naxe xi la ti vinik xchiˀuk ti ˀantze.

100 k'usi ˀayalboxuk ti vinike xi la ti jtotike.
ˀayalbunkutik 'mi ˀoy k'usi chapasik' xiyutkutik vulele xi la xchiˀuk ˀantz ti vinike.

101 muˀyuk k'usi jnaˀ jpaskutik' xkutkutik ti vinike.
xi la yalbik ti jtotik ti vinik xchiˀuk ti ˀantze.

102 ˀa . . . pero maˀuk vinik.
taje pukuj ma taj ˀay ˀutilanoxuke xi la ti jtotike.

103 li yalbekutik mi muˀyuk k'usi xana xapasike mu xabolik xiyutkutike.
moˀoj jaˀ lek ta xkak' ˀavil k'uxi ta pasel xiyute xi la ti vinike.
lik yak'bun kil k'uxi ta pasel.

104 jech xapas k'uchaˀal ta jpase' xiyut ti pukuje xi la yalbe jtotik ti vinike.
jaˀ yuˀun jech laj jpaskutik jech ti k'usi la jyak'bun kil ti pukuje xi la ti vinik.
yalbik yaˀi xchiˀuk ˀantz ti jtotike.

105 veno mi jech la chanike,
stak' jech xapasik jaˀ to te xabolik xi la ti jtotike.

106 pero jaˀ noˀox ˀun ta xakalbe ˀavaˀi mu me saˀ yan ˀantz.
jaˀ noˀox sapas ˀamulik xchiˀuk li ˀantz la jkak'bot ta baˀyele xi la ti jtotike.

107 pero mu xak'opon yan ˀantz.
ti mi yuˀun la k'opon yan ˀantz k'alal ˀoy yajval te xavil k'usi xavaˀi.

The man and the woman were indeed hiding. 98
They were very ashamed in front of Our Father.

"Why are you ashamed?" asked Our Father. 99
"It's nothing, only that a stranger came here.
He came here earlier to leave us a message," said the man and the woman.

"What did the man tell you?" asked Our Father. 100
"'Are you doing anything,' he asked us when he came,"
said the man and the woman.

"'No, there is nothing that we know how to do,'" we said to the man." 101
So the man and the woman said to Our Father.

"Oh, but that wasn't a man. 102
That was that Demon Pukuj who came to torment you," said Our Father.

The man replied: "He said to us: 'If there is nothing you know how to do, 103
you will not multiply.
I'd best show you what to do,' he told us," said the man.
"So, he started to show us what to do.

'Now, you are to do what I do,' the demon said to me," the man said to 104
Our Father.
"That is why we did just what the demon showed us," said the man.
He told this to Our Father in the company of the woman.

"Well, if you learned it that way, 105
You can go on doing it until you have offspring," said Our Father.

"But I tell you, it is only proper to continue if you do not seek 106
another woman
You may only commit sin with the woman I first gave you," said Our Father.

"But don't have an affair with another woman. 107
If you have an affair with a married woman who already has a husband,
then you will pay dearly for it.

108 mi xavaˀi majel,
ˀo mi xavaˀi bojel ta machita.
ˀo mi xavaˀi jomel ta kuchilu.
ˀo mi xavaˀi jomel ta punyal.
ˀo mi xavaˀi tuk'ael ta tuk'.
ˀo mi xavaˀi tuk'ael ta pistola.
ˀo mi xavaˀi tenel ta ton.

109 xavil pukuj la jyak' ˀavil.
jaˀ chask'an chaxchiˀin yaˀi ti pukuje.
xi la ˀalbat ti baˀyel vinik yuˀun jtotik ti voˀnee.

110 jaˀ yuˀun ti jech komem ˀasta ˀora ti mu stak' lek jk'opontik li ˀantz k'alal mi ˀoy yajval.
jtatik li ˀantze jaˀ yuˀun ta jmilan ˀo jbatik.

111 xavil la ti voˀnee jaˀ la ti pukuj la jyak' ˀiluk baˀyel k'uxi ta pasel li jmultike.
jaˀ yuˀun ti ta jmilan ˀo jbatik k'alal mi la jk'opontik mi ˀoy yajval li ˀantze.

112 veno jechot leˀ ˀeke ˀantz.
lek ˀavaˀi la spasbot ti pukuje.

113 te savil k'usi xavaˀi xi la yal ti jtotike.
jaˀ noˀox mi xavaˀi xacham ˀalajel ˀo mi saˀ yan ˀamalal.

114 te xavil mi xalaj ta majel.
ˀo mi moˀoj te xavil mi xasmil ˀamalale k'alal mi la pas ˀamul ta yan vinike.

115 ˀo mi moˀoj te xavil k'usi xavaˀi k'alal xalah ta milel.
mi xavil bojel ta machita.
ˀo mi moˀoje te xavil mi chukbil la nuk' xalah ta ch'ohon.
ˀo moˀoje te xavil mi tuk'ael ta tuk'.
ˀo mi moˀoje mi tuk'ael ta pistola.
ˀo mi moˀoje jomel ta kuchilu.
ˀo mi moˀoje jomel ta punyal.
ˀo mi moˀoje jomel ta naˀuxa.

You might be beaten up. 108
You might be cut up with a machete.
You might be stabbed with a knife.
You might be stabbed with a dagger.
You might be shot with a rifle.
You might be shot with a pistol.
You might be stoned.

You see, it was the Demon Pukuj who taught you. 109
So it is that the demon wants you to walk with him forever."
So it was said to the first man by Our Father long ago.

That is why it remains even now that we should not fall in love 110
with women who have husbands.
Whenever we seek women out, there are bound to be killings.

You see that long ago it was the Demon Pukuj who taught us 111
how to get in trouble.
That is why we kill each other when we have affairs with married women.

"Well, the same goes for you, woman. 112
That which the demon did to you felt good.

You will see what you have gotten yourself in for," said Our Father. 113
"You must understand that you will die an awful death
if you seek out a casual lover.

You will see how hard your husband hits you. 114
Or, even worse, you will find out that your husband will kill you
if you do wrong with another man.

If you do not heed this warning, you should consider the ways 115
you might meet your death.
You might be cut up with a machete.
Or, if not that, you might be choked to death by a rope tied around your neck.
If not that, you might be shot with a shotgun.
If not that, you might be shot with a pistol.
If not that, you might be stabbed with a knife.
If not that, you might be stabbed with a dagger.
If not that, you might be cut up with a razor.

jaˀ ti k'usi xavaˀi xacham ˀoe.
ˀo mi moˀoj mi balch'ujel xavaˀi.
jaˀ ti k'usi xacham ˀoe.

116 ˀo mi lekil chamel xacham ˀo.
ti mi yuˀun lekil chamel la cham ˀoe.

117 yuˀun lek ˀavich'ojbe smelol yuˀun.
mu xanaˀ xapas ˀamul.

118 ti mi yuˀun milel la cham ˀoe;
yuˀun toyol xapas ˀamul."

119 xˀutat la yuˀun jtotik ti baˀyel ˀantz ti voˀne,
k'alal lik ˀo ti baˀyel kirsano,
ti k'alal lik ˀo ti banomil ti mas voˀnee.

120 jaˀ yuˀun ti jech la komem ˀasta ˀora:
k'alal mi la saˀ yan smalal ti ˀantze ta xlaj ta milel yuˀun smalal.

121 jech xtok mi toyol saˀ skumpare ti ˀantze,
ta xlaj ta milel yuˀun skumpare.

122 xavil la li ˀantze pukuje la xchiˀinoj k'ajomal.
la xchiˀinoj jtotik ˀoˀlol k'ak'al.

123 mi tz'eˀbubuj jtotike pukuj xa la xlik xchiˀinik li ˀantzetike.
xavil la ti voˀnee jaˀ la ti pukuj baˀyel la jyak' ˀiluk k'uxi ta pasel ti jmultike.

124 jaˀ yuˀun ti ta jmajan ˀo la jbatik ti ta jmilan ˀo jbatik.
k'alal mi kaˀitik ta xich' k'oponel ta yan vinik mi kantztik.

125 ˀo mi kajniltik ta sk'opon sbaik xchiˀuk yan vinik.
ˀo mi moˀoj mi jaˀ la saˀ yan smalal ta xlaj ta milel li ˀantze.

126 xavil la jaˀ la ti pukuj ta sok joltike;
jaˀ yuˀun ti jech komem ˀo ˀasta ˀora mu stak' jk'opontik yan ˀantz,
ˀi mu xtak' jchiˀintik yan ˀantz.

That is how you will meet your death.
Or, if not that, you might even get thrown to the floor.
That is how you will die.

Otherwise you will die a natural death. 116
Your end will come from an ordinary sickness.

Such will be your reward if you have heeded this warning. 117
Knowing this, you will not be inclined to commit adultery.

Otherwise, your end will be sudden and violent; 118
If so, it will be because of your own sin."

So it was said by Our Father to the first woman, 119
At the time when the first people emerged,
At the time when the earth began in the most ancient times.

And that is why it has stayed that way into the present time: 120
That if a woman seeks another husband, her husband will kill her.

So, also, if a woman looks too eagerly for compadres, 121
Her compadres may be the cause of her death.[4]

You see, it was the Demon Pukuj himself, he alone, who accompanied the woman for a while. 122
For the other half of the day Our Father accompanied her.

When Our Father passes his zenith, the demons begin to accompany women. 123
You see, long ago it was the demon who first showed them how to do sinful things.[5]

That is why we fight with one another and kill one another. 124
When we find out that our women receive compliments from other men.

Or, if our wives talk with other men, 125
Or if they seek lovers, these women will be murdered.

You see, it is because of the Demon Pukuj that we lose our tempers; 126
That is why it remains to this day that we should not speak to other women,
That we should not go around with other women.

127 jaˀ yuˀun mi yilik ta jk'opontik,
ˀo mi yilik jchiˀinotik yan ˀantze,
ta xˀich'vanik
ta ˀit'ixal li kirsanoe.

128 jech' ˀaˀal mu stak' lek k'oponel li ˀantzetike.
mu stak' lek chiˀinel.

129 xavil jaˀ yuˀun ti pukuj xchiˀinojike;
jech' ˀaˀal mu stak' chiˀinel li yan ˀantzetike mu stak' k'oponel.

130 lek xavil jaˀ la ti pukuj baˀyel kobvan ti voˀnee.
jaˀ yuˀun la mu stak' pas jmultik buch'uk noˀox ˀantzilal jtatik,
ˀi xchiˀuk mu stak' jpas jmultik ta satilal.

131 xavil la ti voˀnee k'alal la ti la jyak' ˀiluk' ti pukuje,
lik la k'exavikuk ti vinike ti ˀantze.

132 k'alal la ti laj spas ti smulik xchiˀuk ti pukuje,
k'alal la ti la xchan jech ti vinike.

133 lik la k'exavikuk k'alal la ti k'ot ti jtotik ta stz'elik ti vinike ti ˀantze.
mu xa la stak' ˀaˀyel chaˀik ti ˀantze ti vinike.

134 ta la sk'exavik xchiˀuk ti ˀantze.
k'alal ta sk'exavike, mu la stak' ˀaˀyeluk chaˀik.
moˀoj la ˀun, yaˀik la ti bu ta sk'exavune.

135 pero k'usi xkutik xanaˀ
ta jmak jbatik ˀun xut la sbaik xchiˀuk ˀantz ti vinike.

136 pero ˀak'o xa jmak batik ta jkobtik,
pero mu stak' jech ˀo xijxanavotik xi la ti vinik.
yalbe la sbaik xchiˀuk ti ˀantze.

137 jaˀ lek la jsaˀtik yanal teˀ jmak ˀo jbatik xut la sbaik xchiˀuk ti ˀantze.
lik la smak ˀo sbaik ta yanal teˀ.

That is why, if they see us speak to other women, 127
Or if they see us going around with other women,
It bothers them,
It makes them jealous.

That is why women ought not to receive compliments. 128
They ought not to accept romantic company.

You see, it is because of the demon who goes with them; 129
That is why one ought not to give them compliments.

You see clearly that it was the demon who first made love 130
to a woman long ago.
That is why we ought not to commit sin with just any woman we meet,
Why we ought not to commit sin in public.

You see, long ago when the demon showed them about it, 131
The man and woman started to be ashamed.

When they commited sin in the company of the demon, 132
That was when the man learned how to do it.

The man and woman started to feel ashamed when Our Father 133
approached them.
The man and the woman felt they ought not to come out.

They were both ashamed. 134
They were so ashamed that they felt they ought not go out
from the shadows.
Had they done so, they would have felt even greater shame.

"But what shall we do? 135
We'll cover ourselves," said the man and the woman to each other.

"But even though we cover ourselves while having sex, 136
We still can't walk around like this," said the man.
So the man and the woman said to each other.

"We'd better look for leaves to cover ourselves with," he said to his wife. 137
So, they started to cover themselves with leaves.

138 jaˀ la lik smakik yanal teˀ ti xchakike.
k'alal la ti la smak ta yanal teˀ ti xchakike,
jaˀ to la lok' xanavikuk ti vinik xchiˀuk ti ˀantze.

139 pero maˀ leˀ ne mu stak' jech ˀo xanavik ma li kalab jnich'nabtik ˀune.
ˀa li t'anajtik ˀune xi la ti jch'ulmeˀtike.

140 pero moˀoj yabtel ˀoy xa talem li jk'exole xi la ti jch'ulmeˀtike.
jaˀ lek ta xkak'be yil k'usi xlik xchan spasel li sk'uˀike xi la ti jch'ulmeˀtike.

141 k'alal la ti lik yak' ˀiluk ti jch'ulmeˀtike.
lik la saˀ talel tuxnuk'.

142 jaˀ lek ˀilo ˀavabtel.
jaˀ xaˀabteh ˀo ˀachiˀuk li tuxnuk'.
jaˀ to te xak'uˀilajik xchiˀuk la ˀamalale xi la li jch'ulmeˀtike.

So it was that they started to cover their nakedness with leaves. 138
When they had covered their nakedness with leaves,
It was then that the man and the woman went out to take a walk.

"But my children, my offspring, can't go about like that. 139
They're naked!" exclaimed Our Holy Mother.

"This just won't do. Now the weight of work has come to my successor," 140
said Our Holy Mother.[6]
"I had better teach her so she can start to learn to make clothing,"
said Our Holy Mother.

With that, Our Holy Mother Moon started to teach her. 141
She began by bringing in cotton..

"You had better concentrate on your work. 142
You will be working with cotton.
You will then clothe yourself and your husband," said Our Holy Mother.[7]

FIGURE 3

"You had better concentrate on your work.
You will be working with cotton.
You will then clothe yourself and your husband," said Our
Holy Mother.

143 k'alal xlik ˀapas ta ˀavabtele baˀyel xlik ˀasiun.
chat'ujbe lok'el sbek' li tuxnuk'e.

144 k'alal mi laj ˀasiune,
jaˀ to xlik ˀajax.

145 k'alal mi laj ˀajaxe,
jaˀ to xlik ˀanaun.

146 k'alal mi laj ˀanaune,
jaˀ to xlik ˀapis.

147 k'alal mi laj ˀapise,
jaˀ to xlik ˀani ta komen.

148 k'alal mi laj ˀani ta komene,
jaˀ to xlik ˀavak'be ˀul.

149 k'alal mi ta ˀavak'be ti ˀule,
jaˀ to xlik ˀamuyes ta teˀ ta jolobe.

150 k'alal mi laj ˀamuyes ta teˀ ta jolobe,
chamala xtakij.

151 k'alal mi takij ta jolobe,
chlik ˀachiu.

152 k'alal mi laj ˀachiu ta jolob,
jaˀ to chlik ˀajal.

153 k'alal mi laj ˀajal,
jaˀ to chlik ˀachuk' ˀamutzes.

154 k'alal mi laj ˀamutzese,
chak'iˀ takijuk.

155 k'alal mi takije,
chlik ˀak'uˀinik.

"When you start your work, you begin by fluffing it. 143
You must sort out the seeds from the cotton.

When you have finished fluffing it, 144
Then you start to card it.

When you have finished carding it, 145
Then you start to spin it up.

When you have finished spinning it, 146
Then you start to wind it up.

When you have finished winding it up, 147
Then you place it on the warping frame.

When you have finished placing it on the warping frame, 148
Then you wet it with atole.[8]

When you have finished wetting it with atole, 149
Then you start to stretch it on the sticks of the loom.[9]

When you have finished stretching it on the sticks of the loom, 150
Then you wait until it dries.

When it has dried on the loom, 151
Then you start to separate the strands from one another.[10]

When you have finished separating the strands from one another, 152
Then you start to weave.

When you have finished weaving it, 153
Then you start to wash it to shrink and felt it.

When you have finished shrinking and felting it, 154
Then you stretch it out to dry.

When it is dry, 155
Then you start to make clothes.

156 jaˀ jech ˀo ˀavabtel.
muˀyuk yan ˀavabtel.

157 jaˀ chapas skotol ti k'ak'ale.
jaˀ ˀavabtel ˀo skotol k'ak'al jaˀ to te xak'uˀilajik ˀun kalab.

158 tekeˀ ˀilo ˀavabtejeb ˀune.
jaˀ me chaˀabtej ˀo ˀun.

159 ˀilo ˀapetet,
ˀilo ˀajalabteˀ ˀun,
ˀilo ˀakomen ˀun.
jaˀ me chaˀabtej ˀun.

160 xi la ti jch'ulmeˀtik k'alal la ti yalbe yaˀi ti ˀabtel ti baˀyel ˀantz ti mas voˀne.
ti k'alal lik ˀo ti banomil ta mas voˀnee.

161 jech la la jyal ti jch'ulmeˀtike.
jaˀ yuˀun la jech komem ˀasta ˀora ti ˀoy ti jk'uˀtik komeme.
jaˀ yuˀun ti mu xuˀ t'ant'an xijxanave.
jaˀ yuˀun la ti chijk'exavotik k'alal ch'abal jk'uˀtike.
jaˀ yuˀun la ti jech chanik ˀo ti ˀabtel ti ˀantzetik ˀasta ˀora.

162 xavil la jech la la jyak' ˀiluk ti jch'ulmeˀtik,
ti k'alal la ti lik ˀo ti baˀyel kirsano,
ti k'alal la ti lik boluk talel ti kirsano ti mas voˀnee.

✠ ✠ ✠

163 ti k'alal la ti lik boluk ti kirsanoe,
lik la ˀayanuk bolom,
lik la ˀayanuk ˀok'il.

164 lik la ˀayanuk chonetik.
lik la ˀayanuk k'usitikuk chanulal ta banomil.

165 li bolome jaˀ la baˀyel lok'.
xchiˀuk li ˀok'ile,
xchiˀuk li leone,
xchiˀuk li ˀosove.

That is the task that you will carry with you. 156
You have no other duties.[11]

You must do this every day. 157
It will be your work every day until you have clothed my children.

Well, take care of your tools. 158
You are to work with them.

Take care of your spinning bobbin, 159
Take care of your loom,
Take care of your warping frame.
You are to work with them."

So said Our Holy Mother when she explained her tasks 160
to the first woman long ago
That was when the earth was created in the most distant antiquity.

That is what Our Holy Mother told her. 161
That is why it has remained like that until today, that we have clothing.
That is why we no longer walk about naked.
That is why we feel shame when we have no clothes on.
That is why women keep on learning this kind of work even today.

You see, Our Holy Mother taught it in that way, 162
Back when the first people came forth,
Back when people first began to fill the earth in the most distant antiquity.

✠ ✠ ✠

At the time when people first began to multiply, 163
Jaguars started to be born,
Coyotes started to be born.

Animals started to be born. 164
All the animals there are on the earth started to be born.

The jaguar was the first. 165
He emerged with the coyote,
With the lion,
With the bear.

166 li bolom jaˀ la baˀyel lok'e.
xavil jaˀ la li ˀoy xch'ulelinojik jˀolol li kirsanoe.
xchiˀuk la li ˀok'ile.
jaˀ yuˀun ti baˀyel lok' ti muk'tik chonetike.

167 xavil la ti kirsanoe syakel la ta bolel talel,
k'alal la ti ta xvok' ti kirsanoe.

168 ˀo la yan bolome xch'ulelinoj;
ˀo la yan xch'ulelinoj ˀok'il;
ˀo la ti yane ˀo la xch'ulelinoj saˀben ti kirsanoe.

169 Pero li yan kirsano bu la xch'ulelinoj bolome,
jaˀ la mas jk'ulej.

170 bu la xch'ulelinoj ˀok'ile,
jaˀ la mu masuk jk'ulej.

171 bu la xch'ulelinoj saˀbene,
jaˀ la mas povre ti kirsanoe.

172 bu la xch'ulelinoj vet ti kirsanoe,
jaˀ la mas povre,
koˀol la povre xchiˀuk saˀben.

173 kapal la xtok bu la xch'ulelinoj saˀbene,
mu la jaluk xch'i.

174 ti kirsanoe jaˀ la li ˀoy ta stiˀan viche.
k'alal mi yil ti yajval viche.
ta smil ta tuk' ti saˀbene.

175 k'alal mi cham ta tuk' ti saˀbene,
ˀosib xa la k'ak'al kuxul ti buch'u xch'ulelinoj saˀben ti kirsanoe.
ta xch'ulel ta xcham ta ˀora.

176 jaˀ noˀox jech li vet xtok.
buch'u xch'ulelinoj ti kirsanoe mu jaluk xch'i.

The jaguar was the first one to come into being. 166
So, you see, jaguars came to be the animal-soul companions
of half the people.
The other half had the coyote.
This was because the large animals came first.[12]

You see, the people were occupied in increasing their numbers. 167
So it was when the first people emerged.

Jaguars accompanied some of them; 168
Coyotes accompanied some;
Weasels accompanied others.

But those whom the jaguars accompany, 169
These are the richest.

Those whom coyotes accompany, 170
They are not so rich.

Those whom weasels accompany, 171
These people are poorer.

Those whom foxes accompany, 172
These are the poorest,
Just as poor as those of the weasel.

Furthermore, those human companions of both the fox and weasel, 173
They do not live for very long

There was once a person whose baby chicks had been eaten by some animal. 174
Then the owner of the chicks saw this.
He shot the culprit, a weasel, with a shotgun.

After the weasel died, 175
It was only three days until the owner of the chicks,
whose soul companion had been that very weasel, died also.
He has shot his own animal soul and so died quickly himself.

So also with the fox. 176
He who has the fox as a soul companion does not live very long.

177 jaˀ la li ta stiˀ ˀalak'e.
k'alal mi yil ti yajval ˀalak' ti bu ta stzak ˀalak' ti vete,
ta xlaj ta milel ta tuk'.

178 k'alal mi cham ta tuk' ti vete,
k'ajomal xa ˀoxib k'ak'al kuxul ti buch'u xch'ulelinoj ti vete.

179 mi vinik mi ˀantz jaˀ ti buch'u xch'ulelinoj vet ti kirsanoe.
jaˀ yuˀun ti ˀoy chijcham ta jch'ulelike.

180 xavil la ti voˀnee jaˀ la ti jtotik k'usi la snop.
ti k'usi la chanulal xak' jvayujelintik ti jtotik voˀnee.

181 jaˀ yuˀun la ti jech komem ˀasta ˀora,
ti mu jkotoltikuk jch'ulelinojtik puru bolom.

182 jaˀ ti k'usi chanulal xak' jvayujelintik ti jtotike.
jaˀ yuˀun mu jnaˀtik k'usi jvayujeltik yak'ojbotik ti jtotike,
mi bolom,
mi ˀok'il,
mi vet,
mi saˀben.

183 jaˀ ti k'usi xak' jvayujelintik ti jtotike.
jaˀ yuˀun ti jech komemotik ta ˀorae.

184 xavil ti voˀne ti k'usi lik snop ti jtotik,
k'alal ti lik smeltzan ti banomile.

✠ ✠ ✠

185 xavil la ti voˀnee muˀyuk la vitzetik muk la teˀtik,
puru la stenlej.

186 muk la ton,
puru la banomil.

187 ta yoxibal la k'ak'al lik ch'iuk ti teˀetik.
k'alal la ti ˀul ti nab ti voˀnee.

This one, the fox, likes to eat chickens. 177
When the owner of the chickens sees that the fox is catching his chickens,
The fox quickly meets its end at the point of a shotgun.

Then, when the fox dies of shotgun wounds, 178
He who has this fox as a soul companion lives for only three days.

The person who has the fox as a soul companion may be a man or a woman. 179
In this manner, whoever we are, we die just as our soul companions do.

You see, long ago it was Our Father who thought about all this. 180
Our Father long ago gave us dreams about our animal-soul companions.

That is why it remains the same even to this day, 181
That not all of us have jaguars as animal souls.[13]

There are several kinds of animals that Our Father has given to us 182
as soul companions.
For this reason it is often unclear what soul companions
Our Father has given us,
Whether they be jaguars,
Whether they be coyotes,
Whether they be foxes,
Whether they be weasels.

These, then, are the kinds of soul companions that Our Father provides. 183
That is our heritage, even into our time.

You see, long ago this was what Our Father thought about, 184
At the time when he started to prepare the earth.

You see, long ago there were no mountains, no forests, 185
Only flat land.

There were no rocks, 186
Only the earth itself.

On the third day trees started to grow. 187
This was when the seas dried up long ago.[14]

188 lik la ch'iuk teˀetik;
lik la ch'iˀuk vomoletik.

189 ti ta yoxibal k'ak'ale.
k'alal la ch'i ti teˀtike.

190 jaˀ la te bat nakluk ti chonetik.
jaˀ yuˀun ti ta teˀtik sna li chonetike.

191 veno jech la ti puru batz'i banomile.
ti puru stenleje.

192 mu la xˀul lek ti nabe.
mu la xch'i lek ti teˀetike.
toyol la ta xlom ti banomile.

193 pero k'usi van chkut syihub li banomile xi la ti jtotike.
pero mi moˀoje mu xch'iik ma jnich'nabe xi la ti jtotike.

194 jaˀ lek ta jsaˀbe yoyal ma banomile.
pero mi moˀoje ta xlom tajmek xi la ti jtotike.

195 jaˀ lek ta xkak'be yoyalin ton xi la ti jtotike.
pero ta jlomes yalel.
ta jk'elkik tana bu k'alal xk'ot ta lomel tana xi la ti jtotike.

196 lik la svuy yalel ti banomile.
k'alal la ti la svuy yalel ti banomile,
jlikel la lom yalel ta ˀora ti banomile.

197 k'alal la ti syakel ta slom ti banomile,
jlikel la ch'i talel ton ch'enetik.
jlikel la ˀayan vitzetik.
jlikel la ˀayanuk ˀuk'um.

198 lik la ˀayanuk sat ˀoˀ.
lik la ˀayanuk yochob bu ta xˀoch yalel ˀuk'um.
lik la ˀayanuk xab sventa sna pukuj.

Trees started to grow; 188
Grass started to grow.

This was on the third day of creation. 189
It was when the forest started to be.

The animals went to live there. 190
So it happened that the animals have their homes there in the forest.

But the fact was that there had been only land. 191
It was just flat land.

The seas had not fully dried up. 192
The forests could not grow well.
The surface of the earth was constantly caving in.

"But how am I going to harden the earth?" wondered Our Father. 193
"If I don't do it, my children won't survive," said Our Father.

"It would be better for me to look for supports for the land. 194
If I don't do this, it will surely fall apart completely," said Our Father.

"It would be better for me to place rock supports," said Our Father. 195
"I shall pull things down.
Let's see where the landslides end up," reflected Our Father.

He proceeded to make the earth quake and tremble. 196
Once he had provoked the landslides,
The earth's surface itself quickly collapsed.

Then, as the earth continued to cave in, 197
Suddenly stones and caves emerged.
Suddenly, mountains were born.
Suddenly, rivers were born.

Springs came forth. 198
Sinkholes came forth, places where rivers sink into the earth.
Small cracks for the door to the demon's house began to appear.[15]

199 k'alal syakel xch'i li tonetike li ch'enetike,
lik ˀayanuk nail ch'enetik sventa la sna ˀanjeletik.

200 k'alal la ti ˀayan ti tonetik ti ch'enetike,
jaˀ la sventa yoyal banomil sventa la mu slom ti banomile.

201 jaˀ yuˀun la ˀun ˀoy la ton ch'iem ta banomil,
ˀoy la muk'tik ch'enetik ch'iem ta banomil.

202 jaˀ la ti jtotik jech la la snop ti ˀoy tonetik ti ˀoy ch'enetik.
komem ˀasta ˀorae.

203 jaˀ la ti voˀnee toyol toˀox la slom ti banomile.
ch'abal toˀox la ti tone;
ch'abal toˀox la muk'tik ch'enetik;
ch'abal toˀox la vitzetik.

204 k'alal la ti ˀayan ti vitzetike,
jaˀ la te bat nakluk ti muk'tik chonetik,
ti k'uyepal puru vayujelil ti ta vitzetike.

205 jech la li muk'tik ch'enetike jaˀ la sna ˀanjeletik.
xchiˀuk la li nail ch'enetike.

206 jaˀ yuˀun ti ˀayan la ti vitzetike,
ˀayan la ti muk'tik ch'enetike.

207 veno jech la la snop ti jtotik ti k'alal la lik smeltzan ti baˀyel banomil,
ti mas voˀne ti k'alal la lik ˀo ti banomil yuˀun ti jtotik ta voˀne.

208 jech laj ti jloˀile.

Then, as the rocks and caves kept forming, 199
Caverns for the homes of the earth lords started to form.[16]

When the rocks and caves had been created, 200
They acted as supports for the earth so that the earth would not collapse.

That is why there are rocks in the earth itself, 201
Why there are huge caves lacing the earth.

It happened that Our Father thought there ought to be rocks and caves. 202
And so it has remained to this day.

Long ago, the earth was still unstable. 203
There still were no rocks;
There still were no great caves;
There still were no mountains.

So, when the mountains were formed, 204
The large animals went to live there,
Those who were animal-soul companions found their homes
in the mountains.

So the great caverns came to be the homes of the Earth Lords. 205
So, also, the great caves.

That is why the mountains were created, 206
Why the great caverns were created.

So, all of this is what Our Father decided when he started to prepare 207
the First World long ago,
Back when the earth was created by Our Father, long ago.

So the story ends. 208

1 ˀoy jun kuento ta xal ti mol voˀnee.
jun kuento sventa ˀixim.

2 ˀa ti voˀne lae ˀa ti ˀixime sbek'tal,
la yoˀ to jtotike."

3 xi ti mole ta sloˀilaj ta k'ixin ˀosile;
ti bu loˀilaje.

4 ti k'alal lik yal sloˀile ti mole,
yuˀun ˀoy jun vinik toj toyol ta sjip vaj.

5 ˀaaa . . . pere li vaje mu xtun jiptik xi ti mole.
ˀa ti voˀnee sbek'tal la jtotik.

6 la xi jech la jyalbun kaˀi ti ˀanima jtote xi ti mole.
jaˀ ˀo la ti k'alal la ti lik smeltzanutik ti jtotik ta vinajele.

7 k'alal la li jmeltzaj yuˀune ti jtotike,
lik la saˀ jveˀeltik ti jtotik ta vinajele.

8 la la jyak'be la baˀyel li ˀitaje.
jutuk ˀo la la sloˀik ti ˀitaje.

9 yak'be la ti napuxe.
jutuk ˀo la la sloˀik.

10 yak'be la ti chikarioe;
mu la bu la sloˀik ti sveˀelike.

TEXT 4
About Corn

Manuel López Calixto

Here is a story that an old man told long ago. 1
It is a story about corn.

"Long ago, corn was the body, 2
It was once the thigh of Our Father Sun."

So said the old man who was talking in Hot Country;[1] 3
That was where he spoke.

At the time that the old man started to tell his story, 4
It was because of a man who was wasting tortillas.

"Oh, don't throw away the tortillas," spoke the old fellow. 5
"For once they were part of Our Father Sun's body.

That is what my late father told me," said the old man. 6
"It all came about when Our Father Sun was starting
to make us and shape us.

Once he had created us, 7
Our Father Sun in Heaven sought to provide us with food.

First, he tried giving our ancestors cabbage. 8
But the cabbage didn't appeal to them very much.

He gave them turnips. 9
But these were not very successful either.

He gave them wild sawthistle greens; 10
They refused to eat them at all.

11 veno pero k'usi ta ˀaveˀel chak'anike xi la ti jtotike ta vinajele.
mu jnaˀ xi la ti kirsanoe.

12 ˀaaa . . . pero k'usi ta ˀaveˀelike chak'ane xi la ti jtotike.
pere k'usi lek ta veˀel chaveˀe xutat la ti vinike ti ˀantze.

13 chaˀvoˀik la ti kirsanoe mu la sna k'usi la ta sveˀele.
lik la saˀbe la yan sveˀel xtok.

14 lik la me sjos sbek'tal yoˀ
ˀa li liˀe mi xanaˀ xaveˀ liˀe xutatik la ti ˀantivo kirsanoe.

15 yak'be la ti sbek'tal yoˀe.
jaˀ la sveˀik ta ˀora ti sbek'tal jtotike.

16 ˀaaa . . . pere mi jaˀ xanaˀ sveˀel,
xutat la ti vinike.
xutat la ti ˀance.

17 jaˀ xi la xchaˀvalik ti kirsanoe.
veno mi jaˀ ˀaveˀelik ˀo ˀun xi la ti jtotik ta vinajele.

18 jaˀ xi la.
jaˀ ma leˀ ˀune xiik la ti kirsanoe.

19 jaˀ jnaˀkutik sveˀel xi la.
ˀaaa . . . veno lek ˀoy nich'on xi la ti jtotike.

20 jech'o la xal li ˀixime sbek'tal la jtotik.
sbi yuˀunik li ˀixime xi ti mol ta sloˀilajike.

21 jaˀ me jech kom ti ˀixim voˀnee xi ti xal ti mole.
jech'o la me xal ti puru la me ˀixim ta jveˀtike xi ti mole.

22 yuˀun jaˀ la ti baˀyel kirsanoe.
jaˀ la lek snaˀ sk'anel sveˀelik ti ˀantivo kirsanoetike.

'So, then. What food do you want?' asked Our Father Sun in Heaven. 11
'We don't know,' said the people.

'Come on. What food do you really want?' asked Our Father Sun. 12
'What food would really taste good to you?' he asked the man
and the woman.

And neither of the two people had any clue about what their food should be. 13
So he started to search once again for their food.

He proceeded to scrape off a piece of his body, a part of his thigh. 14
'This, here: Does it appeal to you?' he asked the ancestors.

He gave them his body, his thigh. 15
And they ate the body of Our Father Sun right away.

'Ah, then! Do you think you could get used to this as your food?' 16
So it was spoken to the man.
So it was spoken to the woman.

'Yes,' said the two people. 17
'Good, this is to be your food?' said Our Father Sun in Heaven.

'Yes,' they said. 18
'This is it. No doubt about it,' declared the people.

'Let us make this our food,' they said. 19
'Ah, that's fine, my children,' replied Our Father Sun.

That is the way corn came from the body of Our Father Sun. 20
They came to call it corn," said the old man as he
continued with his story.

"'This is how corn was given long ago,'' said the old man. 21
"That is why corn is our main food," said the old man.

"It is the work of the ancestors. 22
They knew how to choose their food very well, these people of long ago.

23 ti k'alal la lijmeltzaje xi.
jaˀ ˀo la lik sjak' k'usi la jnaˀtik sloˀel,
k'usi la jnaˀtik sveˀel.

24 ˀa ti voˀne lae skotol la sjak' ti jtotik la ta vinajele ti jveˀeltik lae xi.
jech'o la me xal ti puru la me ˀixim ta jveˀtike xi ti mole.

25 pere yuˀun ta skotol banamil ˀoy ti ˀixime xi.
ˀak'o me jkaxlan jaˀ snaˀ sveˀel ˀek li ˀixime.
jaˀ noˀox jaˀ jveˀeltik ta jkotoltik xi ti mole.

26 jech'o xal puru ˀixim ta jveˀeltike.
jaˀ ti ˀantivo kirsano voˀnee jaˀ la sk'an komel ti ˀixime.

27 pero yuˀun jaˀ toh lek snaˀ sk'an hveˀeltik ˀa ti ˀantivo kirsano voˀnee.
jaˀ la st'uj jveˀeltik.

28 ˀa ti jtotik lae la la stak ˀech'el ta paxyal ti vinik lae ti ˀantz lae.
batik la ta paxyal xchaˀvalik la.

29 ˀo la te muk'ta teˀ la staik.
te la k'ot.
chotiˀukuk ta yolon la ti teˀe.

30 te la chotahtik xchaˀvalik.
ta sloˀilajik xchiˀuk yajnil ti vinike.

31 te la me k'ot jun vinik ta stz'elik.
mi liˀ ˀo te xi la ti vinike.

32 ti k'alal k'ot te chot xi la k'otel ta xokon yajnil.
k'usi chapasik xi la.

33 ch'abal xi ti vinike.
ˀaaa . . . xi la ti mu jvuˀlale.

34 mi xanaˀ xak'obvan xutat la ti vinike.
mu jnaˀ xi la.

That is how it was when we were being made," he said. 23
"It occurred to Our Father to ask us about what we wished to eat,
What would be our food.

So it was spoken long ago when Our Father Sun in Heaven 24
asked us about our food.
That is why corn is our main food," said the old man.

"Indeed, corn is found everywhere on earth," he declared. 25
"Even Ladinos like to eat corn.
So it is for all of us. It is our mainstay," said the old man.

"In this manner corn came to be our main food, 26
Thanks to our ancestors of long ago, who asked for corn.

Our ancestors of long ago made a good choice for their food. 27
They were the ones who chose it.

Our Father Sun suggested that the man and the woman walk around. 28
And so the two of them did his bidding and took a walk.

They came across a huge tree. 29
They went up to it.
And they sat down at the foot of the tree.

The two of them were sitting there. 30
The man was talking to his wife.

A strange man approached them there. 31
'Are you here?' asked the stranger.[2]

When he came there he sat down beside the woman. 32
'What are the two of you up to?' he asked.

'Nothing,' said the man. 33
'Oh, I see,' replied the stranger in a knowing voice.

'Do you know how to fuck?' asked the stranger provocatively. 34
'I don't know what you're talking about,' said this man, our ancestor.

35 ˀaaa pere mi xak'ane ta xkak ˀavil xi la.
ˀa veno xi la ti vinike.

36 mu la snaˀ k'usi jaˀ to la me yil tzakxutbat la me ti yajnile.
xiˀ la me tajmek ti vinike ti k'alal la ti ˀak'bat yile.

37 ˀa ti mu jvuˀlale maˀuk la kirsano.
ti tzakvan lae mu pukuj.

38 la ti tzakvan komele maˀuk la kirsano,
mu pukuj la.

39 mi lavil k'usi la jpas xi la ti mu pukuje.
jech la me ti vinik ˀeke lik la me yak' ˀat ˀeke.
jaˀ la me jech la spas ti vinik ˀeke.

40 yuˀun jaˀ la me ti mu pukuj yak' ˀiluk komele ti mas ta voˀnee,
ti k'alal la mu toˀox la snaˀik k'usi ta spasike.

41 jaˀ la mu pukuje jaˀ ta ˀora la yak' ˀiluk.
ti mu pukuj ˀek ˀune.

42 ˀa ti jechuke jaˀ to la mi vul ta sjol stukike.
la ˀun jech'o la xal ti yoˀ la ˀoy la toj chopol ti kirsanoetike.

43 pere yuˀun jaˀ ti mu pukuje.
la jyak' ˀiluk ti voˀne.

44 xi ti mol ta sloˀilajik xchiˀuk sviniktak k'alal la ta skuxik xa ta mal k'ak'ale.
ˀa ti mi yuˀun la toj toyol la ta jiptik li ˀixime xi ti mole.

45 ˀak'o mi xaˀabtej,
mi ˀaˀuk xch'i ti jchobtike xi.

'Ah, but if you like, I'll be glad to show you,' he said. 35
'All right,' said this man, our ancestor.

He didn't know what the stranger was talking about until he 36
saw his wife get fucked by him.
Our forefather was frightened when he was shown this.

The fact is that the stranger wasn't a person. 37
The one who did the fucking was the Demon Pukuj.[3]

So it was that the one who first demonstrated sex was not a person, 38
But the bad Demon Pukuj.

'Did you see how I did it?' the bad Demon Pukuj asked the man. 39
So the man also had sex.
So the man did it also

So it was that the damned Demon Pukuj taught them long time ago, 40
When they still didn't know how to do it.

It was the damned Demon Pukuj who taught them the trick in no time at all. 41
It was the Demon Pukuj himself.

If it had not happened this way, people would have had to think 42
it up on their own.
And because it did happen this way, there are many evildoers
in our midst today.[4]

That was because of that scoundrel Pukuj. 43
He gave instructions long ago."

✠ ✠ ✠

The man who was talking with his fellow workers said these things 44
while they were resting one afternoon.
"The fact is that we do waste a lot of corn," said the old man.

"For this reason, even though you work, 45
Your corn field may not prosper," he said.

46 ˀak'o mi xatz'un ˀep ta chobe,
mu xch'i.

47 pere yuˀun ˀoy ti kastikoe.
pere yuˀun ˀaˀ ta xak' stuk kastiko ti jtotik ta vinajele.

48 jech'o la xal mu la stak jiptike.
mu xavil jaˀ yak'oj ˀixim ti jtotike.

49 vaˀi ˀun mi mu la jlabantike,
jech'o la xal ˀoy la ti kastikoe xi ti mol ti voˀne k'alal ta spasik ti xchobtik.

50 jech'o me xal mu me xajiptik ma li ˀixime xi ti mole.
ˀa la k'usi ˀoy kuˀuntike skotol jaˀ yak'oj ti jch'ultotike xi.

51 ˀa ti kalojtike kuˀuntik,
pere moˀoj.

52 ˀaˀ yuˀun li jch'ultotike xi ti mol ta sloˀilajike.
pero voˀne xa.

"Even though you sow much corn, 46
Perhaps it will not grow.

The reason is that there is punishment. 47
The reason is that Our Father Sun in Heaven himself
put the punishment in place.

That is why we should not waste things. 48
Don't you see that this is so? Our Father Sun has given us corn.

That is why, if we don't behave well, 49
There will be a punishment," said the old man long ago
while they were preparing their cornfields.

"That is why we should not throw away corn," said the old man. 50
"Our Father Sun has given us everything we have, they say.

We have said that it is ours, 51
But it isn't.

It is by the grace of Our Holy Father Sun," said the old man as he was 52
talking with his companions.
So this knowledge was given long ago.

1 ʔa li voʔnee k'alal liʔ toʔox ʔoy ti jtotike,
ʔabtej toʔox la ta la slomes teʔtik.

2 pero to k'alal ta xʔabtej ti jtotike ʔep la ta xak' smachita,
xchiʔuk yek'el ʔep la.
xchiʔuk yasaran ʔep la.
ta jun k'ak'ale ʔep la yabtel ma ti jtotike.

3 pero mu ʔechuk ta xʔabtej ma ti jtotik k'uchaʔal ʔoʔtike.
ʔa li jtotike teʔ la ta spas yasaranain,
pero ti yasaranae te la ta xʔabtej stuk.

4 ʔoy la mu snaʔ xʔabtej yasarana ti jtotik ta la xak'be nukul yasarana.
k'alal mi la jyak'be nukul yasarana ti jtotike lek xa la snaʔ xʔabtej.

5 k'alal muy ta vinajel ti jtotike,
ta ʔox la xak' komel yasarana ʔabtejkutik ʔoe.

6 ʔoy la jun vinik buy ta xavak' ʔayasarana xi la.
ʔa li jtotik ta xkak'be jnich'nab xi la.

7 ʔaʔ la ti vinik mu xavak'be ʔayasarana li ʔanich'nab.
ʔixch'un la ti jtotik.
yochelik la ta loʔil.

8 pero maʔuk lek vinik ti la xchiʔin ta loʔil ti jtotik.
pukuj la.

TEXT 5

About Why We Did Not Receive Our Lord Sun/Christ's Magical Hoe

Xalik López Setjol

Long ago when Our Lord Sun/Christ still lived on earth, 1
He still worked, as we do today, at the task of clearing
underbrush and woods.

When he worked on earth, he was a good hand at using the machete, 2
A good hand with the axe.
A good hand with the hoe.
Every day Our Lord Sun/Christ found himself hard at work.

But Our Lord Sun/Christ did not work exactly as we do. 3
Our Lord Sun/Christ worked at his hoeing,
But the hoe worked there by itself.

If a hoe didn't want to work, Our Lord Sun/Christ would lash it
with a rawhide whip. 4
After receiving the whipping, Our Lord Sun/Christ's hoe
would work just fine.

When Our Lord Sun/Christ rose to the sky, 5
He left the hoe so that we might work.

There was a stranger who asked him, "What did you do with your hoe?" 6
Our Lord Sun/Christ answered: "I have left it with my children."

The man replied: "Don't leave your hoe to your children." 7
And Our Lord Sun/Christ paid close attention to him and obeyed him.
And they continued to talk.

But it was not a good person who spoke with Our Lord Sun/Christ. 8
It was the Demon Pukuj.

9 ˀech'o la xal mu sk'an xkich'tik yasarana jtotik ti pukuje.
ˀaˀ la tzk'an ti ˀabol jbatik.

10 ti pukuje mạnchuk k'usi la jyal ˀechuke,
ch'abal tzotz ˀabtel ti jpastik.

That is why he didn't want us to have Our Lord Sun/Christ's hoe, 9
that magical tool that worked all by itself.
The demon Pukuh wanted us to remain forever poor.

If the Demon Pukuj had not interfered, 10
We would not have to work so hard.[1]

1 ˀoy jun kuento ta t'ul voˀnee.
jaˀ la ti jtotike.

2 yuˀun ta la spas la yav la xchob.
ti jtotike ˀi ta la xbat la ta montanya.

3 ˀi ta la xich' la yek'el.
ta la xich' la smachita.
ˀi ta la xich' la sluk ti jtotike.

4 ˀi ta la xbat ta teˀtik ti jtotike.
ta xbat sjam la yav xchob ti jtotike.

5 veno k'alal la ta xk'ot ta teˀtike ti jtotik la ˀune,
ta la slomesan la ti steˀe.

6 veno k'alal la ta xbat ti jtotike,
lomem la xkom la ti teˀe.

7 vaˀun k'alal la ta sut la talel la ˀune ˀi k'ot la sk'el ti steˀe la ˀune,
ˀi staoj ˀo yav ti steˀe.

8 vaˀajtik ˀo la.
pere k'uchaˀal tajmek leˀe.

9 ti vaˀajtik ti jteˀ.
ti ta jta tajmeke xi la ti jtotike.

10 ˀi slomes noˀox la xtok.
vaˀun sut noˀox la xtok.

11 veno k'alal la bat la jten la xtok ˀun,
vaˀajtik la ti teˀ noˀox la xtoke.

TEXT 6
Of What Happened to Rabbit Long Ago

Marián López Calixto

Here is a story about what happened to rabbit long ago. 1
It's actually about Our Father Sun/Christ as well.

It happened that Our Father was preparing the ground for his cornfield. 2
He was on his way to the woods.

He carried his axe. 3
He carried his machete.
And Our Father carried his sickle.

Our Father headed off to the woods. 4
Our Father was going to clear the land for his cornfield.

So, when Our Father came to the woods, 5
He cut down the trees.

And so, when Our Father went home,[1] 6
He left the trees cut down.

Then, when he returned and surveyed the site of his clearing, 7
He found the site of his trees, all right.

But they were standing up! 8
"But how in the world did this happen?

My trees are standing upright! 9
I see it with my very own eyes," exclaimed Our Father.

And so he cut them down again. 10
And then he went home again.

Then when he went once more to the site of his clearing, 11
The trees were standing upright again!

12 pere k'uchaˀal tajmek leˀe.
veno ta jpastik chab.

13 ta xibat ja jkak' ta chikin-chikin-chikin ˀosil.
kik ti chabe xi la ti jtotike.

14 vaˀun ˀispas la ti chab la ˀune.
bat la yak' ta chikin ˀosil.

15 xchotanan la ti chabe.
vaˀun ti jtotik la ˀune bat la ta sna ˀun.

16 vaˀun tal la me ti k'usi ta xk'ot ta svaˀan la ti teˀ ˀune.
mu t'ul la ta svaˀan ti teˀ ˀune.

17 vaˀun tal la ti mu t'ul la ˀune.
te la me chotol ta taat ti chab ˀune.
ˀi k'ot la ti t'ul la ˀun.

18 k'opoj la k'otel ˀun.
jaˀ la sk'opon ti chab ˀune.

19 lok'an xi la ti mu t'ul la ˀune.
mu la xtak'av ti mu chab la ˀune.

20 hecheˀ
la te vaˀal ti chabe.

21 lok'an.
pere lok'an.
pere lok'an tajmek.
pere mi mu xa ch'un tana.

"But why on earth is this happening? 12
Well, I think I'll just prepare some pine pitch.

I'll put some at each and every little corner of the field. 13
I'll set some pine-pitch traps," said Our Father.[2]

So, he got the soft resin dolls ready. 14
He went to put them at each corner of his field.

He placed several of the pine-pitch people in a sitting position. 15
Then Our Father went home.

Well, the one who had been making the trees stand up came. 16
It was the damned rabbit who made the trees stand up.

Well, the no-good rabbit himself came upon the scene. 17
He found the pitch people sitting there.
That was the scene when the rabbit arrived.

He spoke when he arrived. 18
He spoke to one of the pine-pitch dolls.

"Go away!" said the damned rabbit. 19
The pine-pitch doll did not answer.

It was useless. 20
The resin doll just stood there.

"Get out of here! 21
Beat it!
Scram!" yelled the rabbit.
But the resin doll didn't answer at all.

22 ta me xahputzbe tana xi la ti mu t'ule.
jech la ti chab ˀune mu la xtak'av.

23 pere ta me xajmaj tana chaˀe xi la ti t'ule.
mu la xtak'av ti chabe.

24 ta me xakak'be tana chaˀe xi la ti t'ule.
jech la ti t'ule spujbe la ˀun.

"I'm going to punch you in a minute!" said the bad rabbit. 22
But the pine-pitch doll didn't answer.

"I'm going to hit you in just a minute," said the rabbit. 23
And the pine-pitch doll didn't answer.

"Then I'm going to let you have it this instant," said the rabbit. 24
And so the rabbit gave him a punch.

FIGURE 4

"I'm going to punch you in a minute!" said the bad rabbit.
But the pine-pitch doll didn't answer.

25 jech la ti sk'ob ˀune te la matz'al k'ot ta chab ti sk'obe.
pere koltabun ti jk'obe.
pere koltabun ti jk'obe.

26 ta xakak'be jun jk'ob tana xtok chaˀe.
ˀi yak'be la sjun sk'ob xtok.

27 matz'al la k'ot ti sk'ob la xtoke.
pere koltaun tajmek.
pere koltaun tajmek xi la ti sonso t'ule.

28 ˀi mu la xkol ti sk'obe.
ˀoy kok tana xtok xi la ti t'ule.
ˀi yak' la yok jun.

29 matz'al la k'ot ˀi yak'be la jun yok.
ˀi te la pak'al la kom ta chab ti sk'obe.

30 jech la ti t'ule: koltaun tajmek.
xi la ti t'ule.

31 ta xkak' jol tana.
ˀoy jol xi la ti t'ule.

32 yak' la ti sjole.
te matz'al la kom.

33 pere koltaun tajmek.
pere koltaun tajmek xi la ti t'ule.

34 vaˀun ˀi te la tzakal kom ti t'ule.
jech la ti jtotik la ˀune tal la sk'el ti steˀ la ˀune.

35 veno ch'abal sa bu vaˀal ti jteˀe xi la ti jtotike.
bat la sk'el ti steˀe.

36 k'ot la ti bu spajoj ti chabe.
jaˀ to la yil ti jtotike t'ul.

In that way his front foot got stuck in the pine pitch when he hit it. 25
"Let go of my foot!
Let go of my foot![3]

If you don't, I'm going to let you have it with my other front foot." 26
And he kicked him with his other front foot.

This foot got stuck, too. 27
"Let go of me, I tell you!
Let go of me, I tell you!" said the dumb rabbit.

But his front feet remained useless. 28
"I've got my hind feet, too," said the rabbit.
And he let loose a good kick with his hind foot.

It got stuck and he struck with the other hind foot. 29
And this foot remained stuck there in the pitch.

So the rabbit hollered: "Let go of me, I tell you!" 30
So said the rabbit.

"I'll hit you with my head next. 31
I still have my head," said the rabbit.

He struck with his head. 32
And it got stuck there.

"But let go of me, I tell you! 33
Let go of me, I tell you!" raged the rabbit.

Well, the rabbit remained hopelessly stuck there. 34
Whereupon Our Father came up to see the clearing
where he had cut the trees.

"Well, now, fancy that! No one has stood my trees up," said Our Father. 35
He went to admire his nicely felled trees.

He came to the place where he had put the pine pitch. 36
And then Our Father saw the rabbit.

37 la te pak'al ta chab sta ti jtotike.
veno k'usi chapas leˀ ˀune.
xamala vaˀ tana xi la ti jtotik la ˀune.

38 jech la ti t'ule te la matz'al.
mu la xtak'av.

39 vaˀun k'ot la ti jtotik tzak xch'ut la ti t'ule.
snitbe la xchikin ti t'ule.

40 stok'be la ti xchikine.
jech la ti t'ule nitbat la xchikin.

41 vaˀun ti t'ul la ˀune jatav la ta ˀora.
bat la ta teˀtik ti t'ule.
jaˀ yuˀun la nat la ti xchikine.

42 vaˀun ti jtotik la ˀune bat la sk'el ti steˀlal ˀune.
k'ot la stikbe la sk'ak'al.

43 ˀi stz'un la ti maˀile.
stz'un ti chobtike.
stz'un ti chenek'e.

44 vaˀun k'alal stz'un ti chobtik ˀune,
lik la spasotik ˀune.

45 sbal la ti ˀach'ele,
ˀi svaˀan la jun vinik,
ˀi svaˀan la jun ˀantz,
ti voˀnee.

46 vaˀun k'alal la spasotik ti jtotike,
muˀyuk la ta xbak' ti jk'obtike.

47 jejech la te vaˀal kirsano ˀune.
ˀi mu la jk'antik ti ta xijveˀotike.

Our Father found him there stuck in the pine pitch. 37
"Well, what are you doing there?
You can wait there a bit longer," said Our Father.

And the rabbit remained stuck there. 38
He didn't answer.

Well, Our Father came up and grabbed the rabbit by the stomach. 39
He pulled the rabbit's ears.

He gave his ears a good yank. 40
That is how the rabbit's ears got pulled out nice and long.

Well, the rabbit fled at once. 41
The rabbit disappeared into the woods.
And that is why he has such long ears.

✠ ✠ ✠

Well, Our Father went to see his expanse of felled trees. 42
He set fire to the brush.

He planted squash. 43
He sowed his cornfield.
He sowed his beans.

And, when he had sowed his cornfield, 44
He started to make us.

He molded the clay, 45
And left a man standing there,
And left a woman standing there,
Long ago.

But, when Our Father made us, 46
Our hands did not move.

We, the early people, just stood there. 47
And we did not want to eat.

48 jech la ti jtotike ta la saˀ la talel momoletik.
ˀi ta la xak' jloˀtik ti momole.

49 vaˀun mu la jk'antik ti momole.
pere k'usi ta sk'an ti jnich'one xi la ti jtotike.

50 vaˀun x'ut la ti sbek'tal ˀune.
saˀ la ti sbek'tale
yak'be la ta ye ti yole.

51 jech la ti sbek'tal la ti jtotik ˀune jaˀ ti ˀixime.
k'alal laj la yak'botik ˀune ˀiˀ pere jaˀ la sk'an ti sbek'tal jtotike.

52 jaˀ yuˀun ˀoy ti ˀixim jveˀtike.
jech la xkomtzanoj ti jtotik voˀnee ti ˀoy la ti ˀixime.

53 ˀi la jkak'betik la smuˀul ti ˀixime.
jaˀ la jveˀeltik yak'botik ti jtotike.

54 jech kom ˀo ti ˀixim ˀoye.
laj ˀo ti kuentoe.

So it happened that Our Father found some grass. 48
He gave us the grass to eat.

Well, we did not want the grass either. 49
"Well, what do my children want?" asked Our Father.

Then he thought of his own body.[4] 50
He found a good piece of his own body.
This he put into the mouths of his children.[5]

For this reason, corn is the body of Our Father. 51
Once he had given it to us, how we came to crave Our Father's body!

That is why we eat corn. 52
For Our Father long ago bestowed the gift of corn upon us.

We ourselves must prepare the corn and make it good to eat. 53
It is our food that Our Father gave us.

And so it happened that there is corn today. 54
And that's all there is to the story.

1 jun kuento ta vo?nee.
?oy jun vinik ta xlo?ilaj ta k'ixin ?osil.

2 k'alal lik yal ti slo?ile yu?un la smil tz'unun ti kereme.
ja? te lik slo?il ti vinike.

3 ?a li tz'unune stzual la smoy jtotik ta vinajel.
yu?un ja? jech la jyalbun ka?i ti ?anima jmuk'tote.

4 ?a li tz'unune stzu la jtotik ti vo?nee ti k'alal ta to?ox xanavik ta banamile ti jtotik la ta vinajele.
ja? la stzu ti jch'ultotik ti vo?ne lae xi ti vinike.
jech'o la xal mu la stak' jmiltik xi ti vinike.
?a ti mi la la jmiltike ta la xak'butik kastiko ti tz'unun lae.

5 mu xavil stzu la jtotik ta vinajel ti tz'unune xi ti vinike.
?a ti mi la la jmiltike ta la me sk'as kasaronatik.
ta la me sk'as jmachitatik.
ta la me sk'as kek'eltik ?un.

6 jech'o la me xal ti yo? la mu xtun jmiltike,
yu?un ?oy la xch'ulel ti tz'unune.

7 yu?un stzu la jtotik ti vo?ne lae.
yu?un te la yich'oj ta xanav ti stzue.
jech'o la xal stzu la jtotik sbi ti stz'unune.
?a li tz'unune ?oy la smelol ti vo?nee.

TEXT 7

About Hummingbirds

Manuel López Calixto

There is a story of long ago. 1
I heard it from a man who was talking in Hot Country.[1]

When the story came up, a little boy had killed a hummingbird. 2
And that was what prompted the man to talk.

"The hummingbird was once the tobacco gourd of Our Lord 3
Sun/Christ in Heaven.[2]
My late grandfather told me this was so.

That the hummingbird was Our Lord Sun/Christ's tobacco gourd 4
when he was still walking upon the earth long ago.
It was the tobacco gourd of Our Holy Lord Sun/Christ
long ago," said the man.
"That is why we should not kill it," said the man.
"If we should kill one, the hummingbird will punish us.

Don't you see that the hummingbird is the tobacco gourd of Our Lord 5
Sun/Christ in Heaven?" said the man.
"If we should kill one, it will cause our hoes to break.
It will cause our machetes to break.
It will cause our axes to break.

That is why it is not right to kill it, 6
For the hummingbird has a soul.[3]

It was Our Lord Sun/Christ's tobacco gourd long ago. 7
He would carry this along with him on the road.
That is why the hummingbird is called 'Our Lord Sun/Christ's
tobacco gourd'.
That is the hummingbird's special meaning that comes from long ago.

8 ˀa li bu la mas bik'ite.
    jaˀ la li bik'ital tzue.

9 yan la li bu muk'ta tz'unune.
    yuˀun jaˀ la muk'ta tzu la ne xi ti vinike.

10 pere li tz'unune snaˀ stz'uyultes chobtik.
    k'alal mi lok' stz'utujil ti jchobtike ta xlik ˀok'ikuk li tz'ununetike.

11 pere yuˀun ta la stz'uyultes chobtik ˀun.
    ti k'alal stzijlajet xa la ta spase yuˀun ta me stz'uyultes sbe siyal chobtik.
    ti k'alal tzijlajetik xa ta spasike.

12 pero ˀoy sk'ak'alil ta xˀok' ti tz'ununetike xi ti vinike.
    k'alal ta xlik ˀok'ikuke ta julio ta ˀakosto xi ti vinike.
    pere jaˀ noˀox la chib ˀu ta xˀok'ik.

13 k'alal mi yijub ti jchobtike mu xa bu ta xˀok'ik ˀun.
    jaˀ noˀox k'alal ta stz'utujin ti chobtike xi ti vinike.

14 veno ˀa li mutetike skotol jaˀ la yak'oj ti jtotik ta vinajele xi ti vinike.
    pere mu jnaˀtik sjay lajunebal xa ˀavil ˀech'.
    mu xavil jaˀ ˀo la ti k'alal ta toˀox la xanav ta banamil ti jtotik la ta vinajele xi ti vinike.

There is a small kind of hummingbird. 8
This little bird is called the 'small tobacco gourd'.

It is different from the large hummingbird. 9
This bird is known as the 'big tobacco gourd'," said the man.[4]

"The hummingbird blesses the cornfield for us. 10
When the corn starts to tassel, the hummingbirds start to sing.

What they are doing is blessing the cornfield. 11
When they sing 'tzijlajet,' they are blessing the way of the
tender ears of the new corn.
That is the meaning when they begin to cry 'tzijlajet.'

The hummingbirds have their time of singing," said the man. 12
"They sing in July and August," said the man.
"It is only for two months that they sing.

When the grains of the corn start to mature and grow firm, 13
the hummingbird no longer sings.
It is only at the time of tasseling," said the man.

"So it is that Our Lord Sun/Christ in Heaven has created 14
all these birds," said the man.
"We have no idea how many tens of years ago it all happened.
Don't you see that this happened in that far away time when
Our Lord Sun/Christ in Heaven was still walking
on the earth?" said the man.

1 loʔil yuʔun jtotik cham ta kurus.

2 veno li jch'ulmeʔtik smeʔ vinajele muʔyuk la bu xaʔi k'uxi la xchiʔin yol.
pero mu la snaʔ bu la sta ti yole.

3 ʔentonse laj la saʔ jun takin vach',
pero muʔyuk la yanal.

4 vaʔi ʔun laj la yak'be jtotik rasarena ti vach'e.
ʔaʔ la baʔyel la stzak ti rasarenae.

5 tzako li vach'e.
jk'eltikik mi xkux ʔavuʔun xi la ti smeʔ vinajele.

TEXT 8

Of Our Father Who Died on the Cross

Mateo Méndez Tzotzek

Here is an account of Our Father, who died on the cross. 1

So, then. Our Holy Mother, the Mother of Heaven, did not understand how she became pregnant. 2
She did not know where or how she had conceived her child.

Then she looked for a dry stick, 3
One that did not have any leaves.

Then, without more ado, she presented the stick to Our Father of Nazareth.[1] 4
Our Father of Nazareth was the first one to take the barren branch.

"Take this dry branch. 5
Let's see if it sprouts buds for you," said the Mother of Heaven.

FIGURE 5

"Take this dry branch.
Let's see if it sprouts buds for you," said the Mother of Heaven.

6 pero k'uchaˀal.
k'usi sventa xi la ti rasarenae.

7 ˀech noˀox chatzak yuˀun ta jk'elkik mi xnichin ˀavuˀun xi la ti smeˀ vinajele.
ˀentonse laj la xch'un ti rasarenae.

8 laj la stzak ti vach'e.
te la stzakoj jlikel ta k'ob ti vach'e.

9 pero ta slajeb ˀun muˀyuk bu xnichin yuˀun ti vach'e.
muˀyuk bu xyaxub yuˀun.

10 pero li rasarenae mu snaˀ k'uchaˀal la stzak ti vach'e.
ˀentonse ti smeˀ vinajele la jyil ti muˀyuk bu xnichin yuˀun ti vach'e.

11 la sk'anbe ti rasarenae.
tzako talel li vach'e.

12 ta xkak'bekik li san joseˀe.
ta jk'eltikik mi ˀaˀ xnichin yuˀun li vach'e.

13 voˀote mu xnichin ˀavuˀun xˀutat la ti rasarenae.
ˀentonse laj la yak'be ti san joseˀe.

14 tzako li vach' liˀe.
ta jk'eltikik mi xnichin ˀavuˀun xi la ti smeˀ vinajele.

15 xuˀuk ta jtzak xi la ti san joseˀe.
ˀentonse laj la stzak ti vach' ta sk'obe.

16 k'alal la stzak ti vach'e jlikel la nichin yuˀun ti vach'e.
teke ˀun nichin xa ˀavuˀun li vach'e.

17 ta me xavik'un yuˀun ˀoy xa kol.
pero mu jnaˀ bu jta.
mu jnaˀ k'uxi tal.

"But why? 6
What is this all about?" asked Our Father of Nazareth.

"You only have to take the stick to see if it sprouts for you," 7
said the Mother of Heaven.
So Our Father of Nazareth obeyed her.

He took the barren branch. 8
In fact he took the stick in his hand quite willingly.

But in the end, it did not sprout for him. 9
It did not turn green for him.

But the truth of the matter was that Our Father of Nazareth did not 10
know why he had been asked to take the stick in his hand.
All that mattered was that the Mother of Heaven saw that
the stick did not sprout for him.

She told Our Father of Nazareth to return it to her. 11
"Give the stick back to me," she demanded.

We shall give it to San José. 12
We'll see if it sprouts blossoms for him.

It did not sprout for you," she said to Our Father of Nazareth. 13
Then she gave it to San José.

"Take this stick here. 14
Let's see if it sprouts for you," said the Mother of Heaven.

"All right, I'll take it," replied San José amicably. 15
Then he took it in his hand.

When he took the stick it quickly sent forth living buds. 16
"Well, now, the stick sprouted for you.

You are to marry me because I am with child. 17
But I don't know where I conceived the child.
I don't know how it came to me.

18 k'alal kaˀie te xa ta jch'ut.
ta xbak'.

19 ˀech'o xal ˀun ta xkik' jbatik xchiˀuk li voˀote.
yuˀun ta xkaltik voˀot ˀanich'on liˀ ta jch'ute.

20 ˀaˀ li ch'abal stote.
ˀech'o xal voˀot chakuchin.
ˀech'o xal voˀot chakom ta stot kol xi la ti smeˀ vinajele.

21 veno lek ˀoy mu xaxiˀ.
ta xkik'to xi la ti jtotik san joseˀe.
ˀentonse laj la yik' sbaik xchiˀuk ti smeˀ vinajele.

22 vaˀi ˀun vok' la yol ti smeˀ vinajele.
pero ˀoy xa ˀox la smalal.

23 ˀech'o xal ti xchiˀiltak ti smeˀ vinajele muˀyuk bu xaˀik mi ch'abal toˀox smalal ti k'alal la xchiˀin ti yole.
porke k'alal vok ti yole ˀoy xa ˀox smalal.

24 ˀech'o xal mu snaˀik xchiˀiltak ti smeˀ vinajel mi ch'abal toˀox smalal ti k'alal la xchiˀin yol ti smeˀ vinajele.
ˀentonse la jyik' sbaik xchiˀuk ti san jose.

25 ˀaˀ la ti nichin yuˀun ti vach'e.
mi manchukuk la nichin yuˀun ti vach'e muˀyuk bu xik' sbaik xchiˀuk ti san jose.

26 porke ti rasarenae muˀyuk bu xnichin yuˀun ti vach'e.
ˀech'o xal muˀyuk bu xik' sbaik.

Suddenly I felt it, it was already there in my womb. 18
It was moving in my body.

That is why we are going to get married. 19
Because we will be able to say that it is your child here in my womb.

It doesn't really have a father. 20
That is why you are to be responsible for it.
That is why you are going to be the father of my child,"
said the Mother of Heaven.

"Very well, that's fine. Don't be afraid. 21
I will marry you," said Our Lord San José.
Then he did marry the Mother of Heaven.

So, then. The son of the Mother of Heaven was born. 22
But fortunately she already had a husband, and he,
the newborn, a father.

For that reason, the relatives of the Mother of Heaven 23
never found out that she did not yet have a husband
when the child was conceived.
For, when the child was born, she already had a husband.

For that reason, the relatives of the Mother of Heaven 24
did not know that she did not yet have a husband
when the child was conceived.
That was because she married San José.

For him, the barren branch sprouted. 25
If the stick had not sprouted for him, she would not
have married San José.

As for Our Father of Nazareth, the stick never sprouted for him. 26
That is why they did not get married.

27 ˀaˀ ti manchukuk la nichin ti vach'e,
mu la sbol ti kirsanoe.

28 pero komo nichin la ti vach'e,
ˀech'o la xal ˀibol ti kirsanoetike.

If that stick had never sprouted, 27
Humankind would not have happened at all.

Since the stick did sprout, 28
It happened that humankind did increase.

FIGURE 6

If that stick had never sprouted,
Humankind would not have happened at all.

29 ˀentonse k'alal vok' yol ti smeˀ vinajele ˀoy la xojobal.
chijil xa la xojobal ti yol smeˀ vinajele.

30 mu la sk'anik ti juraxetike.
bat la smilik ti ˀolol xchiˀuk smeˀe.

31 pero li smeˀ vinajel la jyil ti ta smilat xchiˀuk ti yole.
ˀi jatavik xchiˀuk yol.

32 batik la ta yut chobtik.
laj la skuch ˀel ti yole.

Now, when the son of the Mother of Heaven was born, he had a halo. 29
The halo of the son of the Mother of Heaven sparkled brightly.

The Jews didn't like it. 30
They were determined to kill the child and his mother.[2]

But the Mother of Heaven realized that she and her child 31
were going to be killed.
So she fled with her child.

They went off into the cornfield. 32
She carried off her son.

FIGURE 7

Now, when the son of the Mother of Heaven was born, he had
a halo.
The halo of the son of the Mother of Heaven sparkled brightly.

33 te la bat snak' sbaik ta yut chobtik.
te la la jyak' chuˀnuk ti yol ta yut chobtike.

34 pero ti bu la jyak' chuˀnuk ti yole te la tz'uj yalel xchuˀ ti smeˀ vinajel ta yut chobtike.
vaˀi ˀun ti yalel xchuˀ ti jch'ulmeˀtike pas la ta ˀisak'.

35 te la ˀibol ta yut banumil ti ˀisak'e.
ˀech'o xal li ˀisak'e yalel la xchuˀ jch'ulmeˀtik.

36 pero sjunul la banumil xanav ti jch'ulmeˀtik xchiˀuk ti yole.
k'alal ta skuch yol ti jch'ulmeˀtike ta stz'uj yalel xchuˀ ta ˀora.

37 ˀech'osal ti ˀisak'e ˀoy ˀep tajmek ˀoy skotol banumil.
yuˀun xanav skotol banumil ti jch'ulmeˀtike.

38 vaˀi ˀun ti smeˀ vinajele muˀyuk xa bu sut ˀel ti bu vok' ti yole.
bat xanavuk ta skotol banumil xchiˀuk yol.
pero ti yole te skuchoj ta spat.

There they took refuge in the midst of the cornfield. 33
There she nursed her child in the midst of the cornfield.

There, in the midst of the cornfield, some of the Mother of Heaven's 34
milk dripped down onto the earth.
So it was that Our Holy Mother's breast milk became potatoes.

There in the earth the potatoes grew and multiplied. 35
So it is said that potatoes are the breast milk of Our Holy Mother.

Our Holy Mother walked all over the earth with her son. 36
As she was carrying her son, her breast milk kept dribbling out.

That is why there are so many potatoes all over the earth. 37
It is because Our Holy Mother walked all over the earth.

Well, the Mother of Heaven never returned to where her son had been born. 38
She walked all over the earth with her son.
She carried him bundled there, wrapped in a shawl on her back.

FIGURE 8

Well, the Mother of Heaven never returned to where her son had
been born.
She walked all over the earth with her son.
She carried him bundled there, wrapped in a shawl on her
back.

39 veno li juraxe bat saˀ tajmek ti smeˀ vinajele,
pero muˀyuk xa bu sta.

40 muˀyuk xa bu xil bu.
yuˀun snak'oj xa sba lek xchiˀuk yol ti smeˀ vinajele.

41 ˀentonse ti yol smeˀ vinajele ˀich'i.
muˀyuk bu xcham xchiˀuk smeˀ.

42 tekeˀ meˀ ˀaˀ lek batik ti bu li vok'e.
jk'eltikik mi ta to smil ti juraxe.
jk'eltikik mi ta to xiyojtikin.

43 batik meˀ.
hk'eltikik mi ta to smilotik ti hurase.

44 pero mu xaxiˀ meˀ.
batik.

45 ti mi yuˀun chismil ti juraxe mu xicham.
manchuk mi xismil.
mu xicham xi la ti yol smeˀ vinajele.

46 xuˀuk chaˀe.
batik pero ti mi la smilike mu me jventauk.

47 mi xak'ane ˀaˀ lek liˀotik noˀoxe xi la ti smeˀ vinajele.
ˀaˀ lek meˀ batik.

48 ˀa li voˀone kaloj xa chicham.
pero jk'eltikik mi chicham xi la yol ti smeˀ vinajele.

49 xuˀuk chaˀe batik xi la ti smeˀ vinajele.
batik la ti bu vok' yol ti smeˀ vinajele.

50 vaˀi ˀun k'alal k'otik ti bu vok yol ti smeˀ vinajele,
te la k'ot staik ti juraxe.

Now, although the Jews looked diligently for the Mother of Heaven, 39
They didn't find her.

They had no idea how to find her. 40
For the Mother of Heaven had hidden well with her son.

Then the son of Our Mother of Heaven grew up. 41
Neither he nor his mother died.

"Well, Mother, we had better go to where I was born. 42
Let's see if the Jews are still going to kill me.
Let's see if the Jews still know me.

Let's go, Mother. 43
Let's see if the Jews are still going to kill us.

Come now, don't be afraid, Mother. 44
Let's go.

If the Jews do kill me, I won't die. 45
It doesn't matter if they do kill me.
I won't die," said the son of the Mother of Heaven.

"All right, then. Let's go. 46
But if they kill you, don't blame me.

If it pleases you, it would really be better for us just to stay here," 47
said the Mother of Heaven.
"No, Mother, it would be better if we went to our destiny.

I think that I am indeed going to die. 48
So let us go see if I really do die," said the son of the Mother of Heaven.

"All right, then. Let's go," said the Mother of Heaven. 49
And they went back to the place where the Mother of Heaven's
son had been born.

Now, when they came to the place where the Mother of Heaven's 50
son had been born,
There they came upon the Jews.

51 veno ti juraxe yilik ti k'ot ti smeˀ vinajel xchiˀuk ti yole.
bat la smilik ta ˀora ti smeˀ vinajel xchiˀuk yole.

52 vaˀi ˀun ti yol smeˀ vinajele muˀyuk xa bu xjatav.
te ˀimilat ta ˀora.

53 ti smeˀe muˀyuk bu smilat.
te vaˀal sk'eloj.

54 ˀaˀ la mu sk'an ti jurax ti ˀoy xojobal ti yol smeˀ vinajele.
ˀech'o xal la smilik ta persa.
ˀaˀ la smul ti ˀoy xojobal ti ˀolole.

So the Jews saw the Mother of Heaven arrive with her son. 51
And they straightaway went to kill the Mother of Heaven and her son.

But the son of the Mother of Heaven decided not to flee. 52
He was prepared to be killed then and there.

However, his mother was not going to be killed. 53
She stood there watching and waiting.

Now, recall that the Jews didn't like it that the Mother of Heaven's 54
son had a halo.
That is why they felt they had to kill him.
The child's crime was that he had a halo.[3]

FIGURE 9

Now, recall that the Jews didn't like it that the Mother of Heaven's
son had a halo.
That is why they felt they had to kill him.
The child's crime was that he had a halo.

55 pero maˀuk xa la ˀolol.
vinik xa la.
ch'iem xa la.

56 ˀentonse ˀicham la ti yol smeˀ vinajele.
laj la yich' mukel.

57 pero ti yol smeˀ vinajele maˀuk kirsano.
jch'ultotik la.

58 ˀech'o xal ˀoy xojobal,
li kirsanoetik muˀyuk xojobal.

59 ˀentonse ti juraxetik k'alal yilik cham ti jtotike bat smukik ta lum.
pero laj la smukik lek ta lum ti jch'ultotike.

But he was no longer a child. 55
Now he was a man.
Now he had grown up.

Then the son of the Mother of Heaven died. 56
He was buried.

However, the son of the Mother of Heaven was not a mere person. 57
He was Our Holy Father.

That is because he had a halo, 58
Unlike plain people who do not have halos.

Then, when they saw that Our Father had died, the Jews went to bury him. 59
They buried Our Holy Father right in the ground.

FIGURE 10

Then, when they saw that Our Father had died, the Jews went
to bury him.
They buried Our Holy Father right in the ground.

60 te la mukul ˀoxib k'ak'al.
va'ˀi ˀun ti juraxetike te la ta sk'ot sk'elik jujun k'ak'al ti bu mukul
ti jch'ultotike.

61 te la ˀoy mukul ti jch'ultotike.
muˀyuk la bu ta xlok'.

62 pero ti juraxetik xch'unojik xa ti chamem xa ti jch'ultotike.
ˀaˀ la ti te ta xk'ot sk'elik jujun k'ak'al ti bu mukule.

63 k'alal ta xk'otik jujutene te ˀoy mukul.
muˀyuk bu ta xlok'.

64 ˀentonse ta yoxibal k'ak'al lok' ti jch'ultotike.
bat k'alal ta vinajele.

65 vaˀi ˀun ti juraxetike la jyilik lok' ti jch'ultotike.
batik la ta ˀanil bat la stzakik ta ˀora.

66 pero muˀyuk xa la bu staik ta tzakel ti jch'ultotike,
muy la ta ˀora ta vinajel.

67 ti smeˀe te kom ta banumil.
stuk noˀox.
ˀi muy ta vinajel ti jch'ultotike.

68 ˀentonse ti juraxetike la jyilik ti ˀoy xojobal ta vinajele.
pero li xojobal ta vinajele ˀaˀ li jxalik.

69 te ˀoye.
pero chijmuyotik.
ba jmiltik xiikla ti juraxetike.

70 pero k'usi ta xkutik chijmuyotik ˀun xiik ti juraxetike.
ta jpas jtek'obtik xiik la ti juraxetike.

71 ˀentonse lik la spas stek'obik k'uchaˀal ˀeskalera.
vaˀi ˀun muyik la ti juraxetike.

He lay buried there for three days. 60
And each day, the Jews went there to see the place where
Our Holy Father lay buried.

There Our Holy Father lay buried. 61
He had not escaped.

So, the Jews now thought that Our Holy Father was really dead. 62
There they came every day to check up on the burial site.

And every time they came to see, he remained buried there. 63
He did not stir.

Then, on the third day, Our Holy Father emerged from the grave. 64
He arose into heaven.

Now, the Jews saw that Our Holy Father burst forth from the grave. 65
They rushed to recapture him right away.

But they did not manage to overtake Our Holy Father, 66
For he promptly rose up into heaven.

His mother stayed on the earth. 67
She was all alone.
As for Our Holy Father, he ascended to the sky.

Then the Jews saw that there was radiance in the sky. 68
"That radiance in the sky is San Salvador!", they exclaimed.[4]

There he is! 69
So let's climb up!
Let's kill him!" said the Jews to one another.

"But how will we manage to climb up?" wondered the Jews. 70
"Let's make some steps," said the Jews.

"With that, they started to make steps, just like a ladder. 71
And so the Jews climbed up.

72 ta k'unk'un la ta k'unk'un la,
ˀimuyik tajmek ta vinajel ti juraxetike.

73 ˀaˀ la mu sk'anik ti ˀoy ti jtotike.
ˀech'o xal ˀimuy smilik ta vinajel.

74 pero ti juraxetike poˀot xa xk'otik ta ˀoˀlol vinajel,
ti k'alal ˀavan ti ˀanjel,
ˀibalch'ujik skotol ti juraxetike k'alal ta ˀolon.

75 lajik ta majel yuˀun ˀanjel,
li ˀanjeletik mu sk'an xmuy juraxetik ta vinajel.

76 mu sk'an smilik ti jch'ultotike.
ˀech'o xal la smajik ti juraxetike.

77 vaˀi ˀun ti juraxetike muˀyuk bu xmuyik ta vinajel.
te ˀibalch'ujik ta ˀoˀlol vinajel skotol ti juraxetike.

78 pero ti juraxetike muˀyuk bu xcham skotolik.
jlom ˀicham.
jlom muˀyuk bu xcham.

79 ˀentonse ti jtotik ˀoxib k'ak'al te ta vinajel.
vaˀi ˀun ta yoxibal k'ak'al ˀichaˀsut yalel ta banumil ti jch'ultotike.

80 k'alal k'ot ta banumil ti jch'ultotike,
te k'ot sta ti juraxetike.

81 ˀentonse ti juraxetik yilik ti k'ot ta banumil ti jtotik xtoke,
bat smilik.

82 vaˀi ˀun ti jtotike la jyal:
mu xamilikun ta ˀech noˀox.
ˀaˀ lek pasbikun jkurusil.

83 te chicham ta kurus.
ˀaˀ mas lek yuˀun mu jk'an ti ˀech noˀox chamilikune
xi la ti jch'ultotike.

Little by little, little by little, 72
The Jews pressed upwards towards heaven.

The reason was that they didn't want Our Father to live. 73
That was why they climbed up to kill him in the sky.

But, when the Jews had almost reached the center of heaven, 74
The Earth Lords cried out with a loud voice,
And all the Jews were cast down.[5]

They died from the beating that the Earth Lords gave them, 75
For the Earth Lords did not want the Jews to climb up to heaven.

They didn't want them to kill Our Holy Father. 76
That is why they beat them up.

So it was that the Jews did not succeed in climbing up to the sky. 77
All the Jews fell back to earth from where they were
at the center of heaven.

However, not all of the Jews perished. 78
Some died.
Some did not die.

Now, Our Father was there in the sky for three days. 79
But on the third day, Our Holy Father came back down to earth.

When Our Holy Father arrived on earth, 80
There he found the surviving Jews.

When the Jews saw that Our Father had come to earth again, 81
They rushed to kill him.

But Our Father told them: 82
"Don't just kill me outright.
It would be better if you made me a cross.

There I am going to die on the cross. 83
It would be better that way, for I don't want you to kill me
in a common way," said Our Holy Father.

84 ˀentonse ti juraxetike laj la xch'unik.
bat la spasik ti kuruse.

85 vaˀi ˀun k'alal bat spasik kurus ti juraxetike,
te la bat ti jtotik ˀeke.

86 bat la sk'el stuk ti skurusil,
ti k'u smuk'ul ta sk'ane.

87 k'alal syakel ta xˀabtej ti juraxetik te nopol vaˀal ti jtotike.
ta sk'el mi lek ta spasbat ti skurusile.

88 k'alal yil ti te busul ti kamul teˀe,
laj la stzak laj la sjip ˀel ta ˀuk'um ti kamul teˀe.

89 vaˀi ˀun ti kamul teˀe pas ta coy.
skotol ti kamul teˀe.
pero jtotik ta sjip ti kamul teˀ ta ˀuk'ume.

90 ˀentonse k'alal meltzah ti kuruse jyich'ik ˀel la skajanik ˀel ta snekebik ti juraxetike.
la jyich'ik ˀel k'alal k'otik ta yut ch'ulna ta chamoˀ.

91 vaˀi ˀun k'alal k'otik ta yut ch'ulna ti juraxetike.
lik la svaˀanik ti kuruse.

92 pero mu la svaˀik yuˀunik tajmek.
toj ˀol la tajmek ti kuruse.

93 laj la saˀik jun teˀ laj la spajik ta banumil.
snitik ta ch'ojon ti kuruse.

94 ˀaˀ la te la xchukik ti ch'ojon ti bu la spajik ti teˀe.
ˀentonse ti kuruse vaˀi la.
te la la spajik ta yut ch'ulna.

95 vaˀi ˀun ti teˀ ti bu la xchukik ti ch'ojone joybijla ta kaˀ.
ti voˀnee teˀ toˀox li kaˀe.
pero pas ta kaˀ ti teˀe.

So the Jews obeyed him. 84
They went to make a cross.

Now, when the Jews were busy making the cross, 85
Our Father went to the site of their labors.

He went to oversee the making of his own cross, 86
To advise them on how big it should be.

And while the Jews kept on working, Our Father stood close by. 87
He was watching to see that his cross was well made.

When he saw the wood chips lying there, 88
He picked up the wood chips and threw them into the river.

With that, the wood chips turned into fish. 89
This happened with all of the wood chips.
This was the work of Our Father who threw the wood chips into the river.[6]

Then, when the cross was finished, the Jews dragged it along 90
hoisted on their shoulders.
They carried it to the Chamula church.

Then the Jews came into the church. 91
They started to raise up the cross.

But they could not raise it at all. 92
The cross was too heavy.

They found a short stake and drove it upright into the ground. 93
Using this to gain leverage, they pulled on the cross with a rope.

They did it by tying a rope on it there where they had driven in the stake. 94
This is how they made the cross stand upright.
They anchored it there inside the church.[7]

Then, the stake where they had tied the rope turned into a horse. 95
In times long ago, the horse was still a piece of wood, just like this stake.
And it was this very piece of wood that turned into a horse.

96 ˀentonse k'alal vaˀi ti kuruse:
veno chamilikun.
pero mu ta ˀorauk.
ˀaˀ to ta vukubal yernex xi la ti jch'ultotike.

97 baˀyel la jyalbe sbi ti k'ak'al ti k'usi ˀora ta xchame.
laj la yal:
sba yernex.
scibal yernex.
yoxibal yernex.
xchanibal yernex.
svoˀobal yernex.
svakibal yernex.
vukubal yernex ˀaˀ to chamilikun xi la ti jch'ultotike.

98 xuˀuk xiik la ti juraxetike.
laj la xch'unik ti mantal ti juraxetike.

99 ˀaˀ to la smilik ti jtotik ta vukubal yernexe.
vaˀi ˀun ta vukubal yernex la smilik ti jtotike.
te ˀicham ta kurus ta vukubal yernex.

100 pero juraxetik milvanik ti voˀnee.
ˀentonse ti juraxetik ti k'alal yilik cham ti jtotik ta kuruse
ta ˀox xjatavik.

101 pero muˀyuk xa bu xjatavik.
la jyich' tzakel ta ˀora.

102 ˀaˀ la tzakvan ti ˀanjeletike.
muˀyuk xa bu xjatavik ti juraxetike.

103 vaˀi ˀun ti ˀanjeletik ti k'alal la stzakik ti juraxetike.
laj la xchik'ik ta k'ok' ta ˀora.

104 te la ˀicham skotol ti juraxetike.
ˀech'o la xal ˀech snaˀojik li kirsanoetik ta chamoˀe ta xchik'ik
ta k'ok' ti jurax jujun ˀavile.
yuˀun ˀech la spasik ti voˀnee.

Then, when the cross was standing upright, he commanded: 96
"Fine. You are determined to kill me.
But don't do it now.
Wait until the Seventh Friday," said Our Holy Father.

First he told them the name of the day on which he would die. 97
He told them:
"First Friday.
Second Friday.
Third Friday.
Fourth Friday.
Fifth Friday.
Sixth Friday.
Seventh Friday—only then are you to kill me," said Our Holy Father.[8]

"All right," said the Jews. 98
The Jews obeyed his orders.

They did not kill Our Father until the Seventh Friday. 99
And, on the Seventh Friday they killed Our Father.
He died there on the cross on the Seventh Friday.

So it was that the Jews carried out this murder long ago. 100
Once the Jews saw Our Father dead on the cross,
they were going to flee.

But, in the end, they did not succeed in fleeing. 101
They were taken prisoner at once.

The Earth Lords captured them. 102
The Jews were not able to get away.

So it was that the Earth Lords caught the Jews. 103
They lost no time in burning them alive in a great fire.

All the Jews died there. 104
That is why the people of Chamula have the custom of
burning Judas in the fire every year.
It is because the Jews committed these crimes long ago.[9]

1 jun kuento ta voˀnee,
jun kuento ta voˀnee sventa jch'ulmeˀtik ta vinajel.

2 ˀentonse ti jch'ulmeˀtike jaˀ la tz'akal muy ta vinajel.
ˀa li jtotik la ta vinajele.
jaˀ la baˀyel muy ta vinajel ti jtotike.

3 jech ti jtotike:
cham la ti jtotik ta vinajele.

4 k'alal la cham ti skerem ˀole xˀok' xa la tajmek ti jch'ulmeˀtik ta vinajele.
ti k'alal cham ti skerem ˀole.

5 ˀentonse bat la ta mukel ti jtotik ta vinajele,
jech la ti jch'ulmeˀtik ta vinajele ta la xˀok' yuˀun tajmek ti yole.

6 ˀentonse ti jtotik lae ˀech' la ta ˀinyerno ti jtotik la ta vinajele.
ˀentonse ta yoxibal la k'ak'al ˀun ta vinajel xa la ˀoy ti jtotik ta vinajel ne.

7 ˀentonse k'alal la ti yilbe sat ti skerem ˀole lek xa la xaˀiti jmeˀtik ta vinajel.
ˀentonse jlikel la me muy ta vinajel ta ˀora ti jch'ulmeˀtik ta vinajele.

8 bat la sk'opon ti yole.
ˀentonse lik la loˀilajuk xchiˀuk smeˀ ti jtotik ta vinajel.

9 ˀa li ˀoˀote meˀ chaxanav ta ˀak'obaltik xut la smeˀ ti jtotik ta vinajele.
ˀa li ˀoˀone ta xixanav ta k'ak'altik li ˀoˀone xut la ti smeˀe.

TEXT 9

Of Our Holy Mother in Heaven

Manuel López Calixto

This a story of long ago, 1
An account of long ago about Our Holy Mother in Heaven.

Now, Our Holy Mother was not the first one to ascend into the sky. 2
That one was Our Lord Sun/Christ.
Our Lord Sun/Christ was the first to ascend into the sky.

So it was with Our Lord Sun/Christ: 3
Our Lord Sun/Christ in Heaven died.

When her son died, Our Holy Mother in Heaven wept bitterly. 4
This happened when her son died.

When Our Lord Sun/Christ in Heaven went to the grave, 5
Our Holy Mother in Heaven wept bitterly for her son.

After that Our Lord Sun/Christ went to the underworld. 6
Then, on the third day, Our Lord Sun/Christ found his
dwelling place in Heaven.

When she saw the face of her son, Our Holy Mother in Heaven felt happy.[1] 7
So Our Holy Mother in Heaven left at once to take
her own place in the sky.

She went to talk to her son. 8
So Our Lord Sun/Christ in Heaven and his mother started to talk.

"You, Mother, you are going to walk at night," said Our Lord 9
Sun/Christ in Heaven.
"As for me, I am going to walk by day," he said to his mother.

10 pere koˀol chijxanavotik xut la ti smeˀe.
jech'o xal ti yoˀ koˀol ta xanavik xchiˀuk smeˀ ti jtotik ta vinajele xi ti ˀanima jyayae.

11 la jyalbun kaˀi ti loˀile ti voˀnee.
pero jaˀ la ti mas la voˀne tajmek lae ti k'alal la muy ta vinajel ti jtotike.

12 pero mu jnaˀtik sjayibal xa ˀavil.
mu xavil jaˀ ti mas voˀne tajmeke xi ti ˀanima jyayae.

13 ˀentonse jech'o xal k'alal mi li jchamutik ˀoˀtike ta xijbat k'alal ta ˀinyerno mi li chame.
pero yuˀun jaˀ la jech ti jtotik voˀne k'alal cham me ˀech' la ta ˀinyerno.

14 ti k'alal la muy ta vinajel ti jtotik ta vinajele ti voˀne lae xi la jyalbun kaˀi ti ˀanima jyayae.
jaˀ jech muy ta vinajel ti jtotik voˀne lae.

15 jech'o sal ti yoˀ koˀol la ta xanavik xchiˀuk smeˀ ti jtotik ta vinajele.
ˀentonse la li jch'ulmeˀtik ta vinajele ˀoy la smelol yuˀunik li kirsanoetike.

"But we shall walk in the same direction," he said to his mother. 10
That is the reason why Our Lord Sun/Christ in Heaven
and his mother both move in the same way,
according to my late grandmother.[2]

She told me this story a long time ago. 11
It was of course even longer ago when Our Lord Sun/Christ
first ascended into the sky.

We don't really know how many years ago all of this happened. 12
My late grandmother said to me: "Don't you see that this
took place long, long ago?

That is why, when we die, we go to the underworld. 13
The reason is that Our Lord Sun/Christ passed through
the underworld when he died long ago.[3]

Then Our Lord Sun/Christ ascended into the sky long ago," 14
continued my late grandmother.
So it happened that Our Lord Sun/Christ ascended into the sky.

So it is that Our Lord Sun/Christ in Heaven walks together with his mother. 15
That is Our Holy Mother in Heaven's secret wisdom for the people.[4]

1 ˀoy jun kuento sventa jmeˀtik ta vinajel xi.
la jyalbun kaˀi jmeˀ ti kuentoe.

2 ˀi te la jyalbun ta jna.
k'alal lik ˀo ti kuento yuˀun lilok'kutik ta pana ta ˀak'obaltik.

3 ˀi la jkilkutik ti jmeˀtik ˀune.
ˀi jaˀ te lik ˀo ti kuentoe.

4 jech la ti jmeˀtik ti voˀne.
liˀ toˀox la nakal ta banamil ti jmeˀtik ta vinajele.

5 ˀoy la stzek.
ˀi ˀoy la sk'uˀ jech la chak k'uchaˀal voˀotike.

6 vaˀun ˀoy la yol ti jmeˀtik la ˀune,
ˀi spetoj la yol ti jmeˀtik la ˀune.

7 jech la ti yol ti jmeˀtik la ˀune,
ˀi ta la xloˀilaj tajmek ti yole.

8 jech la ti smeˀ ˀune,
ˀi te sk'eloj ti k'usi la ta xal ti yole.

9 jech la ti yole,
te la xvulvun la tajmek.
ta la xal smantale.

10 jech la ti smeˀ ˀune,
ta la stzeˀin tajmek.

TEXT 10

Why the Moon Has Only One Eye

Marián López Calixto

Here is an account of what is said about Our Holy Mother Moon in Heaven. 1
My mother told me this story.

She told it to me at my house. 2
When the story came up, it was because we had gone outside at night.

And we saw Our Mother Moon in Heaven. 3
And that is how the story came up.

This is what happened to Our Mother Moon long ago. 4
Our Mother Moon in Heaven still lived here on earth.

She wore a skirt. 5
She wore clothing just like we do.

Then Our Mother Moon had a son, 6
And Our Mother Moon held her son in her arms.

As for Our Mother Moon's child, 7
He was given to talking a lot.

As for his mother, 8
She listened carefully to what her son said.

As for her child, 9
There was no end to his jabbering.
There was no end to his bossiness.

As for his mother, 10
She was overtaken with laughter.

11 pere k'uchaˀalot tajmek leˀ ˀune.
toj toyol ta xaloˀilaj tajmek xi la ti smeˀe.

12 mu la xaˀi ˀalbel tajmek ti yole.
ˀi xvulvun la tajmek.

13 voˀote meˀ ta xijbatotik ta vinajel.
ˀaˀ li jmariane ta xkom liˀ ta banamile xi la ti yole.

14 pere k'uchaˀalot tajmek leˀ ˀune xalik.
mu ˀanuk xachi tajmek ˀune xi la ti smeˀe.
pere yuˀun jech tajmek xi la ti ˀolole.

15 vaˀun jech ti smeˀe kich'tik pus marian.
tik'o siˀ xi la ti smeˀ ti jmarian ˀune.

16 veno xi la ti jmarian ˀune.
ˀi stik' la ti siˀ ta pus ti kereme.

17 vaˀun jech la ti jxalik ˀune k'uchaˀal ta satik' ti puse.
xi la ti jxalike.

18 yuˀun ta la xich' la pus la jmeˀtik xi la ti jmariane.
ˀa veno xi la ti jxalike.

19 vaˀun jech la ti smeˀ la ˀune batan ta xak'elo ti puse.
xi la ti smeˀ ti jmariane.

20 veno ta xibat ta jk'el xi la ti jmariane.
vaˀun k'ot la sk'el ti pus ˀune.

21 jech la ti jmarian ˀune ˀi sut la talel ta sna ˀun.
tzajub xa me ˀun meˀ.
mi ta xijˀochotik ˀun xi la ti jmarian ˀune.

"But why on earth are you carrying on this way? 11
You're certainly talking a lot," laughed his mother, amused at
the strange child's behavior.

Her son would not pay the slightest attention to what she said. 12
And he continued to mutter lots of strange things.

"You, Mother, you and I are going to go to the sky. 13
And my brother Marián will stay here on earth," said her son.[1]

"But why are you carrying on like this, Xalik?[2] 14
It is not your place to speak like this," said his mother,
utterly exasperated.
"But it is my place to speak the truth," said the child.

Then his mother, ignoring Xalik, spoke to her older son: 15
"Let's take a bath, Marián.
Put some wood in the sweat," said Marián's mother.

"All right," said Marián. 16
And the boy put the wood on the bathhouse hearth.[3]

And so Xalik said, "Why are you putting that firewood in the bathhouse?" 17
So spoke Xalik.

"Because our mother wants to take a bath," replied Marián. 18
"Oh, all right," said Xalik.

And so his mother said to Marián, "Go tend the bathhouse." 19
So said Marián's mother.

"All right, I'll go take care of it," replied Marián. 20
And so he went to take care of the bathhouse.

Then Marián returned to the house to let her know that it was ready. 21
"Now it's ready, Mother.
"Shall we go in?" asked Marián.

22 ˀa mi tzajub xa ˀun.
vaˀun jech la ti smeˀ ti jmariane ˀune:
bu ti jxalik ˀune xi la ti smeˀ ti jmarian ˀune.

23 mu jnaˀ k'uxi bat.
ch'abal liˀe xi la ti jmarian ˀune.

24 vaˀun jech la ti smeˀ ti jmarian ˀune ˀi la jyapta la ˀun:
xalik bu ˀoyot taj ˀune.
laˀ me kich'tik ti pus ˀune.

25 pero k'uxi bat ta ˀavitz'in ˀune xi la smeˀ ti jmarian ˀune.
mu jnaˀ k'uxi bat.
pero liˀ toˀox kile xi la ti jmariane.

26 veno ˀochkutik ˀun chaˀe.
ch'abal bu xtal ta ˀavitz'ine xi la ti jmeˀtik ˀune.
vaˀun ˀochik la ta pus ˀun.

27 te ta xtal tana,
te tz'akal xˀoch tana xi la ti jmarian ˀune.

28 vaˀun naka la ˀoch ta pus ti smeˀ ˀune,
tal la ti jxalik ˀune.

29 meˀ ta xiˀoch ta pus ˀek xi la ti jxalik ˀune.
mu xaˀoch xi la ti jmarian ˀune.

30 meˀ u xak' ˀochkun ta pus ti jmariane xi la ti jxalik.
pere k'uchaˀal mu xatal ta ˀora ˀek ˀune xi la ti smeˀ ti jxalike.

31 ˀana ta xiˀoch kaˀ ˀek ˀun xi la tajmek ti jxalike.
veno ˀochan tal chaˀe.
lok' ˀak'uˀ xi la ti smeˀ ˀune.

32 ˀey malun to me ˀune xi la ti jxalike.
ˀana soban me ˀun xi la ti smeˀ ˀune.

33 veno xi la ti jxalike.
likel la ˀoch ta pus ta ˀora.

"Oh, is it ready to go?" she asked. 22
Then Marián's mother added, with a touch of suspicion:
"Where is Xalik?" asked Marián's mother.

"I don't know what's become of him. 23
He isn't here," said Marián.

Then it happened that Marián's mother called out to Xalik: 24
"Xalik, where are you?
Come on, let's take a bath.

But wherever did your brother go?" asked Marián's mother. 25
"I don't know where he went.
I just saw him here a minute ago," said Marián.

"Well, let's go ahead then. 26
Your brother must not be coming," said Our Mother Moon.
And so they went into the sweat-bath house.

"He'll be along in a little while, 27
Let him come in later," said Marián.

Then, just after his mother had gone into the bathhouse, 28
Xalik appeared.

"Mama, I want to come in the bath house too," insisted Xalik. 29
"Don't come in," said Marián.

"Mama, Marián won't let me come into the bathhouse," complained Xalik. 30
"But why didn't you come on time?" scolded Xalik's mother.

But I want to come in too," insisted Xalik. 31
"Well, come in, then, but hurry up.
Take off your clothes," said his mother.

"Okay, wait for me," said Xalik. 32
"Hurry up, then," replied his mother impatiently.

"All right," said Xalik. 33
And in no time he had taken his place in the bathhouse.

34 vaˀun jech la ti jxalik ˀune voˀon ta xkak' talel job voˀo.
xi la ti jxalike.

35 mala to me ˀun.
sk'an to me xipuch'i xi la ti smeˀ ˀune.

36 vaˀun jech la ti jxalik la ˀune:
likel la yak' la talel ta ˀora li sjob la ti pus ˀune.

37 jech la ti smeˀ ˀune ˀichotol to la ˀun toj k'ak'el la ti sat ˀune.
ˀay, iii . . . k'ak' xa ti jsat ˀavuˀun ˀune.

38 k'uchaˀal mu xamala ˀora ˀune xalik xi la ti smeˀ ˀune.
xˀilin xa la tajmek ti smeˀ ti jxalik ˀune.

39 vaˀun ti smeˀ la ti jxalik ˀune lok' la ta pus ˀun.
ˀi tub xa la ti sate.
ˀi jbejbej xa la ti sat ˀune.

40 vaˀun ˀilok' la talel ˀun.
laj xa ti jsat ˀune marian.
k'el ˀavil ˀun.

41 chopol sjol ta ˀavitz'in ˀune.
laj xa ti jsat ˀune.
tub xa ˀune.
ˀanaˀ k'uchaˀal mu xich'be smelol ˀune xiut la ti jmariane.

42 veno yuˀun jaˀ jech ta jk'an ta ˀasate.
k'el ˀasat ˀune lek xa ˀun.
jaˀ ta jk'an ma leˀ ˀune xi la ti jxalik ˀune.

43 ˀi stzeˀtzun xa la tajmek ti jtotike.
yaˀ la jset jset la ti sat la ˀune.
yuˀun la k'ak' ta pus ti jmeˀtike.

44 vaˀun ti jmeˀtik la ˀune bat la k'alal la ti vinajel.
bat la xchiˀuk ti yol jxalik ˀune.

Then Xalik said, "I am going to toss more hot water on the hearthstones for you." 34
So said Xalik.

"Wait a minute. 35
I haven't had a chance to lie down yet," said his mother.

Then it happened that Xalik did this: 36
Quickly he threw hot water onto the bathhouse hearth.

However, his mother was still sitting up and her eye got burned. 37
"Ay! Eee . . . Eee . . . ! Now you have gone and scalded my eye!

"Why didn't you wait a minute?" screamed his mother. 38
Xalik's mother flew into a terrible rage.

Xalik's mother fled from the bathhouse. 39
For her eye was blinded.
Now she had but one eye.

Once she got out, she yelled: 40
"My eye is gone, Marián!
Come and see!

"Your younger brother is a shithead, a wicked child! 41
My eye is gone!
Now I am half blind!
Why doesn't that child ever learn to behave?" she exclaimed helplessly to Marián.

"Well, as a matter of fact, I like your face that way. 42
Your face looks very pretty now.
I like it like that," said Xalik, rudely asserting his opinion.

Now, indeed, the sun shines very brightly. 43
But, as for his mother, she now has but one eye.
It's because Our Mother Moon was scalded in the sweat bath.

After all of this, Our Mother Moon went up into heaven. 44
She went there with her son Xalik.

45 vaˀun k'alal ta xˀik'un ˀune ch'abal xa la k'ixin ti xojobal ti jmeˀtik la ˀune.
ˀi jaˀ la ti yol la ˀune jaˀ la mas k'ixin tajmek ˀun.
ˀi mas la sak tajmek ti xojobale.

46 veno meˀ a xkal jbel jmantal:
ta jpastik banamil xi la ti jxalike.

47 jecheˀ chaval.
pere k'uchaˀalot yan ˀaba tajmeke xi la ti smeˀe.

48 ˀa jech kal tajmek xi la ti jxalike.
ˀi xbat la ta jujot,
ta xanobal tajmek li jxalike.

49 mu la jaˀuk snaˀ xchoti ti jtotik la ˀune.
puru la xanobal ta spas tajmek.

50 ta la saˀ talel ti pom la sloˀik la ˀune.
puru la pom ta sloˀ ti jtotik.

51 laj ˀo ti kuentoe.

Now when it gets dark, the rays of Our Mother Moon are no longer hot. 45
The truth is that her son is much hotter.
His rays are much brighter.

"Well, Mama, I have a plan: 46
Let us make the earth and act together to set the
order of things," suggested Xalik.

"You're talking nonsense. 47
Why do you go on saying crazy things like that?" asked his mother.

"What I say is just how things will be," said Xalik. 48
And so he set off for each side of heaven,[4]
Xalik went off to travel without end.

Our Father Sun doesn't know how to rest. 49
He is always on the go, traveling constantly.

He goes about looking for incense to eat.[5] 50
Incense is Our Father Sun's only food.

And that's all there is to this story. 51

1 kuento baˀyel kirsano.
veno ti k'alal tal ti baˀyel kirsanoe jch'ultotik la.

2 jun la vinik jun la antz.
sbi la ˀaran la ˀeva la ti baˀyel kirsanoe.

3 ˀentonse ti ˀarane ti evae muˀyuk la snaik.
ta yolon la teˀ ta xvayik komo ti voˀnee.

TEXT II

Of the First People, Who Were Like Gods

Xalik López Castellanos

Here is a story about the first people. 1
When the first people came they were like gods.

There were one man and one woman. 2
The first people were called Adam and Eve.

Now, Adam and Eve didn't have houses. 3
They slept under a tree, for this was long ago.

FIGURE II

Now, Adam and Eve didn't have houses.
They slept under a tree, for this was long ago.

4 ch'abal la vitz,
ch'abal la nail ch'en,
ch'abal la tonetik.

5 solel la parijo ti banumile;
muˀyuk la vitz,
muˀyuk la beˀoˀe,
solel la parijo ti banumile.

6 ˀech'o yal ti ˀarane ti ˀevae ta yolon teˀ ta xvayik,
komo ˀaˀ baˀyel kirsano ti ˀarane ti ˀevae.

7 ˀentonse ti ˀarane ti ˀevae naˀtik k'usi lik snopik;
lik la spasik ˀach'el.
lik la spatik ti ˀach'ele.

8 lik la yak'bik sk'ob sjol sniˀ yok xchikin sat.
skotol la jyak'bik.

9 lek la spasik.
ˀentonse ti ˀach'ele lik la joybijuk ta kirsano.

10 ta xa la k'opoj.
ta ˀora ti ˀach'el toˀoxe pas la ta kirsano.

11 ˀentonse ti jtotik ta vinajele chopol la xil
ti muˀyuk ti vitze,
ti muˀyuk ti tone,
ti muˀyuk ti beˀoˀe.

12 muˀyuk la bu xuˀ xanav ti ˀoˀe.
ch'abal la yochob.

13 mu la xuˀ xnaki ti snich'nabe.
ta la xnojik ta ˀoˀ.

14 ˀa ti ch'abal beˀoˀe,
ti ch'abal vitzetike.

There was not a single mountain, 4
Not a single cave,
Not a single rock.

The earth was just flat; 5
No mountains,
No valleys.
The earth was just flat.

So Adam and Eve slept under a tree, 6
For Adam and Eve were the first people.

So, who knows just what Adam and Eve were thinking? 7
They started to prepare clay.
They started to shape the clay.

They stuck hands, head, nose, feet, ears, and eyes onto it. 8
They stuck on all of these parts.

They did it very well. 9
Then the clay began to turn into people.

Now it spoke. 10
Quickly that which had been clay turned into people.

Then Our Father in Heaven saw that it was wrong 11
That there were no mountains,
That there were no rocks,
That there were no valleys.

That there was no place for the water to go. 12
There was not even a sinkhole.[1]

His children could not survive. 13
For they would be covered with water.

For there were no valleys, 14
There were no mountains.

15 k'alal ta xtal nikel,
toj tzotz la.

16 ta xˀech' ti nikele ˀaˀ la ti ch'abal tone.
ˀentonse ti jch'ultotik ta vinajele lik la slomes ti banumile.

17 tal la jun nikel,
pero toj tzotz la tajmek ti nikel ˀech'e.

18 ˀentonse lom la skotol ti banumile.
ˀech'o xal ˀoy vitzetik,
ˀoy beoˀetik,
ˀoy naˀil ch'en,
ˀoy tonetik.

Then there came an earthquake, 15
  And it was a strong one.

The earthquake happened because there were no rocks; 16
    nothing to serve as an anchor.
  Whereupon Our Holy Father Sun in Heaven started
    to cause the ground to collapse.

There came an earthquake, 17
  But what an earthquake! It was very, very strong!

When it struck, the earth collapsed and crumbled down. 18
  That is why there are mountains,
  Why there are valleys,
  Why there are caves,
  Why there are rocks.

FIGURE 12

When it struck, the earth collapsed and crumbled down.
  That is why there are mountains,
  Why there are valleys,
  Why there are caves,
  Why there are rocks.

19 k'alal toˀox ch'abal tone toj toyol la xˀech' nikel.
jujun la k'ak'al ta xˀech' ti nikele.

20 muˀyuk la ˀol ti banumile.
ˀech'o la xal la jyak' ton ti jch'ultotik ta vinajele.

21 la jyak' ton,
la jyak' vitzetik,

22 la jyak' be-oˀetik,
la jyak' yochobetik.

23 ˀentonse xuˀ xa xanav ti ˀoˀetike.
mu xa xnojik ta ˀoˀ ti kirsanoetike.

24 ˀech la ti nikel xtoke.
muˀyuk xa la bu ta xjelav jujun k'ak'al.

25 mu xa la xnik,
yuˀun ti meˀ nikele toj ˀol xa la ti banumile.

26 pero ti baˀyel toˀoxe muˀyuk la ˀol
ˀaˀ la ti muˀyuk toˀox tone.

27 ˀentonse k'alal la jyak' ton ti jch'ultotike,
ˀalub ti banumile.

28 ta xtal ti nikele,
pero jutuk xa.

29 muˀyuk xa ta xˀech' jujun k'ak'al.
pero ta voˀnee jujun k'ak'al ta xˀech' ti nikele.

30 ˀentonse ti ˀarane ti ˀevae ti bu nakalike,
muˀyuk la bu xlom ti banumile.

31 ti k'alal ˀech' ti nikele te la chotajik ta yolon teˀ
ti k'alal ˀech' ti nikele.

When there were still no rocks in place, earthquakes were commonplace. 19
Earthquakes came every day.

The earth bore no burden of weight. 20
That is why Our Holy Father Sun in Heaven created rocks.

He made rocks, 21
He made hills,

He made valleys, 22
He made sinkholes.

This allowed the water to flow away. 23
So the people were no longer submerged in water.

So also with the earthquakes. 24
They stopped coming every day.

There were no longer so many tremors, 25
For the earth now felt very heavy to the Mother of Earthquakes.[2]

But in the beginning it did not feel heavy to her 26
Because there were still no rocks.

Then when Our Father Sun in Heaven put down the rocks, 27
The earth became heavy and stable.

Earthquakes still come today, 28
But now there are fewer.

They no longer come every day. 29
But long ago earthquakes came every day.

However, at the place and time that Adam and Eve lived, 30
The earth had not yet collapsed.

When the earthquake happened, there they were, sitting at the foot of a tree. 31
That is the way things were at the time of the earthquake.

32 ˀech ti ˀach'el la spasik ta kirsanoe.
ta la chotajik yolon teˀ xchiˀuk ti ˀarane ti ˀevae.

33 pero kirsano xa la ti ˀach'el toˀoxe.
pasem xa la ta kirsano.

34 jun la vinik,
jun la ˀantz.

35 pero ch'abal la sk'uˀik.
t'anajtik la k'ajomal la.

36 makal juteb yatik xchakik,
xchukojik la ta xch'utik.

37 pero mu la snaˀ xveˀik,
mu la snaˀ xk'ejinik,
mu la snaˀik spasik k'in,
mu la snaˀik xˀak'otajik,
mu la snaˀik xvayik,
te la chotajtik noˀox.

38 muˀyuk la ta xvayik skotol k'ak'al,
ˀech la ti banumile muˀyuk la ta xˀik'ub;
sak ˀo la skotol k'ak'al.

39 ta la xbat ti jch'ultotike,
ta la xtal jch'ulmeˀtik,

40 pero koˀol xchiˀuk jch'ultotik ti jch'ulmeˀtike;
muˀyuk la ta xˀik'ub.

41 ˀentonse ti jtotik ta vinajele mu la sk'an ti muˀyuk ta xˀik'ub ti banumile.
mu la xuˀ xvay ti snich'nabe.
ˀaˀ la ti sak ˀo skotol k'ak'ale.

42 ˀentonse ˀik'ubuk ti banumile.
ˀoy xa la ˀak'obaltik,
ˀoy xa la k'ak'altik.

The clay beings they had made were with them. 32
They were sitting under the tree beside Adam and Eve.

But these beings that had once been clay were now human. 33
They had already turned into people.

One was a man, 34
One was a woman.

But they had no clothes. 35
They were just naked.

Their genitals and asses were a bit covered, 36
For they had tied a covering around their waists.

But they did not know how to eat, 37
How to sing,
How to have festivals,
How to dance,
How to sleep,
They just sat there.

They didn't sleep at all, 38
For the earth did not darken;
There was light all day.

Our Holy Father Sun set, 39
Our Holy Mother Moon rose,

But Our Holy Mother Moon and Our Holy Father Sun were just alike; 40
It did not get dark.

Then Our Father in Heaven became displeased that there 41
was no darkness on earth.
His children were unable to sleep.
There was light all day long.

So he caused the earth to get dark. 42
Now there was night,
Now there was day.

43 veno ʔentonse ti k'alal makbat sat ti jch'ulmetike,
jlikel la tal pukujetik.

44 pero mu la bu xʔilik k'uxi tal ti pukujetike.
te xa ʔonoʔox la,
vaʔajtik,
yilik.

45 ʔaʔ la ti makal xa sat ti ti jch'ulmeʔtike mu xa la xʔil ti yalabe.
ʔech'o la xal lok' ti pukujetike.

46 veno ʔech la ti kirsano ti ʔach'el toʔoxe,
ti la spas ti ʔavane ti ʔevae,
vayik la xchibalik.

Then, when the face of Our Holy Mother Moon was veiled, 43
now in the face of darkness,
The demons rushed to the scene.

But the early people did not see how the demons came. 44
They were just there,
Standing,
Watching.

Because Our Holy Mother Moon's face was covered, she could 45
no longer watch over her children.
That is why the demons were able to come out.

So these people who had been fashioned of clay, 46
These whom Adam and Eve had made,
These two slept.

FIGURE 13

Because Our Holy Mother Moon's face was covered, she could
no longer watch over her children.
That is why the demons were able to come out.

47 muˀyuk la bu xaˀi ˀoch svayelik ti chaˀvoˀ kirsanoe.
ˀech la ti ˀavane ti ˀevae vayik la muˀyuk bu xaˀik ˀoch svayelik.

48 ˀaˀ la ti muˀyuk toˀox jch'ultotik ta ch'ulnae.
ch'abal la ch'ulna.
ch'abal la naetik.

49 k'ajomal la ˀoy jch'ultotik ta vinajel xchiˀuk jch'ulmeˀtik.
ˀaˀ noˀox.

50 ˀech'o la xal ˀoy ˀep pukujetik,
k'ajomal jun jtotik ˀoy ta vinajel xchiˀuk jch'ulmeˀtik.

51 ta k'un to la laj lok'uk tal ti jtotiketik ta ch'ulnaetike.
pero ˀoy xaˀox la vitzetik beoˀetik.

52 ˀoy xaˀox skotol,
ti k'alal laj lok'uk ti jtotiketike ta ch'ulnae.

53 ˀentonse ti ˀarane ti ˀevae laj la stzak sbaik.
muˀyuk la bu xaˀik k'uxi stzak sbaik ˀaˀ la ti vayike.
ˀech'o la xal muˀyuk bu xaˀik la stzak sbaik.

These two early people did not realize that they had dropped off to sleep. 47
Adam and Eve also slept without realizing that they were sleeping.

It must be understood that there were still no saints in the church. 48
There was no church.
There were no houses.

There were none present but Our Holy Father Sun in Heaven and 49
Our Mother Moon in Heaven.
No others.

That is why so many demons lurked about, 50
For there was just Our Holy Father Sun in Heaven
with Our Holy Mother Moon.

Later, the saints in the church appeared. 51
By this time, then, mountains and valleys were already in place.

Everything would be in place at that future time, 52
When the saints eventually came to make their home in the church.

However, long before them, when the demons still lurked among us, 53
the time came for Adam and Eve to make love.
But they didn't understand how to start making love,
for they were fast asleep.
That is why they didn't think about having sex.

54 pero ʔaʔ la ti pukujetik la jyal mantale ti la stzak sbaik ti baʔyel kirsanoe.
ʔentonse ti ʔarane ti ʔevae toj lek la yaʔik ti k'alal la stzak sbaike.
jujun xa la k'ak'al ta stzak sbaik ʔaʔ la ti toj lek yaʔiktajmek.

55 veno lik la yalbe ti chaʔvoʔ kirsanoe ʔach'el toʔoxe:
k'alal chavayike xamey ʔabaik xabutz' ʔabaik.
pero toj lek tajmek xi la ti ʔarane ti ʔevae.

56 porke ti kirsano ti ʔach'el toʔoxe mu la snaʔ smey sbaik,
mu la snaʔ sbutz' sbaik,
mu la snaʔ xtajinik,
mu la snaʔ xʔabtejik.
skotol mu snaʔik.

57 ʔentonse laj la xch'unbik smantal ti ʔarane ti ʔevae;
lik la smey sbaik sbutz' sbaik ti ʔach'el toʔoxe.

But then it happened that the demons ordered the first people to make love. 54
Sure enough. Adam and Eve really got into the feeling of making love.
Now they made love every day because it felt very good.

So, they started to tell this to the two people, 55
those who had once been of clay:
"When you are sleeping, hug and kiss each other.
It's very, very nice," said Adam and Eve.

For the clay people didn't know how to hug each other, 56
Nor how to kiss each other,
Nor how to enjoy the foreplay of sex,
Nor how to enjoy the hard work of sex.
They didn't know anything, nor did they know each other.

Then they obeyed Adam and Eve's order; 57
Those who were once of clay started to hug and kiss each other.

FIGURE 14

But then it happened that the demons ordered the first people to
make love.
Sure enough. Adam and Eve really got into the feeling of
making love.
Now they made love every day because it felt very good.

58 veno ˀech la ta k'unk'un la vok' la yolik.
ˀech la lik bolikuk ˀo ti kirsanoetik ta voˀnee.
ta k'unk'un lik bolikuk.

59 pero mu la snaˀik spasik k'in,
mu la snaˀik xk'ejinik,
mu la snaˀik xˀuch'ik pox,
mu la snaˀik xˀak'otajik,
muˀyuk la snaik,
muˀyuk la sk'uˀik,
skotol mu snaˀik.

60 ˀech xtok mu la snaˀik ˀep xveˀik.
jbej la sat ˀixim ta sk'uxik.

61 jbej la ta sob.
jbej la ta ˀoˀlol k'ak'al.
jbej la ta mal k'ak'al.

62 pero ti baˀyele muˀyuk la ˀixim.
ˀaˀ noˀox la ˀoy ˀitaj napux xchiˀuk la chenek'.
ˀaˀ noˀox la.

63 ta k'un to la tal ti ˀixime,
pero ti ˀitaje ti chenek'e ti napuxe,
muˀyuk la bu xˀilik k'uxi tal;
te xa ˀonoˀox la.

64 yilik ˀaˀ la baˀyel lok' ti ˀitaje ti chenek'e;
ti ˀixime ˀaˀ la tz'akal to.

65 puru la ˀitaj ta sloˀik ti kirsanoe ti ˀach'el toˀoxe.
muˀyuk la bu ta sveˀik vaj.

66 ˀaˀ noˀox la ta sloˀik ˀitaj xchiˀuk chenek'.
pero jutuk noˀox la ta sloˀik ti ˀitaje ti napuxe.

67 ˀentonse ti pukujetike lik la smil ti jtotik ta vinajele,
ˀaˀ la ti toˀox xanav ta banamil ti jtotik ta vinajele.
ta k'un to muy ta vinajel xchiˀuk jch'ulmeˀtik.

So, in that way, little by little their children were born. 58
That is how the people of long ago started to reproduce.
They multiplied little by little.

But they didn't know how to have festivals, 59
They didn't know how to sing,
They didn't know how to drink rum,
They didn't know how to dance,
They didn't have houses,
They didn't have clothing,
They didn't know anything.

They didn't know how to eat enough, though. 60
They ate nothing but hard grains of corn.

They would eat one grain. 61
One at noon.
One in the late afternoon.

But in the beginning there was corn. 62
There was only cabbage, turnip greens, and beans.
That was all.

Corn came later, 63
But as for cabbage, beans, and turnip greens,
No one saw how they came;
They were just there.

They saw that cabbage and beans came first; 64
Corn came later.

The people who were once made of clay ate only cabbage. 65
They didn't eat tortillas.

They ate only cabbage and beans. 66
They ate only a little bit of cabbage and turnip greens.

Then the demons plotted to kill Our Father Sun in Heaven, 67
For at that time Our Father Sun in Heaven was still walking on the earth.
Afterwards, he went up to the sky with Our Holy Mother Moon.

68 ˀentonse ti jch'ultotik ta vinajele cham la.
laj la smukik pero muˀyuk la chamem.

69 pero ti pukujetike chamem xa la yilik.
laj xa la smukik ˀaˀ to la xˀilik kuxul la.

70 muˀyuk la chamem.
ta la xanav.

71 veno yilik ti muˀyuk bu xchame,
lik la yak'bik pox yuch' kapal la ta sk'ab pukujetik.

72 laj la yuch' ti jch'ultotike,
pero kapal la ta k'abil yakub la ti jch'ultotike.

73 yal la ta lum junuk ˀora.
ˀentonse ti jch'ultotik ta vinajele toj lek la yaˀi ti pox la jyuch'e.

74 ˀaˀ lek ˀech ta xkak'be yuch' li jnich'nabe.
Moˀoje ˀech ˀo skotol k'ak'al mu snaˀ xk'ejin.
mu snaˀ xˀak'otaj,
mu snaˀ spasik k'in.

75 ˀa lek ta xkak'be yuch' pox.
ta mi la jyuch' poxe ta xispasbun jk'inal.
ta xchanik ta stijik vob ˀarpa xi la ti jch'ultotik ta vinajele.

76 ˀentonse lik la xchanik yuch'el pox ti kirsano ti ˀach'el toˀoxe.
veno k'alal la jyuch'ik pox ti kirsanoe,
snaˀ xa la xk'ejinik;
snaˀ xa la xˀak'otajik;
snaˀ xa la stijik vob ˀarpa;
snaˀ xa la spasik k'in;
skotol snaˀik xa.

Then Our Father Sun in Heaven died. 68
They buried him, but he wasn't really dead.

But the demons *thought* that he was dead. 69
They had already buried him when they saw that he was alive.

He was not dead. 70
He was walking about!

Well, when they saw that he hadn't died, 71
This was when they started to give him rum to drink
mixed with the demons' own piss.[3]

Our Father Sun drank it, 72
And since it was mixed with piss, Our Father Sun got drunk.

He passed out there on the ground for an hour or so. 73
Then, once he came to, Our Holy Father Sun in Heaven recalled
that the rum that he had drunk tasted very good.

"It would be good to give this to my children to drink. 74
If I don't, they will never sing.
They won't know how to dance,
They won't know how to have festivals.

I had better give them this gift of rum to drink. 75
If they drink this rum they will surely have festivals in my honor.
They will learn to play the guitar and harp," mused
Our Holy Father Sun in Heaven.

So, the people who were once made of clay learned to drink rum. 76
This was the trick! When the people finally took to drinking rum,
They at last learned how to sing;
They at last learned how to dance;
They at last learned how to play the guitar and the harp;
They at last learned how to have festivals;
Now they knew everything.

77 pero ˀaˀ la ti la jyuch'ik poxe.
ti manchukuk la jyuch'ik poxe muˀyuk bu la xchanik stijik vob ˀarpa.
muˀyuk bu la xchanik xˀak'otajik xk'ejinik.

78 pero komo la jyuch'ik ti poxe,
ˀech'o xal la xchanik stijel vob ˀarpa,
xk'ejinik,
spasik k'in.

79 veno ˀech la ti baˀyel ti kirsanoe ti ˀach'el toˀoxe:
ˀa li sate koˀol la xchiˀuk sat tz'iˀ.

80 lek la xˀil xanav ta ˀak'obaltik.
koˀol la xchiˀuk k'ak'altik ta xˀil.

81 pero ti jch'ultotik ta vinajele la jyil,
ti koˀol xchiˀuk sat tz'iˀ ti snich'nabe.

82 mu sk'an.
chopol la ta xˀil ta la xˀilbe stak'in ˀanjel ta vitz.

83 ˀaˀ lek ta jmakbe sat.
moˀoje mu xtun xi la ti jch'ultotik ta vinajele.

84 veno ti kirsanoe makbat la sat ta juteb pok'il.
veno k'alal makbat ti sate, mu sa la xˀil sbe ta ˀak'obaltik.

85 mu xa la xuˀ xanavik ta ˀak'obaltik.
ˀech'o la xal mu xˀil sbeik li kirsanoetik ta ˀak'obaltike.
pero ti voˀnee toj lek la xˀilik tajmek.

86 ˀech xtok ti jch'ultotik ta vinajele la jyil ti muˀyuk ˀep ta xveˀ ti kirsanoe.
chopol la ta xˀil.

87 ˀaˀ lek ˀak'o veˀikuk ˀep.
moˀoje muˀyuk ta xˀabtejik ˀep.

This was all thanks to the fact that they drank rum. 77
If they had not drunk rum, they would not have learned
to play the guitar and harp.
They would not have learned how to dance and sing.

But since they did drink rum, 78
That is why they learned to play the guitar and harp,
To enjoy singing,
To have a good time at festivals.

There is something else said about these first people made from clay: 79
These people had eyes just like a dog's.

Their sight was keen when they walked at night. 80
They saw just like during the day.

Indeed, Our Father Sun in Heaven saw this, 81
That his children had eyes just like a dog's.

He didn't like it. 82
It was wrong for them to see the Earth Lord's mountain riches.[4]

"I had better cover their eyes. 83
If I don't, it won't be right," said Our Holy Father Sun in Heaven.

With this, the ancestors had their eyes veiled with a bit of cloth. 84
Thus, with their eyes covered, they couldn't see their way at night.

They could no longer walk at night. 85
That is why the people no longer saw their way at night.
But long ago they could see very well.

Our Holy Father Sun in Heaven also saw that people didn't eat enough. 86
He thought it was wrong.

"It would be better for them to eat plenty. 87
If not, they will not be inclined to work hard.

88 ti mi veˀik ˀepe ta xˀabtejik ˀep,
xi la ti jch'ultotik ta vinajele.

89 ˀech'o la xal toj ˀep ta xveˀik ti kirsanoetik ta chamoˀe.
ˀaˀ la ti ta smantal ti jch'ultotik ta vinajele.

90 ˀaˀ la chopol ta xˀil ti k'ajomal jbej sat ˀixim ta sk'uxe.
ˀaˀ la chopol ta xˀil muˀyuk la ˀep ta xˀabtej ti kirsanoetike.

91 veno ˀech la k'alal ta stz'unbal li ˀixime ta ˀoˀ la tal taˀuk'um la.
kajal la tal ta ba ˀoˀ neneˀ chobtik.

92 bat la stzakik ti neneˀ chobtike.
laj la stz'unik te ta tiˀ ˀuk'um.

93 laj la yak'bik yaˀlel ti yoˀ la mu xtakij ˀoe.
ˀentonse te la ch'i ti neneˀ chobtike.

94 mu la bu xtakij.
te la ch'i.

95 ˀentonse ta k'unk'un la ˀibol ti chobtike.
ˀibol la ˀep tajmek.
ˀibol ˀep ti chobtike.

If they eat a lot, they will work a lot," 88
Surmised Our Holy Father Sun in Heaven.

That is why the people of Chamula eat a lot. 89
It was by the will of Our Holy Father Sun in Heaven.

He saw it as wrong that they ate only one grain of corn at a time. 90
He also saw it as wrong that the people did not work hard enough.

Just then, a seedling corn plant came by way of the river. 91
A little corn seedling was floating by on top of the water.

They went to catch the little maize plant as it floated by. 92
They planted it there at the edge of the river.

They threw water on it so that it would not dry out. 93
Then the little maize plant grew.

It did not wither. 94
There it grew.

So the cornfield grew, little by little. 95
It increased a great deal.
The cornfield prospered.

96 ˀibol ˀep ti kirsanoe.
skotol ˀibol tajmek.

97 ˀentonse ti kirsanoetike ta k'unk'un lik spas snaik.
pero yanalteˀ la ti snaike.

98 pero mu la xtun.
k'alal la mi tal ˀoˀe ta la xˀech'.
mu la smak yuˀun ˀoˀ ti yanalteˀe.

99 ˀech la ti sk'uˀik xtoke.
[jaˀ la ta spasik ta pat teˀ].

So with the people; they increased a lot. 96
Everything and everybody multiplied.

Then, slowly, the people started to build their houses. 97
But their houses were rude structures made of the leaves of trees.

But these [houses] were no good. 98
When the rains came, they leaked.
The leaves did not keep out the water.

The same was true of their clothes. 99
They were made of tree bark.[5]

FIGURE 15

So with the people; they increased a lot.
Everything and everybody multiplied.

100 ta k'unk'un la tal.
ˀaˀ to la ti k'alal tal ti jtotik san juan xchiˀuk xchije.
ˀaˀ to la tal ti sk'uˀik ti kirsanoetike.

101 veno lik spas sk'uˀik ta k'unk'un xchiˀuk yalabik.
pero ta k'unk'un la lik spasik ti sk'uˀike.

102 mu la snaˀik k'usi ta spasik,
porke ti k'alal vok'ike t'anajtik la.

103 muˀyuk la sk'uˀik,
k'ajomal la pateˀ xchukoh ta xch'utik.
ti yoˀ la mu xvinaj ˀo ti sbek'talike.

Slowly, clothing came to be as we know it. 100
But this did not happen until Our Lord San Juan came with his sheep.
Not until that time did the people learn about clothing.

So, he set about making clothing for his children. 101
Ever so slowly, they started to make clothing for themselves.

They had not known how to make it, 102
For when they were created they were naked.

They had no clothes, 103
Just bark tied around their bodies.
That was so that their bodies would not be noticed.

FIGURE 16

Slowly, clothing came to be as we know it.
But this did not happen until Our Lord San Juan came with his
sheep.
Not until that time did the people learn about clothing.

104 ˀentonse k'alal la k'ot ti jtotik san juan xchiˀuk xchije.
yilik la k'uxi k'ot.
yilik la k'uxi lik spas sna.
yilik la k'uxi la sjines vitz.
yilik la ˀoy toˀox nab ti bu la spas ti snae.
yilik la ti k'usi bat saˀ talel ti ton sventa snae.
yilik la ti k'usi ta stij sba stuk ti kampana ti jok'ol ta teˀe.
pero ˀaˀ ti baˀyel kirsano la jyilike.

105 ˀentonse k'alal ti molibe la jyalbe komel ti snich'nabik ti k'uxi ch'iike.
ˀech'o xal snaˀojik skotol kirsanoetik ti k'uxi laj ch'iikuk ti
baˀyel kirsanoetike.

106 k'alal cham ti moletike,
yalojbe xaˀox snich'nabik ti k'us ˀelanil ti voˀnee.

Then, at last, Our Lord San Juan arrived with his sheep.[6] 104
They saw how he arrived.
They saw how he started to make his house.
They saw how he made the hill tumble down in a landslide.
They saw how a lake remained, beside which he built his house.
They saw how he went to look for stones for his house.
They saw how the bell that was hanging in the tree rang all by itself.
That was what the first people witnessed.[7]

Then, when the people grew old, they told their children 105
how they had come to be.
That is why all people have come to know how the first people came.

When the old people died, 106
They had already told their children what things were like long ago.

1 ˀoy jun kuento voˀnee tajmek.
la jyalbun kaˀi ti jtote ti jmeˀe.

2 ˀaˀ la ti ˀantivoetike.
ˀik'ubik la ta ˀosil voˀob la k'ak'al.

3 jech la ti jtotike ta vinajele k'epel toˀos la lek.
sta la ti ˀolol k'ak'al ˀune ˀik'ub la ˀun.

4 ta xa me xijlajotik ˀun xi la ti kirsanoetik ˀune.
k'uxi xa noˀox xijbatotik liˀ ˀune xi la ti kirsanoetike.

5 vaˀun ˀik'ub ti banamil ˀune
laj la svok'anik la ti sbinik ˀune.

6 jech la ti sbinike,
ˀo la ˀep laj la svok'anik ta ˀora.

7 jech ti binike k'alal la ˀik'ub ti ˀosile.
k'opoj la ta ˀora tajmek ti biniketike.

TEXT 12

Of When the Earth Darkened for Five Days

Marián López Calixto

There is a story of long, long ago. 1
My father and mother told it to me.

It was in the time of the ancients. 2
The earth darkened for five days.[1]

The sun was still bright and clear. 3
Then, at midday, it got dark.

"Now we will surely die," said the people.[2] 4
"But how on earth shall we get away?" said the people.

Well, the earth went dark 5
And they broke their pots.[3]

As for the pots, 6
They smashed them fast and furiously.

As for the pots, as the earth went dark, 7
These pots began at once to talk.

8 vaʔun k'alal ti ʔik'ub ʔune lok' la talel ti pukujtik ne.
tal la leon.
tal la mokoch.
tal la bolom.

9 jech la ti povre kirsanoetike lajik la ta tiʔel ta pukuj.
ti kirsanoetike xʔavlajetik xa la tajmek.
ti povre kirsanoetike.

10 ʔi ʔoy la ʔuni ʔololetik;
lok' la xik'ik.

11 ta xa me xachamik ʔun meʔ xi la ti ʔolole.
jech la ti ʔolole lok' la ta pana ta ʔora,
ʔi k'ataj xa la ta mut ti ʔolole.

Well, when it darkened, the demons rushed forth from the broken pots. 8
Lions came forth!
Snakes came forth!
Jaguars came forth!

So it was that the poor people perished in the jaws of the demons. 9
How the people screamed and shrieked!
Pity these poor people!

As for the little children; 10
They sprouted wings.

"Now you will surely die, Mother," said one child. 11
With that, the child went outside at once,
And that child promptly turned into a bird.

FIGURE 17

Well, when it darkened, the demons rushed forth
from the broken pots.
Lions came forth!
Snakes came forth!
Jaguars came forth!

12 jaʔ la kuch yuʔun ti ʔololetike.
ʔa ti smeʔike ti stotike ti ʔololetike,
jaʔ muʔyuk la skuch yuʔun.
jaʔ la te chamik ta snaik ti kirsanoetike.

13 vaʔun k'alal la sakub ti ʔosil ʔune mu xa la junuk ti kirsanoetike.
tuk xa la ti mutetike.
xch'eʔch'un xa la ta teʔtik tajmek.

14 xi la jlom ti mutetike:
voʔone ti jbie bexun xi la ti mute.
voʔone ti jbie karpinteroun.
chaʔtos ʔoy.
tos ti jbie tuktukun,"
xi la ti mutetike.

15 ʔoy jlom ti mut leʔ ʔune:
k'alal ta stonin ti ʔuni mut jlome ta teʔ ta xak' yuni tas ta k'aʔ toj
k'alal bu xa mol ti k'atoje.

16 jaʔ ta xbat tzjom ti teʔe.
jal ta tzjom tajmek.
juju likel ta xtal tzjom ti yuni nae.

17 k'alal mi sta sjomel yuʔun ti snae ta xak' yuni ton.
mu ʔepuk ta xak' ti stone.
ʔuni ʔoxbej k'o.

18 jech'a ʔal jech la spas ti ʔantivoetike.
ti k'ex ti kirsanoetike,
k'exik ʔun.

19 kom lek ta ʔach' ti kirsanoetike.
sakub lek ti banumile.
lok' la talel ti jtotike.
sak jaman xa la talel ti xojobale.

The children survived in that way. 12
However, the mothers and fathers of these children,
They did not survive.
These people perished right there in their houses.

Well, when dawn came upon the earth, there was no longer a single person left. 13
Now there were only birds.
They were already rushing and screeching about the forest.

Some of the birds spoke: 14
"My name is 'jay'," said one bird.
"My name is 'woodpecker'," said another bird.
"Actually, I have two names.
I am also called the 'solitary one'."
So spoke the birds.

One type of bird [the woodpecker] does this: 15
When the female lays her eggs, this little bird makes her little nest in a rotten pine tree.
But it must really be a nice old, rotten pine tree.

Then she goes to peck in the wood. 16
She pecks there for a long time.
She comes very often to peck out a spot for her little house.

When she has finished the hole for her house, she lays her tiny eggs. 17
She doesn't really lay very many eggs.
Never more than three.

Such was the fate of the ancient ones. 18
These people were transformed,
Their nature was changed.

However, people had, once again, the chance to prosper. 19
The earth brightened.
The sun came out.
Its rays came forth in soft white radiance.

20 jech la ti jtotik ta vinajel.
yal la talel ta banumil ta la spas yan ti kirsanoetike,
meltzaj ti kirsanoetike.

21 k'alal spas kirsano ti jtotik ta vinahele puru ta ˀach'el la spas xa baˀyo,
la smeltzaj ti kirsanoe.

22 ch'abal la bu xbak' tajmek.
jecheˀ la te vaˀal chak' chumanteˀ.

23 k'usi ta xkut, xi la ti jtotik ta vinajel ne.
laj la stuki noˀox xtok.

24 smeltzan la yan,
ti k'usi xa la svul ta sjol ti jtotike.

25 laj la sk'asan la skotol ti ˀach'ele.
slilin la skotol tajmek.

26 ti ˀach'eletik ne lik la spas ta ch'uch'ul ti ˀach'ele.
ˀi smeltzan ˀun.

27 k'alal la ti meltzaj yuˀun ti jtotike laj la sk'opon.
laj la spikbe sk'ob.

28 k'alal laj la yaˀi yuˀun kuxul ti ˀach'ele yochel la ta saˀbe sveˀel
ti k'utik momolal.
sta la ta saˀel.

29 laj la stijanbe ta ye ti momoletike,
mu la sk'anik.

30 k'usi ta xkak'be ˀun chaˀe xi la ti jtotik ˀune.
saˀ la talel ˀitaj.
sk'anik jutuk pere jutuk la tajmek.

31 ˀisnop la lek ti jtotike.
ta jbojkik la koˀe xi la ti jtotike.
ˀi sboj la ti yoˀe.

So it was with Our Father in Heaven. 20
He descended to the earth to create another race of people,
To prepare humankind.

When Our Father in Heaven made these people, he made them first from clay, 21
So humankind was prepared.

But it could not move very well at all. 22
Quite badly, it stood like a stump.

"What shall I do?" said Our Father in Heaven. 23
And he destroyed it once again.

With this, he made another try. 24
It was an idea that came to him.

He broke apart all of the clay. 25
He shook the clay all about.

He began to prepare the clay by crushing it. 26
And so he prepared it.

When these beings were created by Our Father, he spoke to them. 27
He felt the pulses of their wrists.[4]

When he realized that the clay beings were alive, he searched for some sort of grass to serve as their food. 28
Eventually, he found it.

He touched the grass to their mouths, 29
But they did not want it.

"What shall I give them, then?" wondered Our Father. 30
He found some cabbage and brought it.
They liked it somewhat, but not very much.

Our Father thought over the matter very carefully. 31
"Let's cut off a part from my thigh," said Our Father.
And so he cut off a piece of his thigh.

32 laj la saʔ bu la lek tajmek ti yoʔe.
laj la sta bu la lek tajmek.

33 ti sbek'tale ʔisjos.
yak'be la ti ʔach'el spasoj ʔune.

34 lek xa la xaʔik ti ʔach'ele.
spojpoj xa la sbaik tajmek.

35 yuʔun jaʔ ta sk'anik ti jbek'tal ʔun chaʔe.
xi la ti jtotik ʔune.

36 jech la ti ʔach'el ʔune k'opoj la likel.
pas la ta kirsano ʔun.

37 jun la ʔantz.
jun la vinik.

38 pasokik k'usi xameltzajik xi la ti jtotike.
veno xi la ti vinike.

39 laj la spasik xchiʔuk ti ʔantz ʔune.
mu la snaʔik k'uxi la ta pasel ti yolike.

40 jecheʔ la te snopnun la ta spasik.
jech la ti ʔantz ʔeke mu la snaʔ ʔek.

41 ʔoy la te bajal jun pukuj ta chukinab.
likel la lok' talel ta ʔora.

42 mi mu xanaʔ voʔote.
pastik ʔavil xi la ti pukuje.

43 pet sut la ʔech'el ti ʔantze.
jech la ti vinik te la bat la sk'el ʔek.

44 xi la pasele xi ti pukuje.
ʔaaa . . . vis ʔelanil ta pasel xi la ti vinike.

He checked to see where the flesh of his thigh was the very best. 32
He found where it was just right.

He scraped off this part of his body. 33
And he gave it to the clay he had made.

That tasted very good to the clay beings. 34
In fact, they fought trying to take it away from each other.

"It must be that they like my body, then." 35
So spoke Our Father.[5]

It happened that the clay soon began to speak. 36
It became human.

One part was a woman. 37
One part was a man.

"Well, let's see what you can do about getting on with your lives," 38
said Our Father.
"Okay," said the man.

With this, they did something together, the man and the woman. 39
It was clear that they did not know how to make their offspring.

In vain they wondered about what to do. 40
Not even the woman knew what to do.

Now the Demon Pukuj was locked there in a jail. 41
He lost no time in getting out.

"Don't you know how to do it? 42
Let's have a lesson," said the demon.

He carried the woman off in an embrace. 43
And the man went to look for himself.

"This is the way it is done," said the demon. 44
"Oh . . . That's the way it is done," said the man.

45 ˀi pas la ti vinik ˀeke.
xchan la me ˀun.

46 jaˀ yuˀun chopol lok' ti kirsanoetike,
ta stzakik chij,
ˀi ta stzakik vuro.

47 toj chopol ta spasik.
mu xtun.

And the man did it too. 45
He learned how.

And that is the reason that people turned out badly, 46
That they are inclined to fuck sheep,
And to fuck burros.

They do much that is evil. 47
It is not proper.[6]

1 ʔa li voʔne k'alal ʔayan ti baʔyel kirsanoe,
pero chavoʔik la.
jun la vinik.
jun la ʔantz.

2 pero ch'abal la sk'uʔik ti buy ta xanavike.
xchiʔuk ta xvayike ch'abal la snaik.
ta nail ch'en la ta xvayik.

3 pero xchiʔuk la ch'abal ta xveʔik.
mu la snaʔik k'usi ta slajesik.

4 ʔa to la tal jun vinik yal mantal ta yoxibal k'ak'al.
mi liʔoxuke xi la ti vinike.
liʔune xi la ti baʔyel kirsanoe.

5 mi la veʔik xi la ti vinike.
muʔyuk xi la ti baʔyel kirsanoe.

6 saʔo me k'usi stak' lajesele xi la ti vinike.
xuʔuk xi la ti baʔyel kirsanoe.

7 ti vinike jujun la k'ak'al ta sjak' mu to snaʔ saʔ sveʔel ti baʔyel kirsanoe.
pero k'alal muʔyuk ta snaʔ saʔel sveʔel ti baʔyel kirsanoe
bat yal ta vinajel ti vinike.
ti mu snaʔ saʔel sveʔel ti baʔyel kirsanoe.

8 yal la talel jtotik sk'el yil ti mu snaʔ sloʔel momol ti baʔyel kirsanoe.
ti jtotik k'alal yal talel sk'el yil ti baʔyel kirsanoe:
k'usi ta xalajesik xi la ti jtotike.
ch'abal xi la ti baʔyel kirsano.

TEXT 13

Of Long Ago When the First People Appeared

Xalik López Sethol

It was long ago when the first people appeared, 1
But there were two of them.
One was a man.
One was a woman.

Now, they wore no clothes when they walked about. 2
Neither did they have houses to sleep in.
They slept in a cave.

Furthermore, they had nothing to eat. 3
They had no idea about what they might eat.

Later, on the third day, a stranger came with an order.[1] 4
"Are you here?" asked the stranger.
"We are here," said the first people.[2]

"Have you eaten?" asked the stranger. 5
"No," said the people.

"Go find something that you can eat," said the stranger. 6
"All right," said the first people.

Every day this stranger came to ask if the first people had learned how to find food. 7
But since they did not know how to find food, the messenger went to the sky to advise Our Father.
He told him that the first people did not know how to find food.

Our Father came down to see if the first people knew how to eat grass. 8
So spoke Our Father when he came down to check up on the first people:
"What are you going to eat?" asked Our Father.
"We have no idea," said the first people.

9 mi la veˀ xi la ti jtotike.
ch'abal xiveˀ xi la ti baˀyel kirsano.

10 yochel la ta saˀel momoletik ti jtotike.
yak'bela sloˀ ti baˀyel jentee.

11 k'alal yil mu sk'an sloˀ momol snich'nab ti jtotike,
la saˀ yan sat teˀ ta muk'ta teˀtik.

12 yak'be la yil sloˀ ti baˀyel jente.
mu la sk'an sloˀ sat teˀ ti baˀyel kirsano.

13 k'alal yil ti jtotik mu k'usi sk'an sloˀ ti baˀyel kirsano,
yochel la ti st'olel sbek'tal slotz'op ti jtotike.

14 k'alal la jyak' sbek'tal slotz'op ti jtotike,
ˀora la ˀilajesik ti baˀyel kirsanoe.

15 ti k'alal laj slok'es slotz'op ti jtotike,
ˀixim la tey la stzak lok'el.

16 ˀora la ˀayan chobtik.
k'alal ˀayan ti chobtike yochel la ta spasel snaik.

17 ti k'alal lok' yiximik ti baˀyel krisanoetik,
ti k'alal sut muyel ta vinajel ti jtotik,
chapal xa la sbinik xchiˀuk setz'ik.
snaˀik xa slakanel sveˀelik k'alal ˀayan ti chobtike.
ven la xkuxet yoˀntonik.

18 xchanik la spasel sk'uˀik.
k'alal xchan spasel sk'uˀike ven lik xkuxet yoˀntonik.
ti k'alal snaˀ xa lik xˀabtejik ti baˀyel krisanoe.[3]

"Have you eaten anything?" 9
"We haven't eaten anything at all," said the first people.

Our Father began to look for grass. 10
He gave it to the first people to eat.

But when he saw that his children did not want grass, 11
He looked for some fruit in the great forest.

He showed the first people how to eat this. 12
But the first people did not want to eat fruit.

When Our Father saw that the first people wished to eat, 13
Our Father began peeling off the flesh from his upper arm.

When Our Father gave the first people the flesh from his upper arm, 14
The first people ate it right away.

When Our Father removed the flesh from his upper arm, 15
That part which he took became corn.

And soon there were born fields of corn. 16
When the fields of corn were born, they began the
construction of their houses.

Then, when at last corn harvest time came for the first people,[3] 17
When Our Father himself had returned to the sky,
They already had their cooking pots and eating bowls ready for use.
They already knew how to cook their food when their
fields of corn gave their fruit.
Their hearts were truly happy.

They learned how to make their clothing. 18
When they had learned how to make their clothing,
their hearts grew happy.
So it was now that the first people had begun learning to work
at their accustomed tasks.

19 ˀora la ˀayan yalak' xchiˀuk stuluk' xchiˀuk xchitom.
yoxchopal stz'unubal la jyich' ti baˀyel krisano.

20 ti k'alal bolaj yalak' xchiˀuk stuluk' xchiˀuk xchitom tal la jun vinik.
sjak' la mi lek yoˀntonik ti baˀyel krisanoe.

21 mi lek ˀavoˀntonik xi la ti vinike.
lek koˀntonkutik xi la ti baˀyel krisanoe.

22 laj la sjak' ti vinik:
buy ta xavak' ˀavalak' xi la ti vinik.
mu jnaˀ xi la ti baˀyel krisano.

23 li ˀavalak'e ta xatiˀik xi la ti vinike.
xuˀuk xi la ti baˀyel krisanoe.
ti k'alal snaˀ xa mi stak' tiˀel kaxlan xchiˀuk tuluk' ti baˀyel krisanoe.

24 la jyic' yan mantal.
ti k'alal snaˀ xa lek stekel ˀabtel.
ti k'alal ˀoy xa chapal ˀabtejeb.
k'usitik ta spasik.

25 ti mantal la jyich'e ti baˀyel krisano.
ˀaˀ la jun vinik ta xal ti mantale.

26 paso ˀavolik xi la ti vinike.
xuˀuk xi la ti baˀyel krisano.

27 k'uxi ta xkut ta jpas ti kole xi la baˀyel krisano.
te xanop ˀachibalik xi la ti vinike.

28 te ta jnopkutik xi la ti baˀyel krisano.
yochelik la ta snopel.

29 k'uxi ta xkutik xiik la.
spasik la lum yolik ti baˀyel krisano.

And soon, chickens, turkeys, and pigs came into being. 19
The first people got animals for breeding stock
for these three kinds of animals.

Then, when their chickens and turkeys and pigs had multiplied, 20
a stranger came.
He asked the first people if their hearts were happy.

"Are your hearts happy?" asked the stranger. 21
"We are contented," said the first people.

Then the stranger asked: 22
"What are you planning to do with your chickens?" he said.
"We don't know," said the first people.

"You are to eat your chickens," said the man. 23
"All right," said the first people.
So it was then that the first people found out that
chicken and turkey could be eaten.

They received another order. 24
This was when they already knew well all of their tasks.
This was when their tools were already set to use.
This was when they knew what to do with them.

The first people received the order. 25
It was a stranger who delivered the order.

"Make your children," said the man. 26
"All right," said the first people.

"How are we to make our children?" asked the first people. 27
"The two of you must think about it," said the man.

"We will think about it," said the first people. 28
With this, they began to think.

"How shall we do it?" they asked each other. 29
And the first people made their child out of clay.

30 yak'beik la sk'uˀ.
xchiˀinik la ta chotlej.

31 pero mu la snaˀ xk'opoj ti yolik.
k'u sˀelan ta spasik.

32 spasik la ˀep ti yolik ti puru lum.
yilik la ti yolik k'u sˀelan ti puru lum ti mu snaˀ xk'opoj.

33 spasik la jtos ˀo.
puru la teˀ la lik spasik.

34 yakbeik la sk'uˀ ti teˀ laj spas yolinike.
ˀaˀ noˀox la jech k'uchaˀal lum ti teˀ la spas yolinik ti baˀyel krisano.

35 ˀecheˀ la cholol.
mu la snaˀ xloˀilaj.
mu la snaˀ xanav.

36 ti k'alal yil ti jtotik ta vinajel ti mu snaˀ xloˀilaj yolik ti baˀyel krisano,
laj la spas ta mantal jun velta vinik ti jtotike.

37 ti vinik tal sjak' k'u sˀelan meltzaj yolik ti baˀyel krisano.
k'alal vul ti vinik ta sjak' ˀel mi laj smeltzanik yolik ti baˀyel krisano.

38 mi laj ˀameltzan ti ˀavolik xi la ti vinike.
la jmeltzan xi la ti baˀyel krisano.

39 k'uxi laj ˀapasik xi la ti vinike.
la jpaskutik lum xchiˀuk la jpaskutik teˀ xi la ti baˀyel krisano.

40 paso xa me yan.
ta xital jk'el ˀok'ob xi la ti vinike.

41 xuˀuk xi la ti baˀyel krisano.
laj to la spas yan lum yolik ti baˀyel krisano.

They dressed this being. 30
They sat down beside it.

But their child did not know how to talk. 31
What were they going to do?

They made lots of children from clay. 32
But they saw that their children, such as they were, would never speak.

So they made another type. 33
They made them out of wood.

They clothed their wooden children in garments made of wool. 34
But their wooden children were just like their clay children.

In vain they stood there in a row. 35
They could not talk.
They could not walk.

When Our Father in Heaven saw that the children of the first people couldn't talk, 36
He once again sent a man with an order.

The man came to ask how the first people were doing with the preparation of their offspring. 37
He came to check up on whether the first people had succeeded in making their children.

"Have you succeeded in creating your children?" inquired the stranger. 38
"We made them," the first people replied.

"How did you make them?" asked the man. 39
"We made them of clay and we made them of wood," said the first people.

"Make another one, now. 40
I will come to check up on things tomorrow," said the man.

"All right," said the first people. 41
And the first people made still another child out of clay.

42 ti k'alal sut ti vinike.
tal la ta yok'omal ti vinike.

43 mi laj ˀapas yan ti ˀolol xi la ti vinike.
la jpas yan xi la ti ˀantze.

44 tzak'o tal ta jk'elkik xi la ti vinike.
yak' la ta ˀilel ti k'u yelan spatoj lum yolin ti ˀantze ti vinike.

45 mu xtun ma li yelan laj ˀapase xi la.
pero k'uxi ta pasel xanaˀ xi la ti ˀantze.

46 vuˀune jnaˀ spasel k'uxi ta ˀutel xi la ti vinike.
pero ˀaˀ to mi muˀyuk to ta sut talel ˀamalal xi la ti vinike.

47 muˀyuk to ta sut talel.
ta la xˀak'in ta chobtik xi la ti ˀantze.

48 pero ta xajavi ti k'alal ta jchanubtasot ta spasel ˀavole xi la ti vinike.
javi la ti ˀantze.

49 ta me jtoy ˀavok xi la ti vinike.
toyo xi la ti ˀantze.

50 ti k'alal ta stik' yat ti vinike mu la xˀoch.
k'alal mu xˀoch yat ti vinike:
malo jlikeluk.
ta jmeltzanot xi la ti vinike.

51 pero ta ˀek'el la ˀisjambe sbek'tal ˀantz ti vinike.
ti k'alal slok'es yek'el ti vinike lek xa la xˀoch yat ti vinike.

52 k'alal sut ti vinike,
jlikel xa la sk'an xtal smalal ti ˀantze.

Then the stranger returned. 42
He came back on the following day.

"Have you made another baby?" asked the stranger. 43
"We made another," replied the woman.

"Bring it to me so we can see it," said the man. 44
The woman showed him how it was, this child that she and
her husband had made out of clay.

The way you did it won't do," he said. 45
"But do you know how it is done?" asked the woman.

"I do know how to do it," said the man. 46
"But I can't teach you until it is certain that your husband
won't be back for awhile," said the man.

"He won't be back for awhile. 47
He's busy weeding in the cornfield," said the woman.

"Now, you must lie down for me to teach you how to make children," 48
said the man.
The woman lay down.

"I'm going to lift up your legs," said the man. 49
"Lift them up," said the woman.

But when the man tried to stick in his cock, it would not enter. 50
When his cock would not go in, he spoke:
"Wait a minute.
I'm going to get you ready," said the man.

And with an axe, the man cut open the body of the woman. 51
When he finished up with the axe job, the man's cock
now slid in quite easily.

Then the stranger left, 52
But the woman's husband soon returned.

53 k'alal vul smalal ti ˀantze,
snaˀ xa la k'usi stak' pasel.

54 ti k'alal xchan spasel yolik ti baˀyel krisano,
chanubtasbilik ta jun vinik.

55 pero ti vinike laj xchanubtas ta spasel yolik ti baˀyel krisano
pero maˀuk la krisano.
ta xalik pukuj la.
pero mu jnaˀtik mi jech.

56 k'alal sjapu spasel snich'on ti baˀyel kirsano,
mu la snaˀ mi chanubtasbil ti yajnile.

57 ti ˀantze muˀyuk la xˀal mi ˀoy ˀay jun vinik chanubtasvanuk.
ˀaˀ noˀox la jyal ti ˀantze vaykutik.
xi la.

58 ti k'alal laj bitziuk muyan talel ta jba xi la ti ˀantze.
xuˀuk xi la ti vinike.

59 muy la ti vinike pero mu la snaˀ k'uxi ta spas.
ti ˀantz la snaˀ k'uxi ta pasel.

60 toyo muyel li koˀe xchiˀuk liˀ ta xatik' ˀochel la vate xi la ti ˀantze.
xuˀuk xi la ti vinike.

61 ti k'usi ˀora lik sjapuiik spasel yolik ti baˀyel krisano,
ta baluneb la k'ak'al k'ot ta vok'el yolik.

62 ti k'alal vok' ti yolike,
xkuxet xa la yoˀontonik.

63 ti k'alal vok' ti yolike,
yochelik la ta spasel yan.

When the woman's husband came back, 53
She already knew all about how it was done.

So the first people learned to make children, 54
As they were taught by the stranger.

But the man who taught the first people to make their children 55
was not a person.
They say it was the Demon Pukuj.
But we don't know if that is really so.

When the first people got the knack of making children, 56
Even then the man did not realize that his wife had been
taught about this.

The woman did not say that there had been a man who had shown her. 57
She just said, "Let's go to bed."
That's all she said.

Then, as they were wriggling and playing around, she said, 58
"Get on top of me."
"All right," said the man.

The man climbed on top, but didn't know what to do. 59
The woman knew full well!

"Lift up my leg and then you slide your cock in here," said the woman. 60
"All right," said the man.

At the time when the first people caught on to the technique 61
of making babies,
The child spent only nine days in the womb.

Once their child was born, 62
Their hearts were happy.

Once their child was born, 63
They began to make others.

64 pero jech la ta baluneb k'ak'al ta xvok' ta jukot,
ti k'alal xchanik spasel ti yolike.

65 ti k'alal mu toʔox snaʔik spasele,
laj toʔox spasik lum.
laj toʔox spasik teʔ.

66 pero mu toʔox xtun.
jecheʔ bat.

67 ʔaʔ to lek lok' ti yolik ti k'alal laj spasik ta sbek'talik.
ch'abal la xchanubtasvan ti vinike.

68 mu snaʔik k'usi ta spas yolik ti baʔyel krisano;
ʔa li baʔyel krisanoe stekel mu k'usi snaʔ spasel.
ʔaʔ to lek to ʔoy jchanubtasvaneje.

69 ti k'alal ʔoy xaʔox jayibuk yolik ti baʔyel krisanoe,
la jyal ti ʔantz k'uxi laj xchanik spasel ti yolike.
ti k'alal la jchantik spasel ʔolole tal jun vinik xi la ti ʔantze.

70 k'usi ʔora ʔay ti vinike xi la smalal ti ʔantze.
jaʔ ʔo ʔay k'alal la ʔay ta ʔak'in chobtik xi la ti ʔantze.

71 k'usi la jyalbot xi la ti vinik.
javlan xiyut xi la ti ʔantze.

72 ta jtoy ʔavoʔ yut xi la ti ʔantze.
ta jtik' talel kat xiyut xi la ti ʔantze.
pero mu xʔoch yat ti vinik xi la ti ʔantze.

73 la jyak'be ʔek'el ta jbek'tal ti vinike xi la ti ʔantze.
ʔaʔ to k'alal la jyak' ʔek'el ti vinik,
ʔaʔ to ʔoch yat xi la ti ʔantze.

74 bu ʔoy ti vinik xi la smalal ti ʔantze.
mu jnaʔ xi la ti ʔantze.

And, as before, the child was born after only nine days. 64
Things were like this when they first learned to make babies.

Until the time that they saw how it was actually done, 65
They were still using clay.
They were still using wood.

But that technique wasn't any good. 66
It was wrong.

Their children didn't come out well until they used their bodies 67
to make them.
But the man had not been shown.

The first people didn't know how to make their children; 68
The first people didn't really know how to do anything.
It was lucky that there was someone to teach them.

Only when the first people already had a number of children, 69
It was then that the woman told how she had learned to make children.
"When we were trying to make children, a stranger came,"
said the woman.

"When did the stranger come?" asked her husband. 70
"When you were out weeding the cornfield," replied the woman.

"What did he say to you?" asked the man. 71
"'Lie down,' he said," replied the woman.

"'I am going to lift your legs,' he said," said the woman. 72
"'I am going to stick my cock into you,' he said," said the woman.
"But the man's cock wouldn't go in," said the woman.

"The stranger struck my body with an axe," said the woman. 73
"Only when he used the axe,
Only then would his cock go in."

"Where *is* this man?" asked her husband. 74
"I don't know," said the woman.

75 mi ˀoy to xavil buy xanav xi la smalal ti ˀantze.
mu̓ˀyuk xa buy xkil xanav xi la ti ˀantze.

76 pero maˀuk jchiˀiltik xi la smalal ti ˀantze.
mu jnaˀ xi la ti ˀantze.

77 mi laj stik' yat ti vinik xi la smalal ti ˀantze.
laj stik' ˀochel.
pero baˀyel laj sboj ta ˀek'el jbek'tal ma ti vinike xi la ti ˀantze.

78 mi ˀip ˀavaˀi xi la smalal ti ˀantze.
muˀyuk ˀip xi la ti ˀantze.

79 mi ˀoy to buy ˀavile mu xa me xavak'be stik' yat ti vinike xi la smalal ti ˀantze.
xuˀuk xi la ti ˀantze.

"Do you still see anything of him?" asked her husband. 75
"No, I don't see him around anymore," said the woman.

"But could he have been anyone we know?" asked the woman's husband. 76
"I don't know," said the woman.

"But did he really stick his cock in?" asked the woman's husband. 77
"He really stuck it in.
But first he cut my body open with his axe," said the woman.

"Did it hurt you?" said the woman's husband. 78
"It didn't hurt," said the woman.

"If you see him again, don't let him stick his cock in you," 79
said the woman's husband.
"All right," said the woman.

1 loˀil yuˀun baˀyel kirsano.

2 veno ti baˀyel kirsanoe ch'abal snaik.
nakalik ta yolon teˀ.

3 ˀech xtok ch'abal toˀox ˀixim.
mu snaˀik sveˀik vaj.
puru momol ta sloˀik,
xchiˀuk sat teˀ,
xchiˀuk sat ˀak'.

4 ˀech' xtok mu la snaˀ xk'opojik lek.
mu la snaˀ xk'ejinik.
mu la snaˀ spasik k'in.
ˀaˀ noˀox la ti ta xanav ta sba banamile.

5 yuˀun muˀyuk toˀox ti jtotiketik ta ch'ulnaetike.
ˀaˀ noˀox ˀoy jun jtotik ta vinajel xchiˀuk ta banamil.

6 ˀech'oxal mu toˀox snaˀik spasik k'in ti baˀyel kirsanoe.
ch'abal toˀox xch'ulna.
ch'abal jtotiketik.
ˀaˀ noˀox nab xchiˀuk teˀtik.

7 ˀech la ti jtotik ta vinajele nakal toˀox la ta banamil;
ta yosil chamulaˀ xchiˀuk la smeˀ.

9 ˀech la ti baˀyel kirsanoe mu snaˀik mi ˀaˀ jtotik ti te nakal ta banamile.
ˀaˀ la ti koˀol xchiˀuk kirsanoe.
ˀech'o xal mu snaˀik mi ˀaˀ jtotik.

TEXT 14

About Why Our Lord Sun/Christ Destroyed the First People with a Rain of Boiling Water

Mateo Méndez Tzotzek

This is what is said about the first people. 1

Now, the first people did not have houses. 2
  They lived under the trees.

They still did not have corn, either. 3
  They did not know about eating tortillas.
  They simply ate grass,
  Along with the fruit of trees,
  Along with the fruit of vines.

Moreover, they could not talk well. 4
  They knew nothing of singing.
  They knew nothing of having festivals.
  They did nothing but rove about on the earth.

For there were still no saints in the churches. 5
  There was but one god in the sky and on the earth.[1]

That is why the first people still knew nothing about having festivals. 6
  They still had no churches.
  Neither did they have saints.
  There was nothing but seas and woods.[2]

This was when Our Lord Sun/Christ in Heaven still lived here on earth; 7
  It was in the land that is now Chamula where he lived with his mother.

So it was that the first people were not aware that Our Lord Sun/Christ 8
    lived here on earth.
  He looked just like a person.
  And so they did not know he was Our Lord Sun/Christ.

9 ˀech'o xal muˀyuk ta sk'oponik,
muˀyuk ta spasik k'in,
ˀaˀ ti koˀol xchiˀuk kirsanoe.

10 ˀentonse ti jtotik nakal ta banamile,
la jyil ti mu snaˀ xk'opojik ti kirsanoetike.
laj la smil ta k'ak'al ˀoˀ.

11 ˀaˀ la mu sk'an ti mu snaˀ xk'opoj yile.
ˀech'o la xal la smil ta k'ak'al ˀoˀ.

12 vaˀi ˀun ti k'ak'al ˀoˀe lok' la ta vitz muy la ta vinajel,
koˀol la xchiˀuk tok muy.

13 ˀentonse k'alal yal talel ti ˀoˀe,
koˀol la xchiˀuk ˀoˀ.
pero k'ok' la tajmek.

14 ˀentonse ti kirsanoetike,
cham la skotolik ta k'ak'al ˀoˀ ti baˀyel kirsanoe.

Therefore, they did not pray to him, 9
Neither did they have festivals in his honor,
Because he looked just like the people themselves.

Now, while Our Lord Sun/Christ was living on earth, 10
He saw that the people could not speak.
So he destroyed them with boiling rain.

He thought their muteness was not good. 11
That is why he destroyed them with boiling rain.

The boiling rain just poured out of the mountains and rose to the sky. 12
It rose just like clouds.

Then when the rain fell, 13
It was just like ordinary rain.
But it was boiling hot.[3]

As for these people, then, 14
All of these first people perished in the rain of boiling water.

1 kuento ta stiˀ yolik ti voˀnee.

2 ˀoy jun mol.
ta xloˀilajik xchiˀuk jun vinik ti mole.

3 ˀa ti voˀne lae toj chopol toˀox la.
ˀa ti antivoe kirsanoetike toj chopol toˀox la
xi la sal stot ti mol voˀnee.

4 ti ˀantivoe kirsanoetike ta la stiˀan toˀox la yolik.
k'alal mi lek xa la, jubem xa la ti yolike.
ta la smilik stiˀik ti ˀolole lek xa muk'e.

TEXT 15

About How the Ancient Ones Ate Their Own Children

Manuel López Calixto

A story about how they ate their children long ago. 1

There was an old man. 2
  This old man was talking with a friend.

"Long ago, times were very bad. 3
  The problem was the ancient people themselves, who were very evil."
  So the old man's father told him long ago.

"The ancient people ate their own children. 4
  They did this when their children were nice and fat.
  They killed their children to eat them, just when they were
    getting nice and big.

FIGURE 18

The ancient people ate their own children.
  They did this when their children were nice and fat.
  They killed their children to eat them, just when they were
    getting nice and big.

5 stak’ xa tiʔel xi la smalal ti ʔantze.
lek xa ʔoy.
mi chamile xi la ti ʔantz ʔeke.

6 moʔoj.
jaʔ lek lakan k’ak’al ʔoʔ xut la yajnil ti vinike.
veno xi la ti ʔantz ʔeke.

7 mu la bu la smilik ti yolike.
kuxul to la jutuk ta stz’ajik ta k’ak’al ʔoʔ.

8 k’alal cham ne laj ta slok’esbik ti sbikil xchitomik lae.
chitom la sbi yuʔunik ti ʔolole.
jaʔ la sveʔelik toʔox la ti mu ʔantivo kirsanoe.

9 mu la sk’an ti jtotik ta vinajele.
leʔe toj chopol xi la ti jtotik ta vinajele.

10 cham la skotol ta sik k’ok’.
laj la skotolik ti ʔantivo kirsanoe.

11 k’alal cham skotol ti chopolike tal la yan sk’exolik ach’,
yan stz’unobal ti kirsanoe.

12 jaʔ to la toj lek tal ti ʔach’ kirsanoe
mu la snaʔ jech ta spasik.
jech ne snaʔ la saʔ sveʔelik ti ʔach’ kirsanoe.

13 k’alal mi ʔalajike ta la stz’itesik.
ta la xak’bik xchuʔ ti yolike.

14 jech la ti vinike ta la xak’be sveʔel ti snich’one.
jech la ti ʔantze ta la spetla ti yole.
ta la xak’be la vaj xveʔ.

15 jaʔ to lek ti jtz’unobe.
xi la ti jtotik ta vinajel.

'Now they will be good,' declared the first woman's husband. 5
'Yes, they're just right.
Why don't you kill them?' suggested the woman.

'No, let's not kill them first. 6
It would be better to boil them alive,' said the man to his wife.
'All right, then,' agreed the woman.

So they did not kill their children beforehand. 7
Even as they still had breath, they stuck them into the boiling water.

When they were dead, they took out their guts as though they were pigs. 8
Indeed, they called their children 'pigs.'
For they were the food of the evil, ancient people.

Our Father in Heaven did not like this. 9
'This is really awful,' said Our Father in Heaven.

They all died of a fever. 10
All of the ancient people perished.

When the evil ones died, there came a replacement, a new batch, 11
Another stock of people.

Things did not get better until a new people came 12
Who did not do evil.
The new people sought proper food.

When their children were born, they took care of them. 13
They nursed them.

As for the men, they provided food for their children. 14
As for the women, they hugged their children.
They gave them tortillas to eat.

'This seed is at last of better quality.'[1] 15
So said Our Father in Heaven.

16 k'ot la jun vinik ta snaik ti ˀach' kirsanoe.
mi liˀote xi la k'otel ti vinike.
liˀune mi la tal vulaˀal xi la ti ˀach' kirsanoe.

17 mu la snaˀ bu tal.
bu la tal xˀutat la ti vinike.
leˀ noˀoxe.
lek ˀoy xi la komel.

18 mi xanaˀ xaˀabtej xi la ti vinike.
jnaˀ xi la ti ˀach' kirsanoe.

19 ta xiˀabtej.
ta jpas jchobkutik xi la ti vinike.

20 mi xavojtikin li ˀixime xi la ti jvulaˀale.
xkojtikin.
jaˀ ta jveˀkutik xi la.

21 jaˀ jnaˀ jveˀ vaj.
jnaˀ jtiˀ chenek'.
jnaˀ jtiˀtik bek'et.
jnaˀ jloˀ ˀitaj.
jnaˀ jloˀ napux xi la.

22 veno lek ˀoy.
paso ˀachobik.
xuˀuk xi la.

23 lek xa la xaˀi ti vinike,
k'alal la ti ˀalbat mantale.

24 chabaj la.
laj la stz'un ˀep xchobik.
stz'un la ˀep xchenek'.
lek la snaˀ xchabajik ti ˀach' vinike.

Soon a stranger arrived at the house of the new people. 16
'Are you here?' said the man as he arrived.
'We are here. Have you come for a visit?' asked the new people.

They did not know where he had come from. 17
'Where did you come from?' the stranger was asked.
'From hereabouts.
Everything is all right. Don't worry,' he declared.

'Do you know how to work?' asked the stranger. 18
'Yes, we know how,' said the new people.

'We work.
19
We take care of our cornfield,' said the new people.

'Do you know about corn?' asked the visitor. 20
'Yes, we know about it.
That is what we eat,' they said.

'We know how to eat tortillas. 21
We know how to eat beans.
We know how to eat meat.
We know how to eat cabbage.
We know how to eat greens,' they said.

'Well, that's good. 22
Tend your cornfield.
All is well,' he said.

Whereupon the people felt happy, 23
For these instructions were given to them.[2]

They broke the ground. 24
They planted many fields of corn.
They sowed lots of beans.
These newly created people learned to till the soil very well."

1 ˀoy jun kuento sventa li jvok'otik ti voˀnee.
jech la ti voˀnee snop la ti jtotik,
yuˀun ch'abal toˀox la ti kirsanoe.

2 vaˀun jech la ti jtotik la ˀune ˀoy la yixim la ˀep tajmek.
vaˀun ˀoy la yuni jay noj la ta ˀixim ti sjaye.
vaˀun sjam la ti sjay la ˀune slok'es la skotol ti yixime.

3 vaˀun tal la jun ti jtotik la ˀune.
tomax la sbi ti jtotik la ˀune.

4 vaˀun snopik la skotolik la ˀun:
mi ta jtanitik ti kalab jnich'nabtike xi la ti jtomax la ˀune.
veno voˀot ta xanop mi ta xatani skotol ta ˀavixime xi la ti sbankil ti jtomaxe.

5 veno k'uchaˀal moˀoj xi la ti jtomaxe.
vaˀun lok' la ta sna ˀun skuch la lok'el la ti sjay ˀune.

6 saˀ la jun spek' sventa la ta skuch la ti yixime.
vaˀun bat la ta kampo ˀun.

7 k'ot la baˀyuk la ta kampoun ˀi snop la lek jlikel la ˀun.
pero k'usi ta xkal tana ˀun xi la ti jtomax la ˀune.
vaˀun ˀi snop la ˀun.

TEXT 16

About the Time When We Were Created Long Ago

Marián López Calixto

There is a story about the time when we were created long ago. 1
This is what Our Father thought about long ago,
When there were still no people.[1]

Well, then, as for Our Father, he had a great deal of corn. 2
He had this little gourd vessel, a gourd full of corn.
He opened up the gourd vessel and he took out all of his corn.

Just then a saint came by. 3
The saint was named Tomás.

So, then, these two thought together about everything: 4
"Shouldn't we do something to spread our children,
our offspring, around?" asked Tomás.
"Very well, then. You are the one who should think about
whether you want to spread around all of your corn,"
replied Tomás's older brother.[2]

"Well, why not?" said Tomás. 5
And out of the house he went, carrying his gourd vessel.

He found a tumpline for carrying his corn.[3] 6
Then he went out into the country.

Soon he came out into open country and immediately started 7
to ponder things over.
"Whatever am I going to do now?" wondered Santo Tomás
Then he thought about it some more.

8 k'opoj la likel ti jtotik tomax la ˀune:
jaman banamil.
jaman vinajel.
jaman nab xi la ti jtotik jtomax la ˀune.

9 jech la ti yixim la ˀune lik la stanik ta skotol la banamil la ˀun.
jech la ti ˀixim la ˀun ti yan la ˀune kajajtik la kom ta ba ˀoˀ la ˀun.

10 vaˀun ti jtotik tomax la ˀune.
vaˀ xi la k'alal laj la yoˀnton la ˀune sk'el la ti sjay la ˀune.

11 jech la ti sjay la ˀune.
ˀuni ˀoxib xa la ˀoy la ta sjay ˀun.

Suddenly Our Lord Santo Tomás spoke: 8
"Open, earth!
Open, heavens!
Open, seas!" said Our Lord Santo Tomás.

With this, his grains of corn began to be scattered across the earth. 9
In this way, also, some of his corn kernels remained floating
on top of the seas.

So it was with Our Lord Santo Tomás. 10
They say that once he had done this [the spreading of corn],
he looked into his seed gourd.

This is how it was with his seed gourd. 11
Only three small grains were left.

FIGURE 19

Suddenly Our Lord Santo Tomás spoke:
"Open, earth!
Open, heavens!
Open, seas!" said Our Lord Santo Tomás.

12 vaˀun jech la ti te kom to la ta sjay la ˀune.
svok' la ti yixim la ˀune ˀi sjip la ˀun.

13 sk'el la spat la ti jtotik tomax la ˀune.
ˀi la jyil la ˀun pasem xa la ta chobtik ti yixime.

14 veno yuˀun jech xakom ˀo leˀe xi la ti jtotik tomax la ˀune.
vaˀun ˀavan la ˀun.

15 ˀuuuh laˀ me xun,
laˀ me lol.

16 laˀ me xunkaˀ,
laˀ me loxa xi la ti jtotik tomax la ˀune.

17 vaˀun k'alal ˀavan la ˀune tal la ti yixim la ˀune.
puru sa la kirsano ˀun.

So it was with the remaining seeds in the gourd. 12
This corn sprouted and he threw it away.

Then Our Lord Santo Tomás looked behind him. 13
He saw that his discarded corn kernels had turned into a field of corn.[4]

"Well, such is to be your destiny," said Our Lord Santo Tomás 14
to those corn kernels.
Then he beckoned them to come back to him.

"Oooo! Come here, Juan, 15
Come here, Lorenzo.

Come here, Juana, 16
Come here, Rosa," said Our Lord Santo Tomás.

When he shouted, his corn came to him. 17
It had turned into people.

FIGURE 20

When he shouted, his corn came to him.
It had turned into people.

18 jlom lae chij.
jlom lae paloma la ˀun.

19 jech la ti paloma la ˀune ta la xk'opoj la ˀun.
ˀo to te kom ma ti ch'uch'ulil ti ˀixime xi la ti paloma la ˀune.

20 vaˀun jech la ti jtotik tomax la ˀune:
te ˀoyuk te.
te xtal ta k'unk'un xi la ti jtomas la ˀune.

21 vaˀun jech la ti mu paloma la ˀune mu la xch'un.
likel la bat ta ˀora.
bat la sloˀan ti ch'uch'ulil ti ˀixim la ˀune.

22 vaˀun jech ti xch'uch'ulil ti ˀixim la ˀune jaˀ la ti ˀololetik la ˀune.
jech la ti paloma la ˀune sut la talel ˀun.
noj xa la lek ti xch'ut la ti paloma la ˀune.

23 k'ot la yalbe la k'otel la ti jtotik tomax la ˀune:
laj xa jloˀ ti ch'uch'ulil ˀixime xi la ti palomae.

24 vaˀun jech la ti jtotik tomax la ˀune ˀilin la ˀun.
k'u yuˀun la loˀ ˀun.
mu la kalbot ti mu xaloˀe xi la ti jtotik tomax.

25 jech la ti jtotik la ˀune smaj la ti palomae.
svelbe la ti sjaye.

26 jech la ti palomae toj vilˀel la ta ˀora.
ta likel noˀox la sjay.
vil ˀo ti palomae.
jaˀ yuˀun ta la xvil ti palomae.

27 ˀi ta la xyal stak' la jtz'untik.
ˀi snaˀ la sloˀ ˀixim.

Some corn turned into sheep. 18
Other corn turned into doves.

So, now the dove spoke. 19
"There are a few pieces of corn left," said the dove.

So, then Our Lord Saint Thomas said this: 20
"Well, there do seem to be some.
They will come along little by little," said Tomás.[5]

So, then, the disobedient dove paid no attention to him. 21
It went away at once.
It went off to eat the little pieces of corn.

It happened that the little pieces of corn were children.[6] 22
And so the dove returned.
The dove had a nice full stomach.

It came back to report to Santo Tomás: 23
"I have already eaten the little pieces of corn," confessed the dove.

Then Our Lord Santo Tomás got angry. 24
"Why did you eat them?
Didn't I tell you not to eat them?" said Our Lord Santo Tomás.

With that, Our Lord Santo Tomás struck him. 25
He hit him with his gourd.

With that, the dove took rapid flight. 26
It fled in no time at all.
The dove was off and gone.
That is why the dove flew away.

Sometimes when this dove flies low, it can be captured and 27
kept as a domestic game bird.
It has the habit of eating corn, so getting caught is a fitting punishment.[7]

28 jech la ti yan ti paloma la ʔune mu la snaʔ k'usi ta spas.
lek la ʔoy yoʔnton.
jaʔ la kom ta xchiʔil jtotik ti palomae.
ti bu mas la leke tajmeke.

29 vaʔun jech la ti ch'uch'ulil la ti ʔixim la ʔune puru neneʔ ʔololetik la ʔun.
vaʔun k'alal ta xvok' ti ʔolol la ʔune ʔi mu la xch'iʔ la ʔun.
ta la xcham tajmek.

30 jaʔ la xch'ulel ti ʔololetik la ti xch'uch'ulil la ti ʔixim la ʔune.
vaʔun jaʔ la ch'i la ti bu la muʔyuk bu la laj ta paloma la ʔune.
vaʔun jaʔ la tal ʔun.

31 pero chopol la tajmek ti sat la ʔune.
jaʔ noʔox la ti yakan ta xanave.
jech la ti sk'obe ch'abal la ʔun.
ʔi mu la k'u xuʔ la xveʔ.

32 ʔi ta xʔabtej ʔi ta xbak.'
toj chopol la ti kirsano la ʔune.

33 vaʔun snop la ti jtotik la ʔune.
pere mu jk'an ma leʔ ʔune.
jaʔ lek ta jnojes ta ʔoʔe xi la ti jtotik la ʔune.
vaʔun skomtzan la ti kirsano la ʔune.

34 muy la ta vinajel ti jtotiketike.
yak' la talel ti ʔoʔ la ʔune.

35 jaʔ la kom ti jtotik tomaxe xchiʔuk jtotik ʔisikro jtotik san pavlo.
ʔoxvoʔ la kom ti jtotiketike.

36 vaʔun xch'ak la sbaik la ʔun.
bat la ta jujot la xokon vinajel.

37 bat la stijik la talel ti nabe smilik la ti kirsanoe.
snetik la talel ti nabe.
vaʔun noj la ti nabe.

But the other dove did nothing bad. 28
It was very agreeable.
So it stayed on as a companion for Our Father.
It was very good and kind.[8]

Now, it happened that the little pieces of corn had all been the souls of unborn human beings. 29
For that reason, when the children were born, they did not grow well.
Many died.

The little pieces of corn had been the souls of little children. 30
Those that the dove had not devoured survived.
Then they grew up.

But their faces were really very ugly. 31
They did little more than crawl about.
They did not have hands.
They could not eat.

They worked, but grew very thin. 32
They did not prosper at all.

So, Our Father started to think things over. 33
"Really now, I don't want this kind of offspring.
I had better drown them," said Our Father.
So he abandoned these people.

The saints went up to heaven. 34
And Our Father caused the rains to come.

However, Santo Tomás, San Isidoro, and San Pedro stayed behind. 35
These three saints stayed behind [on earth].

Then they parted. 36
They went to each side of heaven.[9]

They went to call the seas to kill the people. 37
They pushed the seas inland.
And so the seas swelled.

38 ˀi ˀoy la jun ti vinik la ˀune.
ˀoy la yiloj la jun ch'en.

39 ˀi te la muy ˀun.
bat la stik' la sba ta yut ch'en.

40 ˀi te la nak'al tajmek,
ˀi yil la noj la ta ˀoˀ ti xchiˀiltake.

41 jesus ta xa xicham ˀun xi la ti vinike.
ˀi noj la tajmek ti ˀoˀe.

42 vaˀun jech ti te la nak'al la kom ta ch'en la ˀune,
jaˀ muˀyuk bu la laj ˀun.

43 ˀi te la sk'eloj ti xchiˀiltake vaˀun k'alal la laj ˀune.
te la sk'eloj ti vinike vaˀun.

44 yil la yal talel ti paloma la ˀune.
ˀi te la xvilet ta sk'el la ti kirsano la ˀune,
mi laj ˀo mi mu la bu xlaj.

45 vaˀun jech la ti paloma la ˀune ˀi la jyil ti laj la ˀune.
vaˀun k'ot la yalbe la ti jtotik ta vinajel la ˀune.

46 k'opoj la k'otel ti paloma la ˀune:
mu jnaˀ k'usi ta xkutik.
toj toyol tajmek ti k'aˀal bek'ete pero toj tu tajmek xi la ti paloma la ˀune.

47 vaˀun jech la ti jtotik tomax la ˀune ˀi snop la ˀun.
veno jk'eltikik k'usi ta xkutik xi la ti jtotik tomax la ˀune.

48 vaˀun smil la jkot svakax la ˀun.
xchoˀ la ti svakax la ˀune.

49 vaˀun ti snukulil la ti vakax ˀune takij la lek ˀun.
lik la sjatanan ti snukul la ˀune.
ˀi bol la ˀep tajmek ˀun.

There was one man. 38
He had spied a cave.

He climbed up to it. 39
He went to seek refuge in the cave.

He remained there well hidden and safe, 40
And he watched his friends drown.

"Oh, Jesus, now we are going to die!" said the victims. 41
And with this, the flood filled the land.

Well, the one who was hiding in the cave, 42
He did not die.

He was there watching his friends as they perished. 43
The man just watched them.

He saw a dove swoop down. 44
It had been flying around observing the people,
Whether they lived or whether they died.[10]

The dove saw that they had perished. 45
Then he went to report to Our Father in Heaven.

The dove spoke when he arrived: 46
"I don't know what we are going to do.
There is a great deal of rotten meat down there and
it smells terrible," said the dove.

Then Our Lord Santo Tomás thought things over. 47
"Well, now, let's see what should be done," said Our Lord Santo Tomás.

He then killed a cow. 48
He skinned this cow.

Then the cowhide dried out. 49
He proceeded to cut the hide into pieces.
And suddenly the number of pieces increased.

50 xulem xi la ti jtotik tomax la ˀune.
batan ba tiˀo k'aˀal bek'et xi la ti jtotik tomaxe.

51 vaˀun jech la ti xulem la ˀune likel la bat la ta ˀora.
ˀi k'ataj bat la stiˀ ti k'aˀal bek'ete.

52 vaˀun ti xulem la ˀune laj la stiˀ la skotol ti k'aˀal bek'etetik la ˀune.
vaˀun jech la ti paloma la ˀune yal la talel noˀox la jten xtok ˀun,
vaˀun la jyil la ti ch'abal xa la ti k'aˀal bek'etetik xa ˀune.

53 ˀi k'ot la yal la k'otel ti paloma la ˀune:
xuˀ xa chijyalotik.
lek xa ti banamile xi la ti paloma la ˀune.

54 vaˀun jech la ti jtotiketik la ˀune yalik la talel ˀun.
sk'elik la ti banamil la ˀune.
ˀi mu la k'usi xˀayan ti ta banamil la ˀune.

55 vaˀun jech la ti jtotiketik la ˀune ˀi snop la jten xtok ˀun.
k'usi ta jk'antik xiik la ti jtotiketik la ˀune.

56 voˀone ta xkale baˀyo ta jk'antik li nichime xi la ti xalike.
veno lek ˀoy mi jaˀ chakane xi la ti jtotik san josee.

57 veno jaˀ lek jk'antik xi la skotolik la ˀun.
buch'u baˀyel ta xk'opoj xi la ti jtotik san josee.

58 voˀon ta xik'opoj xi la ti jtotik ta vinajele.
vaˀun k'opoj la ˀun.

59 pasan teˀ.
pasan nichim.
pasan momol.
pasan vinajel xi la ti jtotik ta vinajel la ˀune.

60 vaˀun jaˀ la jech la kom ˀo ti banamile.
laj ˀo ti kuentoe.

"Buzzard!" said Our Lord Santo Tomás, summoning the bird into existence. 50
"Go! Go eat the rotten flesh," commanded Our Lord Santo Tomás.

Then, in no time at all, it happened that the buzzard flew away. 51
Having been so created, it went away to eat the rotten meat.[11]

Then the buzzard went off and finished all of the rotten meat. 52
Whereupon the dove flew down once again to the earth,
And saw that no rotten flesh remained.

And then the dove arrived in heaven with this news: 53
"Now we can go down.
Now the earth is pleasant," said the dove.

With this the saints descended. 54
They surveyed the earth.
And there was no longer anything on the earth.

So the saints considered things once again. 55
"What do we need?" the saints asked one another.

"I think that the first thing we need is flowers," said San Salvador. 56
"All right, that's fine if that's what you want," said Our Lord San José.

"Well, now, we had better state our wishes," said all the saints together. 57
"Who is going to speak his mind first?" said Our Lord San José.

"I am going to speak up," said Our Father in Heaven. 58
And then he spoke:

"Let the trees be created! 59
Let the flowers be created!
Let the grasses be created!
Let the heavens be created!" said Our Father in Heaven.

And is was thus that the earth remained. 60
So the story ends.

1 ˀoy jun kuento ta sba lamal banumil.
lik yal sloˀil jun vinik ta pinka morelia.

2 veno ti voˀne lae ti baˀyel kirsanoe muk' la xch'iik ˀep jabil,
yuˀun la toyol ta stiˀ yolik.

3 mu la xbolik tajmek,
jaˀ la ti ta stiˀik ti yolike.

4 k'alal la vok' ti yolike ta la smalaik ta xch'i vakib ˀu.
k'alal la mi sta vakib ˀue ta la xlik smilik ti ˀolole.

5 k'alal la ta smilik ti ˀolole baˀyel la ta slakanik jun bin k'ak'al ˀoˀ.
k'alal la mi ta xvokan xa ti k'ak'al ˀoˀ sk'eloj ti ˀantze.

6 ta la xak' ˀak'otajuk ti yole.
jaˀ la ti slajeb xa ta spet ti yole.
jaˀ la ti ta xˀoch xa ta veˀlil ti yole.

7 k'alal la mi la jyak' ak'otajuk ti yole,
ta la stz'aj ta k'ak'al ˀoˀ ti yole,
te la xcham ti ˀolol ta k'ak'al ˀoˀe.

8 k'alal la ti la stz'aj ta k'ak'al ˀoˀ yol ti ˀantze,
ˀok' to la ti ˀolol k'alal ˀoch ta k'ak'al ˀoˀ ti ˀolole.

9 k'alal la ti la slok'es yol ti ˀantz ta binal k'ak'al ˀoˀe,
chamem xa la ti ˀolole.

10 k'alal la ti chamem xa ta k'ak'al ˀoˀe yil yol ti ˀantze,
lik la sbojilan ta kuchilu ti yole.

TEXT 17

About How and Why the First People Perished in a Boiling Rain

Xun Méndez Tzotzek

Here is a story about the First Creation. 1
A man on the Finca Morelia began to tell this account.
This is how I remember it.

Well, long ago the people of the First Creation did not live for many years, 2
Because they insisted on eating their own children.

They did not increase at all, 3
Because they persisted in eating their own children.

When their children were born, they let them grow for six months. 4
At six months old, they killed them.

They killed their children by first cooking them in pots of boiling water. 5
While the pot was boiling, the woman faced her child.

She danced with her child. 6
She hugged her child for the very last time.
Her baby was soon to be her meal.

When she finished dancing with her child, 7
She cast her child into the boiling water,
Where her baby boiled to death.

As the woman plunged her child into the boiling water, 8
The child would still be crying.

When the woman pulled her child from the pot of boiling water, 9
The baby was quite dead.

When the woman would see that her child was dead, 10
She diced her child up with a knife.

11 k'alal la ti laj sbojilan ta kuchilu ti yol ti ˀantze,
lik la spas ta tamaliˀ ti yole.
lik la svatz' ta ˀixim sbek'tal ti yole.

12 lek la ta stiˀik ti tamaliˀ ti yolike.
lek la stiˀik ta kalto ti ˀolole.

13 ech la ta spasik skotolik ti kirsanoetike.
mu la xbolik tajmek.

14 pero k'uchaˀal tajmek mu xbolike xi la ti jtotike.
jaˀ lek ta jk'eltik k'uchaˀal tajmek mu xbolike xi la ti jtotike.

15 lik la sk'el k'usi ta spasik ti kirsano mu xbolik tajmeke.
lik la sk'el tajmek jaˀ to la yil ˀoy la jun ˀantz muk' la tajmek xch'ut.

16 lik la sjak' ti jtotike.
sjak'be la ti ˀantze k'usi spas ˀach'ut.
toj muk' tajmeke xi la ti jtotike.
sjak'be la ti ˀantze.

17 tak'av la ti ˀantze:
ˀa . . . ˀolol xi la ti ˀantze.

18 ˀa . . . xi la ti jtotike.
jaˀ xi la ti ˀantze.

19 k'usi ˀora ta xvok' ˀun xi la ti jtotike.
ta xvok' ta jun ˀu xi la ti ˀantze.
ˀa . . . xi la ti jtotike.

20 k'uchaˀal xi la ti ˀantze.
mu k'uchaˀal jech noˀox ta jak' xi la ti jtotike.

21 veno lek ˀoy la jkaˀi xi la ti jtotike.
veno pero k'alal mi vok' li ˀololee ta stak' jk'eltik xi la ti jtotike.

22 veno sta la ti jun ˀue.
bat la sk'el ti ˀolol mi vok'em xae.

When the woman's baby was chopped into pieces, 11
She began making the baby meat into tamales.
She began wrapping the flesh of her child in corn dough.

The people enjoyed eating the baby-filled tamales.[1] 12
The people enjoyed sipping the baby-flavored soup.

This is what all the people did. 13
They did not multiply at all.

"Why aren't they increasing their numbers?" asked Our Father. 14
"I had better go see why they are not multiplying," said Our Father.

So he went to see why the people weren't increasing. 15
He looked around carefully and saw a big-bellied woman.

Our Father questioned the woman. 16
He asked her, "What's wrong with your belly?
It's really very large," said Our Father.
This is what he asked the woman about.

The woman answered: 17
"Oh, I'm with child," said the woman.

"Oh, is that so?" said Our Father.
"That's right," said the woman.

"When is it going to be born?" said Our Father. 19
"It is due in a month," said the woman.
"Oh," said Our Father.

"Why do you ask?" inquired the woman. 20
"No reason. I just asked," said Our Father.

"Well, very well. Now I understand," said Our Father. 21
"Now, when the child is born, I plan to come and see
how things are," said Our Father.

Then a month passed. 22
He went to see whether the baby had been born.

23 veno k'ot la ti jtotik ta sna ti vinike,
ti bu ˀoy nakal xchiˀuk yajnil ti vinike.

24 k'ot la sjak' ti jtotike mi liˀoxuke,
xut la k'otel xchiˀuk yajnil ti vinike.

25 liˀunkutike xi la xchiˀuk yajnil ti vinike.
ˀa . . . xi la ti jtotike.

26 k'usi mantal xi la xchiˀuk yajnil ti vinike.
liˀ tal jak'e mi vok' xa ti ˀolole xi la ti jtotike.

27 ˀa . . . vok' xa xi la ti vinik xchiˀuk ti yajnile.
ˀa . . . xi la ti jtotike.

28 yuˀun tal jk'el k'usi ˀololal xi la ti jtotike.
laˀ ochan talel k'elavil xi la ti vinik xchiˀuk yajnil.

29 veno ˀoch la sk'el ti ˀolole.
ta la xvay ti ˀolol ta teme.

30 ak' la ˀiluk yal ti ˀantz,
k'usi ˀololal ti yole.
yak'be la yil ti jtotike.

31 k'alal la yil ti jtotike:
ˀa . . . kerem la ˀavolike xi la ti jtotike.
Jaˀ xi la xchiˀuk yajnil ti vinike.

32 veno pero le ˀune kerem vok' ti ˀolole.
te xa ta k'unk'un chabolik xi la ti jtotike.

33 veno te chital jk'eloxuk k'usi ˀora,
mi la xch'iˀ xa li ˀolole xi la ti jtotike.

34 teyuk xi la xchiˀuk yajnil ti vinike.
bat la ti jtotike.

He came up to the man's house, 23
To the place where the man lived with his wife.

Our Father came up and politely asked, "Are you here?" 24
So he asked the man and his wife when he arrived.

"Yes, we are here," said the man and his wife. 25
"Oh, I see," said Our Father.

"What do you want?" asked the man and his wife. 26
"I came to ask if your child has been born yet," said Our Father.

"Oh, yes, it is born," said the man and his wife. 27
"I see," said Our Father.

"I came to see how the child is," said Our Father. 28
"Come on in and see for yourself," said the man and his wife.

With that, he went in to see the child. 29
There it was, asleep in its bed.

The woman showed him how big the baby was, 30
What it was like.
She showed him to Our Father.

When Our Father saw it, he spoke: 31
"Oh, the child is a boy," said Our Father.
"That's right," said the man and his wife.

"Good. So, indeed, a child is born. 32
This way you will multiply, little by little," said Our Father.

"Well, I will be back to see you someday, 33
When your child has grown up a bit," said Our Father.

"Very well," said the man and his wife. 34
With that, Our Father left.

35 veno ta jk'elkik bu ta xak'ik tajmek li ˀololetik.
ˀep xa laj vok'uk tajmek kerem tzeb,
pero mu hunuk kuxul xi la ti jtotike.

36 ˀora la jkil xa vok'em jun li kereme,
ta jk'elkik bu ta xak'ik xi la ti jtotike.

✠ ✠ ✠

37 ˀa . . . pero liˀe mu xa sta vakib ˀu xch'i tal kuˀuntik ma koltike.
la jyil xa li ˀajvalile xiik la xchiˀuk yajnil ti vinike.

38 jaˀ lek ta ˀoxib noˀox ˀu xk'ot jtiˀtik ma ˀolole xi la xchiˀuk yajnil ti vinike.
moˀoje ta xilotik ˀajvalil xiik la xchiˀuk yajnil ti vinike.

39 veno k'alal la sta ti ˀoxib ˀue pero xuˀ xa jtiˀtik.
muk' xa jutuk ma li ˀolole.

40 xalakan ˀak'ak'al ˀoˀ tana.
ta jpastik jch'a ta tamaliˀ li ˀolole.
na me taluk ˀajvalil xiik la xchiˀuk yajnil ti vinike.

41 lik la slakanik jun bin k'ak'al ˀoˀ xchiˀuk yajnil ti vinike.
k'alal la vokan ti k'ak'al ˀoˀe xchiˀinolan xa la ta ˀak'ot yol ti ˀantze.

42 k'alal la ti laj xchiˀinolan ta ˀak'ot yol ti ˀantze,
lik la stz'ajik ta k'ak'al ˀoˀ ti ˀolole.

43 k'alal la ti syakel ta stz'ajik ta k'ak'al ˀoˀ,
jaˀ ˀo la k'ot ti jtotike.

44 k'uchaˀal chatz'ajik ta k'ak'al ˀoˀ ti ˀolole xi la ti jtotike.
ˀa . . . yuˀun ta xkak' ˀatinuk yuˀun toj ˀep xa skuchoj ˀik'obal.

45 yuˀun toyol ta xˀok' xchiˀuk ˀik'obal.
mu xa xˀoch svayel xchiˀuk.

46 k'alal mi la jkak' ˀatinuk lek ta k'ak'al ˀoˀe ta xˀoch lek vayel.
ta xvay lek tajmek xi la xchiˀuk yajnil ti vinike.

"Well, I wonder what they are doing with their children? 35
By now, many little boys and girls must have been born,
But none remains alive," said Our Father to himself.

"Now, not so long ago, I actually saw one little newborn boy," 36
said Our Father.
"I wonder what's become of him," mused Our Father.

✠ ✠ ✠

"Oh, but now we can't wait for our child to reach six months of age. 37
The master has already seen him," said the man and his wife.

"Better to wait just three months before we eat him," 38
said the man and his wife.
"Otherwise, the master will catch us," said the man and his wife.[2]

"Good, when he is three months old, we can eat him. 39
Then the child will be nice and big.

You can cook him in your pot of boiling water. 40
We can stuff the child into tamales right away.
If only the master does not appear," said the man to his wife.

The man and his wife began to heated up a pot of boiling water. 41
While the water was boiling, the woman was dancing with her child.

When the woman had finished dancing with her son, 42
She plunged the child into the boiling water.

When she was right in the middle of plunging him into the boiling water, 43
It was then that Our Father arrived.

"Why are you dipping the child in boiling water?" asked Our Father. 44
"Oh, we're giving the dirty thing a bath.

He was fretful because of the dirt. 45
He didn't want to sleep well.

When we bathe him in hot water, he sleeps very well. 46
He really sleeps very well," said the man and his wife.

47 xak'el ˀavil tana ˀun lek ta xvay tajmek xiik la ta xalbik ti jtotike.
pero k'uchaˀal.
cham xa li ˀolol la ˀavuˀunik ta k'ak'al ˀoˀ xkile xi la ti jtotike.

48 moˀoj yuˀun jaˀ k'ixin xa yaˀi li k'ak'al ˀoˀe.
jaˀ vay ˀo xchiˀuk xa.

49 k'el ˀavil tana.
ta xhjlav ta jlikel xi la chalbik ti jtotike xchiˀuk yajnil ti vinike.

50 pero k'el ˀavil k'uchaˀal vi snukulik sk'ob li ˀolol ta k'ak'al ˀoˀe xi la ti jtotike.
ˀa . . . pero leke.
jaˀ li yik'obal bos lok'el ta k'ak'al ˀoˀe xiik la ta xalbik jtotik xchiˀuk yajnil ti vinike.

51 ˀa . . . moˀoj.
cham xa ˀavuˀunik ta k'ak'al ˀoˀ ma li ˀolole.

52 veno tekeˀ la jkiloxuk xa vi sˀelanil chamilik ta k'ak'al ˀoˀ li ˀolole.
jaˀ yuˀun ti muˀyuk junuk kuxul ti ˀololetik tanae xi la ti jtotike.

53 jaˀ lek chaˀatinik ta k'ak'al ˀoˀ ˀek,
k'uchaˀal chaˀatin ˀavuˀunik li ˀololetike.

54 jech chapasik reva.
ta jk'elkik mi xkuch ˀavuˀunik.
chaˀatinik ta k'ak'al ˀoˀ ˀeke xi la ti jtotike.

55 veno k'alal la ti sakub talel ti ta yok'omal,
tal la baˀyel jutuk chakil ˀoˀ.

56 k'unk'untik la lik k'ixinajuk ti ˀoˀe.
lik la k'ak'ubuk ti ˀoˀe k'alal la yaˀik ti kirsano.

57 ta xa xyal talel ti k'ak'al ˀoˀe ta vinajele.
lik la jatavikuk lok'el ta snaik ti kirsanoetik.

"You'll see right away how well he sleeps," they said to Our Father. 47
"But how can that be?
I see full well the child has been boiled to death by
your own hands!" said Our Father.

"Oh, no! The water felt nice and warm to him. 48
He's just asleep, that's all.

You'll see in a minute. 49
He'll wake up right away," the man and the woman said to Our Father.

"But look! Why is the skin of the child's hand there in the boiling water?" 50
asked Our Father.
"Oh, that's all right.
It's just some dirt washed off in the hot water," said the man
and his wife to Our Father.

"Oh, no. That's not right. 51
Your child has been boiled to death.

Very well. Now I have seen you boil your children. 52
That is why there are no children left," said Our Father.

"You ought to boil yourselves, 53
Just as you bathed your children!

You will see what it is like. 54
You will see if you can stand it.
You, too, will bathe in boiling water," said Our Father.

Well, just as it was getting light on the following day, 55
There came the first shower.

Slowly, very slowly, the rain began to grow warmer. 56
The people felt the rain getting hotter and hotter.

Soon boiling rain poured from the heavens. 57
The people began to flee from their houses.

58 batik la ta naˀil ch'en snak' sbaik.
ha' la tznaˀik mi xkolik to lae.

59 te la ˀoyik ta naˀil ch'en ti jˀoˀlol ti kirsanoe.
yaˀuk to la mi xkolik ti yalojike.

60 jaˀ to la yaˀik ˀoch la ti k'ak'al ˀoˀe.
vos la ti naˀil ch'en ta k'ak'al ˀoˀe.

61 te la chamik ta naˀil ch'en jˀoˀlol ti kirsano ta k'ak'al ˀoˀe.
ti jˀoˀlole te la chamik ta snaik.

62 laj la skotol ti kirsano ta k'ak'al ˀoˀe.
jech la chamik ta k'ak'al ˀoˀe ti baˀyel kirsano ti voˀnee.

63 jaˀ la smulik ti ta stiˀik ti yolike,
ti ta spasik ta tamaliˀ ti ˀolole.

64 jaˀ la smulinik ti yoˀ muk' la jaluk xch'iike;
jaˀ la ti toyol ta stiˀik ti yolike jaˀ ti mu xbolik xchiˀuk.

65 mu la snaˀik sk'oponik jtotik.
toj pukujik la.

66 jaˀ la smulinik ti yoˀ chamik ta k'ak'al ˀoˀe.
jech la chamik ti baˀyel kirsano ti voˀnee.

They went to the caves to hide. 58
They thought they still could save themselves.

Half of the people were there in the caves. 59
They still thought they could save themselves.

Then at last they felt the boiling water begin to seep through. 60
The caves collapsed from the boiling rain.

There in the caves half of the people perished, victims of the boiling rain. 61
The other half died in their houses.

All of the people died in the rain of boiling water. 62
That is how the first people died long ago in the boiling rain.

It was their fault for eating their children, 63
For making tamales of their children.

It's their fault that they did not prosper; 64
Because they willfully ate their own children, they did not increase.

They did not know how to pray to Our Father. 65
They were evil.

They alone bear the guilt for the fact that they died in the 66
rain of boiling water.
This is how the first people perished long, long ago.

1 ˀa li maxetike krisano toˀox la ti voˀne.
ti k'alal k'ataj ta max ti krisano yuˀun la chopolik ti krisano.

2 k'usi ta spas ti krisano voˀne.
yuˀun la snaˀ stiˀan yolik ti voˀne.

3 k'usi muk'ul ti yolik ti k'alal ta stiˀik.
muk' xa la ma ti yolik ti k'alal ta stiˀik.
yuˀun la ta xa xal ta saˀ yajnil ti yolik ti k'alal ta smil stiˀik.

4 k'usi ta smilik ˀo ti yolik ti k'alal ta smil stiˀik.
ta teˀ la ta smilik ˀo yolik ti maxetik.
ti k'alal krisano toˀox ti voˀne.

5 mi skotol krisano ti k'ataj ta max ti voˀne.
mu stekeluk.
chamik jlom xchiˀiltak.

6 k'usi laj spas xchiˀiltak ti max k'alal chamik.
ˀaˀ la jyak' kastiko ti jtotik ta vinajel.

7 k'usi kastiko la jyak' ti jtotik ta vinajel.
yak' la kastiko nojel ta ˀoˀ.

8 k'usi ta yalil ti ˀoˀ la jyak' ti jtotik.
ˀaˀ to ta ˀolol vinajel kechel k'ot ti ˀoˀ k'alal cham xchiˀil ti maxetik.

9 jayib k'ak'al ˀi ˀoy tz'anal ti ˀoˀ k'alal cham xchiˀiltak ti max.
liˀ la ˀoy tz'anal ˀoxib k'ak'al ti voˀ.

TEXT 18

Monkeys Were Still People Long Ago

Xalik López Setjol

Monkeys were still people long ago. 1
The people became monkeys because they were evil.

What were the deeds of these people long ago?[1] 2
They used to eat their own children long ago.

What size were their children when they ate them? 3
They were already nearly grown up when they ate them.
For it is said that they were at the age of seeking wives when
they killed them to eat.

How did they slay their children to eat them? 4
The monkeys clubbed their children to death with sticks.
This was when monkeys were still people long ago.

Were all the people changed into monkeys long ago? 5
Not all of them.
Some of their kinsmen simply died.

What happened to these kinsmen of the monkey people who died? 6
Our Lord Sun/Christ in Heaven gave them a punishment.

What punishment did Our Lord Sun/Christ in Heaven give them? 7
He gave them a great flood as punishment.

How great was the deluge that Our Lord Sun/Christ sent down? 8
The waters had reached halfway to Heaven when the kinsmen
of the monkey people died.

For how many days were the flood waters gathered when the kinsmen 9
of the monkey people died?
The flood waters persisted here on earth for three days.

10 bu ʔoy ti max ti ʔaʔ muʔyuk xcham ti k'alal cham xchiʔiltak.
yuʔun la ʔaʔ laj spas skajon ti k'alal yaʔi ta xtal nojel ta ʔoʔ.

11 ti k'alal tal xa ti nojel ta ʔoʔ stik' la sbaik ʔochel ta yut kajon.
ti k'alal syakel xa ta xnoj ti ʔoʔ tey la kuchbil muy ta ba ʔoʔ.
ti k'alal la jyak' nojel ta ʔoʔ ti jtotik.

12 ti k'alal pek'tzaj yal tal ti ʔoʔ,
tey la kajatik yal to ti max xchiʔuk skajonal.

13 ti k'alal ʔul ti ʔoʔ lok' la ta skajonal ti max.
stzan la sk'ok'ik pero mu toʔox la maxuk.
krisano toʔox la ti k'alal ʔech' ti ʔoʔ.

14 ti k'alal skajel ti ba ʔoʔ ti max pero mu la vajuk ta sveʔ.
xchik'oj la ʔixim.
tey la xveʔ ta yut kajon.

15 ti k'alal laj xchik' ʔixim ti max,
ʔoxib toʔox la k'ak'al xk'an stal ti nojel ta ʔoʔ.

16 ti k'alal tzanal xa sk'ok'ik ti max,
yal talel ti jtotik,
tal sk'el ti max.

17 pero mu toʔox maxuk.
krisano toʔox k'alal yal talel ti jtotik.

18 k'usi ta xapas liʔ xi la ti jtotik.
Muʔyuk xi la.
yuʔun noʔox ta jtzan jk'ok' xi la ti max.

19 ʔaʔ noʔox la ti loʔilajik ʔoxbel chanbel,
ʔora la ʔak'bat sne ti max xchiʔuk stzotzil.

20 ti k'alal ʔak'bat sne xchiʔuk stzotzil ti max,
tey la kom ʔo ta teʔtik.

Where were the monkey people who did not die when their kinsmen died? 10
They made a box boat when they realized that the flood waters
were coming.

When the flood came they got inside the box boat. 11
As the flood continued in full force, they floated safely there
on the surface of the water.
So it was when Our Lord Sun/Christ sent the flood.

As the flood waters receded, 12
Down came the monkey people floating there in their box boats.

When the waters evaporated, the monkey people got out of their box boats. 13
They made a fire, these who still were not monkeys.
They were still people when the waters went away.

When they were floating on top of the water, they had no tortillas to eat. 14
They had toasted some dry corn.[2]
There they ate it inside the box boats.

When the monkey people toasted their dry corn, 15
It was still three days before the flood.

When the monkey people lit their fire, 16
Our Lord Sun/Christ descended.
He came down to watch the monkeys.

Remember that they were still not monkeys. 17
They were still people when Our Lord Sun/Christ came down.

"What are you doing here?" asked Our Lord Sun/Christ. 18
"Nothing," they said.
"We're just lighting a fire," said the monkey people.

They had but spoken three or four words, 19
When at once they were given monkey tails and monkey fur.

Once they had monkey tails and monkey fur, 20
There they remained in the woods, forever.

21 muˀyuk xa la xˀak'bat yixim ti max.
muˀyuk xa ta xkak' ˀavixim xi la ti jtotik.
Xuˀuk xi la ti maxetik.

22 tey xa la cha saˀ k'usi stak' loˀel xi la ti jtotik.
xuˀuk xi la ti maxetik.

23 k'alal sut muyel ta vinajel ti jtotik,
yochel la ta saˀel sveˀel k'usi stak' lajesel ta teˀtik ti max.

24 ˀa li maxe krisano toˀox ti voˀne.
ti k'alal k'ataj ta maxe yuˀun la chopol jutuk.

25 stiˀ yolik.
ˀech'o xal la jyich' k'atajesel la max.
manchuk snaˀ stiˀ yolik, muˀyuk xk'ataj ta max.

These monkeys were never given corn again. 21
"I shall never again let you have corn," said Our Lord Sun/Christ.
"All right, then," said the monkeys.

"From now on you can find your food there in the woods," 22
said Our Lord Sun/Christ.
"All right, then," said the monkeys.

When Our Lord Sun/Christ went back up to the sky, 23
The monkeys began searching in the woods for their food.

These monkeys were still people long ago. 24
When they were changed to monkeys it was because they were
inclined to be evil.

They ate their own children. 25
That is why they were turned into monkeys.
Had they not taken to eating their own children, they would
not have been changed into monkeys.[3]

1 jun kuento ta voʔnee.

2 ʔoy jun mol.
ta xloʔilajik ta k'ixin ʔosil ti mole xchiʔuk jun vinik.

3 k'alal lik yalike ti jun kuentoe yuʔun ʔoy ta la staik skechel chuch ta tiʔ teʔtik.
te ʔep busul sbakal.

4 ti chuche ʔa ti voʔnee yuʔun kirsano toʔox la xi ti mole.
jaʔ ʔo la pas ta chuch ti k'alal la ʔech' ti nojelal ta ʔoʔe xi ti mole.

5 ʔa ti voʔnee nojik la ta ʔoʔ ti ʔantivo kirsanoe.
noj la ta ʔoʔ ti snaike.

6 ʔa ti yane te la bajal laj ta sna.
ʔep la ti cham ta snaik.

TEXT 19

His Wife Turned into a Monkey; the Man Became a Squirrel

Manuel López Calixto

Here is a story of long ago. 1

There was an old man. 2
This old man and a companion were talking to each other
in Hot Country.[1]

The story began just after they had found the scraps from a 3
squirrel's meal at the edge of the woods.
There were lots of corncobs piled up.

"The squirrel was a person long ago," said the old man. 4
"He was turned into a squirrel at the time of the flood."

Long ago the ancient people drowned in a great flood. 5
Their houses were filled with water.

There were some who locked themselves in their houses and 6
perished inside.
There were many who died there in their houses.

7 jaˀ xa noˀox la ti buch'u ˀun jatav lok'ele.
bat la saˀik ti bu la toyol ti vitze.
jaˀ xa la te bat snak' sbaik ta jol vitz.

8 te la nakiik ta yolon teˀ.
ˀo la te la staik jun muk'ta tulan.
jaˀ la te nakiik ta yolon ti teˀe.

9 ch'abal xa la ti ˀiximike.
lik la saˀik sloˀik sat tulan.

10 la spasik reva mi stak' la loˀel.
jaˀ to la yaˀik toj lek.
la stak' loˀel.

11 laj la saˀik yan sat teˀ.
ˀo la te la staik sat ˀak'.

There were only a few who managed to flee. 7
They went to seek refuge high on a mountain.
They went to hide there on top of a mountain.

They lived there under a tree. 8
They found there a large oak tree.
They lived there at the foot of the tree.

They no longer had any corn. 9
So they sought acorns to eat.

They tried them to see if they would do as food. 10
At last they determined that they tasted very good.
They would do for food.

They searched for other fruits as well. 11
And they found the fruit of a vine.

FIGURE 21

There were only a few who managed to flee.
They went to seek refuge high on a mountain.
They went to hide there on top of a mountain.

12 jlikel la muy ta teˀ ti vinik.
slilin la yal talel ti sat ˀak'e.

13 laj la sloˀil la xtok ti sat ˀak' lae.
toj lek noˀox la xtok.
jaˀ la sveˀel ˀinatab.

14 k'alal ta xak' ti ˀoˀe ta la xch'i chechev ta yut teˀtik.
bat la saˀik xtok ti checheve.

15 toj lek la yaˀik.
jaˀ la sloˀik xtok.

16 ˀak'o taluk li ˀoˀe mu xicham ˀo xi la ti ˀantivo kirsanoe.
muˀyuk la yatel yoˀontonik.

17 jech la ti ˀoˀe mu la bu ta xˀech' tajmek.
ta la xˀak' sjunul la ˀak'obal sjunul la k'ak'al.

18 ti puru la ˀoˀ ti smal sakub lae.
toj jal la yak' ti ˀoˀ ti voˀnee.

19 ti bu la jujun stenleje solel la nojik xa la ta ˀoˀ.
mu xa la xuˀ xjelavik ta jot vitz.
yuˀun xa la noj stekel ti stenlejale.

20 jun xa la ti muk' ta vitz.
jaˀ xa la noˀox la muk' xmuy ˀech'el.

21 ti bu la muk'tik vitze jaˀ xa la te nakaj ti kom ti kirsanoetike.
ti jayib xa la kuch yuˀunike ti jatovale.
jaˀ la kuxul ˀikom ti k'alal ˀech' ti nojelal ta ˀoˀe.

22 k'alal la ti k'ep lek xa la xaˀik ti kirsanoetike.
xmuyubajik xa la ti muk' la xchamik ˀo la ti ˀoˀe.

23 moˀoj ma liˀe ta xkuch xa kuˀuntik xi la ti kirsanoe k'u la yepal muk' xchamik ˀo ta ˀoˀe.
yuˀun muyik la ta jolvitz ti yoˀ xa la kuxul la komike.

A man would climb the tree. 12
He would shake it so that the fruit of the vine in the tree would fall.

Of this fruit they also ate. 13
They found that it, too, would serve them well as food.
It was the wild grape.

When it rained, mushrooms grew in the woods. 14
So they also went to collect mushrooms.

They tasted good to them. 15
So they ate them as food.

"Let it rain! We will not die," said the ancient people confidently. 16
Their hearts were not sad.

But the rains gave no sign of letting up. 17
It rained constantly every night, every day.

There was nothing but rain, from twilight to dawn! 18
It rained and rained without ceasing long ago!

Every stretch of flat land was now flooded. 19
The water could no longer drain away to the other side of the mountains.
This happened because all of the flat land was flooded.

Soon, there remained but one high mountain peak, 20
The only one that the waters did not reach.

This mountaintop was the only place where these people could take refuge. 21
These were the only people who had gotten away.
It was only these who remained alive when the flood finally subsided.

When they realized that the weather had cleared, the people were happy. 22
They were joyous that they had not died in the flood.

"There's no need to worry. Here we will indeed survive," said those who had not died in the flood. 23
They had climbed to the top of the mountain and thereby remained alive.

24 k'alal la paj ti k'inobal ˀoˀe,
ˀech' xa kuˀuntik li kastikoe xi la ti ˀantivo kirsanoe.

25 k'alal la ˀech' ti nojelal ta ˀoˀe k'ot la jun vinik ta teˀtik.
mi liˀote xi la k'otel.
liˀune xi la ti jnaklejetike ta teˀtike.

26 k'uchaˀal muk' xachamik ˀo ta ˀoˀe xˀutatik la.
muˀyuk lek ˀech' kuˀuntik xi la ti ˀantivo kirsanoe.

27 bu ˀataik ti ˀixime.
k'usi la veˀik xi la ti jvulaˀale.

28 moˀoj.
ˀoy lek jveˀelkutik xi la.

29 pere k'usi la loˀik.
k'usi la veˀik xi la ti jvulaˀal vinike.

30 muˀyuk.
la jloˀkutik sat teˀ xi la.

31 k'usi sat teˀal la loˀik.
la jloˀkutik sat tulan.
la jloˀkutik sat ˀak'.
la jtiˀkutik chechev.
k'usi k'an ta jloˀkutik xi la ti ˀantivo kirsanoe.

32 veno lek ˀoy xi la ti jvulaˀal vinike.
mi jech muyankik ta teˀ ta ˀora xi la.

33 veno xi la.
jlikel la muy ta ˀora.

34 k'ot la stul sat tulan.
sloˀ ta niˀ teˀ.

When the great rainstorm had passed, 24
"Now our punishment has passed!" said the ancient people.

When the flood had receded, a man came out of the woods.[2] 25
"Are you here?" asked the visitor politely.
"We are here," said those who lived on the mountain.

"Why didn't you die in the flood?" he said to them. 26
"We didn't have any problems. We came out of it very well,"
said the ancient people.

"Where did you find corn? 27
What did you eat?" asked the visitor.

"That wasn't a problem. 28
We had very good food," said the ancient people.

"But what did you eat? 29
What did you consume?" asked the visitor.

"No problem. 30
We ate fruits and nuts," they said.

"What fruits and nuts did you eat?" 31
"We ate acorns.
We ate fruits of the vine.
We ate mushrooms.
We ate whatever we wanted," said the ancient people.

"Well, that's fine," said the visitor. 32
"If what you say is true, then be off to climb up in the trees
right away," he said.

"All right," they said. 33
They climbed up right away.

They proceeded to gather acorns. 34
They ate them there in the branches of the trees.

35 ˀaaa . . . jech ˀaval xi la ti vinike.
veno jaˀ loˀanik xi la.

36 veno.
bitan yalel tal xi la ti vinike.

37 k'alal la bit yalele jaˀ ˀo la pas ta chuch.
k'alaluk bit yal talel ta niˀ teˀe xkotkun xa la likel ti vinike.

38 snaˀ to la ti k'uxi ta xanave.
mu xa la stak' xanav ti xvaˀvune.

39 ta la xvaˀi ti yaloje.
kotol la ta xk'ot ta banamil.
mu xa la stak' xvaˀi xanav ti vinik lae.

40 yan la ti yajnile jaˀ la xvavun ta xanav ˀo.
xkotkun la batel ta xanav li ˀantz ˀeke.

41 yan la li vinike jaˀ la pas ta chuch.
yan la li ˀantz jaˀ la pas ta max.

42 mu xa la stak' sk'opojik.
k'alal ta xk'opoje jaˀ xa noˀox la ti stz'ektzun ta spase.
yuˀun la ta xk'opoj la ti yaloje.
mu la stak' xa xk'opoj.
k'ajom xa la ti stz'ektzun xa la ta spase li chuche.

43 yuˀun la ta xk'opoj la ti yaloje.
ta la sk'opon yajnil ti chuche.
mu la xtak'av ti yajnile.
jaˀ noˀox la ti svik vi ˀun la ta xk'opoj li ˀantze.

"Hmmm. You *are* telling the truth," said the man. 35
"Well, go on eating them, then," he said.

"That's just fine. 36
Now, jump down here," said the man.

At the moment when one of them jumped down, he turned into a squirrel. 37
As soon as he had jumped from the treetop, he began
walking on all fours.

He still knew how to walk, 38
But he could no longer walk upright.

It seemed to the creature that he was still walking upright, 39
But he landed on all fours.
The man could no longer walk upright.

Things turned out differently for his wife, who would sometimes 40
walk upright.
Sometimes she would also walk about on all fours.

It was different for the man, who became a squirrel. 41
Different for the woman, who became a monkey.

Neither of them could talk anymore. 42
When he spoke, all that came out of him was "*tz'ek tzun*."
It seemed to him that he was talking.
But he could no longer speak.
Now the squirrel could only chatter, "*tz'ek tzun*."

It seemed to him that he was talking! 43
He would speak to his wife.
But his wife would not answer.
The woman would just screech when she spoke.

44 ja? la pas ta max li yajnile.
li vinike ja? pas ta chuch.

45 jech'o la xal sna? la sk'ux ?ajan li chuche.
yu?un la kirsano la ti vo?nee.

46 yan la li maxe.
mu la sna? la sk'uxel ?ajan.
mu la sna? lek sve?el li vaje.
ja? no?ox la sna? slo?el li sat te?etike li lo?bole li kenyae li ja?ase li pane.
ja? sve?elinoj li maxe xi ti mol vo?ne ta xlo?ilajike.

His wife turned into a monkey. 44
  The man became a squirrel.

That is why the squirrel is fond of tender corn. 45
  It is because he was a person long ago.

The case is different for the monkey. 46
  She does not eat tender corn.
  She does not like tortillas.
  She just likes to eat fruit, bananas, guineos, zapotes, and bread.[3]
  "Monkeys feed on these things," said the old man who
    told this story long ago.

FIGURE 22

His wife turned into a monkey.
  The man became a squirrel.

47 ˀa li mu maxe jaˀ toj chopol xi li mole.
mi la jk'eltike ta ˀora ta spik xchak.
ta sjot'ilan stiˀ schak.
ta la xak' ˀil ti smise.
ta la sk'abtavan.
ta la sjot' yuch' ti meˀ maxe.

48 k'alal la jatavik ˀel ta teˀtike te xa la batik ˀo.
pas ˀo xa la ta xchanul teˀtik ti ˀantivo kirsanoe ti voˀnee.
jaˀ ˀo la ti ˀech' ti nojelal ta ˀoˀe.

49 skotol la ti jayib jatav ˀech'el ta teˀtike jaˀ la pasik ta xchanul teˀtik.
ti bu la muk' xchamik ˀo la ta ˀoˀe,
jaˀ la k'atajik ta chuch,
jaˀ la k'atajik ta max.

50 yuˀun haˀ la smul ti la sloˀik ti sat teˀ ti ˀantivo kirsanoe.
jech'o la xal ˀoy la ta skotol banamil ti chuche ti maxe.

51 jaˀ la toj bij.
mu la snaˀ la xch'i ta bik'ital teˀtik.
puru la ta muk'tik teˀtik ta xanav la ti maxe.

52 yuˀun jaˀ la li toj pukuje.
jech'o la xal ta nom banamil ˀoye.
xi la ta xloˀilaj ti mol voˀnee.

"Those miserable monkeys are really awful," said the old man. 47
"Why, whenever we look at them they touch their asses.
They keep scratching at their assholes.
They show their twats.
They'll even piss on you.
And female monkeys scratch their lice."

When they fled to the woods, they went there for good. 48
The ancient people had already turned into animals of the forest.
It all goes back to what happened at the time of the flood.

All of those who fled into the woods turned into wild animals. 49
Those who did not die in the flood,
They turned into squirrels,
They turned into monkeys.

It was the fault of the ancient people themselves for eating fruits and nuts. 50
That is why there are squirrels and monkeys everywhere.

The monkey is very clever.[4] 51
It doesn't like to live in little thickets.
It lives only in the great forests.

The monkey is also very evil. 52
That is why it lives very far away.[5]
So said the old man who told this story long ago.

1 ˀoy jun kuento sventa k'ak'al ˀoˀ.
ja' toˀox la ti pimero banamile.

2 vaˀun k'alal la ta ti k'ak'al ˀoˀ la ˀune,
jech la ti kirsanoetik la ˀune.

3 k'alal la tal ti k'ak'al ˀoˀ la ˀune,
jatavik la ta ch'en ti ˀantivoetike.

4 vaˀun k'alal la k'ot la ch'en ti kirsano la ˀune:
ˀi ta la k'ak' ta yulemal ti ch'ene.

5 jech la ti k'ak'al ˀoˀ la ˀune:
toj k'ok' la tajmek.

6 ˀoy la xtz'un ˀo xchob ti ˀantivoetik la ˀune.
ta la k'ak' la skotol k'alal la tal ti k'ak'al ˀoˀ la ˀune.

7 ch'abal la ta xˀavan ti ˀanjele.
ch'abal bu ta xˀok' ti mu ta tzinil la ti banamile.
jech la ti ˀantivoetike ta la xˀok'ik tajmek.

8 jech la ti yane bat la ta ˀil chij.
te la laj skotol ti jˀilchij la ˀune.

9 vaˀun ti k'ak'al ˀoˀ la ˀune k'alal la ta ch'en ta syul.
yuˀun ti k'ak'al ˀoˀ la ˀune.

10 jech la ti snaik la ˀune.
k'ak' la skotol ti sna ti ˀantivoetik la ˀune.

TEXT 20

About the Boiling Rain

Marián López Calixto

There is a story of the boiling rain.[1] 1
It was still in the time of the First Earth.

So, at the time the boiling rain came, 2
This is what happened to those people.

When the boiling rain came, 3
The ancestors fled to caves for protection.

So it was when these people reached the cave: 4
They had been scalded by the time they arrived at the cave.

So it was with the boiling water: 5
It was unbearably hot.

Some of the ancestors had been sowing their cornfields. 6
They were all burned to death when the boiling rain came.[2]

The Earth Lords did not shout. 7
They did not cry, for their order was not yet established on the earth.[3]
But the ancestors indeed cried a lot.

Others had gone out to watch their sheep. 8
There they perished, all of the shepherds.

Then the boiling rain reached the caves where others had taken refuge. 9
So it was with the boiling rain.

It even reached their houses. 10
All of the houses of the ancestors burned up.

11 vaˀun jech la ti yan la ˀune sjok'ik la ti banamile.
vaˀun k'alal laj la sjok'ik ti banamil la ˀune smuk la sbaik la ta lum ti ˀantivoetik lae.

12 vaˀun jech la yan la ˀune cham la ˀun.
jaˀ xa noˀox xa la kom ti smukoj la sbaik ta yut lum lae.

13 vaˀun ˀoxib la k'ak'al la yak' la ti k'ak'al ˀoˀe.
jaˀ xa noˀox komik ti ˀantivoetike.

14 vaˀun jech la ti banamil la ˀune,
yuˀun mu la xvaˀi ti banamile.
ch'abal la mas ˀep ti tone.

15 vaˀun jech la ti jtotik la ˀune ˀilin la ˀun.
jaˀ la ˀilin ti jtotik san josee yuˀun la bik'it la yoˀonton.

16 muˀyuk la sperton ti baˀyo jtotik san josee.
k'alal mi ta la xˀilin jutuk ti kirsano lae ta la xak' la kastiko ti jtotike.

17 vaˀun jech la ti banamil la ˀune mu la sk'an la lek la svaˀi.
vaˀun jech la ti jtotik la ˀune ˀilin la tajmek ˀun.

18 taˀlo xa la xaˀi smeltzanel la ti banamil ti jtotik san jose la ˀune.
yuˀun mu la snaˀ la smeltzanel la lek ti banamile.

19 vaˀun jech la ti jtotik la ˀune.
k'alal la meltzajem xa la ta skomtzan ti banamil la ti jtotike san jose la ˀune,
ta la xbat ta vinajel ti jtotik san jose la ˀune.

20 vaˀun k'alal la sut tal la ˀune lomem xa la ˀun sta ti banamil la ˀune.
pere k'usi ta xkut tajmek la ˀune xi la ti jtotik la ˀune.
ta la xat la tajmek yoˀonton ti jtotik san jose la ˀune.

21 vaˀun k'alal vok' ti jtotik jxalik la ˀune ta la xal ti sloˀik.
pere k'uchaˀal ˀun mu smeltzaj ˀavuˀun ti banamile xi la ti jtotik ta vinajele.

Some of them dug graves in the earth. 11
When they finished digging these graves, the surviving ancestors
buried their comrades in the earth.

Then even these survivors perished. 12
They lasted only long enough to bury one another.

For three days, the boiling rain fell. 13
That sealed the fate of the ancestors.

☩ ☩ ☩

Now, as for the earth itself, 14
The surface of the earth would not stand erect,
For there were not many stones.[4]

For this reason Our Lord Sun/Christ got angry. 15
He became angry because Our Lord San José was mean and ungenerous.

Our Lord San José, the first saint, knew no mercy. 16
When the people became disgruntled, he always struck back at them.

For example, there was the case of the earth, which refused to lift itself up. 17
This caused him to get very angry.[5]

Our Lord San José became fed up with trying to make the earth habitable. 18
The reason was that he knew nothing about how to go about
preparing the earth!

This is what happened with Our Lord San José: 19
When Our Lord San José at last thought that he had succeeded in
preparing the earth,
Our Lord San José went away to the sky.

But when he returned, he found that the earth had collapsed. 20
"Now, what shall I do about this?" wondered the saint.
Our Lord San José's heart was very sad.

Then, when Our Lord Salvador was born, he spoke to San José:[6] 21
"Why haven't you succeeded in making the earth habitable?"
asked Our Lord Sun/Christ in Heaven.

22 veno ta jmeltzantik ti banamil xi la ti jtotik jxalike.
veno jmeltzantik ti banamile xi la ti jtotike.

23 la jyalbun jun mol ta pinka.
yuˀun ta jkuchkutik k'ak'al ˀoˀ.
ˀi jaˀ te lik ˀo ti kuentoe.
jaˀ la jech tal ti k'ak'al ˀoˀ lae ti mas voˀne tajmek lae.

24 ch'abal toˀox ˀep ti kirsano.
k'ajomal la ˀoy voˀob yoxvinik ti kirsanoe.

"Well, let us make the earth ready," said Our Lord Sun/Christ in Heaven. 22
"Yes, let us make the earth ready," said Our Lord San Salvador.[7]

An old man on the coffee plantation told this to me. 23
We were carrying hot water.
That is how this story came up,
The account of how the boiling rain came long, long ago.

There were not yet many people around at that time. 24
Maybe there were forty-five, at the most.

2

The Second Creation

1 kuento jch'ulmeˀtik ta vinajel.

2 ti voˀnee ˀoy jun mol nakal ta ˀoxib jok'.
sna' lek ˀilol.

3 ˀentonse voˀne li bat jk'opon mu xˀabolaj xisk'el.
yuˀun ˀip ta xkaˀi.

4 veno k'alal li k'ot ta sna ti mole te chotol k'ot jta.
mi liˀote juntot xkut.

5 liˀune junich'on k'usi chaval xiyut ti mole.
muˀyuk juntot lital jk'oponote.
mu jnaˀ mi mu xaˀabolaj xak'elun.
yuˀun ˀip ta xkaˀi xkut ti mole.

6 veno lek ˀoy chajk'el ta ˀora.
chotlan jlikeluk xiyut ti mole.

7 ˀentonse lichoti jlikel.
veno ta tz'akal lik sk'elun.

8 k'alal laj sk'elune lik kuch'kutik pox.
veno k'alal la jyuch' jbis poxe lik loˀilajuk ti mole.
xi liyalbee:

9 ˀa ti voˀne la ti jch'ulmeˀtike nakal toˀox la ta banumil xchiˀuk la
chaˀvoˀ yalab.
snaˀ la lek xˀabtejik ti chaˀvoˀ yalabe.
snaˀ la stz'un chobik.

TEXT 21

Of Our Mother Moon and Her Two Sons

Xalik López Castellanos

A story of Our Mother Moon in Heaven. 1

Long ago there lived an old man in the hamlet of Oshib Hok'. 2
He was a very good curer.

So I went to talk to him, to see if he would be so good as to cure me, 3
For I was not well.

Well, when I arrived at the old man's house I found him sitting there. 4
"Are you here, Uncle?" I said to him.[1]

"I am here, Nephew. What do you want?" the old man said to me. 5
"Nothing, Uncle. I just came to talk to you.
I wonder whether you would do me the favor of curing me.
For I feel sick," I said to the old man.

"All right, then. That's fine. I'll attend to you right now. 6
Sit down for a minute," the old man said to me.

Then I sat down for a little while. 7
Then he began to cure me.

When he had checked out my problem, we started to drink rum. 8
Well, after we had drunk one glassful, the old man began to talk.[2]
This is what he told me:

Long ago Our Holy Mother Moon lived on earth with her two sons. 9
The two sons knew how to work very well.
They knew how to sow their cornfields.

10 jujun la k'ak'al ta xbatik ta ˀabtel ta xchobik ti chaˀvoˀ yalabe.
veno ti jch'ulmeˀtike te la ta xkom ta sna ta la xnaˀu tuxnuk jich'il la tajmek.

11 ti chaˀvoˀ yalabe ta la xbat ta ˀabtel ta xchobik.
te la ta xˀabtejik sjunul k'ak'al ta xchobik.

12 veno ti chaˀvoˀ yalabe koˀol toˀox la ta sutik talel jujun k'ak'al ta snaik.
koˀol ta xˀabtejik ta xchobik.

13 ˀentonse ta tz'akalpat la jyilik jun spom ˀakov.
ta jun muk'ta tulan nijnij la.

14 ˀentonse ti bankilale la jyalbe yitz'in:
batik ba jloˀtik li spom ˀakove.
te xijtal ˀabtejkutik ta tz'akalpat xi la ti bankilale.

15 batik chaˀe xi la ti ˀitz'inale.
batik la sloˀik ti spom ˀakove.

16 ˀaˀ la muy ta teˀ ti bankilale.
ti ˀitz'inale ˀaˀ la mu xmuy ta teˀ.

Every day the two sons would go off to work in their cornfields. 10
Our Holy Mother Moon would stay at home spinning cotton
into a very fine thread.

Her two sons would go to work in their cornfields. 11
There, they would work all day long in their fields.

Now, her two sons would also come home together every day. 12
For they had worked together in their cornfields.

One day they saw a beehive right behind them. 13
It was hanging there in a huge inclined oak tree.

Then the older brother said to the younger brother: 14
"Let's go get some honey to eat.
We'll get back to work later," said the older brother.

"Why not? Let's do it," said the younger brother.[3] 15
With that they went off to eat honey.

The older brother climbed up in the tree. 16
The younger brother did not climb up in the tree.

17 ti bankilale ˀaˀ la jlikel muy ta teˀ ta ˀora.
ˀentonse k'ot ti bu ti spom ti ˀakove.
veno lik sloˀ ti spom ˀakove.

18 ti ˀitz'inale mu xmuy ta teˀ.
te ta xanav ta yolon teˀ.

19 ta sk'el muyel.
veno ti bankilale syakel xa ta sloˀ ti spom ˀakove.

20 ˀentonse ti ˀitz'inale la jyal:
jipbun talel jutebuk jloˀ,
yuˀun jloˀ kaˀi ˀek xi la ti ˀitz'inale.

The older brother quickly scrambled up the tree. 17
Then he reached the place where the honey was.
He started to eat the honey.

The younger brother did not climb the tree. 18
He was just pacing about at the foot of the tree.

He looked up. 19
Sure enough! There was his older brother happily eating honey.

Then the younger brother spoke: 20
"Throw me a bit to eat.
I want a little too," said the younger brother.

FIGURE 23

The older brother quickly scrambled up the tree.
Then he reached the place where the honey was.
He started to eat the honey.

21 ta xa jip talel tzakome xi la ti bankilale.
ˀentonse laj la stzak ti ˀitz'inale.
te la stzakoh ta sk'ob ti spom ˀakove.

22 laj la sk'el lek.
ˀaˀ to la xˀil smatz'om xa la ti sbankile.

23 jipo xa me talel xi la ti ˀitz'inale.
veno tzako me ta me xtal xi la ti bankilale.

24 veno jipo me tal chaˀe.
ˀatuk noˀox chaloˀ te' xi la ti ˀitz'inale.
ta xa jiptalel yan tzakome xi la ti bankilale.

25 veno lek ˀoy jipo me talel xi la ti ˀitz'inale.
tzako xa me yan xi la ti bankilale.

26 pero smatz'om xa la ti bankilale.
muˀyuk xa la spom.
puru xa la xchabil ta sjip yalel ti bankilale.

27 ˀentonse ti ˀitz'inale la snop.
bat la saˀ talel ˀaj.

28 sut talel xchiˀuk ti yaje.
k'ot la ti bu ta sloˀik ti spom ˀakove.

29 te la choti ta yok teˀ.
lik la sbas ti ˀaje.

30 k'alal laj sbas ti ˀaje,
lik la yak'be yok ti ˀaje xchiˀuk la sne.

31 te la chotol ta yok teˀ ti ˀitz'inale.
syakel xa ta xak'be yok ti ˀaje.

32 lik la yak' ta yok teˀ ti ˀaje.
laj la yak' sjoylej yok teˀ.

"I'll throw you some. Catch!" said the older brother. 21
With that, the younger brother caught it.
He caught the honeycomb in his hand.

He looked at it carefully. 22
Soon he realized that his older brother had already
chewed out the sweetness.

"Throw me some more," said the younger brother. 23
"All right. Catch it when it comes," said the older brother.

"Good. Throw it down, then. 24
It seems you alone are eating it all yourself up there,"
said the younger brother.
"I'll throw you some more. Catch!" said the older brother.

"Okay, that's fine. Throw it down," said the younger brother. 25
"Catch! Here comes some more!" said the older brother.

But the older brother had already chewed it. 26
There was no longer any honey in it.
The older brother had thrown down nothing but wax.

Then the younger brother thought about it. 27
He went to find a reed.

He returned with the reed. 28
He came to the place where they were eating honey.

He sat down at the foot of the tree. 29
He began to cut the reed into small pieces.

When he had cut the reed into small pieces, 30
He formed feet and tails out of the pieces of reed.

The younger brother sat there at the foot of the tree. 31
He was busy forming the feet out of the pieces of reed.

He began to place the pieces of reed at the foot of the tree. 32
He placed them all around the foot of the tree.

33 ti bankilale muyem la ta teˀ ta sloˀ ti spom ti ˀakove.
mu la snaˀ mi ˀoy k'usi ta spas ti yitz'ine.

34 jipo xa me talel yan ti pome xi la ti ˀitz'inale.
veno ta jip yalel tal tzakome xi la ti bankilale.

35 jipo xa me talel yan.
jipo xa me talel yan.
jipo xa me talel yan xi la ti ˀitz'inale.

36 te la chotol ta yok teˀ ˀaˀ la ti mu xmuy ta teˀe.
ˀentonse laj la yak' ti ˀaj ta yok teˀe.
laj la yak' sjoylej yok teˀ.

37 k'alal la jyak' ti ˀaj ta yok teˀe,
jlikel la ˀoch ta lum.
jlikel lik sk'uxbe yiˀbel ti teˀe.
jlikel la joybij ta ba.

38 lik la sk'uxik skotol ti yiˀbel teˀetike.
ˀentonse ta k'unk'un la ˀilom ta teˀe.

39 pero ti bankilale te la ˀoy luchul ta teˀ
ta la sloˀ ti spom ˀakove ˀaˀ to la chaˀi ta xa la slom ti teˀe.

40 k'usi me chapas xi la ti bankilale.
muˀyuk k'usi ta jpas ch'abal.
jipo xa me talel jloˀ ti pome xi la ti ˀitz'inale.
veno tzako me ˀun xi la ti bankilale.

41 ˀentonse ti baetik syakel ta xˀabtejik tajmek ta sk'uxik ti yiˀbel teˀe.
pero ti ˀitz'inale te chotol ta sk'el mi ta xlom ti teˀe.

42 veno k'alal laj sk'uxik skotol yiˀbel teˀ ti baetike,
lom ti teˀe ta jemeltik la.

The older brother was busy up in the tree eating honey. 33
He had no idea that his younger brother was up to something.

"Throw me down some more honey," said the younger brother. 34
"Okay. I'll throw some down. Catch!" said the older brother.

"Throw me down some more now! 35
Throw me down some more!
Throw me down some more!" insisted the younger brother.

He remained sitting there at the foot of the tree for, indeed, 36
he had not climbed the tree.
Then he put the pieces of reed at the foot of the tree.
He put them all around the foot of the tree.

When he placed the pieces of reed at the foot of the tree, 37
Quickly they tunneled into the earth.
Quickly they started to gnaw at the roots of a tree.
Quickly they turned into gophers.

They started at once to eat all the roots of the tree. 38
Then, slowly, the tree began to fall over.

But the older brother was still perched there in the tree. 39
He was still eating honey when he realized that the tree was falling.

"Hey! What are you doing?" asked the older brother. 40
"I'm not doing anything, nothing at all.
Throw me some more honey to eat," said the younger brother.
"Okay. Catch it!" said the older brother.

With that, the gophers continued to work hard at chewing 41
the roots of the tree.
But the younger brother just sat there watching the tree fall over.

Well, when the gophers had chewed up all the roots of the tree, 42
The tree fell down into a gully.

43 bat.
ta luchul bat ti bankilal ta jemeltike.

44 veno k'alal ti yil lom ti teˀ ti ˀitz'inale,
bat sk'el ta ˀora ti sbankil mi kuxule.

45 ˀaˀ to la jyil chamem xa la ti sbankile.
ˀentonse k'alal la la jyil chamem xa ti sbankile bat la ta sna ta ˀora.

46 veno k'alal k'ot ta sna laj la sjak' ti smeˀe:
bu kom ta bankile xi la ti smeˀe.
te kom ta chobtik ta xtajin xˀut la ti smeˀe.

Away it went! 43
And away went the older brother into the gully, still perched up in the tree!

Well, when the younger brother saw the tree fall, 44
He went at once to see if his older brother was still alive.

When he looked, his older brother was already dead. 45
When he saw that his older brother was dead, he went home at once.

Well, when he got home, his mother spoke: 46
"What's become of your older brother?" she asked.
"He stayed to play in the cornfield," he said to his mother.

FIGURE 24

Away it went!
And away went the older brother into the gully, still perched
up in the tree!

47 mi ˀech me xaval ti te ta xtajin kom ta bankile.
mi yuˀunuk la mil xi la ti smeˀe.
moˀoj te kom ta xtajin xi la ti yole.

48 mu jnaˀ mi ˀech xaval ti tey ta xtajin kom ˀabankil ta chobtike.
porke muˀyuk bu ˀech spas ti tey ta xkom tajinuk ta chobtike.
persa koˀol chatalik jujun k'ak'al xchiˀuk ta bankile xi la ti smeˀe.

49 pero tzaˀ yuˀun.
mu xiyak'be jloˀ pom.
stuktuk ta sloˀ ti pome muy ta teˀ.

50 voˀone mu ximuy.
te ˀoyun ta yok teˀ ˀaˀ li toj bik'itune.
ˀechˀaˀal mu ximuy xi la ti ˀitz'inale.

"Is it true what you say, that your older brother stayed to play 47
in the cornfield?
Could it be that you killed him?" asked his mother suspiciously.
"No. He stayed there to play," said her son.

"I'm not sure you're telling the truth, that your older brother 48
stayed to play in the cornfield.
He doesn't usually stay there playing in the cornfield.
You and your older brother always come home together
every day," said his mother.

"But it's his fault. 49
He didn't give me honey to eat.
He ate honey all by himself up there in the tree.

As for me, I didn't even climb up. 50
There I was at the foot of the tree, for I am very little.
That is why I didn't climb up," said the younger brother.

FIGURE 25

"Is it true what you say, that your older brother stayed to play in
the cornfield?
Could it be that you killed him?" asked his mother suspiciously.
"No. He stayed there to play," said her son.

51 ˀentonse yuˀun xa lamil ma ta bankile.
k'uchaˀal ˀech xapas,
xamil ta bankile.

52 mi mu ˀaˀuk ta smalk'inotik.
mi mu ˀaˀuk snaˀ lek xˀabtej.

53 ˀa li voˀote mu xanaˀ xaˀabtej.
puru tajimol chapas k'alal chabat xchiˀuk ˀabankile.

54 ˀora tana ˀun buch'u ta spas ti chobtike xi la smeˀike.
ˀoch la ta ˀok'el ti smeˀik.

55 moˀoh meˀ mu saˀok'.
ta xibat ta ˀora ba jchaˀkuxes ma ti jbankile.

56 ta xak'el ˀavil tana.
xtal.
muˀyuk chamem.
kuxul.

57 pere ˀaˀ ta smul k'uchaˀal mu xiyak'be jloˀ pom.
stuktuk ta sloˀ tajmek ti pome.
puru xa smatz'om ta sjip yalel tal.

58 ˀech' ˀaˀal kap jol.
la jlomes ti teˀe.

59 te luchul bat ti k'alal lom ti teˀe.
ta jemeltik bat.

60 pere mu xaxiˀ meˀ.
ta xibat ta ˀora.
ba jchaˀkuxes ta ˀora.

61 mu xavat ˀavoˀonton meˀ.
ta xtal ma ti jbankile xi la ti ˀitz'inale.

"Then it is true that you have already killed your older brother. 51
Why did you do that?
Why did you kill your older brother?

Don't you realize it was he who fed us? 52
Don't you realize it was he who knew how to work?

You don't know how to work. 53
You do nothing but play when you go out with your older brother.

Now, who will tend the cornfields?" scolded their mother. 54
With that their mother started to cry.

"Now, now, Mother, don't cry. 55
I'll go right away to bring my older brother back to life.

You'll see soon enough. 56
He will come.
He is not dead.
He is alive.

But it's really his own fault, for he gave me no honey to eat. 57
He gobbled up the honey all by himself.
He gave me nothing but the chewed-up honeycomb.

That's why I got mad. 58
That's why I knocked the tree over.

He was perched in the tree when it fell. 59
It fell into a gully.

Don't worry, Mother. 60
I'll be off at once to take care of this.
I'll be off at once to bring him back to life.

Don't let your heart be sad, Mother. 61
My older brother will come back," said the younger brother.

62 tekeˀ me pasbun ˀoxibuk memela ta ˀora xi la ti ˀitz'inale.
k'u sta ˀavuˀun ti memelae xi la ti smeˀe.

63 yuˀun ta xibat jk'el ti bankile.
ˀech ˀaˀal ta xkich' ti ˀoxib memelae.
ˀa ver mi xˀul ˀo ta ˀora ti jbankile xi la ti ˀitz'inale.

64 ˀentonse laj la spas ˀoxib memela ti smeˀe.
veno k'alal meltzah ti ˀoxib memelae bat la sk'el ti sbankile.
laj la yich' ˀech'el ti ˀoxib memelae.

65 tekeˀ meˀ ta xibat ba jkik' talel ti jbankile.
pero mu xa me jk'an xaˀok'.
ta xtal ta ˀora ma ti jbankile xi la ti ˀitz'inale.

66 veno bat la yik' talel ti sbankile.
ˀentonse ti k'alal k'ot ti bu ˀoy ti sbankile,
te la puch'ul k'ot sta javal la.
chamem xa la.

67 veno laj la yak'be ti memela ta sniˀe.
veno ti k'alal la jyak'be ti memela ta sniˀe jlikel ˀichaˀkux.

"All right, then, make me three *memela* tortillas at once," 62
said the younger brother.[4]
"What do you want *memela* tortillas for?" asked his mother.

"I'm going to take care of my older brother. 63
That is why I need to take the three *memela* tortillas.
We'll see if they help my older brother come to quickly,"
said the younger brother.

Then his mother made the three *memela* tortillas. 64
When they were ready, he went to see his older brother.
He carried with him the three *memela* tortillas.

"Well, Mother, I'm going to fetch my older brother. 65
But, really, I don't want you to cry so much.
My older brother will be back very soon," said the younger brother.

With that, he went to fetch his older brother. 66
Well, when he arrived at the place where his older brother was,
He found him lying there on his back.
He was already dead.

Well, he put the *memela* tortillas on his brother's nose. 67
When he had put the *memela* tortillas on his nose,
his brother quickly revived.

68 ta ˀora jlikel la ˀijoybij ta chitom.
ta ˀora:
ti ˀuk ti ˀuk xi xa la ta ˀora ti sbankile.

69 veno k'alal yil chaˀkux xa ti sbankile kontento xa la ti ˀitz'inale.
ˀentonse batik la xchiˀuk ti sbankile.

70 ˀaˀ la jbabe ˀech'el ti sbankile.
pere joybijem xa la ta chitom ti sbankile.

71 ˀentonse ti k'alal k'otik ta snaike,
veno k'el ˀavil ˀun meˀ.
tal xa ma ti jbankile.

72 laj xa jchaˀkuxes talel.
mu xa me jk'an xaˀok' porke ˀul xa me talel ti jbankile xi la ti ˀitz'inale.

In no time he turned into a pig. 68
At once he spoke:
"Oink! Oink!" grunted his older brother right on cue.[5]

When he saw that his older brother had come back to life, 69
the younger brother was happy.
Off he went with his older brother.

His older brother trotted in front of him.[6] 70
But now his older brother had the form of a pig.

Well, when they arrived at their house, the younger brother spoke: 71
"Well now, look here, Mother.
My older brother has come back.

I revived him. 72
I don't want you to cry any longer, for my older brother has come back,"
said the younger brother.

FIGURE 26

In no time he turned into a pig.
At once he spoke:
"Oink! Oink!" grunted his older brother right on cue.

73 ˀentonse ti meˀile laj sjak'be ti sˀitz'inal ˀole:
mi ˀaˀ ˀabankil leˀe xi la ti smeˀe.
ˀaˀ jbankil ma leˀe xi la ti sˀitz'inal ˀole.

74 k'uchaˀal sˀelanil lavut ta bankile xi la ti smeˀe.
veno pere ˀaˀ ta smul ma li jbankile.
xal yuˀun mu xiyak'be jloˀ pom.
pero laj xa jchaˀkuxes meˀ xi la ti sˀitz'inal ˀole.

75 ˀentonse ti sbankilal ˀole te la kotel.
ti ˀuk ti ˀuk xi la ti sbankilal ˀole.

76 pas ˀo la ta chitom ti sbankilal ˀole.
ˀech'a ˀal sbankil jtotik sbi li chitome.

77 ˀoy yasarona sniˀ.
ˀaˀ pas ta yasarona sniˀ ti ˀoxib memelae.

78 ˀech'a ˀal ti chitome setset sniˀ.
porke li memela setset.

79 ˀech'a ˀal ˀaˀ pas ta yasarona sniˀ.
porke li chitome snaˀ xchaˀbaj.

80 snaˀ sjotz' k'onon.
stiˀ ta banumil.

81 ˀech'a ˀal li chitome sbankil.
jmaryan sbi.

Then the mother asked her younger son: 73
"Is that your older brother?" asked the mother.
"Yes, that is my older brother," said her younger son.

"Why did you play this wicked trick on your older brother?" said his mother. 74
"Well, it was my older brother's own fault.
For his own reasons he didn't give me honey to eat.
But I did revive him, Mother," said her younger son.

The older son just stood there. 75
"Oink! Oink!" said her older son.

Her older son had indeed changed into a pig. 76
That is why the pig is said to be the older brother of Our Father Sun.

He has a nose like a hoe. 77
The three *memela* tortillas made a hoe of his nose.

This is why the pig has a round snout. 78
The reason is that the *memela* tortillas were round.

Thus, his nose came to be like a hoe. 79
That is why a pig is so good at rooting around in the dirt,

That is why he is so good at digging out grubworms, 80
He gobbles them right out of the dirt.

So it is that the pig is the older brother of Our Father Sun.[7] 81
His name is Marián.

1 k'alal bik'it kerem ti jtotik bat la paxyajuk ta te'ʔtik.
te la sta jbej ʔakov ti buy ta xanav ta yut teʔtik.

2 k'alal yil ti ʔakov sut la talel yalbe smeʔ ti jtotik.
ʔoy te la jta jbej muk'ta ʔakov xi la ti jtotik.

3 bu to xi la ti jmeʔtik.
nom to jutuk xi la ti jtotik.

4 te la vaʔal ti sbankil ti jtotike.
skuxet xa la yoʔnton sbankil ti jtotik k'alal yaʔi ti ʔoy ʔak'ov ta teʔtik.

TEXT 22

Of Our Father Sun and His Older Brother

Xalik López Setjol

When Our Father Sun was a little boy, he went for a walk in the woods. 1
He found a beehive where he was walking in the woods.

After he had seen the hive, Our Father Sun went back to tell his mother. 2
"I found a huge beehive out there," said Our Father Sun.

"Where?" asked Our Mother Moon. 3
"It's pretty far away," said Our Father Sun.

Our Father Sun's older brother was standing nearby.[1] 4
And his heart became very happy when he heard that there was
a beehive in the woods.

FIGURE 27

Our Father Sun's older brother was standing nearby.
And his heart became very happy when he heard that there
was a beehive in the woods.

5 ti jtotike:
k'usi ta skut ta jk'ok xanaˀ xi la ti jtotike.
mu jnaˀ xi la ti jmeˀtike.

6 ta xibat jk'ok ˀuˀune xi la ti sbankil ti jtotike.
batanik xi la ti jmeˀtike.

7 xuˀuk xi la ti jtotik xchiˀuk sbankil.
ti sbankil ti jtotike skuxet xa la yoˀonton ti k'alal batik ta sk'okel ti ˀakov.
ti bankil ti jtotike.

8 k'alal k'otik ta stz'el ti ˀakov,
liˀ ˀoy ti ˀakov xi la ti jtotik.

9 muykutik bat jloˀtik xi la ti sbankil ti jtotik.
ˀune mu ximuy xi la ti jtotik.

10 ˀuˀne ximuy xi la ti sbankil.
tey ta xkak' yal tal ˀaloˀ liˀe xi la ti sbankil ti jtotike.

11 k'alal k'ot ta sk'okel ˀakov sbankil ti jtotike yochel la ta sloˀel.
ti jtotike vaˀal la ta lumtik ta smala.

12 ch'abal xˀak'bat sloˀ ˀakov ti jtotike.
ˀecheˀ la te vaˀal ta lumtik.

13 stuk la ta sloˀ ti bankilale.
ta la xak' yalel tal ti bankilale.
pero smatz'om xa la la sjip yalel.

14 k'uchaˀal stuk ta sloˀ ˀakov ti jbankile xi la ti jtotike.
ˀaˀ lek ta jpas mentes mi snaˀ slomes teˀ xi la ti jtotike.

Our Father Sun spoke: 5
“But how am I going to break off the hive to get the honey?”
asked Our Father Sun.
“I don’t know,” said Our Mother Moon.[2]

“I’ll get it myself,” said Our Father Sun’s older brother. 6
“Go, then, both of you,” said Our Mother Moon.

“All right,” said Our Father Sun and his older brother. 7
Our Father Sun’s older brother was very happy when
they set off to rob the beehive.
The older brother was in a good mood.

Soon they approached the site of the beehive. 8
“Here is the beehive,” said Our Father Sun.

“Let’s climb up and eat honey,” said Our Father Sun’s older brother. 9
“I can’t climb up,” said Our Father Sun.

“I can climb up,” said his older brother. 10
“I’ll throw it down for you so you can eat it down here,”
said Our Father Sun’s older brother.

Soon Our Father Sun’s older brother succeeded in robbing the hive, 11
and started to eat the honey.
Our Father Sun remained below, waiting.

Nothing was given to him to eat from the hive. 12
In vain he stood waiting there below.

His older brother was feasting on it all by himself. 13
The older brother threw down some honeycomb.
But what he gave him was already sucked dry.

“Why should my older brother be eating all of the honeycomb himself?” 14
wondered Our Father Sun.
“Perhaps I should create a gopher to see if he knows how to
cut down trees,” said Our Father Sun.

15 ˀaˀ to la yil toj lek la snaˀ stz'etel teˀ ti mentese.
spas la yan.

16 k'alal ˀepaj xa ti mentese xˀech' lajesik ˀoˀox.
ta la sk'uxel ti yibel teˀe ti mentesetik.

17 mu la jaluk lom yuˀun ti teˀe,
ti k'alal laj smeltzan mentesetik ti jtotike.

18 bik'ital teˀ la la jyak'be yein.
k'alal yil ti jtotik snaˀ stz'etel teˀ ti mentesetik.

19 yochel la ta sk'anel ˀep ti smatz'omal ˀakov ti jtotike.
tzako xa me tal yan jloˀ spom ˀakove xi la ti jtotike.
xuˀuk xi la sbankil ti jtotik.

20 k'alal ta sloˀ ˀakov sbankil ti jtotike,
mu la snaˀ k'usi ta spas ti yitz'in.

21 sbankil ti jtotike yuˀuˀun bolat.
ˀa li jtotike ˀaˀ lek bij xˀul ta sjol k'uxi ta pasel ti mentese.

22 k'alal yaˀi xˀaplajet xa ti muk'ta teˀ ti sbankil ti jtotike:
k'usi me chapas, k'ox xi la sbankil ti jtotike.

23 muˀyuk k'usi ta jpas xi la ti jtotik.
ˀak'bun xa me jloˀ ˀakove xi la k'alal jlikel xa la sk'an slom ti teˀe.

24 ta to la xak' smatz'om sbankil ti jtotik.
pero julikel xa la ta sk'an ˀakov sloˀ ti jtotike.
k'alal likel xa la sk'an slom.

Soon he saw that the gopher was good at cutting down trees. 15
So he made another one.

Soon the gophers multiplied and they just kept on eating. 16
The gophers chewed away at the roots of the tree.

It was not going to take them long to fell the tree, 17
Once Our Father Sun had created the gophers.

He did this by strengthening their mouths with little sticklike teeth.[3] 18
With this, Our Father Sun saw to it that the gophers really knew
how to cut down trees.

In the meantime, he continued to beg for more honeycomb. 19
"Toss me some more, so I can eat some more honeycomb,"
said Our Father Sun.
"All right," said Our Father Sun's elder brother obligingly.

So Our Father Sun's older brother kept right on eating the honey, 20
Little did he know what his younger brother was up to.

Our Father Sun's older brother was really quite stupid. 21
Our Father Sun, however, was really quite clever in that it
occurred to him how to make the gophers.

When Our Father Sun's older brother heard the sudden cracking noise 22
of the great tree, he spoke:
"What are you doing, little one?" asked Our Father Sun's older brother.

"I'm not doing anything," said Our Father Sun. 23
"Throw me down some more honeycomb to eat," he said,
just as the tree was about to fall.

Even then Our Father Sun's older brother kept tossing him 24
chewed-up honeycomb.
And every little while Our Father Sun kept asking for a bit of
the honeycomb to eat.
So it went, even as the tree was just about to fall.

25 pero muˀyuk la ta sloˀ.
ˀaˀ la sujom ta spasel ti mentese.

26 k'alal lom ti teˀe muˀyuk xa la ˀakov ti jtotike.
laj stzutzes ta loˀel sbankil ti jtotike.

27 pero k'alal lom ti teˀe jchamel la k'ot sbankil ti jtotike.
k'alal yil cham sbankil ti jtotik yochel la ta st'uyanel jboj tzu.

28 k'alal sut ti jtotike stuktuk xa la.
k'alal k'ot ta stz'el smeˀ ti jtotike stuktuk xa la.

29 buy kom ˀabankile xi la ti jmeˀtike.
te to kom sloˀ ˀakob xi la ti jtotik.

But, as always, there was nothing for him to eat. 25
All of which explains why he created the gophers without delay.

When the tree finally fell, Our Father Sun found no honeycomb at all. 26
Our Father Sun's older brother had finished it off.

When the tree finally fell, however, Our Father Sun's older brother 27
came down too, quite dead.
When Our Father Sun saw that his older brother was dead,
he proceeded to hang a gourd there in his place.[4]

When Our Father Sun went home, he was all alone. 28
When he approached his mother's house, he was very much alone.

"What became of your older brother?" asked Our Mother Moon. 29
"He stayed there to eat honeycomb," said Our Father Sun.

FIGURE 28

"What became of your older brother?" asked Our Mother Moon.
"He stayed there to eat honeycomb," replied Our Father Sun.

30 k'alal jalij muˀyuk sk'ot sbankil ti jtotike.
ˀak'o taluk ˀabankile xi la ti jmeˀtik.

31 ˀavan la ti jtotik.
te la tak'av yaˀyelik ti sbankil,
pero muˀyuk xa la tak'av sbankil ti jtotik.

32 ˀaˀ xa la tak'av ti tzu st'uyanoj ti jtotike.
ˀa li sbankil ti jtotike chamem xa la.

33 bat la sk'el sbankil ti jtotike.
te la net'ubil.

34 yochel la ta sk'oponel sbankil ti jtotike.
mu la stak'av.

35 pere ta xviˀnaj jbankile xi la ti jtotike.
ˀaˀ lek bat kich'be tal vaj sveˀ xi la ti jtotike.

36 meˀ ta la xviˀnaj jbankile xi la ti jtotik.
ta la sk'an xbat kak'be vaj sveˀ.
paso ˀoxibuk xi la ti jtotike.

37 xuˀuk xi la ti jmeˀtik.
k'alal ˀoch ta spasel vaj ti jmeˀtik te la vaˀal ti jtotik.

38 bik'itik xapasbe vaj sveˀ ti jbankile xi la ti jtotike.
pero ta xajombe sat yot ti jbankile xi la ti jtotike.

39 k'alal meltzaj ti vaj bat la yak' ti jtotike.
k'alal k'ot ti jtotike ta stz'el sbankil ti jtotike stoybe la sjol.
spak'be la ta sniˀ ti vaje.

40 k'alal laj spak'be vaj ta sniˀ sbankil ti jtotike,
ˀora la k'ataj ta chitom sbankil ti jtotike.

After a long while, Our Father Sun's older brother still had not shown up. 30
"Go fetch your older brother," said Our Mother Moon.

Our Father Sun called out in a loud voice to his older brother. 31
His older brother seemed to be out there somewhere answering him,
But in truth the answer had not come from his older brother at all.

It was in fact the gourd that Our Father Sun had hung up that answered. 32
Our Father Sun's older brother was dead.

Our Father Sun went to see his older brother. 33
There he was, all squashed.

Our Father Sun attempted to talk to his older brother. 34
He did not answer.

"I'll bet my older brother is hungry," said Our Father Sun. 35
"Maybe I should go get him some tortillas to eat," said Our Father Sun.

"Mother, my older brother is hungry," said Our Father Sun. 36
"He wanted me to go get him some tortillas to eat.
Make him three tortillas," said Our Father Sun.

"All right," said Our Mother Moon. 37
As Our Mother Moon started to make the tortillas,
Our Father Sun was standing there.

"Make the tortillas very small so my older brother can eat them," 38
ordered Our Father Sun.
"And make little holes in my older brother's tortillas,"
ordered Our Father Sun.

When she had finished making the tortillas, Our Father Sun 39
went to deliver them.
When Our Father Sun came up to his older brother, he lifted up his head.
He put the tortillas on his nose.

When Our Father Sun had finished pressing the tortillas 40
on his older brother's nose,
Our Father Sun's older brother immediately turned into a pig.[5]

41 pero k'alal k'ataj ta chitom sbankil ti jtotike,
ˀep la lok' maˀ ti chitome.

42 muˀyuk la skuch yuˀun stzakel chitom maˀ ti jtotike.
chib k'ot la sta ta tzakel.
bat la ta teˀtik maˀ ti chitome.

43 k'alal k'ot ta stz'el smeˀ ti jtotik stzakoj la k'otel.
ˀoy xa chaˀkot sbik'tal chitom.

44 k'uchaˀal la ˀavik' talel chitom xi la ti jmeˀtike.
ta xkak'be stiˀ jnich'nab xi la ti jtotike.

45 ˀaˀ ˀech ˀayan ti chitom:
sbankil jtotik k'ataj ta chitom.

46 k'alal manchuk cham sbankil ti jtotike ch'abal chitom.
ˀa li chitome juntotik yaˀyel.
ˀaˀ sbankil jtotik.

As soon as Our Father Sun's older brother turned into a pig, 41
Many, many pigs sprang forth.

Our Father Sun could not catch all of the pigs. 42
He only caught only two of them.
The rest of the pigs escaped into the woods.

As Our Father Sun approached his mother's house, he came along with the two that he had caught. 43
He now had two little pigs.

"Why did you bring the pigs?" asked Our Mother Moon. 44
"I am going to give them to my children to eat," said Our Father Sun.[6]

And that is how pigs were created: 45
Our Father Sun's older brother turned into a pig.

If Our Father Sun's older brother had not died, there would be no pigs. 46
So it is that the pig seems to be like our uncle.
He is the older brother of Our Father Sun.[7]

1 lo?il yu?un xcha?lamal kirsano.

2 ?entonse ti jtotik ta vinajele lik la sjos te? sventa ti xcha?lamal kirsanoe.
te la sjos ti bu nakale.

3 laj la yak'be sk'ob yok sjol.
skotol la jyak'be.

4 k'alal la jyak'be ti sjole yoke lik la sk'opon ti te?e.
va?i?un ti te?e k'opoj la.
lik la lo?ilajikuk xchi?uk ti jtotike.

5 veno ti jtotike laj la yak'be svob ta la sk'el mi sna? la stijel.
pero ti te?e mu la sna? stijel ti vobe.

6 ?ech la ti vobe jbejbej la yak'il.
ma?uk la mero vob.
ko?ol la xchi?uk t'umparax.

TEXT 23

About How the Second People Became Monkeys

Mateo Méndez Tzotzek

This is a story of the second people. 1

Well, Our Father Sun in Heaven decided to carve a wooden stick 2
to make the second people.[1]
He carved it there where he lived.

He gave it hands, feet, and head. 3
He put on everything.

When he had given it head and feet, he started to speak to the stick person. 4
With that, the stick talked.
It began to chat with Our Father Sun.

Well, Our Father Sun gave it a guitar to see if it knew how to play it. 5
But the stick person did not know how to play the guitar.

It happened that the guitar had only one string. 6
It was not a true guitar.
It was a bow with a single string, like the bow of a bow and arrow.[2]

7 ˀentonse ti teˀe laj la stzak ti vobe.
pero mu la snaˀ stijel.
ˀecheˀ la te vaˀal.

8 vaˀuˀun ti jtotike laj la sk'asbe ti sk'obe.
laj la yak'be stz'akavul sk'ob yok.

9 ˀentonse k'alal la jyak'be stz'akavul sk'obe yoke,
lek la ˀak'otajuk jutuk.
pero jutuk noˀox la.

10 vaˀiˀun k'alal la jyil snaˀ xa jutuk xˀak'otaje,
lik la spasbe sna yuˀun la ta sk'an ta stz'un.
te la spasbe sna ti bu nakal ti jtotik ta vinajele.

Then the stick person picked up the mouth bow. 7
But it did not know how to play it.
It just stood there.

Whereupon, Our Father Sun broke the rigidity of the hands of this being. 8
So he gave the stick figure joints in its hands and feet.

Then, once he had given it joints in its hands and feet, 9
It began to dance a little.
But only a little bit, no more.

Well, when he saw that it now knew how to dance a little, 10
He started to create a dwelling for it, for he wanted to encourage it to survive and multiply.
So Our Father Sun in Heaven made it a house right where he himself lived.[3]

FIGURE 29

Then the stick person picked up the mouth bow.
But it did not know how to play it.
It just stood there.

Whereupon, Our Father Sun broke the rigidity of the hands of this being.
So he gave the stick figure joints in its hands and feet.

Then, once he had given it joints in its hands and feet,
It began to dance a little.
But only a little bit, no more.

11 ˀentonse k'alal la spasbe ti snae,
jlikel la ˀibol.
pas la ta kirsano ti teˀ toˀoxe.

12 veno laj la yak'be jbej sat ˀixim.
pero muˀyuk la ta xax.
te noˀox yumoj ˀo.

13 ˀaˀ la te ta xˀipan ˀo.
ˀech'o la xal mu xcham.
ˀaˀ la ˀech kuxul skotol ti kirsanoe.

14 mu la snaˀ xveˀik ˀep.
k'ajomal noˀox la te yipanojik ti jbej sat ˀixime.

15 ˀentonse ti jtotik ta vinajele laj la yil ti mu snaˀ xveˀik ˀep,
mu snaˀik xˀabtejik,
mu la snaˀik spas xchobik,
mu snaˀik stijik lek ti vobe,
mu snaˀik xk'opojik lek.

16 ˀentonse ti jtotike laj la smil xtok ti kirsanoe.
yuˀun la la jyil ti mu snaˀ xˀabteje,
ti mu snaˀ xveˀ ˀepe,
ti mu snaˀ xk'ejine.

17 yuˀun la ˀaˀ ta sk'an ti ˀep ta xveˀik ti kirsanoetike.
ˀech'o la xal la smil.

18 vaˀiˀun k'alal la smil ti kirsanoe noj la ˀoˀ.
laj la yak' ti ˀoˀ jun xamuna.

19 koˀol la xchiˀuk nab.
solel ta ch'ay ti banumile.

20 ˀentonse ti xchaˀlamal kirsanoe cham skotol.
ti nabe te la ˀoy lajuneb k'ak'al.

Once he had built it a house, 11
It quickly multiplied.
That which had been a stick turned into people.

Then he gave them kernels of corn to eat. 12
But they could not chew them.
They just kept them in their mouths without swallowing.

That is how they were able to survive. 13
They did not die.
In this manner they all stayed alive.

But they really did not eat much at all. 14
It was with but a grain of corn that they clung to life.

Soon Our Father Sun in Heaven saw that they were not eating very much, 15
That they did not know how to work,
That they did not know how to tend their cornfields,
That they did not know how to play the guitar well,
That they did not know how to talk well.

So Our Father Sun decided to do away with these people. 16
For he saw that they did not know how to work,
That they did not know how to eat enough,
That they did not know how to sing.

He really wanted them to eat properly. 17
That is why he felt he had to do away with them.

The destruction of these people came as a flood. 18
It rained for a week.

It was like a great sea. 19
The land simply disappeared.

Then the second people died. 20
For the great sea remained for ten days.

21 veno ti jtotik ta vinajele laj la spas kajon.
k'alal noj ti ˀoˀe te la kajal muy ta ba ˀoˀ ta yut kajon xchiˀuk la jun vinik
jun ˀantz.

22 laj la yilik ti la spas kajon ti jtotike.
laj la xchan ti vinike.
laj la spas jun skajon ˀek.

23 k'alal noj ti ˀoˀe ˀoch la ta yut kajon xchiˀuk ti jun ˀantze.
te la kajal muyik ta ba ˀoˀ.
koˀol la muyik xchiˀuk ti jtotike.

24 skotol ti kirsano muˀyuk bu xlok'ike.
te cham skotol ta ˀoˀ.

25 vaˀiˀun ti vinik k'alal muy ta ba ˀoˀ xchiˀuk skajone,
laj la yich' muyel sibak sk'ux sventa la mu xcham ˀo ta viˀnal ti xchiˀil.

26 te la kajalik ta ba ˀoˀ.
te la ta xveˀ xulem ta sba ti kirsanoe.

27 vaˀiˀun ti ˀoˀ ta k'unk'un la yal.
k'alal yal ti ˀoˀe yuˀun la lom ti banumile.
ˀaˀ la te ˀoch ˀel ti ˀoˀe.

28 ˀentonse kom la yochob.
kom la vitzetik.
kom la xaˀab.
kom la nail ch'en.
kom la sna pukujetik.
kom be ˀoˀ.
kom la tonetik.

29 lok' la pukujetike.
lok' la mokochetik.

To survive this, Our Father Sun in Heaven made a box boat for himself. 21
Indeed, a man and a woman also used a box boat like this
to float themselves to safety when the flood came.

They had seen Our Father Sun make his own boat. 22
So the man learned how.
He made a box boat for himself as well.

When the flood came, he got into the box boat with the woman. 23
They floated to the surface of the water.
They floated up just like Our Father Sun.

No one else escaped. 24
All the rest drowned.

When the man and his wife floated up to safety on the surface of the water 25
in their box boat, they came prepared.
The man had brought with him powdered charred corn to eat
so that he and his wife would not starve.[4]

So they floated on the water. 26
And above them hovered hungry buzzards.[5]

Then, little by little, the level of the water went down. 27
When the water at last disappeared it was because the earth caved in,
opening channels and holes.
The water flowed into these openings and disappeared.

With that, the sinkholes came into being.[6] 28
Mountains came into being.
Caves came into being.
Rock-shelter caves came into being.
Dwellings of the demons came into being.[7]
Paths for the waters came into being.[8]
Rocks came into being.

Out came the demons. 29
Out came the snakes.

30 ˀentonse ti jtotike te la chaˀsut ˀel ti bu toˀox nakale.
ˀech ti vinik xchiˀuk ti jun ˀantze koˀol yalik xchiˀuk jtotik.
te la koˀol k'otik ti bu sna ti jtotik.

31 ˀentonse ti jtotike laj la yal:
mi xak'an jchiˀin jbatik xi la ti jtotik ta vinajele.

32 mu jk'an ˀunbi.
ˀaˀ li ta ˀox xamilune xi la ti vinik xchiˀuk ti jun ˀantze.
veno tekeˀ chaˀe xi la ti jtotike.

33 laj la yak'be sne.
laj la yak'be stzotzil.

34 tekeˀ ˀun batan xi la ti jtotike.
jlikel la joybij ta max ti vinike ti ˀantze.
pas la ta max ti xchaˀlamal kirsanoe.

35 ˀaˀ la ti muˀyuk bu xch'unbe smantal ti jtotik ta xchiˀine.
ˀech'o la xal joybij ta max.

Then Our Father Sun went back to where he had been living on earth before. 30
It happened that the man and woman also floated down and settled to earth, just as Our Father Sun had done.
They arrived together at the house of Our Father Sun.

Then Our Father Sun spoke to them: 31
"Shall we go on our way together?" suggested Our Father Sun in Heaven.

"No, we really don't want to. 32
You almost killed us," said the man and the woman.
"Very well, then," said Our Father Sun.

With that, he gave them tails; 33
He gave them fur.

"Very well, then. Be on your way," said Our Father Sun. 34
In an instant the man and the woman turned into monkeys.
The second people became monkeys.

This happened because they did not accept Our Father Sun's invitation to accompany him. 35
That is why they were turned into monkeys.[9]

FIGURE 30

"Very well, then. Be on your way," said Our Father Sun.
In an instant the man and the woman turned into monkeys.
The second people became monkeys.

1 jun kuento ta voˀnee sventa meˀel chon.

2 k'alal lik sloˀil ti mole,
yuˀun ˀayik ta nutzol ti viniketike.

3 ˀentonse k'alal sutik talel ta nutzole ti viniketike,
la staik talel jkot smeˀelik.

4 jaˀ sutik talel ti viniketike.
yuˀun ˀayik ta paxyal xchiˀuk stz'iˀik ti viniketike ta k'ixin ˀosile.

5 mi ta skuxik ta rominkoe ta xbatik ta paxyal.
pero mu skotoluk rominkoe ta skuxik ti jˀabteletike.
k'alal mi ta xlubik tajmek.

6 ˀentonse jaˀ to ta xbatik ta paxyal.
jech ti mole lik yal sloˀil.

7 ˀa ti voˀne lae kirsano toˀox la li meˀel chone xi ti mole.
kirsano toˀox la ma ti voˀnee xi ti mole.

8 pero k'alal la pasik ta meˀel chon ti voˀnee,
jaˀ la ti ˀech' nojelal ta ˀoˀe.

9 ˀentonse k'alal la yilik xa noj tal ta ˀoˀ ti snaike:
jaˀ lek jatavkutik ˀel ta teˀtik xiik la ti ˀantivo kirsanoe.

10 ˀentonse bat la saˀik bu jomol ch'en ta jol vitz.
te la staik ti ch'ene.

TEXT 24

About a Time When Raccoons Were Still People

Manuel López Calixto

This is a story of long ago about raccoons. 1

At the time the old man began to tell this story, 2
The subject came up because some men had gone hunting.

Now, when these men returned from hunting, 3
They brought back with them a raccoon that they had killed.

These men were coming home. 4
They had gone out hunting with their dogs there where they had been staying in Hot Country.[1]

When they had Sundays off from work they would often go out and about. 5
But it was not every Sunday that the workers had a rest day.
It was only when they were very tired.

It was only then that they could go out and relax. 6
It was on such a day that the old man told his story.

✠ ✠ ✠

"Long ago the raccoon was still a person," said the old man. 7
"Long ago they were still people," said the old man.

At the time when they turned into raccoons long ago, 8
It happened because of a flood.

When they saw that their houses were covered with water, they spoke: 9
"It would be better if we fled to the woods," said the ancient people.

Then they went to look for a cave on top of the mountain. 10
There they found the cave.

11 ˀa, pere jaˀ lek ma liˀe xiik la ti ˀantivo kirsanoe.
ta ch'en la bat naklikuk.

12 veno ˀaˀ liˀe mu xijlajutik ma liˀe xiik la ti k'alal staojik xa lek snaike.
ˀora liˀe ˀak'o mi xtal jayibuk ˀu ti ˀoˀe ta xkuch kuˀuntik
ma liˀe xiik.

13 la mu la bu ta xˀat yoˀntonik.
ˀak'o taluk ti ˀoˀe xiik la ti ˀantivo kirsanoetike.

14 ˀo la te tek'ajtik momol.
ˀoy la sjol momole.
jaˀ la lik saˀ sloˀik ti jol momole.

15 ti k'alal laj la ti yiximike lik la saˀ sloˀil ti k'usi xa la stak' la loˀele.
li yoˀ muk' xchamik ˀo ta viˀnale.
puru la jol momol ta saˀ sloˀik ti ˀantivo kirsanoetike lae.

16 ˀentonse k'alal la ˀech' ti k'inobal ˀoˀe.
lek xa la xaˀik ti k'alal ˀech' yuˀunik ti nojelal ti ˀoˀe.

17 ˀentonse te la k'ot jun vinik ta jol ch'en.
mi liˀote xi la k'otel ti vinike.

18 pere muk' la me xˀilik bu tal ti vinik lae.
ˀa liˀ ˀune xˀutik la ti vinike.

19 ˀentonse lik la me jak'batikuk:
k'uchaˀal la talik ta jol ch'ene xˀutatik la ti ˀantivo kirsanoe.
ˀa yuˀun ta xnoj ta ˀoˀ ti jnakutike xˀutik la ti vinike.

20 pere k'usi la veˀik ti k'alal laj ta ˀaviximike xi la ti vinike.
ˀa la jloˀkutik jol momol xˀutik la ti vinike.
mu la snaˀik mi jtotik la ti vinike.

21 veno mi jaˀ ˀaveˀelik ˀo xa li jol momol ne xˀutatik la ti ˀantivo kirsanoe.
ˀa jaˀ pere k'usi yan ta jloˀ ta ˀavaloje xutik la ti jtotike.

"Ah, this is certainly better," said the ancient people. 11
So they set up housekeeping in the cave.

"Well, we won't die here," they said confidently, once they had found 12
a pleasant place to live.
"Now we will survive here, even if it should rain for ever
so many months," said the ancient people.

And their hearts were not sad. 13
"Let the rain come," said the ancient people.

They had various kinds of plants growing there. 14
Among these plants were some that had edible bulbs.
Soon they began to use these bulbs as food.

When they ran out of corn, they began to search for anything 15
that could serve as food.
This was so they would not die of hunger.
Soon the ancient people could find nothing to eat but the bulbs of plants.

Then the persistent rain ended. 16
They felt happy when the flood had at last subsided and left them in peace.

Then a man appeared there by the cave entrance. 17
"Are you here?" said the man when he arrived.

But they did not see where the man had come from. 18
"We are here," they replied to the man.

Then he began to question them: 19
"Why did you come here to this cave?" he inquired of the ancient people.
"Oh, because our houses were flooded," they replied to the man.

"But what did you eat when you ran out of corn?" asked the man. 20
"We ate bulbs of plants," they said to the man.
But they did not know that the man was none other than Our Father Sun.

"Well, is this your food now, these bulbs?" he asked the ancient people. 21
"Yes, it is. What else did you think we were going to eat?"
they responded resentfully to Our Father Sun.

22 ʔa veno lek ʔoy xi la ti jtotike.
pero vinik la yiluk.

23 veno bitanik liʔe xʔutatik la ti ʔantivo kirsanoe.
la la xch'unik.
bitik la ta ba ton.

24 k'alal la ti bitike kotol la k'ot ta banamil.
xchanibal yok sk'otik ta banamil.

25 veno batanik ʔun.
bat saʔ ʔaloʔik ti momol ne xʔutatik la.

26 k'alal la ti ʔalbatik yaʔi ti sveʔelike xkotlajetik xa la ʔel ta teʔtik.
ti k'alal la pasik ta meʔel chon ti ʔantivo kirsanoe.
hech'o la xal snaʔ la sjotz ʔixim.

"Oh, very well, then," said Our Father Sun. 22
But, indeed, he looked just like a man.

"Good, jump over here," he said to the ancient people. 23
They obeyed him.
They jumped on top of a rock.

When they jumped, they landed on all fours. 24
They landed on the ground on all fours.

"Well, be gone, then. 25
Go get your plants to eat," they were told.[2]

When they had been told about their food, they went off walking on 26
all fours into the woods.
This happened when the ancient people turned into raccoons.
This is why, even today, they have the habit of digging up corn plants.

FIGURE 31

When they had been told about their food, they went off walking
on all fours into the woods.
This happened when the ancient people turned into raccoons.
This is why, even today, they have the habit of digging up corn
plants.

27 k'alal ta xkav ti jchobtike,
ja? ?o me ta sjotz jchobtik ti mu me?el chone.

28 k'alal mi tz'unbil xa ?oxe,
ja? ta sa? ?ech'el ti ?ovolile.

29 ta sjotz ?ech'el juju petz,
ti ?ovolile ta sa? ?ech'el.

30 jech'o xal ti yo? la ta sjotz ti ?ixim sk'uxe,
yu?un kirsano to?ox la ti vo?nee xi ti mole.
?entonse pas la ta jotzovil chon sbi ?un.

31 k'alal mi lok' ti ?ajane,
ta sk'ux ?ajan xtok.

32 jech'o xal ta sa? ?ixim sk'uxe,
yu?un la kirsano la ti mas vo?nee xi ti mole.

33 pere mu jna?tik sjay lajunebal xa ?avil ?ech'.
mu xavil ja? ti ?antivo kirsanoetik ja? pasik ta chon ?un.
pero ja? ?o la ti k'alal ?ech' ti nojelal ta ?o?e xi ti mole.

34 pere ja? ti ba?yel ?antivo kirsanoetike.
ja? la pasatik ta me?el chon ti mas la vo?ne tajmeke.

35 pere yu?un mu la sna? xi?ik.
ta la xbatik ta ch'en nakalikuk.

36 ?entonse ja? la mu sk'an ti jtotik ne.
jech'o la xal ti yo? la me k'atajik ta me?el chon la ne
xi ti mol vo?nee.

When the corn seeds sprout, 27
It is then that the raccoon digs up corn.

When the corn has just been planted, 28
It is at this time that it searches out the newly sprouted corn.

It digs up each corn hill. 29
It searches out the newly sprouted corn seeds.

"That is why this one digs out the corn to eat.
Because it was once a person long ago," said the old man.
"Then it turned into the 'digging animal', as it is called.[3]

No sooner do the the ears of tender corn appear, 31
Than it eats the ears, too, just like the newly sprouted seeds.

That is why it seeks out corn to eat. 32
Because it was once a person long ago," said the old man.

"But we don't really know how many tens of years ago this happened. 33
Don't you see that it was the ancient people who turned into animals?
It was at the time of the great flood," said the old man.

"But these were the first, the ancient people. 34
It was they who were transformed into raccoons in the most distant past.

It was because they had no fear. 35
They went to find a cave to see if it might do as a place to live.

But it turned out that Our Father Sun did not like this. 36
That is why they were turned into raccoons."
So said the old man long ago.

1 jun kuento ta voˀnee sventa momolal chobtik.
jun mol ta xloˀilaj.

2 ti k'alal lik sloˀile yuˀun ˀo te jsep chobtik.
tzinil ta momol ti chobtike ta k'ixin ˀosil.
ˀentonse lik yal sloˀil ti mole.

3 ˀa ti voˀne lae ta la sk'opojik toˀox la ti momole.
jaˀ jec la jyalbun kaˀi ti ˀanima jmuk'tote xi ti mole.

4 k'alal la ta xˀak'inta xchobike ti ˀantivo kirsanoetike,
ta la sk'anbe parte jtotik ta vinajel ti momolae.

5 k'alal la ta xˀak'intaik ti xchobike ta la xk'opoj ta yut xchobtik ti krisanoe.
ˀavaˀi bu ti kirsanoe xiik la ti ˀantivo kirsanoetike.

6 ˀentonse bat la sk'elik ti bu la vulajetike,
k'alal la k'otike ch'abal la kirsano.

7 pere k'alal la ta xk'opojike koˀol la xchiˀuk kirsano.
yaˀluk ta xk'opojik la ti mu momole.
pere k'usi xanaˀ ti jvulajetike xˀut la sbaik ti ˀantivo kirsanoetike.

8 k'alal la sutik ˀel ta yak'inta ˀel ti xchobike la la snupik ta be jun vinik
ti ˀantivo kirsanoe.
ˀentonse k'oponatik la:

TEXT 25

Of Olden Days When Weeds Could Speak

Manuel López Calixto

Here is a story of long ago about weeds that grow in the cornfields. 1
An old man told it to me.

He began to talk when we were working together detasseling corn.[1] 2
[This job went along with weeding,] for there are really a lot of
weeds in the cornfields in Hot Country.
That was what got the old man started telling the story.

"In olden days, weeds could speak. 3
This is what my late grandfather told me," said the old man.

"When the ancestors worked at hoeing their cornfields, 4
The weeds went to complain to Our Father Sun in Heaven.

As the ancestors worked at hoeing their cornfields, 5
it seemed as though there were strangers talking there
in the midst of the corn plants.
'Didn't you hear someone talking?' said the ancient people.

With that, they went to check out the whereabouts of the visitors, 6
But when they got to where the noise seemed to be coming from,
there was no one there.

When the noise came, it sounded just like people talking. 7
So it seemed to them when the strange weeds talked.
'But who can these visitors be?' the ancestors asked one another.

When they were going home from hoeing their cornfields, 8
the ancient people came across a man in the road.
He spoke to them like this:

9 bu la ˀayik xˀutatik la ti ˀantivo kirsanoe.
mu la snaˀik mi jtotik la ta vinajel ti vinik la snupik ta bee.

10 ˀa li ˀaykutik ta ˀak'in.
ˀaˀ kak'intik jchobkutik xˀutik la ti vinik la snupik ta bee.

11 ˀa veno xi la ti vinike.
mi muk' bu xavaˀik xk'opoj ti momole xi la ti vinike.

12 ˀaˀ la jkaˀikutik xiˀik la ti ˀantivo kirsanoe.
koˀol xchiˀuk kirsano ta sk'opon tajmek kaˀikutik xˀut la ti vinike.

13 ˀa jaˀ jech la jyalbun kaˀi xi la ti vinike.
yuˀun ta la xabojik li momole jaˀ la mu sk'an.
pero ˀoˀone laj xa kalbe yaˀi xi la ti vinike.

14 k'alal mi la xboj te mu xachamee.
xkut komel ti momole xi la ti vinike.
ˀa veno xi la ti ˀantivoe.

15 pere li jbek'tal ne jaˀ me chapojbikun tajmek ˀun xi la komel ti vinike.
ˀak'o mi mu sk'an bojel ti momole.

16 pere laj xa jkalbe yaˀi komel li momole:
jaˀ lichamil chamilbun ti jbek'tale.
jech'o xal ti yoˀ chavik'ik bojele xˀut la momol ti vinike.

17 ˀentonse pere ˀoxuk me chapojbikun ti jbek'tale xi la ti vinike.
pere jech'o sal ti yoˀ chakalbik
xˀutatik ti ˀantivo kirsanoe.

18 veno lek ˀoy xˀutik la ti vinike.
mu la snaˀik mi jch'ultotik la ta vinajel ti vinike.
ˀa ti yalojike xchiˀilik la ti vinike.
pere ti vinike jtotik la ta vinajel ˀun xi ti mole ˀa ti voˀnee.

'Where have you been?' he asked the ancestors. 9
But they did not realize that the man whom they had met on the road
was Our Father Sun in Heaven.

'We've been out hoeing. 10
We were cleaning our cornfields,' they said to the man they met
on the road.

'I see,' said the man. 11
'Did you hear the weeds talk?' said the man.

'Yes, we certainly did,' said the ancestors. 12
'We heard them speaking clearly, just like people,' they said to the stranger.

'Ah, that is the same story I have heard,' said the man. 13
'For you were cutting the weeds up and they did not like it.
But now I have cut a deal with the weeds,' declared the man:

'When they cut you up, you will not die. 14
That is the agreement I made with the weeds,' said the man.
'We understand,' replied the ancestors.

'But as for my body, you must defend it faithfully,' the man declared. 15
'Even if the weeds don't want to be hoed out.'

'So, I have spoken to the weeds: 16
You have killed my body in the past, and might also kill me today.
Because of this you must allow yourselves to be cut,'
said the man to the weeds.[2]

'But you people, you are the ones who must defend my body for me,' 17
said the man.
'That is why I am telling you this.'
So it was said to the ancient people.

'Very well,' said the men. 18
But they did not realize that the stranger was Our Father Sun in Heaven.
They thought he was one of their own kind.
But the man was really Our Father Sun in Heaven,"
said the old man long ago.

19 ta toˀox la xk'opojik ti momole yuˀun mu la sk'an bojel.
jlikel la bat sk'anbe parte jtotik ta vinajel ti momole.

20 pere te k'alal ta xavich' bojel pere mu xacham ˀo xˀutat la ti momole.
ta xa la xˀok'lajetik tajmek ti mu momole.

21 ti k'alal la ti mu la bu xpojatike,
ti yoˀ la ta sk'anik partee yuˀun la ta smilik yaˀi ti chobtike.

22 ˀentonse ti jtotik ta vinajele:
te k'alal jaˀ li chamilbun li jbek'tale.
xˀutat la ti mu momole.

23 jech la ti k'alal ta xkak'intatik ti jchobtike,
yuˀun ta la jpojtik ti sbek'tal jtotike ti k'alal ta xkak'intatike xi ti mole.

24 jaˀ la me jech ti voˀnee xi ti mole.

"'The weeds declared that they did not want to be hoed. 19
So the weeds lost no time in lodging a complaint with
Our Father Sun in Heaven.

'Come, come. Don't worry. Sure, you will get cut up a bit, but that 20
won't be the end of you,' he said to the weeds.
And the wretched weeds sobbed for fear they would die.

Since the weeds felt that they had no hope for survival, 21
They went to plead that it was unfair, for, in truth, they really wanted
to kill the corn in the field.

Then Our Father Sun in Heaven spoke: 22
'Come, come, now. What you really want to do is to kill my body.'
Thus it was said to the wretched weeds.

So it is when we weed our cornfields. 23
We are defending the body of Our Father Sun when we
do the weeding," said the old man.

"So it was established long ago," said the old man. 24

FIGURE 32

So it is when we weed our cornfields.
We are defending the body of Our Father Sun when we do
the weeding," said the old man.

1 kuento jtotik san juan ta chamoˀ.

2 veno ti voˀne ti k’alal lik spas sna ti jtotik san juan ta chamoˀ.
vokol ta sta yav sna.

3 baˀyel bat spas sna ta yak’ol xitalaˀ.
ta yav jteklum ta k’ixin ˀosil.

4 pero la jyil toj k’ixin ti banumile.
muˀyuk la spas ti snae.
mu xch’i xchij.

5 muˀyuk jamal ti banumile.
muˀyuk bu xveˀ ti xchije.

6 jech xtok toyol jinich’.
mu xch’i ti xchije.
ta xtiˀvan jinich’.

7 jech’a ˀal muˀyuk spas ti sna ta yak’ol xitalaˀe.
komo la jyil toj k’ixin ti banumile.

8 pero ˀabtej xa ˀox ˀep.
laj xa skuch ˀep ton.
laj xa slikesbe spasel ti sna.

9 ta k’un to la jyil mu xuˀ xveˀ xchij.
ta xcham ta k’ok’.
ta xcham ta jinich’.
mu xkuch yuˀun ti xchije.

TEXT 26

About How Our Lord San Juan Made His Home in Chamula, I

Xalik López Castellanos

This is a story of Our Lord San Juan of Chamula.[1] 1

Well, long ago Our Lord San Juan made his home in Chamula. 2
But it was no easy task to establish his home.

He planned to live just above a place called Xitalá. 3
This is known in Tzotzil as the Place of Our Ceremonial Center
in Hot Country.[2]

But he found that the land was too hot. 4
So he did not make his home there.
His sheep did not thrive there.

The land was not open and level. 5
So his sheep had no place to graze.

There were also too many ants. 6
His sheep could not thrive.
The ants bit them.

That is why he did not make his home near Xitalá. 7
For he realized that the land was simply too hot.

But he had already worked a great deal. 8
He had carried many rocks.
He had begun to build his house.

But soon he noticed that his sheep refused to eat. 9
They suffered from the heat.
They suffered from the ants.
His sheep could not stand the heat.

10 ˀentonse lik snop bat saˀ yan yav sna.
bat k'alal ta jol ch'umtik ta nopol yaˀal ˀichin.

11 ta bat spas ti sna ti jtotik san juane ˀaˀ mas sik ti banumile.
pero komo ti xchije mu la sk'an xveˀ ta xˀat yoˀonton.
mu sk'an xnaki tey ti xchije.

12 veno ti yitz'in jtotik san juan laj la yal:
ˀa li chije mu me sk'an xveˀ
ta me xˀat yoˀonton.
moˀoje ta me xcham skotol xi la ti yitz'in jtotik san juane.

13 pere k'uchaˀal ta xcham.
yuˀun muˀyuk ta xavak'be ˀoˀ yuch'.
yuˀun muˀyuk chabat ˀasaˀbe lek sveˀel xi ti bankilale.

14 pere k'usi ta xkut.
ta hk'el lek.
ta xkak'be lek ˀoˀ yuch'.
ta jsaˀbe lek sveˀel xi la ti ˀitz'inal san juane.

15 pero k'uchaˀal ta xˀat yoˀonton.
k'uchaˀal mu sk'an xveˀ.
k'uchaˀal puru vayel ta spas.

16 ˀaˀ lek ta xibat jsaˀ yan yav jna.
liˀe yuˀun mu sk'an xnaki ti jchije xi la ti bankilal san juan.

17 veno ˀoˀot k'usi chanop
voˀone mu jnaˀ xi la ti ˀitz'inal san juan.
veno bat la saˀ yan yav sna.

18 pero bu ta xibat.
bu ˀoy lek ti banumile.

19 veno, ta jnop lek xi la ti bankilal san juan.
veno laj la snop lek ti bu ˀoy ta xbat spas ti sna.

So he began to think about looking for another site for his home. 10
He then went to a land called Jol Ch'umtik, which is near
the hamlet of Yaʔal Ichin.[3]

Our Father San Juan went to make his home where the land was cooler. 11
However, even there, his sheep did not do well and their hearts were sad.
His sheep did not want to live there.

Presently, the younger Lord San Juan spoke up: 12
"My sheep refuse to eat.
Their hearts are truly sad.
This won't do. They're all dying on me," declared the younger
Lord San Juan.[4]

"But why are they dying? 13
Perhaps you don't give them enough water to drink?
Perhaps you don't find good pasture grass for them?"
speculated the elder San Juan.

"What am I to do? 14
I take good care of them.
I give them plenty of good water to drink.
I find good pasture for them," responded the younger San Juan.

"But why are their hearts so sad? 15
Why don't they want to eat?
Why do they do nothing but sleep?

I had better go look for another site for my house. 16
My sheep just don't want to live here," concluded the elder San Juan.

"Well, what do you think?" asked the elder San Juan. 17
"I really don't know," said the younger San Juan.
And so it was that they finally decided to look for another place to settle.

"But where shall I go? 18
Where can there be good land?

I shall give it a lot of thought," said the elder San Juan. 19
With that, he thought very seriously about where he would make his home.

20 veno te k'alal ta xibat.
mu jnaˀ k'uchaˀal mu la jnop lek.
mu la jk'el lek ti bu ˀoy lek ti yav jnae.

21 leˀe jecheˀ li ˀabtej.
jecheˀ la jkuch ton xi la ti bankilal san juan.

22 veno batik la xchiˀuk ti yitz'ine xchiˀuk ti xchije.
yil xa bu ˀoy ta xbat spas ti snae.

23 veno ti k'alal la k'ot ti bu ˀoy ta spas ti snae.
ˀoy la jun muk'ta vitz.

24 te la bat sk'el ti yav snae.
te la vaˀi ta jol vitz.

25 veno liˀe haˀ liˀ ta hpas ti hnae.
haˀ sa noˀos slaheb ti banumil ˀoye.
muˀyuk sa bu sibat yan," si la ti htotik san huan.

"Well, then, I think I'll be off to look around. 20
I wonder why I didn't think it over better to start with.
I didn't look very carefully for a good house site.

In those other places, I worked for nothing. 21
I carried rocks in vain," said the elder San Juan, sadly.

They went then, he and his younger brother and his sheep. 22
He now had in mind just where he would build his house.

Soon he arrived at the new house site. 23
It was right by a large mountain.

He went there to check the site out. 24
He stood there gazing at it from the top of the mountain.

"Good! This is it! Here I will build my house. 25
This is *the* place, at last.
I shall go nowhere else."

FIGURE 33

"Good! This is it! Here I will build my house.
This is *the* place, at last.
I shall go nowhere else."

26 veno ˀoy la nab te ta yok vic.
muk'ta nab la ˀoy.

27 veno ti jtotik san juane lik la sjines ti vitze.
jin la batel ta ˀora ti vitze.
jaˀ la jyules ti nabe.

28 veno ti k'alal jin ti vitze jlikel la ˀul ti nabe.
veno ti k'alal ˀul ti nabe, lik la spas ti parijo ta ˀasarona.

29 pero stuktuk la xˀabtej ti jtotik san juane.
veno lik la snop bat la saˀ svinik yuˀun ta skoltaat ta ˀabtel.
veno ti yitz'ine jaˀ la bat sk'el chij.

30 ˀoˀote kitz'in chabat ta ˀilchij.
pere laˀ me ˀavak'be ˀoˀ yuch'.
ti chije lek me xak'el.

31 voˀone ta xibat ta ˀabtel.
ta xibat jsaˀ steˀel jnatik xi la ti bankilal san juane.
veno bat la saˀ ti steˀel snae.

32 baˀyel la lik saˀ ston sventa spak'bal sna.
bat la ta teˀtik saˀ ti tone.
sjunul la k'ak'al te ˀoy ta teˀtik ta saˀ ti tone.

33 bat xa la jtotik bat ti bu ta xvaye.
ˀoy la jun muk'ta tulan ti bu ta spas ti snae.
ˀaˀ te ta xvay ti bu ˀoy ti muk'ta tulane.

34 veno ta yok'omal ta jun k'ak'al bat skuchik tal ti ton xchiˀuk ti svinike.
ti k'alal k'otik ti bu ˀoy ti tone la stzobik.
skotol la sbusanik ta jmoj ti tone te ta teˀtik.

Now, there was a lake at the foot of the mountain. 26
It was really a large lake.

Whereupon, Our Father San Juan began to cause the mountain to collapse. 27
In no time at all, a great landslide happened.
And with that, the lake vanished.

In an instant, just as the mountain collapsed, the lake dried up. 28
And, once the lake had vanished, he began to level the surface of
his house site with a hoe.

At this time, our Father San Juan was working all alone. 29
So it occurred to him that it would be good to find workers
to help him with his task.
His younger brother would then be free to tend the sheep.

"You, little brother, you are going to watch the sheep. 30
Come along and see that they get water.
See that you tend the sheep well.

As for me, I'm going to get to work. 31
I'm going to look for beams for our house," said the elder San Juan.
And with that, he was off to find the house beams.

But first of all, he had to look for stones for the walls of his house. 32
He went into the forest to gather stones.
He spent the entire day in the woods, looking for stones.

At dusk, Our Father found a place to sleep. 33
In this place, back at the house site, there was a great oak tree.
He slept there by this great oak tree.

So, he spent all of the next day hauling rocks with his helpers. 34
When they got to where the stones were, they heaped them up into a pile.
They piled the stones up, right there in the forest.

35 veno ti svinike ˀaˀ la smak ˀel ton.
muˀyuk bu la skuch ˀel ti tone.
ta xanav ˀel stuk chak k'uchaˀal junuk chij.

36 pero ˀep la ti ton tajmeke.
ˀoy la yan mu sk'an xanav ˀel ta be.
ta la xjatav batel ta teˀtik.

37 ta la xbat ta ˀanil ti vinik sciˀuk hun steˀ.
ta xbat smak talel ti ton.

38 pero mu la sk'an xanav ˀel ti tone.
mu la sk'an xbat ta ch'ulna.

Then his helpers began to herd the stones along. 35
They did not carry the stones.
They walked along by themselves, just like sheep.[5]

But there were ever so many stones! 36
And some of them refused to walk along on the road.
They would flee into the woods.

Whereupon one of the herdsmen would take off after them with his staff.[6] 37
He would go to round the stones up.

However, some of the stones simply did not want to walk. 38
They did not want to go to the site of the church.

FIGURE 34

Then his helpers began to herd the stones along.
They did not carry the stones.
They walked along by themselves, just like sheep.

39 yan la tuk' ta xanav ˀel ta be.
yan la mu sk'an xanav ˀel.
ta la snak' sba ta xokon be.
vokol la ta xk'ot ti bu ta spas sna ti san juane.

40 veno ti k'alal la xk'ot ti tone ta la stij kampana.
ˀoy la jun muk'ta kampana te la jok'ol ta muk'ta tulan ti bu ta spas sna ti san juane.
pero ti kampanae te la stij sba stuk ti k'alal ta xa k'ot ti tone.

41 pero ti vinik ta smak ˀel ti tone jch'ultotik.
maˀuk kirsano.

42 ˀech ti san juane ˀaˀ jbaˀbe ta xanav ˀel.
ˀaˀ jtz'akal pat to xanav ˀel ti ton xchiˀuk jun vinike.
ˀaˀ ta sk'el mu xjatav ti ton ta be.

43 veno ti k'alal k'ot ti ton,
lik ˀochuk ta ˀabtel ti jtotik san juan xchiˀuk ti svinike.
lik sbis ta sna ti k'u smuk'ul ta spase.

44 ti k'alal laj sbis ti yav snae,
lik sjok'be yav ton ti bu ta smukik ti tone.

45 veno k'alal laj sjok' be yav ti tone,
lik yak' yalel ti tone.

46 ˀaˀ ta xˀabteh stuk ti san juan xchiˀuk ti svinike.

47 veno k'alal mu xa sta ta ˀak'el ti tone,
ta sjip muyel.
te ta stzak ta ˀak'ol ti jtotik san juane.

48 pero ti tone muk'.
jun metro spatil.
jun metro spimil.
toj muk' ti tone.

Some walked obediently along the road. 39
Others refused to walk.
They went to hide beside the road.[7]
So it was with great effort that sufficient stones were forced
to go to the future site of San Juan's house.

When the stones finally arrived, the bell rang. 40
This was a large bell that hung there on a large oak tree
at the future site of San Juan's house.
This bell tolled all by itself when the stones arrived.

But in truth the herdsmen responsible for all of this were saints. 41
They were not people.[8]

San Juan walked first in line. 42
Behind him came other saints, herding the stones.
It was their job to see that the stones did not flee.

When the stones finally got there, 43
Our Lord San Juan set to work with his helpers.
He began to measure how big he was going to make his house.

When he had finished measuring out the site of his house, 44
He started to dig out a foundation, a place to anchor the stones.

Then, when they had dug out the foundation trench, 45
They began to lower the stones into position.

All of this happened when San Juan worked alone with his workers. 46

Now, when they could no longer reach far enough to set the stones in place, 47
They threw them up.
San Juan himself stood above to catch them.

But these were no ordinary stones! They were huge! 48
One meter to a side.
One meter thick.
They were very large indeed.

49 pero ti jch'ultotike muʔyuk ʔol ta xaʔi.
ta ʔora ta sjip muyel ta ʔak'ol.

50 jech ti jtotik san juan:
ta ʔora ta stzak ti tone.

51 pero ti bu ta spas sna ti san juan ʔoy ʔoʔ ta ʔolon.
komo ʔoy toʔox nab tey.

52 komo la jyil ti jtotik san juan mas lek ti banamile.
mas lek xch'i xchij.
muʔyuk jinich'.
muʔyuk k'ak'al maʔuk k'ixin ʔosil.
toj lek ti banumile.
toj lek xch'i ti snich'nabe.
ʔech'a ʔal te la spas ti sna ta sba ti nabe.

However, for the saints, they were not heavy. 49
They threw them up effortlessly.

Likewise for San Juan, the receiver: 50
In no time and with little effort he caught the stones.

Now, at the site of San Juan's house, there was a water supply 51
down the slope to the west.
Indeed, the former lake was still there, although reduced in size.

Our Lord San Juan found that the land was good. 52
His sheep would prosper.
There were no ants.
There was no intense heat, for it was not Hot Country.
The land was very good.
His children would thrive.
That is why he built his house there above the lake, to the east.[9]

FIGURE 35

. . . the land was good. . . .
His children would thrive.
That is why he built his house there above the lake, to the east.

53 veno ti xchije mu?yuk xa ta x?at yo?onton.
lek xa ?oy ta xve?ik ti xchij ti jtotik san juan.

54 veno ti san juan te naki xchi?uk yitz'in,
pero ti sna ti vo?ne ta vitz.

55 te ?oy sna ta tzonte? vitz.
pero ?ora mu?yuk xa te sna ta tzonte? vitz.

56 te xa ?oy sna ta chamo?.
jech'a ?al sbi san juan chamula.
sna?oj skotol jkaxlanetik ta jo?bel k'alal ta tuxta.

57 pero toj vokol ta sta yav sna ti jtotik san juan ti vo?ne.

So his sheep no longer had sad hearts. 53
The sheep of Our Lord San Juan now ate well and prospered.

So, with this, San Juan and his younger brother took up residence 54
in this place,
Whereas before they had lived in the wilderness.

They once had a home on Tree Moss Mountain. 55
But now Tree Moss Mountain was no longer to be their abode.[10]

They would now have a permanent residence in Chamula. 56
That is why they call it San Juan Chamula.
Even the Ladinos, all of them from San Cristóbal to Tuxtla Gutiérrez,
know about this.

So it happened long ago that with great effort, Our Lord San Juan 57
found a site for his home.

1 loˀil yuˀun jtotik san juan.

2 veno ta voˀne ti jtotik san juane ta ˀox la spas sna.
ta ˀox la xnaki te ta xitalaˀ ta yosil jyan lum.

3 yuˀun la jyil mu sk'an xveˀ ti xchije yuˀun la k'ixin ti banumile.
ˀech'o la xal mu sk'an xveˀ ti xchije.

4 ˀentonse k'alal yil ti mu sk'an xveˀ ti xchije bat saˀ yan yav sna.
pero koˀol bat xchiˀuk xchij.

5 pero ti ta xitalaˀe laj xa ˀox slikes ti snae.
laj xa skuch ˀep ton.
pero k'alal yil ti mu xveˀ ti xchije te la skomes ti yav snae xchiˀuk jun skampana.

6 yuˀun la toj muk' ti skampanae,
ˀech'o la xal te kom ˀo ta yut ˀoˀ ti skampanae.

7 k'alal mi sta ˀoˀlol k'ak'ale ta la stij ti kampanae.
pero te la ta yut ˀoˀ ta stij.

8 ˀentonse bat saˀ yan yav sna ta belel tzimajobel.
lik la spas sna te ta belel tzimajobel.

9 laj xa skuch ˀep ton sventa sna.
pero ta tz'akal la jyil muˀyuk jamal ti banumile.
muˀyuk la bu xuˀ xveˀ ti xchije.
veno bat la saˀ yan ti yav sna xtoke.

TEXT 27

About How Our Lord San Juan Made His Home in Chamula, II

Mateo Méndez Tzotzek

This is a story about Our Lord San Juan.[1] 1

Now, a long time ago San Juan was planning to build his home. 2
He was living there in Xitalá, in another town.[2]

He noticed that his sheep did not want to eat because the land was very hot. 3
That is why his sheep did not want to eat.

When he saw that his sheep did not want to eat, he went to look for 4
another location for his home.
He took his sheep with him.

There in Xitalá, he had already started his house. 5
He had already carried many stones.
But when he saw that his sheep would not eat, he abandoned
that house site and also a bell.

Since this was a very large bell and hard to carry, 6
He left his bell there in a small lake.

To this day, the bell rings every day at noon. 7
And it rings as though the sound were coming from within
the water itself.[3]

He then went on to look for another house site on the road to Simojovel.[4] 8
And he set about building his house there by the road to Simojovel.

He had already carried many rocks for his house. 9
After a while, he saw that the land was too heavily wooded.
His sheep could not find good pasture.
So he went on to look for another house site.

10 pero ti jtotik san juane ʔoy la yitz'in.
ʔaʔ la te kom ta sbelel tzimajobel.
te la ʔoy nakal ta ʔora ta sbelel tzimajobel ti yitz'in jtotik san juane.

11 vaʔi ʔun ti jtotik san juane bat la saʔ yav sna.
ta jol ch'umtik ta sbelel san ʔanteres.

12 te la bat saʔ ti yav snae.
te la bat xchiʔuk xchij.
pero ti yitz'ine te la kom ta belel tzimajobel.

13 veno ti jtotik san juane te la lik spas ti sna ta jol ch'umtike.
te ta mero jol vitz.

14 pero laj xa ʔox slikes ti snae.
laj xa skuch ʔep ti tone.

15 pero ti xchije mu la sk'an xveʔ tajmek.
ta la xʔat yoʔonton jujun k'ak'al.

16 ʔech la ti jtotik san juane ta la xʔat yoʔnton,
ʔaʔ la ti la jyil ti mu sk'an xveʔ ti xchije.

17 bat saʔ yan yav sna xtok.
bat la k'alal ta ʔoʔlol banumil.
smixik la banumil sbi.
ʔaʔ la te bat saʔ ti yav snae.

18 pero baʔyel la k'ot ta kuchulumtik xchiʔuk xchij.
ti xchije ta la xveʔ jutuk.
ti banumile lek la jamal.
xuʔ la xveʔ ti chije.

19 pero ti jtotik san juane laj la yil ti banumil ʔoy la xch'ixal.
mu la sk'an.

Now, Our Lord San Juan had a younger brother.[5] 10
He decided to stay there by the road to Simojovel.
And so, even into our time, the younger brother of Our Lord San Juan
is to be found living there on the road to Simojovel.

However, Our Lord San Juan the Elder set out to find still 11
another house site.
This one was in Jol Ch'umtik, near the road to San Andrés Larraínzar.[6]

He went there to look for a site for his house. 12
He took his sheep with him.
But his younger brother stayed there by the road to Simojovel.[7]

So, Our Lord San Juan started to build his house there by Jol Ch'umtik. 13
There it was, right on top of the mountain.

He had already started his house. 14
He had already carried many stones.

But his sheep refused to eat anything. 15
Their hearts were sad every day.

Naturally, Our Lord San Juan's heart was sad, too, 16
When he saw that his sheep refused to eat.

He went to look for still another site for his house. 17
He traveled toward the center of the earth.
It is called the navel of the earth.[8]
That is where he went to seek a site for his home.

He first arrived with his sheep at the hamlet of Kuchulumtik.[9] 18
His sheep ate a little bit.
And the land was nice and open.
It seemed that the sheep would do well.

But then Our Lord San Juan noticed that the land had many thorny bushes. 19
He did not like this.

20 k'alal mi vok' ti kirsanoetike.
yuˀun la xal ta xlok' ti snich'nab ti jtotik san juane.
mu la sk'an.

21 ti xchije lek la xveˀ,
pero ˀaˀ la ti banumil ˀoy xch'ixale.
ˀaˀ la mu sk'an ti jtotik san juane.

22 veno bat la saˀ yan yav sna.
te la bat ti bu ˀoy ti nabe.
te la bat xchiˀuk xchij.

23 k'alal la k'otik xchiˀuk ti xchije lek la xveˀ tajmek ti xchije.
veno ˀaˀ liˀ chinakie yuˀun toj lek xveˀ ti jchije xi la ti jtotik san juane.

24 veno bat la spaj svaxton ta ˀoˀlol nab.
vaˀi ˀun ti svaxtone lek la te vaˀal ta ˀoˀlol nab.
muˀyuk la bu xlom.

"But what will become of people when they come to be?" he wondered. 20
For it was Our Lord San Juan's plan to bring forth his children in this place.
No, this site would not do.[10]

Although his sheep found good grazing, 21
The land had lots of thornbushes.
This Our Lord San Juan could not abide.

So he set off to find still another site for his house. 22
He went to a place where there was a lake.
He went there with his sheep.

When he arrived with his sheep, they found that the grass was good. 23
"So, here I shall make my home, for my sheep have good pasture,
said Our Lord San Juan.

With that, he plunged his staff into the center of the lake. 24
Indeed, his staff stuck straight up there in the center of the lake.
It did not fall over.

FIGURE 36

With that, he plunged his staff into the center of the lake.
Indeed, his staff stuck straight up there in the center of the lake.
It did not fall over.

25 ˀentonse ti jtotik san juane:
li˚ chinaki xchiˀuk jchije.
yuˀun li jchije toj lek xa xveˀ tajmek.
ˀech xtok lek xch'i li jnich'nabe.
toj lek jamal ti banumile.
ˀaˀ lek liˀ chinakie xi la ti jtotik san juane.
k'alal la jyil ti lek ti banumile.

26 laj la slok'es ti svaxton ta ˀoˀlol nabe.
vaˀi ˀun ti jtotik san juane bat la sjemes talel ti vitze.

27 ˀentonse ti vitze jem la.
skotol ta la bat ta sba nab,
skotol ti lume.

28 veno ti nabe ch'ay la.
takij la.

29 ˀentonse te la lik spas sna ti jtotik san juan ta ba nabe.
pero ch'abal xa la ti nabe.
ˀech'o xal te la spas ti snae.

30 veno k'alal lik spas ti snae la saˀ svinik ti jtotik san juane.
vaˀi ˀun ti viniketike bat la sbojik ti ton ta teˀtike.

31 bat ˀo la sbojik ti ton ta ˀichintone.
pero mu la sk'an bojel ti tone.

32 ˀik'opoj la ta ˀora:
voˀon ˀichintonun.
mu xabojikun xi la ti tone.

33 ˀentonse ti viniketike xiˀik la tajmek.
mu la bu xbojik.
te la kom ti tone.

34 ˀaˀ la ti k'opoje.
mu la sk'an xbat ta ch'ulna ti tone.

Then Our Lord San Juan spoke: 25
"I shall live here with my sheep.
For my sheep seem to be grazing happily.
My children will surely do well here.
The land is nice and open.
This is the place for me to settle, right here," said Our Lord San Juan.
So he said when he saw that the land was good.

He took his staff out of the center of the lake.[11] 26
And with this, Our Lord San Juan caused the nearby mountain to collapse.

So the mountain slumped. 27
It all slid into the lake,
All of it, in a great landslide.

Then the lake disappeared. 28
It dried up.

Then Our Lord San Juan began to build his house on top of the lake site. 29
But there was no longer a lake.
That is how he was able to build his house there.

When Our Father San Juan began to build his house, he looked for helpers. 30
The helpers set about cutting stone in the wilderness.

They went to cut stones from the quarry at Owl Rock.[12] 31
But the stones refused to be cut.

Right away it spoke: 32
"I am Owl Rock.
Don't cut stones from me," said the rock.

With that, the workers became very frightened. 33
They didn't cut a single stone from there.
The rock remained there, untouched.

It had spoken. 34
This rock did not wish to be incorporated into the church at all.

35 chaˀton la sbi.
ti ta ˀox sbojik ta ˀichintone koˀol xchiˀuk stanal choˀ.

36 ti yan tonetik bat la saˀik ta teˀtik.
pero batz'i ton la.
sakil ton.

37 ˀentonse k'alal meltzajem xa ti tone bat la smak talel chak k'uchaˀal chij.
bat la stuk ti jtotik san juane.
pues ti tone ta xanav stuk k'uchaˀal chij.

38 ˀentonse k'alal k'ot skotol ti tone lik slatz ti tone.
pero ˀaˀ la ta slatz ton stuk ti jtotik san juane.

39 vaˀi ˀun k'alal meltzajem xa ti snae ta xnaki xchiˀuk xchij.
pero ti xchije slekoj nakal te ta xokon sna.

It was made of basalt. 35
That stone they were planning to quarry at Owl Rock was of
the same type as that used to make grinding stones.

They finally had to find other stones in the woods. 36
These were "true stone," as it is known.
It was white limestone.

When these rocks were ready to go, he went to herd them like sheep. 37
Our Lord San Juan went to do this himself.
They walked along for him, just like sheep.

When all the rocks had arrived, he began to stack them up. 38
Our Lord San Juan built them up all by himself.

So it was that when his house was finished, he lived there with his sheep. 39
But the sheep lived apart in a separate space right there beside his house.

40 ʔentonse ti jtotik san juane la sbiin san juan chamula.
ʔech'o xal ti snich'nabe chamula sbi.

41 k'alal tzutz ti sna ti jtotik san juane la spas k'in sventa sna ta ventikuatro junio.
yuʔun ʔech la spas ti voʔnee.
ʔech'o xal ti kirsanoetike snaʔojik ta spasik k'in ta ventikuatro junio.

42 vaʔi ʔun k'alal meltzajem xa sna ti jtotik san juane yal la ti jtotik jesukristo.
ta vinajel yalel.

43 ti jtotik jesukristoe te la stzob sbaik ta ch'ulna xchiʔuk san juan.
pero k'alal yal talel ta vinajele jesukristo la sbi.
pero k'alal te xa ta ch'ulnae sbi san machyo.

Then Our Lord San Juan named the place San Juan Chamula. 40
That is why his children are called Chamulas.

When Our Lord San Juan finished his house, he had a fiesta 41
in honor of his house on June 24.
That is what he did long ago.
And so, to this day, people have a festival each June 24.[13]

When Our Lord San Juan's house was ready, Our Lord 42
Jesus Christ descended.
He came down from heaven.

Our Lord Jesus Christ came to join San Juan there in the church. 43
When he came down from heaven, he was the one known as Jesus Christ.
But his image in the church is called San Mateo.[14]

FIGURE 37

Then Our Lord San Juan named the place San Juan Chamula.
That is why his children are called Chamulas.

1 jun kuento ta voˀnee.
ˀoy jun kuento sventa vinik.
jun vinik ta xloˀilajik ta k'ixin ˀosile.

2 yuˀun ˀo te jun kerem toj lek snaˀ syakel ch'o ta yut k'ajbentik.
ti kerem sotzlebe.
yuˀun toj lek snaˀ syakel ch'o jech ti vinike lik yal sloˀil.

3 ˀo la me jech ti voˀnee:
bat la ta yak ch'o ti vinik lae.

4 jaˀ la ti mas voˀne kirsanoetike,
jaˀ la ti ˀantivoetike.

5 bat la ta yak ch'o ta ch'entik.
bat la sk'el ta yok'omal ti xch'oe.

6 te la tik'il la sta.
ta yut spetz' la sta.

7 bat noˀox la sk'el yan ti spetz'e.
te la tik'il la sta yan xtok ti xch'oe.
toj lek la muk'tik ti xch'oe.

8 lek sa la saˀi ti vinike ti k'alal la sta ti xch'oe.
bat la sk'el yan ta jbej vitz ti xch'oe,
yuˀun ˀo la te syakojan yan ti xch'oe.

9 k'alal la k'ot ta stzel ti spetz'e jaˀ to la yil jun la smuk'ul chon te tik'il.
la sta ta yut ti spetz'e.

TEXT 28
The Earth Lord's Daughter

Manuel López Calixto

There is a story of long ago. 1
  It is a story of a man who was one of our ancestors.
  Someone told it to a group of companions in Hot Country.

The subject came up because there was a little boy who was 2
    good at trapping rats in the dry corn fodder.
  It was a little boy from Zinacantán.[1]
  Indeed, the boy knew how to trap rats so well that the man
    felt like telling the story.

So it happened long ago: 3
  A man once went to trap rats.

He was one of the people of long ago, 4
  One of the ancient ones.

He went out to set traps by the rat holes. 5
  He went out the next day to see if he had caught any rats.

He found some rats trapped there. 6
  He found them inside his traps.

Then he went to check out his other traps. 7
  He found some other rats trapped there.
  These rats were fine ones, nice and big.

The man was very happy to have found these rats. 8
  So he went to check out his catch on another hill,
  For he had the custom of placing his rat traps there as well.

As he drew closer to the trap, he saw a huge snake trapped inside. 9
  He found it there inside the trap.

10 toj xiˀel la k'ot ti vinike.
ta˒ox la smil ti chone.

11 k'alal la ti taˀox la smile jaˀ to la yil lik la me k'opojuk ti chone:
mu xamilun xi la ti chone.
mi mu xak'an xbat ta ˀavak'un ta jna xi la ti chone.

12 k'alal la lik k'opojuke lik la pasuk ta jkaxlan ti chone.
jech la ti vinik ˀeke la la xch'unbe smantal ti chone.

13 bat la yak' ta sna ti chon lae.
skuchoj la ˀel ta spat ti vinike.

14 pere koˀol la xchiˀuk jkaxlan yiluk.
pero k'alal la ta xk'opoje ta batz'i k'op ta la xal kaˀitik la ti sk'ope.

The man was very much afraid as he came near. 10
Indeed, he was planning to kill the snake.

Just as he was about to kill it, he noticed that the snake began to speak: 11
"Don't kill me!" said the snake.
"Wouldn't you please take me to my home?" asked the snake.

As it spoke, the snake began to change into a Ladino. 12
So it was that the man obeyed the snake's command.[2]

He obliged and took the snake to its home. 13
The man carried it on his back packed in a net suspended
from a tumpline.

Now, in truth, it looked just like a Ladino. 14
However, when it spoke, it spoke in Tzotzil, thus
making its speech intelligible.[3]

FIGURE 38

Just as he was about to kill it, he noticed that the snake began
to speak:
"Don't kill me!" said the snake.
"Wouldn't you please take me to my home?" asked the snake.

15 jech la me ti vinike la la sjak'be:
bu to ta ˀanae xut ti jkaxlane.

16 ˀaaa . . . pere yuˀun toj nom to ma ti jnae xi la ti jkaxlane.
jech'o xal mi xaˀabolaj xakuchun ˀel ta jna xi la.

17 ta xahtoj xi la.
veno xi la ti vinike.

18 skuchoj lae.
bat la yak' k'alal ta sna.

19 ˀo la te staik jun muk'ta ch'en.
jaˀ jna liˀe xi la ti jkaxlane.

20 jech la ti vinike k'ot la stij ti ch'ene.
jaˀ to la yil ti k'alal la ti jambate koˀol la xchiˀuk yut na.

And so the man asked it a question: 15
"Where is your house?" he said to the Ladino snake.

"Oh, my house is very far away," answered the Ladino snake. 16
"That is why I am asking you the favor of carrying me home," he said.

"I will pay you," he said. 17
"All right," said the man.

He carried the creature on and on. 18
He proceeded to carry it home.

They soon came upon a huge cave. 19
"This is my house," said the Ladino snake.

So the man went up to knock at the mouth of the cave. 20
It was only when the door was opened that he realized
it looked just like the interior of a house.

FIGURE 39

"Oh, my house is very far away," answered the Ladino snake.
"That is why I am asking you the favor of carrying me home,"
he said.

21 mi la tal xˀutat la ti vinike.
li tal yuˀun tal kak' ˀatot xi la k'otel ti vinike.

22 ˀaaa . . . veno, lek ˀoy xi la ti yajval ch'ene.
veno ˀochan tal xˀutat la ti vinike.
ˀoch la ˀel ta yut na.

23 veno kolaval ta la ˀavak' ˀuˀune xi la ti jkaxlane.
mi xak'an junuk ˀavajnil xˀutat la ti vinike.

24 veno xuˀuk mi chavak'bune xi la ti vinik ˀeke.
veno t'ujo bu junukal chak'an xˀutat ti vinike.

25 la la jyik' talel skotol yantzikil nich'nab ti jkaxlane.
veno bu junukal chavik'e xˀutat la ti vinike.
ˀaaa . . . jaˀ ta xkik' ˀel liˀe xi la ti vinik ˀeke.

26 ˀaaa . . . veno ˀik'o ˀel xi la ti jkaxlane.
yak' la talel yantzil nich'on.

27 jaˀ ˀatojol ma liˀ ne xˀutat la ti vinike.
ˀu . . . lek xa la xaˀi ti vinike ti k'alal la ˀak'bat ti yajnile.

28 toj lek la sak ti yajnile meko ˀantz la.
toj lek la sak tajmek.

29 toj ˀalak la sba tajmek yil ti yajnile.
koˀol la xchiˀuk xinulan ˀantz yiluk ti yajnil lae,
ti ˀak'bat la lok'el ta ch'ene.

"Have you come?" the occupants said to the man. 21
"I have come. I have brought your father home," said the man
as he stepped forward.

"Ah, very well," said the mistress of the cave.[4] 22
"Good. Come in," she said to the man.
And he went into the house.

"Good. Thank you for bringing me home," said the Ladino snake. 23
"Might you like a wife?" he asked the man.

"Sure. Why not, if you feel like giving me one," said the man. 24
"Okay, then. Choose the one you like," he said to the man.

With that, the Ladino called all of his daughters. 25
"Well, which one do you want to marry?" he said to the man.
"Umm . . . I'll take this one here," said the man.

"Very well, then. Take her," said the Ladino. 26
And he gave him his daughter.

"Here is your pay for helping me," he said to the man. 27
And the man felt very happy now that he had been given
a wife as a reward.

His wife was nice and white, a very fair woman. 28
She was indeed very, very white.[5]

His wife seemed very beautiful to him. 29
She looked exactly like a Ladino woman,
This one who was given to him in the cave.

30 ˀa li ch'en la ne jaˀ la sna ti ˀanjel lae.
jech la ti chone ˀanjel la yajval banamil la.

31 jech'o la xal ti jlikel la pas ta jkaxlane.
yuˀun yajval banamil la ti jkaxlan la yiluke.

Now, in reality, this cave was the house of the Earth Lord. 30
The angel-snake was truly an Earth Lord.

That is why the snake turned so quickly into a Ladino. 31
Because Earth Lords look just like Ladinos.

FIGURE 40

Now, in reality, this cave was the house of the Earth Lord.
The angel-snake was truly an Earth Lord.

32 k'alal la sut ˀel ta sna ti vinike ˀoy xa la yajnil k'otel ta sna.
yik'ojbe xa la k'otel yantzil nich'on ˀanjel ti vinike ˀantivo kirsanoe.

33 k'alal la k'ot ta snae xiˀ la ti smeˀe.
xiˀ la ti stote.

34 bu la ta talel li xinolan ˀantze xˀutat la ti skerem ˀolike.
moˀoj yuˀun bat kak' jun vinik jkaxlan ta sna xˀut la stot smeˀ ti vinik lae.

35 ˀaaa . . . veno xi la ti stot smeˀe.
pere k'uxi tal ti jkaxlane.
pere bu lok' talel xi la stot smeˀ ti vinik lae.

36 ˀaaa . . . ˀa ti k'alal li k'ot ta stz'el ti jpetz'e jaˀ to kil te tik'il ta yut ti jpetz'e.
pere li xiˀ tajmek yuˀun xi la ti skerem ˀolike.

37 jaˀ to me kil lik k'opojuk ti chone.
mi la tal xi la likel.
li tal xˀut la ti vinik ˀeke.

When the man went home, he returned as a married man. 32
The man who was one of the ancient people had taken as a wife
the daughter of the Earth Lord.

When he got home, his mother was frightened. 33
His father was frightened.

"Where did you find this Ladino woman?" they asked their son. 34
"I didn't exactly find her. It was because I did a Ladino man
the favor of returning him to his home," the man said
to his father and mother.

"Oh, really, now," said his parents. 35
"But how did the Ladino appear?
Where did he come from?" inquired the man's parents.

"When I came up to my trap, I saw a snake there inside my trap. 36
It scared me to death!" said their son.

"Soon I noticed that the snake began to talk. 37
'Have you come?' asked the creature.
'I have come,' I said in reply.

FIGURE 41

When the man went home, he returned as a married man.
The man who was one of the ancient people had taken as a
wife the daughter of the Earth Lord.

38 mi xak'an xbat ta ˀavak'un ta jna xiyut ne.
veno xuˀuk xkut ˀek ˀun.

39 vaˀi ˀun li bat kak' k'alal ta sna ti jkaxlane.
k'alal li k'ot kuˀune kolaval ta la vak' ˀune xiyut ti jkaxlane.

40 jaˀ te la jta talel ti kajnile xi la ti vinike.
jaˀ te la jyak'bikun talel xˀut la ti stot smeˀe.

41 ˀay pere toj ˀalak sba tajmek xi la stot smeˀ ti vinike.
lek xa la saˀik ti ˀoy yajnil ti skerem ˀolike.

42 jech la me ti smeˀe la la sjak'be k'usi la sveˀel ti yalibe:
k'usi la snaˀ xveˀ.
k'usi la snaˀ stiˀel ti yajnil skerem ˀole.

43 mi xanaˀ xaveˀ vaj xˀut la.
ˀaaa . . . ˀaˀ jna xi la ti yajnil skerem ˀole.

44 mi xanaˀ satiˀ ˀalak' xˀut la.
ˀaaa . . . ˀaˀ jnaˀxi la ti yajnil skerem ˀole.
skotol jnaˀ sveˀel xi la ti ˀantze.

45 jnaˀ spasel vaj.
jnaˀ spakanel ma li vaje xi la ti yalibe.
lek xa la xaˀi stot smeˀ ti vinike.

46 k'alal la ta spas ti vaje jun la yepal ta spas.
juteb k'ol la ti yixime pere toj ˀep la ta xlok' yuˀun ta pasel.

47 ti yot lae toj lek la xbol yuˀun ti ˀixim ti ˀantz lae.
ˀak'o la mi juteb xa la ti yixime ta la xbol tajmek yuˀun ti ˀixim laˀe.
ta la xbol yuˀun ti chenek'e.
ˀak'o mi juteb xa la ti sveˀeltike ta la xbol yuˀun ti sveˀeltike lae.

‘Would you mind taking me to my house?’ he said to me. 38
‘All right,’ I said.

Then I went to take the Ladino home. 39
When we got there, the Ladino said, ‘Thank you for bringing me home.’

And it was there that I found my wife,” said the man. 40
“They gave her to me there,” he said to his parents.

“Ah! But she really is pretty,” said the man’s parents. 41
They felt very happy that their son had a wife.

Then the man’s mother asked her daughter-in-law about food: 42
What sort of food she was accustomed to,
Whether her daughter-in-law knew how to eat meat and beans.

“Do you know how to eat tortillas?” she asked. 43
“Oh, yes, I do,” said her son’s wife.

“Do you eat chicken?” she asked. 44
“Oh, yes, I do,” said her son’s wife.
“I eat everything,” said the woman.

“I know how to make tortillas. 45
I know how to pat and shape tortillas,” said the daughter-in-law.
And this pleased the man’s parents very much.

When she made tortillas she made lots of them. 46
She had but a little bit of dough, but she made it stretch a long way.

In this way, the woman made her corn increase so that it produced 47
many tortillas.
Even though she had but a little bit of corn, she made it increase
in volume a great deal.
She also made the beans increase.
Thus, even though the household had but a little bit of food,
she made that food increase.

48 k'alal la mi bat la saˀ talel ˀajane jun la yepal ta xtal yuˀun.
k'alal la mi bat sk'aj talel ti ˀajane jun la me yepal xtal yuˀun.

49 pere mu la me bu ˀep ta sk'aj ti ˀajane.
jaˀ noˀox la me chaˀ ch'ix ta saˀ talel ti yajane.
pere jun la muk' ta nutiˀ ta xtal yuˀun ti ˀajane.

50 ti chenek' lae:
k'alal la ta stul ti xchenek' chaˀbej ta sat ta stul talel,
pere jun la me yepal ta xbat ti chenek'e.

51 jech la me ti vinike la la me jyut ti yajnile.
ˀaaa . . . pere muˀyuk ˀep la jsaˀ talel xi la ti ˀantze.

52 jech la ti mu vinike xˀilin xa la tajmeke ti smalale.
jech la ti vinike jlikel la la smaj ti yajnile.
yuˀun ˀaˀ ˀoy la smul spas ˀepajuk ti ˀajane.

Whenever she went out to get sweet corn, she would bring back plenty. 48
Whenever she went out to harvest sweet corn, she returned with lots and lots.

She really did not harvest many ears of corn. 49
She would actually only pick two ears of sweet corn.
But when she returned she had a large carrying net full of sweet corn.

And so it was with the beans: 50
When she went to pick beans she picked only two pods,
But these few beans became many.

For her seeming wastefulness, the man scolded his wife.[6] 51
"Ah, but I gathered a very little bit," said the woman.

So it was that this ungrateful and mean man, her husband, became furious. 52
It was because of this that he hit her.
His wife's only fault had been her success in causing the corn to increase.

FIGURE 42

So it was that this ungrateful and mean man, her husband, became furious.
It was because of this that he hit her.
His wife's only fault had been her success in causing the corn to increase.

53 jech ti yajnile ta sniˀ la k'ot ti mahele.
toj lok'el ta xch'ich'el ti sniˀe.

54 te la chepel ti jun nutiˀ ti yajane.
la la stzak jch'ix ti yajane.

55 la la skus ˀo sniˀ ti ˀixim lae.
jaˀ la me xch'ich'el sniˀ ˀanjel ma li tzahal ˀixime.

56 jech la me ti k'alal la laj ta majel ti ˀantze,
jlikel la me tal ˀik'vanuk ti stot.
stot la ti ˀantze.

57 lek toˀox la me k'epel ti vinajele.
ta ˀora la me tal ti toke.
ta ˀora la me tal ti ˀoˀe.

58 k'alal la ti tal la jutuk ti ˀoˀe,
jaˀ ˀo la me lok' ti ˀanjele ta stz'el sna ti vinik lae.
sjisluj la ti ˀanjele.

59 jaˀ ˀo la bat ti yajnile ti k'alal la ˀavan ti ˀanjele.
jaˀ ˀo la yik' ˀech'el ti yantzil nich'one.

60 ti k'alal laj ta majele ti stzebe,
jlikel la me tal yik' ˀech'el ta ˀora ti stzeb lae.

61 jech la ti ˀantze yuˀun jaˀ la stot ti ˀanjele.
jech'o la xal ti jlikel la me tal ˀik'ate;
yuˀun jaˀ la me stot ti ˀantz lae.

62 jech la ti ˀantzee,
yuˀun ˀanjel la me ˀeke.
jech la ti ˀantze:
ˀoy xa la yalab kom ti ˀantze.

63 ta la skomtzan li yalabe,
stukik la kom ti ˀoltike.

He landed a blow against his wife's nose. 53
This caused blood to flow profusely from her nose.

One of the nets of sweet corn was close by. 54
From it she grabbed an ear of corn.

She wiped her bloody nose with this ear of corn. 55
This is why red corn is known as blood of the Earth Lord's nose.[7]

After the woman had suffered this awful beating, 56
Her father came at once to take her away.
It was the woman's father himself.

At that time the sky had been completely clear. 57
Suddenly the clouds gathered!
Suddenly the thunderstorm broke!

When it had just started to rain a little, 58
A great bolt of lightning struck close to the man's house.
How the thunder crashed!

At the very moment when the thunder sounded, the man's wife vanished. 59
Right then, the Earth Lord came to rescue his daughter
and take her away.[8]

No sooner had his daughter suffered the beating, 60
Than he quickly came to carry his daughter away.

Indeed, the woman's father was none other than an Earth Lord. 61
That is why she was rescued so quickly;
Because he was the woman's father.

As for the woman, 62
She, too, was an Earth Lord.
However, the woman's situation was complicated:
She had borne human children.

She left her children, 63
And the children were forced to fend for themselves, all alone.

64 k'alal ta xˀok'ik ti yalabe,
jlikel la ti xtal sk'el ta ˀora ti yole.

65 k'uchaˀal chaˀok'ike xˀut la ti yalabe.
yuˀun ta xiviˀnaj tajmek xi la ti ˀoltike.

66 mu xaˀok'ik ta jsatik tal sbinal ˀaveˀelik xi la komel ti smeˀike.
vaˀun ti smeˀik lae bat la saˀbe tal sbinal sveˀel ti yalabe.

67 sut la tal ti smeˀike.
tal yak'be sbinal sveˀel ti yalab lae.

68 ˀa li liˀe.
jaˀ me sjayil la ˀavotik, ma liˀ ˀune.
jaˀ me sbinal ˀaveˀelik ma liˀ ˀune.
ˀa li liˀe jaˀ me sbinal ˀapaninik ma liˀ ˀune.
xˀut la komel ti yalabe.

69 k'alal mi laj ta ˀavotike,
jaˀ chanujanik la jayike.

70 k'alal mi laj ta ˀachenek'ike,
jaˀ chanujanik ti sbinal ˀachenek'ike xi la ti smeˀik.

71 k'alal mi laj ta ˀaveˀelike,
xanujanik me sbinal ta ˀachenek'ike.
xanujan me sjayil ta ˀavotike.
xanujan me sbinal ta panine
xi la komel ti smeˀike.

72 k'alal la mi laj ti yotike,
ta snujananik ti sjayil la ti yotike.

73 k'alal la mi laj ti xchenek'ike,
ta snujananik ta ˀora ti sbinike.

74 k'alal la mi laj ti yotike,
ta ˀora la ta snujananik ti sjayil la ti yotike.

When her children began to cry, 64
She lost no time in returning to take care of her little ones.

"Why are you crying?" she asked her children. 65
"Because we're very hungry," said the children.

"Don't cry. I'll bring pots of food for you," said their mother. 66
Then their mother went to fetch pots of food for her children.

Presently their mother returned. 67
She gave the food pots to her children.

"I have some things for you here. 68
Here is a tortilla gourd for you. Here it is.[9]
Here is a food pot for you. Here it is.
Here is a corn-cooking pot for you. Here it is."
So she said to her children.

"When you run out of tortillas, 69
You must turn your tortilla gourd upside down.

When you run out of beans, 70
You must turn your bean pot upside down," said their mother.

"When you run out of food, 71
You must turn your bean pot upside down.
You must turn your tortilla gourd upside down.
You must turn your corn pot upside down."
So their mother left instructions.

When they ran out of tortillas, 72
They were to turn their tortilla gourd upside down.

When they ran out of beans, 73
They were to lose no time in turning their cooking pots upside down.

When they ran out of tortillas, 74
They were to lose no time in turning the tortilla gourd upside down.

75 k'alal la mi la snujanike,
ta la xk'ojilanik ti sbinal sveˀelik lae.

76 k'alal la mi laj xk'ojilane,
ta la slik xchotan ti sbinal sveˀele.

77 jaˀ to la xˀil nojik xa la sbel ti sbine;
nojik xa la sbel ti sjaye.

78 ˀoy xa la yotil.
ˀoy xa la xchenek'ul ti sbine.
jaˀ la me jech ta xveˀik ˀo ti yalabe.

79 jech la me ti stotik la ti ˀoltike:
bu chata ti vaje xˀut la ti snich'nabe.
la la sjakbe ti bu la ta stae.

80 jech la me ti ˀoltike lik la me yak'ik ˀiluk ti sjayil yotike.
lik la me yak'ik ˀiluk ti sbinal xchenek'e.

81 pere k'uxi ta xlok' talel jaˀ ˀa vuˀunik xi la ti stotike.
pere k'uxi ta xlok' talel ti chenek'e xi la ti stotike ti ˀololetike.

82 jech la me ti ˀololetike la la me jyak'bik ˀiluk sbinal sveˀelik.
ti ˀoltike la la me jyak'bik ˀiluk sjayil ti yotike.

83 k'alal la jyil yuˀunik ti stotike,
lik la me spojanbe sjayil yot,
lik la me spojanbe sbinal ti sveˀele ti snich'nabe.

84 k'alal la ti laj spojanbe,
lik la me svok'anbe ti sbinal xchenek'e,
lik la me svok'anbe sjayil ti yote.

85 k'alal la vok'bat ti sbinaltak sveˀelike ta xchamik ta viˀnal ti ˀoltike.
toj ˀabol ti sbaik ti ˀoltik lae.

86 jech la me ti smeˀike tal la me sk'el ti yalabe ta ˀora.
ti k'alal la jaˀ o ch'abal te ti stotike.

When they had turned them upside down, 75
They were to beat on their food containers like a drum.

When they had finished drumming on them, 76
They were to place the food containers upright.

They were to do this until they saw that their pot was full; 77
And that their gourd was full.

Then they would have tortillas. 78
Then they would have beans in their pot.
And in this way her children had food to eat.

Then it happened that the children's father discovered this and spoke: 79
"Where did you find those tortillas?" he asked his children.
He asked them where they had found them.

So the children began to show him their tortilla gourd. 80
They began to show him their bean pot.

"But how do you get the food to appear for you?" asked their father. 81
"Where do the beans come from?" the father asked his children.

So the children showed him their food pot. 82
The children showed him their tortilla gourd.

When their father had seen their possessions, 83
He snatched away their tortilla gourd,
He snatched away his children's food pot.

When he had taken them away, 84
He hastened to break the bean pot,
He hastened to break the tortilla gourd.

With the children's food containers broken, the children were dying of hunger. 85
The fate of the children was very sad.

However, the mother came at once to look in on her children. 86
This happened when their father was not there.

87 tekee mu xaˀok'ik.
te ta xital kik'ot ta ˀora ta na xi la komel ti smeˀik lae.

88 k'alal la tal yik' ti yole jlikel la me tal ta ˀora ti toke.
jlikel la me tal ti tok ta vinajele,
ta ˀora la me tal ti ˀoˀe.

89 k'alal la me ta xak' jutuk ti ˀoˀe,
jaˀ ˀo la me lok' ti ˀanjele.
sjisluj la me ti ˀanjele.
jaˀ ˀo la me tal yik' ti yalabe ti ˀantze.

90 k'alal la me ti sut talel ta ˀabtel ti vinike,
ch'abal xa la ti snich'nabe k'ot stae.

91 k'usi bat ti jnich'nabe xi la ti vinike.
ˀentonse bat ta k'alal ta sna smeˀ ti vinike.
bat la sjak'be ti smeˀ lae.

92 mi mu xa bu xavilbun sk'ote xˀut la ti smeˀe.
ch'abal xi la ti smeˀ ti vinike.
ˀaaa . . . pere jaˀ li la vutilane xi la smeˀ ti vinike.
naˀ mu ˀaˀi xa yik' smeˀ ma ti ˀololetike xi la syaya ti ˀololetike.

93 veno te k'alal xi la ti vinike.
k'usi xa la ta xkut ti yuˀun laj xa la yik' ˀech'el ti smeˀe.

94 snaˀ xa la ti vinike ti k'alal la bat ti snich'nabe.
snaˀ xa la tajmek ti vinike.

95 k'alal bat ti yajnile jech la ti vinike;
stuktuk xa la kom ta sna ti vinike.

96 pere yuˀun jaˀ ti la smaje.
jech'o la xal ti yoˀ la jatav ˀech'el ta sna ti ˀantze.

"Now, now, don't cry. 87
I have come to take you home with me right away,"
their mother told them.

At the time when she came to carry her children away, 88
it clouded over very quickly.
The clouds gathered quickly in the sky,
And in a moment the rain came.

When it had begun to rain a little, 89
The Earth Lord appeared in a flash of lightning.
The Earth Lord roared in a clap of thunder.
And with this, the woman rescued her children.

Soon, the man returned from his work. 90
He realized that his children were no longer there.

"Where did my children go?" wondered the man. 91
Then he went to his mother's house.
He went to ask his mother.

"Have you by any chance seen my children around here?" 92
he asked his mother.
"No," said the man's mother.
"Ah, but come to think of it, you did quarrel with their mother,"
recalled the man's mother.
"I think that their mother felt like taking the children away,"
added the children's grandmother.

"Well, never mind," said the man. 93
"But now what can I do since their mother has taken them away?"

Now the man regretted that the children had gone away. 94
Now he missed them very much.

With his wife gone, the man had to accept his fate; 95
He found himself all alone in his house.

It was all because he had hit her. 96
That is why the woman fled to her former home.

97 yuˀun toj pukuj la ti vinike.
jech'o la xal ti sut la ˀel ta sna,
yuˀun toj toyol la smajvan ti vinike.

98 ti k'alal la laj ta majele jaˀ la la skus ˀo xch'ich'el sniˀ ti ˀajane.
jech'o la xal ti yoˀ la ˀoy tzoj ti ˀixime [xi ti vinike].[10]
yuˀun jaˀ la me xch'ich'el sniˀ ˀanjel ti voˀne lae.
ˀa li tzajal ˀixime.

99 xi ti vinik ta sloˀilaj ti voˀnee.

It was all because the man was thoroughly evil. 97
That is why she went home,
For he had really beaten her up.

It was when she suffered a beating at his hands that she wiped 98
her bloody nose with the ear of corn.
That is why there is red corn.
It is from the blood of the Earth Lord's daughter from long ago.
That is where red corn came from.

That is how the storyteller told it long ago. 99

1 ʔoy jun kuento sventa ʔantz voʔne.

2 jech la ti mu ʔantze ch'abal la smalal.
ʔi ta la sk'an tajmek ti smalale.

3 vaʔun ti mu ʔantz la ʔune,
ʔi ta la xvay,
ʔi ch'abal la smalal.
ʔi ta la sk'an tajmek ti ʔate.

TEXT 29

Of A Poor, Wretched Woman Who Had No Husband for Herself

Marián López Calixto

There is a story about a woman of long ago. 1

It concerns a poor, wretched woman who had no husband for herself. 2
And she really wanted a husband of her own very much.[1]

Now, as for the poor woman, 3
She would retire to sleep,
But she had no husband to accompany her.
All the same, she had great desire for sex.

FIGURE 43

There is a story about a woman of long ago.

It concerns a poor, wretched woman who had no husband for herself.
And she really wanted a husband of her own very much.

4 vaˀun ta la xbat la koral ˀitaj.
ta saˀ la talel sjol ˀavanux ta ˀitajtik ti mu ˀantze.

5 vaˀun k'alal la ti xvay ti mu ˀantz.
jech la ti sjol yalvanux ˀune ta la xak'be ta smis ti mu ˀantze.

6 ˀi lek xa xaˀi tajmek ti sjol ˀalvanuxe.
ˀi ta la xˀok' ti smu mise.

7 jech la ti ˀantze pere toj lek tajmek.
xi la ti mu ˀantze.

8 ˀi ta xalbe la xchiˀiltak:
maˀ la vinik jaˀ toyol ta xvay.
xi la ti mu ˀantze.

9 ˀa . . . pere k'uchaˀal mu xasaˀ ta ˀamalale xi la ti xchiˀile.
pere ch'abal tajmek ti vinike xi la ti mu ˀantze.

10 vaˀun ti voˀne la ˀune ch'abal toˀox ti vinik la ˀune.
jech la ti ˀantze jujun la lak'obaltik ta spajbe ta smis ti sjol ti ˀalvanuxe.

11 vaˀun yaˀik la ti xchiˀiltak la ˀune.
jech la ti xchiˀiltak la ˀun ˀiyaˀik la ˀun.

12 pere k'usi taje ˀo mi ˀoy ˀoch mu tz'iˀ xi la ti vinik ˀune.
vaˀun ˀiyaˀi la me ˀun.

13 jech la ti vinik ˀune.
k'unk'un la lik ta stem ti vinike.

14 mi ta xibat ba jk'el xi la xchiˀuk yajnil ti vinike.
vaˀun, batan xi la ti yajnil ti vinik la ˀune.

So, she made her way to the enclosed vegetable plot. 4
The woman went to get a long white radish root that was growing
there among the cabbage plants.

Then the wretched woman went back to bed. 5
And, with the radish root in hand, the horny woman
proceeded to masturbate.

She liked the feel of the radish very much; 6
So much, in fact, that she became very wet.

The woman would say, "Ah, this is very nice." 7
These were the disgusting woman's words.

She would say to her friends: 8
"My man doesn't pay attention to me."
So the poor woman spoke of her plight.[2]

"Oh, then, why not get a husband all for yourself?" suggested her friends. 9
"But there aren't nearly enough men," said the poor, wretched woman.

And, indeed, long ago there were still not enough men.[3] 10
And so every night the woman would resort to masturbating
with the long radish.

As fate would have it, her relatives [who were also sleeping there] 11
heard something.
Her relatives heard some funny sounds.

"What is it? Has the damned dog gotten into the house?" said the man. 12
And he proceeded to listen very carefully.

This is what the man did. 13
The man slowly and quietly got out of bed.

"I'm going to see what's going on," said the man to his wife. 14
"Go, then," said the man's wife.[4]

15 vaˀun ti vinik.
bat k'unk'un la tajmek ti vinike.
vaˀun k'ot la ta stz'el stem ti mu ˀantz la ˀune.

16 jech la ti vinik la ˀune:
yaˀi la ti stuk ti mu ˀantz la ˀune.
likel la bat ta stem ti vinik la ˀune.

17 vaˀun k'ot la yalbe ti yajnil la ˀune:
naˀtik k'usi ta spas, pere stuktuk te ˀoy ta tem ti kavron ˀantze xi la ti vinike.

18 vaˀun k'alal la sakub la ˀune bat la sk'elbe la stem ti mu ˀantz la ˀune.
bat saˀbe la ti k'u la xi ta spas ti mu ˀantze.

19 vaˀun ˀisaˀbe la ˀun ˀi ch'abal la.
pere buy xi la ti vinike.
ˀisaˀbe la tajmek ti k'u la xi ta spajbe la ta xchake.

20 vaˀun ˀistabe la ˀun.
jaˀ la ti sjol ti ˀalvanux la ˀune.

21 jech la ti sjol ˀalvanuxe toj tu la tajmek koˀoltik la chak chamem tz'iˀ.
ti jol ˀalvanuxe toj tu xa la tajmek.

22 vaˀun ti vinik la ˀune saˀ la ˀich'.
jech' ti ˀich'e ˀisbonbe la ta sjol ti ˀalvanuxe.

23 vaˀun vayik la ˀun.
ˀi jaˀ noˀox jech la spas noˀoxtok.

24 veno ti vinik la ˀune ta xa la yaˀibinoj ti k'usi ta spas ti mu ˀantz la ˀune.
vaˀun jech la ti mu ˀantze.

25 ˀiyaˀik ta stzak ti sjol ti yalvanux la ˀune.
ˀiyak'be la xtok.

26 vaˀun lek la jlikel la ˀun jech la ti mu ˀantz la ˀune ˀiˀok' la me ˀun.
k'usi la pas ˀun xi la ti vinike.

This is what the man did. 15
The man proceeded ever so slowly.
Whereupon, the man sneaked up close to the poor woman's bed.

This is what the man discovered: 16
He realized that the poor woman was in bed alone.
So the man returned at once to his own bed.

Then he spoke to his wife: 17
"Who knows what she's doing, but the bitch is there all alone
in bed, doing something," said the man.

Well, at dawn he went to inspect the wretched woman's bed. 18
He went to see what the wretched woman had been doing.

Well, he looked around and there was nothing to be found. 19
"But where can it be?" said the man.
And he looked around for whatever it was that she had stuck in her twat.

Then he found it. 20
It was a long white radish root.

The radish root smelled terrible, just like a dead dog. 21
The radish root really stank a lot.

Well, then the man went to find some chili peppers. 22
He coated the entire radish with chili.

Then they all went to sleep. 23
And she proceeded to engage once again in her customary activity.

The man had discovered what the disgusting woman had been up to. 24
But, unaware of this, the poor woman went on doing her thing.

They heard her take the radish root. 25
And she stuck it in once again.

Well, in no time at all the wretched woman screamed. 26
"What's happening to you?" inquired the man.

27 ch'abal yuˀun. k'ux tajmek jch'ut.
ˀuuu, ˀuuuuu xi la ti mu ˀantze.

28 ˀaltik chal ti k'ux ti xch'ut ˀune.
jaˀ la ti smis la ˀune toj k'ux la tajmek ˀun.

29 ˀa pere k'usi la pas ˀun xi la ti vinik la ˀune.
mu jnaˀ tajmek toj k'ux tajmek ti jmise xi la ti puta ˀantz ˀune.

30 k'usi spas ta ˀamis ˀune xi la ti vinike.
mu jnaˀ k'usi ta spas xi la tajmek.

31 vaˀun,
ta xa xicham,
ta xa xicham,
ta xa xicham.

32 ti ˀay ˀay ˀay.
toj k'ux,
toj k'ux,
toj k'ux xi la ti mu ˀantze.

33 vaˀun ˀi jaˀ la cham ˀo ti sk'uxul la ti smis ˀune.
ˀi laj la ti smu chak ˀo taj yalel ˀun.

34 jaˀ la ti ˀantivoetik la ti voˀnee.
jaˀ la ta xchaˀ lomal.
toj chopol toˀox ti kirsanoetike.

35 jaˀ jech laj ˀo ti kuentoe.

"Nothing. It's just that I have a bad stomachache. 27
Oooh! Oooh!" yelled the poor woman.

But to tell the truth, it was not so that she had a stomachache. 28
It was in fact her cunt that was causing her pain.

"But what on earth has happened to you?" asked the man. 29
"I don't know why my cunt hurts so much," yelled the wretched bitch.

"What's wrong with your cunt?" asked the man. 30
"I don't know what happened!" she replied hysterically.

Then she exclaimed: 31
"I'm dying!
I'm dying!
I'm dying!

Ay! Ay! Ay! 32
It hurts so much!
I can't stand it!
It's unbearable!" said the wretched woman.

So it happened that she died then and there from the pain in her cunt. 33
Her evil crotch did her in, just like that.

Such were the doings of the early people. 34
It was in the time of the Second Creation.[5]
People were still very bad back then.

And so the story ends. 35

1 ˀoy jun kuento sventa vinik ta lajebal voˀnee.

2 jech la ti vinike ˀoy la jun yajnil.
toj lek la ti ˀantze,
mu la bu ch'aj.

3 ˀi toj lek la spas la vaj,
ˀi sob la ta xlik ti ˀantze.

4 jech la ti ˀantz ˀune:
taat la ta chamel ti povre ˀantze.

5 jech la ti vinike:
ˀi saˀ la ti jˀilole.
laj la yoˀnton ti puru la saˀ jˀilole.

6 jech la ti povre ˀantz ne cham la ˀun.
mu la bu ˀech' la yuˀun ti chamele.

7 ˀa ti vinik lae ˀoy la jun snich'on.
ˀa ti snich'on lae.

8 ˀuni kerem la snich'on ti vinike.
jech la snich'on ti vinik lae cham la.

9 tekeˀ ˀun chaˀe cham xa ti jnich'one.
jechun ˀek ˀun chaˀe chamkun ˀek xi la ti vinike.

10 jech la ti vinike.
puru la ˀok'el ta spas la jujun la k'ak'al la ti vinike.

TEXT 30

Of a Man Who Went to the Underworld

Marián López Calixto

This is a story of long ago about a man who went to the underworld. 1

Now this man had a wife. 2
She was a very good woman,
Not lazy at all.

She made tortillas very faithfully, 3
And she got up early every morning.

But such was this woman's fate: 4
Sickness fell upon this poor woman.

So the man did this: 5
He sought out a curer.
Then more and more curers until he finally gave up, for it was in vain.[1]

So the poor woman died. 6
She was not able to recover.

The man, now a widower, had a son. 7
And this was the fate of his son.

The man's child was but a little boy. 8
And it happened that the man's child also died.

"So fate would have it!" exclaimed the man. 9
"Why not me? I, too, should die," said the man.

So the man began to take this very course. 10
The man spent all day, every day, crying.

11 pere maˀ ti kajnile,
ta xibat ba jk'el xi la ti vinike.
vaˀun ti vinik la ˀune bat la sk'el ti yajnile.

12 laj la sman la skantila.
sventa la ta jtob sentavo ti kantilae.
ˀep la tajmek la sman ˀech'el ti kantilaetike.
puru la sera la sman ˀech'el ti vinik.

13 vaˀun ti vinik la ne bat la ta lajebal.
ˀoy jun ch'en.
te la la sta jech,
te la ˀoch ta ch'en ˀun.

14 jech la ti skantila ne,
laj la stzan la chaˀbej ti skantilae.

"But my wife, my wife, 11
I must go to see her," he mourned.
So the man decided to go see his wife.

He proceeded to buy candles. 12
The candles were of a size and type valued at twenty centavos.
The man bought lots of these candles to take with him.
The candles for his trip were made of pure beeswax.[2]

And with that, the man departed for the underworld.[3] 13
There was a cave.
The man found it there,
And he entered the cave.[4]

Now, of the candles he had with him, 14
He lit two of them.

FIGURE 44

And with that, the man departed for the underworld.
There was a cave.
The man found it there,
And he entered the cave.

15 vaˀun ˀoch la ˀech'el ti mu vinike.
bat bat la tajmek ti mu vinike.
jun la xemana ta xanav ta yut lum ti mu vinike.

16 vaˀun bat la tajmek.
k'ot la ta sbe ti jtotik ta vinajel ne.
vaˀun ˀi te la sta ti jtotik san pekro ne.

17 k'u chasaˀ liˀ ˀune xi la ti jtotik ta lajebal ˀune.
yuˀun ˀoy chamem kajnil xi la ti vinik ˀune.

18 pere mi stuk ta xcham ta ˀavajnile xi la ti jtotik ta lajebal ˀune.
pere yuˀun ta xibat ba jk'el tajmek ti kajnile xi la ti vinike.

19 veno batan ˀun chaˀe mi mu xak'an xach'ie.
laj me kalbot xi la ti jtotik ta lajebal ˀune.

20 pere muk' bu jal ta xibat.
ta noˀox chipaj chib k'ak'al.
vaˀun ta xisut tal ta ˀora xi la ti vinike.

21 veno batan ˀun chaˀe xi la ti jtotik ta vinajel ne.
jech la ti vinik ˀune bat la ˀun.
veno ˀi k'ot la ˀun.

Then the wretched man proceeded into the earth. 15
This unfortunate man walked and walked.
This misguided man walked within the earth for a week.[5]

He went on and on. 16
Presently he reached the path of Our Father Sun in Heaven.
And there he found Our Lord San Pedro.[6]

"What are you looking for here?" asked the Lord of the Underworld. 17
"My wife is dead," said the man.

"But is it only your wife who is dead?" inquired the Lord of the Underworld, thinking that the man was dead also. 18
"Yes, it is only she who is dead, not I, but I want very much to see my wife," said the man.

"Well, go ahead then, if you no longer wish to live. 19
Now I have warned you," said the Lord of the Underworld.

"But I don't plan to stay long, 20
I'll only be here a couple of days.
Then I'll be coming back without delay."

"Well, go on then," said the Lord of the Underworld. 21
With that, the man departed.
Presently he reached his destination.

22 mi liˀ ˀote xi la ti vinike.
liˀ ˀune.
k'u chasaˀ leˀ ne xi la ti yajnil ti vinik ˀune.

23 pes muˀyuk.
li tal jk'el to.
k'uxot ta koˀnton tajmek xi la ti vinik ˀune.

24 pere k'uchaˀal la tal ˀun xi la ti yajnil ti vinik ne.
veno tekeˀ la tal xa leˀ ne.

25 pere mu xa bu chasut maˀ le ˀune.
ta xa xatal jchiˀin jbatik xi la ti yajnil ti vinik ne.
veno xi la ti vinike.

"Are you here?" said the man. 22
"I am here.
What are you seeking here?" said the man's wife.

"Well, nothing, really. 23
I came to see you.
I missed you a lot," said the man.

"But why did it ever occur to you to come?" asked the man's wife. 24
"But that's beside the point now that you've already come.

But it is truly the case that you are not going to return. 25
Pretty soon you will come here forever to keep me company,"
said the man's wife.
"Good," said the man.

FIGURE 45

"Are you here?" said the man.
"I am here.
What are you seeking here?" said the man's wife.

"Well, nothing, really.
I came to see you.
I missed you a lot," said the man.

26 vaˀun ti yajnil ti vinik ˀune:
teke ˀ ˀun
koman liˀ ta jna ne.

27 ta xibat ta pus ta ˀanil xi la ti yajnil ti vinike.
ta xibat ˀek xi ti mu sonso vinik ˀeke.

28 moˀoh koman liˀ to e.
chital ta jlikel.

29 lakano hveˀeltik.
t'ujo chenek' liˀ ta bine.
k'alal mi la lakan ˀune mu me xavuch'ta ˀun xi la ti yajnil ti vinik ˀune.
veno xi la ti vinike.

30 vaˀun ti sveˀel ti mu sonso vinik ˀune.
k'alal la tomaj sveˀel ti ˀanima ˀune.

31 jech la ti mu sonso vinik ˀune laj la svuch'ta ti sbine.
k'alal svuch'ta ti sbine jech la ti sveˀel ti yajnil ti ti vinike.

Then the man's wife spoke: 26
"All right, then, if your mind is made up.
Go ahead and stay here in my house.

I am going to take a sweat bath now," said the man's wife. 27
"I will take one too," said the wretched, foolish man.[7]

"No, you stay here. 28
I'll be back in a minute.

Tend our food. 29
Sort the beans here in the pot.
When you put them on to cook, don't blow on them."
"All right," said the man.

Well, this is what happened to the food that the poor, foolish man was tending. 30
It happened just as the dead woman's food started to bubble in the pot.

Then it happened that the poor, stupid man blew on the pot. 31
It was the pot that contained his wife's food.

FIGURE 46

Then it happened that the poor, stupid man blew on the pot.
It was the pot that contained his wife's food.

32 k'alal la vul ta ˀich' pus ti ˀantze.
mi taˀaj ti jveˀeltike xi la ti ˀantz ˀune.

33 taˀaj,
pero vilanuk lok'el skotol xi la ti mu sonso vinik ˀune.

34 ˀaaa . . . pere k'uchaˀal la vuch'ta lok'el ˀun xi la ti ˀantze.
la jvuch'ta ˀun bi.
yuˀun ch'ay ta koˀnton xi la ti mu sonso vinike.

35 jech la ti sveˀelik ˀune pas la ta vov.
veno tekeˀ ˀun chaˀe.
jlakantik yan xi la ti ˀantz ˀune.

36 lakano xi la ti mu vinike.
vaˀun taˀaj la ti sveˀelik ˀune,
veˀkutik ˀun chaˀe xi la ti ˀantz ne.

37 k'alal la nojik ti vinike xchiˀuk yajnil ˀune.
vaykutik ˀun xi la ti ˀantz ˀune.

38 vaˀun jech la ti mu sonso vinik ˀune.
ta la xak' yaˀi la ˀat ˀun.

39 vaˀun jech la ti mu sonso vinik ˀune.
bat ta spik ti yajnil ˀune.

40 jech la ti yajnil ne.
pas la ta chitom.

Presently the woman returned from taking her sweat bath. 32
"Is our food cooked?" asked the woman.

"It is cooked. 33
But all of it flew out of the pot," said the wretched, stupid man.

"Ah, but why did you blow on it?" said the woman. 34
"I blew on it.
I forgot," said the wretched, stupid man.

Thus their food turned to flies.[8] 35
"Well, never mind.
Let's cook something else," said the woman.

"You cook it this time," said the man. 36
Soon their food was done,
And the woman announced: "Let's eat."

When the man and his wife had eaten their fill, the woman spoke. 37
"Let's go to bed," suggested the woman.

So it was that the wretched, foolish man succumbed. 38
For he felt like having sex.

So the wretched, stupid man proceeded. 39
He cuddled up and touched his wife.

His wife responded this way: 40
She turned into a sow.

41 buy ˀot kajnil xi la ti mu sonso vinik ˀune.
ˀi laj la snob la sk'ok',
jaˀ to la yil puru la bak.

42 jech la ti mu sonso vinik ˀune xiˀ la tajmek.
jatav la talel ta sna ti mu sonso vinike.

43 vulbat me meˀ xi la ti mu vinike.
laˀ me kol.
mi la tal.

44 li sut talel xi la ti smeˀ ti mu vinike.
ˀi xˀok' xa la tajmek ti mu sonso vinike.

45 te la jkil maˀ ti kajnile xi la ti mu vinike.
mi ta la vil ˀun kol xi la ti smeˀ ti mu vinike.

"Where are you, woman?" asked the wretched, stupid man. 41
He then stirred the fire to life,
And it was then that he saw that she was nothing but bones.

With that, the poor, stupid man became very frightened.[9] 42
The poor, stupid man fled all the way to his home on earth.

"I am back, Mother," said the man. 43
"Come, my son.
Have you returned?" she asked.

"I have returned," the wretched man said to his mother. 44
And then the poor, wretched man began to cry and cry.

"I saw my wife there," said the wretched man. 45
"Did you see her, Son?" asked the wretched man's mother.

FIGURE 47

"Where are you, woman?" asked the wretched, stupid man.
He then stirred the fire to life,
And it was then that he saw she was nothing but bones.

46 te la jkil tajmek.
joˀoj la jkil xa ti kajnile xi la ti mu sonso vinike.

47 jech la me ti mu vinik ˀune.
ˀipaj la me ˀun.

48 te k'alal maˀ liˀ ne ta xicham.
toj kux tajmek ti jole xi la ti mu vinike.

49 ta xa xicham maˀ liˀe.
mu xa xak'elikun.
ta xa xicham xi la ti mu vinike.

50 ˀa ti mu vinik ˀune cham la ˀun.

51 jech la ti smeˀ ti mu sonso vinik ˀeke.
tekeˀ,
cham ti kole.
xicham ˀek xi la ti mu ˀantz ˀeke.

52 jech la ti smeˀ ti mu vinike.
k'alal cham ti yole ta la xˀok' tajmek.

"I really saw her! 46
I actually saw my wife!" said the foolish man.

And this is what happened to the wretched man. 47
He got sick.

"It's no use. Now I am dying. 48
My head aches so that I can hardly stand it," said the wretched man.

"Now I am going to die. 49
Don't take care of me any more.
Now I am done for," said the wretched man.

And with that, the ill-fated man indeed died. 50

Then it happened that the mother of the poor, foolish man spoke: 51
"What is to be done?
My son is dead.
Now I might as well die, too," said the poor woman.

And with that spoken, the mother of the wretched man consoled herself. 52
When her son died she wept bitterly.

1 jun kuento ta voˀnee.
ˀoy jun vinik ta sloˀilaj ta k'ixin ˀosil ti vinike.

2 ti k'alal lik sloˀile yuˀun ˀo te luchul mu tararan ta ba ton.
ˀentonse lik yal sloˀil ti vinike.

3 ˀa li mu tararane ˀa ti voˀne lae kirsano toˀox.
la spas ta ta mu tararane xi ti ˀanima jmuk'tote.

4 xi ti vinike.
jaˀ jech la jyalbun kaˀi sloˀil ti ˀanima jmuk'tote xi ti vinike.

TEXT 31

Why the Damned Buzzard Has a Red Neck

Manuel López Calixto

This is a story of long ago. 1
There was a man who told it in Hot Country.

When he began to tell this story there was a disgusting buzzard 2
that was perched there on top of a rock.
That was what got his story started.

"'The damned buzzard was still a person long ago. 3
He turned into a damned buzzard,' said my late grandfather."

So the man spoke. 4
"That is what my late grandfather told me in his story," said the man.

FIGURE 48

"'The damned buzzard was still a person long ago.
He turned into a damned buzzard,' said my late grandfather."

5 ˀa ti ˀantivo kirsano lae
ti k'alal ta xbat ta chobe mu la sk'an xchaˀbaj.

6 ti vinik lae k'alal la k'ot ta yabtele:
ta la xk'ot spuch'an sba ta yolon teˀ.

7 ˀentonse te la tal ti mu xuleme.
te la me xvilet tal ta vinajel.

8 k'alal la xvilet tal yile ˀentonse lik la sk'opon ti xuleme:
mi xak'an yalan talel xˀut la ti mu xuleme.

9 ˀentonse jlikel la me yal talel ta ˀora ti mu xulem lae.
jaˀ to la me yil te la me kotol.
k'ot ta stz'el ti vinike.

"This is about one of the ancient people." 5
When he went to the cornfield he didn't feel like doing his hoeing.

He would do this upon reaching his cornfield: 6
He would stretch out on his back in the shade of a tree.

Soon a wretched buzzard appeared.[1] 7
He came swooping down from the sky.

When he saw the buzzard come swooping down, the man spoke to him: 8
'Why don't you land here?' he suggested to the damned buzzard.

Then the damned buzzard swooped down at once. 9
The man saw him standing there.
He landed close to the man.

FIGURE 49

Soon a wretched buzzard appeared.
He came swooping down from the sky.

10 ˀentonse lik la k'opojuk:
k'usi chaval xi la k'otel ti xuleme.

11 ˀa mi xak'ane laˀ jel jk'uˀtik xi la ti vinike.
veno mi jech xavale.
laˀ jeltik chaˀe xi la ti mu xuleme.
veno jeltik chaˀe xi la ti vinike.

12 ˀentonse k'alal la ta xloˀilajike jaˀ ˀo la me jelta ti sk'uˀe.
ti k'alal la laj yoˀntonik ta loˀile jaˀ to la me yaˀi ti vinike ˀoy xa la sk'uk'umal.
jech la ti xuleme jaˀ la pas ta vinik.

13 ˀentonse laj xa me jeltik ti jk'uˀtik ne.
xˀut la sbaik xchiˀuk vinik ti xuleme.

14 k'alal chasaˀ ˀaveˀele jaˀ chak'el ti bu ta xlok' ti ch'aˀile xi la ti xuleme.
ˀentonse la la xch'un ti vinike.

15 lek xa la xaˀi ti k'alal jelta ti sk'uˀe.
xvilet xa la likel ti vinike xuleme.

16 jech la ti xulem toˀoxe jaˀ la pas ta vinik ne.
lek xa la xaˀi ˀek ti k'alal pas ta vinike.

17 jlikel ta chabaj ta ˀora ti xulem la ˀeke.
ˀentonse k'alal la laj ti xchobe bat ta na ti vinik xulem lae.

18 k'alal la k'ot ta nae ta la sk'elat tajmek,
yuˀun ˀoy to la jutuk sk'uk'umal sjol yakan.
jech'o la xal ti yoˀ la ta sk'elat te.

19 ˀentonse lik la jak'batuk:
k'uchaˀal ˀoy sk'uk'umal ti sjol ˀavakane.

Then the buzzard started to speak: 10
'What's on your mind?' asked the buzzard as he approached.

'What would you say to our changing places with each other?' said the man. 11
'Fine. If you really mean what you say.
Come on! Let's change places,' said the wretched buzzard, obligingly.
'Okay. Let's change places,' replied the man.

Then, as they talked, they changed clothes. 12
When they finished talking, the man could feel that he now
had a coat of feathers.
As for the buzzard, he turned into a man.

'Well, we've done it. We've changed clothes with each other.' 13
That was what the man and the buzzard said to each other.

'When you look for food, just go where the stench rises,' said the buzzard. 14
And the man paid heed to what he said.

He was very happy to have changed places with the buzzard. 15
The man-buzzard quickly flew away.

So, the one who had formerly been a buzzard was now a man. 16
He, too, was happy with the exchange of places now that he
had become a man.

The buzzard started right in to break the soil with his hoe. 17
And when he finished working in the cornfield,
this man-buzzard went home.

When he reached the house, he received a lot of stares, 18
For he still had a few feathers on his knee.
That is why he was the object of such close inspection.

Then his wife asked him the obvious question: 19
'Why do you have feathers on your knee?'

20 ˀentonse lik la yal sloˀil ti xuleme:
pere yalel la jyalbun ti vinike:
mi xak'an laˀ jel k'uˀtik xiyute
xi la ti vinik xuleme.

21 ˀentonse k'alal la sakub ta yok'omale snaˀoj la me talel sna ti vinik lae.
jech la ti yajnile ta la sap spanin ta sob ˀiklumantik.
ti ˀantze jaˀ to la me yil xvilil xa la tal ti mu tararane.

22 luchul la k'ot ta sapob panin.
jaˀ la tal sloˀ ti panine.

23 jech la ti ˀantze,
xiˀ la tajmek ti yajnil toˀox la ti vinik lae.
ˀentonse mu la snaˀ mi smalal toˀox la ti mu tararane.

24 jech la ti ˀantze ˀoy la slakanoj k'ak'al ˀoˀ.
jaˀ la la smalbe ta sjol ti mu tararane.
toj tzajubel la sjol ta k'ak'al ˀoˀ.

25 k'ot la ti mu tararan lae:
ti yoˀ la tal sloˀ ti panine,
yuˀun ta la xviˀnaj.
jech'o la xal tal sloˀ ti tok'on ˀixime,
yuˀun mu la snaˀ saˀel sveˀel ta teˀtik.
jech'o la xal tal sloˀbe spanin ti yajnile,
yuˀun kirsano la ti mu tararane.

26 ti yoˀ la tzoj la sjole.
yuˀun ˀak'bat la k'ak'al ˀoˀ ta sjol ti voˀne lae.

27 jech'o la xal ti yoˀ tzoj ti sjole ˀa li mu tararane.
vinik toˀox la ti voˀnee.
xi ti ˀanima jmuk'tote.
xi ti vinike.

Then the buzzard replied: 20
'The man who spoke to me said this:
'If you'd like to . . . come, let's change clothes,' he suggested to me.
That is what the man who had formerly been a buzzard said.

Then, at dawn on the following day, the buzzard who had 21
formerly been a man felt like coming home.
His wife was rinsing corn very early in the morning.
Suddenly she saw a disgusting buzzard come flying up.

He came and perched where she was rinsing the cooked corn. 22
Indeed, he had come to eat the cooked corn.

As for the woman, 23
She, the one who had been the man's wife, was terrified.
She did not realize that the wretched buzzard was in fact a
transformation of her husband.

Now this woman had some boiling water. 24
She threw it on the head of the wretched buzzard.
With that, his head was scalded by the boiling water.

So it happened that the red-headed buzzard came into being: 25
As for why he came to eat the cooked corn,
It was because he was hungry.
That is why he came to eat the softened kernels of corn,
For he still could not cope with finding his food in the wild.
That's why he came to eat up the corn that his wife had cooked
to make tortillas,
For the wretched buzzard's nature was still partly human.

All of this explains why his head is red, 26
For he had hot water thrown on his head long ago.

'That is why the damned buzzard has a red head. 27
He was once a man long ago.'
That is what my late grandfather told me."
So the man spoke.

28 ˀa ti mu baˀyel kirsanoetike toj chopol toˀox.
la ta la sk'oponik mu xulem.

29 pere yuˀun toj ch'ajik la ta ˀabtel ti mu kirsano lae.
jaˀ la ta sk'an ti mu la bu ta xˀabtejike ti ˀantivo kirsanoe.

30 pere mu jnaˀtik sjay lajunebal xa ˀavil ˀech'.
mu xavil jaˀ ti baˀyel kirsanoetike xi ti vinike.
mu jnaˀtik mi ta k'ixin ˀosil mi ta sikil ˀosil xi.

"The ancient people had no principles at all! 28
Imagine talking to a damned buzzard!

The truth is that these worthless people were very lazy about their work. 29
They didn't want to work.

Who knows how many tens of years ago all of this happened? 30
Don't you see that these were the ancient people?
In fact, we don't even know whether this happened in Cold Country
or Hot Country."[2]

1 ˀoy jun kuento sventa xulem ta voˀnee.
tz'akal kirsanoetik.

2 ˀoy la jun vinik bat la ta chob.
jech la ti vinike.

3 toj ˀep la yoxil ti vinike.
toj ˀep xa la chabaj tajmek,
ˀi taˀ lo xa xaˀi ti ˀabtele.

4 ˀoy la tal la jun xulem ta vinajel.
yalan tal xulem.

5 xˀut ti vinike.
yaˀi la ti xuleme.
yal la talel ti xuleme.

6 k'usi chak'an xi la ti xuleme.
mi xak'an jeltik k'uˀtik xi la ti vinike.
veno jeltik chaˀe xi la ti xuleme.

7 jech la ti vinike muˀyuk la bu yaˀi.
jel ti sk'uˀ ti vinike,
jaˀ to la yaˀi xulem xa la ti vinike.

8 jech la ti vinike likel la vil ta ˀora.
bat la ti vinik ne.

9 vaˀun ti xulem ne ta la kom ˀabtejuk ta yosil ti vinike.
jech ti xuleme te la ta xˀabtej ˀun.

10 vaˀun mal ti k'ak'al ne jech la ti xulem ˀune tal la ta sna ˀun.
k'ot la ta na.

TEXT 32

Of How the Buzzard Got to Be Like He Is

Marián López Calixto

There is a story about how, long ago, the buzzard got to be like he is.[1] 1
It is about the second people, who came after the most ancient ones.

There was a man who went to his cornfield. 2
This is that man's story.

The man had a lot of land. 3
He had already broken a lot of the land for planting,
But now he was sick of working.

There was a buzzard who flew down from the sky. 4
He swooped down to earth.

The man spoke to him. 5
The buzzard listened.
The buzzard came down to him.

"What do you want?" asked the buzzard. 6
"What would you say to changing clothing?" asked the man.
"Okay, let's change, then," said the buzzard.

Well, the man didn't fully realize what he was doing. 7
The man changed clothing with the buzzard,
And, indeed, soon the man felt as though he was a buzzard.

With that, the man promptly flew off. 8
The man departed.

Now, the buzzard stayed in the man's place to work his land. 9
The buzzard continued working there.

Well, in the afternoon the buzzard went to the man's former home. 10
He arrived at the house.

11 li tal xa me xi la xulem ne.
la ˀ me xi la ti ˀantze.

12 mu la snaˀ mi xulem ti smalale.
k'alal la choti ta xila ti xuleme.

13 k'uchaˀal ˀoy stzatzal la ˀavakane xi la ti ˀantze.
yuˀun laj jel k'uˀkutik xchiˀuk ta ˀamalale xi la ti xuleme.

14 ˀaaa . . . xi la ti ˀantze.
jech ti ˀantze ˀixiˀ la tajmek.

15 ˀa ti xuleme loˀilaj la ˀun.
jech ta ˀamalale mu sk'an xˀabtej xi la ti xuleme.
toj ch'aj tajmek ta ˀamalale xi la ti xuleme.
jech'al ˀun laj jelkutik ti jk'uˀkutik ˀune xi la ti xuleme.

16 vaˀun k'alal la sakub sob la lik ti ˀantz.
sap la spanin ti ˀantze.

17 jech la ti ˀantz ne la jyak' la yixim komel ta bin.
ˀoch la ta yut na.
bat la slup la talel yaˀal.

18 k'alal la lok' ta pana ti ˀantze.
jaˀ to la yil te la luchul ta bin ti xuleme.
jech la ti xulem ne jaˀ smalal ti ˀantze.

19 jech la ti ˀantze ˀoch la ta yut na ta ˀora.
ˀo la ta slakanoj k'ak'al ˀoˀ.
ˀistzak la lok'el ta ˀora ˀiyak'be la ˀun.
toj tzajubel la ti sjol ti xulem ne.

20 k'alal la bat ti xulem ne toj tzoj xa la sjol ˀun.
ˀi bat la ˀun.

"I have come," said the buzzard. 11
"Come, then," said the woman.

She did not realize that the one who seemed to be her husband 12
was in fact the buzzard in human clothing.
Then he came and sat down in a chair.

"Why do you have hair on your feet?" asked the woman. 13
"It's because I changed clothes with your husband," said the buzzard.

"Oh, I see," said the woman hesitantly. 14
The woman was indeed very frightened.

The buzzard continued talking. 15
"It seems that your husband did not want to work," said the buzzard.
"Your husband is very lazy," said the buzzard.
"That is why we changed clothing," said the buzzard.

Well, when the first light of dawn showed on the next day, 16
the woman got up.
The woman rinsed and drained her corn.

Then the woman put her corn in the pot and left it outside. 17
Then she went into the house.
She went in to bring water.

Then the woman came back outside. 18
It was then that she saw a buzzard perched there on the pot.
And this buzzard was none other than her husband.

The woman promptly went back into the house. 19
She had some water boiling in there.
She got it, brought it out, and tossed it right on him.
With that, the head of the buzzard turned bright red.

When the buzzard left, his scalded head was very, very red. 20
And so he departed.

21 ja' jech ti vo'nee.
pas ta xulem ti kirsanoe.

22 pero kom 'o 'ech ti xuleme.
ja' yu'un toj tzoj tajmek ti sjole ti xuleme.

23 ja' jech laj 'o ti kuentoe.
toj chopol ti tz'akal kirsanoetike.

That is how it was long ago. 21
This person turned into a buzzard.

And that was the origin of buzzards. 22
And that is why buzzards have red heads.

So the story ends. 23
The people who came after the most ancient ones were very bad indeed.

1 ʔa li voʔne ʔoy toʔox pukuj ta la smilvan.

2 ʔoy la homal jun nail ch'en.
 ʔaʔ la tey ta xlok' talel ti pukuj.

3 ti pukuje mu la x'ak' jelavuk krisano.
 ta be ta la smil ta machita ti pukuj.
 ta smilan krisanoe.

TEXT 33

Of War and Peace with the Chief of Guatemala

Xalik López Setjol

Long ago there lived a demon who was a real killer.[1] 1

There was a narrow gorge with a cave opening on the side. 2
It was there that the Demon Pukuj would appear.

The Demon Pukuj wouldn't let people pass by. 3
There by the road the Demon Pukuj would kill them with his machete.
There he would slay his victims.

FIGURE 50

There was a narrow gorge with a cave opening on the side.
It was there that the Demon Pukuj would appear.

4 yuˀun ta la xbat yak' ta tiˀel ta vatemal.
ti k'alal ˀep xa cham ti krisano.

5 ˀoy la ˀoxib viniketik lek la tzotzik sch'ulel.
batik jk'eltikik k'usi sˀelan ti pukuje xiˀik la ti viniketik.

6 sjak'be la sbaik k'usi xch'ulelik jujun ti viniketike.
ti jun vinike k'ok' la sch'ulele.
ti xchibal vinike sutum ˀik' la sch'ulel.
ti yoxibal vinike sk'ak'ayat la sch'ulel.
koˀol la tzotz sch'ulelik yoxibalik ti viniketik.

7 ˀa la tal sk'el yil k'usi ˀelan ti pukuj la smilvan.
ti k'alal bat sk'elik ti pukuje ti viniketik yich'oj ˀech'el yak'teˀ.

8 k'alal k'otik ti viniketik ti buy ta xlok' talel ti pukuj.
ˀora la lok' tale ti pukuj k'alal k'ot ti viniketik.
xvil xa la tal ti pukuj.

9 pero k'alal ta smilvan ti pukuj ta machita.
pero mu la stae ta machita ti viniketik.

10 ti viniketik ta sak'abe ˀak'teˀ ti pukuj.
pero ˀaˀ la tae ta ˀak'teˀ ti pukuje.

11 pero toj tzotz la ti pukuj.
snaˀ la xvil.
pero muˀyuk la stabik ta machita ti viniketik.

12 ˀaˀ la ta persa ta sta ta ˀak'teˀ ti pukuj ta juˀech'el.
pero ˀora la lubtzaj ti pukuj.
mu xa la toyoluk xvil muyel.

13 ti k'alal lubtzaj ti pukuje yak'be la yepal ti viniketik.
sjisbe ti ˀak'teˀ.
ˀora la cham ti pukuj.

14 k'alal cham ti pukuj ˀisk'oˀbeik la sjol.
yochelik la ta schik'ik' la ti k'ok' ti stzotzil sjol ti pukuj.

He would then carry them off to Guatemala to be eaten. 4
Great numbers of people were perishing in this way.

Now, there lived in Chamula three brothers who had very strong souls.[2] 5
"Let's go see what this demon is like," the brothers said.

The men asked one another what sort of soul each possessed. 6
One brother had fire as his soul.
The second brother had a whirlwind for his soul.
The third man had a wasp for his soul.[3]
The souls of the three men were equally strong.

They finally came to see for themselves what the killer-demon was like. 7
When they went to see the demon, they all carried their staffs.[4]

Soon the brothers came to the place where the demon was known to appear. 8
He came out at once when the men arrived.
The demon came leaping out at them.

But when the demon tried to kill them with his machete, 9
He could not strike the men with his machete.

The men struck at the demon with their staffs. 10
And their staffs hit the demon.

But the demon was incredibly strong. 11
He would fly and swoop about.
But he could not touch the men with his machete.

Each time, without fail, the blows of the staffs fell upon the demon. 12
And soon the demon grew tired.
He could no longer swoop out of the way.

Just as soon as the demon grew tired, the brothers overwhelmed him with blows. 13
They dashed him to pieces with their staffs.
In no time, the demon fell.

As soon as he died, they bashed in the demon's head. 14
They proceeded to burn the fur off the demon's head in the fire.

15 ti k'alal laj xchik'ik ta k'ok' ti pukuj,
yochelik la ta snopel buy ta xak'ik ti pukuj.

16 ˀaˀ la ti bankilal vinik:
ˀochkutik ˀech'el li buy lok' talel pukuj xi la.
bat jk'eltikik mi ˀoy to yan pukuj tey tik'il ta yut ch'en xi la ti bankilal vinik.

17 xuˀuk xi la ti chib ˀitz'inal.
ˀora la ˀochik ˀech'el ta yut ch'en ti viniketik.

18 ch'abal xa la staik pukuj ta yut ch'en ti viniketike.
ˀaˀ xa noˀox la ˀoy te staik bolom xchiˀuk ˀok'il ta yut ch'en.

19 ti bolom mu la snaˀ k'usi xˀal.
xchiˀuk ti ˀok'il mu la snaˀ k'usi xˀal.

20 muˀyuk la smilik.
tey la laj skomtzanik ti viniketik.

21 xanavik ˀech'ele ta yut ch'en.
pere mu la jaluk.
k'otik la ta jun likel.
ti k'alal k'otike tuk la sna ˀajvalil.

22 lital ta lumal xˀutik la ti ˀajvalil ta vatemal.
k'usi tal ˀasaˀ xi la ti ˀajvalil ta vatemal.

23 yuˀun ta kak' k'usi liˀ.
mi xtun ˀavuˀun xi la ti viniketik.

24 buy laj ˀata xi la ti ˀajvalil ta vatemal.
teye la jnup ta be xi la ti viniketik.

25 buy beel laj ˀanup xi la ti ˀajvalil ta vatemal.
tey la jnup ta jun muk'ta be xi la ti viniketik.

26 pere ˀaˀ jmuchachu laj ˀamilbun xi la ti ˀajvalil ta vatemal.
muˀyuk jmil ˀamuchachu xi la ti viniketik.

When they finished burning the demon, 15
They consulted about where they were going to dump
the demon's corpse.

The oldest brother spoke: 16
"Let's go into the place where the demon came out.
Let's go see if there are still other demons inside the cave,"
said the oldest brother.

"All right," said the two younger brothers. 17
And in no time at all the men went into the cave.

However, they did not find any more demons inside the cave. 18
All they found were a jaguar and coyote inside the cave.

However, the jaguar could not assist them in their quest. 19
Neither did the coyote know anything about it.[5]

So, they did not kill them. 20
The brothers just left them there.

They walked deep into the cave. 21
But not for long.
Soon they got to where they were going.
They came right to the home of the chief.

"We have come to your country," they said to the chief of Guatemala. 22
"What are you seeking?" asked the chief of Guatemala.

"We have come to deliver something here. 23
It may be of interest to you," said the brothers.

"Where did you find it?" asked the chief of Guatemala. 24
"We found it there in the road," said the brothers.

"On what road did you find it?" asked the chief of Guatemala. 25
"We found it there on the main road," said brothers.

But it is my boy whom you have killed," said the chief of Guatemala.[6] 26
"We didn't kill your boy," said the brothers

27 ˀaˀ jmuchachu ˀuˀun xkojtikinbe sat ti jmuchachue xi la ti ˀajvalil ta vatemal.
mi ˀaˀ amuchachu k'usi ta xavalbun xi la ti viniketik.

28 te jchukot xi la ti ˀajvalil ta vatemal.
Chukun xi la ti viniketik.
oˀot ventaot k'usi ta xanop xi la ti viniketik.

29 persa ta jchukot xi la ti ˀajvalil ta vatemala.
xuˀuk xi la ti viniketik.

30 ti k'alal ˀoch ta chukel ti viniketike.
pero mu la jaluk.
ˀora la lok' la stuk.

31 ti k'alal lok' ta chukel ti viniketike.
bat la xanavikuk ta tiˀ kavilto.
bat la xanavikuk ta ch'ivit.

32 pero toj lek la kontento yoˀontonik xchiˀuk svobik ti ˀoxib viniketike.
pero koˀol la xcholetik ta xanavik.

33 pere k'alal ˀilat yuˀun ti ˀajvalil ta vatemal:
k'uxi lok' ti viniketik xi la ti ˀajvalil.

34 pero ˀora la ˀistik' ta chukel jun velta.
k'alal ˀoch ta chukel ta xchibal velta ti viniketik tey xa la ˀoy soltaroe.

35 ta xchabivan ti soltaroe.
muˀyuk la xˀilik k'uxi lok' ta chukinab ti viniketik.
ti k'alal yilike ta xa la xanav ta ch'ivit ti viniketike.

36 ti ˀajvalil ta vatemala mu la snaˀ mi lok'em xa ta chukel ti viniketik;
k'alal yilike ta ch'ivit xa la ta xanavik yoxibalik.

"Why, it *is* my boy, for I recognize his face," said the chief of Guatemala. 27
"If it is your boy, what of it?" replied the brothers.

"I am going to take you as prisoners," declared the chief of Guatemala. 28
"Capture us, then," said the brothers.
"Do as you see fit," said the brothers.

"I must take you as prisoners," said the chief of Guatemala. 29
"All right, then," said the brothers.

Then the men entered prison. 30
But not for long!
In no time at all, they succeeded in setting themselves free.

Once the men were out of prison, 31
They marched without fear in front of city hall.
They paraded through the central plaza.

The three brothers were really quite happy as they strolled with their guitars.[7] 32
They strolled along, single file.

But when the chief of Guatemala spotted them, he spoke: 33
"How did those men escape?" he exclaimed.

He immediately put them in prison once again. 34
This time there were guards to tend them where they were
imprisoned for the second time.

The soldiers kept watch over them. 35
But they did not see how the men escaped from prison.
They simply saw the men strolling once again around the plaza.

As for the chief of Guatemala, he did not realize that the men 36
had escaped from prison, either;
Not until he and his men saw the three of them walking fearlessly
around the plaza.

37 ti k'alal yilik mu stak' chukel ti viniketik.
stzob la sbaik stekel k'u yepal ti jvatemaletik.
sk'el yilik k'usi ˀelan ti viniketik mu stak' chukel.

38 ti k'alal tzobol xa stekel svinik ti ˀajvalil ta vatemal:
k'el ˀavilik ˀoy liˀ ˀoxib vinik.
ˀaˀ laj smil ti jmuchachu xi la ti ˀajvalil.
pere mu stak' chukel xi la ti ˀajvalil ta vatemal.

39 k'usi ta xavalbun xi la ti viniketik.
muˀyuk k'usi la xkal xi la li ˀajvalil ta vatemal.
ˀaˀ noˀox ta jchukot xi la ti ˀajvalil.
xuˀuk xi la ti viniketik.

40 ˀoch la ta chukel ti viniketik.
pero muˀyuk la xˀilik k'uxi lok' ta chukel ti viniketik.

41 k'alal yilike jun ˀo xa la kaya.
xcholetik lok'el talel xchiˀuk svobik.

42 k'alal kuch yuˀun ˀoxib velta chukel ti viniketik ˀaˀ xa la baˀyel k'opoj:
mi ta xˀavat ˀavoˀonton cham ˀamuchachu xi la ti vinik.
ta xkat koˀonton xi la ti ˀajvalil ta vatemal.

43 ta xˀavat ˀavoˀonton ke ta xaval ˀuˀun laj jmil ˀamuchachu xi la ti viniketik.
ˀaˀ lek milun xi la ti viniketik.

44 pere mu ta tuk'uk ta xamilun xi la ti viniketik.
ta xatzob ˀasiˀik.
ta k'ok' ta xik'ak'.
ˀaˀ to ta xicham xi la ti viniketik.

Soon it became evident that the men could not be kept in prison. 37
All the Guatemalans assembled.
They were perplexed about why they were unable to
hold the men as prisoners.

And when the Guatemalan chief's men were all assembled, he spoke: 38
"Listen well, all of you. We've got these three men here.
They are the ones who killed my boy," said the chief.
"But we don't seem to be able to hold them captive,"
said the chief of Guatemala.

"What have you to say to us?" asked the brothers. 39
"I have nothing to say to you.
Only be assured that I shall hold you as prisoners," said the chief.
"So be it," said the brothers.

So the brothers landed in prison once again. 40
But their captors did not see how the brothers managed to
escape yet again.

When they saw them, they were already in the street again. 41
They were strolling along, single file, playing their guitars.

After the brothers had endured imprisonment three times, 42
the first brother spoke:
"Do you mourn the death of your boy?" asked the brother.
"Yes, I am sad," said the chief of Guatemala.

"Perhaps you are sad for you think we killed your boy?" said the brothers, 43
speaking together.
"Better, then, for you to kill us," said the brothers.

"Don't bother with shootings," said the brothers. 44
"You should gather wood for a fire.
We shall burn," said the brothers.
"That is how we shall die," said the brothers.

45 xuˀuk xi la ti ˀajvalil ta vatemal.
ora la ˀistzob siˀik.
ti k'alal laj stzob siˀik ti jvatemaletik skuxet xa la yoˀntonik.

46 k'alal yil tzobol xa siˀ ti viniketik:
xuˀ xa xicham xi la.
xuˀuk xi la ti ˀajvalil ta vatemal.

47 bitziik la ta lumtik ti viniketike.
k'alal bitziik ta lumtik ti viniketike yak'beik la siˀ ta sba.

48 k'alal laj yak'beik siˀ ta sba ti viniketik,
yak'beik sk'ak'al xchiˀuk kasolina k'uchaˀal stzan ti k'ok'.

49 ti k'alal ta xa stzan ti k'ok'.
tey xa la tzobol stekel ti k'uyepalik ti jvatemal.
ta sk'el yilik ti k'usi ˀelan ta xcham ti ˀoxib viniketik.

50 ti k'alal tzan ti k'ok' muˀyuk la sk'ak' ti viniketike.
ˀaˀ noˀox la k'ajomal tzaub ta k'ok'.

51 ti k'alal ta xa sikub ti k'ok' tey la vitzajtik kom ti viniketik.
k'alal sikub ti k'ok' ta la ˀoxib tzajakil kotz.
ta la stam k'aˀep ti k'ok'.

52 k'alal syakel ta stam k'aˀep ti kotze.
pere mu la snaˀ ti ˀajvalil ta vatemala mi ˀaˀ k'ataj ta kotz ti viniketik.
ti k'alal syakel ta stam k'aˀep ti ˀoxib kotzetike.

53 pero ti k'alal laj stam k'aˀep ti kotz.
ˀora la vaˀi ti viniketik.

54 ti k'alal vaˀi ti viniketike,
ˀora la cham stekel svinik ti ˀajvalil ta vatemal.

"All right," agreed the chief of Guatemala. 45
And at once they gathered the firewood.
When they had finished gathering the firewood, the Guatemalans were feeling quite happy.

When the brothers saw them gathering the firewood, they spoke: 46
"Now it is time for us to die," said the brothers.
"Very well," said the chief of Guatemala.

They laid the brothers down on the ground. 47
When the brothers were lying on the ground, they piled wood on top of them.

When they had piled the wood on top of the brothers, 48
They lit the fire with gasoline so that it would be sure to burn well.

Then the fire was started. 49
Everyone in Guatemala was there.
They were going to watch the three brothers burn to death.

When the fire was lit, it did not burn the brothers up. 50
They just turned red, illuminated in the glow of the coals.

As the fire died down, the brothers just remained there, piled together. 51
When the fire was dead, three red roosters appeared.
They were pecking around in the remains of the fire.

The roosters just kept pecking in the remains of the fire. 52
But the chief of Guatemala did not realize that the brothers had turned into roosters.
It seemed to him that they were just three roosters pecking gently in the remains of the fire.

Finally, the roosters stopped pecking around in the rubbish. 53
They rose up once more as men.

When these men rose to their full height, 54
It was then that all of the Guatemalan chief's men suddenly died.[8]

55 ti k'alal cham stekel svinik ti ˀajvalil,
ˀora la k'opoj ti viniketik.

56 mi ta toˀox xavilbajinun jun velta xi la ti viniketik.
moˀoj xa xi la ti ˀajvalil ta vatemal.

57 mi ta xavilbajinune ta jmilot ta ˀora xi la ti viniketik.
mu xamilun xi la ti ˀajvalil ta vatemal.

58 muˀyuk ta jmilot mi mu xa xapas ˀech jun velta.
xamilbun ti jvinik xi la ti viniketik.
muˀyuk xa ta jmil ˀavinik xi la ti viniketik.

59 ˀa li ˀuˀune mu jk'an xavilbajinun xi la ti viniketik.
xkuch kuˀun stekel k'usi xak'an xapas xi la ti viniketik.
muˀyuk xa ta xkilbajinot xi la ti ˀajvalil ta vatemal.

60 ti k'alal ta sloˀilajik ti ˀajvalil ta vatemal xchiˀuk li ˀoxib viniketik.
pero stuktuk xa kuxul ti ˀajvalil.

61 ti svinike chamem xa,
stekel svinik ti ˀajvalil.

62 ti k'alal stuk xa kuxul ti ˀajvalil ta vatemal.
ta xa la xˀat ˀoˀnton ti ˀajvalil ta vatemal.

63 ta jkuxajes ˀavinik mi muˀyuk xa ta xbat ˀamilbun jvinik xi la ti ˀoxib viniketik.
ˀavokoluk kuxajesbun ti jvinike.
ta jtojot k'u yepal ta xak'an ˀatojot xi la ti ˀajvalil ta vatemal.

64 muˀyuk xa ta xbat jmil ˀavinik xi la ti ˀajvalil ta vatemal.
xuˀ ˀechuk xi la ti ˀoxib viniketik.
ˀora la ˀiskuxajes soltaro xchiˀuk viniketik.

Once all of the chief's men had perished. 55
The brothers lost no time in speaking.

"Well now, do you plan to keep on harrassing us?" asked the brothers. 56
"Never again," said the chief of Guatemala.

"If you keep on tormenting us, we will kill you at once," said the brothers. 57
"Don't kill me," said the chief of Guatemala.

"We won't kill you if you promise not to repeat what you have done. 58
You have killed our people," said the brothers.
"I will never kill your people again," said the chief of Guatemala.

"We don't want you to threaten us ever again," insisted the brothers. 59
"For we will defeat you in anything you try to do to us," said the brothers.
"I won't bother you any longer," said the chief of Guatemala.

That was the substance of the chief of Guatemala's conversation 60
with the three brothers.
Indeed, the chief was the only one of his countrymen who was still alive.

His men had already died, 61
Each and every one of the chief's men.

Now the chief of Guatemala was the only survivor. 62
No wonder that the chief of Guatemala found himself with a heavy heart!

"We will bring your people back to life if you promise not to kill 63
our people any longer," said the three brothers.
"Please, restore my people to me.
I will pay you as much as you wish," said the chief of Guatemala.

"I won't attack your people ever again," promised the chief of Guatemala. 64
"All right, then," said the three brothers.
And at once, they brought his soldiers and his people back to life.

65 ti k'alal kuxaj ti soltaro xchiˀuk k'u yepal gente:
pero ta jpastik lek ˀun.
ti lital jmeltzan ti k'op ta vatemal xi la ti viniketik.
xuˀuk xi la ti ˀajvalil ta vatemal.

66 laj la stzakik ta ˀun ti muˀyuk xcham ta chukel ta k'ok' ti viniketik.
ˀaˀ lah stzakik ta ˀun ti snaˀ skuxaje krisano ti ˀoxib viniketik.
laj stzakik ta ˀun ti mu stak' chukel ti ˀoxib viniketik.
laj stzakik ta ˀun mu k'usi snaˀ spas ti viniketik.
laj stzakik ta ˀun ti kataj ta kotz ti viniketik.
laj stzakik ta ˀun ti k'aˀep laj stam ti kotz.
laj stzakik ta ˀun ti k'aˀep cham ˀo ti krisano ta vatemal.

67 k'alal laj smeltzanik ti ˀun:
k'u yepal ta xak'an ˀatojol xi la ti ˀajvalil ta vatemal.

68 muˀyuk ta jk'an jtojol xi la ti viniketik.
muˀyuk k'usi xtun kuˀun tak'in xi la ti viniketik.

69 k'alal ˀul ta sna ti viniketik.
muˀyuk xa la sjalij ta sna.

70 ˀaˀ xa noˀox la ˀech yal ti k'usitikuk laj spasanan.
ti buy k'alal xanav.

71 k'alal la jyal ti k'usitik laj spas,
bat la ta yibel vinajel.

72 pero mu xa snaˀ xcham ti ˀoxib viniketik.
batemik ta yibel vinajel.

When his soldiers and who knows how many people were revived, 65
the brothers spoke:
"Let us make a treaty.
That was our purpose in coming to Guatemala in the first place,"
declared the brothers.
"All right," agreed the chief of Guatemala.

So, they wrote on the paper that neither fire nor prison could bring 66
death to these men.
They wrote on the paper that these three brothers knew how to
revive people from the dead.
They wrote on the paper that these three brothers could not be
imprisoned.
They wrote on the paper that these brothers could do no evil.
They wrote on the paper that these brothers had turned into roosters.
They wrote on the paper of how the roosters had pecked around
in the remains of the fire.
They wrote on the paper that the people of Guatemala had died
from the magical power of the rubbish of the fire.[9]

Once they had prepared this treaty, the chief of Guatemala spoke: 67
"How much do you wish me to pay you?" inquired the chief
of Guatemala.

"We don't want any payment," the brothers replied. 68
"Money is of no use to us," said the brothers.[10]

Whereupon, the brothers went home. 69
But they did not linger long at home.

They simply stopped to report their many adventures, 70
Those things that had happened during their wanderings.

Once they had told of what they had done, 71
They went to dwell at the edge of heaven.[11]

These three brothers had now become immortal.[12] 72
They have gone to dwell at the edge of heaven.

73 k'alal mi sta yan leto ti bak'ine ta sut talel ti ʔoxib viniketik.
batemik ta yibel vinajele.

74 ta xtal skolta ti chamula ti viniketik.
batemik ta yibel vinajele.

75 chamula.
ʔa li voʔne ʔoy toʔox lek tzotz ti chamula.
ta ʔorae mu xa jnaʔtik mi ʔoy tzotz ti chamula.

If in the future another war comes, these three brothers will return. 73
They have gone to dwell at the edge of heaven.

Certainly, these three brothers will come back to help the Chamulas. 74
For they have gone to dwell at the edge of heaven.

These are Chamulas. 75
In time past, Chamulas were still good and strong.
In our time, it is no longer so clear that the Chamulas are strong.

1 ˀoy jun kuento sventa xinlan xchiˀuk stz'iˀ.
ˀa ti ˀantz lae k'alal la tal la ti ˀoˀe yuˀun ta la xnoj ta ˀoˀ.

2 vaˀun jech la ti ˀantz la ˀune:
ta xa xijchamotik xi la ti ˀantze.

3 vaˀun jech ti kirsano la ˀune:
veno te k'alal.
ta xijchamotik xi la ti ˀantivoetike.

4 vaˀun ˀik'ub la tajmek ti vinajele,
tal la ti toke,
vaˀun tal la tajmek ti ˀoˀ ˀune.

5 voˀlajuneb la k'ak'al la yak' ti voˀe.
pero tzotz tajmek ti ˀoˀe.

6 vaˀun k'alal xa la ta xa xyal talel ti voˀ ˀune,
vaˀun k'opoj la jun jtotik ta ba tok.

7 pere mu xˀilik ti k'usi la ta xˀok'e.
vaˀun ˀisk'elik la tajmek.

8 pere bu taje jesus xi la sk'elik la ti vinajele.
ˀi mu la xvinaj ti k'u la xi ta xk'opoj lae.

9 k'elo me ˀabaik.
ta xa me xachamik.
kokorin kokorin kokorin xi la ti jtotik la ta tok ˀune.

10 jech la ti kirsanoe ta la xjatavik la ta yok teˀ.
ta yut ch'en ti ˀantivoe.

TEXT 34
On the Origin and Nature of Ladinos

Marián López Calixto

This is a story about a Ladino woman and her dog. 1
This woman was about to drown when the great flood came.[1]

This is what happened: 2
"Soon we will all die!" the woman exclaimed.

And this is what the people said: 3
"Well, what's to be done about it?
Our time has come to die," the ancient ones declared.

Then the heavens darkened, 4
The clouds gathered,
And the great deluge began.

It rained for fifteen days. 5
It rained very hard.

Then, in the midst of the great deluge, 6
The voice of a god spoke from above the clouds.

But they could not see what it was that seemed to be crying out at them. 7
Desperately, they looked about.

"Where is that coming from, in the name of Jesus?" they said as they gazed at the sky.[2] 8
But they could not make out who it was that spoke.

"Watch out! 9
You are now going to die.
Kokorín! Kokorín! Kokorín!" said the voice of the god from the clouds.[3]

Some people ran to seek refuge under the trees. 10
Other ancestors sought shelter in caves.

11 vaʔun laj la skotol ti ʔinyoetike.
k'ajomal xa la kom jun ti xinlan la ʔune.

12 vaʔun k'alal laj la skotol ti ʔantivoetik,
yal la talel ti jtotik la ʔune.
vul la sk'el la mi laj la skotol ti snich'on.

13 ʔi mu la sk'an ta stiʔvan ti snich'on ti jtotik la ʔune.
mu la sk'an ta stiʔ sbaik ti snich'on ti jtotike.

14 vaʔun jech la ti ʔantivoetike chamik la ta ʔoʔ.
yak' ti ʔoʔ jale.

15 vaʔun k'alal la yak' ti ʔoʔ la ʔune,
yal la talel ti jtotike.
tal la sk'el mi laj ti yolike.

16 vaʔun k'alal yal talel ti jtotik ʔune,
jech la ti yol ʔune muʔyuk la bu laj skotolik;
kuxul to la kom jun ti yol ti jtotik ʔune.

17 jech la ti jtotik k'alal la yal la talel la ʔune.
te la sta ti jun xinlan xchiʔuk stz'iʔ ʔune.
te la chotol ta jol vitz ti xinlan xchiʔuk la stz'iʔe.

18 vaʔun jech la ti jtotik la ʔune:
ʔoch la ʔech'el ta ʔoʔ ti jtotike.

19 k'usi chapas liʔe xi la ti jtotike.
muʔyuk yuʔun noj ta ʔoʔ ti banamile xi ti xinlane.

20 k'uxi la kol.
muk' bu xalaj ta ʔoʔ ʔune xi la ti jtotike.

21 muk' bu xilaj.
liʔ li muy talele.

Finally, all the Indians died. 11
There was but one person, a Ladino woman, left.

Then, when all of the ancient ones had perished, 12
Our Father Sun/Christ descended.
He came to see whether all of his children had died.[4]

Our Father did not like their habit of consuming the flesh 13
of their own children.
Our Father did not want his own children to eat one another.

That was why the ancestors died in the flood. 14
He sent a great deluge that seemed never to end.

Then, in the midst of the downpour, 15
Our Father descended.
He came to see if all of his children had indeed perished.

Once Our Father had come down to earth, 16
He noticed that not all of his offspring had died;
One of his children was still alive.

That is what happened when Our Father descended. 17
He found a Ladino woman with her dog.
There they were, sitting at the top of a mountain, this Ladino woman
and her dog.[5]

Our Father did this: 18
Our Father moved through the water so that he stood before her.

"What are you doing here?" asked Our Father. 19
"Nothing, really. It's just that the flood was covering the earth,"
said the Ladino woman.

"How did you save yourself? 20
Aren't you going to drown in the flood?" asked Our Father.

"No, I don't plan to die. 21
I came up here for that reason.

22 jaˀ skuchun talel ti jtz'iˀe.
jaˀ yuˀun liˀ li kom jchˀiuk ti jtz'iˀe xi la ti ˀantze.

23 ˀa veno koman chaˀe.
ta jk'elkik k'usi ta xapas xi la ti jtotike.

24 vaˀun jech la ti xinlan la ˀune.
lik la sk'opon ti stz'iˀe.
k'uxi ta xijbatotik ˀun jtz'iˀ xi la ti ˀantze.

25 jech la ti stz'iˀ ˀune.
k'opoj la ˀune:
mu jnaˀ k'uxi ta xijbatotik xi ti tz'iˀe.

26 vaˀun jech la ti mu tz'iˀ la ˀune.
ta la xtajin tajmek.

27 vaˀun ˀa ti mu ˀantz la ˀune.
stzak la ti smu tz'iˀ la ˀune.
svalk'un la ti stzeke.

28 jech la ti yuni tz'iˀ laˀe.
skakan la ˀochel ta xchak ti mu ˀantze.

29 vaˀun jech la ti stz'iˀ la ˀune.
mu la snaˀ la ta xak' ti ˀate.
jecheˀ la te xˀiˀun ta spas.

30 vaˀun jech la ti mu ˀantz la ˀune.
sk'opon la ti smu tz'iˀ lae.
mi mu xanaˀ xavak' ˀat xˀut la ti smu tz'iˀe.

31 jech la ti tz'iˀe,
mu la xtak'av.
k'ajomal la ta sk'elvane.

32 vaˀun jech la ti mu ˀantz la ˀune ˀa ti smu tz'iˀ la ˀune.
spak'olan la be xchak ti tz'iˀe.

My dog carried me to safety. 22
And here I stayed with my dog," said the woman.

"Good enough. Stay here, then. 23
Let's see what becomes of you," said Our Father.

Now, this is what the Ladino woman did: 24
She began conversing with her dog:
"What is to become of us, my little doggie?" asked the woman.

Now, this is how the dog responded. 25
He spoke:
"I have no idea what is to become of us," replied the dog.

Then the foolish dog did this. 26
He began to frolic about happily.

Then the disgusting woman made her move. 27
She grabbed up her dog.
And she lifted up her skirt.

And this is what happened to her little doggie. 28
She stuck him right up there close to her ass.

But the dog was bewildered. 29
He had no clue how to fuck her.
Frustrated and confused, he stood there whining.

But the disgusting woman continued her efforts. 30
She spoke to the poor, wretched dog.
"Don't you know how to fuck?" she demanded of the poor creature.

It was the dog's turn to respond, 31
But he did not answer.
He just sat there looking around.

Then the disgusting woman forced her poor dog into action. 32
She pressed the dog right up there against her cunt.

33 vaˀun jech la ti tz'iˀ la ˀune k'alal la pak'bat la ti xchake:
lik la me yat ti tz'iˀe.
spak'pun xa la ti chak ti tz'iˀe.

34 vaˀun jech la ti ˀantz la ˀune.
lek me xatik' talel xi la ti mu ˀantze.
veno xi la ti tz'iˀe.

35 jech la ti tz'iˀe:
muˀyuk la bu mas nat ti yat ti tz'iˀ lae.

36 vaˀun jech la ti mu ˀantze la ˀune ti stz'iˀ lae.
snitbe la yat ti stz'iˀe.
toj lok'el la talel sbok ti stz'iˀe.

37 vaˀun jech ti tz'iˀ la ˀune.
k'alal la lok' la mas nat ti yat ti stz'iˀ ˀune.

38 jech la ti stz'iˀe:
xchuk la sba ti yat ti tz'iˀe.

39 vaˀun jech ti mu ˀantz la ˀune.
matz'iˀ la ti yat ti tz'iˀ ta xchak la ti mu ˀantz la ˀune.

40 jech la ti mu ˀantze.
snit la lok'el.
snit la lok'el ti yat ti tz'iˀ ˀune.
vaˀun lok' la yat ti tz'iˀ ˀune.

41 jech la ti tz'iˀe:
sk'el la ti yate.
lok'em xa la ti sboke.
yoˀ la ˀoy sbok ti tz'iˀ la ˀune.

42 vaˀun la ti mu ˀantz la ˀune,
ˀayan la ti yol ˀune.

43 k'alal la vok' ti yole neneˀ jkaxlan la ˀun.
yuˀun la ˀoy ti jkaxlan la ˀune.

Now, this is what happened when she pressed the dog up against her cunt: 33
Sure enough, the dog started to get a hard-on.
And the woman helped him along with little pats on the butt.

So the woman spoke: 34
"Poke it right in," said the disgusting woman.
"All right," said the dog.

But the dog's problem was this: 35
The dog didn't have a cock that was long enough.

So the disgusting woman went to work on the dog. 36
She pulled away at the dog's cock.
And with these efforts, she managed to jerk his knot into place.[6]

Such was the dog's fate. 37
For sure, he ended up with a longer cock.

But worse was in store for the dog: 38
The dog got hopelessly hung up with his knot when he was fucking

The wretched woman was, of course, directly to blame. 39
The dog's dick was stuck there in the disgusting woman's cunt.

The woman finally solved the problem. 40
She pulled away at it.
She struggled to pull the dog's cock out.
Finally, the dog's cock popped out.

The dog did this: 41
He looked at his cock.
He saw that a large knot had now emerged.
That is how dogs came to have cock knots.

As for this wretched woman, 42
She became pregnant.

When she gave birth, she had a little Ladino boy. 43
And that is where Ladinos came from.[7]

44 jech la ti jtotik la ˀune snop la ˀun:
pere k'usi ta xkal liˀ ˀune.
mi ta jpas yan ti jnich'one ˀo mi moˀoj xa xi la ti jtotik.
ˀi snop la lek ti jtotike.

45 veno tekeˀ.
ta jpas yan mi jaˀ to mas leke ta xbat kuˀune xi la ti jtotike.

46 vaˀun spasotik la ˀun.
smeltzanotik la ˀun.

47 veno k'alal la li jmeltzajotike la ˀune,
mu la xijk'opoj la lek.
puru la tzeˀej ta jpastik la ˀun.

48 jech la ti jtotik la ˀune.
bat la saˀ talel la sbek'tal.

49 veno vul la ˀun.
yak'botik la ta ketik ti sbek'tal la ti jtotike.

50 k'alal laj la kich'tik ˀune jaˀ la jam la ti ketike.
ta la xijloˀilaj likel.
ta la xijk'elvan.
ta la xijsanav.
xijtzeˀlaj la likel.

51 jaˀ ta sk'an ti jbek'tal ˀun chaˀe.
xi la ti jtotike.

52 vaˀun k'alal la meltzaj la yuˀun ti yol la ti jtotik la ˀune.
ta la sk'el la ti k'usi la ta spas la ti snich'one.
vaˀun jujun la k'ak'al ta xtal la sk'el ti yol la ˀune.

53 k'alal la ta xk'ot sk'el ti yol la ˀune,
muˀyuk la k'usi ta spas.

With these events in mind, Our Father reflected: 44
"What am I to do?
"Shall I create some other children or do the Ladinos suffice?"
wondered Our Father.
Our Father thought about this very carefully.

"Well, my mind is made up. 45
I will try another round to see if it comes out better," said Our Father.

With that, he made us. 46
He created us.

But, this was what happened once he had created us. 47
We did not talk well.
We did nothing more than laugh.[8]

And this is how Our Father responded. 48
He sought out his own body to give to us.

So he appeared before us. 49
Our Father placed his own body in our mouths.[9]

When we received it, it was as if our mouths opened to allow our 50
true nature to express itself.
We soon found pleasure in speaking with one another.
We gained sight of one another.
We walked.
We soon came to enjoy life and the company of one another.

"So, it seems that they like my body." 51
So said Our Father Sun/Christ.

Then the following came to pass once Our Father had helped 52
his children to become more fully human.
He came to check up on what his children were doing.
Every day he would come to look in on his offspring.

He would come by to check on his children, 53
And usually found them doing nothing wrong.[10]

54 tal noˀox la jten ti jtotik la ˀune.
ch'abal toˀox la k'usi ta spas ti snich'on la ˀune.
nopol toˀox la ta xˀech' ti jtotike.

55 vaˀun tal la ti slajeb la jten ti jtotik la ˀune.
nom xa la ˀech' ti jtotik la ˀune.
yuˀun xa la stzak xa la sbaik la ti yol la ˀune.

56 chopol xa la ti snich'one.
mu xa la sk'an la xˀech' ti jtotik la ˀune.

57 ta nom xa ta xˀech' ti jtotike.
mu xa la sk'an snopolik ti jtotike.

58 jech la ti jtotik xa la ˀune:
k'unk'untik xa la bat ta vinajel ti jtotik.

59 vaˀun tal to ta slajeb ti jtotike.
ta nom xa la tajmek la ta sk'elvan la talel ti jtotike.

60 vaˀun tal xa la ta slajeb xa la tajmek.
tal ti jtotik xa la ˀune.
ta vinajel xa la ˀoy ti jtotike.

61 jaˀ to vi tana ˀune.
te ˀoy ta vinajel ˀun.

62 k'alal la kom xa la yuˀun la ˀune:
ˀoy xa la jkaxlan,
ˀoy sa la ˀinyo.

63 chib la kom jkaxlan.
chib la kom ˀinyo.

64 vaˀun naka tzaj xa la li jbolotik la ˀune.
ˀi parte la spasoj la ti sak la ti sbek'tal ti yalab snich'nab la ˀune.

Then once again Our Father came by. 54
And once again he found his children doing nothing unseemly.
In those days Our Father passed by very close to us and to the earth.

Then, Our Father passed by one last time. 55
This time Our Father Sun/Christ passed by and observed them
at some distance.[11]
For now his children were having sex.

His children now had the knowledge of evil. 56
Our Father no longer wished to come close to us.[12]

Our Father now passes by only at a distance. 57
Our Father no longer wished to come close to us.

So it was that Our Father did this: 58
Slowly, Our Father withdrew his presence from the earth
and went to the sky.

That is how Our Father acquired the custom of letting us know 59
his presence from the very edge of heaven.
It is now from this great distance that Our Father watches over us.

His radiance now comes from the very edge of heaven.[13] 60
Our Father's presence now shines from there.
Our Father is now in heaven.

So it is today. 61
There he is in the sky.

This is how things remained according to his will: 62
That there are Ladinos.
That there are Indians.

Two Ladinos remained. 63
Two Indians remained.

Slowly, we who are Indians began to multiply. 64
And apart from us, those of his children, his offspring, who have
white bodies, they too began to multiply.

65 jun la yoˀnton la muy ta vinajel ti jtotike.
bat la ˀun,
yal la komel ti smantale:

66 pere mu xatiˀ ˀabaik ˀun xi la ti jtotike.
ˀey xijxiotik la ˀek ˀun.

67 ˀi voˀotik laj la jch'untik ti mantal.
muˀyuk la ta jtiˀ jbatik.
lek la ta xijloˀilajotik.

68 vaˀun jech la ti jkaxlan la ˀune:
ta la sk'oponvan.
k'alal ta la sk'oponvan ti jkaxlane mu la xkaˀitik.

69 jech la ti jkaxlan la ˀeke.
ta la sk'oponat la ta sak sbek'tal la ˀeke,
mu la xaˀik ˀek.

70 jaˀ noˀox la ta xijtzeˀinotike.
ˀi mu la xkaˀbe jbatik ti k'optike.
ˀi jaˀ la ta sk'an ti jtotike.

71 laj ˀo ti kuentoe.

Our Father was happy with the state of the world. 65
He departed forever,
And he left these orders:

"Now, don't eat one another," said Our Father.[14] 66
"Very well," we said in reply.

We have heeded that order. 67
We do not eat one another.
We speak to one another with respect.

As for the Ladinos, it is not so clear: 68
Men and women speak suggestively to each other.
When they speak in this disrespectful manner, we don't understand why they do this.[15]

It may be the same for the Ladinos. 69
When those with white bodies hear us speak,
They don't understand our manner of speaking either.

We just laugh, all of us. 70
We do not understand each other's language.
That is how Our Father wished it to be.[16]

So the story ends. 71

The Third Creation

3

1 lo'il yu'un yoxlamal kirsano.

2 veno ti yoxlamal kirsanoe 'ach'el la laj la spat ti jtotike.
laj la yak'be sk'ob yok sat.
va'i 'un pas la ta kirsano ti 'ach'ele.

3 'entonse ti 'ach'ele 'a' la toj lek sna' spas k'in.
'a' la toj lek sna x'ak'otajik.
'a' la toj lek sna' x'abtej.

TEXT 35

Of the Third People

Mateo Méndez Tzotzek

This is a story about the Third People: 1

Now, Our Father Sun/Christ made these people of the Third Creation 2
from clay.
He put on the hands, the feet, the face.
Then the clay turned into a person.

These clay people knew very well how to put on a good fiesta. 3
They knew how to dance very well.
They knew how to work very well.

FIGURE 51

These clay people knew very well how to put on a good fiesta.
They knew how to dance very well.
They knew how to work very well.

4 ˀentonse ti jtotike bat la saˀbe sveˀel.
laj la saˀbe sat toj,
laj la saˀbe sat tulan,
laj la saˀbe momoletik.

5 mu la sk'an sloˀik ti kirsanoe.
pero k'usi ta xkak'be xveˀ xi la ti jtotike.
laj la snop.

6 ˀaˀ lek ta xkak'be jutebuk jbek'tal.
ˀa ver mi sk'an stiˀ xi la ti jtotike.

7 laj la sjos ti sbek'tale.
laj la yak'be ta ye ti kirsanoe.

8 veno ti kirsanoe laj la stiˀ ta ˀora.
batz'i toj mu la yaˀi tajmek ti sbek'tal jtotike.

9 pero ti sat teˀetike mu la sk'an sloˀik.
yan la ti sbek'tal jtotike.
ˀaˀ la toj mu yaˀik tajmek.
ˀech'o la xal li ˀixime sbek'tal la jtotik.

10 ˀentonse ta yoxlamal kirsano lik la ti jtotik ta ch'ulna.
ˀaˀ la ti laj yilik xa ti lek snaˀik spasik k'ine,
lek la snaˀik xˀak'otajik.

11 ˀech'o xal muˀyuk xa bu xcham.
yuˀun la toj lek xa snaˀik sk'oponik ti kirsanoe.

12 ˀentonse ti jtotik ta vinajele laj la yil ti bu xbol ti snich'nabe.
pere k'uchaˀal tajmek ti mu xbolik ti jnich'nabe.

13 ˀaˀ lek ˀak'o taluk li juraxe.
ˀaˀ snaˀ k'uxi spas.
ˀaˀ ta xˀak' ˀiluk xi la ti jtotike.

So Our Father went to find for food for them. 4
For them, he sought pinecones,
For them, he sought acorns,
For them, he sought grass.

The people refused to eat what he offered. 5
"But what shall I give them to eat?" said Our Father Sun/Christ.
He thought about it.

"Why not offer them a little bit of my own body?" thought Our Father. 6
"Let's see if they want to eat that," said Our Father.

So he scraped off a piece of his body. 7
This he placed in the mouths of the people.

Well, the people ate it up at once. 8
Our Father's body tasted delicious to them.

On the other hand, they did not want to eat the fruits and plants of the forest at all. 9
This was not the case with Our Father's body.
It tasted delicious to them.
This is why we speak of corn as being the body of Our Father Sun/Christ.

Then the people of the Third Creation acquired the custom of keeping images of saints in the church. 10
The saints noticed that the people knew how to put on a good fiesta,
That they danced with enthusiasm.

That is why they were not destroyed. 11
The reason was that these people honored the saints with respect.[1]

Then Our Father in Heaven was concerned about whether his children had multiplied. 12
"But how can it be that my children do not multiply?

It would be best if Judas came. 13
He knows how to do it.
He can show them how," said Our Father.[2]

14 vaˀi ˀun ta bat la ti juraxe.
laj la yak' ˀiluk ti k'uxi ta spasik ti kirsanoe.

15 veno ti kirsanoe toj lek la yaˀik.
ˀech la lik spasik.
pero jurax la la jyak' ˀiluk ti yoˀ k'uxi ta xbol ti kirsanoe.

16 ti jtotike laj la yak' ˀasarona ˀek'el machita.
lik la ˀabtejikuk ti kirsanoe ti yoxlamal kirsanoe.

17 lik la spas xchobik pero ti kirsanoe muˀyuk bu ta xˀabtejik.
te la ta xˀabtej stuk ti ˀasaronae ti ˀek'ele ti machitae.
ti vinike te la chotolik.

18 ˀentonse ti ˀanjeletik laj la yilik ti muˀyuk ta xˀabtejik ti viniketike.
mu la sk'an.

19 bat la yalbe ti jtotik ta vinajele.
pero li ˀotike xkaltik chopol li mu xˀabtejik li viniketike.
ˀaˀ noˀox stuk ˀasarona ta xˀabteje.
muˀyuk lek.

20 ˀaˀ lek ˀak'o ˀabtejikuk.
moˀoje mu xask'oponik.

21 ˀaˀ li muˀyuk ta xlubine.
ˀech'o xal mu xask'oponik xi la ti ˀanjeletike.

22 xuˀuk chaˀe.
ˀak'o ˀabtejuk xi la jtotik ta vinajele.
veno ti kirsanoe lik la ˀabtejikuk skotolik.

With that, Judas appeared. 14
He showed them exactly how to reproduce.

Sure enough, the people thought it felt just fine. 15
So they started to have sex.
But it was none other than Judas who showed the people how to increase their numbers.

Our Father gave them hoes, axes, and machetes. 16
And so the Third People also learned how to work.

They began to cultivate their cornfields, but the people themselves did not really work. 17
The hoes, axes, and machetes worked there alone.
The men just sat there.

It was the Earth Lords who noticed that the men were not working. 18
They disapproved of this.

They went to tell Our Father in Heaven. 19
"Look. We think it is very bad that the men do not work.
The hoe simply works there by itself.
That is not right.

It would be better if you made them work. 20
Otherwise they will not pray to you.

The problem is that they will never get tired. 21
That is why they won't want to pray to you," said the Earth Lords.

"Very well. 22
Let's make them work," said Our Father in Heaven.
With that, he ordered the people to work, all of them.

23 ˀech'o la xal k'alal ta xˀoch ta ˀabtel ti kirsanoetike ta sk'oponik jtotik:
kajval jesus.
k'usi xavak'bun kajval,
k'usi xak'elanbun jesus
xiik ti kirsanoetik ti k'alal ta xˀochik ta ˀabtele.

24 yuˀun ˀanjel la jyal ˀech.
ˀech'o la xal snaˀik sk'oponik jutuk jtotike.
yuˀun ˀanjel la jyal ˀech ta sk'opon jtotik ti kirsanoe.

For that reason people now pray to Our Father when they start to work: 23
"My Lord, Jesus.
What will you bestow upon me, my Lord?
What will you grant me, Jesus?"
That is what the people pray when they begin their labor.

The Earth Lords were responsible for promoting this custom. 24
This is why these people learned to pray a little to Our Father.
These people learned to pray to Our Father because the
Earth Lords went to tell on them.

1 loˀil yuˀun t'ul teˀtikal chij.

2 veno ti voˀne ti jtotik ti k'alal nakal toˀox ta banumil xchiˀuk smeˀe,
bat spas schob ta teˀtik.

3 la slomes ˀep teˀetik ti bu ta spas ti schobe.
pero ˀep la slomes ti teˀe.

4 sjunul k'ak'al ta xˀabtej ta teˀtik.
k'alal bat ta yok'omale vaˀal k'ot sta skotol ti teˀe.

5 pero k'uchaˀal vaˀi skotol li teˀetike li vomoletike.
buch'u tal svaˀan,
ˀo mi vaˀi stuk xi la ti jtotike.

6 te la ta xk'opoj stuk ti jtotik,
ti k'alal k'ot ta yabtel ti bu la slomes ti teˀetike.

7 pero stuktuk la ta xˀabtej ti jtotike.
muˀyuk la svinik.

8 ˀentonse ti jtotike lik ˀabtejuk.
lik slomes ti teˀ xtoke.

9 te ˀabtej sjunul k'ak'al ta teˀtik.
pero la slomes ˀep ti teˀetike ti ˀak'etike.
vaˀun ta mal k'ak'al sut batel ta sna ti bu nakale.

10 ˀentonse ta yoxibal k'ak'al bat ta ˀabtel xtok.
bat slomes ti teˀetik xtoke.

TEXT 36

About How Rabbit and Deer Got Their Short Tails and Long Ears

Mateo Méndez Tzotzek

A story about rabbit and deer.[1] 1

Well, a long time ago, when Our Father still lived on earth with his mother, 2
He went into the forest to prepare his cornfield.

He cut down many trees where he was going to make his cornfield. 3
He really cut down a lot of trees.

Everyday he would go there to work in the forest. 4
And every time, when he arrived on the following day, he would
find all of the trees standing up again.

"But why are all of the trees and weeds standing up again? 5
Who came to stand them up again?
Or did they stand up by themselves?" wondered Our Father.

These things Our Father considered when he was all alone, 6
When he arrived at the site where he had been cutting down trees.

But Our Father was working all alone. 7
He had no helpers.

Then Our Father started in to work. 8
He began to fell the trees once again.

All day he worked there in the forest. 9
For he had many, many trees and vines to clear away.
Then, in the afternoon, he returned to his home, his dwelling.

Then, on the third day, he went to work once again. 10
He went to cut down trees once again.

11 pero k'alal k'ot ta yoxibal k'ak'al ti bu ta slomes ti teʔe,
va'ʔal k'ot sta skotol ti teʔ xtoke.

12 pero k'uchaʔal tajmek ta xvaʔi ti teʔe.
k'uchaʔal mu xcham.
ʔecheʔ ti chiʔabtej jujun k'ak'ale.

13 ʔaʔ lek chital jchabi.
ʔa ver buch'u ta svaʔan ti teʔe.
ʔo mi ta xvaʔi stuk tanae.

14 slajeb k'ak'al chiʔabtej.
slajeb k'ak'al ta lomes ti teʔe.
ʔok'om chital jchabi leʔe xi la ti jtotike.

15 vaʔi ʔun ti jtotike.
lik la slomes ti teʔ xtoke.
lik ʔabtejuk xtok.
sjunul k'ak'al te la slomes ti teʔe.

16 pero te ʔo noʔox la la slomes ti bu la slomes ta baʔyel k'ak'ale.
ʔaʔ te ta xʔabtej jujun k'ak'al.

17 pero k'alal ta xk'ot jujun k'ak'al ti bu ta slomes ti teʔe,
vaʔal ta xk'ot sta jujun k'ak'al.
jujun la ak'obal ta xvaʔi ti teʔe.

18 pero k'uchaʔal tajmek ta xvaʔi ti teʔ jujun ʔak'obale
xi la ti k'alal xk'ot ti bu ta slomes ti teʔe.

19 ta la ta xk'opoj stuk ti jtotike,
ti k'alal ta xk'ot ta yabtele.

20 ʔentonse ta xchanibal k'ak'al bat xchabi ti teʔe.
bat sk'el ti k'uxi ta xvaʔi ti teʔe.
te bat chotiuk ti bu la slomes ti teʔe.

But when he arrived on the third day at the site of his clearing, 11
He arrived to find all the trees standing up in place.

"But how can it be that the trees are standing up? 12
Why don't they die?
It is in vain that I work every day.

I'd best come to check up on things, 13
To find out who it is that is causing the trees to stand upright again.
Or could it be that they stand up by themselves?

Until evening I will work. 14
Until evening I will clear this forest.
Tomorrow I will come to check up on what has happened,"
said Our Father.

With this, Our Father proceeded. 15
He began to fell trees once again.
He started in to work once again.
So he worked for a whole day, clearing the forest away.

He cut trees in the very same place where he had cut them the first day. 16
There he worked every day.

But as surely as he came every day to his clearing, 17
Every day he would find them standing in place once again.
Every night the trees righted themselves.

"But how can it be that the trees stand up every night?" 18
That is what he said when he arrived at the clearing.

Our Father once again found himself wondering, 19
Thinking to himself as he came to the site of his labors.

Then, on the fourth day, he went to keep watch at the site of the trees. 20
He went to uncover the mystery of the magical return of the trees.
He proceeded to find a good hiding place to sit and keep watch
at the site where he had felled the trees.

21 ˀentonse k'alal k'ot ti t'ule ti teˀtikal chije ti chak lakanteˀe ti sk'ak'al yate ti chanul ˀakove.
lik k'opojuk ti t'ule ti teˀtikal chij.

22 ti k'alal k'otik ti bu lomem ti teˀe,
lik k'opojikuk ti t'ul xchiˀuk ti teˀtikal chije.
lik la yal:

23 yukan teˀ.
yukan ˀak'.

24 yukan teˀ.
yukan ˀak'.

It was then that the rabbit, the deer, the hornet, the tarantula-killer wasp, 21
and the common wasp arrived.[2]
The rabbit and the deer began to talk, totally unaware that
they were being observed.

When they arrived at the site of the fallen trees, 22
The rabbit and the deer began to speak together.
They began to chant these words:

"Rise up, tree![3] 23
Rise up, vine!

Rise up, tree! 24
Rise up, vine!

FIGURE 52

It was then that the rabbit, the deer, the hornet, the tarantula-killer
wasp, and the common wasp arrived.
The rabbit and deer began to talk, totally unaware that they
were being observed.

25 yukan teˀ.
yukan ˀak’ xi la ti t’ule ti teˀtikal chije.

26 te la kotolik ti bu lomem ti teˀe.
ti chak lakanteˀe ti sk’ak’al yate ti chanul ˀakove muˀyuk la xk’opojik.
ˀaˀ noˀox te la skolta sba ta svaˀanel ti teˀe.

27 ˀentonse ti jtotik k’alal yil k’ot ti t’ule ti teˀtikal chije vaˀi la ta ˀora.
vaˀi ˀun k’alal yaˀi k’opoj ti t’ule ti teˀtikal chije.
bat la stzak ta ˀora ti t’ule ti teˀtikal chije.

28 laj la stzakbe sne ti t’ule tuch’ la.
laj la snitbe xchikin ti t’ule ti k’alal syakel ta xk’opoje.

29 ˀech’o la xal toj nat xchikin ti t’ule;
yuˀun la la snit ti jtotike.

30 ˀech la ti snee tuch’ la.
ˀech’o la xal toj komkom sne ti t’ule.

31 ˀech li teˀtikal chije tuch’ la sne ˀek.
ˀech’o la xal toj komkom sne ti teˀtikal chije.

32 k’alal ta xchikin ˀinitbat.
ˀech’o la xal li teˀtikal chije toj nat xchikin ˀek.
koˀol xchiˀuk t’ul.

33 pero ˀaˀ la ta smul ti t’ule ti teˀtikal chije.
ˀaˀ la ti ta svaˀan ti teˀe.

34 ˀech’o la xal ˀinitbat xchikinik.
ˀaˀ ta smul stuk.

35 ti schak lakanteˀe,
ˀaˀ noˀox ˀimich’bat ti xch’ute.

36 xchiˀuk ti sk’ak’al yate,
ˀaˀ noˀox ˀimich’bat ti xch’ute.

Rise up, tree! 25
Rise up, vine!" chanted the rabbit and the deer.

There they stood, all the culprits, right there in the clearing. 26
As for the hornet, the tarantula-killer wasp, and the common wasp,
they did not talk.
They just helped in righting the trees.

When rabbit and deer appeared, Our Father stood up at once. 27
He had heard rabbit and deer speaking their magical words.
So he went at once to capture rabbit and deer.

He grabbed rabbit's tail and cut it off. 28
Then he pulled rabbit's ears, for he kept right on uttering
the magical words.

That is why rabbit has very long ears; 29
It is because Our Father pulled them.

As for his tail, he cut it off. 30
That is why rabbit's tail is very short.

As for the deer's tail, he cut it off too. 31
That is why deer's tail is very short.

At this same time, his ears got a good yank. 32
That is why deer's ears are very long, too.
Just like those of rabbit.

But rabbit and deer have only themselves to blame. 33
It was they who righted the trees.

That is why their ears were pulled. 34
It was their own fault.

As for the hornet, 35
It just had its stomach squished.

As for the tarantula killer wasp, 36
It just had its stomach squished.

37 xchiˀuk chanul ˀakov,
laj la set’be xch’utik ta sniˀ yich’ak ti jtotike.

38 ˀech’o la xal li chak lakanteˀ li k’ak’al yate, li chanul ˀakove toj bik’it la xch’utik.
pero jtotik la smich’be xch’ut ti chonetike.

39 pero ˀaˀ la ta smul stukik ti chonetike.
ˀaˀ la ta smul ti ta svaˀan ti teˀetike.

40 k’alal syakel ta xk’opojik ti t’ule ti teˀtikal chije,
jlikel la vaˀi skotol ti teˀetike.

41 ti k’alal la jyal,
yukan teˀ,
yuk’an ˀak’e
jlikel la la jvaˀiuk ti teˀetike ti ˀak’etike.

42 ˀech’o xal ti jtotik la jyil ti t’ul ti teˀtikal chij ta svaˀan ti teˀetike.
ˀech’o la xal la snitbe xchikin xchiˀuk sne.
pero yuˀun ˀaˀ ta smul stukik ti chonetike.

43 vaˀi ˀun k’alal laj snitbe xchikin ti t’ule ti teˀtikal chije chak lakanteˀe ti k’ak’al yate ti chanul ˀakove,
laj la skolta batel.
laj la yak’be sbi t’ul teˀtikal chij chak lakanteˀ k’ak’al yat chanul ˀakov.

44 ˀech’o la xal ˀoy sbi li t’ule li teˀtikal chije li chak lakanteˀe li k’ak’al yate, li chanul ˀakove.
yuˀun jtotik la jyak’be sbi.

45 pero ti voˀnee ta svaˀanan teˀetik:
yuˀun toj toyol smanyaik.
yuˀun la xˀutilanik ti jtotike.
yuˀun mu sk’anik ti ta spas xchob ti jtotik ta teˀtike.
ˀech’o la xal bat svaˀanik ti teˀetike.

So with the common wasp, 37
Our Father cut his stomach with his fingernail.

For this reason, these wasps and hornets all have very small middle bodies. 38
It was Our Father who squished the stomachs of these creatures.

But these creatures have only themselves to blame. 39
They were guilty of righting the trees.

When rabbit and deer were in the midst of speaking words of power, 40
The trees quickly stood up again.

When they said, 41
"Rise up, trees,
Rise up, vines,"
The trees and vines quickly stood up.

In this way, Our Father caught rabbit and deer in the very act of righting the trees. 42
That is why he pulled their ears and tails.
But, of course, it was the animals' very own fault.

After pulling the ears of the rabbit and deer and pinching the middles of wasps and hornets, 43
He released all of them.
He named them in this manner: rabbit, deer, hornet, tarantula-killer wasp, and common wasp.

That is why they are so named to this day: rabbit, deer, hornet, tarantula-killer wasp, and common wasp. 44
Our Father gave them their names.

But it was long ago, when they righted the trees, that Our Father punished them: 45
For these creatures were very devious.
For they drove Our Father crazy with annoyance.
For they didn't want Our Father to prepare his cornfield in the woods.
That is why they insisted on making the trees spring up again.

46 ˀentonse k'alal laj skolta ˀel ti t'ule ti teˀtikal chije lik ˀabtejuk ti jtotike.
lik slomes ti teˀetike.

47 pero muˀyuk xa la bu xvaˀi teˀe ti ˀak'e.
laj la spas ti xchobe.
laj la stz'un ti xchobe.

48 pero ti t'ule, ti teˀtikal chije ti chanul ˀakov ti chak lakanteˀe ti k'ak'al yate,
muˀyuk xa la bu xk'otik svaˀanik ti teˀetike.

49 pero te kuxulik.
muˀyuk bu xchamik ti t'ule ti teˀtikal chije.
ˀaˀ noˀox ti mu xa sk'an xbatike yuˀun ta xiˀik xa.

50 vaˀi ˀun ti jtotike la sk'opon sbaik xchiˀuk ˀanjeletik.
pero te la loˀilajik ti bu ta spas xchob ti jtotike.

51 veno mi xak'an xatz'unubin ti chonetike,
yuˀun ta jk'an ta jmil kaˀi xi la ti jtotike.

52 veno lek ˀoy ta jtz'unubinikik.
a ver mi sch'i xi la ti ˀanjeletike.

53 ˀentonse laj la stz'unubin ti t'ule ti teˀtikal chije.
laj la yik' ˀel ta sna ti t'ule ti teˀtikal chije.

54 ta la stz'unubin ta sna ti ˀanjeletike.
ˀech'o la xal ti t'ule ti teˀtikal chije stz'unub ˀanjeletik.

55 pero li chanul ˀakove li chak lakanteˀe li k'ak'al yate maˀuk la stz'unub ˀanjel.
ˀech noˀox xchanul banumil.

56 muˀyuk yajval.
muˀyuk ta sk elat yuˀun ˀanjeletik.
xuˀ xcham ta teˀtik.

After he released rabbit and deer, Our Father began to work. 46
He resumed his labor of clearing brush.

But the trees and vines no longer resisted his will. 47
He succeeded in making his cornfield.
He succeeded in sowing his cornfield.[4]

As for rabbit, deer, hornet, tarantula-killer wasp, and common wasp, 48
They no longer came to right the trees.

But they were still alive. 49
The rabbit and deer did not die.
It's just that they were were no longer interested in their old tricks,
for they were afraid.

Our Father consulted with the Earth Lords. 50
They all talked together at the site of Our Father's cornfield.

"Well, do you think these animals should be allowed to survive 51
and multiply?
For my part, I feel like doing away with them altogether,"
said Our Father.

"Why not give them a chance? We'd like to give them a try. 52
We'll see whether or not they survive," said the Earth Lords.

With that, they sowed the breeding stock of rabbit and deer. 53
They invited rabbit and deer to come and live near their own house.

The Earth Lords gave them a chance to live near their own home. 54
That is how rabbit and deer came to be the responsibility
of the Earth Lords.[5]

But the wasps and the hornets are not the charges of the Earth Lords. 55
They are just creatures of the earth.

They have no patron. 56
They are not cared for by the Earth Lords.
They simply die in the woods and no one notices.

57 ˀaˀ noˀox ti t'ule ti teˀtikal chije ˀoy yajvalik.
mu xuˀ xchamik ta teˀtik.

58 xuˀ xchamik pero ˀaˀ to ti mi la jyal mantal ti ˀanjeletike.
pero mu la jyal mantal ti ˀanjele mu xcham li t'ule li teˀtikal chije.
yuˀun ˀoy yajval.

It is only the rabbit and deer who have patrons. 57
They do not simply die in the woods.

They can die, but not until the Earth Lords want them to. 58
As long as the Earth Lords don't give this order, rabbits and deer
will not die.
The reason is that they have a patron who watches over them.[6]

1 ˀa li voˀne ˀoy jun vinik stz'un xchob ta teˀtik.
pero ta la xch'ay ti xchob.

2 k'alal bat sk'el xchob ti vinik ch'ayem la ti xchob.
buch'u ta xˀelk'an ti jchob xi la ti vinik.

3 tey la yikta komel xchob ti vinik.
sut talel ta sna ti vinik.

4 ti k'alal bat sk'el xchob ta xchibal velta ti vinik.
ta xa la stzutz ta ch'ayel stekel ti xchob.

5 buch'u ta xˀelk'an ti jchob xi la ti vinik.
ˀaˀ lek ta jmeltzan junuk chab.
ta jak'be ˀok'om buch'u ta xˀelk'an ti jchob xi la ti vinik.

TEXT 37

Adventures of Coyote and Rabbit, I

OF THE BEESWAX DOLL AND THE CORN THIEF

Xalik López Setjol

A long time ago there was a man who sowed his cornfield in the woods. 1
 But his cornfield was being destroyed.

When he went to check up on his cornfield, it was stripped bare. 2
 "Who can be stealing from my cornfield?" said the man.

He felt like giving his cornfield up for lost. 3
 The man went back home.

Then the man went for a second time to check up on his cornfield. 4
 This time the loss of his cornfield was complete.

"Who can be stealing from my cornfield?" wondered the man. 5
 "I'd best make an image out of beeswax.
 And then I will ask this image tomorrow who has been stealing
  from my cornfield," said the man.

FIGURE 53

"Who can be stealing from my cornfield?" wondered the man.
 "I'd best make an image out of beeswax.
 And then I will ask this image tomorrow who has been stealing
  from my cornfield," said the man.

6 ˀi smeltzan la chab ti vinik.
tey la laj svaˀal komel ta xchikin xchob ti chab laj smeltzan ti vinik.

7 ti k’alal lah smeltzan chab ti vinik:
yalbe la mantal ti chab.

8 mi ˀoy buch’u tal ˀavil mu me xak’opon xi la ti vinik.
xuˀuk xi la ti chab.

9 mu la snaˀ ti vinik buch’u ta xˀelk’an ti xchob.
bat la ti jˀelek chobtik ta yut chobtik.
teye xa la vaˀal ti chab ta chikin chobtik.

10 k’usi ta xapas xi la ti jˀelek chobtik.
mu la xtak’av ti buch’u ta sk’opon ti jˀelek.

11 ti jˀelek’ chobtike ˀaˀ la ti t’ul.
ti buch’u ta sk’opon ti t’ul ˀaˀ la ti chab teye vaˀal ta chikin chobtik.

12 ti k’alal tey vaˀal ti chab ta chikin chobtik.
pero pas la ta simaron ti t’ul.
ta la xˀilin.
ˀaˀ la ta xˀut ti chab tey vaˀal ta chikin chobtik.

13 ti k’alal mu xtak’av ti chab,
solel k’ak’ub ta ˀil ti t’ul.

14 k’uchaˀal ti mu xatak’av xi la ti t’ul.
ta jmajot tana xi la ti t’ul.

15 ti k’alal k’ak’ub ta ˀil ti t’ul,
smah la ti chab.

16 k’alal laj smaj ti chab ti t’ul,
tey la pak’tzaj ti sk’ob.

He proceeded to make this image in the form of a doll. 6
The man left the doll that he had made standing there in the corner of his cornfield.

Now, once the doll was finished, the man did this: 7
He spoke to the doll.

"If anyone shows up, you are not to talk to them!" ordered the man. 8
"Okay," said the wax image.

The man did not know who had been stealing from his cornfield. 9
But presently the corn robber stole into the cornfield.
The wax doll was standing there in the corner of the cornfield.

"What are you doing here?" asked the corn thief. 10
The one to whom the thief spoke did not answer.

The corn robber himself was a rabbit. 11
The one to whom the rabbit was talking was the beeswax image standing in the corner of the cornfield.

The beeswax image just stood there passively in the corner of the cornfield. 12
This made the rabbit furious.
He really got angry.
He scolded the wax doll who stood there silently in the corner of the cornfield.

When the wax image refused to answer, 13
The rabbit became even more furious.

"Why won't you answer me?" said the rabbit. 14
"I'm going to hit you in a minute," said the rabbit.

Having gotten himself into such a fit of rage, 15
He struck the wax image.

And once the rabbit had delivered the blow to the image, 16
His paw got stuck there.

17 k'ucha'al la tzakbun ti jk'ob xi la ti t'ul.
stuk la tey xvulvun ti t'ul.
mu la xtak'av ti chab.

18 koltao jk'ob mi xak'an xi la ti t'ul.
mi mu xak'an xakolta ti jk'ob ta jmajot ta jun jk'ob xi la ti t'ul.

19 yak' la jun sk'ob ti t'ul.
tey la pak'tzaj xchibal sk'ob ti t'ul.

20 ti k'alal pak'tzaj xchibal sk'ob ti t'ul:
k'ucha'al la tzak xchibal jk'ob xi la ti t'ul.
ta me xkak' pujel ta tek'el xi la ti t'ul.

21 yak' la ti pujel ta tek'el.
pak'tzaj la yok ti t'ul.

22 k'alal pak'tzaj jun yok ti t'ul suj la sba ta 'iline.
ta me xkak' jun kok xi la ti t'ul.

23 yak' la xchibal yok ti t'ul.
tey la pak'tzaj.

24 ti k'alal pak'tzaj xchibal yok' ti t'ul,
suj la sba ta 'ilinel.

25 ti k'alal tey xvulvun ti t'ul,
'a' 'o la tey tal 'ok'il.

"Why did you grab my paw?" asked the rabbit. 17
The rabbit was there sputtering and fuming.
And the wax image did not answer.

"Let go of my paw, if you please," said the rabbit. 18
"If you won't let go of my paw, I'll hit you with my other paw,"
demanded the rabbit with mock courtesy.

So he gave it to him with his other paw. 19
Now both of the rabbit's paws were stuck there.

Now, with both of his paws stuck there, the rabbit spoke: 20
"Why did you go and grab both my paws?" said the rabbit.
"I'm going to kick you for sure," continued the rabbit.

With that he gave him a kick. 21
And the rabbit's back paw got stuck.

Since his back paw was now stuck, his anger reached a fever pitch. 22
"I'm going to give you another kick," threatened the rabbit.

So he struck with his other back paw. 23
And it got stuck there, too.

Now, with both back paws stuck, 24
The rabbit's rage increased even more.

The rabbit was there sputtering and fuming, 25
Whereupon a coyote came by.

26 jak'be kaˀtik k'usi la spas ti t'ul xvulvun xi la ti ˀok'il.
k'usi ta xapas xi la ti ˀok'il.
yuˀun laj stzakun jun vinik liˀ vaˀal xi la ti t'ul.

27 k'uchaˀal laj stzakot ti vinik xi la ti ˀok'il.
yuˀun ˀoy stzeb ti vinik.
yuˀun la ta xak'bun kik'be ti stzeb ti vinik.
ˀech'o la xal laj stzakun xi la ti t'ul.

28 bu ˀoy stzeb ti vinik xi la ti ˀok'il.
te ˀoy ta sna xi la ti t'ul.

29 mi xak'an xavich'ote xi la ti t'ul.
mu jk'an xi la ti ˀok'il.

30 pero toj lek xi la ti t'ul.
manchuk ˀoy kajnile ta xkik' xi la ti t'ul.

"I think I'll ask rabbit what he's doing there, carrying on like that," 26
said the coyote.
"What are you up to?" inquired the coyote.
"Well, this man standing here grabbed me," said the rabbit.

"Why did the man grab you?" asked the coyote. 27
"The reason is that the man has a daughter.
The man wanted to give me his daughter's hand in marriage.
That's why he grabbed me," said the rabbit.[1]

"Where does the man's daughter live?" asked the coyote. 28
"She's there at his house," said the rabbit.

"Wouldn't you like to marry her?" said the rabbit. 29
"No, I don't want to," said the coyote.

"But she's very pretty," said the rabbit. 30
"If I weren't already engaged, I would marry her myself," said the rabbit.

FIGURE 54

"I think I'll ask rabbit what he's doing there, carrying on like
that," said the coyote.
"What are you up to?" inquired the coyote.
"Well, this man standing here grabbed me," said the rabbit.

31 ˀa li ˀoˀote ch'abal ˀavajnil.
xuˀ xavich' xi la ti t'ul.
xuˀuk xi la ti ˀok'il.

32 pero mi ˀoˀot ta xavich' ti tzeb pero ˀoˀot xakom xi la ti t'ul.
xuˀuk xi la ti ˀok'il.
ˀaˀ la ˀistik' ˀochel sk'ob ti ˀok'il.

33 ti k'alal laj stik' sk'ob xchiˀuk yok ti ˀok'il.
ti k'alal laj stik' sk'ob ti ˀok'il.
skuxet xa la yoˀnton ti t'ul.

34 tik'o xa ˀochel ˀavoke xi la ti t'ul.
xuˀuk xi la ti ˀok'il.
stik' la ˀochel yok ti ˀok'il.

35 ti k'alal laj stik' yok ti ˀok'il,
skuxet a la yoˀnton ti t'ul.

36 toj lek ti ˀavajnil chata xi la t'ul.
xuˀ ˀechuk xi la ti ˀok'il.

37 skuxet xa la yoˀnton ti ˀok'il,
ti k'alal ta xˀak'bat yajnil yuˀun ti vinik.

38 ˀaˀ la tey pak'al kom ti ˀok'il.
ti k'alal laj xch'un loˀlae.

39 ti k'alal bat sk'el xchob ti vinik,
ˀaˀ la tey pak'al tee ti ˀok'il.

40 k'usi ta xapas xi la ti vinik.
muˀyuk xi la ti ˀok'il.

41 k'usi ta xasaˀ xi la ti vinik.
muˀyuk k'usi ta jsaˀ xi la ti ˀok'il.

42 yuˀun ˀoy stzeb jun vinik ta xˀalik;
yuˀun la ta xak'bikun kich'.

"And you, you don't even have a wife. 31
You can marry her," said the rabbit.
"Very well," said the coyote.

"However, if you are going to marry the girl, you have to stay right here," 32
said the rabbit.
"Very well," said the coyote.
So the coyote stuck in his front paw.

Then he stuck in his back paw with the front paw. 33
Then he stuck in his other front paw.
With this, the rabbit was delighted.

"Stick in your other foot," said the rabbit. 34
"Okay," said the coyote.
The coyote stuck in his other foot.

When the coyote had finished getting his last paw stuck, 35
The rabbit was delighted.

"Ah, what a pretty wife you are to have," said the rabbit. 36
"That's great," said the coyote.

The coyote had become quite happy, 37
For the man was going to present him with a wife.

But the coyote remained stuck there. 38
He had allowed himself to be deceived.[2]

Now, when the farmer went to check up on his cornfield, 39
He found the coyote stuck there, completely immobilized.

"What are you up to?" asked the man. 40
"Oh, nothing," said the coyote.

"What are you looking for?" asked the man. 41
"I'm not looking for anything," said the coyote.

"They say a certain man has a daughter; 42
And that he is going to present her to me as a wife."

43 buch'u la jyal xi la ti vinik.
ˀaˀ la jyal ti t'ul xi la ti ˀok'il.

44 buy laj ˀata ti t'ul xi la ti vinik.
ˀaˀ li pak'al la jta li buy pak'alun xi la ti ˀok'il.

45 ˀaltik chaval xi la ti vinik.
ˀoˀot lavelk'an ma ti jchobe xi la ti vinike.
muˀyuk k'usi ˀelk'an xi la ti ˀok'il.

46 ti ˀok'il k'alal ˀaˀ tey pak'al ta chab tae,
ˀaˀ laj yich' kastiko.

47 ti k'alal la jyich' kastiko ti ˀok'il:
mu sachik'bun ti jchake xi la ti ˀok'il.

48 pero k'uchaˀal lavelk'an ti jchob xi la ti vinik.
muˀyuk ta xiˀelk'an.
ˀaˀ noˀox la jyak'un komel ti t'ul xi la ti ˀok'il.

49 k'uxi bat ti t'ul xi la ti vinik.
liˀ yal batel ta ˀolon xk'ux ˀajan xi la ti ˀok'il.

50 pero ta xbat ˀavak' kil buy laj sk'ux ˀajan ti t'ul xi la ti vinik.
xuˀuk ta xbat kak' ˀavil xi la ti ˀok'il.

51 mi muˀyuk xaˀelk'aj xi la ti vinik.
muˀyuk xiˀelk'aj xi la ti ˀok'il.

52 ta jk'elkik k'us ˀelan ˀave xi la ti vinik.
k'elo ˀavil xi la ti ˀok'il.
sjach' la schaˀye.

53 ti k'alal laj sk'elbe ye ˀok'il ti vinik,
skoltabe la yok xchiˀuk sk'ob ti pak'al ta chab.

54 k'alal kol ti ˀok'il,
k'ak'em xa la ta k'ok' xchak.

"Who told you that?" asked the man. 43
"The rabbit told me," said the coyote.

"Where did you meet the rabbit?" asked the man. 44
"I found him stuck here where I'm stuck now," said the coyote.

"You are surely lying," said the man. 45
"You've simply been stealing from my cornfield," said the man.
"But I haven't stolen anything," said the coyote.

Now, since the coyote was the one who was stuck in the beeswax, 46
It was his fate to receive the punishment.

As the coyote received his punishment, he spoke: 47
"Don't burn my ass!" yelled the coyote.

"But why did you steal from my cornfield?" said the man. 48
"But I've stolen nothing at all.
The rabbit just left me here," said the coyote.

"Where did the rabbit go?" asked the man. 49
"He went down that way to eat your sweet corn," declared the coyote.

"Well, then, how about showing me where the rabbit ate my tender corn," ordered the man. 50
"All right, I'll show you," said the coyote.

"Truthfully, now, wasn't it you who stole my corn?" asked the man. 51
"No, I really didn't rob you," said the coyote.

"Let's see what your mouth looks like," said the man. 52
"Look all you want," said the coyote.
And with that he opened wide his muzzle.

When the man finished examining the coyote's gaping jaws, 53
He released the coyote's front and back paws, which were stuck in the beeswax image.

Now, when the coyote was at last free, 54
He already had his ass good and scorched.

55 k'alal kol ti ˀok'il,
bat la yak' ta ˀilel ti buy laj sk'ux ˀajan ti t'ul.

56 ti k'alal yil ti vinik buy laj sk'ux ˀajan ti t'ul:
ba saˀo tal ti t'ul xi la ti vinik.
ˀa li ˀoˀot chopolot laj ˀach'un loˀlael xi la ti vinik.

57 xuˀuk xi la ti ˀok'il.
bat la saˀ talel buy bat ti t'ul.

58 k'alal bat saˀ talel t'ul ti ˀok'il,
chopol la yoˀnton ti ˀok'il.

59 k'uchaˀal laj jch'un ti loˀlael xi la ti ˀok'il.
k'ak' ti jchak xi la.

60 ti k'alal sta ta saˀel t'ul ti ˀok'il,
k'usi ta xapas xi la ti ˀok'il.
ta jpas jna xi la ti t'ul.
syakel la ta saˀ jobel ti t'ul.

When the coyote was at last free, 55
He went to show the man where the rabbit was munching on sweet corn.

When the man finally spied the rabbit eating the sweet corn, he spoke: 56
"Go fetch the rabbit," said the man.
"You were really stupid to believe his lies," said the man.

"Very well," said the coyote. 57
And he went off to fetch the rabbit.

Now, as the coyote set off to bring the rabbit back, 58
He was resentful and angry.

"Why did I believe his lies?" wondered the coyote. 59
"My ass got burned," he reflected.

Then the coyote found the rabbit, 60
"What are you up to?" asked the coyote.
"I'm making my house," said the rabbit.
The rabbit was busy looking for nesting grass.

61 ˀa li ˀoˀte k'usi ta xasaˀ xi la ti t'ul.
mu ˀyuk k'usi ta saˀ xi la ti ˀok'il.

62 yuˀun noˀox tal kik'to xi la ti ˀok'il.
k'uchaˀal xi la ti t'ul.
yuˀun ˀoy ti k'in.
bat jk'eltik ˀavil xi la ti ˀok'il.

63 bu ˀoy ti k'in xi la ti t'ul.
leˀ ˀoy ta sna vinike xi la ti ˀok'il.

64 k'usi k'inal xi la ti t'ul.
k'in jnupunel.
bat jk'eltik ˀavil xi la ti ˀok'il.
xuˀuk xi la ti t'ul.

"And what are you looking for?" asked the rabbit. 61
"I'm not looking for anything," said the coyote.

"Actually, I came to get you," said the coyote. 62
"Why?" asked the rabbit.
"Because there's a party going on.
Let's go check it out," said the coyote.

"Where's the party?" asked the rabbit. 63
"It's at some guy's house down the way," said the coyote.

"What sort of a party is it?" asked the rabbit. 64
"It's a wedding party.
Let's go check it out!" said the coyote.
"Why not?" agreed the rabbit.

FIGURE 55

"And what are you looking for?" asked the rabbit.
"I'm not looking for anything," said the coyote.

65 k'alal k'otik ti bu ˀoy k'in,
ch'abal la k'in.

66 ˀaˀ la te ˀoy ti vinik yajval chobtik.
ta xmalavan.

67 ti k'alal k'ot ti t'ul.
mu la snaˀ mi ta x'ich' tzitzel ti la jyelk'an chobtik.

68 ti k'alal k'ot ti t'ul ta stz'el ti vinik,
tzak xi la yajval ta ˀora.
xˀavet xa la ti t'ul.

69 ti k'alal ta xchik'bat xchak ta k'ok' ti t'ul:
liˀ ˀoy ti tzitzel xi la ti vinik.

70 k'uchaˀal la velk'an jchob xi la ti vinik.
muˀyuk xkelk'an ˀachob xi la ti t'ul.

71 liˀe buch'u la jyelk'an xi la ti vinik.
mu jnaˀ xi la ti t'ul.

72 mi mu xanaˀ liˀ ˀoy ti tzitzel xi la ti vinik.
yuˀun mu jnaˀ xiˀabtej.
ˀech'o xal ta xiˀelk'aj xi la ti t'ul.

73 ti k'alal la jyich' chik'bel ta k'ok' xchak ti t'ul:
batan ta ˀuk'um sikubtaso ˀachak jch'ajiluˀ xi la ti vinik.

74 xuˀuk kolaval xi la ti t'ul.
ti k'alal bat ta ˀuk'um.

75 ti k'alal k'ot ta ˀuk'um ti t'ul,
yochel la lek ta ˀatimol ta ˀuk'um ti t'ul.

76 ti k'alal bat ta ˀuk'um ti t'ul,
tey la nabal batel ta patil ti ˀok'il.

When they reached the place where the party was supposed to be happening, 65
There was no party at all.

There was the man who owned the cornfield. 66
He was waiting for them.

Now the rabbit appeared on the scene. 67
But he did not realize that he was going to be punished for stealing corn.

Now the rabbit came up close to the man. 68
And the owner of the cornfield lost no time in grabbing him.
Then the rabbit began to yell.

When the rabbit's ass had been burned in the fire the man spoke: 69
"Here is your punishment," said the man.

"Why did you steal from my cornfield?" asked the man. 70
"I didn't steal your corn," said the rabbit.

"Who, then, did steal my corn?" asked the man. 71
"I don't know," said the rabbit.

"If you don't know, we'll find some more punishment," said the man. 72
"Okay, I did it. It's because I don't know how to work.
That's why I steal," confessed the rabbit.

Then, when the rabbit's ass had been burned in the fire, the man spoke: 73
"Go to the river and cool your ass, good-for-nothing," said the man.[3]

"Very well. Thank you," said the rabbit. 74
Whereupon he proceeded to the river.

Then the rabbit reached the river, 75
He plunged in to take a good bath in the river.

But, while the rabbit had been making his way to the river, 76
There, right behind him, followed the coyote.

77 ti k'alal syakel ta ˀatimol ti t'ul.
tey la kolol sat ti ˀok'il k'alal ta xˀatin ta ˀuk'um ti t'ul.

78 ˀochan talel liˀ,
ˀatinkutik xi la ti t'ul.

79 xuˀuk xi la ti ˀok'il.
ti k'alal yil lek ta xˀatin ti t'ul.

80 ti k'alal ˀoch ta ˀuk'um ti ˀok'il,
mu la snaˀ xˀatin ta ˀuk'um.
ˀora la ˀoch voˀ la sniˀ ti ˀok'il.

81 ti k'alal ˀoch voˀ ta sni ti ˀok'il,
cham ti ˀok'il.

82 ti k'alal cham ti ˀok'il,
xi la ti t'ul.
ˀora la lok' ta ˀuk'um ti t'ul.

83 k'alal cham ti ˀok'il,
bat yal ti t'ul ti cham ta ˀuk'um ti ˀok'il.

84 k'alal k'ot ti t'ul ta sna ti vinik,
yich' la jun velta kastiko ti t'ul.

85 ti k'alal cham ti ˀok'il.
yich' la nitbel xchikin.
ˀoˀote ta mul ti cham ˀok'il xi la ti vinik.

86 ti k'alal laj nitbatuk xchikin ti t'ul,
koltaat la.
bat ˀel ti t'ul teˀtik.

The rabbit kept right on bathing. 77
But the coyote stared at him enviously, watching the rabbit
enjoy his bath in the river.

"Come on in here! 78
Let's have a swim!" said the rabbit.

"All right," said the coyote. 79
The thought of joining the rabbit seemed very pleasant as he
watched him bathing.

Once the coyote plunged into the river, 80
It turned out that he had no idea how to swim in a river.
And in no time at all, water got in the coyote's snout.

Now, once the coyote's snout was full of water, 81
The coyote drowned.

And once the coyote was dead and gone, 82
The rabbit got scared.
At once he climbed out of the river.

Now, once the coyote was dead, 83
The rabbit went to report that the coyote had drowned.

And once the rabbit reached the man's house, 84
To his great surprise, the rabbit received yet another punishment.

It was all because of the coyote's death. 85
For this crime, he received a stout yank on his ears.
"It's your fault that the coyote died," said the man.

And once the rabbit had had his ears yanked, 86
He was released.
The rabbit fled into the woods.

1 ˀoy jun kuento yuˀun ˀok'il xchiˀuk t'ul ˀi jun svob.

2 vaˀun tal la ti ˀok'il la ˀune.
ˀi jun la svob ˀi tal la ˀune.

3 vaˀun k'ot la ta ˀolol be la ˀun.
vaˀi la k'otel ti ˀok'il la ˀune ˀi stij la ti svob lae.
pero ti svob la ˀune toj chopol la ta stij tajmek ˀun.

4 vaˀun ˀoy la te nopol la te jnaklej la ˀun.
ˀi ˀoy la yuni tz'iˀ la ˀun.

5 jech la ti tz'iˀ la ˀun,
yaˀi la ti toj chopol ta la tij ti svob la ˀune.

6 vaˀun jech la ti tz'iˀ la ˀunc.
lok' la sk'elbe ti tz'iˀ la ˀune.

7 jech la ti tz'iˀ la ˀune.
tiˀvan la ˀun.

8 vaˀun k'alal ta tiˀvan ti tz'iˀ la ˀune yaˀi la ti ˀok'il la ˀune.
ˀi jatav la ta ˀora.
likel la bat ta yan be ti ˀok'il la ˀune.

9 jech la ti svobe xchuk la ta sne ta ˀora.
bat la ta jun be xtok.
ˀi k'ot la stij la ti svob la xtok ˀune.

TEXT 38

Adventures of Coyote and Rabbit, II

OF MUSIC, DANCE, AND FIESTA TIME

Marián López Calixto

Here is a story about a coyote and a rabbit and a guitar. 1

Well, the coyote came along. 2
He appeared with his guitar.

Soon he arrived at the middle of the road. 3
Well now, as he arrived he was playing his guitar.
But, in truth, he was really playing his guitar very badly.

Well, there was a neighbor who lived very close. 4
He had a little dog.

Now, as for this dog, 5
The sound of the guitar playing seemed just awful to him.

And this is what the dog did. 6
The dog went out to see what was going on.

And the dog did this. 7
He started to bark.

Now, scarcely had the dog begun to bark, when the coyote heard him. 8
He ran away at once.
Immediately the coyote went away by another road.

He quickly tied the guitar to his tail. 9
He turned off on still another road.
And presently started to play his guitar once again.

10 vaˀun te la tal la ti t'ul la ˀune.
jech la ti t'ule jaˀ la ti nat la ti xchikin la ˀune.
koti la ˀoy la spixol la yilel la ˀune.

11 vaˀun ti ˀok'il la ˀune ˀi xiˀ la ˀun,
yuˀun xkoˀolaj la chak kirsano la yilel ˀun.

12 jech la ti svob la ˀune.
sjip la komel ˀun.

13 vaˀun ti t'ul la ˀune,
k'opoj la ˀun:
k'uchaˀal ta xaxiˀe jun tot ˀok'il xi la ti t'ule.

14 vaˀun jech la ti t'ul la ˀune mu la snaˀ xiˀ.
jun la yoˀnton bat sk'opon sbaik xchiˀuk ti ˀok'ile.

15 jech la ti ˀok'il la ˀune mu la sk'an k'oponel la ˀune.
ta la xˀilin la ˀun.

16 povre jun tot t'ul mu jk'an ta xak'oponun ˀavokoluk,
pere ta me xajtiˀ tana xi la ti ˀok'il la ˀune.

17 k'u yuˀun toj toyol ta xaˀiline.
mi yuˀun ta jpastik leto.
moˀoj xi la ti t'ul la ˀune.

18 moˀoj.
ta xajtiˀ tana xi la tajmek ti ˀok'ile.

19 vaˀun jech la ti t'ul la ˀune xiˀ la ˀun.
mu xatiˀun.
mu xatiˀun.
mu xatiˀun.

20 tijo noˀox ti vobe.
ta xiak'otaj ˀun.
ta jvalk'un ti jne ˀune xi la ti t'ule.

Soon a rabbit came along. 10
The rabbit had very long ears.
In fact, they were standing straight up in such a way that it seemed
he had a hat on.

Then the coyote got scared, 11
For the rabbit looked exactly like a person.

Now, this is what happened to his guitar. 12
He tossed it aside.

As for the rabbit, 13
He spoke up:
"Why are you scared, Uncle Coyote?" said the rabbit.

It happened that this was a very fearless rabbit. 14
He sauntered up cheerfully to talk to the coyote.

Well, it turned out that the coyote wasn't interested in talking. 15
He became angry.

"Pity on you, Uncle Rabbit. Wise up! Please, I don't want you to talk to me, 16
But I really do feel like eating you up right now," said the coyote.

"But why are you so angry? 17
Do you want us to fight?
Surely that can't be," said the rabbit.

"No, *you've* got the wrong idea. 18
I intend to eat you up this instant," said the coyote.

With this the rabbit became frightened. 19
"Don't eat me!
Don't eat me!
Don't eat me!

Just play your guitar. 20
I'm going to dance.
I'm going to party," said the rabbit.[1]

21 veno,
muk' ta xajtiˀ chae xi la ti ˀok'il la ˀune.

22 jech la ti t'ul la ˀune lik la ˀak'otaj ˀun la ˀun.
stoy xa la ti xchake,
spik xa la ti snee,
slilin xa la ti yoke.

23 vaˀun jech la ti ˀok'il la ˀune.
ch'ay la ta yoˀnton la kansonal ta sk'an yak'ot ti t'ul la ˀune.

24 ˀa jun tot t'ul k'usi ta ˀavak'ot ta xak'an ˀune xi la ti ˀok'ile.
k'usi ˀak'otal ta xatij chae xi la ti t'ule.

25 muˀyuk sbi ti vobe xi la ti ˀok'ile.
mi mu xanaˀbe sbi ta vob chae xi la ti t'ule.

26 mu jnaˀ k'usi sbi.
jaˀ noˀox ta jtije xi la ti ˀok'ile.

27 ˀa ti sbi ta vobe ˀok'il xi la ti t'ule.
ˀa veno lek ˀoy xi la ti ˀok'ile.
stij la ti svob la ˀune.

"Very well, 21
I'll not eat you, then," said the coyote.

With that, the rabbit started to dance. 22
Now he raised his ass,
Now he touched his tail,
Now he shook his paw.

And this is what happened to the coyote. 23
He forgot which dance tune the rabbit wanted him to play.

"Ay, Uncle Rabbit, which dance tune do you want?" asked the coyote. 24
"Well, which ones do you know how to play?" asked the rabbit.

"But the tunes I know have no names," said the coyote. 25
"You mean to say you don't know the names of your tunes?"
said the rabbit.

"I really don't know their names. 26
I just play them," said the coyote.

"Let's call it the 'coyote song,'" suggested the rabbit. 27
"Good, that's fine!" said the coyote.
And so he played his guitar.

28 jech la ti t'ul la ˀune.
jun la yoˀnton ta xˀak'otaj la ˀun.

29 vaˀun jech la ti t'ul la ˀune.
snop la ta sjol ˀun.

30 lik la xuxubajuk la xchak.
xun, xun, xun,
lech ˀul xi la xchak ti t'ul la ˀune.

31 jijola tal me kirsano.
ˀay ˀavaˀi ta xpiubaj xi la ti ˀok'ile.

32 buy.
k'elo la ˀapate xi la ti t'ul ˀune.

And the rabbit joined right in with the spirit of things. 28
  Happily, he danced about.

Then the rabbit did this. 29
  He thought of a plan.

He started right in to whistle a rhyme out of his ass. 30
  "John, John, John,
  A spoonful of atole," farted the rabbit.[2]

"God damn it! Here come some people! 31
  Hey, listen! They're whistling," said the coyote.

"Where are they?" he continued. 32
  "Look behind you," said the rabbit.

FIGURE 56

And the rabbit joined right in with the spirit of things.
  Happily, he danced about.

33 vaˀun ti ˀok'il la ˀune.
sk'el la ti spat la ˀune.

34 vaˀun k'alal la sk'el la spat ti ˀok'il la ˀune,
vaˀun ti t'ul la ˀune jatav la ta ˀora ˀun.
loˀlavan la ti t'ul la ˀune.

35 vaˀun ti ˀok'il la ˀune.
jecheˀ chaval ˀun cae.
pere ta xajtiˀ tana ˀun chae.
pere ta persa chajmil tana ˀun xi la ti ˀok'il ˀune.

36 kap la me sjol ˀun.
bat la ba snutz la ti t'ul la ˀune.
ta jmil tana xi la ti ˀok'ile.

37 vaˀun ti t'ul la ˀune.
jelav la ta jot ˀuk'um.

38 vaˀun ti ˀok'il la ˀune,
ˀok' la tajmek yuˀun pojbat la ti svob ˀune ti ˀok'il lae.

39 bit la jelavel ta jot ˀuk'um ˀa ti t'ul la ˀune.
te la spetoj ti svob.

40 vaˀun ti t'ul la ˀune.
ta la xˀak'otaj la tajmek.

41 vaˀun ti ˀok'il la ˀune.
ˀilin la tajmek.
bat la tzakvanuk ta ˀora ti t'ul la ˀune.

42 mu xamilun k'il leˀ kexue.
jaˀ ta xatiˀ xi la ti t'ule.

43 buy ti kexue xi la ti ˀok'il ˀune.
leˀ chavile batan ta ˀora xi la ti t'ule.

And this is what the coyote did. 33
He looked right behind him.

When the coyote had turned around to look behind him, 34
It was at that very moment that the rabbit fled.
And this is how the rabbit tricked him.

With that, the coyote swore vengeance. 35
"Well, you lied to me.
But I'm going to eat you up.
I have no choice but to kill you at once," said the coyote, as though the rabbit were still there.

He proceeded to become enraged. 36
He stormed off to chase the rabbit.
"I'm going to kill him as soon as I can!" exclaimed the coyote.

Now, as for the rabbit, this is what he was up to. 37
He had jumped across to the other side of the river.

As for the coyote, 38
The coyote yelled and hollered in frustration, for he needed to protect his guitar and therefore could not wade across the river.[3]

Finally, he took a leap across the river to where the rabbit was. 39
He carried his guitar safely embraced in his arms.

As for the rabbit, 40
He was dancing merrily.

And the coyote did not take long to respond. 41
He became furious.
He rushed at once to grab the rabbit.

"Don't kill me. Look here at this cheese. 42
That's what you can eat," said the rabbit.

"Where is the cheese?" asked the coyote. 43
"There it is! Go and get it," said the rabbit.

44 jech la ti ˀok'ile.
jaˀ la toj bolat.
ˀi ch'un noˀox la tajmek ti k'usi ta xal la ti t'ule.
vaˀun bat la ti ˀok'il la ˀune.

45 bu ti kexu ˀune xi la ti ˀok'ile.
leˀe batan xi la ti t'ule.

46 pere k'uxi la xkut ˀun.
te tik'il ta ˀoˀ ˀune xi la ti ˀok'ile.
mi mu xanaˀ.

47 moˀoh.
baˀyo ta xavuch' skotol li ˀoˀe.
vaˀun ta slok' talel ti kexue xi la ti t'ule.

48 vaˀun ti bolat ˀok'il ˀune.
ˀi xch'un la ˀun.
bat la yuch' ti ˀoˀ la ˀune.

49 lik la yuch' ti ˀoˀ lae.
vaˀun noj la ti xch'ut la ˀune.

50 mu xlaj tajmck ti ˀoˀc.
jaˀ xa ti jch'ut ta xa xjat tajmeke xi la ti ˀok'ile.

51 ˀuch'an xa tajmek ˀun.
ta xa xlaj xi la ti mu t'ule.

52 ˀi xch'un la xtok.
yuch' la ti ˀoˀe.

53 vaˀun noj la ti xch'ute.
ˀi mu xa la xuˀ la xanav.

54 ˀay mu xa jk'an ˀun.
ta xa xicham xi la ti mu sonso ˀok'ile.

And this is what the coyote did. 44
He was unbelievably stupid.
He simply believed everything that the rabbit said.
So the coyote went off to check things out.

"Where is the cheese?" said the coyote. 45
"There it is! Go get it!" said the rabbit.

"But what am I going to do. 46
It's in the water," said the coyote.
"Didn't you know that?"

"Come, come, you haven't got a problem. 47
First, you should drink all the water.
Then the cheese will appear," said the rabbit.

With that, the poor, stupid coyote proceeded. 48
He swallowed the whole story.
He went off to drink the water.

He had begun to drink the water. 49
But then his stomach got full.

"The water isn't about to disappear. 50
And it seems that my stomach is going to burst," said the coyote.

"Come, come, now! Keep on drinking. 51
It's just about gone," said the mischievous rabbit.

And he believed him once again. 52
He drank up all the water.

By this time, his stomach was bloated. 53
Indeed, he could no longer walk.

"Oh, I don't like this anymore. 54
I think I'm about to die," said the bad, dumb coyote.

55 jecheˀ la ta xkal ˀun.
jaˀ la jmeˀtik la yak'oj la talel la sat ˀune xi la ti mu t'ul la ˀune.

56 veno tiˀun.
laˀ liˀe xi la ti mu t'ul la ˀune.

57 jech la ti ˀok'il la ˀune.
ˀi mu xa la xanav.
toj noj xa la ti xch'ute.

58 vaˀun ti t'ul la ˀune.
bat la ta sch'en snak' sba.

59 sk'el la k'otel ti stase.
ˀi ch'abal la ˀun.
lok' la ta ˀora saˀ la talel ti stase.

60 vaˀun sut la talel ˀun.
k'ot la ta xch'en.

61 ˀi mu la snaˀ mi k'uxul ti ˀok'il la ˀune.
jun la yoˀnton ti t'ul.
ˀi k'alal sta la ti stas ˀune vay la ˀun.

62 vaˀun jech la ti ˀok'il la ˀune.
k'ot la ta xch'en ti t'ul la ˀune.

63 jech la ti ˀok'ile.
yutz'i la tz'el be yav yok ti t'ule.

64 jech la ti ˀok'il la ˀune.
stabe la sna ti t'ul la ˀune.
ˀi likel la k'ot ta sna ˀun.

65 vaˀun jech la ti ˀok'il la ˀune.
mu la k'usi yal ˀun.
ˀi yaˀi ti te la tik'il te ta xch'en la ˀune.

"I told you a lie! 55
It's simply the image of Our Mother Moon reflected there!"
said the clever rabbit.

"Come on now, eat me! 56
Come here," taunted the mischievous rabbit.

By this time the coyote was sorely afflicted. 57
He could no longer walk.
His stomach was hopelessly bloated.

And, as for the rabbit, this is what he did. 58
He ran off to hide in his burrow.

When he got there, he looked at where his nest should have been. 59
And it was not there.
He went out to look for more material for his nest.

Then he returned. 60
He reached his burrow.

He did not realize that the coyote had in fact survived. 61
The rabbit's heart was happy and carefree.
And when he reached his nest, he slept.

And this is what the coyote did. 62
He found his way to the rabbit's burrow.

And this is how he did it. 63
He just sniffed the trail from the tracks the rabbit left in his path.

And this is what happened next to the coyote. 64
He found the rabbit's house.
He got there in no time.

And this was the next event in coyote's adventure. 65
He did not say anything at all.
For he realized that the rabbit was there in his burrow.

66 jech la ti ˀok'ile.
bat la saˀ la talel ta ˀora ti xuch'e.
k'ot la ta yok toj stzob talel ˀep tajmek.

67 vaˀun k'ot la ta stiˀ xch'en ti t'ul ti ˀok'il la ˀune.
bat la yak'be ti xuch'e ˀi smeltzan la ˀun.

68 vaˀun te la bat ba xchotan ti xuch'e.
vaˀun lok' la talel ti t'ul la ˀune.

69 jech la ti t'ule.
makal xa la ti sbe ˀune.

70 jech la ti t'ul la ˀune.
mu la xlok' ˀun.

71 te la matzal ti sjole.
sluch la ta sjol ti t'ule.

72 vaˀun te la matz'al la ti sjole.
ˀi snit ˀi snit ˀi snit tajmek.
mu la xt'ol ti sjole.

73 vaˀun te la nak'al ti ˀok'il la ˀune.
likel la bat ta ˀora ba stzak ti t'ule.

74 jech la ti ˀok'il la ˀune,
veno mu xa chakolta.
jmilot to ta jyalel xi la ti ˀok'ile.

75 vaˀun bat la ta ˀora.
vaˀun ti ˀok'il la ˀune bat la stzak ti sveˀele.
vaˀun ti t'ul la ˀune laj ˀun.

76 povre kuni veˀel.
ta xibat ba jvoˀote xi la ti ˀok'ile.

So the coyote did this. 66
He went immediately to look for pine resin.
Presently he came to the foot of a pine tree where a great deal of resin had accumulated.

Then the coyote went right up to the door of the rabbit's burrow. 67
He intended to arrange the resin just right.

With this, he went to set down the resin in its place. 68
Then the rabbit came out.

This was the fate that awaited the rabbit. 69
He could not get out, for the hole was blocked.

This was the rabbit's fate. 70
His hole was plugged up, and he could not get out.

His head got stuck there. 71
The resin was simply plastered to his head.

Well, his head stayed there, stuck. 72
He pulled and pulled and pulled.
But his head did not budge.

Well, the coyote was hidden there. 73
He rushed to grab the rabbit.

Then the coyote said, 74
"Good, now I shall not let you go.
I plan to kill you right away," said the coyote.

So he rushed up at once. 75
The coyote went to grab his dinner.
Well, the rabbit was done for.

"My fine little dinner. 76
I am going to roast you," said the coyote.

77 vaˀun stzan la ti sk'ok' la ti jtiˀval la ˀune.
sa˚ la siˀ.
vaˀun ˀan xa la skotol ti siˀ la ˀune.

78 jech la ti st'ul la ˀune.
te la bajal la ta bin.

79 jech la ti st'ul la ˀune,
slok'es la ˀun.

80 saˀ la jun teˀ ti ˀokile.
xchuk la ta ˀak' ti sveˀele.
ˀi stik' la ta k'ok' ti st'ule.

81 vaˀun jech la ti st'ul la ti ˀok'il la ˀune.
k'alal la taˀaj la ˀune stik' la ta sbin.

82 vaˀun ti ˀok'il la ˀune:
vaˀun bat la saˀ la talel ti xchiˀil la ˀun.

83 vaˀun ti ˀok'il la ˀune:
mu la bu sta talel ti xchiˀiltak la ˀune.

84 vaˀun vul la sk'el ti sveˀel la ˀune.
ch'abal xa la ˀun.

85 k'uxi bat ti jveˀel ˀune xi la ˀok'ile.
ˀi te la ch'ay ˀo ˀun.

With that, the beast built a fire. 77
He found firewood.
And soon the wood had formed nice coals.

Such was the rabbit's plight, 78
He was imprisoned in the pot.

And this is what happened to the rabbit, 79
The coyote took him out alive.

The coyote looked for a roasting stick. 80
He bound his food onto the stick with a vine.
Then he put it into the fire.

Now, as for the coyote's rabbit dinner, this was what happened. 81
Once the coyote thought that the rabbit was roasted, he returned him to the pot.

Whereupon, the coyote did this: 82
He went to call his friends.

And this was the coyote's luck: 83
He did not find his friends.

He returned and went to check up on his food. 84
And it was gone!

"What became of my food?" yelled the coyote. 85
He had indeed lost it.[4]

1 ˀoy jun kuento voˀnee sventa ˀantz.

2 jech la ti ˀantze.
sob la lik.

3 jech la ti smalale.
yuˀun ta la xbat ta ˀabtel ta kankuk ti vinike.

4 jech la ti ˀantze.
ˀik' to lok' ta pana ti ˀantze lae.
bat la sap talel la spanin la ti ˀantze.

TEXT 39

Kidnapped by a Demon

Marián López Calixto

Here is a story of long ago about a woman. 1

So the woman's story begins. 2
  She had gotten up very early.

It was for the sake of her husband. 3
  It seems that he was going to work in Cancuc.[1]

This is what the woman did to start with. 4
  The woman went outside while it was still dark in the early morning.
  She went out to rinse her cooked corn.[2]

FIGURE 57

This is what the woman did to start with.
  The woman went outside while it was still dark in the early morning.
  She went out to rinse her cooked corn.
  . . .
  "Ay!" she exclaimed; but one word, and that was all she said.

5 jech la ti vinike.
puch'ul to la ta stem.
muˀyuk to la ta xlik ti vinike.

6 jech la ti ˀantz ˀune:
ay xi la jbel ti ˀantze.

7 jech la ti vinik ˀune:
k'usi la pas xi la ti vinike.

8 jech la ti ˀantze,
mu xa la bu stak'.

9 jech la ti vinike.
lik la ta ˀora,
lok' la sk'el ta pana ti yajnil ti vinike.

10 buy ˀot.
k'uxi la bat xi la ti vinike.

11 jech la ti yajnil ti vinik la ˀune.
ch'abal xa la ˀun.
k'uxi bat ti kajnil ˀune xi la ti vinike.

12 veno k'alal sakub ti banamil ˀune la jyalbe la ti xchiˀiltak ˀune.
ya mu jnaˀ k'uxi bat ti kajnil ˀune xi la ti vinike.

13 jech la ti xchiˀiltak ˀune:
ba jsaˀtik ˀun chaˀe.
pere k'uxi bat ta ˀavajnil ˀune xi la xchiˀiltake.

14 mu jnaˀ k'uxi bat ti kajnile.
mi xaˀabolaj ba jsaˀtik ti kajnile xi la ti vinike.
veno batik ˀun chaˀe xi la ti vinike.
vaˀun batik la ˀun.

15 pere k'uxi chijbatotik ˀun.
pere la jnop voˀne ba jsaˀtik ta xab.
pere jaˀ me pukujuk ˀay stzak ma ti kajnile xi la ti vinike.

And what of the man? 5
He was still lying there in bed.
The man had not yet gotten up.

What of the woman? 6
"Ay!" she exclaimed; but one word, and that was all she said.

Then up spoke the man. 7
"What happened to you?" asked the man.

As for the woman, 8
She did not, indeed *could* not answer him.

So the man did this. 9
He rushed to get up,
He went outside to check up on his wife.

"Where are you? 10
Where did you go?" asked the man.

What of the man's wife? 11
She was nowhere to be seen.
"What has become of my wife?" wondered the man.

Well, at dawn he spoke to his relatives. 12
"My goodness! I don't know what happened to my wife!" said the man.

Then his relatives replied: 13
"Let's go look for her, then.
What has become of your wife?" inquired his relatives.

"I don't know where she went. 14
Won't you please help me look for her?" pleaded the man.
"Let's be off, then," said the man.
With that, they departed.

"But where to?" someone asked. 15
"Well, let's go look for her over by the sinkhole.
I've got a hunch that it was a demon who kidnapped my wife,"
said the man.[3]

16 veno batik.
ba jsaʔtik ta xab ʔun chaʔe xi la skotolik la ti xchiʔiltak ʔune.

17 vaʔun batik la ʔun.
bat la saʔik ta xab ta nail ch'en.
ch'abal la.

18 pere ch'abal ma ta ʔavajnile xi la skotolik ʔun.
teke ʔun chaʔe.
bat ʔo ta jyalel ti kajnile xi la ti vinike.

19 vaʔun lok' la jun ʔu.
tal la ti yajnil ti vinik ʔune.

20 vaʔun ti yajnil ti vinik ʔune.
ta ʔak'obaltik la tal ti yajnil ti vinik ʔune.

21 jech ti mu ʔantz ne.
jaʔ to la yaʔik ti smalal ti mu ʔantz la ʔune.

22 meʔ k'usi liʔ javale.
lok'an tal ta ʔora xi la ti vinik ʔune.
mu jnaʔ k'usi liʔ puch'ule xi la ti vinike.

23 jech la ti smeʔ ti vinik la ʔune bat la.
ba spik sk'elbe la ti sate.

24 jech la ti smeʔ ti vinik ʔune la jyojtikin.
ti k'usi la te javal ta pana ʔune,
jaʔ la yil ti yajnil ti skerem ʔol ʔune.

25 laʔ kol ʔa la jaʔ ta ʔavajnil ʔune.
pere buy lok' talel ta ʔavajnile xi la ti smeʔ ti vinike.

26 jech la ti smeʔ ti vinik ʔune la sk'opon la ʔun:
mi voʔot tzeb xi la ti ʔantz ʔune.

"Well, let's be off. 16
Let's go look in the sinkhole," said the people in the search party.

With that, they went there. 17
They went to look in a cave at the bottom of a sinkhole.
But she wasn't there.

"But your wife is not here," they all said. 18
"Well, what's to be done about it?
My wife seems to have disappeared for good," the man replied.

So a month passed. 19
And the man's wife returned.

This was her story. 20
It was by night that the man's wife returned.

This was how the poor woman made her appearance.[4] 21
The poor woman's husband heard some strange noises.

"Mother, what's that lying on its back? 22
Come out, quick!" said the man.
"Who knows what it can be, lying there," said the man.

With that, the man's mother went out to see. 23
She looked at it and touched its face.

Then the man's mother recognized her. 24
She realized that the one lying there faceup was indeed her daughter-in-law.
She saw that it was her son's wife.

"Come, son, it's your wife. 25
But wherever can she have come from?" said the man's mother.

So the man's mother spoke to her daughter-in-law: 26
"Is it you, girl?" she asked.

27 jech la ti mu ˀantz ˀune.
laj la yik’ik ˀochel ta yut sna ti vinike.
ˀa li jaˀ li kajnil xkil ˀune xi la ti vinike.

28 lah la sk’oponik ti mu ˀantze,
jech la ti mu ˀantze mu la xtak’av.

29 pere k’uchaˀal mu sk’an xtak’ave xi la ti vinike.
pere naˀtik.
haˀ yuˀun nan makal xa ye xi la ti vinike.

30 jech la ti vinike.
saˀ la ˀaxux ˀi moy.
laj la yak’be la ta sat ta sjol ti mu ˀantze.

31 jech la ti mu ˀantze,
jun la smu tzijil ti smu bek’tal lae.

32 laj la yutzil ti sk’ob la ti mu vinike.
jun la stuil tajmek ti sk’obe.

33 vaˀun jech la ti ˀantz ˀune:
laj la smakik la ta rin ta teˀ ti mu ˀantze.

34 vaˀun ti mu ˀantz ˀune,
mu la xk’opoj tajmek.
pasem la ta ˀumaˀ ti mu ˀantze.
vaˀun ti mu ˀantz la ˀune.

35 k’alal la ˀik’ub ti banamil la ˀune,
jech la ti vinike ˀune mu la xvay tajmek ˀun.
puru la chik’inajel ta spas tajmek.

36 puru jlikel ˀun vaˀun tal la ti pukuj ˀune.
jech la ti pukuj ˀune k’ot la ta sna ti vinike.

37 ti pukuj lae.
te la sbuslajet la ta na ti pukuje.

And this is what happened then to the poor woman. 27
They dragged her into the man's house.
"Sure enough. I see that it is indeed my wife," declared the man.

They spoke to the poor woman, 28
But the poor woman did not answer.

"But why doesn't she want to answer?" wondered the man. 29
"Who knows?
It seems that she has been struck dumb," said the man.

And the man did this. 30
He found some garlic and tobacco.
He put these things on the face and head of the poor woman.[5]

As for this poor woman, 31
In truth, her repulsive body smelled horrible.

The unfortunate man smelled her hand. 32
Her hand stank horribly.

So the woman's story goes on: 33
They covered the poor naked soul with a burlap-bag.[6]

As for the poor woman, 34
She was absolutely incapable of speaking.
The poor woman had been struck dumb.
That was the fate of the poor woman.

Soon, night fell. 35
But the man was utterly unable to sleep.
He just lay in bed sweating.

In a little while the demon came. 36
The demon came right up to the man's house.

This was what the demon did. 37
He swooped over, trying hard to make his way into the house.

38 vaˀun ti mu pukuj la ˀune.
bat la ˀun.

39 jech la ti mu ˀantz la ˀune,
ˀi k'opoj la ˀun k'alal la sakub ti ˀosile.

40 jech la ti mu vinike,
ˀi la sk'opon la ti yajnil la ˀune.
k'u ˀaˀelan ˀun xˀut la ti yajnil ti mu vinik lae.

41 jech la ti yajnil ti mu vinik la ˀune.
ˀi k'opoj la ˀun.

42 pere k'alal la ta xk'opoj ti ˀantze la ˀune,
puch'ul la ta xk'opoj.
ti la xˀal ti sloˀil lae.

43 ta jkuch kaˀi ˀoˀ xi la ti mu ˀantze.
ˀuch'an mi ta xˀech' ˀavuˀun.

44 k'usi ti ˀipe xi la ti mu vinike.
jaˀ k'ux tajmek ti jch'ute xi la ti mu ˀantze.

45 jech la ti mu vinike:
saˀbe la spoxil ti yajnil ti mu vinike.
vaˀun stabe la ti sposil ti yajnil ti mu vinik la ˀune.

46 jech la ti mu vinik la ˀune.
yak'be ti spoxil ti yajnil ti mu vinik la ˀune.

47 jech la ti spoxil ti yajnil ti mu vinike la ˀune.
jaˀ la ti yibel ti makome.

48 veno ˀi k'opoj la ˀun.
la jyal ti k'us ˀelan ti yil,
ti k'alal la ti k'ot ta sna ti mu pukuj la ˀune.

49 la jkil ma li k'ote xi la ti mu ˀantze.
k'us ˀelan la ˀavil ˀun xi la ti vinike.

However, this was what happened to the demon. 38
He went away without being able to enter.[7]

As for the poor woman, 39
She was at last able to speak when dawn came the next day.

As for the bewildered man, 40
He spoke to his wife.
"How are you?" the bewildered man asked his wife.

This was what the bewildered man's wife did. 41
She spoke up.

But even as the woman spoke, 42
She was speaking while lying flat on her back.
The words came with difficulty.

"I'm thirsty," said the poor woman. 43
"Drink, then, if you think it will help.

What's wrong with you?" asked the unfortunate man. 44
"What really hurts me most is my stomach," said the poor woman.

And the bewildered man proceeded to do this: 45
The man went to find some medicine for his wife.
At last, the bewildered soul found the remedy for his wife.

With this, the bewildered man's mission was accomplished. 46
The bewildered man gave his wife the medicine.

And this was the medicine that the bewildered man's wife received. 47
It was a tea made from the roots of wild blackberries.[8]

Then she spoke. 48
She described what she had seen,
All that had happened when she was taken to the dwelling of the demon.

"I saw it all when I got there," declared the poor woman. 49
"What was it like? What did you see?" asked the man.

50 k'alal li k'ote petbil li yal ta xab.
jech ti mu pukuje ˀoy xik'.
spetojun yalel.

51 veno k'alal ti li k'ote jech ti xchiˀiltak ti mu pukuje.
mi tal xa ti jveˀeltike xi ma ti mu pukuje.
xi la ti mu ˀantze.

52 jech la ti mu pukuje k'alal la k'ot ti ˀantze:
mi ta jtiˀtik ˀo mi ta jkobtik xi la ti mu pukuje.
moˀoj ta jkobtik xi la ti xchiˀiltake.

53 jech la ti ˀantze.
petat la ˀech'el ta tem.

54 voˀon ta xikob van baˀyuk xi la ti mu pukuje.
veno kob vanan baˀyuk xi la ti mu pukuje.

55 jech la ti mu pukuje.
laj la yak' la ti ˀate.

56 jech la ti mu pukuje k'alal ta la xˀak' ti ˀate:
mi ta jkolta tal skotol ti kate xi la ti mu pukuje.
moˀoj mu xakolta tal skotol xi la ti mu ˀantze.
veno moˀoj chaˀe xi la ti mu pukuje.

57 jech la ti ˀantze.
toj muk' la yaˀi ti yat ti mu pukuje.

58 jech la ti mu pukuj lae,
puru la sesina ti smu veˀelike.

59 jech la ti siˀike,
puru la sat toj.

60 k'alal ta la xveˀik,
ti mu pukuje chotol la ta stem.

"I was carried in his arms down into a sinkhole. 50
The wicked demon had wings.
He carried me in his winged arms as we descended.

When we arrived, the relatives of the wicked demon spoke. 51
'Has our dinner come?' asked the demons."
So spoke the poor woman as she told her story.

One wicked demon came up to the woman and spoke: 52
"Shall we eat her or fuck her?" asked the awful creature.
"Let's not eat her. Let's fuck her," said his friends.

And this is what happened to the woman then. 53
She was carried off to bed.

"Well, I'll be the first to fuck her," said one wicked demon. 54
"Good. Go ahead and be the first to fuck her," said the other damned demons.

And with that, the wicked demon went ahead and did it. 55
He fucked her.

This is what happened as the wicked demon was fucking her: 56
"Shall I take my cock out now?" asked the awful creature.
"No, don't take it out all the way," said the poor woman.
"Okay, then, I won't," said the wicked demon.

Such was the woman's state of mind. 57
Frankly, she was enjoying the feeling of the demon's big cock a whole lot.[9]

Now, the demons had other odd habits.[10] 58
Consider their awful food: they had only dried beef jerky.

Consider their firewood, 59
For this, they used only pinecones.

Their eating habits were also strange, 60
They would eat as they sat on the bed.

61 k'alal ta la xveˀike,
jech la ti ˀantze ˀak'bat la sveˀel.

62 jech la ti sveˀel ti mu ˀantze,
puru la bek'et voˀbil ta k'ok'.

63 jech la ti mu ˀantze.
mu la sk'an stiˀ ti mu bek'ete.
toj tu la tajmek.

64 jech la ti mu pukuj la ˀune.
k'uchaˀal mu xak'an xaveˀe xi la ti mu pukuj.
laj xa jtiˀne xi la ti mu ˀantze.

65 jech la ti mu pukuje.
ˀi saˀbe la ti sveˀele.

66 jech la ti ˀantz ˀune.
te la snak'oj ta sk'uˀ ti sveˀel ti mu ˀantze.

67 jech la ti mu pukuje.
ta la la stabe ti sveˀel ti mu ˀantze.

68 ˀa li liˀ xkil ˀune xi la ti mu pukuje.
yuˀun ˀat ta xak'an ma leˀe xi la ti pukuje.

69 jech la ti mu pukuje.
pet sut la ˀech'el ta tem ti mu ˀantze.
bat la skob ti ˀantze.

70 jech la ti ˀantze:
mu jk'an mu jk'an xi la ti ˀantze.

71 ke mi mu xak'an xi la ti pukuje.
ˀi yak'be la ˀat ti mu ˀantze.

72 jech la ti mu ˀantz la ˀune.
likel la ˀayan la yol ta ˀora.

That was just how they ate, 61
It was there on the bed where the woman was offered food.

As for the food that the poor woman was offered, 62
It was just roasted meat.

But the poor woman responded in this manner. 63
She refused to eat the putrid meat.
It stank horribly.

Then the wicked demon spoke. 64
"Why don't you want to eat?" asked the awful creature.
"I already ate some," said the poor woman.

Then the wicked demon did this, for he did not believe her. 65
He looked for the food that he had given her.

And this is what the woman had done. 66
The poor soul had hidden her food there in the folds of her clothing.

And this is what the wicked demon did. 67
He found the poor woman's food.

"I see it here in your skirt," said the wicked demon. 68
"I'll bet you'd rather have my cock stuck in there," said the awful creature.

And this is what the wicked demon did. 69
He grabbed up the poor woman in his arms and carried her off to bed.
Then he proceeded to bang the woman.

Then the woman shouted. 70
"I don't want it! I don't want it!" the woman pled.

"Oh, so you don't want to do it?" taunted the demon. 71
And with that he stuffed his cock into the wretched woman.

And this was the poor woman's fate. 72
She became pregnant right away.

73 lok' la ˀoxib xemuna ˀi vok' la yol ti mu ˀantze.
jech la ti yol ti mu ˀantze mu kerem.

74 la k'alal la vok' ti yol ti ˀantze,
likel la bat ta ˀora ta nab.

75 jech la ti nene pukuje,
likel la vil ˀech'el ta ˀora.

76 k'alal la sut talel ti yol ti mu ˀantze,
likel la ch'i talel ta ˀora.

77 li tal xa me xi la vulel ti yol ti mu ˀantz lae.
mi la tal ˀun kol si la ti mu ˀantz ˀune.

78 jech la ti mu ˀantz ˀune:
ta la xtal la yaˀi ta sna ti mu ˀantz la ˀune.

79 jech la ti smalal ti mu ˀantz la ˀune.
ta la stzak la mi lok' la ti yajnil ˀune ti mu pukuje.

80 jech la ti mu pukuje:
bat la ta paxyal ta teˀtik ti mu pukuj.

81 jech la ti mu pukuje la ˀun jal.
la ch'abal bu xtal stot ti mu neneˀ pukuje.
jech la ti mu neneˀ pukuj ˀune.

82 ˀoy la te la jun la ton ta xab.
jech la ti mu neneˀ pukuj ˀune.
laj la spet la ti ton ˀune.

83 teke ˀun chaˀe ta jpet kaˀtik li tone xi la ti yol ti mu ˀantze.
petoˀ ˀun chaˀe mi xlik ˀavuˀune xi la ti ˀantze.
veno xi la ti mu neneˀ pukuje.

84 jech la ti ton la ˀune.
ˀi lik la yuˀun la ˀun.

Within three weeks the poor woman's child was born.[11] 73
The wretched soul's demon-child turned out to be a boy.

Soon after the woman's demon-child was born, 74
He went off straightaway to the sea.

That's what the demon-child did. 75
He flew away, vanishing from sight at once.[12]

Then the poor woman's son returned. 76
He grew up very quickly.

"Now I have come back," said the poor woman's son upon returning. 77
"Have you come back then, sonny boy?" asked the wretched soul.

Such was the poor woman's state of mind: 78
A great yearning to go home had overcome the poor, wretched soul.

But, the poor woman's demon husband didn't care about her feelings. 79
The demon-husband would grab his wife whenever she tried to leave.

Then, one day the wicked demon did this: 80
The awful creature went for a walk in the woods.

The wicked demon-husband stayed there for quite a while. 81
The father of the dreadful demon-child did not seem to be coming home.
So this is what the dreadful demon-child did.

There was a rock there, in the cave. 82
And this is what the dreadful demon-child did with it.
He lifted it up in his arms.

"Now, then, don't worry. I'm going to see how heavy this rock is," 83
said the child of the poor woman.
"Pick it up, then, if you can budge it," said the woman.
"All right," said the dreadful demon-child.

And so it happened with the rock. 84
In no time at all he lifted it up.[13]

85 muˀyuk mas ˀol ma li tone xi la ti mu neneˀ pukuje.
petun kaˀtik ˀek ˀun chaˀe xi la ti smeˀ ti mu neneˀ pukuje.
veno xi la ti neneˀ pukuje.

86 jech la ti mu neneˀ pukuj la ˀun.
vil la ˀech'el la ta ˀora.

87 jech la ti smeˀ ti mu neneˀ pukuje,
balch'uj la ta teˀtik la ˀun.
makal la k'ot ta k'obteˀ ti mu neneˀ pukuj la ˀune.

88 jech la ti mu neneˀ pukuj la ˀune.
chotol la k'ot la ta teˀtik.

89 jech la ti mu neneˀ pukuj la ˀune.
muˀyuk bu la cham.

90 jech la ti mu neneˀ pukuj la ˀune.
lik la ta vil ch'el noˀoxtok.

91 bu ta ˀanae meˀ xi la ti mu neneˀ pukuj la ˀune.
jaˀ liˀ ma ti jnae xi la ti mu ˀantze.
veno xi la ti yol ti mu ˀantze.
veno k'alal la k'ot ti mu ˀantz la ta sna ˀune.

92 jech la ti smalal ti mu ˀantze.
k'alal k'ot ta sna la ti mu pukuje.

93 bu bat ti kajnile xi la ti mu pukuje.
ˀi saˀ la tajmek ti yajnil lae.

94 jech la ti neneˀ pukuj la ˀune.
k'alal la k'ot ti smeˀ ti neneˀ pukuj la ˀune.
jatav la ta ˀora tajmek ti yol ti mu ˀantz la ˀune.

95 jech la ti neneˀ pukuj ˀune.
laj la ta tiˀel yol ti mu ˀantz la ˀune.

"This rock doesn't weigh very much at all," said the dreadful demon-child. 85
"Then see if you can pick me up, too," suggested the mother of the
dreadful demon-child.
"All right," said the demon-child.

And the dreadful demon-child did this. 86
He flew away immediately, carrying his mother in his arms.

And as for the dreadful demon-child's mother, 87
She fell from his arms into the woods.
It seems that the dreadful demon-child had crashed against
the branch of a tree as he was flying.

And as for the dreadful demon-child himself, 88
He landed in a sitting position in the woods.

And, furthermore, the dreadful demon-child survived. 89
He did not die.

So the dreadful demon-child made another try. 90
Off he flew once again with his mother.

"Where is your house, Mother?" asked the dreadful demon-child 91
when they were airborn.
"That's my house, right down there," said the poor woman.
"Okay," said the poor woman's son.
Well, with that, the unfortunate woman finally reached her house.

Now, as for the poor woman's demon husband, 92
This was what happened when the awful demon got home.

"Where did my wife go?" roared the awful demon. 93
He looked all over for his wife.

And this is what the demon-child had been up to. 94
The demon-child helped his mother to get home.
Whereupon, the poor woman's son fled immediately.

And, as for the demon-child, this was his sad fate. 95
The poor woman's demon-child died, bitten to death by his angry father.[14]

96 vaˀun ˀa ti mu ˀantz la ˀune ˀi cham la ˀun.
muˀyuk xa la bu ˀech' la yuˀun ti mu ˀantz lae.

97 jech ti kuentoe.
jaˀ la jyalbun kaˀi ti jyayae.
jaˀ smeˀ ti jmeˀe.

98 k'alal lik ˀo ti kuentoe.
yuˀun la te la k'ot la pukuj ta sna la ti jyayae.

99 mu jnaˀ mi pukuj liˀ tal ta jnae xi ti jyayae.
jaˀ yuˀun te lik ˀo ti kuentoe.

Likewise, the poor woman died also. 96
The wretched soul did not recover.

And that's the story, as I know it. 97
My grandmother told it to me.
She was my mother's mother.

As for the way the story came up, it was this way. 98
A demon had been lurking around my grandmother's house.

"It seems to me that a demon has been around my house," 99
said my grandmother.
And that is how the story came to be told.[15]

1 ˀoy jun kuento sventa vinik.
bat ˀatinuk ta ˀuk'um ti vinike.

2 jech la ti vinike.
ta la xˀabtej la ta k'ixin ˀosil ti vinike.
vaˀun bat la ta ˀatimol ˀun.

3 vaˀun k'alal la k'ot ti vinike.
ˀichot xi la k'otel ti vinike.
ˀi slok' la sk'uˀ ti vinike.

4 vaˀun ti vinik la ˀune.
jaˀ to la yaˀi likel ˀoch ta chon ti vinike.

5 vaˀun ti mu chon la ˀune.
likel bik'at ti vinike.

6 jech la ti vinike ˀavan to la ˀun:
ˀuuuuu . . . xi la ti vinike.

7 jech la ti mu chone.
likel la ˀoch ta voˀo ti ˀayine.

8 jech la ti vinik la ˀune.
tiˀat la ta ˀayin ti vinike.
ˀi lok' la jun xemuna.

9 jech la ti vinike.
ˀi te la kuxul ta yut sch'ut ti mu chone.

TEXT 40

OF A MAN WHO WAS SWALLOWED BY A WATER MONSTER

Marián López Calixto

This is a story about a certain man. 1
This man went to bathe in the river.

This is that man's story. 2
He was working in Hot Country in the Pacific Lowlands.
And he went to wash off in the river.

Well, this is what happened when the man got there. 3
He sat down when he arrived there.
He took off his clothes.

Then this happened to him. 4
Presently, the man had the sudden sensation that he had entered the body of some animal.

This damned monster had shown up. 5
And the man was promptly swallowed up, just like that!

Even then, as he was being swallowed, you could still hear the man screaming, just like this: 6
"Uuuuu . . . !" the man cried.

And the damned animal did this. 7
The water monster immediately plunged into the water.[1]

Such was the man's fate. 8
He had been eaten up by the water monster.
And so a week passed.

Such was the man's fate. 9
He was alive there in the belly of the damned monster.

10 vaʔun ti vinik la ʔune.
ʔi te la javal ta yut xch'ut chone ti mu vinik la ʔune.

11 veno jech la ti vinik la ʔune ʔoy la skuchilu ʔun.
ʔi saʔ la ti skuchilue.

12 ya pere ʔoy me jkuchilu yaʔel xi la ti vinike.
ʔi saʔ la ti skuchilue.
ʔi spik la ti xch'ute.
vaʔun ʔi ta la sta ti skuchilu ʔune.

13 ʔi yaʔi la lok' ta tiʔ voʔo ti mu chon ʔune.
jech la ti vinik la ʔune ʔi yaʔi la k'ixin ti k'ak'al la ʔune.

14 vaʔun jech la ti skuchilue ʔi slok'es ta ʔora ʔun.
vaʔun ʔan la xi te javal ti mu chon la ʔune.
jech la ti vinik la ʔune ʔisboj la ta ʔora ʔun.

15 vaʔun jech la ti mu chon ʔune.
likel la ʔoch ta voʔo ta ʔora ti mu chone.

16 vaʔun ti vinik la ʔune ʔi te la javal.
la kom ta tiʔ voʔo ti vinike y laj yil la ti banamile.

17 jech la ti vinik la ʔune ʔichoti la ʔun ʔi sk'el ti banamile.
jaʔ to yil ʔi te la chotol ta tiʔ voʔo ti vinike.

18 jech la ti vinik la ʔune.
solel la spok la sba ta voʔo ti vinike ʔa ti mu sbek'tal lae.
solel la spich'il ta sim ti mu chon ta sbek'tal la ti vinike.

19 jech la ti vinik la ʔune.
lik la spok sba ti vinike.

Now, then, the man's fate unfolded some more. 10
The unfortunate man lay there on his back inside the belly
of the monster.

Now, it happened that the man had a knife on him. 11
And he set about to look for it.

"Hey, it seems I've got my knife with me," declared the man. 12
And he set about looking for it.
He felt around by his waist.
And sure enough, he found his knife.

At this point, he became aware that the damned monster had come 13
out of the water to lie on the shore.
He knew this was so, for he could feel the heat of the day
through the animal's body.

So, he lost no time in taking out his knife. 14
It seemed to him that the monster was lying there resting.
So the man quickly cut a gash in its body.

Then the damned monster responded. 15
The awful creature quickly plunged back into the water.

But as for the man, he found himself lying there on his back, 16
liberated from the monster's belly.
The man was left there on the shore, and he saw that he
was on firm land.

So the man sat up, and stared around him at the landscape. 17
Soon the man realized that he was sitting on the riverbank.

This is what the man did. 18
The man just wanted to wash off his mangled body in the river water.
Indeed, the man's body was just covered with clumps of slime
that had been left from the insides of the damned monster.

So the man did this. 19
The man proceeded to wash himself off.

20 vaˀun ti sbek'tal la ti vinike:
solel la ti yakane tiˀbil xa la tajmek.
tuk xa la sbakil ti yakane.

21 jech la ti svexe.
k'uxbil xa la tajmek svex ti vinike.

22 vaˀun tal la ta chobtik ti vinike.
ˀi t'ant'an la tal ti vinike.
jech la ti sbek'tale ta la xlok' la xch'ich'el ti vinike.

23 vaˀun k'ot la ti vinik ˀune.
k'ot la sk'opon xchiˀiltak.

24 vaˀun mi liˀote xi la k'otel ti vinike.
liˀune k'uxi la tal ˀun xi ti schiˀiltak ˀune.

25 muˀyuk.
yuˀun ˀo jkuchilu.
jech ti jkuchilu ˀune la jsaˀ ˀun.
ˀi te la jta ti jkuchilu ˀune.

26 vaˀun kaˀi ti li lok' ta tiˀ voˀo ˀune.
jech ti jkuchilu ˀune la jlok'cs ta ˀora ˀun.

27 kaˀi ti mu chon ˀune te haval ta tiˀ voˀo ˀune.
jech ti jkuchilu ˀune la jboj ti mu chon ˀune.

28 kaˀi li lok' ta xch'ut ti mu chon ˀun,
pere muˀyuk li cham ˀun.

29 jaˀ noˀox ti jbek'tale.
ta xˀavan tajmek ti kakane.

30 mu jnaˀ mi xkuch' kuˀun ti yakanele.
mu jnaˀ mi ˀoy xpoxil xkal ˀune.

31 jech ti kakane tuk xa sbakil.
yavlo mi ˀo bu jtatik ti spoxil ˀune xi la ti xchiˀiltak ˀune.

Now, as for the man's body, it was not in good shape. 20
His legs were just horribly chewed up.
His legs were nothing but bones.

And as for his trousers, 21
The man's trousers had been almost completely chewed up.

In this pitiful condition the man came to the cornfield. 22
The man appeared naked.
The man's body was streaming with blood.

So the man arrived. 23
He appeared and greeted his companions.

So it went: "Are you here?" the man said as he arrived. 24
"We are here. But what are *you* doing back here?" asked his companions.[2]

"It's okay. 25
I had my knife with me.
I searched for it.
And, sure enough, I found my knife.

Then I realized that the monster had gone ashore. 26
So I lost no time in getting out my knife.

I realized that the damned monster was beached on the shore. 27
So, with my knife, I cut the bastard open.

Then I realized that I had really escaped from the monster's belly, 28
That I had not died.

But my body in fact feels like it is going to die. 29
My legs are shot through with pain.

I wonder whether I will ever survive with my legs in this shape. 30
I wonder if there is any cure that can make them get better.

Why, my legs have become nothing but bones," lamented the poor man. 31
"Son of a bitch! Where can we find some medicine to cure him?"
said his comrades.

32 vaˀun jech la ti vinik la ˀune.
skuchik la talel ta sna ti vinik.
ˀi mu xa la xanav lek ti vinike.

33 vaˀun k’ot la ta sna ti vinike la ˀune.
jech la ti yajnil ˀune ˀi xiˀ la tajmek.

34 vaˀun bul batik me xi la k’otel ti vinike la ˀune.
laˀ me buch’un ˀuxuk taj ˀune xi la ti ˀantz la ˀune.

35 voˀon kutik.
liˀ tal kak’ ta ˀamalale xi la ti vinik ˀune.

36 ˀa, pere k’uchaˀal k’usi la spas xi la ti yajnil ti vinikˀune.
pes muˀyuk jech la ˀamalale yuˀun bat ˀatinuk ta ˀuk’um.

37 vaˀun la jyalbun ˀun:
ta xibat ta ˀatimol xiyut la ˀamalal ˀune.
vaˀun batan ˀun chaˀe xkut la ˀamalal ˀune.

38 vaˀun bat ˀun.
muˀyuk bu xtal ta ˀamalal ˀune.

39 la jmalakutik la jmalakutik.
ch’abal bu xtal ta ˀamalal ˀune.

40 vaˀun libatkutik jk’elkutik ta ˀamalal ˀune.
lik’otkutik ta stz’el voˀun ˀi muˀyuk ta ˀamalal ˀune.
ˀi lisutkutik talel ˀun.

41 veno tekeˀ ˀun chaˀe.
k’uxi ti bat ti vinik ˀune xichikutik ˀun.

42 vaˀun lok’ jun xemuna ˀun.
jaˀ to me kilkutik ˀun xvaˀbun talel ta ˀamalal ˀune.

Well, the man's story proceeded like this. 32
They carried the man home.
The poor guy could no longer get around very well.

Soon the man reached home. 33
And his wife . . . she was horrified!

Their encounter happened like this: "We have arrived," announced the men when they got there. 34
"Come forward, then. Who are you?" inquired the woman.

"It's just us. 35
We have come to bring your husband home," replied the men.

"Really? Why? What happened to him?" inquired the man's wife. 36
"Well, not much. It's just that your husband went to wash off in the river.

This is what he said to us: 37
'I'm off to take a bath in the river,' your husband told us.
'Fine, be off. Good-bye,' we said to your husband.

With that, he departed. 38
But then your husband did not return.

We waited and waited. 39
But your husband just didn't come back.

So we went to check up on your husband. 40
We went over there close to the river, but your husband was nowhere to be seen.
So we went back to our camp.

'Well, well. What's to be done? 41
What's become of the guy?' we said to each other.

Then a week passed. 42
It wasn't until then that we saw your husband staggering toward us.

43 pere bu xa noˀox lok' talel ˀun leˀe xichikutik ˀun xi la ti vinik ˀune.
va ˀun yalbukutik ˀun libat ˀatinkun.
stiˀun mu chon.
li ˀoch ta yut xch'ut ti mu chone xi la ˀamalal ˀune.
xi la ti vinike.

44 jech la ti vinik ˀune.
ˀi te la skomtzan ti vinike.

45 vaˀun ti vinik la ˀune muˀyuk la ˀech' yuˀun.
cham la ti vinike.

46 ˀoy la yuni vorxa.
jech la ti svorxae k'uxbil xa la ta chon.
ti syavil stak'ine.

47 jech la ti sniˀ sk'obe ch'abal xa la sbek'tal;
puru xa la sbakil ti sk'obe.
jun xa la stuˀil tajmek ti vinike.

48 jech la ti vinike te la nakal ta pat vitz ti vinike.
yuˀun tal la saˀ abtel ta k'ixin ˀosil ti vinike.

49 vaˀun jaˀ jech laj ˀo ti kuentoe.
la jyalbun kaˀi jun chiˀil ta chanun ta jlumal.
ˀi jaˀ te lik ˀo ti kuentoe.

50 k'alal lik ˀo ti kuentoe yuˀun ˀoy srevista ti mastaroe.
ˀi la jk'elkutik ˀun.
jaˀ jech li kuento lik' ˀoe.
laj ˀo.

'But where on earth can he be coming from,' we said to each other," 43
the men reported.
"'Then he said to us, 'I went to bathe.
A goddamn monster attacked me.
I ended up in the bastard's belly,' said your husband."
That is what the men told to the victim's wife.

And so the man's story continues. 44
They left the man there at home.

But the man's affliction did not pass. 45
The man died.

He had once carried a little bag in his hand. 46
But this bag had been chewed up by the monster.
It had been his coin purse.[3]

That is why his fingers no longer had any flesh on them; 47
His hands had become nothing but bone.
And indeed, the man's whole body stank of rotten flesh.

Now, this man who was the victim came from the hamlet of Pat Vitz. 48
This man had gone to Hot Country to get work.

And that's the end of this story. 49
A friend told it to me at school there in Chamula Center.
It was there that the subject came up.

When the subject came up, it was suggested by a magazine that 50
the schoolteacher had.
We were looking at it.[4]
That is the way the story came up.
And that's the end.

1 ˀa li voˀne ˀoy la jun kerem ta xanav ta be.
tey la snup ta be jun vinik.

2 buy chabat xi la ti vinik.
yuˀun ta jsaˀ ˀabtel xi la ti kerem.

3 mi ˀoy xa la ta ti ˀabtel xi la ti vinik.
muˀyuk la jta ˀoy kabtel xi la ti kerem.

4 ˀoy kabtel mi xak'an xi la ti vinik.
xuˀuk xi la ti kerem.

5 pero mu ta ˀorauk xi la ti vinik.
buy ˀora ˀoy ˀavabtel xi la ti kerem.

6 k'alal ta ˀoxib k'ak'al xi la ti vinik.
tey xajak' buy xbat ti jna xi la ti vinik.

TEXT 41

On the Adventures of Xun beyond the Sea

Xalik López Setjol

Long ago there was a boy who was walking along the road.[1] 1
There he met a certain man.

"Where are you going?" asked the man. 2
"I'm looking for work," replied the boy.

"Have you found work yet?" asked the man. 3
"No, I haven't found any work at all," said the boy.

"I can give you work if you want it," said the man. 4
"All right," answered the boy.

"But not right now," said the man. 5
"Then when will there be work?" asked the boy.

"In three days," said the man. 6
"Then you are to ask how to get to my house," said the man.

7 buy xbat ti ʔana xi la ti kerem.
ʔa tey xbat ti bu ʔoy mar muerte sine xi la ti vinik.

8 ti k'alal ta xajak' buy xbat ti jna xi la ti vinik,
ʔaʔ ta xajak' bu ʔoy ti mar muerte sine.
ʔaʔ tey nakalun xi la ti vinik.

9 xuʔuk xi la ti kerem.
k'usi ʔabi xi la ti kerem.

10 ʔuʔun reyun xi la ti vinik.
ti k'alal ta xajak' ti jna:
bu ʔoy sna ti rey xachi xi la ti vinik.

11 xuʔuk kolaval xi la ti kerem.
muʔyuk vokol xi la ti vinik.

12 ti k'alal sta yabtel ti kerem xkuxet xa la yoʔnton.
sut la vayuk ta sna.

"But where is your house?" asked the boy. 7
"It's there by the Dead Sea of Sine," said the man.[2]

"When you inquire about the location of my house," explained the man, 8
"You are to ask, 'Where is the Dead Sea of Sine?'
Right there is where I live," said the man.

"All right," said the boy. 9
"But what's your name?" asked the boy.

"I am a king," said the man. 10
"When you inquire about the location of my house, you are to say this:
'Where is the house of the king?' you are to ask," said the man.

"All right. Thank you," said the boy. 11
"You're welcome," said the man.

Since the boy had found work he was very happy. 12
He went back home to rest.

FIGURE 58

"But where is your house?" asked the boy.
"It's there by the Dead Sea of Sine," said the man.

13 ˀoxib la k'ak'al te ˀoy ta sna ti kerem.
ti k'alal sakub ti xchanibal k'ak'al sob lok' batel ta ˀabtel ti kerem.

14 ti k'alal bat ta ˀabtel ti kerem:
yich' la batel sk'u xchiˀuk jun smachita.

15 ti k'alal bat ta ˀabtel ti kerem.
xkuxet xa la yoˀnton.

16 ti k'alal ta xanav ti kerem.
xkuxet la yoˀnton.
pere sjunul la k'ak'al ta xanav ti kerem.

17 ti k'alal mi ˀik'ub ˀosil,
ta la xch'amun la ti buy ta xvay ti kerem.

18 ti k'alal sakub ta yok'omal,
sob la ta xlok' ta sanavil ti kerem.

19 ˀaˀ la ˀech jujun k'ak'al.
ven sob ta xlok' ta xanavil ti kerem.

20 ˀaˀ la ˀech jujun k'ak'al.
ti sjunul k'ak'al ta xanav.

21 ˀaˀ la ˀech jujun k'ak'al.
ta xch'amun ta xvay ti kerem.

22 ti k'alal lok' ta xanavil ti kerem pere bik'it la.
pero tey la ˀich'i ˀech'el ti buy ta xanav ˀech'el ta be ti kerem.

23 ti k'alal xanav xa nat ti kerem snup la jun vinik.
buy chabat xi la ti vinik.
yuˀun ta xibat saˀ abtel xi la ti kerem.

24 buch'u sna ta xabat ta saˀ ˀabtel xi la ti vinik.
ta sna rey ta xibat ta saˀ abtel xi la ti kerem.

He stayed at his house for three days. 13
When the fourth day dawned, he set out early for his work.

Upon setting out for his task, the boy did this: 14
He took along his clothing and his machete.

Upon setting out for his task, the boy felt good. 15
His heart was happy.

As he traveled, the boy was content. 16
His heart was happy,
Even though the boy spent all of each day on the open road.

When it grew dark, 17
The boy would ask permission to sleep at someone's house.

And when the following day would dawn, 18
The boy would set out early on his way.

That was how each day passed. 19
The boy would start his journey nice and early.

That was how each day passed. 20
He would walk all day, every day.

That was how each day passed. 21
The boy would ask for a place to sleep in someone's home.

When the boy set off on his journey he was very small. 22
But as he traveled, he grew up.[3]

After he had traveled a very long way, he met a man. 23
"Where are you going?" asked the man.
"I'm trying to find work," said the boy.

"In whose house are you planning to find work?" asked the man. 24
"I'm going to find work in the house of the king," said the boy.

25 k'usi ta xanaʔ mi ʔoy ʔabtel ti rey xi la ti vinik.
yuʔun la jnup ta be.
la jyalbun ʔoy yabtel xi la ti kerem.

26 k'usi xbat sbe xi la ti kerem.
liʔ ta xabat ta norte xi la ti vinik.

27 xuʔ ʔechuk kolaval xi la ti kerem.
muʔyuk vokol xi la ti vinik.

28 ti k'alal laj snup ta be vinik ti kerem,
laj sjak'be k'u snatil snamal sk'an xk'ot ta sna ti rey.

29 sk'an jun toston xi la ti vinik.
xuʔuk xi la ti kerem.

30 ti k'alal k'ot ta sna rey ti kerem.
chanib la velta laj sjak' ta be.

31 ti k'alal laj sjak' ta xchibal velta ti kerem,
yuʔun tey laj snup ta be jun vinik.

32 buy ta xabat xi la ti vinik.
ta xibat ta saʔ ʔabtel xi la ti kerem.

33 buch'u yabtel xi la ti vinik.
ʔaʔ yabtel rey xi la ti kerem.

34 k'u snamal sk'an xik'to xi la ti kerem.
sk'an chib tak'in xi la ti vinik.

35 k'usi xbat sbelil sna ti rey xi la ti kerem.
liʔ xbat ta norte xi la ti vinik.

36 xuʔ ʔechuk xi la ti kerem.
pere yak'be la yepal xanavil ti kerem.

"How do you know whether the king has work for you?" asked the man. 25
"Because I met him on the road.
He told me he had work," said the boy.

"Which way is it to his house?" asked the boy. 26
"It's this way, to the north," said the man.

"All right, thank you," said the boy. 27
"You're welcome," replied the man.

When the boy had met this man on the road, 28
He also asked him how much farther it was to the king's house.

"You still have a *tostón* to go," said this man.[4] 29
"Very well," said the boy.

In order for the boy to reach the house of the king, he would have to ask for a lot of help. 30
Four times on his journey he would have to ask for directions.

Now, the boy asked for advice for the second time. 31
For he met another man on the road.

"Where are you going?" asked the man. 32
"I'm going to find work," answered the boy.

"Who is going to give you work?" inquired the man. 33
"It's the king who has work," said the boy.

"How far do I still have to go?" asked the boy. 34
"You still have two *reales* to go," said the man.[5]

"Which is the road to the king's house?" asked the boy. 35
"It is there to the north," said the man.[6]

"All right," said the boy. 36
And with this, the boy took courage for his journey.

37 ti k’alal laj snup ta be jun vinik ti kerem ta yoxibal velta.
buy xbat sna ti rey xi la ti kerem.
liˀ xbat ta norte xi la ti vinik.

38 k’usi ta xbat ˀasaˀ ta sna ti rey xi la ti vinik.
yuˀun ta xibat ta saˀ ˀabtel xi la ti kerem.

39 k’usi ˀabtelal ˀoy yuˀun ta sna rey xi la ti vinik.
mu jnaˀ xi la ti kerem.

40 ti k’alal laj sjak’ ta yoxibal velta ti kerem.
pero muk’ xa la jutuk ti kerem.

41 ti k’alal ta xa la xk’ot ta sna rey,
ti kerem lek xa muk’ta xa.

42 la spas ta jun vinik.
ti k’alal ta xa xk’ot ti kerem.

43 ˀoy la tey k’ot sjak’ ta sna ti vinik:
buy xbat sna ti rey xi la ti kerem.
li ˀoy ta jech mar xi la ti vinik.

44 k’usi ta xbat ˀasaˀ xi la ti vinik.
yuˀun ta xibat ta yabtel xi la ti kerem.

45 pero ch’abal yabtel xi la ti vinik.
pero yuˀun la jyalbun ti ˀoy yabtel xi la ti kerem.

46 buy la k’opon xi la ti vinik.
tey laj jk’opon ta be xi la ti kerem.

47 bat jak’o ˀavaˀi mi ˀoy yabtel ti rey xi la ti vinik.
xuˀuk xi la ti kerem.

48 pero mu xajelav xi la ti vinik.
k’uchaˀal mu xijelav xi la ti kerem.

Then the boy met still a third man on the road. 37
"Where is the house of the king?" asked the boy.
"It's there to the north," replied the man.

"But what are you looking for at the house of the king?" asked the man. 38
"I'm going to find work," said the boy.

"What kind of work is there at the house of the king?" asked the man. 39
"I don't know," answered the boy.

And at the time of this third encounter, the boy had changed. 40
The boy was growing up to be a man.

By the time he got to the house of the king, 41
The boy was already a full-grown man.

He had become a man. 42
So the boy had changed upon reaching his destination.

Finally, he reached the house of a man to whom he asked the 43
following question:
"Where is the house of the king?" asked the boy.
"It's there beyond the sea," said the man.

"What do you seek there?" asked the man. 44
"I'm going there to find work," said the boy.

"But he doesn't have work," said the man. 45
"But he told me that he indeed does have work," said the boy.

"Where did you talk to him?" asked the man. 46
"I talked to him on the road," said the boy.

"Go, then, and find out for yourself whether the king has work," 47
said the man.
"All right," said the boy.

"But you'll never get across there," said the man. 48
"But why can't I get across?" asked the boy.

49 ta mar mu xajelav xi la ti vinik.
ta jpastik reva xi la ti kerem.

50 pero ˀecheˀ chabat.
ch'abal yabtel ti rey xi la ti vinik.

51 pero la jyalbun ti ˀoy yabtel ti k'alal la jnup ta be xi la ti kerem.
mi persa ta sba ta k'elavil mi ˀoy yabtel ti rey pero mu xuˀ xabat ta ˀora xi la ti vinik.

52 k'usi ˀora xuˀ xibat xi la ti kerem.
ˀaˀ lek ta xamala ti k'alal ta stail ta ˀatimol ti stzebetik ti rey xi la ti vinik.

53 k'usi ˀora ta xtalik ta ˀatimol ti stzebetik rey xi la ti kerem.
ta baluneb ˀora ˀik'luman ta xtalik ta ˀatimol ti stzebetik ti rey ˀok'om xi la ti vinik.
xuˀuk ta jmala ˀok'om xi la ti kerem.

54 pero jayib ˀoy stzebetik ti rey xi la ti kerem.
ˀoy chanib stzebetik ti rey xi la ti vinik.

55 pero ta ˀukub ˀora ˀik'luman ta xabat ˀok'om xi la ti vinik.
xuˀuk xi la ti kerem.

56 pero baˀyel ta xasaˀ ˀarukal buy ta xanak' ˀaba xi la ti vinik.
xuˀuk xi la ti kerem.

57 ta vaxakib ˀora ta xak'ot ta stiˀil ti mar xi la ti vinik.
xuˀuk xi la ti kerem.

58 ti k'alal ta xtalik ta ˀatimol ti stzebetik ti rey pero nak'alot xaˀox xi la ti vinik.
xuˀuk xi la ti kerem.

59 pero muˀyuk ta xbat ˀajak'be mi ˀoy yabtel stot ti stzebetik ti rey xi la ti vinik.
xuˀuk xi la ti kerem.

"You can't go across the sea," said the man. 49
"But even so, I'd like to try," said the boy.

"But you go in vain. 50
The king has no work," said the man.

"But he told me that he had work when I met him on the road," 51
said the boy.
"Even if you insist on going to see if the king has work for you,
you cannot go right now," said the man.

"Then when can I go?" asked the boy. 52
"You should wait until the daughters of the king come to bathe,"
said the man.

"When do the king's daughters come to bathe?" said the boy. 53
"The daughters of the king come to bathe tomorrow night at
nine o'clock," said the man.
"All right, then, I'll wait until tomorrow," said the boy.

"But how many daughters does the king have?" asked the boy. 54
"The king has four daughters," said the man.

"But you must go tomorrow night at seven o'clock," said the man. 55
"All right," said the boy.

"But first you should look for a little cranny where you can hide," 56
advised the man.
"All right," said the boy.

"At eight o'clock you will arrive at the edge of the sea," said the man. 57
"All right," said the boy.

"And when the daughers of the king come to bathe, you should 58
remain hidden," said the man.
"All right," said the boy.

"But you should not go to ask the king's daughters if their father has work," 59
said the man.
"All right," said the boy.

60 pero ti k'alal ta slok' sk'uˀ ti stzebetik ti rey ta xak'el buy ta xak' sk'uˀ jujunik
xi la ti vinik.
xuˀuk xi la ti kerem.

61 ˀoy jun tz'akal ta xˀul talel ti stzeb ti rey.
ˀaˀ ta xak'el buy ta xak' sk'uˀ xi la ti vinik.
xuˀuk xi la ti kerem.

62 k'alal mi ˀavil lek buy ta xak' sk'uˀ ti stzeb rey.
ti tz'akal ta xˀul talel ti stiˀil ti mar.
ˀaˀ to xbat ˀanak'be sk'uˀ xi la ti vinik.
xuˀuk xi la ti kerem.

63 ˀaˀ mukil stzeb rey ti tz'akal ta xˀul ta ˀatimol ta mar xi la ti vinik.
ˀaˀ ta xbat ˀanak'be sk'uˀ xi la ti vinik.
xuˀuk xi la ti kerem.

64 pero mu ta ˀaniluk ta xabat ˀanak'be sk'uˀ stzeb ti rey xi la ti vinik.
xuˀuk xi la ti kerem.

65 ta xamala ti k'alal ta stik' ˀochel sjol ta yut voˀ ti stzebetik ti rey xi la ti vinik.
xuˀuk xi la ti kerem.

66 jun la k'ak'al te ˀoy ti kerem ta sna ti vinik.
tey la loˀilajik.
tey la vay ti kerem ta sna vinik.

67 ti k'alal sakub ta yok'omal:
ta xibat ˀun xi la ti kerem.

68 malo jlikeluk veˀkutik xi la ti vinik.
xuˀuk xi la ti kerem.

"But when the king's daughters take off their clothes, you should notice 60
where each one leaves her clothes," said the man.
"All right," said the boy.

"Now, there is one of the king's daughters who will arrive later. 61
You should take particular notice where this one leaves her clothes,"
said the man.
"All right," said the boy.

"Then, once you have found out where the king's daughter leaves her 62
clothing, you'll be all set.
You will know which one she is, for she will be the last one to arrive
at the seashore.
Only then should you hide her clothing," advised the man.
"All right," said the boy.

"Of the king's daughters, she will be the youngest and also the last to 63
get to the seashore to bathe.
It is her clothes you are to hide," said the man.
"All right," said the boy.

"Now, you should not hide the king's daughter's clothes right away," 64
said the man.
"All right," said the boy.

"You should wait until all of the king's daughters have their heads totally 65
immersed in the water," said the man.
"All right," said the boy.

The boy spent a whole day in the man's house. 66
The two of them spent the time talking together.
And the boy spent the night at the man's house.

When the next day dawned, the boy spoke: 67
"Now, I shall go," said the boy.

"Wait a minute. Let's have breakfast," said the man. 68
"All right," said the boy.

69 ti k'alal laj veˀikuk:
k'uxi ta jtoj ti veˀel xi la ti kerem.

70 muˀyuk ta xatoh.
ˀamoton ta xˀak'bot xi la ti vinik.
xuˀuk kolaval xi la ti kerem.

71 ti k'alal laj veˀikuk:
ta xibat ˀun xi la ti kerem.
batan chabanukot ˀech'el xi la ti vinik.

72 ti k'alal bat ti kerem:
pero lek me xanak' ˀaba ti k'alal ta xtalik ta ˀatimol ti stzebetik rey
xi la ti vinik.
xuˀuk kolaval xi la ti kerem.

73 ti k'alal syakel xa ta xanav ti kerem:
pero k'alal mi la k'ot ta sna ti rey pero mu xaxiˀ.
lek tzotz xapas ˀaba xi la ti vinik.
xuˀuk kolaval xi la ti kerem.

74 ti k'alal ta xanav ti kerem.
pero ˀanilal ta xanav.

75 ti k'alal ta xa xk'ot ta stiˀil mar ti kerem.
snak' la komel yikatz.

76 ti k'alal laj snak' yikatz ti kerem,
saˀ la ti buy lek snak' sba ti kerem.

77 ti k'alal laj snak' sba ti kerem.
muˀyuk la ta sbak' ti kerem.
ˀaˀ noˀox la ta sk'el yil ti k'usi ta xlok' talel ti stzebetik ti rey.

78 ti k'alal sta ti baluneb ˀora,
talik la ta ˀatimol ti xtzebetik ti rey.

79 ti k'alal ˀulik ta stiˀil mar ti stzebetik ti rey,
ˀora la ˀislok' sk'uˀik.

When they had finished eating, the boy spoke: 69
"What do I owe you for the meal?" asked the boy.

"You don't owe anything. 70
It was given to you as a gift," said the man.
"All right. Thank you," said the boy.

And when he had finished eating, the boy spoke: 71
"Now I'm on my way," said the boy.
"Go, then. Take care," said the man.

And as the boy left, the man spoke: 72
"Remember to hide yourself well when the king's daughters
come to bathe," said the man.
"All right. Thank you," said the boy.

And as the boy was walking away, the man spoke: 73
"But when you come to the house of the king, don't be afraid.
You'll be up to the task," said the man.
"All right. Thank you," said the boy.

Then the boy walked. 74
He walked quickly.

Soon the boy arrived at the edge of the sea. 75
He hid his bundle of belongings.

When the boy had hidden his bundle, 76
He looked for a good place to hide.

Then the boy hid. 77
He did not move.
He just watched to see whether the king's daughters were actually
going to show up.

When it was just nine o'clock, 78
It was then that the king's daughters arrived to bathe.

When the daughters of the king reached the edge of the sea, 79
They took off their clothes.

80 ti k'alal laj slok' sk'uˀik stzebetik ti rey,
pero ta ˀora la laj stik' ˀochel sjol ta yut voˀ.

81 ti k'alal laj stik' ˀochel sjol ta yut voˀ stzebetik ti rey,
bat la ti kerem stzakbe talel sk'uˀ ti stzeb ti rey.
bat la snak'be.

82 ti k'alal laj snak'be sk'uˀ stzeb rey ti kerem,
bat la snak' sba.

83 ti k'alal laj ˀatinikuk stzeb rey,
lek la nak'al ti kerem.

84 ti k'alal laj ˀatinikuk stzebetik ti rey,
pero ta ˀora la ta slap sk'uˀ.

When the daughters of the king had taken off their clothes, 80
  They quickly went to dunk their heads in the water.

When the daughters of the king had dunked their heads in the water, 81
  The boy went to grab the clothes of the youngest daughter of the king.
  He went to hide them.

When the boy had hidden the clothes of the daughter of the king, 82
  He went to hide himself.

While the daughters of the king were still in the midst of their bathing, 83
  The boy remained well hidden.

When the daughters of the king had finished bathing, 84
  They quickly put on their clothes.

FIGURE 59

When the daughters of the king had dunked their heads in the
    water,
  The boy went to grab the clothes of the youngest daughter of
    the king.
  He went to hide them.

85 ti k'alal mi laj slap ti sk'uˀ stzebetik ti rey,
pero ta ˀora la ta xbat ta sna.

86 pero ˀoxib noˀox la.
ti baˀyel laj ˀatinikuk.

87 ˀaˀ la baˀyel bat ta snaik.
pero yuˀ la ˀaˀ baˀyel laj sjapu ˀatimol,
ti ˀoxib.

88 ti jun laj snak'be sk'uˀ ti kerem,
ˀaˀ la tz'akal laj sjapu ˀatimol.

89 ti k'alal laj ˀatinuk ti mukil,
nak'al xaˀox ti sk'uˀ

90 ti k'alal yil ch'abal sk'uˀ ti mukil,
yochel la ta saˀel.

91 ti k'alal ta saˀ sk'uˀ ti stzeb rey,
bat la skuch talel yikatz ti kerem.

92 ti k'alal laj skuch yikatz ti kerem,
sjapula xanavil ta be.

93 ˀaˀ la tey ta xanav batel,
ti bu ˀoy ta saˀ sk'uˀ ti stzeb rey.

94 ti k'alal k'ot ti kerem ta stz'el ti stzeb ti rey,
ti buy ta saˀ sk'uˀ.

95 k'usi ta xasaˀ xi la ti kerem.
yuˀun ta jsaˀ jk'uˀ xi la ti stzeb rey.

96 buy la vak' ˀak'uˀ xi la ti kerem.
liˀ laj jkomtzan k'alal li ˀoch ta ˀatimol xi la ti stzeb ti rey.

97 mi ˀoy ˀachiˀil xi la ti kerem.
ˀoy ˀoxib jvixobtak, pero jelav xa xi la ti stzeb rey.

When the daughters of the king had finished putting on their clothes, 85
They went home, wasting no time on the way.

But there were only three who did this. 86
These were the first to finish bathing.

These first ones went home. 87
For these were the first ones to emerge from their bath,
These three.

The one whose clothes the boy had hidden, 88
This one was the last to come out of the surf.

And when the youngest sister had finished bathing, 89
Her clothes had already been hidden.

When the youngest sister found that her clothes were gone, 90
She started to look for them.

When the king's daughter was looking for her clothes, 91
The boy went to pick up his bundle.

When the boy had picked up his bundle, 92
He set off along the road.

He went walking along there, quite nonchalantly, 93
At the place where the king's daughter was looking for her clothes.

And then the boy approached the king's daughter, 94
Right there where she was looking for her clothes.

"What are you looking for?" asked the boy. 95
"I'm looking for my clothes," said the king's daughter.

"Where did you leave your clothes?" asked the boy. 96
"I left them here when I went to bathe," said the king's daughter.

"Do you have anyone with you?" asked the boy. 97
"I have three older sisters, but they have already gone,"
said the king's daughter.

98 buy bat ti ˀak'uˀ xi la ti kerem.
mu jnaˀ xi la ti stzeb rey.

99 mi xak'an xaˀabolaj xakolta ˀun ta saˀel ti jk'uˀ xi la ti stzeb rey.
xuˀuk xi la ti kerem.

100 skolta la sba ta saˀel k'uˀil ti kerem.
pero jal la muˀyuk staik ta saˀel ti k'uˀil.

101 ti k'alal muˀyuk ta staik ta saˀel ti sk'uˀ ti stzeb ti rey.
ta xˀilin ti jtot mi muˀyuk jta ti jk'uˀ xi la tzeb rey.

102 ti k'alal ta xa xˀok' ti stzeb rey,
bat la ti kerem ti buy laj snak'ojbe sk'uˀ ti stzeb rey.

103 ti k'alal k'ot ti kerem ti buy snak'ojbe sk'uˀ ti stzeb rey:
mi ˀak'uˀ liˀ xi la ti kerem.
bu ˀoy xi la ti stzeb rey.

104 liˀ ˀoy xi la ti kerem.
ˀora la bat sk'el sk'uˀ ti stzeb rey.

105 ti k'alal sta ti s'kuˀ stzeb ti rey:
ˀaˀ jk'uˀ ma liˀ xi la.

106 ti k'alal sta ti sk'u stzeb to rey,
ˀora xa la laj slap sk'uˀ ti stzeb rey.

107 ti k'alal laj slap sk'uˀ ti stzeb re,
xkuxet xa la yoˀnton.

108 kolaval laj kolta ˀun ta saˀel jk'uˀ xi la ti stzeb rey.
muˀyuk vokol xi la ti kerem.

"But what happened to your clothes?" asked the boy. 98
"I don't know," said the king's daughter.

"Would you want to help me look for my clothes?" asked the king's daughter. 99
"All right," said the boy.

The boy helped her look for her clothes. 100
But a long time passed and they did not find the clothes.

It seemed that they were not going to find the king's daughter's 101
clothes at all.
"My father will get angry if I don't find my clothes,"
said the king's daughter.

With that, the king's daughter started to cry, 102
So the boy went to the place where he had hidden the king's
daughter's clothes.

When he came to where he had hidden the king's daughter's clothes, 103
he spoke quite innocently:
"Are these your clothes?" asked the boy.
"Where are they?" asked the king's daughter.

"Here they are," said the boy. 104
The king's daughter went at once to see if they were her clothes.

And when the king's daughter at last found her clothes, she spoke: 105
"Yes, these are my clothes," she said.

And when the king's daughter found her clothes, 106
The king's daughter put on her clothes at once.

And when the king's daughter had put on her clothes, 107
She was indeed relieved, her heart rested.

"Thank you for helping me find my clothes," said the king's daughter. 108
"It was nothing," said the boy.

109 manchuk laj ˀakolta ˀun ta saˀel ti jk'uˀ ta xismil ti jtot xi la ti stzeb rey.
ˀaˀ lek ta xibat jchiˀnot ti buy ta xabat xi la ti stzeb rey.

110 xuˀ ˀechuk mi xak'an xbat jchiˀin jbatik xi la ti kerem.
ta jk'an xi la ti stzeb.

111 buy chabat ti ta ˀora xi la ti stzeb rey.
ta xibat saˀ ˀabtel ta sna ti rey xi la ti kerem.

112 pero ˀaˀ jtot xi la ti stzeb rey.
buy to sna ti ˀatot xi la ti kerem.

113 tey ta hot stiˀil ti mar xi la ti stzeb rey.
pero ˀaˀ tey ta xibat xi la ti kerem.

114 pero muˀyuk yabtel ti jtot xi la ti stzeb rey.
pero la jyalbun ti ˀoy yabtel xi la ti kerem.

115 pero mu xuˀ xajelav ta mar xi la ti stzeb rey.
ta jpaskik reva mi xijelav xi la ti kerem.

116 yuˀun toj ˀabol jba.
ch'abal jtak'in xi la ti kerem.
ˀech'o xal ta saˀ ˀabtel xi la ti kerem.

117 buy laj ˀak'opon ti jtot xi la ti stzeb rey.
tey laj jk'opon ta stz'el jna xi la ti kerem.
ˀech'o xal ta xibat ta persa xi la ti kerem.

118 xuˀ xabat.
pero ta xkik' jelavel xi la ti stzeb rey.

119 xuˀuk mi xaˀabolaj xi la ti kerem.
xuˀuk xiˀabolaj xi la ti stzeb ti rey.

120 pero ta xamuy ta jnekeb xi la ti stzeb rey.
xuˀuk xi la ti kerem.
muy la ta snekeb stzeb rey ti kerem.

"If you hadn't helped me find my clothes, my father would have 109
killed me," said the king's daughter.
"I would like to accompany you to wherever you are going,"
said the king's daughter in deep gratitude.

"All right. If you like, we will go together," said the boy. 110
"I'd like that," said the girl.

"Where are you going now?" asked the king's daughter. 111
"I'm going to find work in the house of the king," said the boy.

"But he is my father," said the king's daughter. 112
"But which is the way to your father's house?" asked the boy.

"It's there on the other side of the sea," said the king's daughter. 113
"Good. That's where I'm going," said the boy.

"But my father doesn't have work for you," said the king's daughter. 114
"But he told me that he did have work," said the boy.

"But you have no way to get across the sea," said the king's daughter. 115
"I'd like to try. Let's see if I am able to cross," said the boy.

"The fact is that I'm very poor. 116
I have no money.
That's why I'm looking for work," said the boy.

"Where did you talk to my father?" asked the king's daughter. 117
"I talked to him right there by my house," replied the boy.
"That's why I really must go," insisted the boy.

"It's all right for you to go. 118
But I will take you across," said the king's daughter.

"All right, if you would be so kind," said the boy. 119
"All right. I would be happy to," said the king's daughter.

"But you must get up on my shoulders," said the king's daughter. 120
"All right," said the boy.
With that the boy climbed up onto the shoulders of the king's daughter.

121 k'alal muy ta snekeb stzeb rey ti kerem,
ta ˀora la batik.
pero jlikel la k'otik ta jech mar ti stzeb rey xchiˀuk ti kerem.

122 ti k'alal k'otik ta jech mar ti stzeb rey,
tey la kom ti kerem.

123 liˀ ta xakom xi la ti stzeb rey.
mu xuˀ koˀol ta xijbat xi la ti stzeb rey.
xuˀuk xi la ti kerem.

124 ta xˀilin jtot ti k'alal koˀol ta xijbat xi la ti stzeb rey.
ˀaˀ lek tz'akal ta xak'to xi la ti stzeb rey.
xuˀuk xi la ti kerem.

125 tey la kom ti kerem ta jech mar.
stuk la bat ti stzeb rey.

126 ti k'alal jalij jutuk te ˀoy ti kerem,
bat la ta sna ti rey.

127 ti k'alal k'ot ta sna rey ti kerem:
mi liˀ ˀoyote xi la ti kerem.
liˀ ˀoyun xi la ti rey.

128 k'usi tal ˀasaˀ xi la ti rey.
yuˀun tal jak' mi ˀoy ˀavabtel xi la ti kerem.

129 muˀyuk ˀabtel xi la ti rey.
pero la valbun ti ˀoy ˀavabtel xi la ti kerem.

130 buy laj kalbot xi la ti rey.
tey laj ˀavalbun ti k'alal laj nupot ta be xi la ti kerem.

131 k'uxi la jelav tal ta mar xi la ti rey.
li xanav jelavel la xi la ti kerem.

When the boy had climbed up onto the shoulders of the king's daughter, 121
They went off quickly.
In no time at all the king's daughter and the boy reached
the other side of the sea.[7]

And when the king's daughter reached the other side of the sea, 122
the edge of beyond,
The boy stayed there.

"You are going to stay here," said the king's daughter. 123
"We cannot go together," said the king's daughter.
"All right," said the boy.

"My father would get angry if we were to go together," 124
said the king's daughter.
"It would be better for you to arrive later," said the king's daughter.
"All right," said the boy.

And the boy stayed there on the shore of the other side of the sea. 125
The king's daughter went on alone.

And when the boy had been there for a little while, 126
He proceeded to go to the house of the king.

And when the boy came to the house of the king, he spoke: 127
"Are you here?" asked the boy.
"I am here," said the king.

"What did you come looking for?" asked the king. 128
"I came to ask if you have work," said the boy.

"I don't have any work," said the king. 129
"But you told me that you did have work," said the boy.

"Where did I tell you that?" demanded the king. 130
"You told me when I met you there on the road," said the boy.

"How did you cross the sea?" asked the king. 131
"I simply walked across it," lied the boy.

132 buch'u laj yik'ot jelavel tal xi la ti rey.
li jelav talel jtuk xi la ti kerem.

133 buch'u la jak'be buy ta jna xi la ti rey.
muˀyuk buch'u la jak'be xi la ti kerem.

134 k'usi tal ˀasaˀ xi la ti rey.
yuˀun tal jsaˀ ˀavabtel xi la ti kerem.

135 pero mu jnaˀ mi xuˀ ˀavuˀun ˀabtel xi la ti rey.
ta xuˀ kuˀun ˀabtel xi la ti kerem.

136 ta xabat ˀok'om ta baluneb ˀora xi la ti rey.
xuˀuk xi la ti kerem.

137 muˀyuk abtel ta ˀora xi la ti rey.
xuˀ ˀechuk xi la ti kerem.

138 buy chavay xi la ti rey.
liˀ ta jch'amun ˀana xi la ti kerem.

139 muˀyuk lek jna xi la ti rey.
pero mu jnaˀ buy ta xbat vaykun xi la ti kerem.

140 ti rey mu la xˀak' lek ta ch'amunel sna.
tey la vay ti kerem ta sna ti rey.

"Who brought you across?" asked the king. 132
"I came across alone," said the boy.

"Whom did you ask how to get to my house?" demanded the king. 133
"I didn't ask anybody," said the boy.

"What did you come looking for?" asked the king. 134
"I came looking for work," said the boy.

"But I don't know if you are able to do the work I have in mind," 135
said the king.
"I am able to work," said the boy.

"You will go to work tomorrow at nine o'clock," said the king. 136
"All right," said the boy.

"There is no work right now," said the king. 137
"All right, then," said the boy.

"Where are you going to sleep?" asked the king. 138
"Here, if you will lend me your house," said the boy.

"My house is no good," said the king. 139
"Then I don't know where I am going to sleep," said the boy.

The king did not lend his house willingly. 140
But there in the house of the king the boy slept.

141 ti k'alal vay ti kerem,
bat la k'elvanuk ti tzeb rey.

142 ta xˀilin ma jtote xi la ti stzeb rey.
k'uchaˀal ta xˀilin xi la ti kerem.

143 ˀaˀ mu sk'an ti liˀ latal ta ˀabtel xi la ti stzeb rey.
ta la me sk'an smilot yaˀi me jtote xi la ti stzeb rey.

144 k'uchaˀal ta xismil xi la ti kerem.
ˀaˀ la mi mu tzutz ˀavuˀun ˀabtel ti ˀok'ome xi la ti tzeb rey.
jpaskik xi la ti kerem.

145 mu xaxiˀ.
ta xibat jkoltaot xi la ti stzeb rey.
xuˀuk xi la ti kerem.

146 ti k'alal sakub ta yok'omal,
ˀak' bat la spiko spala ti kerem.

When the boy was asleep, 141
  The king's daughter went to look for him.

"My father is angry," said the king's daughter. 142
  "Why is he angry?" asked the boy.

"My father doesn't want you to come to work here," 143
    said the king's daughter.
  "My father wants to kill you," said the king's daughter

"Why does he want to kill me?" asked the boy. 144
  "Only if you don't finish your task tomorrow . . . ,"
    said the king's daughter.
  "Well, let's give it a try," said the boy.

"Don't be afraid. 145
  I'm going to help you," said the king's daughter.
  "All right," said the boy.

When the next day dawned, 146
  The boy was given a pick and shovel.

FIGURE 60

When the boy was asleep,
  The king's daughter went to look for him.

147 ti k'alal la jyich' spiko spala ti kerem,
ˀak'bat la sveˀel.

148 ti k'alal laj veˀuk ti kerem,
batan ta ˀabtel xi la ti rey.

149 ba saˀo tal choy xi la ti rey.
xuˀuk xi la ti kerem.

150 pero ˀoxib metro snatil ta xajok' ti banumil xi la ti rey.
ˀaˀ tey chata ti choy xi la ti rey.
xuˀuk xi la ti kerem.

151 ˀoxib me ta xasaˀ talel ti choy xi la ti rey.
xuˀuk xi la ti kerem.

152 k'usi ˀabi xi la ti rey ti k'alal bat ta saˀ talel choy ti kerem.
jxun jbi xi la ti kerem.

153 pero sujom me ˀaba ta ˀabtel xi la ti rey.
pero mu me jaluk ta xabat ta ˀabtel xi la ti rey.

154 jayib noˀox ˀora ti chiˀabtej xi la ti kerem .
chib noˀox ˀora ta xaˀabtej xi la ti rey.
xuˀuk xi la ti kerem.

155 ti k'alal sjapu ˀabtel ti kerem,
toj lek la k'un ti banumil.

156 mu la sta chib ˀora ta sta ti ˀoxib metro.
pero muˀyuk la ti choy ti k'alal tzaki sjok'el ti ˀoxib metro.

157 ti k'alal ta xa sta ti ˀora.
bat la k'elvanuk ti stzeb rey.

158 mi ˀata ti choy xi la ti stzeb rey.
ch'abal xi la ti kerem.

When the boy had received his pick and shovel, 147
The boy was given his food.

When the boy had eaten, 148
"Go to work," said the king.

"Go bring some fish," commanded the king. 149
"All right," said the boy.

"But you are to dig a hole in the ground three meters wide," said the king. 150
"There you will find the fish," said the king.
"All right," said the boy.

"You are to find three fish," said the king. 151
"All right," said the boy.

"What is your name?" asked the king when the boy set out to find the fish. 152
"My name is Xun," said the boy.

"Well, you must work quickly," said the king. 153
"You are not to tarry too long at your task," said the king.

"How many hours am I to work?" asked the boy. 154
"You are to work just two hours," said the king.
"All right," said the boy.

And when the boy began his task, 155
The earth was very soft.

It did not take two hours to reach the three meters. 156
But there were no fish when he reached the depth of three meters.

Well, soon the allotted time was up. 157
Whereupon, the king's daughter came to check up on things.

"Did you find the fish?" inquired the king's daughter. 158
"None at all," said the boy.

159 k'u snatil sk'an stz'aki ti ˀoxib metro xi la ti stzeb rey.
tz'aki xa pero muˀyuk ti choy xi la ti kerem.

160 pero ta xˀilin ti jtot mi c'abal xata ti coy xi la ti stzeb rey.
ˀaˀ lek ta jkoltaot ta saˀel ti choy xi la ti stzeb rey.
xuˀuk mi xaˀabolaj xi la ti kerem.

161 k'alal ˀoch ta saˀel choy ti stzeb rey.
pero aˀa la ˀora ˀista ta saˀel ti choy.

162 ti k'alal sta choy ti stzeb rey:
batan ta ˀora xi la ti stzeb rey.
xuˀuk xi la ti kerem.

163 k'alal ta saˀ choy ti stzeb rey,
jukot la ta sta ta jumoj piko.
ti kereme ˀaˀ la mu sta ta saˀel choy.

164 ti k'alal k'ot ti kerem ta sna ti rey.
sk'an to la jlikel sta ˀora.

165 ti k'alal k'ot ti kerem:
mi ˀata ti choy xi la ti rey.
jta xi la ti kerem.

166 mi la saˀ ˀatuk xi la ti rey.
laj saˀ jtuk xi la ti kerem.

167 lek xanaˀ ˀabtel xi la ti rey.
jnaˀ ˀun jutuk xi la ti kerem.

168 veno lek ˀoy kuxo xi la ti rey.
xuˀuk xi la ti kerem.

169 mi chaveˀ xi la ti rey.
xuˀuk xi la ti kerem.

"How much do you lack to reach the full three meters?" 159
asked the king's daughter.
"I've dug the hole as deep as I was supposed to, but there are
no fish," said the boy.

"But my father will be angry if you find no fish," said the king's daughter. 160
"It will be better if I help you find the fish," said the king's daughter.
"That's fine, if you would be so kind," said the boy.

With that, the king's daughter began to look for the fish. 161
Within an hour she found the fish.

And when the king's daughter had found the fish she spoke: 162
"Go at once and make your appointed appearance,"
said the king's daughter.
"All right," said the boy.

When the king's daughter was looking for the fish, 163
She indeed found one with each blow of the pick.
But it was she, not the boy, who found the fish.

Soon, the boy arrived at the king's palace. 164
In fact, he got there before the time limit of two hours.

And this is what happened when the boy got there: 165
"Did you find the fish?" asked the king.
"I found them," said the boy.

"Did you find them all by yourself?" asked the king. 166
"I found them all by myself," said the boy.

"You obvioiusly know how to work very well," said the king. 167
"Yes, I know a little," said the boy.

"Good. That's fine. Take a rest," said the king. 168
"All right," said the boy.

"Do you want to eat?" asked the king. 169
"All right," said the boy.

170 k'alal laj veˀuk ti kerem:
ba vayan xi la ti rey.
xuˀuk xi la ti kerem.
bat la vayuk.

171 ti k'alal sakub ta xchibal k'ak'al.
sob la lik ti kerem.
sjak' la yabtel.

172 ta xabat ta saˀ siˀ xi la ti rey.
xuˀuk xi la ti kerem.
bat la ta saˀ siˀ ti kerem.

173 ti k'alal bat ta saˀ siˀ ti kerem:
pero mu me jaluk ta xasaˀ ti siˀ xi la ti rey.
xuˀuk xi la ti kerem.

174 hayib ˀora ti saˀ ti siˀ xi la ti kerem.
chib noˀox ˀora ta xasaˀ ti siˀ xi la ti rey.
xuˀuk xi la ti kerem.

175 k'uyepal ta jsaˀ ti siˀ xi la ti kerem.
ta xasaˀ ˀoxib ta mula xi la ti rey.
xuˀuk xi la ti kerem.

176 ti k'alal ta saˀ siˀ ta teˀtik ti kerem,
bat la ti stzeb rey.

177 mi tz'ak'i ti siˀ ˀoxib ta mula xi la ti stzeb rey.
sk'an to jutuk xi la ti kerem.

178 pero ta xa sta ti ˀora xi la ti stzeb rey.
ˀaˀ lek ta jkoltaot xi la.

179 xuˀuk mi sk'an xaˀabolaj xakoltaun xi la ti kerem.
ta xajkolta xi la ti tzeb rey.

When the boy had eaten, the king spoke: 170
"Go and rest," said the king.
"All right," said the boy.
And he went to sleep.

And then the second day dawned. 171
The boy got up early.
He asked about his work.

"You will go gather firewood," commanded the king. 172
"All right," said the boy.
And he went to look for firewood.

And as he was setting out to look for firewood, the king spoke: 173
"You are not to look for firewood very long," said the king.
"All right," said the boy.

"How many hours do I have to look for firewood?" asked the boy. 174
"You will look for firewood for only two hours," said the king.
"All right," said the boy.

"How much firewood should I get?" asked the boy. 175
"You should get three mule-loads," commanded the king.
"All right," said the boy.

When the boy went to look for firewood in the forest, 176
The king's daughter went also.

"Have you gotten the three mule loads of firewood?" 177
asked the king's daughter.
"I still need to get a little more to reach the amount that has been
required of me," said the boy.

"But your time is about up," said the king's daughter. 178
"It would be better if I helped you," she said.

"All right. Since I have not reached my quota, I would be grateful 179
for your help," said the boy.
"I will be glad to help you," said the king's daughter.

180 ti k'alal mi muʔyuk stz'ak'i ti siʔ ta xʔilin ti jtot xi la ti stzeb rey.
pero jutuk xa la sk'an stz'ak'i ti siʔ.

181 ti k'alal tz'ak'i ti ʔoxib ta mula ti siʔ:
batan ta ʔanil xi la ti stzeb rey.
xuʔuk xi la ti kerem.
pero ʔanil la bat ti kerem.

182 k'alal k'ot ti kerem ta sna ti rey:
mi tz'ak'i ti ʔoxib ta mula ti siʔ xi la ti rey.
tz'ak'i xi la ti kerem.

183 bat jk'eltikik xi la ti rey.
xuʔuk xi la ti kerem.
bat la sk'elik ti siʔ mi tzak'al.

184 ti k'alal yil tzak'al ti ʔoxib mula siʔ ti rey.
jun xa k'alal kom ʔavabtel xi la ti rey.
xuʔ ʔechuk xi la ti kerem.

185 toj lek xanaʔ xaʔabtej xi la ti rey.
xiʔabtej ʔun jutuk xi la ti kerem.

186 bat veʔkutik xi la ti rey.
xuʔuk xi la ti kerem.
veʔik la.

187 ti k'alal laj veʔukuk:
bat vayan xi la ti rey.
xuʔuk xi la ti kerem.

188 ti k'alal bat vayuk ti kerem:
sob me xalik ʔok'om xi la ti rey.
xuʔuk xi la ti kerem.

"If you don't finish gathering the firewood, my father will be angry," 180
said the king's daughter.
And now they lacked only a little bit to finish the appointed task.

And when they had finished gathering the three mule loads of firewood 181
the king's daughter spoke:
"Go very quickly to your appointed meeting," said the king's daughter.
"All right," said the boy.
The boy went quickly.

And when he arrived at the house of the king, the king spoke: 182
"Have you collected the required three mule loads of firewood?"
asked the king.
"I have collected them," said the boy.

"Let's go see," said the king. 183
"All right," said the boy.
They went to see if all the firewood was there.

And then the king saw that all three of the mule loads of firewood 184
were there.
"Now but one more day of work remains for you," said the king.
"All right," said the boy.

"You know how to work very well," said the king. 185
"I work a little," said the boy politely, trying not to seem proud
of his accomplishment.

"Let's go eat," said the king. 186
"All right," said the boy.
And they ate.

And when they had finished eating, the king spoke: 187
"Go and rest," said the king.
"All right," said the boy.

And as the boy went off to rest, the king spoke: 188
"You are to get up early tomorrow," said the king.
"All right," said the boy.

189 ti k'alal sakub ta yoxibal k'ak'al.
sob xa la lik ti kerem.

190 k'usi ti ˀabtel ta xibat xi la ti kerem.
ta xabat ta skuchel ti siˀ ˀay ˀasaˀ volje xi la ti rey.
xuˀuk xi la ti kerem.

191 pero baˀyel ta xabat ˀatzak tal ˀoxib mula xi la ti rey.
xuˀuk xi la ti kerem.
bat la stzak talel ti mula ti kerem.

192 ti k'alal bat stzak mula ti kerem:
pero mu me jaluk ta xatzak ti mula xi la ti rey.
xuˀuk xi la ti kerem.

193 jayib ˀora ta xisut talel xi la ti kerem.
ta xasut talel ta baluneb ˀora xi la ti rey.
xuˀuk xi la ti kerem.

194 tey la yaˀbinoj ti stzeb rey k'usi ta sal ti stot.
ti k'alal bat ti kerem ta stzakel ti mula.
ti kerem ˀanil la bat.

195 ti k'alal k'ot ti kerem ta stzel ti mula.
ˀoy la ˀep ti mula.
pero jlikel ti jtzak ti mula xi la ti kerem.

196 ti k'alal sjapu stzakel,
mu la stak' tzakel ti mula.

197 yak'be la yipal stzakel ti mula.
pero mu la junuk sta tzakel ti mula.

198 ti k'alal mu stak' tzakel ti mula,
yat la yoˀnton.

199 bat la k'elvanuk ti stzeb rey.
ti k'alal k'ot ti stzeb rey,
xkuxet xa yoˀnton ti kerem.

And then the third day dawned. 189
The boy got up early.

"What work am I to do?" asked the boy. 190
"You are going to haul the firewood that you collected yesterday," said the king.
"All right," said the boy.

"But first you are to bring three mules," said the king. 191
"All right," said the boy.
And the boy set off to bring the mules.

When the boy was setting off to bring the mules, the king spoke: 192
"Don't take too long to catch the mules," said the king.
"All right," said the boy.

"When should I come back?" asked the boy. 193
"You should come back at nine o'clock," said the king.
"All right," said the boy.

Now the king's daughter was there listening to what her father said. 194
And then the boy went off to catch the mules.
The boy went off at once.

Then the boy came up to where the mules were. 195
There were lots of mules.
"In no time I'll be able to catch the mules," the boy said to himself.

He tried to catch them, 196
But he could not catch the mules.

He tried ever so many times to catch the mules. 197
But he didn't succeed in catching a single mule.

When he realized that he could not manage to catch the mules, 198
His heart was very sad.

Now, the king's daughter went again to see how things were going. 199
When the king's daughter arrived,
The boy's heart was relieved.

200 mi laj xa ˀatzak ti mula xi la ti stzeb rey.
pero mu stak' tzakel xi la ti kerem.

201 tzako talel li ˀalasu.
ta jkoltaot ta stzakel ti mula xi la ti stzeb rey.

202 xuˀuk mi xaˀabolaj xi la ti kerem.
ta xakolta yuˀun.
ta xa sta ti ˀora xi la ti stzeb rey.

203 ti k'alal ˀaˀ sjapu stzakel mula ti stzeb rey.
ˀaˀ la ˀora ˀista ta tzakel ti mula.

204 ti k'alal sta ta tzak mula ti stzeb rey:
muykutik ta ˀora xi la.
xuˀuk xi la ti kerem.

205 xkuxet xa la yoˀnton ti k'alal muy ta mula ti kerem.
yochelik la ta loˀil xchiˀuk stzeb rey.

"Have you caught the mules?" asked the king's daughter. 200
"I can't catch them," said the boy.

"Get me your lasso. 201
I'm going to help you catch the mules," said the king's daughter.

"All right, if you would be so kind," said the boy. 202
"I'll be happy to help you.
Your time is about up," said the king's daughter.

Then the king's daughter began to catch the mules. 203
Quickly she succeeded in catching the mules.

Then, when the king's daughter had caught the mules, she spoke: 204
"Let's mount one of them and ride back together," she said.
"All right," said the boy.

The boy's heart was full of joy when he mounted the mule. 205
And he and the king's daughter began to talk to each other,
mounted together on the mule.

FIGURE 61

The boy's heart was full of joy when he mounted the mule.
And he and the king's daughter began to talk to each other,
mounted together on the mule.

206 k'uxi xbat ˀana xi la ti stzeb rey.
xi xbat ta ˀoˀlol banumil xi la ti kerem.
pero ˀaˀ tey ta xibatkutik xi la ti stzeb rey.

207 k'uchaˀal xi la ti kerem.
yuˀun mu sk'an ti jtot liˀ ˀoyot xi la ti stzeb rey.

208 k'uchaˀal mu sk'an ˀatot ti liˀ ˀoyun xi la ti kerem.
mu jnaˀ xi la ti stzeb rey.

209 ti laj yal ti jtote ta la xasmil xi la ti stzeb rey.
k'usi la jmul ta xismil ti ˀatot xi la ti kerem.

210 yuˀun la ˀaˀ mu sk'an liˀ ta xaˀabtej xi la ti stzeb rey.
ˀaˀ lek batik bu ˀoy ˀana xi la.

211 xuˀuk mi xaˀabolaj savik'on ˀech'el ta jna xi la ti kerem.
ta xiˀabolaj.
mu jk'an liˀ ta xacham xi la ti tzeb rey.
jlikel to la stalelik ti stzeb rey xchiˀuk ti kerem.

212 bat xa ti kajˀabteltik xi la ti rey.
pero laj xa yik' ˀech'el jtzebtik xchiˀuk jkot jmulatik xi la ti rey.

213 ˀaˀ lek ta xibat jta ta be xi la ti rey.
ˀaˀ lek bat tao ta be xi la ti yajnil ti rey.
tal la ta ˀora ti rey.

214 ti k'alal yil ta stot ti stzeb rey:
tal xa ti jtot xi la ti stzeb rey.
ˀaˀ lek la jpastik ta ch'ulna ti mula xi la ti stzeb.

Which is the way to your house?" asked the king's daughter. 206
"It's that way, at the center of the earth," said the boy.[8]
"Let's go there," said the king's daughter.

"Why?" asked the boy. 207
"Because my father doesn't want you to be here," said the king's daughter.

"Why doesn't your father want me to be here?" asked the boy. 208
"I don't know," said the king's daughter.

"Only that my father said he was going to kill you," said the king's daughter. 209
"What wrong have I done that would make your father want to
kill me?" asked the boy.

"It's just that he doesn't want you to work here," said the king's daughter. 210
"We had better go off to your house," she said.

"That's fine, if you will do me the favor of taking me to my home," 211
said the boy.
"I will do you the favor.
I don't want you to die here," said the daughter of the king.
So the boy and the king's daughter quickly departed for the boy's home.

"Now our worker has left," declared the king. 212
"Now this no-account scoundrel has carried off our daughter and
one of our mules," said the king.

"I'm going to take off this minute and intercept them on the road," 213
said the king.
"Yes, indeed! Go catch them on the road," said the king's wife.
The king set off to pursue them.

When the king's daughter saw that her father was coming, she spoke: 214
"My father's coming," said the king's daughter.
"We had better turn the mule into a church," said the king's daughter.

215 ˀa li ˀuˀune ta jpas jba ta jmeˀ valalupa xi la ti stzeb rey.
ˀa li ˀoˀote ta xamuy ta jol ch'ulna.
ta xbat ˀatij kampana xi la ti stzeb rey.
xuˀuk xi la ti kereme.

216 ti k'alal mi ˀul ti jtot,
pero mu me xaval ˀabi xi la ti stzeb rey.
xuˀuk xi la ti kereme.

217 k'alal ˀul talel ti rey,
mu xa la la stak' ˀojtikinel bu ˀoy ti stzeb xchiˀuk ti smula.

218 ˀaˀ xa noˀox la te ˀoy ti kerem.
ta xa xmuy ta stijel ti kampano.

219 k'opoj la ti rey:
mi ˀoy ˀavil k'uxi bat jun kerem xchiˀuk jun tzeb kajajtik ta mula
xi la ti rey.

220 muˀyuk la xtak'av ti kerem.
yo soy kampanero xi la ti kerem.

221 ˀavokoluk ˀalbun mi ˀoy ˀavaˀi jelav ti kerem xchiˀuk ti kerem.
yo soy kampanero xi la ti kerem.

222 ˀavokoluk xavalbun mi ˀoy jelav ti kerem xchiˀuk ti jun tzeb kajajtik ta mula
xi la ti rey.
yo soy kampanero xi la ti kerem.

223 k'alal muˀyuk xtak'av ti kerem,
tey la sut ti rey.

224 mu la snaˀ mi stzeb ti tey tik'il ta yut ch'ulna.
mu la snaˀ mi ˀaˀ smula.
ti kerem laj sk'opon mu la snaˀ mi ˀaˀ yaj ˀabtel.

"As for me, I am going to turn myself into the Virgin of Guadalupe," 215
said the king's daughter.
"As for you, you should climb into the tower of the church.
You will ring the bell," said the king's daughter.
"All right," said the boy.

"Now, when my father comes along, 216
You should not say who you are," ordered the king's daughter.
"All right," said the boy.

When the king arrived, 217
He could not recognize his daughter and his mule.

There was no one there but a young man. 218
He was just then climbing up to ring the bell.

The king spoke: 219
"Have you seen which way a boy and a girl mounted on a mule went?"
asked the king.

The boy did not answer. 220
"I am a bell ringer," the boy at last replied [in Spanish].

"Please tell me if you noticed a boy passing by here recently," said the king. 221
"I am a bell ringer," said the boy [in Spanish].

"Please do me the favor of telling me if a boy and a girl mounted 222
on a mule passed by here," said the king.
"I am a bell ringer," said the boy [in Spanish].

Now, when it turned out that the boy refused to give a helpful answer, 223
The king turned back.

He did not realize that his daughter was there in the church. 224
Nor did he realize that the church itself was his mule, transformed
into the church.
Nor did he recognize that the person to whom he had spoken was
none other than his former workman.

225 ti k'alal sut ti rey,
ˀora la talik ti stzeb rey xchiˀuk ti kerem.

226 ti k'alal k'ot ti rey ta sna:
mi ˀata ti jtzebtik xi la ti yajnil ti rey.
muˀyuk jta xi la ti rey.

227 ˀaˀ xa noˀox te laj jta ch'ulna.
tey tik'il jmeˀtik valalupa xi la ti rey.
xchiˀuk jun kerem ta xa xmuy ta stijel kampano xi la ti rey.

228 pero ˀaˀ kaj ˀabteltik ti ta xa xmuy stij kampano xi la ti yajnil ti rey.
ti jmeˀtik valalupa tey laj ˀata ˀaˀ jtzebtik xi la ti yajnil ti rey.
ti ch'ulnae ˀaˀ jmulatik xi la ti yajnil.

229 ˀuˀun ta xibat jta ta be jun velta xi la ti yajnil ti rey.
batan xi la ti rey.
tal la ti yajnil ti rey.

230 ti k'alal sta ta be ti stzeb,
pero mu xa la stak' ˀojtikinel ti stzeb rey.
ˀaˀ xa noˀox la te ˀoy jun kerem vaˀal ta xˀak' yaˀlel nichim.

231 mi ˀoy ˀavil jelav jun kerem xchiˀuk jun tzeb xi la ti yajnil ti rey.
kajajtik ta mula xi la ti yajnil ti rey.
yo soy jardinero xi la ti kerem.

232 ˀavokoluk ˀalbun k'uxi bat ti jun kerem xchiˀuk jun tzeb kajajtik ta mula
xi la ti yajnil rey.
yo soy jardinero xi la ti kerem.

233 yuˀun ˀaˀ jtzeb ti liˀ jelav xchiˀuk jun kerem kajajtik ta mula xi la ti
yajnil ti rey.
pero yo soy jardinero xi la ti kerem.

When the king had turned back, 225
It was then that the king's daughter and the boy continued
on their journey.

When the king got home, his wife asked him: 226
"Did you find our daughter?" said the king's wife.
"I didn't find her," said the king.

"I just found a church. 227
The Virgin of Guadalupe was there inside," said the king.
"And there was a boy climbing up to ring the bell," said the king.

"But it was our workman who was climbing up to ring the bell," 228
said the king's wife.
"The Virgin of Guadalupe you encountered was our daughter,"
said the king's wife.
"The church was none other than our mule," said the king's wife.[9]

"I shall go to find them on the road this time," said the king's wife, 229
displeased with her husband's incompetence.
"Go, then," said the king.
With that, the king's wife set off on her own journey.

When at last she came to where her daughter was, 230
It was not possible to recognize the daughter's true identity
or anything else about her.
There was just a boy standing there watering flowers.

"Have you seen a boy and a girl pass by?" asked the king's wife. 231
"They were riding a mule," said the king's wife.
"I am a gardener," said the boy [in Spanish].

"Please tell me which way a boy and a girl mounted on a mule went," 232
insisted the king's wife.
"I am a gardener," replied the boy [in Spanish].

"My concern is about my daughter and a young man who recently 233
passed by here mounted on a mule," repeated the king's wife.
"But I am a gardener," repeated the boy [in Spanish].

234 ti k'alal muˀyuk xtak'av ti kerem,
tey la sut ti yajnil ti rey.

235 ti k'alal sut yajnil ti rey,
ˀora la talik ta ˀanil stzeb ti rey xchiˀuk ti kerem.

236 ti k'alal k'ot ta sna ti yajnil ti rey:
mi laj ˀata ti jtzebtik xi la ti rey.
muˀyuk jta xi la ti yajnil ti rey.

237 pero ˀaˀ jtzebtik tey laj ˀata nichimetik xi la ti rey.
ti kerem laj ˀak'opon pero ˀaˀ ti kaj ˀabteltik xi la ti rey.

238 ˀaˀ lek ta xibat jta ta be jun velta xi la ti rey.
bat paso ˀavil mi xata ta be xi la ti yajnil ti rey.
ˀora la tal ti rey ta xchibal velta.

239 ti k'alal k'ot ti rey ti bu ˀoy ti stzeb,
ch'abal xa la k'usi ˀoy.
ˀaˀ xa noˀox la tey la ˀuk'um.

240 ti k'alal k'ot ta tiˀ ˀuk'um ti rey,
jkot xa noˀox lakarto tey laj sta.
mu xa la snaˀ k'uxi bat ti stzeb ti rey.

241 ti k'alal muˀyuk sta ti stzeb rey,
tey la sut ˀech'el ta sna.

242 ti k'alal k'ot ta sna ti rey:
mi ˀata xi la ti yajnil ti rey.
muˀyuk la jta xi la ti rey.

243 ˀaˀ xa noˀox la jta jkot lakarto ta ˀuk'um xi la ti rey.
ti ˀuk'um laj ˀata ˀaˀ jtzebtik xi la ti yajnil ti rey.

When it turned out that the boy would not give a helpful reply, 234
The king's wife gave up and went home.

Now, once the king's wife departed for her home, 235
It was then that the king's daughter and the boy continued
on their own journey.

When the king's wife got home, the king asked: 236
"Did you find our daughter?" said the king.
"I didn't find her," said the king's wife.

"But the flowers you saw were none other than our daughter," 237
said the king.
"The boy you talked to was our workman," said the king.

"I had better go once again to find them on the road," said the king. 238
"Go and see if you can find them on the road," said the king's wife.
And so the king set off for the second time.

Now, once the king reached the places on the road where his daughter 239
might conceivably be,
There was absolutely no one, nor anything unusual, to be seen.
There was nothing there but a river.

When the king reached the bank of the river, 240
He found nothing but an alligator.
The king did not know that this was what had become of his daughter.

Upon not succeeding in finding his daughter, 241
He returned home once again.

When he got home, the king's wife asked: 242
"Did you find her?" asked the king's wife.
"No luck this time, either," replied the king.

"All I found was an alligator in the river," said the king. 243
"The river and the alligator that you found were none other than
our daughter," said the king's wife, wisely.

244 tey xbatuk.
mu xa jventatikuk xi la ti rey.
xuˀ tey batuk xi la ti yajnil ti rey.

245 ti k'alal sut stot ti stzeb rey,
xkuxet xa la yoˀnton.

246 ti k'alal ˀul ti kerem ta sna stot smeˀ:
bu la ˀay xunito xi la ti stot xchiˀuk smeˀ.

247 li ˀay ta saˀ abtel xi la ti jxun.
pero tey la jta talel kajnil xi la ti jxun.

248 ti k'alal laj xchiˀin ta loˀil stot xchiˀuk smeˀ ti jxun,
pero ˀora la laj spas sna ti jxun.

249 pero chib la laj spas sna ti jxun.
pero mu la koˀoluk xchiˀinob sbaik.

250 ti k'alal laj smeltzan snaik ti jxun xchiˀuk reˀina.
mu la snaˀ ti jxun mi xuˀ xchiˀin sbaik xchiˀuk ti reˀina.

251 lek la xkuxet yoˀnton ti jxun,
smeltzan la lek syenta.

252 ti k'alal meltzaj syenta ti jxun,
saˀ la smosov.

253 ti k'alal sta smosov ti jxun,
smeltzanbe la sna ti smosov.

254 ti k'alal meltzaj sna ti smosov,
yak'be yabtel ti smosov.

255 ti reˀina stuk la nakal sna.
ti reˀina ˀaˀ la laj smeltzan sna ti smula.

"Let her be gone, then. 244
She is no longer important to us," said the king.
"Yes, let her be gone," said the king's wife.

Once the king, the father of the fugitive girl, had gone back home again, 245
He was much relieved and happy to forget this unfortunate affair.

When the boy reached his parents' home, they spoke: 246
"Where did you go, little Xun?" asked his father and mother.

"I went to find work," said Xun. 247
"And there I found my wife and brought her with me," said Xun.

Xun finished talking the matter over with his mother and father, 248
And Xun lost no time in building his house.

But Xun built not one, but two houses. 249
For they were not yet living together.

And then Xun finished his house and the queen's house.[10] 250
He did not know whether or not he would be able to find a way
to live with the queen.

Xun's heart was very happy, 251
He built a nice store.[11]

When Xun had finished building his store, 252
He went to look for servants.[12]

When Xun had found servants, 253
He built a home for his servants.

And once the house for his servants was ready, 254
He gave these servants work.

The queen lived alone in her house. 255
The queen even built a shed for her mule.

256 ti k'alal stuktuk kujul ti reˀina:
ta xibat jk'opon ti reˀina xi la ti smosov ti jxun.
yuˀun ta jk'an ta xkik' xi la smosov ti jxun.
k'opono xi la ti jxun.

257 ti k'alal ta sk'oponik ti reˀina,
mu la snaˀ xˀilin ta k'oponel.

258 ta sakik' xi la mosov ti jxun.
xuˀuk xi la ti reˀina.

259 pero ta xaˀabtej jlikeluk xi la ti reˀina.
xuˀuk xi la smosov ti jxun.

260 k'usi ˀabtelal ta jpas xi la smosov ti jxun.
ta xasuk' jbintik xi la ti reˀina.

261 ti k'alal ta suk' bin smosov ti jxun,
yochel la ta slapel k'uchaˀal pixolal.

262 ti k'alal laj slap ti bin smosov ti jxun:
k'usi laj ˀapas xi la ti reˀina.
yuˀun la jlap bin xi la ti smosov ti jxun.

263 pero ˀora tana leˀ ˀune mu xa me jk'an xajmalalin xi la ti reˀina.
sutan batel ta sna ti jxun xi la ti reˀina.
xuˀuk xi la ti smosov ti jxun.

264 ti k'alal k'ot smosov ti jxun,
slapoj xa la k'otel bin.

265 k'usi laj ˀapas xi la ti jxun.
yuˀun la jyalbun suk' bin ti reˀina xi la smosov ti jxun.

266 k'uchaˀal ta xasuk' bin xi la ti jxun.
yuˀun la baˀyel ta jsuk' bin.
ˀaˀ la tz'akal ta xkik' jbakutik xi la smosov ti jxun.

267 ti k'alal slapoj xa bin ti jun mosov,
bat la jun ˀo mosov.

Now, once the queen was settled alone in her house, this happened: 256
"I am going to talk to the queen," said Xun's servant.
"I want to marry her," said Xun's servant.
"Go talk to her," said Xun.

And when such talk came to her attention, 257
She did not reject the proposal at all.

"I want to marry you," said Xun's servant. 258
"All right," said the queen.

"But first you must perform a task," said the queen. 259
"All right," said Xun's servant.

"What task am I to perform?" asked Xun's servant. 260
"You are going to wash some cooking pots," said the queen.

And when Xun's servant had washed the pot, 261
He put it on his head like a hat.

After he had put the pot on his head like a hat, the queen spoke: 262
"Whatever did you do?" she said.
"I just put the pot on my head like a hat," said Xun's servant.

"Well, then, I no longer want you for a husband," said the queen.[13] 263
"Go back to Xun's house," said the queen.
"All right," said Xun's servant.

When the servant got back to Xun's house, 264
He still had the pot on his head.

"What on earth happened to you?" asked Xun. 265
"It's just that the queen told me to wash a pot," said Xun's servant.

"Why did you have to wash the pot?" asked Xun. 266
"The reason was that my assigned task was to wash the pot.
Afterwards, we were going to get married," said Xun's servant.

Now, once the first servant had ended his quest wearing a pot on his head, 267
Another servant went to see the queen on the same errand.

268 ti k'alal k'ot ti xchibal mosov.
liˀ ˀoyune xi la ti reˀina.
k'usi tal ˀasaˀ xi la ti reˀina.

269 yuˀun tal jk'oponot xi la ti mosov.
k'usi ta xaval xi la ti reˀina.

270 yuˀun tal jak'bot mi xak'an xkik'to xi la ti mosov.
xuˀuk xi la ti reˀina.

271 pero baˀyel ta xiveˀkutik xi la ti reˀina.
xuˀuk xi la ti mosov.

272 ba tzako tal vasija ta jpol jk'obtik xi la ti reˀina.
xuˀuk xi la ti mosov.

273 ti k'alal bat stzak talel vasija ti mosov,
yochel la ta slapel k'uchaˀal jun pixolal.

274 ti k'alal ˀoch ta yut sna reˀina ti mosov,
sjol xa la ta snuk vasija ti mosov.

275 k'uchaˀal vi ˀelan chapas xi la ti reˀina.
muˀyuk xi la ti mosov.
pero mu jk'an jmalalinot xi la ti reˀina.

276 k'alal mu jk'an jmalalinot xi la ti reˀina,
kexav la ti mosov.

277 bat la yoxibal mosov.
ta jk'an ta xkik'ot.
xuˀuk xi la ti reˀina.

278 veˀkutik ta ˀora xi la ti reˀina.
ta sijvayˀutik ta ˀora xi la ti reˀina.
xuˀuk xi la ti mosov.

279 toj ˀanil la veˀ ti mosov.
jutuk la mu cham k'alal ta xveˀ.

The second servant arrived. 268
"Here I am," said the queen.
"What did you come looking for?" asked the queen.

"It's just that I came to talk to you," said the servant. 269
"What do you wish to say?" asked the queen.

"It's just to ask you if I may marry you," said the servant. 270
"All right," said the queen.

"But first let's have something to eat," suggested the queen. 271
"All right," replied the servant.

"Go and bring a vessel of water so we can wash our hands," said the queen. 272
"All right," said the servant.

But when he went to fetch the vessel, 273
He proceeded to put it on like a hat.

And when the servant entered the queen's house, 274
The servant's head was stuck in the neck of the vessel.

"Why are you doing that?" asked the queen. 275
"I've no idea," said the servant.
"Then I want nothing to do with you as a husband," the queen declared.

Once the queen had said, "I don't want you as a husband," 276
The servant felt ashamed.

Then the third servant went on the same quest. 277
"I want to marry you," said the servant.
"All right," said the queen.

"Let's eat right away," said the queen. 278
"Then we'll go to bed right away," said the queen.
"All right!" said the servant.

The servant ate as fast as he could. 279
He almost died from eating so fast.

280 ti k'alal jutuk mu cham ti mosov:
pero mu jk'an xatal ˀasibtasun xi la ti reˀina.

281 batan mu jk'an jun vinik chopol xi la ti reˀina.
xuˀuk xi la ti mosov.

282 sut la ti mosov.
bat ta sna ti jxun.

283 k'usi laj ˀapas xi la ti jxun.
jutuk mu licham xi la ti mosov.

284 yuˀun la jyak'bun jveˀel ti reˀina xi la ti mosov.
k'uchaˀal toj chopol ti reˀina xi la ti jxun.

285 ta xibat jk'oponkik ˀuˀun xi la ti jxun.
batan xi la ti smosovtak.
ˀa li ˀuˀune mu xa jk'an xi la smosovtak ti jxun.

286 ti k'alal bat sk'opon reˀina ti jxun.
ˀora la laj yik' sbaik xchiˀuk reˀina ti jxun.

287 ti mosov laj snuptanik palta.
baˀyel ˀislap bin;
ta xchibal ˀislap vasija;
ta yochibal jutuk mu cham.
ˀoch bakil choy ta snuk.

After the servant came close to dying, the queen spoke: 280
"I don't like for you to frighten me that way," said the queen.

"Away with you! I don't want such a foolish man!" said the queen. 281
"All right," said the servant.

The servant departed. 282
He went to Xun's house.

"What happened to you?" asked Xun. 283
"I almost died," said the servant.

"It's just that the queen gave me something to eat," said the servant. 284
"Why do you suppose the queen is behaving so strangely?"
asked Xun.

"Perhaps I should go talk to her," said Xun. 285
"Go, then," said the three servants.
"We no longer want to have anything to do with her,"
announced Xun's servants.

Then Xun went to propose to the queen. 286
Xun and the queen got married at once.

As for the servants, they ran into problems of their own making. 287
The first one put the cooking pot on his head;
The second one put the water vessel on his head;
The third one almost died.
A fish bone got stuck in his throat.

1 loˀil yuˀun jkaxlan ta jobel.

2 vaˀi ˀun ti voˀnee ˀo li jkaxlanetike tz'iˀ la stotik.
tal la jun xinlan xchiˀuk jkot stz'iˀ.

3 ˀaˀ la ti voˀnee puru la jobeltik toˀox ti banumile.
muˀyuk toˀox la naetik.

4 ˀentonse ti tz'iˀe lik la yak'be ˀat ti yajvale.
veno ti xinlane laj la skolta sba.

6 ˀentonse ti tz'iˀe lik yak' ˀat.
te la kotol ta smala ti xinlane.

6 vaˀi ˀun laj la spasik ˀep ta velta.
veno ti tz'iˀe kom la snich'on ta xinlan.

7 ˀentonse ti xinlane ˀayan yol.
vok' la ti yole.
pero jkaxlan xa la vok'.

8 veno k'alal vok' yol ti xinlane,
lik la spas sna xchiˀuk ti stz'iˀe.
ta k'unk'un la lik bolikuk tajmek ti jkaxlanetike.

9 ˀech'o la xal ti jkaxlanetike mu snaˀ sk'exavik.
xuˀ sk'opon sbaik ta be.
xuˀ smeyik baik ta be.
xuˀ sbutz' sbaik ta be.
yuˀun la tz'iˀ stotik ti voˀnee.

TEXT 42

Of the Stinking Ladino Woman and Her Dog

Mateo Méndez Tzotzek

Here is what is said about the Ladinos of San Cristóbal. 1

Long ago, the Ladinos had a dog for their father, and this is 2
how it happened.
It happened when a Ladino woman came along with her dog.[1]

Now, long ago there were still open grasslands all over the earth. 3
There were still no houses; times were different.[2]

It was at this time and place that the dog started to fuck his mistress. 4
Indeed, the stinking Ladino woman encouraged him and helped him.

Then and there, the dog fucked her. 5
The stinking Ladino woman was there waiting for him
on her hands and knees.

Well, they did it lots and lots of times. 6
And sure enough, he got the Ladino woman pregnant.

Now, the stinking Ladino woman had her baby. 7
Her child was born.
And he turned out to be the ancestor of Ladinos.

Well, as soon as the Ladino woman's child was born, 8
She and her dog set up housekeeping.
Slowly but surely the Ladinos began to multiply.

That is why Ladinos have no shame. 9
They flirt and speak with each other on the road.
They hug and put their arms around each other in public.
They even kiss each other in public.
This is all because they had a dog for a father long ago.[3]

10 ʔaʔ la ti voʔnee puru la jobeltik ti banumile.
ʔech'o la xal la sbiin joʔbel.

11 ʔech'o la xal li jkaxlanetike mu snaʔ xiʔik,
toj tzotzik tajmek,
xuʔ smajik li jchamoetike.

12 li jchamoetike maʔuk ta tz'iʔ stotik.
ʔech'o la xal toyol sk'exavik.
toyol xiʔik yuʔun jkaxlanetik.
mu snaʔik xk'opojik ti kastiya.

Long ago the land was an expanse of grass. 10
That is why they called their town Hobel [San Cristóbal],
for it means "grass."

This story explains also why Ladinos have no fear, 11
Why they are powerful,
Why they harass and hit Chamulas.[4]

The Chamulas do not have a dog as their father. 12
That is why they are more self-conscious and proper in their behavior.
They are also afraid of Ladinos.
Perhaps it is because the Indians do not speak Spanish.

1 ˀoy jun loˀil yuˀun kaxlanetik ti voˀne,
    bu talik.

2 veno ti voˀne lae ˀaˀ li jkaxlanetik.
    jaˀ la baˀyel la jyak'be xch'ulel li jkaxlanetik ti jtotike.
    jaˀ la baˀyel ta spat ti ˀach'el.

3 k'alal la ti la spat ti baˀyel vinike,
    jaˀ to la lik spat ti jun tz'akal vinike.

4 k'alal la ti laj spat ˀach'el ti jtotik,
    k'alal la ti laj slok' ta chak k'uchaˀal santo ti ˀach'ele.
    jaˀ to la lik yak'be xch'ulel ti ˀach'el.

5 k'alal la ti meltzajtik ta banomil.
    ti ˀach'el spatoj ti jtotike.
    jaˀ la baˀyel laj yak'be xch'ulel ti bu baˀyel la spate.

6 lik la sjuch' ta ˀox juch'tael.
    ti k'alal la lik yak'be ti xch'ulel ti baˀyel vinike.

7 k'alal la ti laj yak'be xch'ulel ti jun baˀyel vinike,
    jaˀ to la lik yak'be xch'ulel ti jun tz'akal vinike ti tz'akal spat ti ˀach'ele.
    jaˀ la tz'akal la jyak'be xch'ulel ti tz'akal vinike.

8 k'alal la ti la jyak'be xch'ulel ti jtotike,
    lik la pasuk ta viniketik ti ˀach'el toˀox,
    lik spat ti jtotike.

TEXT 43

Of the Great Stone Stairway to Heaven

Xun Méndez Tzotzek

There is an account of long ago about Ladinos, 1
About where they came from.

Long ago there were only Ladinos and Our Father. 2
It happened that Our Father Sun/Christ first gave souls to the Ladinos.
It happened shortly after he had molded them from clay.

When he had formed the first person,[1] 3
Only then did he begin to make the second person.

After Our Father Sun had formed them from clay, 4
The clay came out looking just like little dolls.
It was then that he began to give their souls to the clay images.

This happened at the time when we were being placed on the earth. 5
It was then that Our Lord Sun/Christ molded the clay.
The first of these images to whom he gave a soul was the first
whom he had made.

He began by rubbing and rubbing the molded image, over and over. 6
In this manner, he proceeded to give a soul to the first person.[2]

When he had placed a soul in the first person, 7
It was then that he began to place a soul in the second person,
the second one he had formed from clay.
Just as this image was the second one in Our Father Sun's order of
creation, so it was the second to receive a soul.

When Our Father Sun had finished giving these beings their souls, 8
That which had formerly been only clay began to change into people,
That which Our Father Sun had first wrought from clay.

9 k'alal la lik pasuk ta kirsano ti cha?vo? viniketike,
ko?ol la ta xanavik.
ko?ol la ta x?abtejik.
ko?ol la ta xk'opojik.

10 ta puru kastiya ti cha?vo? viniketik.
ti vo?ne lae jmoj to?ox la ti k'op ta puru kastiyae.
mu?yuk to?ox la ti batz'i k'ope.

11 lik la boluk ti kirsanoe.
k'alal la bol ti kirsanoe jmoj la ta xk'opojik ta puru kastiya.

12 k'alal la ti jmoj ta xk'opojike lik la snop sk'opik.
mi xak'anike ba jtatik la jtotik ta ?ak'ole xiik la.

13 pero k'usi xkutik chijmuy.
xana? ?un xiik la.

14 ja? lek la? jpastik tek'obal.
yo? chijmuy ?o jtatik ta k'oponel ti jtotike xiik la ti kirsanoetike.

15 pero k'usi xkutik xana? xkak'tik ti tek'obale xiik la.
ja? lek la jpastik muyel tek'obal siminto pilal xiik la ti kirsanoetike.
lik la spasik ti tek'obal simintoe.

16 k'alal la ti ?ochik ta spasel ti tek'obal pilal simientoe,
yan la ta sjuy meskla.
yan la ta sa? talel ton.
yan la ta slatz muyel ti tonc.

17 xkechel to?ox la ta meltzanel muyel ti tek'obal pilal simintoe k'alal la ta xlaj ti tone.
tzako me tal ton.
tzako me tal meskla.

18 laj me ton.
sa?o xa me tal.

When the two images began to become human, 9
They walked alike.
They worked alike.
They talked alike.

Indeed, both people spoke only Spanish. 10
Long ago, Spanish was still the only language.
Tzotzil, the true language, did not yet exist.[3]

The people began to multiply. 11
As they multiplied, they talked alike, in just one language, Spanish.

Since they had but one common language, the people talked among themselves and got ideas. 12
"Shall we go find Our Father Sun up above?" they wondered.

"But how shall we climb up? 13
Any ideas?" they asked among themselves.

"Come, it would be best to make a stairway. 14
We can climb up and find Our Father Sun and talk to him," said the people.

"But how shall we build a stairway?" they asked. 15
"It would be best to build up a stairway of stone and mortar," said others.
So they began to build the stone stairway.

As they began to make the great stone stairway, 16
Some prepared the mortar.
Some gathered stones.
Some put the stones in place, layer by layer, higher and higher.

The great stone stairway was still not finished when they ran out of stones. 17
"Bring more stones!
Bring more mortar!

The stones are all gone! 18
Bring some more!

19 laj me meskla.
juyo xa me talel xiik la.

20 ˀak'o xa me muyel talel.
laj xa me meskla.
ˀak'o xa me muyel talel xiik la,
jmoj la ti sk'opik ta xk'opojike.

21 ti tek'obal la ta spasike jlikel la muy yuˀunik.
yantik xa la xmuy yuˀunik jujun k'ak'al ta pasel ti tek'obal pilal simentoe.

22 jaˀ la ti jmoj ti sk'opike.
jmoj la xaˀik ti k'ope.

23 veno pero leˀ ˀune mu xtun ma li jmoj sk'opik ˀune.
xi la lik snop ti jtotike.

24 k'elavil ˀun sk'an xa xistaik ˀun xi la ti jtotike.
moˀoje mu xtun li jmoj ta xk'opojike.
xi la lik snop ti jtotike.

25 jaˀ lek ta jelbe ma sk'opike.
ta jk'elki mi xaˀik ta sk'opon sbaik tana ˀun.
ta jk'eltik mi xaˀik k'alal k'usi ta xˀalbe sbaike k'usi ta spasike
xi la ti jtotike.

26 k'alal la sjelta k'op ti jtotike syakelik la ta ˀabtel,
ti k'alal la ti syakelik ta spasik ti tek'obal pilal simientoe.

27 k'alal la jel ti k'ope mu xa la xaˀik k'usi la ta xˀalbe la sbaik.
ti k'alal la ta xˀabtejike mu xa la xaˀik ti k'usi ta sk'anbe sbaik.

28 ti k'alal la ta smeltzanik ti pilal tek'obale te la kechi yuˀunik smeltzanel.
jaˀ la ti mu xa la xaˀik ti k'usi la ta xˀalbe la sbaike.
jaˀ la ti laj sjel ˀep k'op ti jtotike.

The mortar is all gone!
Make some more!" they said. 19

"Come build it up! 20
The mortar is all gone!
Come build it up!" they said to each other with full understanding,
For the language that they spoke was the same.[4]

The stairway they were building quickly grew upward. 21
Different people came every day to help build the great stone stairway.

They all spoke the same language. 22
They understood the same tongue.

"Well, it simply won't do for them to speak the same language." 23
So said Our Father Sun when he started to think about it.

"Just look! They've almost reached me," exclaimed Our Father Sun. 24
"No, it won't do for them to talk alike."
So said Our Father Sun when he started to think about it.

"It would be better for me to change their languages. 25
We'll see if they understand each other when they talk now.
We'll see if they understand each other when talking among themselves
about what they are doing," said Our Father Sun.

When Our Father Sun changed the languages, the people were right 26
in the middle of their work,
It was when they were in the midst of building the great stone stairway.

When their language changed, they could no longer understand 27
what they were saying to one another.
As they worked, they no longer understood what their companions
were asking for.

Just as they were in the midst of building the stairway, they abandoned it, 28
half-finished.
This happened because they no longer understood what they were
saying to one other.
This happened because Our Father worked great changes in language itself.

29 ja? la ti lik yak' puru batz'i k'op chijk'opojtik,
ti k'uyepaltik ?inyotike.

30 ja? yu?un la ti ta puru batz'i k'op la chijk'opojotik,
ti k'uyepal ?inyotik lae.

31 xavil la ja? la tz'akal ?och xch'ulel,
ba?yel totik ku?untik la ti vo?nee.

32 ja? yu?un la kich'tik ch'akel ti k'u la yepal snich'nab ti tz'akal vinike.
ja? la kom ta ?inyo sbi.

33 yan la ti ba?yel.
?och xch'ulel ti ba?yel vinike.
ja? la kom ta kaxlan.
ja? la yich' komel ti ba?yel k'op.

34 ti puru kastiya to?ox la ti xk'opojik ti vo?nee.
ja? yu?un la ti ja? la kom ta j?espanyol sbi li jkaxlanetike.

35 ja? ti ja? ta xk'opoj ta puru kastiyae.
ja? yu?un la ti ja? la ta persa ta jchantik li kastiyae.

36 xavil la ti vo?ne ja? la ba?yel k'op la jyak' komel ti jtotik vo?nee.
ja? yu?un ja? no?ox la jun k'op kastiya.
ta persa ta s?ich' chanel li kastiyae.

37 xavil la li jkaxlanetike ja? ta puru kastiya ta xk'opojik.
ja? ti ja? ba?yel la jyak'be xch'ulel ti jkaxlan ti jtotike.

38 k'alal la ti jel ti k'ope lik la xch'ak sbaik ti kirsanoetike.
tanijik la;
yan la ?olon;
yan la ?ak'ol la jbatikuk.

It happened that he started to oblige us to speak nothing but Tzotzil, 29
the true language,
Those of us who are Indians.

It is for that reason that we only speak Tzotzil, the true language, 30
Those of us who are Indians.

You see, it happened that their souls entered their bodies second 31
in the order of creation,
The bodies of those ancient ones, our forefathers.[5]

Those of us who were the children of the second person were separated 32
from the others.
We were left with the name of "Indians."

It was different with the first person. 33
It was this one who was the first to receive a soul.
It was this one who was left with the name of "Ladino."[6]
It was this one who received the first language.

Everyone still spoke just Spanish in ancient times. 34
That is why it happened that Ladinos are also called "Spaniards."

They speak only Castilian. 35
That is why we are obliged to learn Spanish.[7]

You see, it was the first language that Our Father Sun assigned to 36
the ancestors long ago.
It is for that reason that there is but one common language, Spanish.
All are thus obliged to learn Spanish.

You see, the Ladinos speak only Spanish. 37
That was because Our Father Sun first gave souls to the Ladinos.

When Our Father Sun changed the languages, people began to split up. 38
They scattered;
Some went to the lowlands;
Others, like ourselves, scattered here and there in the highlands.

39 jaˀ la jmoj la xch'ak sbaik ti bu la koˀol ti sk'opike.
slekoj la xch'ak sbaik ti bu la koˀol ti sk'opike.

40 jaˀ la ti mu la xaˀibe sba sk'opike.
jaˀ yuˀun la tana ti sleklekoj ti batz'i k'optik komem ˀasta ˀora.

41 ta jujun lum ti ˀoy jbatz'i k'optik,
ta skotol banomile.

42 k'ajomal jkaxlanetik jun noˀox k'op.
ta xk'oponik ta kastiya.

43 k'u yepal puru ˀindijena ta puru batz'i k'op ta xk'opojik.
skotol ˀindijena.

44 veno k'alal la ti la xch'ak sbaik ti kirsanoetik ta voˀne lae,
bat la saˀ yosilik bu la xuˀ spas naik ti jchop la ti kirsanoe.
jech la ti jkaxlanetike slekoj la bat saˀ yosilik bu xuˀ xnakik.

45 veno sta la ti yosilike.
te la lik spas naik.
te la bolik

46 k'alal la ti bolike lik la snopik ti jkaxlanetik xkaltike.
pero li sbi la ta kastiyae jˀespanyol la sbi.

47 veno ti jˀespanyole lik la yutilan ti kirsano ˀindijenae.
lik la tzakik ta ˀabtel.

48 k'alal la ti ta xˀabtej ti ˀinyoe mu la xˀak'bat skux k'alal ta xlube.
ˀak'o la chak yuch' yaˀi ˀoˀ mu la xˀak' yuch' ti ˀoˀe.

Those who went off together were those who had the same language. 39
The different groups were divided according to those who had
the same language.

So it is true that different groups did not understand one another. 40
That is why we remained separate, very separate, those of us who
still speak Tzotzil, the true language, today.

In all lands there are those of us who speak our native languages, 41
All over the earth.

It is different with the Ladinos; they all speak but one language. 42
They speak Spanish.

As for those who are Indians, they speak only their native languages. 43
This is true of all native peoples.

So then, when the people split up long ago, 44
The different groups of people went separately to find land
to build their houses.
So it was that the Ladinos went separately to look for land
where they could settle.

So it was that they found their homelands. 45
There they began to build their houses.
There they multiplied.

When they had multiplied, it seems to me that the Ladinos began to 46
reflect upon who they were and what they should do.
Indeed, the correct name of those whom we call "Ladinos"
ought to be "Spaniards."

Now, then, soon thereafter the Spaniards began to harass the native people. 47
They began to oblige them to do forced labor.

When the Indians worked, they were not given rest periods 48
when they grew tired.
Although they were thirsty, they did not permit them to drink water.

49 jaˀ to la mi sta ti ˀorae jaˀ to la ta xkux ta ˀabtel.
pero k'alal ta ti ta xˀabteje mi vayi la jlikeluk ta ˀabtel lek la jun majel ta xˀich'.
k'alal mi vayi la ta ˀabtel jlikel ti ˀinyo vinike.

50 jech la jujun k'ak'al la spasbat.
ti ˀilbaj ta xˀutilan la tajmek ti k'alal la ta xˀabteje.

51 jech la xtok k'alal la ta xˀich'ik ˀoˀe.
muˀyuk la bu ta xˀich'ik ˀoˀ ta ch'ulna.
ch'abal la ch'ulna.

52 k'ajomal la ta xˀak'bat smarkail chak k'uchaˀal kaˀ.
ˀilbaj toˀox la yutilan ti ˀindijenaetik ti ˀespanyoletik ti voˀne lae.

Only when their work time was over could they rest from their labor. 49
And if they chanced to fall asleep during their assigned work time,
they were sure to receive a beating.
This was their fate if the Indian workers should fall asleep.

This was what happened to them in the daily round of their labor. 50
The Spaniards watched over them and tormented them a lot
while they were working.

Their hateful ways carried over into the manner in which they feigned 51
to baptize the people.
They didn't really baptize them in the churches.
There were no churches.

Instead, what really happened was that they did nothing more 52
than brand them, just like horses.
Indeed, the Spaniards of long ago humiliated and mistreated the Indians.

FIGURE 62

Instead, what really happened was that they did nothing more
than brand them, just like horses.
Indeed, the Spaniards of long ago humiliated and mistreated
the Indians.

53 ˀentonse taˀlo xaˀi ti jtotik.
mu la sk'an ti ˀabol la jbatik ta majel.
ti ˀabol la jbatik ta ˀutel yuˀun ti jˀespanyole.

54 k'alal la ti taˀlo xaˀik ti jtotike lik la ti letoe.
lik la spasik leto xchiˀuk ˀinyo ti jˀespanyole.
jaˀ la la spasik ti letoe.
laj la spasik chanvikuk ˀaˀvil ti puru leto lae.
jaˀ la la spasik ti letoe.

55 vokol la meltzaj ti k'ope.
jaˀ la meltzaj yuˀun ti kuch yuˀun pas leto.

Soon, Our Father Sun felt that there had been enough of this. 53
He didn't want us to be abused and hurt by whippings.
Nor to be humiliated by threats and scorn from the Spaniards.

When Our Father Sun felt that there had been enough of this, 54
the warfare began.
The Spaniards began to make war on the Indians.
They were the ones who made war.
Indeed, it was a war that lasted for perhaps four years.
It was they, the Spaniards, who made war.

It was hard to solve these problems. 55
The one who managed to do so was one who suffered through the
fighting and triumphed.

56 ti mikel ˀidadkoe jaˀ la la skomtzan ta lek ti k'ope.
jaˀ la ta xch'ay ti ta toˀox la xkich' jmarkailtik.
jaˀ lik yak' ˀiluk ta xkich'tik ˀoˀ ta ch'ulna.
lik la yak' ˀiluk ta jk'opontik jtotik.
lik la yal k'uxi ta jpastik resal.
lik la yak' ˀiluk k'uxi chijˀabtej.
lik la yak' ˀiluk chanvun.
lik la yak' ˀiluk skotol.

57 k'usitikuk ˀabtelel ti mikel ˀidadkoe.
jaˀ la smeltz'an ti k'op voˀne lae.
jaˀ la la skomtzan ta lek ti k'ope.
jaˀ la snutzik sutel ti jˀespanyoletike ti bu la la sta ti yosilik ti jˀespanyol ti voˀne lae.
jaˀ la ti sutik batel ti ta ˀaspanya sbi ti lume.

58 jaˀ yuˀun la ti ta xlok' sk'inal ta jujun ˀaˀvil, ta vaklajuneb semiembre.
ti k'uxi la ti chan ta tuk' ti don mikel ˀidadko lae.
xavil jaˀ la la skomtzan ta lek ti banomil ti voˀne lae.

It was Miguel Hidalgo who prevailed and caused peace to come.[8] 56
He stopped the old custom of branding us as though we were horses.
He began to show them how to baptize us in the church.
He began to show us how to pray to our Father Sun.
He began to tell us what we should say in prayers.
He began to show us how to work.
He began to show us how to read and write.
He began to show us everything.

It was Miguel Hidalgo who accomplished these good works. 57
It was he who settled the conflict a long time ago.
It was he who resolved the problems.
It was he who hunted and chased the Spaniards back to their
ancestral homeland, where they really belonged.
It was he who forced them to return to Spain, as their country is called.

That is why they celebrate his fiesta every year on the 16th of September. 58
That is when Don Miguel Hidalgo was shot to death.
You see, he left the earth in good condition long ago.

FIGURE 63

It was Miguel Hidalgo who prevailed and caused peace to
come.
He stopped the old custom of branding us as though we were
horses.
He began to show them how to baptize us in the church.

The Fourth Creation

4

1 ˀoy jun kuento sventa ˀixim ta mas voˀnee.

2 ˀoy la jun ˀantz bat la chobtik.
bat la saˀ talel ˀajan ti ˀantze.
vaˀun ti ˀantz ˀune laj la saˀ talel la ˀox ch'ix ti ˀajane.

3 jech la ti ˀajane.
ˀi ta la bol la stukik ti ˀixime.

4 vaˀun ˀa ti ˀantz ˀune ˀoy la smalal.
jech la ti smalal ti ˀantz ˀune.
batem la ta kutz siˀ ta teˀtik ti vinike.

5 veno k'alal la vul kutz siˀ ta teˀtik ti vinike:
jech la ti ˀantz ne lakal xa la ti ˀajan ˀune.

6 veno k'alal la vul la ta kutz siˀ ti vinik ˀune:
bu la ta talel li ˀajan ˀune xi la ti vinike.
leˀ la jta talele xi la ti ˀantz ˀune.

7 k'uchaˀal la k'aj talel tajmek ˀepe xi la ti vinike.
muˀyuk bu ˀep la jk'aj talel tajmek ˀune xi la ti ˀantz ˀune.

8 k'u yuˀun la kaj talel tajmek ˀepe.
k'alal mi tal ti viˀnale mu xa bu ta jtatik ti ˀixime.
kavron mu jventa kot xi la ti vinik ˀune.

SECTION I

Earth Lords, Demons, and Heroes

TEXT 44

Of the Earth Lord's Daughter

Marián López Calixto

Here is a story about corn in ancient times. 1

There was once a woman who went to the cornfield. 2
This woman had gone to gather ears of tender corn for cooking.
Indeed, the woman harvested three ears of corn.

Now, as for these ears of corn, this was what happened. 3
This corn multiplied of its own accord.

Now, this woman had a husband. 4
And this was what the woman's husband was up to.
This man had gone to the woods to fetch firewood.[1]

Well, when the man came back from fetching firewood in the forest, 5
this was what he found:
The woman had already set the corn to cook.

Well, upon returning from bringing the firewood, he spoke: 6
"Where did you get the roasting ears?" inquired the man.
"Oh, I gathered them over there in the field," responded the woman.

"But why did you harvest so many?" accused the man. 7
"Really, I didn't get many ears at all," responded the woman.

"But why did you harvest so much? 8
When we are hungry, then there won't be any corn left for us to eat.
Hell! It won't be may fault!" railed the man angrily.

9 jech la ti ˀantz ˀune ta la xˀokʼ tajmek ˀun.
jech la ti vinik ˀune laj la yakʼ la majel.

10 jech la ti mu vinik ˀune:
la stijbe la ta sniˀ ti povre ˀantz ˀune.

11 jech la ti ˀantz ˀune:
lokʼ la xchʼichʼel la sniˀ ˀep tajmek ti povre ˀantze.

12 kʼalal la ta xˀokʼ ti povre ˀantz ˀune,
jech la ti yixim ˀune laj la skus ta sniˀ ti ˀantze.

13 ˀa ti mu vinik ˀune toj kʼulej tajmek;
ti mu sonso vinik ˀune.

14 ti xchob ti mu vinik ˀune toj lekik la tajmek.
ˀoy la ˀep yixim.
ˀi ˀoy la ˀep la schenekʼ.

15 vaˀun kʼalal laj la smaj ti yajnil ti mu vinik ˀune:
likel la tal ta ˀora tajmek ti toketike.
likel la vol xi la ta ˀora ti toketike.

16 noj la ti tok.
la vul ta sna ti mu vinik ˀune.

17 jech la ti mu vinik ˀune:
tal xa ti toke xi la ti mu vinik ˀune.

18 vaˀun kʼalal la noj tajmek ti tok ˀune,
tal la xojobal ta yut na ti ˀanjele.

19 jech la ti ˀantze ˀanjel la ˀek ˀun.
jaˀ yuˀun ti ˀanjeletik tal la yikʼ ˀel ti ˀantze.

With that, the woman fell to weeping inconsolably. 9
And with that, the man gave her a beating.

This is what the ungrateful man did: 10
He gave the poor woman a punch in the nose.

This is what happened to the woman: 11
Blood came gushing out of the woman's nose.

Whereupon the poor woman wept, 12
And with an ear of corn the woman wiped off her injured nose.[2]

Now, this evil man was very rich and fortunate; 13
But he was in fact stupid and ignorant.

In truth, the evil man's cornfield was abundant and prosperous. 14
He had a lot of corn.
And he had lots of beans.[3]

Therefore, soon after this evil man had struck his wife: 15
Quickly, instantly, the thunderclouds gathered.
Quickly, it is said, the thunderclouds amassed.

Clouds engulfed everything. 16
It was then that the wicked man came up to his house.

This is what the wicked man said: 17
"Now the thunderclouds have come upon us," observed the wicked man nonchalantly.

But, once the place was engulfed with clouds, 18
The Earth Lord himself struck as a lightning bolt, right inside the house.

Now, it must be remembered that the woman herself was of the family of Earth Lords. 19
Indeed, the lightning bolt was a sign that the Earth Lords had come to carry the woman home.

20 veno jech la ti ˀantze ˀoy la yalabtak:
jun la tzeb.
jun la kerem.

21 tekeˀ ˀun kol xi.
me xaveˀik ˀune.
ta me xak'ojik la jayik ˀune xi la ti ˀantz ˀune.

22 ˀey xi la ti ˀololetik ˀune.
jech la ti ˀololetike ta la sk'ojik yuni binik k'alal mi laj la ti yuni veˀelike.

23 jech ti sbinike ta la xlok' la talel la ˀep tajmek ti yuni veˀelike.
jech la ti stotik ti ˀuni ˀololetike muˀyuk xa la ta xˀak' batik sveˀelik.

24 vaˀun ti stotik ti ˀololetike:
pere bu ta xveˀik tajmek ti jnich'one xi la ti mu vinike.

25 jech la ti ˀuni ˀololetike ˀa ti yuni binik snak'ojik la.
mu la bu ta xˀak'bik la yil ti sbinike.

26 pere bu chaveˀik tajmek xi la ti vinike.
muˀyuk xi la ti ˀuni ˀololetike.

27 veno kavron ta jk'elkik bu ta xveˀik xi la ti mu vinik ˀune.
jech la ti mu vinik ˀune.
laj la yil bu ta staik ti sveˀel ti ˀuni ˀololetik ˀune.
ˀora la jkil xa xi la ti mu vinik ˀune.

28 jech la ti mu vinik ˀune k'alal la muˀyuk la te ˀoy ti snich'on ˀune.
jech la ti vinik ˀune.
ˀoch la ta yut sna ta ˀora ti vinik ˀune.
bat la veˀun ˀek' ˀun.

Now, this woman had her children to think about: 20
One was a girl,
One was a boy.

"Don't worry, children. 21
You will have plenty to eat.
You have only to tap on these gourd bowls."

"Okay, fine," replied the children. 22
And the children had only to tap on their little vessels whenever
they were in need of a little food.[4]

Sure enough, good little meals, in generous supply, appeared for them 23
out of these vessels.
It was also the case that the children's food supply was not available
for their father's use.[5]

The children's father wondered about this: 24
"Where can my children be getting all this food?" said the
wicked man to himself.

It was, indeed, the case that the children had carefully hidden 25
their little pots.
They did not show these vessels to him at all.

"But where can all this food you're eating be coming from?" 26
inquired the man.
"Who knows?" responded the little children.

"Well, damn it, we'll find out where their food supply is coming from," 27
railed the wicked man.
And this is what the wicked man did.
He finally found out where the children went to get their food.
"Now I've found out," declared the wicked man.

Now, this is what the wicked man did one day when his children were away. 28
This is just what he did.
The man sneaked quickly into the house.
He also ate his fill from the children's magical supply.

29 k'alal la noj ti mu vinik ˀune.
yochel la ta svok'el ti yuni binik ti ˀun ˀololetik ˀune.

30 k'alal la ˀoch ta yut sna saˀ la ti yuni binike.
ˀi ch'abal la ti sbinike.

31 vaˀun ti smeˀ ti ˀuni ˀololetike tal la ˀun.
mi ˀoy to ta veˀelike xi la smeˀ ti ˀololetike.
muˀyuk xa.
jech ti kuni binikutike xa xvok'bunkutik.

32 veno tekeˀ ˀun chaˀe.
batik ta vinajel xi la ti ˀantz ˀune.
lek ˀoy meˀ xi la ti ˀololetike.

33 jech la ti ˀantze:
laj la yak' la komel la yixim ta sna ti smalale.

34 jech la ti ˀantz ˀune:
tekeˀ ˀun kol.
ˀak'o sveˀ ma ti jch'ich'el jniˀe xi la ti ˀantze.

35 jech la ti ˀantze:
laj la yak' la komel la ti yixim ti ˀantz ˀune.
puru la tzoj tajmek ti ˀixim ˀune.

36 jech la ti ˀixim ˀune ti puru la tzoj tajmeke,
jaˀ la xch'ich'el la sniˀ ti povre ˀantz ˀune.

37 jech'al ˀun jech la kom ti ˀiximetik ˀune:
ˀoy la jlom tzoj.
ˀi ˀoy la jlom sak.

38 jech la ti sake jaˀ la yaˀlel la sat.
ˀa ti tzoje jaˀ la xch'ich'el la sniˀ ti povre ˀantze.

39 jech la ti vinike:
bat xa ti kajnile xi la ti mu vinike.
ta la xˀok' ˀek ˀun.

Once he was full, the wicked man did this. 29
He set about to break the children's little food pots.

When they got home they looked for their little pots. 30
But the pots where nowhere to be found.

Then the children's mother appeared. 31
"Do you still have enough to eat?" inquired the children's mother.
"Not any longer.
For our little pots got broken."

"Well, it doesn't matter, anyway. 32
We shall be going away to the sky," announced the woman.
"That's fine, Mother," said the children.

This is what the woman did: 33
She left some corn there in her husband's house.

This is what the woman said: 34
"It's okay, my little ones.
Let him eat the blood of my nose," declared the woman.

This is what the woman did: 35
The woman left the corn for him.
And, indeed, the corn was totally red.

Really! The corn was as red as could be, 36
For it bore the blood from the poor woman's nose.

That is why, to this day, corn is of two types: 37
There is a red variety.
And also a white variety.

The white type is from the tears from the woman's eyes. 38
The red type is from the blood of the poor woman's nose.

As for the man, he spoke in this manner: 39
"Now, alas, my wife is gone," lamented the wicked man.
And he fell to weeping as well.

40 tekeˀ ma liˀe.
ta xa xicham.
bat xa ti kajnile xi la ti mu vinike.

41 jech la ti yajnil ti mu vinik ˀune.
toj k'on la tajmek la ti sjole ti yajnil ˀune.

42 ˀa ti yajnil ti mu vinik lae ˀanjel.
jech chaˀal ˀun ti bat la ta vinajel ˀun.

43 jech la ti mu vinik ˀune:
bat la sk'an la talel sna ti ˀanjele.
k'ot ta sna ti ˀanjele.

44 bul bat me kajval xi la k'otel ti mu vinik ˀune.
laˀ me k'usi chak'an xi la ti ˀanjele.

45 muˀyuk.
liˀ li tale yuˀun ta jk'an kajnil xi la ti mu vinike.

46 ˀa moˀoj ˀunbi saˀbil chamaj.
lek to koˀntone la jkak'bot ta ˀavajnile.
pero liˀ ne muˀyuk xa ta ˀavajnil ˀune xi la ti ˀanjel ˀune.

47 pere ˀak'bun tajmek xi la ti mu vinik ˀune.
lok'an ˀavokoluk xi la ti ˀanjele.

48 veno tekeˀ ˀun chaˀe.
te k'alal xi la ti mu vinike.

49 jech la ti mu vinik ˀune:
puru la ˀok'el ta spas tajmek ti vinike.

50 ˀi puru la ˀok'el cham ˀo.
ti mu vinik ˀune cham la ˀun.

51 k'alal la cham ti mu vinike ˀa ti smu sat lae toj sit la tajmek.
situb la ta ˀok'el.

"Oh, woe is me! 40
I am going to die!
Now, alas, my wife is gone!" cried the wicked man.

Now, the wicked man's wife was no ordinary mortal. 41
His wife had very blond hair.

The reason was that she was of the family of the Earth Lord. 42
That is why she was able to go away to the sky.[6]

As for the wicked man, this is what he did: 43
He set off for the Earth Lord's house to ask that his wife
be returned to him.
And he arrived finally at the Earth Lord's house.

"I am here, my lord," announced the man upon his arrival. 44
"Come forward, then. What is your business?" asked the Earth Lord.

"Nothing much, really. 45
I've just come here to ask for my wife back," declared the man.

"Oh, but that's out of the question, for you picked a fight and struck her. 46
I was once a person of good will and I gave you a wife.
But as of right now, she is no longer your wife," he explained.

"Please, please give her back to me," implored the wicked man. 47
"Get out of here, please," replied the Earth Lord.

"Well, there is nothing more to be said. 48
That's the way things are," said the wicked man.

As for this wicked man, this is what he did: 49
The man fell to weeping inconsolably.

Indeed he got sick from pure grief and crying. 50
The wicked man finally died.

As he lay dying, his evil eyes became very swollen. 51
They became swollen from so much crying.

52 k'alal la cham la ti smalal ti ˀantz ne.
ˀi yal la talel la sna ti ˀanjele ˀantz ne.

53 jech la ti yixim ˀune,
ti k'u la yepal ti xˀojtikin la ˀune laj la sk'elan la li yixim ˀune.
jech la ti ˀixim ˀune puru la tzoj tajmek.

54 jech la ti yane:
k'uchaˀal toj tzoj tajmek ti ˀavixime xi la ti yane.
yuˀun la smajun.
jech'aˀal ˀun toj tzoj kixim ne xi la ti ˀantze.

Once the woman's husband was dead, she appeared again. 52
She came back down to earth from the home of the Earth Lord.

Now, as for the corn variety that bears her name, 53
She presented this corn as a gift to all the people she knew.
And this corn she gave them was the pure red variety.

Some people on earth asked the Earth Lord's daughter: 54
"Why is your corn so very red?" they inquired.
"The reason is that my husband hit me.
That is why my corn is so red," explained the woman.

1 kuento vinik ta sk'an sk'ulejal ta ch'en.

2 veno ti vinike toj ʔabol la sba.
ch'abal la stak'in.
ch'abal la yixim.
ch'abal la sk'uʔ.

3 ʔentonse ti vinike lik la snop:
pero k'uchaʔal toj ʔabol jba tajmeke.
k'usi chiveʔ ti mi jmolibe.
buch'u chiyak'be jtak'in.
buch'u chiyak'be jk'uʔ.

TEXT 45

OF A MAN WHO SOUGHT RICHES FROM THE EARTH LORDS

Xalik López Castellanos

This is the story of a man who sought riches in a cave. 1

Now, this man was very poor. 2
He had no money.
He had no corn.
He had no clothing.

The man started to think out loud: 3
"Why am I so poor?
What am I going to eat when I grow old?
Who will give me money?
Who will provide my clothing?

4 kajval.
jesus.
jch’ultot xi la ti vinike.
te la chotol ta xokon sna ta la xˀok’.

5 tekeˀ chibat ta ch’en.
chibat jk’opon ˀanjel.
ˀaˀ mas lek ˀaver mi xiyak’be stak’in.

6 ta juevex sob chibat.
pero muˀyuk chiveˀ ˀoxlajuneb k’ak’al.

7 ta xak’elavilik.
mi lok’ xulem leˀ ta vitze,
mi lok’ ti xuleme yuˀun xa li cham xˀut la xchiˀiltak ti vinike.

8 ˀentonse ti vinike te la bat ta vitz ti bu ˀoy ti ch’ene.
te la ˀoy ti ˀoxlajuneb k’ak’al le.
muˀyuk la ta xveˀ.

My God! 4
Jesus!
Holy Father!" exclaimed the man.
He sat there beside his house and cried.

"Well, I'm going to go to the cave. 5
I'm going to go talk to the Earth Lord.
I'll see if he will give me money.[1]

I will leave early Thursday morning. 6
And for thirteen days I will fast.

There you should take notice. 7
If you see buzzards there on the mountain,
If you see buzzards it will be a sign that I have died," said the man to his relatives.

With that, the man set off for the mountain where the cave was located. 8
There he stayed for thirteen days.[2]
He ate nothing.

FIGURE 64

"My God!
Jesus!
Holy Father!" exclaimed the man.
He sat there beside his house and cried.

9 veno ti xchiˀiltake ta la sk'elik mi ta xlok' ti xulem ta vitze.
k'alal la lok' jun xemuna muˀyuk la ta xlok' xulem.

10 naˀ mi kuxuluk ti jmikele.
muˀyuk ta xlok' xulem xi la ti xchiˀiltak ti vinike.

11 ˀentonse tz'aki la ti ˀoxlajuneb k'ak'ale sut la talel ta sna ti vinike.
pero k'alal la sut talel ta snae ta xa la xk'unib ta be.
mu xa la xuˀ xanav.

12 k'alal la tz'aki ti ˀoxlajuneb k'ak'ale laj la yich' ti sk'ulejale.
mu la bu xcham ti vinike.
kuch la yuˀun ti ˀoxlajuneb k'ak'al muˀyuk xveˀe.

13 ˀentonse k'alal la jyich' ti sk'ulejale ˀoch batel ta yut ch'en.
pero ˀoch la batel tajmek ta yut.

14 ˀentonse k'ot la ti bu stiˀ sna ti ˀanjele.
laj la stij ti tiˀ nae.
veno tal la jun jkaxlan sjam ti tiˀ nae.

15 liˀ ˀoye malaˀo.
jlikeluk ta xa xtal.
chotlan te ta xila
xˀutat la ti vinike.

16 veno lek ˀoy liˀ ta jmalaˀe xi la ti vinike.
mu la bu xchoti.

17 te la vaˀal jlikel pero ta xa ˀox la xchoti.
ˀentonse muˀyuk la bu xchoti.
keji la ti bu stiˀ sna ti ˀanjele.

18 ˀa ti chotiuk la ti vinike te la tzakal kom ta ton.
mu xa la bu sut talel ta sna.
pero komo muˀyuk bu xchoti ˀech'o xal sut ˀel ta sna.

Now, his relatives kept checking to see if buzzards appeared on the mountain. 9
At the end of a week no buzzards had appeared.

"Miguel might still be alive. 10
There are no buzzards to be seen," speculated the man's relatives.

At the end of the thirteen days the man was returning to his home. 11
But on the way home, he became weak.
He could no longer walk.

Now, it was upon the last and thirteenth day of his fast when he received what would become the source of his riches. 12
He did not die.
He survived the thirteen days of fasting.

In order to secure his riches the man had gone into the cave. 13
He had to go far into the depths of the cave.

Soon he came to the Earth Lord's front door. 14
He had just knocked on the door.
Whereupon, a Ladino servant came to open the door for him.

"He [the Earth Lord] is here. Wait a minute. 15
He will come soon.
Have a seat and make yourself comfortable,"
That was what the Ladino servant said to the man.

"Very well. I'll wait here," said the man. 16
But he did not sit down.

He stood there for a minute and was about to sit down. 17
But he had second thoughts about sitting down.
He simply knelt down by the Earth Lord's door.

If the man had sat down, he would have remained there stuck forever to the stone.[3] 18
He would not have been able to go home.
However, since he did not sit down, he was eventually able to go home.

19 ˀentonse k'alal tal ti ˀanjele te kejel ti vinike.
k'usi chaval xˀutat la ti vinike.

20 muˀyuk.
yuˀun li tal jk'oponot yuˀun toj ˀabol jba tajmek xi la ti vinike.

21 pero ˀentonse k'usi chak'an ˀun chaˀe xˀutat la ti vinike.
mu jnaˀ k'usi xˀak'bune xi la ti vinike.

22 pero ˀalbun k'usi chak'ane xˀutat la ti vinike.
tekeˀ chaˀe ta jk'an ˀixim xi la ti vinike.
veno lek ˀoy xi la ti ˀanjele.

23 laj la yak' jun mol ˀasarona mu xa la xtun.
mu la sk'an stzak lek ti vinike.

When the Earth Lord came, the man was kneeling there. 19
"What do you wish to say?" he said to the man.

"Not much. 20
I have just come to talk to you because I am so poor," said the man.

"But, come now, get to the point. What do you want?" the Earth Lord asked. 21
"Not much, really. I was just wondering how you might help me," explained the man.

"But come to the point! Tell me, what do you wish?" was the Earth Lord's response. 22
"Well, I need some corn," answered the man.
"Very well. That can be arranged," said the Earth Lord.

And with that, he gave the man an old, worn-out hoe. 23
In truth, the man did not accept it very eagerly.

FIGURE 65

When the Earth Lord came, the man was kneeling there.
"What do you wish to say?" he said to the man.

24 ˀentonse laj la yich' ˀasarona ti vinike.
bat la ta sna xchiˀuk ti yasaronae.

25 veno tekeˀun batan.
pero mu me xak'el ˀapat xˀutat la ti vinike.

26 veno bat ta sna ti vinike.
laj yich' ˀel ti ˀasaronae.

27 k'alal k'ot ta snae la jyak' ta skajon ti ˀasaronae.
xch'ata ta pom.
ti vinike vay.

28 k'alal la julav ta poˀot ˀoˀlol ˀak'obal.
ˀaˀ to la xaˀi ta la xbak' ti skajone.
k'usi ti ta xbak' ta jk'ajone xi la ti vinike.

29 lik la sk'el ti skajone.
laj la sjam ti skajone.
ˀaˀ to la xˀil noj ta tak'in ti skajone.

But the man did finally take the hoe. 24
He then started for home carrying his hoe.

"All right, now, be on your way. 25
But you must not look back," he heard as he was leaving.

With that, the man went home. 26
He carried his hoe with him.

When he got home he put his hoe in a wooden chest.[4] 27
And he carefully burned incense as an offering to his new possession.
Then he went to sleep.

It was shortly before midnight when he woke up. 28
He realized that something was rustling in his wooden chest.
"What's that noise in my chest?" the man wondered.

He got up to check his chest. 29
He opened up his chest.
It was then that he saw that his chest was full of money.

FIGURE 66

He got up to check his chest.
He opened up his chest.
It was then that he saw that his chest was full of money.

✠ ✠ ✠

There was a snake curled up there.
It was sleeping on top of the coins.

30 ta la spuch'an sba jun chon.
xvay ta sba ti tak'ine.

31 toj xiˀel la k'ot ti vinike:
ˀentonse pero maˀuk chon xi la ti vinike.

32 laj la stzak ti chone.
laj la yak' ta jun skajon.

33 porke ti bu la jyak' baˀyele noj xa ta tak'in.
ˀech'o xal la jyak' ta jun ˀo kajon.

34 ˀentonse kontento xa la ti vinike.
mu xa la bu xvay.

35 k'alal la sakub ˀoy sa la ˀep stak'in.
noj la chib kajon.

36 kon ˀese pas ˀo la ta jk'ulej.
laj la sman skaˀ;
laj la sman yosil;
laj la spas sna.

37 veno ti stak'ine bol la tajmek.
jujun la k'ak'al ta xlok' ti tak'in te ta skajone.

There was a snake curled up there. 30
It was sleeping on top of the coins.[5]

At first the man was terrified, but then he reflected: 31
"This must be something other than an ordinary snake," said the man.[6]

So he picked it up. 32
Then he put it into another chest.

The reason for this was that the place where he had originally placed 33
the hoe was now full of money.
That is why he placed the snake in another chest.

The man was overjoyed. 34
He could not get back to sleep.

By dawn he already had lots and lots of money. 35
He had two chests full of it.

With that turn of fate, he became wealthy. 36
He bought horses;
He bought land;
He built a house.

Well, his wealth continued to increase without end. 37
Each and every day money appeared there in his chest.

1 lo?il yu?un pukuj ta belel tuxta.

2 veno, ta von?nee ?oy la cha?vo? moletik bat la xchonik xonobil ta tuxta.
k'alal ta tzutzukoj ta xbat xchonik ti xonobil xchi?uk ti nukule.

3 ti jun mole xonobil ta xchon.
ti mun mole nukul ta xchon.

TEXT 46
Of the Heroes of Bell Cave Who Slew the Demon Pukuj

Xalik López Castellanos

This is an account of the Demon Pukuj who lived on the road 1
to Tuxtla Gutiérrez.

Long ago there were two old men who went often to sell sandals 2
in Tuxtla Gutiérrez.
When they had finished making them, they would go off to sell them.

One old man sold sandals. 3
One old man sold the leather straps.[1]

FIGURE 67

Long ago there were two old men who went often to sell sandals
in Tuxtla Gutiérrez.

4 ˀentonse ti moletike yabinojik ti mu xuˀ xjelavik ta belel tuxtae.
te la xcham skotol ti kirsanoetik ti k'alal ta xbatik ta tuxtae.
ˀech xtok ti kirsanoetik ta tuxta ti k'alal ta xtalik ta joˀbele.

5 mu xuˀ xjelavik,
te la xchamik skotolik ta belel tuxta.

6 ˀoy la te jun muk'ta ch'en ta belel txuta.
kampana ch'en la sbil.
te la nakal ti pukuje.

7 mu la xuˀ xjelav skotol ti kirsanoe.
te la xchamik ta be.
ti pukuje te la nakal ta mero jol ch'en.

8 k'alal la ta xbat xchonik ˀisak' ton ˀalak' ˀitaj ti jchamoˀetike,
te la xchamik skotol ta be.
mu la xjelavik.
te la xcham xchiˀuk sk'aˀik.

9 ˀech ti kirsanoetik ta tuxta ti k'alal ta xbat xchonik manta k'uˀiletik
chamaro pixolal.
te la xchamik ta be.

10 ti mantae ti chamaroe ti pixolale ti k'uˀiletike ti atz'ame te la busul skotol
ta nail ch'en.
k'alal ta xbat chonilajikuk ti kirsanoetike.

11 mu snaˀik mi ˀoy k'usi te ta be.
ti pukuje ta ˀak'ol to ˀoy.

Now, these old men had heard it said that one could not get through 4
safely via the Tuxtla road.
It was said that everyone died there when they were going to Tuxtla.
The same thing happened to those who were traveling from Tuxtla
to San Cristóbal.[2]

You simply couldn't get through, 5
Everyone died on the Tuxtla road.

Now, there was a huge cave that lay close by the Tuxtla road. 6
It was called Bell Cave.
That was where the Demon Pukuj lived.[3]

Not a soul was able to get by that place. 7
They would die right there on the road.
The Demon Pukuj lived right there at the mouth of the cave.

Whenever Chamulas would pass by there on their way to sell 8
potatoes, eggs, or cabbage,
They would all perish right there on the road.
They could never get through.
They just died right there together with their horses.

The same thing happened to the people of Tuxtla who took the road 9
up to the highlands to sell cloth, clothing, tunics, and hats.
They would die right there on the road.

Their cloth, tunics, hats, clothing, and salt would end up strewn in a 10
pile at the cave entrance.
This happened whenever merchants passed by there.

Newcomers did not realize what peril lay waiting for them 11
there by the road.
The fact was that the Demon Pukuj lived right there,
just above the road.

12 k'alal ta xa xk'ot ti kirsano ti bu ti xch'en ti pukuje.
ta la xbat spajbe ti kirsanoe.

13 xjumum xa ˀel xchiˀuk yesparo.
ta la spajbe ti kirsano ta mero yoˀontone.

14 k'alal mi laj spajbee xchechet xa la muyel xchiˀuk yesparo.
ta la xyal talel xtok.
ta la xpajbe yan xtok.

15 ta xyal ta xmuy.
ˀech'o xal te la xcham skotol ti kirsano ta bee.
xbat ta ˀora ta pukuj xchiˀuk ti yesparoe.

It would always happen this way whenever people would come along 12
the road near the Demon Pukuj's cave.
He would leap out to impale the people.

He would come roaring out with his sword. 13
He would stick the people right in the heart.

Once he had impaled them, he would drag them up with his sword, 14
as if they were skewered upon it.
Then he would slam them down again.
And once again, he would pierce them through.

Down and up again. 15
That is how all the people met their end there on the road.
The Demon Pukuj would leap out to assault them with his sword.

FIGURE 68

It would always happen this way whenever people would come
along the road near the Demon Pukuj's cave.
He would leap out to impale the people.

16 ʔentonse k'alal bat ti chaʔ voʔ moletike laj la yich'ik ʔel yakteʔik yek'elik.
ti jun mole ʔak'teʔ la jyich' ʔel.
ti jun mole ʔek'el la jyich' ʔel.

17 ʔentonse batik la xchonik ti xonobile ti nukule.
pero yabinojik la ti ʔoy ti pukuj ta bee.
yabinojik ti te la xcham skotol ti kirsanoe.

18 pero mu la xch'unik ti ʔoy pukuj ta bee.
batikik ta jk'eltikik mi melel ti ʔoy ti pukuj ta bee xiʔik la ti moletike.
batik la.

19 ʔentonse ti moletike ta la xloʔilajik ʔel ta be.
ti mi yuʔun tal ti pukuj tanae me me xaxiʔ.
te me vaʔalan ʔaʔ noʔos xajip ta ʔora la ʔavikatze xi la ti jun mol
ti ʔyo yak'teʔe.

20 moʔoj k'uchaʔal chixiʔ.
ti mi yuʔun tale ta xkak'be jchibaltik xi la ti jun mol ʔoy yek'ele.
veno lek ʔoy mu me xaxiʔ xi la ti jun mol ti ʔoy yak'teʔe.

21 ʔentonse ti k'alal ta xa la xk'otik ti bu xch'en ti pukuje
jaʔ to la xaʔik ti xjumum xa la talel ti pukuje.

22 jlikel la la sjip yikatzik ta ʔora ti moletike.
laj la spas kurus ta banumil ta ʔora xchiʔuk ti yakteʔe.

23 k'alal yal talel ti pukuj xchiʔuk ti yesparoe,
ʔaʔ la k'ot spajbe ti kurus ta banumile.

24 ti mole muʔyuk la bu xʔich' ʔesparo.
ʔaʔ la yich' ʔesparo ti banumile.
ti moletike te la nopol vaʔalalik ti bu la spasik kurus ta banumile.

Now, when the two old men who are the subject of this account set out, 16
they carried with them their clubs and axes.
One old man carried a club.
One old man carried an axe.

They had set out to sell their sandals and leather straps. 17
They had heard that there was a demon by the road.
They had heard that everyone died there on the road.

But, in fact, they did not believe that there was such a demon by the road. 18
"Let us go see if it is true that the Demon Pukuj lives by the road,"
said one of the old men.
With that, they set out.

Now, these old men were talking together as they traveled 19
"If this demon really does attack us, don't be afraid.
Stand up to him and throw down your pack," advised the old man
who carried the club.

"You're right. Why should we be afraid?. 20
If he comes out, the two of us will attack him," said the old man
who had the axe.
"That's the spirit! Don't be afraid!" said the old man who had the club.

Pretty soon they reached the vicinity where the demon's cave was located. 21
Then they heard the Demon Pukuj coming towards them, making
a dreadful roaring sound.

At once the old men threw down their packs. 22
At once they traced a cross on the ground with their clubs.[4]

And, sure enough, when the demon leapt upon them with his sword, 23
It stuck where the cross had been traced in the earth.

The old men were not impaled. 24
It was the earth that received the sword's blow.
The old men remained standing right there where they had traced
the cross in the earth.

25 k'alal la la spajbe jmoj ti yesparo,
la jyich' jmoj ˀak'teˀ ti pukuje.

26 vuruto xi la ti pukuje.
xchechet xa la muyel xtok.
k'alal ta xyal jutene ta xˀich' jumoj ˀak'teˀ.

27 k'alal mi la jyich' jumoj ˀak'teˀe,
vuruto xi la ti pukuje.

28 schechet xa la muyel.
ta la sut yalel xtok.
xjumum xa la yalel xchiˀuk ti yesparo.

29 ˀaˀ la te tuk' ta xbat ti bu kurus ta banumile.
ti moletike te la nopol vaˀalik.

Once the Demon Pukuj's sword blow was deflected to where the cross 25
had been traced,
It was the demon himself who caught a good blow from the man's club.

"Assholes!" screeched the demon.[5] 26
Then he staggered up, attempting to use his wings to rise into the air.[6]
When he descended, he received another clubbing.

Then, once he had received this clubbing, 27
The Demon Pukuj once again screeched, "Assholes!"

Once again he staggered up. 28
Then down he came.
He descended once again, with a roaring and swishing sound,
wielding his sword.

And sure enough, once again, the sword blow struck the place where 29
the cross had been traced in the earth.
And, just as surely, the old man remained right there, standing safe
and unharmed.

30 yantik la spek'tzaj.
yantik la spek'tzaj ta jumoj ʔak'teʔ.
jumoj ʔak'teʔ tajmek.

31 k'alal mi la yich' ʔak'teʔe vuruto xi la ti pukuje.
k'alal mi la jyich' jumoj ʔak'tee.

32 ta k'unk'un la pek'tzaj.
mu la xtoy muyel.
ʔentonse lubtzaj la.
mu xa la xmuy.

33 te la balch'uj ta sba ti kurus banumile.
te la la jyich mas ʔak'teʔ tajmek.

Again and again, the demon swooped. 30
And again and again, the blows fell upon him.
Indeed, he took a terrible beating.

As he was receiving the clubbing, the demon shrieked, "Assholes!" 31
That was how he carried on when he was being beaten up.

Slowly but surely, they laid him flat. 32
He could not get up.
He grew tired.
He could no longer rise.

He fell there, right on top of the cross which had been traced in the earth. 33
There he received still more clubbing.

FIGURE 69

Again and again, the demon swooped.
And again and again, the blows fell upon him.
Indeed, he took a terrible beating.

34 vuruto vuruto vuruto xi xa la ti pukuje.
mu xa la bu xmuy.
te la cham ti bu ti kurus banumile.

35 soban ˀun kavron.
laˀ kolta ˀaba.
mi mu xavil cham xa la ˀatote xi la ti mol ˀoy yak'teˀe.

36 veno xi la ti mol ˀoy yek'ele.
bat la ta ˀora.

37 laj la yak'be ˀek'el ta mero snuk' ti pukuje.
toj lik'el la k'ot sjol.

38 laj la yak'be yan ta sk'ob ta yok ta sch'ut.
laj la sboj tajmek.

39 jlok'esbetik li yoˀntone.
moˀoje ta xchaˀkux xi la ti jun mol ˀoy yak'tee.

40 ˀaˀ lek jlok'esbetik xi la ti mol ˀoy yek'ele.
lik slok'esbik ti yoˀnton.

41 k'alal la lok' ti yoˀntone laj la yak'bik ˀatz'am.
ˀech ti bu lok' ti yoˀntone laj la yak'bik ˀatz'am.

42 tana ˀun ta xkichbekik ˀel ti sjole ti yoˀntone.
ta xijbat kak'tik ˀiluk ta tuxta.
baˀyel chijˀech' ta soktom.
ta tz'akal chijbat ta tuxta.

43 ta jkuchtik ˀel ti sjole ti yoˀntone.
ta xbat kak'tik ˀiluk k'alal ta tuxta.

44 ta xbat kalbetik ti ˀajvalil ti laj xa jmiltik ti pukuj ta bee.
ti xuˀ xa xbat ti kirsano ta jobele.

"Assholes! Assholes! Assholes!" screeched the demon. 34
But he could no longer rise.
There he died, where the cross had been traced in the earth.

"Hurry up, you bastard!" the old man shouted to his idle companion. 35
"Come, give me a hand!
"Don't you see that your own father is dead?" chided the old man who had the club.[7]

"All right," agreed the old man with the axe. 36
And he went quickly to his task.

He started right to work hacking away at the demon's neck. 37
In no time at all, his head rolled off.

He continued hacking away at his hands, his feet, and his stomach. 38
He cut fiercely into the corpse.

"Let's take his heart out. 39
If we don't, he might come back to life," insisted the old man with the club.

"You're right. Let's cut his heart out," agreed the old man with the axe. 40
So they began to cut out his heart.

When the heart was removed, they put salt on it.[8] 41
They put salt on the empty body cavity, also.

"Very well, now. Let's take his heart and head along with us. 42
Let's take it to Tuxtla to show it off.
First, we'll pass through Chiapa de Corzo,
Then we'll proceed to Tuxtla.

We'll take his head and his heart. 43
Let's give the folks in Tuxtla a look at them.

Let's go tell the governor that we have slain the demon who lived by the road.[9] 44
And that people can now travel safely to San Cristóbal.

45 ˀa ver mi xch'unik;
ˀech'o xal ta xkich'betik ˀel li sjole li yoˀntone xiik la ti moletike.

46 laj la xkuch ti yikatzike,
ˀaˀ to la skajanik ti sjol pukuj ta sba yikatzike.

47 ti jun mol ˀoy yakteˀe ˀaˀ la la skuch ˀel sjol pukuj.
ti jun mol ˀoy yek'ele ˀaˀ la skuch ˀel yoˀnton pukuj.

48 laj la yak'ik ta sba yikatzik.
batik la.

49 vaˀi ˀun k'alal k'otik ta soktome.
laj la yalbik ˀajvalil ta soktom.

We'll see if they will believe us; 45
All the better reason to take along his head and his heart,"
said the old men.

They took up their packs, 46
And on top of one of them, they mounted the head of the demon.

The old man with the club carried the demon's head. 47
The old man with the axe carried the demon's heart.

They finally secured them in place on top of their packs. 48
With that, they set off.

Whereupon, they reached Chiapa de Corzo. 49
They notified the mayor of Chiapa de Corzo about what had transpired.

FIGURE 70

The old man with the club carried the demon's head.
The old man with the axe carried the demon's heart.

50 lital kalkutike laj xa jmilkutik ti pukuj ta bee.
li? laj kich'bekutik talel sjole xchi?uk yo?ntone xiik la ti moletike.

51 k'usi la vut.
la milik ?un.
k'uxi la jelavik talel.

52 ?a li kirsanoetik ta xbatik ta jobel mu xjelavik.
te ta xchamik ta persa skotol kirsanoetik.
mu xjelavik.

53 ?a? xukne muk xaxi?ik xi la ti ?ajvalil ta soktome.
mu?yuk xixi?kutik ?unbi.
la jmilkutik xiik la ti moletike.

"We came to tell you that we have killed the Demon Pukuj who
lived by the road. 50
We have brought along his head and his heart," said the old men.

"What are you saying? 51
That you killed him once and for all?
How on earth did you make it through?

Why, people traveling to San Cristóbal haven't been able to get by! 52
They've all died there without exception!
No one has been able to get through at all!

And you, weren't *you* scared?" inquired the mayor. 53
"We weren't afraid at all.
We simply killed him," said the old men.

FIGURE 71

"We came to tell you that we have killed the Demon Pukuj who
lived by the road.
We have brought along his head and his heart," said the old
men.

54 tekeˀ kolavalik tajmek.
la ˀabolajik la jamik ti bee.

55 tekeˀ chijbat k'alal ta tuxta.
ba kak'tik ˀiluk yuˀun kovyerno.
yuˀun melel la milik ti pukuje.
muˀyuk xaxiˀik.
ba jk'opontik ti kovyerno ta tuxta xi la ti ˀajvalil ta soktome.

56 batik la ˀep jkaxlanetik xchiˀuk ti ˀajvalil ta soktome.
k'otik la ta tuxta.
laj la sk'oponik ti ˀajvalile.

57 liˀ tal chaˀvoˀ moletike.
laj xa la smilik ti pukuj ta bee.

58 pero naˀ mu meleluk ti la smilike,
liˀ yich'ojbik talel sjole yoˀntone.
laˀ k'el ˀavil xi la ti ˀajvalil ta soktome.

"Well, thank you very much. 54
You did the favor of opening the road," said the mayor.

"I think I'll go with you to Tuxtla! 55
The state government should hear about this!
For you have truly killed the Demon Pukuj.
Don't be afraid!
We'll go to inform the governor in Tuxtla!" declared the mayor of
Chiapa de Corzo.

Many Ladinos went along with the mayor to present the heroes. 56
They arrived in Tuxtla.
They informed the governor:

"Two old men have come. 57
They have killed the Demon Pukuj who lived by the road!

In case there is any doubt that they have killed him, 58
They have brought along his head and heart.
Come and see for yourself," said the mayor of Chiapa de Corzo.

FIGURE 72

"In case there is any doubt that they have killed him,
They have brought along his head and heart.
Come and see for yourself," said the mayor of Chiapa de
Corzo.

59 buʔoy.
ta jk'elkik xi la ti kovyerno ta tuxtae.

60 liʔ ʔoye.
la jkuchkutik talel ta sba kikatzkutik,
yuʔun li tal jchonkutik xonobil xchiʔuk nukul liʔ ta ʔalume.

61 bak'in ʔun te jtakutik pukuj ta be.
pero muʔyuk xixiʔkutik.
la jmilkutik.
ʔech'o xal la jkich'bekutik talel ti sjole ti yoʔntone.

62 ʔay povre moletik la ʔabolajik la milik ti pukuje.
tekeʔ chotanik jlikeluk xi la ti ʔajvalil ta tuxtae.

63 xuʔuk,
chichotikutik.
ʔech xtok chilubkutik xa tajmek xiik la ti moletike.
te la chotiik jlikel.

64 tekeʔ ʔuch'anik juteb pox.
kolaval la ʔabolajik la jamik ti bee.

65 ʔech xtok, k'uxi chak'an ʔatojolik.
chajtojik.
ʔa ver k'usi chak'anik xi la ti kovyerno ta tuxtae.

66 voʔot k'uxi chatojunkutike xiik la ti moletik.
veno chajtojik 20 pexu jujun.
batz'i kolavalik tajmek ti lajamik ti bee.

67 ʔech xtok li sjol pukuje liʔ ta xkom xchiʔuk yoʔntone xi la ti kovyerno ta tuxtae.
te la kom ti sjol pukuj xchiʔuk ti yoʔntone.

"Where is this proof? 59
Let's see it!" said the governor of Tuxtla.

"Here it is. 60
We carried his head and heart on top of our packs,
For we were actually on our way to sell sandals and leather here in your town.

We had just set out on our way when we met the Demon Pukuj on the road. 61
We weren't afraid at all.
We simply killed him.
That's how we were able to bring his head and heart along with us," said the old men.

"Oh! Dear old fellows! What a great favor you did for us by slaying this demon. 62
Come, sit down for a while," said the governor of Tuxtla.

"We'll be glad to, 63
We'll sit down for a bit.
We're pretty tired, to tell the truth," said the old men.
So they sat down to relax for a little while.

"Well, now, have a little drink of rum.[10] 64
Thanks very much for doing the favor of opening the road.

Also, what would you like as payment? 65
We want to pay you, of course.
Think about what you might like," said the governor of Tuxtla.

"Well, whatever you might want to give us," said the old man. 66
"We'll pay you twenty pesos each.
This is as a token of our deep gratitude to you for opening the road.

As for the head and heart, they will stay here," said the governor of Tuxtla. 67
And the head and the heart of the demon indeed remained there.

68 ˀentonse k'alal laj yuch'ik pox ti moletike,
k'alal laj yich' ti stojolike,
batik la.
bat la xchonik ti xonobile ti nukule.

69 pero laj la stzob sba skotol ti kirsano ta tuxta.
ti k'alal k'otik ti moletik xchiˀuk ti sjol pukuj xchiˀuk ti yoˀntone.
koˀol la xchiˀuk jun k'in.

70 laj la stzob sba skotol ti kirsanoetike,
k'alal laj yaˀi ti kirsanoetik ta tuxta ti xuˀ xa xbatik ta jobele.
kontentoik xa la.

71 pero jchamoˀetik la la smilik ti pukuj ta belel tuxtae.
pero ˀep la cham ti kirsano ta belel tuxtae.

72 pere muˀyuk buch'u smil yuˀunik ˀaˀ to k'ot ti chaˀvoˀ moletike.
k'alal cham ti pukuje xuˀ xjelav skotol ti kirsano ta jobel ta xbat ta tuxta.
muˀyuk xa bu ta xiˀik.

Then, after the old men had drunk ceremonial shots of rum, 68
After they had received their reward,
They departed.
They went to sell their sandals and leather.

Whereupon all the people of Tuxtla got together to celebrate. 69
It was in honor of the old men who came into town bearing
the head and heart of the demon.
It was like a festival!

All of the people of Tuxtla got together to celebrate. 70
At last, the people of Tuxtla found out that they could get through
to San Cristóbal.
Now their hearts were happy!

But bear in mind that it was Chamulas who killed the Demon Pukuj 71
who lived by the road to Tuxtla!
Many were the people who had perished on this very road to Tuxtla!

There was no one up to the task of slaying this demon until the 72
two old men came along.
Once the demon was dead, people from San Cristóbal could get
through once again to Tuxtla.
They were no longer afraid.

1 ʔa li voʔne k'alal la jyak'ik leto ti soltaro.
ʔoy la mu snaʔ xcham ti soltaro,
ti jayib soltaro mu snaʔ xcham.

2 pero k'alal ch'abi ti leto,
ʔoch la ta yut nail ch'en ti soltaro.
ti jayib mu snaʔ xcham ti soltaro.

3 ti k'alal ʔoch ta yut nail ch'en ti soltaro,
tey la yiloj jun vinik.

4 ti k'alal yil ti vinik buy ʔoch ti soltaro,
bat la sk'el yil ti vinik.

5 ti k'alal k'ot ti vinik ti buy ʔoch ti soltaro:
k'usi ta chasaʔ xi la ti soltaro.
yuʔun tal jak'bot buy ta xabat xi la ti vinik.
yuʔun liʔ ta xivay ta nail ch'en xi la ti soltaro.

6 k'uchaʔal liʔ ta xavay ta nail ch'en xi la.
yuʔun li lubtzaj ta xanavil xi la ti soltaro.

7 buy k'alal ʔay xanavan talel xi la ti vinik.
stekel banumil li xanav xi la ti soltaro.
yuʔun ʔay jkolta ta smakel bek'tuk ti jchiʔil ta soltaroil xi la ti soltaro
ta montonya.

8 buy kom ti ʔachiʔil xi la ti vnik.
ʔa li jchiʔile bat ta slumal xi la ti soltaro ta montonya.

TEXT 47

Of an Encounter with the Soldier on the Mountain

Xalik López Setjol

It was long ago when certain soldiers were involved in warfare. 1
Some of these soldiers were immune from death,
These soldiers were among the number who would not die.[1]

When the war was over, 2
These soldiers entered a cave.
These soldiers were among the number who would not die.

When the soldiers went in the cave, 3
A man saw them there.

When the man saw where the soldiers entered the cave, 4
He went to take a look.[2]

When the man reached the place where the soldiers had entered the cave, 5
this is what happened:
"What are you looking for?" said one of the soldiers.
"I came to ask you what you're up to and where you're going,"
said the man.
"I'm going to sleep here in this cave," said the soldier.

"Why are you going to sleep here in this cave?" he asked. 6
"I got tired from my journey," said the soldier.

"Where have you come from on your journey?" asked the man. 7
"I've traveled all over the earth," said the soldier.
"I've been helping to protect my comrades from gunfire,"
said the soldier there on the mountain.[3]

"Where did you leave your comrades?" asked the man. 8
"My comrades went to their own villages," said the soldiers.

9 ˀa li ˀune ˀaˀ jlumal liˀe xi la ti soltaro ta montonya.
ˀa li ˀune koˀol nakalunkutik xchiˀuk jbankil xi la ti soltaro ta montonya.

10 buch'u ti ˀabankil xi la ti vinik.
ˀaˀ jbankil ti san juane xi la ti soltaro ta montonya.

11 ti k'alal laj sk'opoj soltaro ta montonya ti vinik:
ta xibat xi la ti vinik.

12 batan pero chabanukot ˀech'el xi la ti soltaro.
xuˀuk kolaval xi la ti vinik.

13 k'alal bat ta sna ti vinik:
xtal me ˀaˀulanun k'alal ta ˀoxib ˀavil xi la ti soltaro ta montonya.
xuˀuk xi la ti vinik.

14 ti k'alal k'ot ta sna ti vinik toj lek la xkuxet yoˀnton.
ti vinik buch'u laj sk'opon soltaro ta montonya pero mu xa la snaˀ stae ta chamel.

15 tzatzub la lek sbek'tal ti vinik laj sk'opon soltaro ta montonya.
yalbe snich'nab ti vinik

"As for me, this mountain is my home," said the soldier. 9
"Here in the mountain I live together with my elder brother,"
said the soldier there on the mountain.

"Who is your elder brother?" asked the man. 10
"My elder brother is San Juan," replied the soldier on the mountain.[4]

And when the soldier on the mountain had finished talking, the man spoke: 11
"I am going," said the man.

"Go then, but take care," said the soldier. 12
"All right. Thanks," said the man.

As the man was starting to go home, the soldier on the mountain 13
spoke once again:
"Come to see me three years from now," he said.
"All right," said the man.

When the man got home, he was happy and relieved. 14
Indeed, this man who had spoken with the soldier on the mountain
now found himself immune from illness.

The body of the man who had spoken with the soldier on the mountain 15
grew strong.
That is what the man told his children.[5]

1 ˀoy jun kuento la sk'opon pukuj jun vinik.

2 veno ti voˀne lae ˀoy la jun vinik la snup ta be pukuj.
k'alal la ti snup sbaik ta be xchiˀuk pukuj ti vinike, lik la schiˀin sbaik ta loˀil.

3 lik la sjak'be stak'in ti pukuje.
jeˀ xkale mi mu xavak'bun ˀatak'in.
yuˀun ch'abal jtak'in tajmek.
yuˀun toj povreun tajmek xˀut la pukuj ti vinike.

4 ˀa . . . pero mi chijbat jchiˀin jbatike.
ta xakak'be jtak'in xi la ti pukuje.
veno ta xibat jchiˀinot mi chavak'bun ˀatak'ine xi la ti vinike.

TEXT 48
About a Man Who Made a Pact with the Demon Pukuj

Xun Méndez Tzotzek

There is a story about a man who made a pact with the Demon Pukuj. 1

Well, long ago there was a man who met the Demon Pukuj on the road. 2
Once the demon and the man had met on the road, they began talking as they walked along.

He lost no time in requesting money from the Demon Pukuj.[1] 3
"I say, now, won't you let me have some of your money?
For I have no money.
For I am very poor," said the man to the demon.

"What would you say if we became companions?" proposed the Demon Pukuj. 4
"Then I will give you some of my money," said the Demon Pukuj.
"Certainly, I'll go along with you if you will give me some of your money," replied the man.[2]

5 pero k'u yepal chak'an ti tak'ine xi la ti pukuje.
ta jk'an ˀep tajmek xi la ti vinike.

6 pero k'usi sjalil chak'an ˀalajes xi la ti pukuje.
jayib ˀaˀvil xa chak'an ˀalajes xi la ti pukuje.

7 ta jk'an syenuk ˀaˀvil xi la ti vinike.
veno pero mi tzaki ta sien ˀaˀvil ˀune ta me xbat kik'ot ta na ˀun
xi la ti pukuje.

8 veno li jtak'ine manchuk mi xalajes tajmek.
pero mu xlaj ta lajesel tajmek xi la ti pukuje.
pero jaˀ ta jk'an tajmek ˀunbi xi la ti vinike.

9 veno yak' la jun moral tak'in ti pukuje.
nojesbat la smoral ti vinike.

"How much money do you have in mind?" asked the Demon Pukuj. 5
"I want a lot," replied the man.

"But for how long do you want it?" inquired the Demon Pukuj. 6
"For how many years do you want this deal to last?" continued the Demon Pukuj.

"I want it for one hundred years," said the man. 7
"Very well, but after one hundred years, I shall come to call you away without fail," replied the demon.

"Now, my money is limitless, such that you may even spend it lavishly. 8
Even then, it will never be used up," explained the Demon Pukuj.
"Yes, indeed. That's the kind of deal I want," said the man enthusiastically.

With that the Demon Pukuj gave him a bagful of money. 9
When he emptied the bag into his own carrying bag, it was filled to the top.

FIGURE 73

"How much money do you have in mind?" asked the Demon Pukuj.
"I want a lot," replied the man.

10 veno tekeˀ ˀun batan,
ˀich'o batel ti jtak'ine xi la ti pukuje.

11 pero mi tz'aki ta syen ˀaˀvil ˀune te me xamala ˀun.
te me chibat kik'ot talel xi la ti pukuje.

12 veno k'alal la ti bat ta sna ti vinike toj lek xa la xaˀi:
toj kontento xa la ti yoˀntone.
lek xa la xaˀi ti ˀep ti stak'ine.

13 k'alal ti k'ot ta sna ti vinike:
k'ot la yalbe yaˀi ti yajnile.

14 jˀuˀune ˀantz ˀoy xa ˀep jtak'in xˀut la k'otel ti yajnile ta nae.
bu la ta ˀep ˀatak'in xi la ti yajnile.
muˀyuk.
yuˀun la jnup ta be pukuj xˀut la ti yajnile.

15 k'usi la valbe ti pukuj ˀune xi la ti yajnile.
muˀyuk.
k'alal la jnup jbakutik ta bee bu chabat xiyut ti pukuje.

16 ta xibat ta jna xkut ti pukuje.
ˀa . . . xi ti pukuje.

17 mi me xavak'bune ˀatak'in.
yuˀun ch'abal jtak'in tajmek.
yuˀun toj povreun taj yalel xkut ti pukuje.

18 veno pero mi xbat jchiˀinbatike,
ta xakak'be jtak'in.
jˀune toj ˀep jtak'in tajmek.

19 manchuk mi xalajes tajmek ˀep.
pero mu xlaj ta lajesel ma jtak'in ˀuˀune xiyut ma ti pukuje.
xˀut la k'otel yajnil ti vinik ta nae.

"Well, then, be on your way, 10
Take my money and be off," said the Demon Pukuj.

"But after one hundred years exactly, you must be expecting me. 11
Then I shall come to call you away, wherever you may be,"
said the Demon Pukuj.

Well, as he was going home, the man felt very happy: 12
His heart was pleased.
He felt happy to have so much money.

Now, when the man reached his house, this is what happened. 13
He explained things to his wife.

"Dear wife of mine, I now have lots of money," he declared to his wife 14
when he got home.
"Wherever did you find so much money?" asked his wife.
"It was not difficult.
I met the Demon Pukuj on the road," he told his wife.

"What did you say to the Demon Pukuj?" asked his wife. 15
"Not much.
When we met on the road, the demon asked me, 'Where are you going?'

'I'm going home,' I told the demon. 16
'I see,' said the demon.

'Will you give me some of your money? 17
In truth, I have no money at all.
In truth, I am very poor,' I said to the demon.

'But if we should become companions, 18
I will give you some of my money.
I happen to have a great deal of money.

It is limitless, such that you may spend it freely. 19
Even then, it will never be used up,' the Demon Pukuj told me."
This is what the man said to his wife when he got home.

20 jaˀ yuˀun la jk'anbe stak'in ti pukuje xˀut la yajnil ti vinike.
pero ˀep ˀaˀvil la jak'anbe jlajestik stak'in ma ti pukuje xˀut la yajnil ti vinike.

21 jayib ˀaˀvil la k'anbe ˀun xi la yajnil ti vinike.
ˀa . . . la jk'anbe sien ˀaˀvil ta jlajesbatik stak'in ma ti pukuje xˀut la yajnil ti vinike.

22 pero k'alal la mi tz'aki ta sien ˀaˀvile ta la xtal yik'un ti pukuje.
ta la xbat jchiˀin xˀut la yajnil ti vinike.
ˀa . . . xi la ti yajnile.

23 pero toj lek xa la xaˀik xchiˀuk yajnil ti vinike.
toj ˀep ti stak'inike.

24 veno ta xibat ta jobel.
xbat saˀ talel k'usitikuk jlajestik xˀut la yajnil ti vinike.

25 xuˀuk.
batan xi la yajnil ti vinike.

26 yich' la batel ˀep ti stak'in ta jobele.
bat la ti vinik ta jobele.

"That is how I asked the Demon Pukuj for money," said the man to his wife. 20
"But we will have many years to enjoy the money I got from
the demon," said the man to his wife.

"For how long a term did you get the money?" asked the man's wife. 21
"Oh, I asked for one hundred years in which to enjoy the
demon's money," said the man to his wife.

"But after one hundred years, the Demon Pukuj will come to call me away. 22
I will then go with him," said the man.
"I see," said his wife.

The man and his wife were very happy. 23
For they had lots and lots of money.[3]

"Well, I'm going to San Cristóbal. 24
I'm going to look for something good for us to eat," said the man
to his wife.

"Very well, then. 25
Good-bye," said the man's wife.

He took a lot of money with him to San Cristóbal. 26
Off he went to San Cristóbal.

27 k'alal la ti ta xanav ti vinik ta kayae.
te la snup ta be skumpakre ti vinike.

28 mi la tal ta jobel kumpakre xˀut la skumpakre ti vinike.
li tal kumpakre.
mi la tal ˀek kumpakre xi la skumpakre ti vinike.

29 li tal kumpakre.
mi mu xak'an ˀak'uch'tik jutebuk pox xˀut la ti skumpakree.

30 moˀoj kumpakre.
muˀyuk stojol kuˀun xi la ti skumpakree.

31 moˀoj kumpakree,
batik.
ta kuch'tik ˀavaˀi junuk kuarta, kumpakre.
jˀuˀune ˀoy ˀep jtak'in tajmek xˀut la ti skumpakree.

Soon enough, the man found himself walking down the street. 27
There the man came upon his compadre.

"Did you come to San Cristóbal, compadre?" the man said to him. 28
"Yes, I came, compadre.
Did you also come, compadre?" said the man's compadre.[4]

"I came, compadre. 29
Wouldn't you like to have a little drink?" he asked his compadre.

"No, thanks, compadre. 30
I have no money to buy it with," said his compadre.

"That doesn't matter, compadre, 31
Let's go.
Let's sample a cuarta, compadre.[5]
I do have a lot of money," said his compadre.

FIGURE 74

Soon enough, the man found himself walking down the street.
There the man came upon his compadre.

32 xuˀuk ˀun chaˀe kumpakre xi la ti skumpakree.
yik'oj la batel ta kantina ti skumpakree.

33 k'alal la k'ot ta kantina xchiˀuk skumpakre ti vinike.
k'ot la sk'an jun kuarta pox ta xˀak'be yuch' ti skumpakree.

34 k'alal la ti te chotajtik ta xˀuch'ik ti pox ta mexa xchiˀuk skumpakre ti vinik.
lik la loˀilajikuk xchiˀuk ti skumpakree.

35 bu la ta ˀun kumpakre xi la ti skumpakre.
moˀoj kumpakre.
la jnup ta be pukuj xˀut la ti skumpakree.

36 k'u xayut ti pukuj ˀune xi la ti skumpakree.
bu chabat xiyut ma ti k'alal la jnup jbakutik ta bee.

37 lik jak'be ti pukuj ˀune kumpakre:
mi mu xavak'bun ˀatak'in yuˀun toj povreun tajmek.
yuˀun ch'abal jtak'in tajmek xkut ma ti pukuj ˀune kumpakre.
xˀut la ti skumpakre ti vinike.

38 k'u xayut ti pukuj ˀune kumpakre xi la ti skumpakre ti vinike.
veno te xakak'be jtak'in mi xbat jchiˀin batike xiyut ma ti pukuj ˀune kumpakre.
xˀut la skumpakre ti vinike.

39 jech'jal ˀun ˀoy ˀep tajmek ma ti jtak'in ˀune kumpakre.
xˀut la skumpakre ti vinike.

40 veno k'u sjalil la k'anbe ˀun kumpakre xi la ti skumpakree.
moˀoj ˀun bi, kumpagre la jk'anbe sien ˀaˀvil.

41 la valbe yaˀi ti pukuj ˀune kumpakre xi la ti skumpakree.
ˀaˀ jech ˀunbi kumpakre xi la ti vinike.

"Very well, then, compadre," said his compadre. 32
And with that, he took his compadre off to a bar.

Now, soon the man and his compadre reached the bar. 33
He went up and ordered a *cuarta* of rum and offered his compadre
a drink.

Soon, the man and his compadre found themselves seated there at a table, 34
drinking rum.
The two began to talk.

"Where did you find all this money, compadre?" said his compadre. 35
"I'll tell you, compadre.
I met the Demon Pukuj on the road," he said to his compadre.

"What did the Demon Pukuj say to you?" said his compadre. 36
"'Where are you going?'" he said when we met on the road.

"With that, I put the question to him, compadre: 37
'Won't you give me some of your money, for I am very poor?
I have no money at all,' I said to the Demon Pukuj, compadre."
So spoke the man to his compadre.

"What did the Demon Pukuj say to you, compadre?" inquired his compadre. 38
"'Well, I will give you some of my money if you will agree to become
my companion,' the Demon Pukuj told me, compadre."
So spoke the man to his compadre.

"So that's why I have so much money, compadre." 39
So spoke the man to his compadre.

"Well, for how long was the term of the loan?" the man asked his compadre. 40
"Well, compadre, I borrowed it for one hundred years."

"Is that what you agreed to with the Demon Pukuj, compadre?" 41
asked his compadre.
"That's right, compadre," said the man.

42 ˀa . . . moˀoj ˀunbi kumpakre.
mi jech la k'anbe sien ˀaˀvile.
pero mu ˀaviluk la k'anbe.
jechuke kumpakre jechuke.
la k'anbe sien k'ak'al chalajesbe stak'in ti pukuje.
jechuke kumpakre xi la skumpakre ti vinike.

43 pero la k'anbe sien ˀaˀ vil chavale.
pero mu ˀaˀviluk.
taje sien k'ak'al noˀox chalajesbe stak'in ma ti pukuj.
taje kumpakre xi la ti skumpakre vinike.

44 pero mi jech xanaˀ ˀun kumpakre xi ti vinike.
ˀa . . . jech xi la ti skumpakre.
te xamala ˀavil k'alal mi tz'aki ti sien k'ak'ale.
ta xtal yik'ot ma ti pukuje xi la ti skumpakre vinike.

45 pero mi jech tajmek xanaˀ ˀun kumpakre xi la ti vinike.
yan la sba k'ot ta yoˀnton jutuk ti vinike.

46 veno k'alal la ti laj yuch'ik pox xchiˀuk skumpakre ti vinike laj la xch'ak sbaik.
sut la batel ta sna ti vinike.

47 k'alal la ti k'ot ta sna ti vinike.
lik la loˀilajikuk xchiˀuk yajnil ti vinike.

48 te la jta jkumpakretik ta joˀbel xˀut la ti yajnile.
pero li sibtas jutuk ma ti jkumpakretike xˀut la ti yajnile.

49 k'uchaˀal chasibtas jkumpakretik xi la yajnil ti vinike.
ˀa . . . yuˀun la kalbe yaˀi mi xak'an xkuch'tik pox kumpakre,
xkut ti jkumpakretik.

50 moˀoh kumpakre.
ch'abal stojol kuˀun xiyut ti hkumpakretike.

"Oh, no! It can't be, compadre! 42
Did you really agree to a term of one hundred years?
Those weren't really years you agreed to.
Would that they were, compadre! Would that they were!
You actually agreed to one hundred *days* as the term of your loan
from the Demon Pukuj.
Would that it were otherwise, compadre," said the man's compadre.

"You say you agreed to a term of one hundred years. 43
But those weren't *years* at all.
It was only for a term of one hundred days that you negotiated
the loan from the Demon Pukuj.
That's how it is, compadre," said the man's compadre.

"Are you sure of all this, compadre?" asked the man. 44
"Yes, it's true," said his compadre.
"You'll see for yourself at the end of the one hundred days.
The Demon Pukuj will come to call you away," said the man's compadre.

"But are you absolutely certain about this?" asked the man. 45
The man was getting a little worried.

Well, when the man and his compadre had finished drinking their rum, 46
they went their separate ways.
The man went home.

Soon the man reached his house. 47
He and his wife began talking together.

"I met our compadre there in San Cristóbal," he said to his wife. 48
"Our compadre gave me a bit of a scare," he said to his wife.

"How did our compadre scare you?" asked his wife. 49
"Well, I asked him: 'Would you like a drink, compadre?'
That's what I asked our compadre.[6]

'No, compadre. 50
I don't have anything to buy it with,' our compadre said to me.

51 mu yu?unuk ?o?otuk chaman.
?u?un ta jman kumpakre,
xkut ti jkumpakretik.

52 u?une ?oy ?ep tak'in ku?un kumpakre xkut ti jkumpakretike.
bu la ta xiyut ti jkumpakretike.
mu?yuk kumpakre yu?un la jkanbe stak'in pukuj la jnup ta be xkut ti jkumpakretike.

53 k'usi lavalbe ti pukuj ?une kumpakre xiyut ti jkumpakretike.
la jkalbe mi mu xavak'bun ?atak'in.
yu?un ch'abal jtak'in toj povreun tajmek xkut ma ti pukuj ?une kumpakre,
xi la kalbe ma ti jkumpakretike ?une.
x?ut la yajnil ti vinike.

54 veno li yalbe ti jkumpakretik jayib ?avil la k'anbe stak'in ti pukuje.
xiyut ti jkumpakretike.
la jk'anbe sien ?avil xkut ti jkumpakretike.

55 mi jech lavalbe ya?i ?un ta june xiyut ti jkumpakretike.
jech la jkalbe ya?i ma ti pukuj ?unbi xkut ti jkumpakretike.

56 ?a . . . mo?oj ?unbi.
mechuk lavalbe ya?i.
jechuke sien k'ak'al la valbe ya?i ti pukuj.
jechuke.

57 pero sien ?avil la k'anbe ?une,
pero mu ?aviluk ma taje.
sien k'ak'al no?ox chalajesbe stak'in pa ti pukuj taje,
xiyut ma ti jkumpakretike.
x?ut la yajnil ti vnike.

58 mu jay bel yu?un xa xtal yik'un ma ti pukuje x?ut la yajnil ti vinike.
yan xa la sba yo?nton ta xbat xchi?uk pukuj ti vinike.

'You won't have to buy it. 51
I'm going to buy it, compadre.'
That's what I said to our compadre.

'I've got lots of money, compadre,' I said to our compadre. 52
'Where did you get it, compadre?' our compadre asked me.
'Well, compadre, the fact is that I borrowed it from the Demon Pukuj
when I met him on the road,' I explained to our compadre.

'What did you say to the Demon Pukuj?' our compadre asked me. 53
'I said to him, won't you give me some of your money?
I'm very poor; I have no money,' I said to the Demon Pukuj, compadre.'
That's what I told our compadre."
So spoke the man to his wife.

"So our compadre asked me: 'Well, what was the term of the loan of the 54
Demon Pukuj's money?'
That is what our compadre asked me.
'I agreed to a term of one hundred years,' I told our compadre.

'Did you really agree to that?' our compadre asked me. 55
'That's what I agreed to,' I told our compadre.

'Oh, it can't be! 56
That wasn't the deal you cut with him at all.
In reality, you made a deal with the Demon Pukuj for a term of
one hundred days.
That's it, like it or not.

You thought you agreed to a term of one hundred years, 57
But they weren't *years*!
It was only for one hundred *days* that you contracted with the
Demon Pukuj!'
So our compadre told me."
So the man said to his wife.

"It's really not long at all before the Demon Pukuj comes to take me away," 58
the man said to his wife.
He was indeed upset at the thought of having to go off with the
Demon Pukuj.

59 veno ti yajnile lik la snop.
yalbe la ti smalale.

60 mu xapas sonso xˀut la ti smalale.
pero k'usi xkutik xanaˀ ˀun xi la ti vinike.

61 moˀoj xi la ti yajnile.
k'eltik ˀavile.
mu xaxiˀ yuˀun xi la ti yajnile.

62 k'alal xa xtal yik'ot ti pukuje batik ta kutz siˀ xi la yajnil ti vinike.
veno tz'aki la ti sien k'ak'ale sob la batik ta kutz siˀ xchiˀuk ti yajnile.

63 k'alal la ti sutik talel ta kutz siˀe muˀyuk xa la xkuch talel siˀ yajnil ti vinike.
yuˀun la sboj sba ta ˀek'el yajnil ti vinike.

64 k'alal la ti k'ot ta snaike bat la puch'uluk ta stem yajnil ti vinike.
k'alal la ti te puch'ul ta tem yajnil ti vinike.
te la chotol ta yut na ta smala ti pukuje.

65 k'alal la k'ot ti pukuje te la chotol tae ta yut na ti vinike.
k'uxi ˀun.
mi mu chijbat ˀun xi la k'otel ti pukuje.

66 veno tak'av la ti vinike.
pero k'u sta ˀun.
ˀip chaˀi kajnil.
yuˀun la sboj sba ta ˀek'el xi la ti vinike.

67 mi ˀep laj xi la ti pukuje.
ˀu . . . toj ˀep yayij tajmek ma li kajnile.
ˀep la sboj sba ta ˀek'el tajmek xi la ti vinike.

68 bu yayijem.
ta jk'elkik xi la ti pukuje.

Well, his wife set herself to thinking. 59
She spoke to her husband.

"Don't be stupid!" she said to her husband. 60
"But what do you think we can do?" asked the man.

"You might be surprised," declared his wife. 61
"We'll see.
Don't worry about it," said his wife cryptically.

"When the time comes for the demon to call you away, we will go to gather firewood," said the man's wife. 62
So, indeed, at the end of the one hundred days, the man and his wife departed early that morning to gather firewood.

When they returned from gathering firewood, the man's wife did not carry a load of firewood. 63
The reason was that she had cut herself with the axe.

When they got home the man's wife went to lie down in bed. 64
The man's wife lay there stretched out in bed.
He himself sat there in the house waiting for the Demon Pukuj.

When the Demon Pukuj arrived he found the man sitting there inside the house. 65
"Well, how are you?
Shall we be off?" asked the Demon Pukuj when he arrived.

"All right," answered the man. 66
"But I've got a problem.
My wife is sick.
She cut herself with the axe," said the man.

"Is she badly hurt?" inquired the Demon Pukuj. 67
"Oh! My wife is hurt very badly!
She cut herself very badly with an axe," explained the man.

"Where is the wound? 68
Let's have a look at it," said the Demon Pukuj.

69 liˀe.
toj ˀep li yayij tajmek xi la ti ˀantze.

70 svalk'unbe la sk'uˀ ti ˀantze.
sk'elbe la ti bu yayijem yuˀun ti ˀantze.

71 yak'be la la yil syayijemal ti ˀantze.
sk'el la ti pukuje.

72 ˀuj pero toj ˀep yayij tajmek xi la ti pukuje.
toj ˀep xi la ti vinike.
te la puch'ul ta tem ti ˀantze.

73 veno saˀo talel xepuˀ,
ta jpox,
ˀavil ta ˀora.
ta xkol ta ˀora xi la ti pukuje.

74 veno jech la ti vinike saˀ la talel ti xepuˀe.
yak'be la ti pukuje.

75 k'alal la stzak xepuˀ ti pukuje:
saˀo talel junuk xupiteˀ xi la ti pukuje.

76 xuˀuk xi la ti vinike.
saˀ la talel xupiteˀ ti vinike.

77 liˀe xˀut la ti pukuje.
veno xi la ti pukuje.

78 xamala ˀavil.
ta jpoxta.
ˀavil ta ˀora ta xkol ta ˀora kuˀun xi la ti pukuje.

79 veno,
ˀabolajan poxtabun xˀut la pukuj ti vinike.

"Here it is. 69
It's really a nasty cut," declared the woman.

The woman pulled up her clothes. 70
And the Demon Pukuj looked at where she was wounded.

The woman showed him where she had cut herself. 71
The Demon Pukuj looked at it.

"Oh! You really did cut yourself!" said the demon. 72
"She really did!" said the man.
And the woman lay there stretched out on the bed.

"Go get some tallow, 73
I'm going to cure her,
You'll see in a minute.
She'll be better right away," said the Demon Pukuj.

So the man went to fetch the tallow. 74
He gave it to the demon.

Once the demon had the tallow, he spoke again: 75
"Go get a piece of charcoal," ordered the Demon Pukuj.

"All right," said the man. 76
And he fetched a piece of charcoal.[7]

"Here it is," he said to the demon. 77
"Very well," said the demon.

"Wait and see. 78
I will cure her.
You'll see right away that she will get better in no time, thanks to my efforts," said the Demon Pukuj.

"Very well, 79
Please cure her for me," said the man to the demon.

80 veno lik la spoxtabe syayijemal yajnil ti vinike.
lik la snojesbe ta xepuˀ ti bu yayijem ta ˀek'ele.
snojesbe la lek ta xepuˀ ye.
ti k'u snatil la sboj ta ˀek'ele.

81 k'alal la ti la snojesbe ta xepuˀ ti ye yayijem ˀantze:
k'el ˀavil.
xkale kol xa kuˀun.

82 xuˀ xa xanav.
xuˀ xa xlik.

83 spas reva xanavuk xi la ti pukuje.
lik la ti ˀantze.

84 k'alal la ti lik ti ˀantze lik la ta pana k'aˀbinuk.
k'alal la ti laj k'aˀbinuk ti ˀantze ˀoch la ta yut na.

85 k'alal la ti ˀoch ta yut nae sjak' la ti pukuje:
veno k'us aˀiel.
mi xuˀ xaxanav xi la ti pukuje.

86 mu xuˀ.
chiˀipaj mas.
ta slok' yaˀlel tajmek xi la ti ˀantze.

87 ta jk'eltik xi la ti pukuje.
k'el ˀavil.
ta xipuch'i xi la ti ˀantze.

88 puch'i la ti ˀantze.
sk'el la ti pukuj bu la spoxta ta xepuˀe.

89 ˀuj jaˀ to la yil staoj la yav syayijemal.
ta la slok' yaˀlel mas.

Well, with that, he began to put medicine on the wound of the man's wife. 80
He began to fill the axe wound with tallow.
He filled up the opening of the wound with tallow.
He applied it all along the axe cut.

When he had applied the tallow poultice to the opening of the woman's wound, he spoke: 81
"See there, now.
I think I've cured her already.

Now she can walk. 82
Now she can get up.

Let's have her give it a try," said the Demon Pukuj. 83
So the woman got up.

When she got up, she went outside to pee. 84
Once she had peed, she came back to the house.

When she had come back in the house, the Demon Pukuj spoke to her: 85
"Well, how are you?
Can you walk?" he asked her.

"No, I can't. 86
I'm getting worse.
There is a whole lot of bloody fluid oozing out," said the woman.

"Let's have a look," said the Demon Pukuj. 87
"Take a look.
I'm going to lie down," said the woman.

So the woman lay down. 88
And the demon looked at the place where he had applied the poultice of tallow and charcoal.

"My God!" he exclaimed when he saw the site of the wound. 89
"There is even more runny stuff coming out!

90 tzako xa talel xepuˀe.
ta jpoxta.
xakik’ mi xkol to xi la ti pukuje.

91 lik la xchaˀ nojesbe ta xepuˀ ye syayijemal ti ˀantze.
jaˀ to la yil mu la xpak’i ti xepu ti xepuˀ jaˀ la ti yaˀlel ta xlok’ talele.

92 veno tekeˀ koman poxtao.
xakik’ mi xkole xi la ti pukuje.

93 jaˀ li toj ˀep yayijem tajmeke xi la ti pukuje.
jaˀ li ta xlok’ yaˀlel tajmeke.
mu xpak’i li spoxile xi la ti pukuje.

94 tekeˀ koman.
muk’ xa xbat jchiˀin batik.
jaˀ li toj ˀep yayijem tajmek la ˀavajnile xi la ti pukuje.

95 jech la kom ˀo ti vinike.
muk’ la xbat schiˀin ti pukuje.
muk’ la xbat stojbe ti stak’ine.
jech la te yich’ojbe komel stak’in pukuj ti vinike.

96 jaˀ la spasik kanal xchiˀuk yajnil ti vinik.
k’alal la sbis ta yayijemal smis yajnil ti vinike.

97 jech la spasik ˀo ta kanal stak’in ti pukuje.
jech la muk’ xbat xchiˀin ˀo pukuj ti vinike.

98 jaˀ la ti kom spoxtabe syayijemal ti yajnile.
jaˀ la ti ta xlok’ yaˀlel tajmek syayijemal yajnil ti vinike.

Bring me more tallow poultice, quick! 90
I'll cure her.
I'll come to fetch you when she gets better," said the demon to the man.

He then began once again to fill up the opening of the woman's wound with tallow. 91
But soon he saw that the tallow did not stay in place well because of the fluid that kept running out.

"Very well, then. Keep on taking care of her. 92
I will come to fetch you when she gets better," said the demon to the man.

"She really is very badly wounded," admitted the Demon Pukuj in parting. 93
"There is lots of fluid flowing out of the wound.
The poultice won't stick," said the demon to the man.

"So stay here, then. 94
You are not going to go with me at this point.
Your wife is really very badly injured," said the Demon Pukuj.

So it turned out that the man stayed there. 95
He did not have to accompany the Demon Pukuj.
He did not go to pay off his debt.
That was how the man was able to keep the demon's money.

The man and his wife won out in the end. 96
They deceived him with the false "wound" of the man's wife's pussy.[8]

So it was that they were able to win the demon's money. 97
So it was that the man did not go off to accompany the Demon Pukuj.

He stayed right there taking care of his wife's wound. 98
And, indeed, the fluid continued to stream out of the man's wife's wound.

99 jech la ti pukuj k'alal la sut batel ta sna ti pukuje.
yan la sba yoˀnton muˀyuk la sta batel xchiˀil.

100 jech la kom ˀo.
jech la jyal jun vinik ta pinka yosilal tapachula.

Now, as for the Demon Pukuj, he went home. 99
He was upset that he had not succeeded in finding a human companion
to take away with him.

That's how it turned out. 100
That's how a man told it to me on a coffee plantation near Tapachula.

1 la jyalbun ka?i ti kuento?e jun vinik ta slo?ilaj ta sbelel jobel ti vo?ne.
?a li ?o?one xi la jnup ta be mu pukuj xi.
yu?un li bat ta kuch yakilo? xi.

2 ?aaa pero ?o?one mu jna? xixi?.
ta ?ak'obaltik chixanav.
pero li ?o?one jun junun ta xixanav ta ?ak'obaltik xi.

3 ja? to me kil xva?vun tal jun jkaxlan ta be.
va? xi vulel ta jtz'el.

4 xi bu chabat xi la.
?aaaa . . . ta xibat ta santa marta x?ut la.
?aaaa . . . veno xi la.

TEXT 49

Of an Encounter with the Old Red Man, Who Was Actually the Demon Pukuj

Manuel López Calixto

A man who was talking on the road to San Cristóbal some time ago 1
told me this story.
"Me," he began, "I once met the damned Demon Pukuj himself
on the road," he declared.[1]
"It happened when I was going to get a load of cane beer," he said.

"Oh, as for me, I wasn't afraid of anything. 2
I was always willing to walk at night.
I would travel all alone, all by myself at night," he said.

"Then once I saw a strange Ladino coming along the road.[2] 3
He approached me.

He spoke: 'Where are you going?' he asked. 4
'Oh, I'm on my way to Santa Marta,' was my friend's reply.[3]
'Oh, I see,' he said.

5 ˀa li ˀoˀote k'usi ˀabi xˀut la.
ˀa li ˀoˀone tzajal tatilun xi la ti mu pukuje.
ˀaaa . . . veno xi la ti vinike.

6 ˀa li ˀoˀote k'usi ˀabi xi la ti mu pukuje.
ˀaaa . . . tzajal tatilun jbi ˀek xi la ti vinike.
ˀaaa . . . xi la ti mu pukuje.

7 pero bu ˀoy ti tzajal tatile xi la ti mu pukuje.
ˀaaaa liˀ ˀoye xi la ti vinike.

8 jlikel la slok'es yat ti vinike.
yak'be la yil ti yate.

'And you? What's your name?' asked my friend. 5
'Oh, me? I'm the Old Red Man,' replied the Demon Pukuj.
'Oh, I see,' replied my friend.

'And you? What's your name?' inquired the Demon Pukuj. 6
'Oh, me? My name is Old Red Man also,' said the man.[4]
'Oh,' said the Demon Pukuj.

'But come now, I don't see him. Where is the Old Red Man?' 7
asked the Demon Pukuj.
'Oh, here he is,' said the man.

Quickly, the man whipped out his cock. 8
He showed him his cock.

FIGURE 75

"'And you? What's your name?' asked my friend.
'Oh me? I'm the Old Red Man,' replied the Demon Pukuj.
'Oh, I see,' replied my friend."

9 aaa . . . pere koˀol jbitik xi la ti mu pukuje.
jech la ti mu pukuje jaˀ la schiˀil yil ti yaloje.
yuˀun la jaˀ la ti tzoj la li snukulil la li yate.
jech' ˀo la xal ˀaˀ la schiˀil ti yaloje xi.

10 ti k'alal bechebat yil la ˀate a xˀal la schiˀil yil.
ti yaloje ti k'alal ˀak'bat yil ti ˀate.

11 ˀentonse jaˀ ta jpojvan ma ti kate xi ti vinike.
manchuk xvul ta jole la skuchun ˀel ma ti mu pukuje xi.

12 ˀaaa ˀa li ˀak'teˀe toj lek la me snaˀ spojvan xtok ˀeke xi ti vinike.
k'alal mi xijxanavotik ta ˀak'obaltike toj lek la me stak' chiˀinel xtok xi.

13 yuˀun jaˀ la li ˀik' ˀeke.
jech' ˀo la xal ti yoˀ la lek snaˀ spojvan ˀeke.

14 yuˀun jaˀ la li lek ˀik' ˀeke.
jech' ˀo la xal jaˀ la xchiˀil xˀil ˀek ˀun k'alal la mi te la jelbunojtik ˀeke.
toj lek la me spojvan ˀek xi ti vinike.

15 ˀak'o mi jun junutik k'alal mi ˀoy ta kak'teˀtike k'alal mi kak'betik yil li ˀate mu stzakvan ˀel xi.
aaa . . . pere ti mi mu vul ta ˀa jole jaˀ la schiˀilutik ˀunbi . . .
mi la laj vak'be yil la ˀate ˀaˀ xa la schiˀil yil ti yaloje xi ti vinik voˀnee.

16 nakalun ta tiˀ nok'tik xi.
ta belel sananteres xi.

'Oh, so we've got the same name,' said the Demon Pukuj. 9
So it was that the Demon Pukuj thought he saw his likeness
in this guy's cock.
For, sure enough, the foreskin of his cock was red.
That is why the Demon Pukuj thought he saw his likeness in it.

"When your cock is pointing straight out, it looks to him as though he 10
is seeing his buddy, his own likeness.
This is what he thinks whenever he sees a cock.[5]

That is how I defended myself with my cock," said the man. 11
"If I hadn't come up with this plan, why the damned Demon Pukuj
would have carried me off," he said.

"Oh, by the way, something else that's good for fending off the 12
Demon Pukuj is a black walking club," said the man.
"When you go out walking at night, it's good to take one along
as well," he said.[6]

"The reason is that it is black, too, like the Demon Pukuj. 13
That's why it is also useful as a defense.

The reason is that it's good and black. 14
That's why the Demon Pukuj sees his image in it when it is
hanging there on our shoulder.[7]
So it's also really good for defense.

Even if we're all alone, if we have with us a good, black walking club, 15
and also take care to flip him a good look at our cock,
there's no way the Demon Pukuj will try to grab us," he said.
"Oh, but if you don't trick him into believing, hey, we're all buddies,
watch out!
But if you've taken care to flip him your dick so it seems to him that
he's found a new friend, then you're safe," said the man.

"I live in a placed called Ti' Nok'tik," he said. 16
"This is on the road to San Andrés Larraínzar," he said.

17 pere ˀoy xa ta 18 ˀavil ti la jyalbun kaˀie ti vinike.
ˀa ti k'alal la snup ta be ti pukuje.
jaˀ la mas voˀne la tajmek ne.

18 jaˀo ti k'alal ta toˀox jchon yakiloˀe xi.
ˀa ti voˀnee ˀaˀ toˀox kabtel ti puru chon yakiloˀ.

19 ta jpas toˀox tajmek.
jech' ˀo xal ti k'alal ta ˀak'obaltik ti xanobale xi.

20 k'alal mi li k'ot ta jnae ta jkux jun k'ak'al.
ta jna ta rominko ˀun ta xibat jchon ta jlumaltik ˀun xi.
ˀa li chon yakiloˀe.

21 toj tzotz tajmek li xanobale xi.
ˀa ti voˀne le toj ˀutz toˀox ti yakiloˀe.
jun tzajal k'ibe toston xi.

22 jaˀ skuchabil kikatz.
k'alal mi li bat jkuch talele chanib tzajal k'ib jyakiloˀe.
ta jkuch talel ta jpat ti jyakiloˀe.
pere junjun chixanav tajmek xi.

23 ta jujun meke ta jkuch tal chanchan tzajal k'ib xi ti vinike.
ˀa li ta chanibe chib pesu stojol ti yakiloˀe.

24 pero jaˀ toˀox ti mas voˀnee xi.
ti k'alal ˀutzik toˀoxe ti voˀnee.

It was about eighteen years ago that this guy told me this. 17
About how he met the Demon Pukuj on the road.
This was really a long time ago.

"It was when I was still in the business of selling cane beer," he said. 18
"Back then, I still made a living by just selling cane beer."

I did a lot of this kind of buying and selling thing back then. 19
That's why I had to travel so much at night," he said.

"When I'd get home, I would rest for a day. 20
I'd be at home on Sunday and go to Chamula Center to sell cane beer," he said.
That's what the cane beer seller said.

"Travel was rough back then," he said. 21
"And cane beer was still very cheap back then.
It cost only fifty centavos per red clay jug.[8]

All of my cargo was hauled by me, myself. 22
Whenever I'd make a trip, I'd bring back my four clay jugs of cane beer.
I'd have this cane beer on my back.
I did a lot of traveling all alone," he said.

"On every trip I would carry back four red clay jugs," said the man. 23
"Four jugs of cane beer would cost me two pesos.

That was the way things were long ago," he said. 24
"Long ago when things were still cheap."

1 kuento t'ul te?tikal chij.

2 veno ti t'ule ?oy la spixol.
ti te?tikal chije ch'abal la spixol.

3 vo?one ch'abal jpixol xi la ti te?tikal chije.
k'ucha?al ch'abal ?apixol xi la ti t'ule.
na?tik k'ucha?al xi la ti te?tikal chije.

4 ?entonse mi xak'ane ta xakak'be ?ach'amun jpixol.
vo?one mu xu? lek xixanav xchi?uk jpixol.
ja? li toj bik'itune xi la ti t'ule.

5 ?entonse mi chavak'bun jch'amune cha?e lek ?oy.
vo?one toj mas muk'un tajmek.

6 mu xistaik ta tzakel.
toj mas tzotz chixanav xi la ti te?tikal chije.

7 veno vo?ote toj mas muk'ot tajmek.
toj mas tzotz xaxanav.
mu xastaik ta tzakel xi la ti t'ule.

8 ?entonse laj la yak' spixol ti t'ule.
laj la yak'be ti te?tikal chije.

TEXT 50

On How the Rabbit Lost His Hat and Got His Long Ears

Xalik López Castellanos

This is a story about a rabbit and a deer. 1

Now, the rabbit had a hat. 2
The deer had no hat.

"I have no hat," declared the deer. 3
"Why haven't you got a hat?" asked the rabbit.
"I've no idea," responded the deer.

"Well, if you wish, I'll loan you *my* hat. 4
I really can't walk very well with my hat on.
For in truth I am very small," declared the rabbit.

"Very well, then. If you'll loan it to me, that will be just fine. 5
I really am much bigger than you, so it suits me better.

With it on, hunters won't even be able to catch me. 6
I'll be able to travel without danger," said the deer.[1]

"Indeed, you are much, much bigger than I am. 7
You'll manage to get about without having anyone bother you.
They'll never be able to catch you," said the rabbit.

With this, the rabbit gave him his hat. 8
He lent his hat to the deer.

9 veno ti te'tikal chije bat la xchi'uk ti spixole.
ti t'ule ch'abal xa la spixol kom.

10 veno k'alal bat ta sna ti t'ule ch'abal xa spixol.
'a ti stot ti t'ule la la sjak'.

11 bu 'oy ta 'apixole xi la stot ti t'ule.
te kom ku'un ta te'tik.
yu'un ch'ay ko'onton skich' talel xi la ti t'ule.

12 'entonse batan ta 'ora.
ba 'ich'o talel ta 'apixole xi la stot ti t'ule.

13 pere ta 'orae mu jk'an xibat xkich' talel ti jpixole.
yu'un ta xibat vaykun ka'i tajmek xi la ti t'ule.

14 pere k'ucha'al toj toyol vayel chava'i xi la stot ti t'ule.
yu'un 'oy jun tzeb.

Then the deer went off with his hat. 9
And now the rabbit found himself without any hat at all.

So, when the rabbit went home with no hat on, 10
The rabbit's father inquired about what had happened.

"Where's your hat?" asked the rabbit's father. 11
"It got left in the woods.
I forgot to bring it with me," replied the rabbit.

"Then be off right away. 12
Go fetch your hat!" ordered the rabbit's father.

"I don't feel like going to get my hat right now. 13
I feel more like going to sleep," declared the rabbit.

"But why are you so sleepy?" insisted the rabbit's father. 14
"Well, there is this girl . . .

FIGURE 76

Then the deer went off with his hat.
And now the rabbit found himself without any hat at all.

15 ta ˀak'obaltik ta jchaˀbikutik.
ˀech'o xal ta xivay kaˀi tajmek xut la stot ti t'ule.

16 ˀentonse yuˀun la ch'ay naˀ ta pixol.
ˀeche chaval ma ti te kom ta teˀtike xi la stot ti t'ule.

17 moˀoj te kom kuˀun ta teˀtik.
pere ˀaˀ lek chibat ta ˀora ba kich' talel xi la ti t'ule.

18 veno bat la yich' talel spixol ti t'ule,
ti bu ta xloˀilajik xchiˀuk ti teˀtikal chije.

19 k'ot la ti bu ta xloˀilajike.
te la choti ti t'ule.

20 ta la smala ti teˀtikal chij mi ta xtal xchiˀuk ti spixole.
ˀentonse ti t'ule te la smala.
te la smala tajmek mi ta xtal ti teˀtikal chij xchiˀuk ti spixole.

21 ˀentonse ti teˀtikal chije muˀyuk xa la bu xk'ot xchiˀuk ti pixolale.
ˀentonse ti t'ule sutbatel.
pere ch'abal xa spixol.

22 k'alal k'ot ta sna la sjak' ti stote,
bu ˀoy ta pixole.

23 mu jnaˀ mu xa bu ˀijta.
naˀ mu yuˀunuk xa li yelk'anbik xut la stot ti t'ule.

24 komo ke la jyelk'anik ˀapixol kavron xi la ti stot ti t'ule.
jlikel la la snitbe schikin ti snich'one.
snitbela tzotz tajmek.

25 ˀechaˀal ti t'ule toj natik xchikin tajmek.
ˀech kom ˀo vaˀalik xchikin.

Last night we spent the night together. 15
That's why I'm so sleepy," explained the rabbit to his father.

"So *that's* how you lost your hat. 16
You were lying when you said it got 'left in the woods,'" said the rabbit's father knowingly.

"No, it really got left in the woods. 17
But perhaps I *should* go get it and bring it back," said the rabbit.

With that, the rabbit went to fetch his hat, 18
To the place where he had been talking to the deer.

He got to the place where they had been talking. 19
The rabbit sat down right there.

He was waiting for the deer to come along with his hat. 20
There the rabbit waited for him.
He wanted to see if the deer would come along with his hat.

But the deer did not appear with his hat. 21
With that, the rabbit went back home.
But he no longer had his hat.

When he got home his father asked him, 22
"Where's your hat?"

"I don't know. I couldn't find it. 23
Perhaps they've stolen it from me," said the rabbit to his father.

"What do you mean 'they've stolen it from you,' you son-of-a-bitch?" raged the rabbit's father. 24
In no time at all he yanked hard on his son's ears.
He yanked them with all his might.

And that is why the rabbit has such long ears. 25
That is how he ended up with long ears that stand straight up.

1 ˀoy jun kuento voˀnee sventa vinik laj ta tiˀel.
ta pinka la ti ˀech' ti kuentoe.
xi la jyalbun kaˀi jbankil.

2 ˀoy la jun vinik bat la ta paxyal ta teˀtik.
veno k'alal la k'ot ta teˀtik la ti vinike.
jaˀ to la yaˀi xˀavet la ta teˀtik ti pukuj laˀe.
ˀuuuuuu. . . . xi la ti jvalopat ˀok'e.

3 jech la ti vinike:
ˀi stak'be ti jvalopat ˀok'e.
ˀuuuuu . . . xˀut la ti vinike.

4 jech la ti vinike:
ˀoy la yuni tuk'.

5 jech la ti stuk'e:
te la stzakoj.

6 ˀuuuuuu xi la xtok ti jvalopat ˀok'e.

SECTION 2

Spooks, Witches, Souls, and Bad Neighbors

TEXT 51

Bitten to Death by the Backwards Wailing Man

Marián López Calixto

There is a story of long ago about a man who died, bitten to death by a monster. 1
It happened down on the coffee plantations.
My older brother told me about it.

A certain man had gone for a walk in the woods. 2
Now, when he was well within the forest, it all began.
It was then that he heard a monster crying out from the forest.
"Uuuuuuuuh!" cried the Backwards Wailing Man.[1]

This is what the man did: 3
He mocked the Backwards Wailing Man defiantly
"Uuuuuuuu!" answered the man.

As for this man: 4
He had his trusty gun.

As for his gun: 5
He had it right there with him.

"Uuuuu!" cried the Backwards Wailing Man once again. 6

7 jech la ti mu vinike:
ʔistak'be la tajmek ti jvalopat ʔok'e.

8 jech la ti vinike:
ʔi ʔavan la tajmek.

9 vaʔun ti jvalopat ʔok' laʔune:
ʔuuuuu! xi la.
ʔi te xa la vaʔal la stz'el ti vinike.

10 jech la ti vinike:
xʔavet xa la tajmek.

11 li laj xa, li laj xa,
xi la ti mu vinike.

12 jech la ti mu vinike.
yak'be la ti tuk'e!

As for this unfortunate man, he was feeling overly confident: 7
He continued to answer and mock the Backwards Wailing Man defiantly.

This is what the man did: 8
He wailed back in a loud voice, mocking the monster.

Then, the Backwards Wailing Man responded: 9
"Uuuuuu!" he cried.
And then, suddenly, there he was, standing right next to the man!

And this is what the man did: 10
He started to yell for help at the top of his lungs.

"I'm done for! I'm done for!" 11
This is what the poor man yelled.

Then the poor man did this:[2] 12
He fired a shot!

FIGURE 77

As for this unfortunate man, he was feeling overly confident:
He continued to answer and mock the Backwards Wailing
Man defiantly.

13 jech la ti stuk' ti mu vinike la ʔune:
k'alal la yak'be ti tuk'e.

14 jech ti mu jvalopat ʔok'e:
ʔoch la ti bek'tuk ta sk'ob ti mu jvalopat ʔok'e.

15 vaʔun ti pukuj la ʔune:
k'alal la laj ta tuk' ti jvalopat ʔok'e.

16 jech la ti bek' tuk'e:
ʔoch la ta sk'ob ti mu jvalopat ʔok'e.

17 jech la ti sk'obe ti mu jvalopat ʔok' lae:
laj yil la ti lok' la ti xch'ich'el ti sk'obe.
laj la slek' ta ʔora ti sk'obe.

18 jech la ti sk'ob ti mu jvalopat ʔok'e:
likel la kol ta ʔora.

19 vaʔun jech la ti vinik la ʔune:
laj la ta tiʔel ta jvalopat ʔok' ti vinike.

20 veno jech la ti vinike:
xʔavet xa la tajmek.

21 jech la ti vinike:
ʔoy la jun la xchiʔil.

22 jech la ti xchiʔile:
likel la bat ta ʔora ta sna ti xchiʔil lae.

23 vaʔun ti xchiʔil ti vinik la ʔune:
k'ot la yalbe ti xchiʔiltak ti vinik lae.

24 laj xa me ta ʔavole.
te xa stiʔet,
xi la k'otel ti vinike.

As for the foolish man's gun: 13
He fired it once at the monster.

As for the Backwards Wailing Man himself: 14
The gunshot went right through the paw of the Backwards Wailing Man.

Such was the monster's fate: 15
The Backwards Wailing Man was wounded.

Then, the bullets: 16
They went right through the paw of the Backwards Wailing Man.

Now, the fate of the paw of the Backwards Wailing Man: 17
He noticed that blood was pouring out.
So he proceeded to lick his wounded paw.

This was what happened to the paw of the evil Backwards Wailing Man: 18
It got better in no time.

But this is what happened to the man: 19
This man was fatally wounded from the Backwards Wailing Man's attack.

This is what the man did as he lay dying: 20
He cried out in desperation.

As for the victim: 21
He had a friend who heard his cries.

As for this friend: 22
He promptly went to the home of his companion who had been attacked.

So the man's friend did this: 23
He went to inform the victim's relatives of his fate.

"Your son has just died. 24
He has been eaten up."
So this man announced when he arrived.

25 vaˀun ti smeˀ la ti vinik ti laj ta tiˀel ta teˀtik la ˀune:
bat la ta ba stij talel la soltaro.
ti smeˀ la ti vinik ti laj la ta tiˀel ta teˀtike.

26 jech la ti soltaro:
tal la chib ta siento ti soltaroe.

27 vaˀun jech la ti soltaro ˀune:
k'otik la ta teˀtik laˀun.

28 vaˀun jech la ti soltaro ˀune:
ˀavan la ta teˀtik ti soltaroetike.
vaˀun ˀuuuuuu! xi la ti soltaroetike.

29 vaˀun jech la ti jvalopat ˀok' la ˀune:
ch'abal la bu la stak' ti jvalopat ˀok'e.

30 ˀuuuuu! xi la jten xtok.
vaˀun ˀi yaˀi la ti jvalopat ˀok' la ˀune.

31 jech la ti soltaroe.
uuuu xi la tajmek ti soltaroetike.

32 jech la ti jvalopat ˀok'e:
ˀi ˀavan la ˀun.
vaˀun uuuu . . . xi la ˀun.

33 jech la ti soltaro la ˀune:
ˀi stak'bik la tajmek ti jvalopat ˀok'e.

Then the mother of the man who had been eaten up in the woods 25
did this:
She went to mobilize the soldiers.
That is what the mother of the man who was eaten up in the woods did.

As for the soldiers: 26
Two hundred soldiers appeared on the scene.

As for the soldiers: 27
They reached the forest.

As for the soldiers: 28
These soldiers cried out in the forest.
It was like this: "Uuuuuuu!" cried out the soldiers.

But, as for the Backwards Wailing Man: 29
The Backwards Wailing Man did not respond.

"Uuuuuu!" the soldiers repeated once again. 30
But this time the Backwards Wailing Man heard.

Once again the soldiers uttered their challenge: 31
"Uuuuuh!" cried the soldiers in a loud voice.

So the Backwards Wailing Man did this: 32
He cried back at them.
It was like this: "Uuuuh!" he wailed in reply.

Now, the soldiers: 33
They answered the Backwards Wailing Man with a loud voice.

34 vaˀun jech la ti soltaro une:
ya'i la tal ti jvalopat ˀok'e.

35 jech la ti soltaroe:
st'omes la ti stuk'ike.

36 vaˀun jech la ti valopat ˀok' la ˀun:
likel tal ta ˀora.
ˀuuuu . . . xi la tal ta ˀora tajmek ti jvalopat ˀok'e.

37 vaˀun ti soltaro la ˀune:
laj la skotol ti sbek't stuk'ik ti soltaroetike.

38 jech la ti jvalopat ˀok' ˀune:
laj yil la yuˀun laj xa ti sbek' la stuk'ik ti soltaroetike.

39 vaˀun ti jvalopat ˀok' la ˀune:
yal la talel ta teˀ ta ˀora ti jvalopat ˀok'e.

Now, the soldiers: 34
They heard the Backwards Wailing Man coming towards them.

So it was with the soldiers: 35
They fired their guns.

Now, the Backwards Wailing Man: 36
He charged!
"Uuuuh!" roared the Backwards Wailing Man as he fell upon them.

As for the soldiers: 37
All the bullets of the soldiers' guns had already been fired.

But, as for the Backwards Wailing Man: 38
He knew that the soldiers' ammunition was spent.

Now, the Backwards Wailing Man: 39
The Backwards Wailing Man suddenly dropped down out of a tree.

FIGURE 78

Now, the soldiers:
They heard the Backwards Wailing Man coming towards them.

40 jech la ti soltaroetike:
jatav la ta ˀora ti yane.

41 jech la ti yane:
laj ta tiˀel.

42 jech la ti jvalopat ˀok'e:
toj natil la tajmek ti sjole.

43 jech la ti sjole:
jaˀ la ta xchuk ˀo jnuk'tik.

44 jech la ti soltaroetike:
laj la skotolik.

45 k'alal la ta stiˀotike:
ta la xlok' la jk'uˀtik.
t'an t'an la ta stiˀotik.

46 chaˀjot la sat.
ta la xveˀ xchaˀbotal ti yee.
k'alal ta la xveˀe ta la stzaˀan tajmek.

47 laj ˀo ti kuentoe.

As for the soldiers: 40
Some were able to get away.

As for the others: 41
They were eaten up!

This is what the Backwards Wailing Man was like: 42
His hair was very long and stringy.

As for his hair: 43
Even now he uses it to strangle us with.

And that was the fate of the soldiers: 44
They all died in this manner.

And so today, when he attacks us: 45
He snatches away our clothing!
He eats us up, stark naked!

He has faces on both sides of his head. 46
He can eat with both mouths at once.
And even as he eats, he shits continuously.

So the story ends. 47

1 ˀoy jun sloˀil sventa jlakanton ta chiapa.
ta xal li kirsanoetike toj chopol la.

2 ˀi mu la xvinaj mi vinik ˀo mi ˀantz li kirsanoe,
ˀi jmoj la sjolik.
ˀi jmoj la sk'uˀik.
ˀi jmoj la stzekik.
ˀi mu la jnaˀtik mi ˀantz ˀo mi vinik.

3 jaˀ yuˀun jech ta xal ti kirsanoetike:
te ta lakantone ta xtiˀvan,
yuˀun la xchanul teˀtik ti kirsanoetike.

TEXT 52

On the Lacandon People of Chiapas, Who Are Like Beasts of the Jungle

Marián López Calixto

This is an account of the Lacandon people of Chiapas. 1
    People say they are very bad.[1]

One cannot tell if a person is a man or a woman. 2
    They have the same hairstyles.
    They have the same clothes.
    They wear the same tunics.
    One doesn't know if it's a man or a woman.

For this reason, this is what people say: 3
    There in the land of the Lacandons they bite,
    For those people are no more than beasts of the jungle.

FIGURE 79

One cannot tell if a person is a man or a woman.
    They have the same hairstyles.
    They have the same clothes.
    They wear the same tunics.
    One doesn't know if it's a man or a woman.

4 vaˀun ti stz'iˀik la ˀun leon,
ti skatuik la ˀun jaˀ la bolom.
ta la xalik la ˀun.

5 yuˀun ch'abal tz'iˀ,
mi katuuk la,
yuˀun ch'abal la ta jmoj.
puru la chonetik la ta stz'unik ti jlakantonetike.

6 vaˀun mi mu la bu yak'bik la ti sveˀel la ti leone ti bolome ta la xtiˀvan.
toj pukuj la tajmek ti stz'iˀike.

7 jaˀ jech xtok ch'abal la yalak'ik,
mu k'usi xˀayan.
puru la teˀtik tajmek la ti snaike.

8 ˀi ch'abal la k'usi ta smilik ˀo ti chonetike.
jaˀ noˀox ta puru t'umpurax.
ˀi ta spasik la yolob sventa la stuk'ik ˀun.
jech la ti kirsanoetik la ˀune.

9 k'alal ta la xik' la sbaik ˀune,
ta spikbe la sbaik la yatik mi ˀantz ˀo mi vinik.

10 jech la ta la saˀ la yajnilik la ti kirsano la ˀune,
ta la sjak'be sbaik mi vinik ˀo mi ˀantz ti kirsanoe.

11 ˀa ti mi ˀantz la ˀune k'uchaˀal ta xajak'e,
mi ta xak'an xi la ti jlakantone.

12 ˀa ti mi ta jk'el mis xi la ti vinik ti buch'u ta saˀ yaˀi yajnil la ˀune.
jec la ti buch'u ta sjak'be mi vinik ˀo mi ˀantz lae ˀite la sjam li stzeke.
ta la xak' la ˀiluk ti yat ˀune.

What's more, for dogs, they keep lions, 4
For cats, they keep jaguars.
That's what people say.

Indeed, they have no dogs, 5
Not even cats,
Nothing of the sort.
The Lacandons raise nothing but wild animals.

What's more, if their lions and jaguars are not fed, they bite. 6
Their dogs are very mean.

And they don't even keep chickens, 7
For they have no place to hatch their chicks.
This is because these people themselves live in the depths
of the jungle.[2]

They have no way to kill wild animals efficiently. 8
They possess only bows.
For guns, they possess only arrows.
That is what these people are like.

When they want to marry, 9
They feel around in each others' crotches to find out if they are
men or women.

When people wish to find mates, 10
They ask each other if they are men or women.

If the person is a woman, she says: "Why are you asking? 11
Might you be interested in me?" says the Lacandon.

"Might I see if you have a cunt?" says the man who is seeking a wife. 12
Then the one who has asked if the person is male or female
opens up his tunic then and there.
He displays his cock.

13 vaˀun mi ˀantz la ˀune,
te xa la kitzil ti smis la ˀune.
ˀa ti mi la jyil la ti buch'u la ta sjak' bu ˀantz la ˀune lek xa la xaˀi ˀun.

14 ˀi ta la xbat smey la ta ˀora.
vaˀun k'alal la tem ta xbat ta ˀora la ˀun.

15 ˀa ti mi ta sloˀlavan la ˀune.
k'alal ta la sjam ti stzek ˀla ˀune stzeˀin ta la sk'el la ti buch'u ta sk'an yajnil la ˀune.

16 vaˀun mi svalk'un la ˀune tuk la sbek' yat te la bulul ˀun.
jech la ti sbek' yat lae xkoˀolaj la chak yat jum mol vakax ti vinik la ˀune.
ˀay mu ˀat ˀoy ˀavuˀun xi la xal ti ta sk'an yajnil ˀune.
jech mi ˀantz la ˀune ta la spikbe sbaik xchakik.

17 mi ˀantzot li voˀote ˀo mi vinikot mu jnaˀ xi ta xalik ti jlakanton la ˀune.
ˀak'o mi ˀantz la ˀoy yisim.
jaˀ yuˀun mu la xˀil sbaik mi ˀantz ˀo mi vinik ti kirsano la ˀune.

18 yoˀ la sbi ti lakantone yuˀun la la slakan puru la ton.
ti yaloje ston la ˀalak' ti tone.
vaˀun slakanik la ˀun.

19 vaˀun ˀoy la jun xchiˀil ˀun la jyil la ti ton la slakan ti xchiˀil la ˀune.
k'uchaˀal la lakan ti tone.
mu xavil mi mu tonuk xi la ti xchiˀiltak la ˀune.

20 vaˀun jech la ti buch'u la slakan to ton la ˀun ˀay, mu jlakantonun ˀun chaˀe xi la ˀun.
yoˀ lakanton la sbi ti kirsano la ˀune.

21 ta xalik li kirsano ta chamulaˀe:
jtival xiik yuˀun mu snaˀik mi lek ˀo mi chopol ti kirsanoe.

Then, if the person he is speaking to is a woman, 13
There will now be a nice furrowed cunt in view.
Then, when the one who has been asking if she is a woman sees this, he feels very happy.

Straightaway, he will embrace her. 14
Straightaway, he will take her to bed.

But it's always possible that she might give him false illusions. 15
It sometime happens that when she opens up her tunic, she gets the last laugh at the moment the petitioner gets a good look.

She will lift up her tunic and there in full view will be his balls bulging out. 16
What turned out be a man will have balls as big as those on the dick of a bull.
"Oh, you've got a damned dick," says the petitioner.
If on the other hand, the person turns out to be a woman, they go right to it, feeling up each others' crotches.

"Are you a woman or a man? I've no idea," the Lacandons say to each other. 17
Even if they are women, they have beards.
That is why one can't tell if a person is a woman or a man.

Now, the reason Lacandons are called Lacandons is that they cook nothing but stones.[3] 18
They take stones to be chicken eggs.
And they boil them as food.

There was once one of those people who saw that his friend was boiling stones. 19
"Why did you set the stones to boil?
Can't you see that they're nothing but damned stones?" said his friend.

With this, the one who was boiling the stones explained,: Oh, I'm nothing but a poor stone cooker." 20
That is why these people are called Lacandons.

This is what the Chamulas say about them: 21
They say they are like wild animals, for they aren't sure whether these people are good or evil.

22 jech ta xalike ti ye lae ˀe toj nat,
ˀi toj muk' la ti xchikine.

23 vaˀun k'alal la ta xich'ik la ti ˀoˀe ta vok' jun muk'ta teˀ.
ˀi muˀyuk la skumpakreik.
ˀi te noˀox la stukik ta xak'bik ta yich' ˀoˀ ti snich'on ˀune.
ch'abal la ch'ulna k'usi xich'ik ˀo la ti ˀoˀe.

24 vaˀun k'alal mi mu sk'an la lek ti yolik la ˀune muˀyuk xa la bu ta xak'bik la xchuˀ.
vaˀun mi cham la ˀune mu la bu ta smukik.

25 te la sjipik la ˀech'el ta k'aˀ beˀotik ti yolik la ˀune.
vaˀun mi k'aˀ la ˀune ta la xtal xulemal.

26 ti ˀolole koˀol chak junuk tz'iˀ.
ta sjipik ti yolike.

27 jech la ti yatik ti kirsano la tey la ˀune toj natik.
yat jmol vuro ti yat ti jlakantone.

28 jech la ti smisik ti ˀantzetik la ˀeke:
toj nat la timil tajmek.

29 laj ˀo ti sloˀil jlakanton ˀune.

They say they have great long mouths, 22
And that their ears are very big.

When it is time for baptizing their children, they do it with a big stick. 23
And they don't even have compadres.
They just stand there alone when their children are baptized.
There isn't even a church to use for baptisms.[4]

What's more, if it turns out that they don't like their children very much, 24
they don't even nurse them.
And when they die, they don't even bury them.

They toss their children away to rot in the streams. 25
When they have decayed, the buzzards come.

They treat their children like any old dog. 26
They toss their children away.

As for their cocks, these people have great long ones. 27
The Lacandons have got dicks just like an old jackass's.

As for the cunts of the women, it's the same story: 28
They are stretched long and wide.

That is the end of the account of the Lacandons. 29

1 jmololtik yuˀun jˀak' chamel.

2 ˀoy jun kuento sventa jun jmololtik jˀak' chamel.
jech li jmololtike jˀak' chamel ta xˀak' xuvit.

3 ˀoy la jech la jun antz xchiˀuk la smalal ti ˀantze.
vaˀun ti ˀantz la ˀune batik la ta slumal ti jmololtik ta chon k'uˀil la.

4 jech la ti smalal ti ˀantz la une yuˀun toyol ta sk'anbe la stojol la ti k'uˀil la ˀune.
vaˀun jech la ti jmololtike yuˀun yalel la ta sk'an stojol la ti k'uˀile.
mu la sk'an sman toj toyol la ti stojole.

5 vaˀun ti ˀantz la schiˀuk smalal la ˀune mu la xˀak'ik ti k'uˀil la ˀune.
moˀoj molol.
mu xlok' venta yuˀun toj tzotz ti ˀabtele.

6 jaˀ yuˀun ˀun mu xkak'.
mi ta xavich'e chanib pexu, jaˀ noˀox lajeb ˀo xi la ti vinike.
ˀa moˀoj ˀunbi molol toj toyol tajmek xi la ti jmololtik la ˀune.

7 vaˀun ti yajval k'uˀil ˀune lajyutik ˀun yuˀun ˀoy la spersail xa yalesbe la stojol ti k'uˀil la ˀune.
jech ti jmololtike ta chib pexu la ta sk'an ti k'uˀile.

TEXT 53
About Tenejapanecos, Who Engage in Witchcraft

Marián López Calixto

About Tenejapanecos who engage in witchcraft.[1] 1

This is an account of a Tenejapaneco who was a witch. 2
In particular, it concerns a Tenejapaneco man who had the ability
to cast worms into the bodies of others.

Now, there was once a Chamula couple, a woman and her husband. 3
They had gone to the land of the Tenejapanecos in order to
sell clothing there.[2]

Now, it happened that the woman's husband was trying to get a high price 4
for the clothing.
It was also the case that the Tenejapaneco who was interested wanted
to pay less for it.
He refused to buy it at the high price that was asked.

Well, the Chamula woman and her husband refused to bargain further 5
on the sale of the clothing.
"No deal, Tenejapaneco.
For there would be nothing to compensate us for our hard work.

That's why I refuse to sell at that price. 6
If you buy it at four pesos, fine, it's a deal," said the Chamula man.
"No way, Chamula, no way. It's too much," said the Tenejapaneco.

With this, the sellers of the clothing became angry, for they had already 7
agreed to lower the price of the article.
In fact, the Tenejapaneco declared that he wanted the clothing
for only two pesos.

8 vaˀun ti ˀantz xchiˀuk smalal ˀune lajyutik la ti jmololtike.
ˀa k'u yuˀun yalel ta xak'anbe stojol ti k'uˀile.
mi mu vinikotot sonso xˀutik la ti jmololtike.

9 vaˀun jech la ti jmololtik la ˀune ˀilin la ˀek ˀun.
veno mi ta xavutune jmololtik.
mu me yuˀnuk ta xakelk'anbe ta ˀak'uˀike.

10 pere xanaˀ xa me mi lajkak'bot ti chamel.
yalel me saˀbil ˀavuˀunik xi la ti jmolol la ˀune.
jˀak' chamel xiike la ti vinik la xchiˀuk la yajnil ti vinike.

11 vaˀun jech la ti vinik la ˀune sutik la talel ta snaik ˀun.
vaˀun jech la ti jmololtik la ˀune likel la bat ta sna ˀun.

12 vaˀun ti vinik xchiˀuk yajnil la ˀune lok'ik la talel ta slumal jmololtik ˀun.
jech la ti jmololtik ˀay xa la yak' ti ˀak'bil chamel ta be la ˀune.

13 vaˀun jech la ti vinik xchiˀuk yajnil ˀune te la chotol la.
staik ta be jun bin.

14 jech la ti bine ta la xlok' xch'aˀilal ta be.
ˀay k'usi liˀ ˀune ta xlok' xch'aˀilale xi la ti vinik la ˀune.
xiˀ la ˀun.

Whereupon the Chamula woman and her husband argued with the Tenejapaneco. 8
"Why do you want to pay so little for the clothing?
Are you even a man, you ass?" they said to the Tenejapaneco.

With this the Tenejapaneco became furious in return. 9
"Hey, are you picking a fight with me, Chamulas?
It's not as though I have stolen your clothing.

But keep in mind that I might well cast a spell upon you. 10
It seems to me you are seeking just that," said the Tenejapaneco.
"You are nothing but a witch," retorted the man and his wife.

With that, the man and his wife started for home. 11
And so, also, the Tenejapaneco lost no time in setting out for his house.

Then, soon, the man and his wife were on their way out of the land of the Tenejapanecos. 12
But the Tenejapaneco had already set the stage for casting a curse on them as they traveled on the road.

Well, it happened that the man and his wife sat down to rest a while from the journey. 13
And they found a clay pot right there in the road.

As for the pot, it was spewing a trail of smoke along the road. 14
"What can this be that is spewing smoke?" wondered the man.
He was terrified.

15 vaˀun k'alal la ˀech' ˀune ti bin la ˀune toj t'omel la ˀun.
k'alal la t'om la ˀune puru la xuvit sotz' la lok' ta bin la ˀune.

16 jech la ti vinik xchiˀuk yajnil ˀune xiˀik la tajmek ˀun.
ˀay ˀay ˀay k'usi xa la lom ˀune xi la ti vinik xchiˀuk la yajnil la ˀune.

17 vaˀun ti xuvit la ˀune mu la bu la yilik la tik'il la tal ta snutiˀ ti ˀantze.
vaˀun ti sotz' la ˀun ˀi ti xuvit lae te la tik'il la tal ta nutiˀ.

18 vaˀun la jech la ti ˀantz la ˀune schik' ta k'ok' ti snutiˀe.
pere mu xa la bu cham ti mu chonetik la ˀune.

As they passed by the clay pot, it seemed to explode and roar. 15
And once it had exploded, worms and bats came out of the pot.

Needless to say, the man and his wife were terrified. 16
"Ay! Ay! Ay! What was that that exploded?" exclaimed the man and his wife.

Now, they did not notice that the worms had gotten into the woman's carrying net. 17
Indeed, both bats *and* worms got into the woman's carrying net and rode safely in this manner to the couple's hamlet.

When she discovered this, the woman burned up her carrying net. 18
But in no way did this do away with the damned creatures.

FIGURE 80

As they passed by the clay pot, it seemed to explode and roar.
And once it had exploded, worms and bats came out of the pot.

19 vaˀun jech la ti xuvite ti sotz' la ˀune te la tik'il ta skoral chij.
jech la ti xuvite tik'il la k'ot ta sniˀ.
ti sotz' la ˀek ˀune stiˀ la chij.

20 vaˀun jech ˀo kom ˀo ti ˀoy schanul sniˀ ti chij ˀune.
yuˀun la yak'be la schanul sniˀ ti chij ti mu jmololtik.

21 jaˀ to vi tana ˀune ˀoy ta xjat'isaj li chije.
k'alal mi jat'isaj ˀune ta xlok' talel ta ˀora xuvite.

22 jech' ti sotz'e ta stiˀ chij chitom,
skotol la k'usi ˀoy ta banamile.
k'alal la ta kaˀ ta ˀalak' ta tz'iˀ ta stiˀ ti sotz' la ˀune.

23 pere jech la ti jmololtik la ˀun puru la ˀich' la stik'oj ta bin.
jech la ti xuviteˀ ˀixim la yak'oj tal ta bin la ˀun.

24 vaˀun jech la ti ˀantze cham la xchiˀuk la smalal.
ti povre kirsanoe.

25 jech la ti ˀantz cham ˀoe.
puru la xuvit la lok' ta sniˀ ta sbek' sat ta ye la ti xuvite.

26 jech' la ti vinik la ˀek ˀune:
ti chamel la ˀak'bat ti povre vinike.

27 puru la ta sotz' xlaj ta tiˀel tajmek la ˀek ˀun.
pero jujun la ˀak'obaltik ta xtal ti pepen sotz'e.
ta la xlaj ta tiˀel ti vinike.

28 vaˀun saˀ la yaj ˀilol ti vinike.
pero mu la xˀech'e yuˀun.

29 cham la ti vinike.
cham la ti ˀantze.

The worms and bats also found their way into the sheep pen. 19
That is how the worms got into the nostrils of the sheep.
And the bats also bit the sheep and caused them to bleed.[3]

In this way the sheep became infested with nose worms. 20
For the damned Tenejapaneco had caused the nose worms to afflict the sheep through witchcraft.

So it is that, even today, sheep sometimes sneeze.[4] 21
When they sneeze, that is a symptom that worms will start to come out of their noses.

As for bats, they will attack sheep and pigs, 22
Any creature that lives on earth.
Bats will even attack cattle, chickens, and dogs.

This is all on account of the Tenejapaneco who put the chile in the clay pot. 23
In this act of witchcraft they also put corn worms into the pot.

Because of this the man and woman became ill. 24
Poor souls!

So it happened that the woman died. 25
There were lots of worms, nothing but worms, that came out of her nose, her eyeballs and mouth.

The man did not fare much better: 26
The poor man also became afflicted with an illness caused by witchcraft.

It was just bats, nothing but bats, that bit him and caused him affliction! 27
Every night the butterfly bats would attack him.
And so the man became desperately ill from the bat bites.

So the man went off to find a curer. 28
But the affliction did not pass.

The man died. 29
The woman died.

30 vaˀun jech la ti chonetik la skuyoj la talel la ti jmololtik la ˀune.
naka jtza la ˀepaj tajmek ti mu chonetik.

31 vaˀun kap la sjol ti jmololtik la ˀune.
stij la talel k'ujab xtok ti jmololtik la ˀune.

32 vaˀun jech la ti kirsano ta chamula la ˀune ˀi kap la sjol ˀek ˀun.
bat la ba saˀ la talel jun la jˀak' chamel ta san vartol la ˀun.
vaˀun sta la ti vinik la ˀune.

33 jech la ti jsan vartol la ˀune yak'be la ˀak'chamel ti jmololtike.
jaˀ la ta spoj ti chamula la ˀune.
yuˀun ta xa la xcham la ˀep tajmek ti kirsanoetik ta chamulae.

34 vaˀun ti ta la xcham ti kirsanoetik ta chamulae yuˀun talem xa la xch'ojon ta vinajel.
sk'elaj xa la ti xch'ulel ti bu ta xˀak' xch'ojon.
ti xch'ulel ti jmololtik la ˀune.

35 vaˀun jech la ti jsan vartol la ˀek ˀune.
bat la be stuch'be la xch'ojon ti jmololtik la ˀune.

36 yuˀun ta la xlaj la ti kirsano ta chamulae.
ta k'ulob la ta xlaje ti kirsanoetike.

37 vaˀun ti povre san vartol la ˀune spas la ti pavore.
kuch la yuˀun spojel ti kirsanoˀe.

So it was that the Tenejapanecos loosed these plagues on the earth. 30
These awful creatures just multiplied and will be with us forever.

The reason that all of this happened was that the Tenejapaneco got angry. 31
The Tenejapanecos proceeded to turn loose all manner of misfortune.

As for the people of Chamula, they, too, got angry. 32
They went to seek the services of a witch in Venustiano Carranza.
And finally they located a man who would help them.

This man from Venustiano Carranza invoked witchcraft against the Tenejapanecos. 33
In this manner he sought to protect the Chamulas.
For many, many Chamulas had already died.

The reason for the misfortune that the Chamulas suffered was that the cord of their destiny in the sky had become exposed. 34
Since their soul chord had become exposed and vulnerable, the Tenejapanecos lurked there to molest it.
That is what the souls of the Tenejapanecos were up to.[5]

As for the defender from Venustiano Carranza, he was able to perceive what was going on. 35
He intervened by severing the soul cord of the Tenejapanecos.

This was done because so many Chamulas were suffering misfortune. 36
People were dying in great numbers.

So, this humble man from Venustiano Carranza had the kindness to help. 37
He assumed the burden of the defense of the people.[6]

1 ˀoy jun kuento sventa potz'lom voˀne.

2 ˀoy la jun vinik.
nakal la ta teˀtik ti vinike.

3 vaˀun ˀa ti vinik ˀune k'alal la ˀik'ub ti ˀosil ˀune ˀi vayik la ˀun.
jaˀ to la yaˀik la ti potz'lom la ˀune.
ta la xˀok' ta teˀtik ˀun.

4 bu tal ti kirsano taje xi la ti vinik.
vaˀun jech la ti vinik ˀune bat la sk'el ti bu ˀok' la ti potz'lom ˀune.

5 k'alal la xk'ot la ti vinik ˀune.
sk'el la sk'el la.
ch'abal la.

6 pero buy ti kirsano ˀune xi la ti vinik ˀune.
ˀi tzan la ti sk'ok'e.

7 jech la ti mu potz'lom ˀune k'alal la k'ot la ti vinik ˀune.
jech la ti mu potz'lom ˀune tzin xi la ˀun k'alal k'ot la ti vinik ˀune.

8 sk'el la tajmek.
laj yil la ˀun te la chotol la yok tulan ti potz'lom la une.

9 ˀa ti mu potz'lom la ˀune ˀox kot.
la te chotajtik ta yok la tulan ti mu potz'lom la ˀune.

TEXT 54

Of an Encounter with a Potzlom, the Soul of a Witch

Marián López Calixto

This is an account of long ago about an evil spirit called Potzlom.[1] 1

Once there was a man. 2
This man lived in the woods.

Now, it had gotten dark and the man had gone to sleep. 3
It was then that he heard the Potzlom.
It was wailing in the woods.

"Where can the sound of people's voices be coming from?" 4
wondered the man.
Then the man went to see where the wailing of the Potzlom
had come from.[2]

The man got to the place from which the sound had seemed to come. 5
He looked and looked.
There was nothing.

"But where can the person be?" wondered the man. 6
With that, he lit a match.

As for the Potzlom, this was what it was up to when the man arrived. 7
The Potzlom was crouching there as the man drew near.

He stared and stared at it. 8
He saw the Potzlom sitting there at the foot of an oak tree.

In fact, there were three Potzloms. 9
The three disgusting creatures were sitting there at the foot of
the oak tree.[3]

10 jech la ti vinik la ˀune sut la talel tajmek.
ma'ˀuk ne kirsano ta xˀoc ta teˀtike xi la vulel ti vinike.

11 jech la ti mu vinik laj layibel la sat.
ˀa ti sat lae toj ˀik' tajmek.
toj tzoj la tajmek ti sbek' la ti sat.

12 ˀa ti sbek'tale xkoˀolaj la chak tz'iˀ.
ˀa ti tzatzal lae ˀik' la tajmek.

13 jech la ti vinik ˀune sut la talel ta ˀora ta sna ˀun.
lek la jlikel k'ot ta sna ti vinik ˀune.

14 jech la ti potz'lom ˀune te la k'ot ta sna ti vinike.
jech la ti potz'lom ne te la k'ot la ˀok'uk la sna ti povre vinike.

15 ˀa ti mu potz'lom la ˀune.
ta la xˀok' ta jujun la chikina ti mu potz'lom ne.

16 jech la ti vinik xiˀ la tajmek.
ti povre vinike.

17 jech la ti vinik ˀune la sjak'be la jtotik.
jech la ti vinik ˀune la jyaˀi la ti k'u la xi la ti jtotik ˀune.

18 jech la ti jtotik ˀune laj la yal,
ti k'u la xˀut ti pukuje,
k'u la xˀich' laj ˀo ti potz'lome.

19 vaˀun la jyal ti jtotik ne:
mi mu xanaˀike malik la ti ˀak'obaltik.
ta xtal jaˀ noˀox meltzano ˀabaike.

20 jech me ta tuk'ike pokik ta ˀaxux ta moy.
jech me ti stakail ˀune puru me tzatzal la lotz'opik ta xavak'ik.

So the man turned back at once. 10
"That was no person I heard wailing in the woods," the man announced when he got home.

The man had actually seen its face. 11
Its face was black, pitch black!
Its eyeballs were red, very red!

Its body was just like a dog! 12
Its hair was black, pitch black!

This is why the man lost no time in going home. 13
The man went home in no time at all.

As bad luck would have it, the Potzlom followed the man home. 14
It happened that it went there to wail at the poor man's house.

This is what the Potzlom did. 15
The Potzlom went to wail at each corner of the house.

That's why the man was terrified. 16
The poor man was in bad shape.

So the man prayed to Our Lord Sun/Christ, seeking his help. 17
So the man heard what Our Lord Sun/Christ said.

So Our Lord Sun/Christ explained to him, 18
How to fight off the demonic creature,
How to do away with the Potzlom once and for all.

Our Lord Sun/Christ told him this: 19
"If you are not certain what action to take, wait until nightfall.
When it gets dark, make yourselves ready.[4]

You must wash your guns in garlic and tobacco water. 20
For the wadding, you must use only underarm hair.

21 pere mu me xalap ˀak'uˀik ˀun.
t'ant'an me xalok'ik ˀun.
ˀa ti me ˀalapojik ta ˀak'uˀike ta xˀilvan xi la ti jtotike.

22 veno xi la ti vinike.
jech la ti vinike.
ˀislok' la sk'uˀ ti vinik la ˀune.

23 k'alal la slok' la ti sk'uˀ ˀune bat la ta pana ˀun.
te la chotol ta pana ti vinike.

24 jech la ti potz'lom ˀune tal ˀun.
k'ot ta tiˀna ˀun.
ˀi sk'el la k'otel ta tiˀna ˀun.

25 k'alal la laj yoˀnton la sk'el la ti tiˀna ˀune bat la ta yok' kurus.
sbis la k'otel la sat.

26 k'alal la laj yoˀnton la sbis la ti sate ˀi ˀoch la ta ˀak'ot ta yok la ti kuruse.
k'alal ta xˀak'otaj la ti potz'lome jech la ti vinike laj la yak'be la ti tuk'e.

But don't put on any clothes. 21
You must go out naked.
If you put on clothes, you will be seen," said Our Lord Sun/Christ.

"All right," said the man. 22
And the man proceeded to do this.
The man stripped off his clothes.

When he had taken off his clothes, he went outside. 23
The man sat there outside, stark naked.

Sure enough, the Potzlom came. 24
It came right up to the door of the house.
It simply stood there staring at the door when it arrived.

When it stopped staring at the door, it went before the patio cross shrine.[5] 25
Upon reaching that spot, it made the sign of the cross on its face.

When it had finished crossing itself, it began dancing before the 26
patio cross shrine.
As the Potzlom was dancing, the man shot his gun at it.

27 k'alal laj layak'be la ti tuk'e xˀavet xa la tajmek ti mu potz'lome.
k'alal la laj ti mu potz'lom ˀune.
jech la ti vinike bat la smil ta ˀora ti mu potz'lome.

28 jech la ti mu potz'lom ˀune likel la ch'ay ta ˀora.
jech la ti mu potz'lom ˀune.
likel la ch'ay ta ˀora ti mu jˀak'chamele.

29 jech la ti vinike ˀune la jyil la ti bu la ch'ay ti mu potz'lom ˀune.
jech la ti vinik ˀune.

30 ˀi stzak la talel la smachita ti vinike.
laj la yak'be la machita ti banamil ˀun.

31 ta yok'omal la ˀun jech la ti vinik ˀune:
bat la sk'el ti bu layak'be la machita ti banamil ˀune.

As soon as he had fired this shot, the Potzlom began to howl like crazy! 27
Soon the Potzlom lay dying.
With that, the man rushed over to finish off the Potzlom.

However, the Potzlom vanished in no time at all! 28
That's what became of the Potzlom.
In no time at all, this evil, witchlike creature vanished.[6]

The man took note of just where the Potzlom had vanished. 29
And this is what the man did.

The man fetched his machete. 30
He struck the ground in that very place with his machete.

The next morning the man did this: 31
He went out to see the place where he had struck the ground
with his machete.

FIGURE 81

As soon as he had fired this shot, the Potzlom began to howl like
crazy!
Soon the Potzlom lay dying.
With that, the man rushed over to finish off the Potzlom.

32 ja? to la yil ko?oltik la xchak chitom ti potz'lome.
veno, cham xa xi la ti vinik.

33 jech la ti potz'lom ?une stzakoj la talel ti vinike.
laj la xchik' ta k'ok' ti xch'ulel ti j?ak'chamel ?une.

34 ?a ti mu potz'lom la ?une sme? la.
?oy la xchu?.

35 ?a ti j?ak'chamel ?une lok'.
la ?oxib la k'ak'al cham la ti j?ak'chamel ?une.

36 jech la ti xchi?il bat la ta jun la na sa? ti jchamel ?une,
ti bu la ?oy la ?ipik ti kirsanoetik ?une.

37 jech la ti potz'lom ?une te la sta ti jchamel ?une.
jech la ti potz'lom ?une ?och la ta yut na.

38 bat la slok'esbe la sch'ich'el ti jchamel ?une.
jech la ti potz'lom ?une ?oy la slimite sventa la yavil ti ch'ich'el.
va?un laj la slok'esbe la ti xch'ich'el ti povre jchamel ?une.

39 jech la ti potz'lom la ?une.
ta la sk'opon la sbaik ta be xchi?uk la xchi?iltak ti potz'lom la ?une.

40 k'uxi ?un chi?iltik xi la ti potz'lom la ?une.
mi la ta talel ti vo?e xi la ti mu potz'lom la ?une.

41 laj.
mi chavuch' xi la ti xchi?il ti mu potz'lom la ?une.
?aaa . . . tana xi la ti xch'ulel ti mu j?ak'chamel ?une.

It was then that he saw the corpse of the Potzlom had reappeared, 32
transformed to look just like a pig.[7]
"Good! She's finally dead!" declared the man.

The man scooped up the corpse of the Potzlom. 33
He burned it up, attempting thereby to kill the witch's soul
once and for all.

It turned out that the Potzlom was female. 34
She had breasts.

So this witch's soul departed. 35
In three days this witch's soul was dead.

But as bad luck would have it, this witch's remaining soul companions 36
went on to harass another household with sickness,
Causing sick people there to become even sicker.[8]

It happened that the Potzlom was pleased to find a sick person there. 37
So the Potzlom entered the house.

She went to take blood from the sick person. 38
The Potzlom had a bottle in which to keep the blood.
And she proceeded to take the blood from the poor sick person.

This is what the Potzlom did. 39
The Potzlom spoke with her friends on the road.[9]

"How are you, comrades?" asked the Potzlom cheerfully. 40
"Did you bring along some water to drink?" replied her Potzlom
comrades cheerfully.[10]

"Yes, I did. 41
Would you like to drink some?" she asked her fellow Potzloms.
"Ah, yes, indeed!" responded the soul mates of the damned witch.

42 k'alal ta la xlaj ti yoʔntonik la ʔune,
ta la xjoyibajik la ta be ti mu potz'lom la ʔune.

43 jaʔ jech laj ʔo ti kuentoetik ʔune.
ja jech la jyalbun ti jyayae.
jech ti kuentoe te ʔech' la ta paraje minax ti voʔnee.

When they had finished drinking, 42
These Potzloms whirled around like dervishes there on the road.[11]

So the story ends. 43
My grandmother told it to me.
As for the story, it really happened in Minash hamlet long ago.

1 lo?il yu?un ch'ulelal.

2 va?i li jch'ultote liyalbe xie vaychinaj la jten ta svayel.
bat la ta be.
k'alal k'ot ta bee muy la ta te?.

3 k'alal la yil tal ti kirsanoe yal la ta ?ora.
sti? jlikel.
la lastzak ta ?ora.

4 pero ti yo?ontone ti yok'e mu?yuk la bu sti?be skotol.
juteb no?ox la la sti?be.

TEXT 55

The Perils of an Animal Soul as Revealed in a Dream

Xalik López Castellanos

This is a story about soul affliction.[1] 1

Well, my godfather told me of what was once revealed to him in a dream. 2
He was walking in the direction of the road.
When he reached the road, he climbed up into a tree.[2]

Just as soon as he saw some people coming, he immediately climbed down from the tree. 3
He bit his victims to death in one swift attack.
Then he lost no time in seizing the bodies of the victims.

But he took out just the heart and the tongue, not the whole body. 4
Actually, he bit off only a few parts.

FIGURE 82

But he took out just the heart and the tongue, not the whole body.
Actually, he bit off only a few parts.

5 laj la skuch ˀel ta xch'en.
k'alal la k'ot ta xch'ene laj la yak'be jujutiˀ ti xchiˀiltake.

6 yuˀun la ta xˀich' ta k'ux ti xchiˀiltake.
ˀech'o la xal laj yak'be jujutiˀ jujun ti xchiˀiltake.

7 ta la xiˀik ta xbat saˀ sveˀelik.
jujunla ˀak'obal ta xlok' saˀ ti sveˀelik.

8 pero puru la kirsano ta stiˀ.
te la xk'ot jujun ˀak'obal ti bu ti muk'ta teˀe.

9 ˀentonse ti kirsanoetike laj yaˀik ti ˀoy bolom ta bee.
bat la smilik ti bolome.

10 ta ˀak'obaltik la bat smilik.
laj la yich'ik ˀel stuk'ik.

11 k'alal la k'otik ti bu ˀoy ti bolome te la k'ot staik luchul la ta teˀ.
k'alal la k'otik ti jmilvanejetike laj la stzan sjokoik sk'elik la muyel ta teˀ.

12 laj la yilik ti te luchul ti bolome.
laj la yak'bik tuk'.

13 ˀentonse ti jch'ultote laj la yil ti ta xa xˀak'bat ti tuk'e,
jlikel ta choti k'alal la t'om ti tuk'e.

14 laj la smak ta be ti bek' tuk'e.
stzakoj la k'ot ta sk'ob ti bek' tuk'e.

15 t'om la ˀotro jmoj ti tuk'e.
laj la smak ta be ti bek' tuk'e.
laj la stzak ta sk'ob.

These morsels he carried off to his cave. 5
When he got to his cave, he gave each of his family and friends
a little bite to eat.

You see, he really cared about his fellow jaguars. 6
That's why he gave a bite to eat to each of his companions.

You see, they were afraid to go out and find food for themselves. 7
So, every night, he would go out to find food for them.

But it was humans in particular that he chose to attack. 8
That's what he would do every night when he went there to the place
by the big tree.

Soon, people found out that there was a jaguar that was hanging around 9
by the road.
These people set out to do away with the jaguar, once and for all.

One night they went to kill him. 10
And with them they carried their guns.

When they got to the jaguar's favored spot they spied him there 11
sitting in the tree.
When the stalkers came to that place, they turned on their flashlights
and saw that he was, indeed, up there in the tree.

They spied him sitting up there. 12
So they fired and let him have it with their guns.

My godfather realized that he was being shot at, 13
So, he crouched down quickly as soon as the guns fired.

He was able to divert the gunshot. 14
He stopped it by putting out his hand to shield his body.[3]

Once again the guns fired. 15
He diverted the gunshot once again.
Again, he stopped it with his hand.

16 t’om la ˀotro jmoj ti tuk’e.
mu’yuk xa la bu smak yuˀun ta be ti bek’ tuk’e.

17 k’alal ˀoch ta xch’ilteˀ ti bek’ tuk’e.
k’alal ˀoch ti bek’ tuk’ ta xch’ilteˀe jlikel la la sbul stzotzil ta ˀora.

18 laj la sukbe ti bu ˀoch ti bek’ tuk’e.
jaˀ la ti yoˀ mu xlok’ ˀo ti xch’ich’ele.

19 t’om ˀora jmoj ti tuk’e.
laj la smak ta be ti bek’ tuk’e.
ta la stzak ta be ti bek’ tuk’e.

20 ˀentonse yaˀi la ti mu xa snaˀ yuˀun smak ta be ti bek’ tuk’e.
jatav la yal la ta teˀ.

21 bat la ta yut teˀtik.
muˀyuk la bu xcham.

22 ˀentonse k’alal laj yil ti jatav ˀel ta yut teˀtike julavla.
solel xa la xniknun tajmek.

23 xiˀ la tajmek.
pero ti bek’tal ne te la puch’ul ta ba tem.

24 jaˀ noˀox ti xch’ulel ˀisibtas sate.
ti sbek’tale lek ta xvay ta tem.

25 vaˀi ˀun ti jch’ultot k’alal la sakube k’ux la sjol tajmek.
k’ak’al sik xa la sbek’tal tajmek.

26 mu xa la xuˀ xlik ta stem.
jutukuk xa la mu cham.

27 chib xemuna te ta stem.
te kol ta k’unk’un.

And again the guns fired! 16
But this time he was unable to block the gunshot from hitting his body.

It was then that the shot hit him in the ribs. 17
Once the gunshot had hit him in the ribs, he pulled out some
of his own hair.

With this he plugged up the wound where the gunshot had ripped 18
through his rib cage.
This kept the wound from bleeding.

And again the guns roared! 19
This time he blocked the gunshot.
He was able to stop it from hitting his body.

But at this point, he realized that he could no longer avoid the bullets. 20
He scrambled down the tree to run away.

He took off and ran deep into the woods. 21
And in the end, he did not die.

When my godfather saw that he [the jaguar] had fled into the woods, 22
he woke up from his dream.
He found himself deep in a fit of trembling and shaking.

He was terrified! 23
But his own body was, in fact, in his own bed.

Indeed, it was only his soul that frightened him in his dream, as though 24
the jaguar were alive before his very eyes.
His own body was sleeping soundly in his own bed.

Now, when morning came, my godfather had an awful headache. 25
And he felt severe chills through his whole body.

He was not even able to get out of bed. 26
He, in fact, came within a hair's breadth of dying.

He spent two weeks there in bed. 27
There he recovered, little by little.

28 muʔyuk xa la bu xveʔ chanib k'ak'al.
ja' xa noʔox la ta xʔuch' jutuk ʔul.

29 ʔech la ti sk'obe laj la poj ʔun koʔola xchiʔuk k'ak' ta k'ok'.
solel la lok' skotol ti snukulil ti sk'obe.

30 chanib xemuna muʔyuk xʔabtej.
pero xiʔ la tajmek.
jaʔ la ti jutukuk xa mu chame.

31 ʔentonse k'alal kole loʔilaj.
liyalbe.

32 ʔa li voʔone li ʔipaj.
jutukuk xa mu licham.
muʔyuk xa bu xiveʔ chanib xemuna.

33 ʔech li jk'obe solel lok skotol snukulil.
pero k'ux tajmek xi ti jch'ultote.

34 k'uchaʔal la ʔipaj ʔun xkut ti jch'ultote.
yuʔun libat ta be jti kirsanoʔ.
pero ta tz'akal ʔun taʔox xismilik.

35 jaʔ ti kirsanoetike lajyaʔi chopol ti bee.
laj la yaʔik ti ʔoy bolom ta bee.

36 bak'in ʔun bat smilik ti bolome.
pero voʔon jch'ulelʔun.
ʔech'o xal jutukuk xa mu licham.

37 liyak'bik ʔep tuk' tajmek pero muʔyuk bu xk'ot.
jelav ta jxokon ti bek' tuke.

For four days he couldn't even eat much of anything. 28
He was only able to drink a bit of corn gruel.

As for his hands, the skin was completely gone, as though they had been burned. 29
Why, all the skin just peeled off!

For four weeks he was unable to work. 30
You can imagine how scared he was.
He came ever so close to dying.

Then, when he recovered, he talked about his experience. 31
This is what he told to me.

"I have been sick. 32
In fact, I came close to dying.
I couldn't even eat for four weeks.

As for my hands, the skin peeled off completely. 33
And the pain was something terrible," said my godfather.

"Why did you get sick?" I asked my godfather. 34
"It was because I had been attacking people and eating them up along the road.
And later, because of this, they were going to kill me.

You see, the people realized that the road was dangerous. 35
They heard that there was a jaguar that lived by the road.

So, as time went on, they set out to kill the jaguar. 36
But, you see, he was my own animal-soul companion.
That is why I came so close to dying.

They shot at me many times but they never managed to hit me directly. 37
The shots went right by me.

38 ʔech xtok la jtzak ta jk'ob ti bek' tuk'e.
ʔech'o xal poj li jk'obe lok' skotol snukulil xiyut ti jch'ultote.

39 pero voʔne tajmek liyalbe.

And I was even able to block some of the shots with my hands. 38
That is why my hands were like raw meat, with all the skin peeled off,"
my godfather explained to me.

This is what he told me long ago. 39

1 ˀoy jun kuento sventa saˀben.

2 ˀa ti ˀuni saˀbene toj chopol sjol.
ˀa ti mi kutike ta stiˀ kalak'tik.
toj chopol tajmek.

3 ˀo jun ˀantz laj yut ti ˀuni saˀbene yuˀun la tiˀbat la svich ti ˀantze.
vaˀun la jyut la ti ˀuni saˀben ˀune.
k'alal la yut ti saˀbene tal la tiˀbatuk ti yalak' ti ˀantze.

4 ˀa ti ˀuni saˀbene mu snaˀ stiˀ muk'ta ˀalak.
puru ˀuni vich ta stiˀ.

5 toj toyol ta xˀoch ta yut na ta xˀelk'an tzotz.
ta xˀelk'an jit'ak' sventa stas k'alal ta xˀak' yuni ˀole.
ˀi ta xˀelk'an tak'in.

6 jech ti mi stiˀ ti ˀuni vich ˀune,
k'ajomal ta stiˀbe yuni jol ti ˀuni viche.
k'ajomal ta stz'utzbe xch'ich'ele.

7 k'alal mi ˀoy yole ta xˀich' ˀechel sventa sveˀel yuni yol.
ti ˀuni saˀbene.

8 k'alal mi ˀoy ston kalak'tike ta sloˀ.
pero mu yuˀunuk ta xvok' juteb noˀox ta sjom.

TEXT 56

She Killed Her Animal-Soul Companion and Thus Killed Herself

Marián López Calixto

This is a story about a weasel.[1] 1

The weasel is a devious creature. 2
If we scold it, it will eat our chickens.[2]
It is a creature of very ill humor.

There was once a woman who got angry with a weasel because it was eating the woman's baby chicks. 3
That's right, she got really mad at the little devious weasel.
She ranted and raved at the weasel, for it was sneaking up to eat her chickens.

Now, this little fellow, the weasel, doesn't bother with big chickens. 4
It prefers to eat just baby chicks.

It is also fond of sneaking into houses to steal wool. 5
Females will even make off with already spun wool yarn to line their nest when they give birth.
They will even steal coins to put in the nest.

When they eat baby chicks, this is how it happens. 6
They will eat just the tiny heads of the chicks.
They will just suck out the blood.

If the culprit is a mother weasel, she will then take them off to feed them to her babies. 7
That's what these weasel creatures will do.

When our chickens lay eggs, they will eat them up. 8
So that they will not break, the thief will make only a little hole in the egg.

9 k'alal mi laj yuch' komel ti ston ti ˀalak' ˀune te ta skomtzan.
k'alal xa k'eletuk xa spat.
toj chopol sjol maˀ ti saˀbene.

10 ˀa ti ˀuni saˀbene ˀa ti jtos bie k'ak'et.
ˀoy chaˀtos sbi.

11 pero toj chopol tajmek ta spas.
ˀa ti mi la vute ta stiˀ jvichtik.
ta slajes skotol tajmek ti vichetike.

12 vaˀun k'alal mi vok' ti yuni ˀole ta saˀ talel puru tzotz yuni tas.
k'alal mi ch'i ch'i ch'i tajmek ta xˀik' la ˀel ˀun.

13 ˀa ti mi mu xanav xˀil ti yuni ˀole ta xkuch ˀech'el ˀun ti yalamtake.
ta la stz'ot ta sne.

Once it has sucked out the liquid from the eggs, it just leaves the remains there. 9
Once the egg is abandoned, there is no longer anything left but the shell.
What a strange and devious creature the weasel is.

In fact the little beast has two names: "weasel" and "evil tempered one." 10
These are its two names.

And, sure enough, it does much that is evil. 11
And if you get mad at it, it will eat up your baby chicks.
It will eat up every last baby chick.

Now, when its babies are born, the mother will go to fetch wool to line her little nest. 12
And when the babies grow up, up, up . . . she will lead them out of the nest.

And if she sees that they can't get around very well, she will carry them. 13
She does this by wrapping her tail around them.

FIGURE 83

And if she sees that they can't get around very well, she will carry them.
She does this by wrapping her tail around them.

14 k'alal mi laj la stz'ot ta snee ta xkuch ˀech'el ˀun.
ba yak' ta ch'en ˀun.
ˀi te la ta saˀbe sveˀel ˀun.

15 k'alal la mi ch'i ti yol ˀune ˀi te la ta sjatavanuk ˀun.
jech' ti saˀbene ta xˀalaj ta ch'en ˀo ta k'a na ˀo ta yut lum.

16 pere ti ˀuni saˀbene ˀune xch'ulel kirsanoetike.
ˀoy te jun ˀantz ˀa ti xch'ulel lae saˀben.

17 la jech la ti saˀben ˀune toj toyol la ta stiˀ vich.
ˀa ti yajval ti ˀalak' ˀune laj la yut ti ˀuni saˀben ˀune.

18 ˀa ti saˀben lae tal la stiˀ la vich.
laj la skotol ti svich ti mu ˀantz ˀune.

19 jech la ti mu ˀantz ˀune la jyil la ti bu la ˀoch ti ˀuni saˀben ˀune.
jech la ti mu ˀantz ˀune bat la saˀ ti saˀben ˀune.
ti bu la ˀoch ti saˀben ˀune.

20 ˀi jech la ti mu ˀantz ˀune laj la sjok'be la sna ti saˀben ˀune.
jech la ti saˀben ˀune lok' la talel yuˀun ti mu ˀantz ˀune.

21 k'alal la lok' la talel ti ˀuni saˀben ˀune laj la yak'be teˀ ta sjol ti ˀuni saˀben ˀune.
k'alal la cham ti ˀuni saˀben ˀune laj la sbal ta kas y la la xchik' ta k'ok'.

22 jaˀ jech laj
ˀo ti kuentoe.

Once she has wrapped her tail around them, she is able to carry them about. 14
She will go to deposit them in an underground den.
It is here that she will bring food to them.

Now, once her babies have grown up, they will go off on their own. 15
But she actually gives birth in a den, or in the rubble of a tumbled-down house, or in a burrow in the ground.

You see, this little fellow, the weasel is actually an animal-soul companion of people.[3] 16
And the very woman [who is the subject of this account] had had a weasel as her animal-soul companion.

Now, this weasel was really a terrible baby-chicken thief. 17
So, the owner of the chickens became furious with the little beast.

This weasel came and ate up the baby chicks. 18
She ate all of the poor woman's chicks.[4]

It turned out that the poor, stupid woman took note of where the weasel went in to take cover. 19
So the unfortunate woman went to search for the weasel.
She went right to where the weasel had taken cover.

And then the poor woman dug the weasel out of its den. 20
And, sure enough, she succeeded in flushing the weasel out.

And when the little creature emerged, she clubbed the weasel on the head with a stick. 21
Then, when the little weasel was dead, she dowsed it with fuel oil and burned it up.

That is the end of the story. 22
[And that was the end of the woman].[5]

1 ˀoy jun kuento sventa vinik voˀnee.
ˀoy jech la xloˀilaj jun vinik ta pinka vitoria.

2 yuˀun k'alal lik ti kuentoe.
jech ti vinik toyol ta xlik yat tajmek.

3 vaˀun ˀoy jun vinik ˀun:
ˀoy ta me jech jun vinik voˀnee toj toyol ta xlik tajmek ti yate.
vaˀun ˀoy la me jech ti ˀantivo voˀne leˀe xi ti vinike.

4 jaˀ la jech ti mu vinike ch'abal la yajnil.
vaˀun bat la ta ˀuk'um xchuk' la sk'uˀ ti mu vinik la ˀune.

5 jech la ti mu vinik la ˀune.
ˀi te la xpipun ta voˀo ti mu vinike.
ˀi ta la stzebin ˀun.

6 muˀyuk bu la yil tal ti mu ˀantze.
jaˀ to la yaˀi te xa la xvulvul ta tz'el ti vinike.

7 jech la ti vinik ˀune ˀistak'be la ˀun:
ˀoy buch'un ˀot xi la ti vinik ˀune.
voˀonun.
k'usi chapas xi la ti mu ˀantz la ˀune.

8 muˀyuk.
bu chabat xi la ti vinike.

TEXT 57
OF AN ENCOUNTER WITH THE SNAKE-WOMAN

Marián López Calixto

There is a story about a man who lived long ago. 1
A man told it to me there on the Finca Victoria.[1]

This is how the story came up. 2
There was a man in the camp who got super erections all the time.

Then a certain man who was one of our companions spoke up: 3
"There was once a guy long ago who was always getting hard-ons.
You know, even the ancestors got them," said the man.

Now, it happened that this poor guy had no wife. 4
This fellow had gone to the river to wash his clothes.

And this was what happened to the poor guy. 5
It all started as this poor guy was whistling happily by the river.
He was washing his hair.

He didn't notice that a wicked woman had appeared. 6
That is, not until he heard her muttering to herself near him.

So the man spoke up to her: 7
"Hey, who are you?" asked the man.
"It's just me.
What are you up to?" the wicked woman inquired.

"Not much. 8
Where are you going?" asked the man.

9 muˀyuk bu chibat.
liˀ li tal jk'elote xi la ti mu ˀantz la ˀune.

10 pere k'uchaˀal ˀun.
mi xak'an jkik' jbatik xi la ti kerem ˀune.
moˀoj mu jk'an xi la ti mu ˀantze.

11 vaˀun ti vinik la ˀune bat la smey ti mu ˀantze la ˀune.
jech la ti mu ˀantz la ˀune
lek la xaˀi meyel ti mu ˀantz la ˀune.

12 vaˀun ti vinik la ˀune:
buy nakalot ˀun xi la ti vinik.
leˀ nakalune xi la ti mu ˀantze.

13 mi xak'an chijbatotik ta jna xi la ti vinike.
veno batik chaˀe.
bu to ta ˀana ˀune xi la ti mu ˀantz ˀune.
leˀ toe mi xak'an xijbatotik xi la ti vinike.

14 jech la ti mu ˀantze toj lek la tajmek ti smu sate.
jech la ti mu ˀantz ˀune ˀibatik la xchiˀuk la ti vinike.

15 vaˀun ˀiloˀilaj la ˀun.
pere ˀalbun tajmek kaˀi bu nakalot xi la ti vinik ˀune.
ˀana k'uchaˀal ˀun xi la ti mu ˀantz la ˀun.

16 vaˀun ti ˀantz la ˀune batik la sciˀuk ti vinik la ˀune.
jech la ti vinik ˀivayik la xchiˀuk ta tem ti mu ˀantze.

17 vaˀun jech la ti vinik la ˀune.
ta xak' la yaˀi ˀat ti vinike.

18 jech la ti vinik la ˀun ˀispikbe la xchuˀ ti mu ˀantz la ˀune.
ˀi jaˀ to yaˀi ta la xbak' la ti mu ˀantze.

"I'm not going anywhere. 9
I came to see you," answered the wicked woman.

"But why would you do that? 10
Could it be that you might like for us to have some fun together?"
inquired the young man.
"No, I wouldn't want that," answered the wicked woman flirtatiously.

And with that the man went right over to embrace the wicked woman.[2] 11
And this is how the hussy responded:
This hussy really got into it. She enjoyed the embrace very much.

Then the man spoke up: 12
"Where do you live?" inquired the man.
"Right over there," replied the hussy.

"What would you say to coming over to my house for awhile?" 13
proposed the man.
"Fine, let's go.
Where is your house?" the hussy inquired.
"It's over there, just waiting for you to say that you wish to go with me,"
said the man eagerly.

Now, this hussy had a wickedly beautiful face. 14
So, indeed, the man and the woman went off together.

They continued to talk together. 15
"Please, now, tell me where you are from?" asked the man.
"Oh, why should you want to know?" replied the hussy.

With that the woman went off with the man. 16
And soon, the man and the woman were in bed together.

You can well imagine what was on the man's mind. 17
The man was feeling hot and horny and ready to have sex.

The man had just begun fondling the woman's breasts. 18
It was then that he heard strange noises and felt odd movements
coming from the wicked woman's body.

19 jech la ti vinik la ʔune:
k'usi chapas taje xi la ti vinik la ʔune.

20 vaʔun jech ti mu ʔantz la ʔune:
ti chijil chij xi la smu ne ti mu ʔantz la ʔune.

21 jech la ti vinik likel la ʔavan ta ʔora.
ʔi sk'el la.
jaʔ to la yil ʔi mokoch' la te javal ta tem,
ti mu ʔantz toʔoxe.

22 jech la ti vinike xʔavet xa la tajmek:
ti ʔuuu . . . ʔooo . . . ʔaaa.
k'usi liʔ ta jteme.

23 mu chon mu chon mu chon.
mokoch' mokoch'.

Whereupon the man spoke: 19
"Hey, what are you up to?" he demanded.

So the wicked woman replied: 20
"Ti chijil chij," rattled the awful tail that the hussy had grown.[3]

In no time at all, the man began to yell in fear. 21
He checked out what was there beside him.
And, sure enough, he saw a full-grown rattlesnake lying there in bed,
Right where the wicked woman had been before.

Now the man began to shout with terror: 22
"Uh! Oh! Ah!
What's this in my bed?

A fucking animal! A fucking beast! A fucking monster! 23
A snake! A snake!

FIGURE 84

In no time at all, the man began to yell in fear.
He checked out what was there beside him.
And, sure enough, he saw a full-grown rattlesnake lying there in bed,
Right where the wicked woman had been before.

24 ˀuuuh . . . ta xa stiˀun,
ta xa stiˀun,
ta xa stiˀun xi la ti vinike.

25 vaˀun jech la ti mu ˀantz la ˀune:
ˀi ta la slok'es ti yoke.

26 jaˀ la ti mu ˀantz la leˀe:
pero spas xa ta chon ti mu ˀantze.

27 vaˀun jech la ti mu chon ˀune lok' la ta tem.
xi la lok'e:
jech la ti vinike xiˀ la tajmek.

28 vaˀun ti vinike lik lik la ta ˀora saˀ la stik'.
jech la ti stuk'e yak'be.
jech la ti stuk' la ˀune ˀi mu la xt'om.

29 vaˀun ti smachita la ˀune k'ot la ta sjol ti mu chone.
jech la ti chone cham la ˀun.

30 vaˀun jech la ti mu chon la ˀune chamem xa la yilel ˀun.
vaˀun ˀi te la kuxul ˀun.

31 jech la ti vinik la ˀune.
ˀispet la ˀech'el la ta kampo ti vinike.

32 lajuneb la viniketik la yajval ti mu chon la ˀune.
ˀibat sjipik ta kampo ti mu mokoch'.
vaˀun ˀi te la sjavanik komel ti mokoch' la ˀune.

33 ta yok'omal la ˀun jaˀ to xaˀik.
ˀi te la ta xˀavan ta kampo ti mu ˀantz la ˀune.

34 jech la ti mu ˀantz lae:
ti ˀur ˀur ˀurur . . .
ˀu, ˀu, ˀu, ˀuj.
ti ˀeeeev xi la ti mu mokoch'e.

Oh! It's about to bite me! 24
It's about to bite me!
It's about to bite me!" yelled the man.

Indeed, the awful snake-woman was doing this: 25
She was flicking her tongue in and out like a snake.

Sure enough. This was what the evil woman was up to: 26
She had turned into a snake.

Then the awful snake-woman rose up from the bed. 27
This was how she looked:[4]
The man was terrified!

With that, the man hastily looked for his gun. 28
He took a shot at her.
But the gun would not fire!

Then he found his machete and struck her in the head. 29
With that, he felt sure that she was dead.

But the awful creature only seemed to be dead. 30
She was still alive!

Therefore, the man hastened into action. 31
The man picked up the awful snake and hauled it away to the bushes.

In truth, it took ten men to get the job done.[5] 32
They went to throw the awful snake away in the bushes.
There they left the awful snake, cast away.

It was not, however, until the next day that they heard more noises. 33
There was the damned snake-woman yelling from the bushes.

This is how the damned snake-woman sounded: 34
"Ti ur, ur, ur, ur.
U, u, u, uj.
Ti eeev," yelled the damned snake-woman.

35 vaˀun ti vinik la ˀune ˀibat sk'el la xtok ˀun.
ˀibat la sk'el.

36 ya pere yuˀun kuxul ma ti mu ˀantze xi la ti vinik.
ˀibat ta sk'el jaˀ to la yil kuxul la ti mu ˀantze.

37 jech la ti mu ˀantze ˀi ta javal ta kampo.
ta xˀavan.

38 ˀi maˀuk xa la mokoch'.
la spasoj xa la sba ti mu ˀantze.
jaˀ xa la noˀox xa la mokoch' la ti smu hole.

39 ˀi te la patal ta kampo ti mu ˀantze.
xi la spasoj la sbae.

40 ti ˀay ˀay, ˀay . . .
ti jole ti jole ti jole.
toj k'ux tajmek xi la ti mu ˀantze.

41 vaˀun ˀibat ta tiˀ vinik la ˀune ˀi te la javal ti mu ˀantze.
ˀi smilik la tajmek.

42 jech la ti mu ˀantze cham la ˀun.
ˀi smukik la ta lum.

43 vaˀun k'alal la mukul xa la ta lum ti mu ˀantz ˀune,
ˀital jun vinik ta chob.

44 jech la ti vinike ˀichabaj la ta ˀora.
ˀisyales la ti yasarina la ˀune.

45 jech la ti vinik la ˀune:
k'alal la snik la lok'el ti yasarina ˀune,
jaˀ to la yil puru la mokoch' la lok' la talel ta banamil la ˀune.

So the man went once again to see what was going on. 35
He went to see what she was up to.

"I think that damned snake-woman is alive," declared the man. 36
He went to see and, sure enough, he saw that the damned
snake-woman was alive.

The wretched creature was just lying there in the field. 37
She was yelling and carrying on.

But it was no longer just a snake! 38
The damned snake-woman had transformed herself once again,
so that her body was now that of a woman.
Now it was only her awful head that was snakelike.

There was the awful creature lying face downward in the field. 39
She had transformed herself just like that!

"Ti ay! ay! ay! 40
My head! My head! My head!
It hurts horribly!" said the awful snake-woman.

Then the man went to where the awful snake-woman lay. 41
He and his companions killed her, once and for all.

Then the awful snake-woman died. 42
And they buried her once and for all.

Now, once the awful snake-woman had been buried, 43
A man came along to cultivate the soil for his cornfield.[6]

The man started right in, breaking the earth with his hoe. 44
He dug his hoe into the earth.

This is what happened to the man: 45
When the man had finished making a cut with his hoe,
He saw snakes come out of the earth in that very place. Nothing but
snakes and more snakes!

46 vaˀun jech la ti vinik la ˀune jatav la ta ˀora.
ˀi xˀavet xa la tajmek ti vinik:
laˀ xapojikun laˀ xapojikun laˀ xapojikun xi la ti vinik la ˀune.

47 jech la ti vinik la ˀune.
laj la ta mokoch' ˀa ti vinik la ˀune.
ˀitiˀat la ti mokoch'.

48 jaˀ jech laj ˀo ti kuentoe.
jech loˀilaj ti vinike ta pinkae.

Needless to say, the man lost no time in running away as fast as he could. 46
The man was hollering and bellowing at the top of his voice.
"Help! Help! Help!" he shrieked.

But the man's fate was sealed. 47
He died from the snakes' attack.
He was bitten by the snakes.

So the story ends. 48
This is how the man on the coffee plantation told it.

1 ˀa li voˀne ˀoy jun vinik.
ta xanav ta be xchiˀuk jkot skaˀ ti vinike.

2 k'alal ta xanav ti vinik snup la jun ˀantz ta be.
ti buy ta xanav.

3 buy ta xabat xi la ti ˀantz.
ta xibat ta jna xi la ti vinik.

4 buy la lik talel xi la ti ˀantz.
li lik talel ta pinka xi la ti vinik.

5 k'usi ˀay ˀasaˀ xi la ti ˀantz.
li ˀay ta ˀabtel xi la ti vinik.

6 bak'in ta xak'to xi la ti ˀantz.
ta xik'ot liˀ ta jun xemun xi la ti vinike.

TEXT 58

Of the Troubles of Men Who Have Turned into Women

Xalik López Sethol

Once, long ago, there was a certain man.[1] 1
He was walking along the road accompanied by his horse.

As this man was walking along, he met a woman on the road, 2
Right there where he was walking along.

"Where are you going?" inquired the woman.[2] 3
"I'm going home," said the man.

"Where are you coming from?" asked the woman. 4
"I'm coming home from the coffee plantation," answered the man.

"What were you doing there?" asked the woman. 5
"I went there to find work," replied the man.

"Perhaps you will get home someday," said the woman obliquely. 6
"I should be getting home about a week from now," said the man.

7 mu xak'an jun ˀamoton.
ta xkak'bot xi la ti ˀantz.

8 k'usi jmoton ta xavak' xi la ti vinik.
xkuxet xa la yoˀnton ti vinik.

9 ti ˀamoton ta xkak' ˀaˀ ta xkak'bot ti k'usi ˀoy kuˀun xi la ti ˀantz.
mu jnaˀ mi ˀech xaval xi la ti vinik.
ˀech xkal xi la ti ˀantz.

10 yuˀun ta jk'upin ˀavat xi la ti ˀantz.
xuˀuk mi ˀech xaval xi la ti vinik.
ˀech xkal xi la ti ˀantz.

"Would you like a little gift? 7
I'll give it to you," offered the woman.

"What sort of gift do you have in mind?" inquired the man. 8
Indeed, the man was already feeling quite happy about the state of affairs.

"The gift I propose to give is just something that I have and plan to give to *you*," declared the woman. 9
"I wonder if what you say can be true," said the man.
"Yes, I'm telling the truth," said the woman.

"The fact is, I'd love to enjoy your prick for a little while," said the woman. 10
"Well, fine, if you really mean it," said the man.
"I really do," insisted the woman.

FIGURE 85

"Would you like a little gift?
I'll give it to you," offered the woman.

⁜ ⁜ ⁜

"What sort of gift did you have in mind?" inquired the man.

11 pero buy xuˀ xkak' ti ˀat xi la ti vinik.
xuˀ xiˀoch ta yut teˀtik xi la ti ˀantz.
xuˀ ˀechuk xi la ti vinik.

12 ˀora la ˀochik ta yut teˀtik ti vinik xchiˀuk ti ˀantz.
ti k'alal ˀochik ta yut teˀtik ˀora la laj yak' ˀat ti vinik.

13 ti k'alal ta xˀak' ˀat ti vinik toj lek ti ˀavat xi la ti ˀantz.
ˀa li jmalale mu ˀechuk xˀak' ˀat xi la ti ˀantz laj snup ta be ti vinike.

14 ti k'alal laj yak' ˀat ti vinik mu xabat xi la ti ˀantz.
ˀabtejkutik liˀ ta lukar xi la ti ˀantz.

15 mu jk'an.
naka me smilun ˀamalal xi la ti vinike.

16 ta la xbat ti vinik.
ti k'alal laj yak' ti ˀat ti vinik.
mu la snaˀ ti chopol ti ˀantz laj yak'be ˀat ta be.

17 k'alal ta xk'abin ti vinik.
ch'abal xa la yat ti vinik.

18 pero chopol xa la yoˀnton ti vinik.
k'alal ch'abal yat ti vinik.

19 ˀaˀ xa la ˀech ti vinik k'uchaˀal ˀantz.
ti vinik ˀoy xa la smis k'uchaˀal ˀantz.

20 ti vinik k'alal ˀayan smis ti ta la snup ta be jkot vakax.
pero ven sak ti vakax ta snup ta be ti vinik.
ti k'alal ta snup ta be vakax ti vinik ˀoy xa la smis k'uchaˀal jun ˀantz ti vinike.

21 ti k'alal ˀayan smis ti vinik,
ˀora la stae ta chamel ti vinik.
k'alal stae ti chamel ti vinik saˀ la yajˀilol.

"But where can we go to fuck?" asked the man. 11
"We can go into the woods," suggested the woman.
"Then let's be about it," said the man.

With that, the man and the woman went right into the woods. 12
Once they were in the woods, the man lost no time in fucking her.

As the man was fucking her, the woman declared, "Your prick is just fine. 13
My husband can't screw like this," said the woman that the man
had met on the road.

When he had finished fucking her, the woman said, "Don't go. 14
Let's keep on working at our task right here," declared the woman.

"I'm not interested. 15
What if your husband just decides to kill me?" said the man.

With this, the man set off on his way. 16
This was just after the man had finished fucking.
He didn't know that the woman he had been fucking by the road
was, in fact, a bad woman.

The man discovered this when he took a piss. 17
The man discovered that he no longer had a dick.

With this, the man's heart grew very sad. 18
For the man realized that he did not have a dick.

The man was now like a woman. 19
He now had a cunt just like a woman.

Now, this man who had grown a cunt met a cow standing in the road. 20
But this cow the man met was no ordinary cow; she was pure white.
And when the man met the cow, of course, he was already in the
odd position of being a man who had a cunt,
just like a woman.

Now once this man had grown a cunt, 21
It became certain that the man had been bewitched.
Realizing that he had been bewitched, the man sought out a curer.[3]

22 ti k'alal sta ti jˀilol ti vinik:
k'usi laj ˀapas xi la ti jˀilol.
yuˀun ˀoy laj kak'be ˀat jun ˀantz xi la ti vinik.

23 bu ˀoy ti ˀantz laj ˀavak'be ˀat xi la ti jˀilol.
leˀ laj jnup ta teˀtik xi la ti vinik.

24 pero ˀaˀ jun pukuj tey laj ˀanup ta be xi la ti jˀilol.
yuˀun mu jnaˀ mi pukuj xi la ti vinik.

25 pero stak' meltzanel xi la ti jˀilol.
ˀabolajan meltzanun xi la ti vinik.
xuˀuk xi la ti jˀilol.

26 k'uyepal ta xajtoj xi la ti vinik.
muˀyuk ˀep ta xatojun xi la ti jˀilol.

27 k'alal laj yich' tukulanel ti vinik bat la xanavuk ta be.
k'alal ta xanav ta be tey la snup ta be ti vakax.
xˀak'e jelavuk ti vinik.

28 ti k'alal ta xanav ti vinik pero ˀoy la smis k'uchaˀal jun ˀantz.
ti k'alal snup ta be vakax ti vinik tzaksut la ti meˀ vakax.

29 ti k'alal laj stzak vakax ti vinik laj la sjis ta lum.
ti k'alal lom ta lum ti vakax ˀora la ˀayan yat ti vinik.

30 ti k'alal ˀayan yat ti vinik yak'be ˀat ti vakax.
ti k'alal la xak'be ˀat vakax ti vinik pero mu xa la vakaxuk.
ˀora la k'ataj ta ˀantz ti vakax.

✠ ✠ ✠

31 pero chib ti vinik;
ˀech k'ataj ta ˀantz.

32 ta be ti buy ta xanav ta jun ˀo lum ti jun vinik.
ˀaˀ la snaˀbe smelol.
laj smeltzan sba ti ch'abal xa yat ti vinik.

Once the man found a curer, the curer spoke: 22
"What have you been up to?" inquired the curer.
"Well, there was this woman that I fucked," answered the man.

"Where did you find this woman that you fucked?" asked the curer. 23
"I met her there in the woods," replied the man.

"But it was undoubtedly a demon that you met instead," said the curer. 24
"Oh, but I didn't realize that it was a demon," replied the man.

"Well, this problem can be fixed up," said the curer. 25
"Please cure me, then," pleaded the man.
"All right," said the curer.

"How much must I pay you?" asked the man. 26
"Oh, you won't have to pay me much," replied the curer.

Once the man had received his treatment, he once again took to the road. 27
As he was walking along the road he met the above-mentioned cow.
The man was about to pass her.

As he was walking he still had his cunt, just like a woman. 28
Now, when he met the cow, the man reached for her.

Once the man had grabbed the cow, he threw her to the ground. 29
Once the cow fell to the ground, the man started to grow back his cock.

Once he had grown back his cock, he fucked the cow. 30
Once the man had fucked the cow, she was no longer so cowlike.
Indeed, she quickly turned into a woman.[4]

Now, there were, in fact, two other men who had similar experiences; 31
That is, that they turned into women.

One case concerned a man who was traveling in another community. 32
This one knew how to remedy his problem.
This man cured himself of the dilemma of suddenly being
without a cock.

33 pero ˀaˀ la mu snaˀbe smelol ti jun vinik.
ˀaˀ la cham.

34 ti k'alal k'ot ta na ti vinik ta la xˀat yoˀnton.
k'uchaˀal ta xavat ˀavoˀonton xi la yajnil ti vinik.
ch'abal ta xkat koˀnton xi la ti vinik.

35 mi xak'an xaveˀ xi la ti ˀantz.
mu jk'an xiveˀ xi la ti vinik.

36 k'uchaˀal xi la ti ˀantz.
yuˀun noj to jch'ut xi la ti vinik.

37 pero ˀaltik la ta xa ti noj xch'ut ti vinik.
yuˀun la ta xat yoˀnton ti vinik ch'abal yat.
ti ˀaˀ ˀoy smis k'uchaˀal ˀantz.

38 ti k'alal vay ti vinik mu xa la sk'an xchiˀin ta vayel yajnil ti vinike.
koˀol jchiˀin jbatik ta vayel xi la yajnil ti vinik.
mu jk'an xi la ti vinik.
xuˀ noˀox liˀe xi la ti vinik.

39 ti k'alal ˀoch svayel ti vinik bat la spik ˀat yajnil ti vinik.
pero ti k'alal laj spikbe yat smalal ti ˀantz muˀyuk la xaˀi ti vinik.

40 ti k'alal sakub ˀosil ta yok'omal,
pero ch'abal xa la xˀak'be veˀuk smalal ti ˀantz.
sob xa la lok' batel.
bat yalbe stot ch'abal yat smalal ti ˀantz.

41 ti k'alal k'ot ta sna stot ti ˀantz chopol jmalal xi la ti ˀantz.
k'usi laj spas ˀamalal xi la stot ti ˀantz.
yuˀun ch'abal xa yat xi la ti ˀantz.

Then there was another man who was not so lucky in finding the 33
secret for a cure.
This one died.

When the second of these men got home one day, his heart was sad. 34
"Why is your heart sad?" inquired the man's wife.
"My heart is not really sad," the man responded obliquely.

"Do you want something to eat," asked his wife. 35
"No, I don't feel like eating," said the man.

"Why is that?" asked his wife. 36
"Because my stomach is full," replied the man.

But, the fact of the matter was that the man was lying about having 37
a full stomach.
In truth, his heart was sad because he had no prick.
Indeed, the truth of the matter was that he had a cunt, just like a woman.

When the man went to bed, he no longer had any desire to sleep 38
with his wife; not this man.
"Let's cuddle up together in bed," suggested the man's wife.
"I don't feel like it," said the man.
"I'm comfortable as is," said the man.

Now, when the man had fallen asleep, his wife proceeded to grab for 39
his cock.
Now, when the woman tried to grab her husband's cock, the man
did not respond.

Then the next day dawned, 40
Indeed, the woman no longer felt like feeding her husband his breakfast.[5]
She left the house very early.
The woman was going to tell her father that her husband no longer
had a cock.

When the woman got to her father's house, she announced, 41
"My husband is no good."
"What has your husband done?" inquired the woman's father.
"The problem is that he hasn't got a cock anymore," declared the woman.

42 k'uchaˀal ch'abal yat ˀamalal xi la stot ti ˀantz.
mu jnaˀ k'uchaˀal xi la ti ˀantz.

43 ˀo xa smis k'uchaˀal ˀuˀun xi la ti ˀantz.
ˀaˀ lek ta jk'eltik k'usi sˀelan smis ti ˀamalal xi la stot ti ˀantz.
xuˀuk xi la ti ˀantz.

44 ti k'alal xuˀuk xi la ti ˀantz laj stzob sba vakib viniketik ta sk'elal ti vinik k'u sˀelan smis ti k'atajem ta ˀantz.
ti k'alal laj sk'elbeik smis ti vinik k'atajem ta ˀantz tae la ta k'exlal ti vinik.
te la cham ˀo ta k'exlal ti vinik.

45 ti k'alal laj sk'elbe smis ti vinik sjak' la smuniˀ ti vinik k'usi laj spas ˀayan ˀamis.
xi la muniˀ ti vinik.
yuˀun laj jnup ta be jun ˀantz xi la ti vinik.

46 k'usi laj spasbot ti ˀantz xi la smuniˀ ti vinik.
yuˀun laj kak'be ˀat xi la ti vinik.
ˀaˀ tey jmis xi la ti vinik.

47 pero muˀyuk la jal skuch yuˀun ti vinik ˀoy smis.
cham la ta jun xemuna.

48 ˀoy jun vinik bat saˀ yajnil ta jun ˀo lum.
ti k'alal mu skan snop ti vinik ta la sk'an ta sut ta slumal.

49 ˀaˀ la ta skomtzan ti yajnil.
stuk la ta sut ta slumal ti vinik.

50 muˀyuk la ta xˀik' ˀechel ti yajnil.
ti k'alal sut ta slumal ti vinik pero muˀyuk la xˀalbe yajnil.

"Why hasn't your husband got a cock anymore?" asked the woman's father. 42
"I've no idea," replied the woman.

"He's got a cunt just like me," announced the woman. 43
"Well, we'd best go see about your husband's cunt," said the
woman's father.
"All right, then," replied the woman.

Once the woman had agreed to this, six men assembled to check out 44
the matter of the man's cunt, of the man who had changed
into a woman.
When they examined the cunt of the man who had changed into
a woman, this man was overcome by embarrassment.
Indeed, the shame of it was soon to kill him, then and there.

When they had finished examining the man's cunt, the man's father-in- 45
law asked him, "What did you do to grow your cunt?"
This was what the man's father-in-law asked.
"Well, I met this woman along the road," replied the man.

"What did this woman do to you?" asked the man's father-in-law. 46
"Well, the fact is, I fucked her," said the man.
"That must be why I've got my cunt," suggested the man.

But it was not for long that this man who had a cunt could stand the 47
stress of it all.
He died within the week.

✠ ✠ ✠

There was yet another man who went to find a wife in another town.[6] 48
In time, this man no longer felt like staying there and he wanted to
go home to his own town.

He left his wife there. 49
Straightaway he returned to his own town.

He did not take his wife with him. 50
When the man left for home, he didn't even tell his wife the truth.

51 ta xibat ʔulan kamiko xi la ti vinik.
ti k'alal sut ta slumal ti vinik.

52 ti k'alal lok' ta sna ti vinik pero lek la skuxe yoʔnton ti vinik.
ti k'alal ta xanav ti vinik mu la snaʔ mi ch'abal xa yat.
ʔoy xa la smis k'uchaʔal jun ʔantz.

53 ti k'alal ch'abal yat ti vinik k'abin.
yat la jutuk ʔoʔnton.
pero tey la sut ta be ti vinik ti k'alal ch'abal yat.

54 ti k'alal ta k'ot ta xa k'ot ti vinik ta sna:
k'usi laj ʔapas xi la ti viniketike.
muʔyuk k'usi la jpas xi la ti vinik.

55 ʔoy xa smis k'uchaʔal jun ʔantz.
mu la sk'an xʔal ti vinik ʔoy xa smis k'uchaʔal jun ʔantz.

56 ti k'alal k'ot ta sna ti vinik meltzanbil xa la sveʔel yuʔun yajnil.
k'usi ta xak'an ta ʔora mi baʔyel ta xaveʔ
mi baʔyel ta xijvayotik xi la yajnil ti vinike.
ʔaʔ baʔyel ta xiveʔ xi la ti vinik.

57 ti k'alal ta sveʔ ti vinik t'uyul la ta ba k'ok' ti yat.
ti k'alal laj veʔuk ti vinik mutz'o ʔasat xi la ti yajnil.
xuʔuk xi la ti vinik.

58 ti k'alal laj smutz' sat pero jlikel laj smutz' sat ti vinik.
vik'o ʔasat xi la yajnil ti vinik.
xuʔuk xi la ti vinik.

59 ti k'alal laj svik' sat ti vinik ʔi xa la yat.
muʔyuk xa la smis ti vinik.

"I'm going to visit a friend," said the man. 51
This was what he said when he was going to depart for home.

When the man left for home, he felt very happy; that was his state of mind. 52
As the man traveled, he did not realize that he no longer had a cock.
That he now had a cunt, just like a woman.

Now, in this condition, without a cock, he went to take a piss. 53
He was, of course, a little sad at what he discovered.
So this man, finding himself without a cock, decided to turn around and go back where he had come from.

Now, once the man had reached home, this is what happened: 54
"What have you been up to?" inquired the other men.
"I haven't been up to anything," answered the man.

Indeed, he had a cunt, just like a woman. 55
He didn't feel like telling anyone that he now had a cunt, just like a woman.

When this man reached his home, his wife already had his dinner ready. 56
"What do you feel like doing now?
Do you want to eat first?
Or should we go to bed first?" inquired his wife.
"Oh, I feel like eating first," responded the man.

When the man was in the midst of his meal, his prick appeared dangling from the ceiling, just above the fire. 57
When the man had finished eating, his wife said: "Close your eyes."
"All right," agreed the man.

And, right away, he closed his eyes. 58
"Now open your eyes," commanded the man's wife.
"All right," agreed the man.

And, upon opening his eyes, he found that he now had his prick again. 59
He no longer had a cunt.

60 ti k'alal ˀoy xa yat ti vinik:
vaykutik jlikeluk xi la yajnil ti vinik.
xuˀuk xi la ti vinik.

61 ˀora la vayik ta k'ak'altik xchiˀuk yajnil ti vinik.
ˀora la ˀiyak' ˀat ti vinik.

62 k'alal ta xak' ˀat ti vinik,
xkuxet xa la yoˀnton yajnil ti vinik.

Once the man had his prick back, his wife spoke: 60
"Let's go to bed for awhile," said the man's wife.
"Good idea," said the man.

So the man and his wife lost no time in going to bed in the 61
very light of day.
And the man proceeded without delay to fuck her.

And as he fucked her, 62
His wife's heart became, once again, very happy.

1 ˀa li voˀne ˀoy la jun vinik snaˀ snutz teˀtikal chij.
ˀoy la chaˀkot stz'iˀ.

2 pero nom la ta xbat snutz teˀtikal chij ti vinik.
pere tey la ta xvay ta teˀtik ti vinik,
ti buy ta xbat snutz ti teˀtikal chij.

3 pere ˀecheˀ la ta xch'ay sk'ak'al ti vinik.
mu la xcham ti teˀtikal chij ti k'alal ta xˀak'be tuk'.

4 k'uchaˀal mu xcham ti teˀtikal chij xi la ti vinik.
jnaˀtik k'uchaˀal xi la ti chib xchiˀil.

5 ti k'alal mi ˀaˀ ta xˀak' tuk' ti xchiˀil ti vinik.
ta la xcham ti teˀtikal chij.
ti jun vinik mu la xcham yuˀun teˀtikal chij ti k'alal ta xˀak'be tuk'.

6 ˀaˀ la ˀech ta juten.
ti mu xcham ti teˀtikal chij.

7 k'alal ch'abal xcham ti teˀtikal chij yuˀun ta tuk' laj la xchuk stz'iˀ ti vinik.
sut la tal sk'el yajnil mi stuktuk.

8 pere k'alal tal sk'el yajnil ti vinik laj la xchuk komel ta be stz'iˀ ti vinik.
k'alal ta xa xk'ot ta sna ti vinik nak'al xa la ta xanav.

9 k'alal k'ot ta sna ti vinik muˀyuk la xk'opoj.
ta la xaˀi mi ˀoy buch'u tey.

TEXT 59

Of an Unfaithful Wife Who Goes to the Grave with Her Lover

Xalik López Setjol

Long ago there was a man who went often to hunt deer. 1
He had two dogs.

This man would wander great distances on his deer-hunting trips. 2
He would sleep right there in the woods,
Right where he had gone deer hunting.

But on one of these hunting trips it turned out that the man's days were spent in vain. 3
The deer simply wouldn't die when he shot at them.

"How can it be that the deer won't die?" exclaimed the man. 4
"Who knows why?" replied his two friends.

As for the man's friends, they had no problems when they took a shot. 5
The deer would always die at their hand.
But this one man could never manage to kill a deer when he took a shot.

So it was with every time he shot. 6
No deer would die at his hand.

When it became clear that he was having no success at deer hunting, the man tied his dogs up. 7
He thought he would go home to see if his wife was indeed all alone.[1]

When he went on this trip to check up on his wife's activities, the man left his dogs tied up by the road. 8
This permitted the man to slip up to his house quietly, without being noticed at all.

As he approached his house, he did not speak to announce his arrival. 9
He wanted to observe unnoticed, if someone else was there.

10 k'alal ya?i te la ?oy ta xlo?ilaj jun vinik ta sna ti vinik yalbe la xchi?il:
te ?oy jun vinik ta jna xi la ti vinik.

11 la? jmalatik xkojtikintik xi la ti vinik.
xu?uk xi la ti vinik.

12 tey la ta smala?ik k'usi ?ora ta xlok'.
tey la ya?binojik.

13 k'alal ta x?ak'ik ?at tey la ya?binojik ta xlo?ilajik.
k'usi ta x?alik ti ?antz k'alal ta x?ich' at.

14 ?o?ot toj lek xana? xavak' ?at xi la ti ?antz.
?a li jmalale ?a? mu sna? lek x?ak' ?at xi la ti ?antz.

15 ?a li ?o?te ta jk'anot lek xi la ti ?antz.
xu? ?echuk xi la ti vinik k'alal ta x?ak' ?at.
tey la ya?binoj smalal ti ?antz k'usi ta spas.

16 k'alal laj yo?nton ?ak' ?at ti vinik ta xik'abin xi la.
k'abinan xi la ti ?antz.

As soon as the man heard a strange man talking in his own house, 10
he whispered this to his companions:
"There's some guy there in my house," said the man.

"Let's wait awhile to see if we recognize who he is," suggested the man. 11
"All right," replied his friends.

There they waited quietly for him to come out. 12
There they were, listening, trying to make out what was going on.

As they proceeded with their lovemaking, they spoke to each other 13
as the visitors listened.
They heard what the man and woman said as they were fucking.

"You are truly a first-class lover," declared the woman. 14
"My husband is no good at fucking," continued the woman.

"I love you a lot," said the woman. 15
"It's mutual," replied the man as he poked it to her.
And right there, close by, the woman's husband was able to find out
exactly what she was up to.

When the man finally finished fucking, he said, "I've got to take a leak." 16
"Go ahead and pee," replied the woman.

17 liʔ ma sk'abin jmala xi la ti ʔantz.
xuʔuk xi la ti vinik.

18 ti k'alal ta sk'abin ti vinik tey la vaʔal smalal ti ʔantz.
ti smalal ti ʔantz tzakxutbe la yat ti vinik.

19 bojxutbe la ta kuchilu.
ti k'alal laj sboj ʔat ti smalal ti ʔantz sut la batel ti nutz teʔtikal chij.
pere ti ʔat laj sboj ti vinik yich'oj batel ta teʔtik ti buy bat snutz teʔtikal chij.

20 pere ti k'alal laj yich' bojbel yat ti vinik ʔorala ʔicham.
k'alal cham ti vinik k'usi ʔapas xi la ti ʔantz.
pere ti vinik mu xa la xtak'av.
chamem xa la.

"Right there is where my husband pees," said the woman helpfully. 17
"Fine," replied the man.[2]

And, as the man was peeing through a crack in the wall, the woman's husband was standing right there, outside the house. 18
The woman's husband grabbed hold of the other guy's dick.

He lopped it off neatly with his knife. 19
Once the woman's husband had cut the guy's dick off, he left quietly to return to his deer hunting.
But the man took care to take the severed dick with him to the woods to where he was hunting deer.

Now, once the other man had his penis lopped off, he proceeded to die in no time at all. 20
As he lay dying, the woman asked, "What happened to you?"
But the man could no longer answer.
He was already dead.

FIGURE 86

"Right there is where my husband pees," said the woman helpfully.
"Fine," replied the man.

21 k'alal yil cham vinik ta sna ti ˀantz:
yochel la ta smukel ˀanima ti ˀantz.
k'alal laj smuk ta xa la sakub.

22 pere mu la nomuk laj smuk ˀanima ti ˀantz.
yolon la stem laj smuk.

23 ti k'alal sakub muˀyuk la k'usi ta xˀal ti ˀantz ti smalal ti ˀantz.
k'alal ta snutz teˀtikal chij tey la yich'ojbe yat ti vinik laj skobe.

24 pero ˀora xa la sta ti teˀtikal chij.
yak'be la tuk'.

25 ti k'alal la jyak'be tuk' teˀtikal chij ti vinik
cham la ti teˀtikal chij.
k'alal cham ti teˀtikal chij xkuxet xa yoˀonton ti vinik.

26 tey la ˀixchoˀik ta teˀtik ti teˀtikal chij.
tey la ˀistzan sk'ok'ik ta teˀtik.

27 ti viniketik tey la ˀisvoik ti teˀtikal chij.
stiˀik ti viniketik.

28 tey la yich'oj ti ˀat.
ˀisvo la ta k'ok'.
yich'be tal stiˀ yajnil.

29 ti k'alal ˀul ta sna ti vink muˀyuk la k'usi ta xˀal.
lek la yoˀnton ti k'alal la jyak'be stiˀ ˀat yajnil ti vinik.

30 pero slekoj la xch'akoj talel sveˀel yahnil ti vinik.
slekoj la xch'akoj talel sveˀel snich'nab ti vinik.

When the woman saw that her lover had died, she did this: 21
The woman proceeded to bury the corpse.
When she had finished burying it, morning was already dawning.

Now, this woman did not bother to bury the corpse very far away. 22
She buried it right under the bed![3]

When the day dawned, the woman's husband said absolutely nothing to her.[4] 23
As he set off once again to hunt deer, he carried with him the dick of the man who had been having sex with his wife.

In no time at all he came upon a deer. 24
He fired a shot.

No sooner had the man shot the deer 25
Than the deer dropped in its tracks.
And when the deer died, the man felt very happy.

They skinned the deer right there in the woods. 26
Right there in the woods they built a fire.

Right there, they roasted the deer meat. 27
Then the men ate their fill.

Then and there the man took out the severed dick that he had brought with him. 28
He roasted it over the fire.
Then he put it away to take home for his wife to eat.

When the man got home, everything seemed to be normal. 29
The man's wife was delighted when he gave her the roasted dick to eat.

However, the man had been careful to keep his wife's food separate from the rest. 30
The man had carefully set aside the portion of food that was intended for his children.

31 ti k'alal la jyakbe stiˀ ˀat yajnil ti vinike ta ˀora la ta sk'an stiˀ ti snich'nab.
malo? jlikel xi la ti vinik.
liˀ ˀoy ma ˀavunike xut la snich'nab.

32 ti k'alal ta stiˀ at yajnil ti vinik mi ta te xatiˀ jutebuk xi la ti ˀantz.
moˀoj jtiˀoj xa xi la ti vinik.

33 ti k'alal laj stiˀ ˀat ti ˀantz ˀora la la jyak' ˀuch' voˀ.
yuch' la voˀ ti ˀantz.

34 pero mu la sbalin ta jutuk ti voˀ.
ˀep la la jyuch' voˀ ti ˀantz.

35 ti k'alal la jyuch' ˀep voˀ ti ˀantz te la cham ˀo.
t'om la sch'ut ta voˀ ti ˀantz.

36 ti k'alal cham yajnil ti vinik la jyalbe xchi'il ta naklej.
laˀ k'el ˀavil cham kajnil xi la ti vinke.
t'om sch'ut ta voˀ ti kajnil xi la ti vinik.

37 k'uchaˀal toj ˀep la jyuch' voˀ xi la ti xchiˀiltak ta naklej ti vinik.
yuˀun laj kak'be stiˀ ˀat xi la ti vinik.

38 buy laj ˀata ti ˀat la ˀavak'be stiˀ ti ˀavajnil xi la ti xchiˀiltak ta naklej ti vinik.
yuˀun ˀoy jun vinik ta xˀak'be ˀat ti kajnil xi la ti vinik.

39 buch'u vinikal xi la ti xchiˀil ta naklej ti vinik.
mu jnaˀ buch'u vinikal xi la ti vinik.

40 mi xak'an xavojtikinik liˀ ˀoy mukul xi la ti vinik.
bu ˀoy mukul xi la ti xchiˀil ta naklej.
liˀ ˀoy mukul ta yolon jtem xi la ti vinik.

41 laˀ jotztik xi la ti xchiˀiltak ta naklej ti vinik.
xuˀuk xi la ti vinik.

Just as soon as the man had given his wife the roasted dick to eat, 31
his children immediately asked for something to eat, too.
"Wait just a minute," said the man.
"Here's your food," he said to his children.

As the man's wife was eating her dick meat, she asked him, 32
"Wouldn't you like a bit to eat, too?"
"No, thanks. I've already eaten some," he replied.

When the woman had finished eating her dick meat, she had a 33
sudden craving for water.
So the woman drank some water.

But a little water would not quench her thirst. 34
The woman proceeded to drink a great deal of water.

Once the woman had gulped down a lot of water, she died then and there. 35
The woman's stomach burst from so much water.

Once the man's wife had died, he told his neighbors about it. 36
"Come and see. My wife died," announced the man.
My wife's stomach burst," said the man.

"Why on earth did she drink so much water?" asked the man's neighbors. 37
"It's because I gave her dick meat to eat," explained the man.

"Where did you get the dick meat that you fed your wife?" asked the 38
man's neighbors.
"It came from a man who was fucking my wife," said the man.

"Who was it?" asked the man's neighbors. 39
"I have no idea who the guy was," said the man.

"If you would like to know who he was, he's buried right here," 40
said the man.
"Where is he buried?" asked the neighbors.
"He's buried right here under the bed," replied the man.

"Come on. Let's dig him up," suggested the man's neighbors. 41
"Not a bad idea," replied the man.

42 yochelik la ta sjotzel ti ˀanima ti xchiˀil ta naklej ti vinik.
ti k'alal laj sjotzik ti ˀanima yochelik la ta sk'elel buch'u vinikal.

43 ti k'alal ta sk'elik mu xa la stak' ˀojtikinel buch'u vinikal.
ˀaˀ xa noˀox la yilik ti bojbil yat ti vinik.

44 ti k'alal laj sk'el yilik ti ˀanima mu xa stak' ˀojtikinel buch'u vinikal.
laj schaˀmukik jun velta.

45 ti k'alal laj smukik ti ˀanima pero koˀol xa laj smukik xchiˀuk ti ˀantz
t'om ta voˀ.
ti k'alal laj smukik ti ˀanima vinik xchiˀuk ti ˀantz.

46 pero ˀora laj saˀ yan yajnil ti vinik.
ti ˀantz la jyik' ti vinik ˀaˀ toj lek.
mu la snaˀ saˀ yan vinik ti ˀantz.

47 ti k'alal lek yajnil ti vinik persa xa la ta sta ti teˀtikal chij ti k'alal ta xbat snutz.
ti k'alal chopol yajnil ti vinik mu la sta ti teˀtikal chij.
ti k'alal mi sta pero mu la xcham ti teˀtikal chij ta tuk'.

With that, the man's neighbors started in to dig up the corpse. 42
Once they had dug up the corpse, they tried to determine the man's identity.

Once they had taken a look, they could no longer make out who the man was. 43
All they could see at this point was that the man indeed had had his dick cut off.

Soon they finished examining the corpse and determined that it was no longer possible to identify the man. 44
With that, they buried him again.

When they buried the dead man, they buried him together with the woman who had burst from drinking so much water. 45
When they buried the corpse, the dead man was in the company of his lover.

Now, this man lost no time in finding another wife. 46
The woman he finally married was very good and moral.
This woman had no eye for other men.

So it is that when a man has a good and faithful wife, he will always have good luck at deer hunting. 47
If the man's wife is unfaithful, he will not succeed in bagging any deer.
He might find deer, all right, but his gunshot will be powerless and impotent as a weapon for killing them.

1 veno ˀoy jun vinik ta ˀox saˀ yajnil.
bat sjak' ti tzebe.

2 pero k'alal k'ot ta sna ti tzebe laj la sbaj stiˀ sna.
mu la sk'an smalal.

3 ˀentonse ti kereme te sut talel.
pere ta la xˀik' yaˀi tajmek ti tzebe.
yuˀun la ti tzebe toj lek la tajmek.
ˀech'o la xal ta la xˀik' yaˀi xchiˀuk.

4 k'alal la sut ˀel ti kerem ta snae,
sut la ˀel ta xˀok',
yuˀun la jyil ti tzeb toj leke.

5 ˀentonses ti kereme la snop ti k'uxi xuˀ xbat yutilan ta ˀak'obaltike.
laj la saˀ sjimjimteˀ.
laj la xchuk ch'ojon.
laj la spas reva mi xˀok' ti steˀe.
laj la sjimolan.
ˀentonse lek la xˀok' ti sjimjimteˀe.

6 veno lek ˀoy.
xˀok' ti jteˀe.
ˀa ver mi mu xiˀ ti tzebe xi la ti kereme.

7 laj la saˀ xepuˀ xchiˀuk xch'ailal semet.
baˀyel la la jyak'be xepuˀ ti sate.
la la sjaxbe lek xepuˀ ti sate.

TEXT 60

Abducted by a Demon Lover

Xalik López Castellanos

Now, there was once a man who was trying earnestly to obtain a wife, 1
but with no success.
He went to her home to present a formal petition for her
hand in marriage.[1]

But when he reached the girl's home, the front door was locked. 2
She didn't want a husband.[2]

The young man had no choice but to retreat. 3
But he remained determined to marry this girl.
For indeed, this girl was very attractive.
That is why he was set on marrying her.

As the young man was returning to his own home, 4
He actually wept on the way,
For he thought the girl was exceptionally attractive.

Then it occurred to the young man what he might do to force her 5
to change her mind that very evening.
He found a bull-roarer.
He tied it to a cord.
He tested it out to see if the wooden piece would make a good
wailing sound.
He gave it a test spin.
And sure enough, his bull-roarer wailed admirably.[3]

"Now, this is great! 6
My bull-roarer makes a fine wailing sound.
Let's see if it gives the girl a good scare," said the young man to himself.

He also got some tallow and soot from the bottom of a tortilla griddle. 7
First he put the soot on his face.
Then he rubbed the tallow all over his face.

8 jaˀ to la sjaxbe xch'ailal semet.
sjaxbe la lek tajmek.
ˀentonse ti sate solel la ˀik' ˀik' tajmek.

9 laj la xchuk tzajal pok'il ta snuk'.
laj la slap spisol xchiˀuk spantalon.

10 ˀentonse bat la xchiˀuk ti sjimjimteˀe.
te la tuk' bat ta sna ti tzebe.

11 ˀentonse k'alal la xa xk'ot ti vinik ta sna ti tzebe:
te la smala jlikel ta xokon na.
ta la smala ta xlok' k'abinuk ti tzebe.

12 ˀentonse k'alal lok' k'abinuk ti tzebe.
bat ta ˀora ti vinik xchiˀuk ti sjimjimteˀe.
bat stzak ta ˀora ti tzebe.

13 ti jimjimjim xi xa la ti sjimjimteˀe.
laj la stzak ti tzebe.
ta la sk'abin ta ˀamak' ti tzebe.

14 ti ˀay ti ˀay li bat xa ˀun xut la xchiˀiltak ti tzebe.
ti ˀay ti ˀay xi xa la ti tzebe.

15 bat la ta ˀora xchiˀuk ti vinike.
li bat xa ta pukujˀun xi xa ti tzebe.
bat la ta ˀora xchiˀuk ti pukuje.

16 vaˀiˀun ti pukuje smeyoj la batel ti tzeb k'alal ta snae.
sjimjun xa la ˀel ti steˀe.

17 bat xa ta pukukuj ti jvixtike.
ti ˀus ti ˀus xiik ti yitz'inab ti tzebe.
te la vaˀalik ta koryol.

Then he rubbed in the soot from the tortilla griddle. 8
He blended it in very well.
With this treatment, his face had become totally black.

He tied a red bandanna around his neck. 9
And put on his hat and his trousers.

Then he set off with his "humming stick." 10
He went straight to the girl's house.

Now, this is what happened when the young man got to the girl's house: 11
He waited there beside the house.
He waited for her to come out and pee.

Presently, the girl did come out to relieve herself. 12
The man leapt out at once, whirling his "humming stick."
He lost no time in grabbing her.

"Heem, heem, heem," wailed his "humming stick." 13
And then he grabbed the girl,
Just as the girl was peeing there in the courtyard of the house.

"Ay, ay, ay! I've been kidnapped!" cried the girl to her relatives. 14
"Ay, ay, ay!" shrieked the girl.

And, indeed, her abductor lost no time in running away with her. 15
The girl was in the throes of panic and continued to yell, "I've been kidnapped by the Demon Pukuj!"
And she was indeed being taken off by the Demon Pukuj.

Well, now, the Demon Pukuj carried the woman off, embraced in his arms to his own house. 16
And his bull-roarer hummed as they went along.

"Our older sister has been kidnapped by the Demon Pukuj! 17
Sic 'm! Sic 'm!" yelled her younger brothers to the dogs.
But the brothers themselves remained standing there helplessly under the front eaves of the house.

18 k'alal k'ot ta snae la jyik' batel ta stem.
laj la spajbe ta ˀora ti yate.

19 ˀay ˀay ˀay xi la ti tzebe.
mu xaˀok' nich'on.
mu xaˀok' nich'on.
ˀok'om ta xibat jkomesot ta ˀana.

20 jaˀ noˀox ta jpas reva mi leke.
mu xaxiˀ xi la ti vinike.

21 ˀentonse ti tzebe ˀoch la svayel.
muˀyuk xa la bu ta xbak'.

22 ˀentonse ti vinike laj la stzan skantin.
ta la sk'el mi yuˀun cham ti tzebe.
jaˀ la ti muyuk' ta xbak'e.

23 ˀech'o xal la stzan skantin.
veno laj la sk'el.
muˀyuk la chamem ti tzebe.

24 ˀentonse yuˀun ta sk'an yan ˀat chaˀe.
xi la ti vinike.

25 lik la yak'be yan ˀat xtok.
laj la yak'be tajmek.
ti tzebe te la talel ta ba tem.

26 vaˀiˀun ti vinike chik'inaj la.
tz'uj la yalel xchik' ta sat ti tzebe.
veno julav la ti tzebe.

27 taloˀun pukuj taloˀun pukuj xi la ti tzebe.
xamala jlikel xamala jlikel mu xaˀok xi la ti vinike.

When the abductor reached his house he took her to his bed. 18
In no time, he impaled her with his dick.

"Ay, ay, ay!" cried the girl. 19
"Don't cry, daughter of mine.
Don't cry, my dear.
Tomorrow I plan to take you home.

I'm just trying a little sample to see if it's good. 20
Don't be afraid," said the man reassuringly.

With that, the woman fell sound asleep. 21
She no longer stirred in the slightest.

Then the man lit his lantern. 22
He wanted to see if perhaps the girl had died.
For, indeed, she scarcely moved at all.

That is why he lit his lantern. 23
Well, he checked her out.
And the girl was not dead.

Then the man said to himself: "Maybe the problem is that she wants some more sex." 24
That is what the man speculated.

He proceeded to fuck her once again. 25
He really poked it to her.
There she was, flat on her back on top of the bed.

Now, in the midst of all this, the man started to sweat. 26
His sweat dripped down onto the girl's face.
And with this, the girl woke up.

"Enough, demon!! No more, demon!" cried the girl desperately. 27
"Wait a minute! Wait a minute! Don't cry," replied the man.

28 porke ti tzebe mu snaˀ mi ˀaˀ ti vinik ˀay k'anvanuke.
ta k'un to la jyil ta ˀaˀ ti vinik ˀay k'anvanuke.
ˀaˀ to ti chik'inaje la jyojtikin.
ˀaˀ ti vinike.

29 chik'inaj tajmek.
lok' la skotol ti sbon sate.
lok' ti xepuˀe ti xch'aˀilal semete.

30 ˀech'o xal la jyojtikin ti tzeb.
maˀuk ti pukuje.

31 ˀi voˀot kaˀ maryan.
ˀa ti xkal voˀone pukuj ne.
liyik'batel ta xch'en ˀanimal.

Indeed, the girl had not realized that this man was the one who had sought permission to marry her. 28
Slowly she came to realize that he was indeed her suitor.
Only when he began sweating did she recognize that it was none other than he.
It was that very man!

He really sweat a lot. 29
Off came the coloring from his face!
Off came the tallow and soot from the tortilla griddle!

In this way, the girl was able to recognize who he was. 30
And that he was not, in fact, the Demon Pukuj.

"Oh, it was really *you*, Marián! 31
I was just *sure* it was the Demon Pukuj,
And that he had carried me off to some animal den.

FIGURE 87

"Oh, it was really *you*, Marián!
I was just *sure* it was the Demon Pukuj,
And that he had carried me off to some animal den."

32 mu xak'exav laj xa ˀapas ta reva ti jbek'tale.
pere xkal voˀone pukuj ne.

33 muˀyuk bu kaˀi k'uxi lital.
muˀyuk bu kaˀi k'uxi li vul ta ch'en xi la ti tzebe.

34 moˀoj voˀon jmaryanun mu xaxiˀ.
ˀok'om chijbat jk'opontik ˀatot ˀameˀ yuˀun chakik'.
mu ˀecheˀuk chakutilan xi la ti vinike.

35 mu xak'exav xi la ti tzebe.
ˀentonse ˀech la jyik' sbaik xchiˀuk ti vinike.

36 chik'inaj la ti k'alal syakel ta xˀabtej ta sba ti ˀantze.
ˀech'o xal lok' skotol ti sbon sate.

37 ˀentonse k'alal lok' skotol sbon sat ti vinike ti ˀantze la jyojtikin.
ˀaˀ kirsanoe.
maˀuk pukuj.

38 vaˀi ˀun ti vinike ˀabtej la ˀep tajmek.
yuˀun la ti ˀantze toj lek la tajmek.
ˀech'o la xal ˀep ˀabtej.

39 vaˀi ˀun k'alal lub ta ˀak' ˀat ti vinike ˀivayuk xchiˀuk ti ˀantze.
veno k'alal sakub ta yok'omale bat sk'opon li smuniˀe.
bat xchiˀuk ti ˀantze.

40 veno ti smuniˀe la sjak':
k'uchaˀal la la ˀavik'bun ˀel li jtzeb ta ˀak'obaltike xi la stot ti tzebe.

41 pere k'elavil tata mo kuˀun ta jmul.
k'uchaˀal lok' k'abinuk la ˀanich'one.
la jyak'bun kil li sbek'tale.

But, really, don't have regrets about taking advantage of me. 32
I thought all the time that you really were the Demon Pukuj.

I have no idea how I got here. 33
I don't know how I got to this cave," declared the girl.

"Come, come, now. It's really me, Marián. Don't be afraid. 34
Tomorrow, I'll go to talk to your parents about marrying you.
I have not caused you all this hassle and trouble without sincere intentions of marrying you," said the man.

"Don't worry about it anymore," replied the girl. 35
And with that, the two of them decided to get married.

He had worked up a powerful sweat when he was in the midst of his labors on top of the woman. 36
That is how the stain washed off his face.

Then, when all of the stain came off his face, the woman recognized him. 37
He was indeed a person.
No way was it the Demon Pukuj.

Well, in truth, the man got quite a workout. 38
For the woman was very, very attractive.
That's why he worked so hard!

Finally, when the man got tired of fucking, he went to sleep beside the woman. 39
And then, when the next day dawned, he went to speak with his father-in-law.
He went to see him with the woman at his side.

Whereupon, the father-in-law asked: 40
"Why did you abduct my daughter in the middle of the night?" demanded the girl's father.

"Look at it this way, sir.[4] It wasn't really my fault. 41
Why did your daughter provoke me by going out to pee?
She really gave me quite a nice show of her body.

42 ˀech'o xal ˀun ta jpas kaˀi mi tun kuˀun la ˀanich'one.
la jkik' ˀel ta jch'en xi la ti pukuje.

43 pere maˀuk pukuj kirsano.
ˀaˀ noˀox ta sk'an ta xˀal ˀecheˀ.

44 veno k'usi ta jtoj la ˀanich'one xi la ti pukuje.
batan ta tzoˀ kavron xi la stot ti tzebe.

45 jlikel la smaj ti pukuje.
te la balch'uj ti pukuje.

46 k'alal yil laj ta majel smalal ti ˀantze bat ta ˀanil jlikel.
ˀijatav.
te batla ta teˀtik.

47 ˀech ti vinik jatav.
muˀyuk bu la stoj ti yajnile,
mu la snaˀik k'uxi bat.

Therefore I felt the need to sample her, to see if your daughter 42
could suit my tastes.
So I took her to my cave," said the demon insolently.

(But, it will be recalled, he was no demon, but rather, a person. 43
He just felt like talking in a teasing, bantering manner.)

"Well, then, how much bride-price would you like me to pay 44
for your daughter?" asked the former demon.
"Go to hell, you son of a bitch," replied the girl's father.

And in a flash, he landed one good blow at the former demon. 45
It knocked the former demon flat, right then and there.

When the woman saw her new husband receive this pounding, 46
she got out of there fast.
She fled.
She took off into the woods.

The man eventually fled as well. 47
He never did pay for his wife,
And no one ever found out what became of him.

1 ˀoy jun kuento sventa jxanobaletik ta voˀnee.

2 jech la ti moletike ta la xbatik ta xanobal ta katarina.
ti moletike ta la saˀik ta ˀech'el yikatzik.
ta la xbat ba xchonik ta katarina.

3 ti k'utiksi la ta smanik la ˀech'ele ˀun,
vaˀun ta la xbatik ˀune.

4 ta la xˀich'ik la ˀech'el yaˀalik.
ti bu la ta xtakij yoˀntonik la ta be la ˀune ta la xˀuch'ik ti yaˀalik la ˀune.

5 vaˀun laj la ti ˀoˀ ˀune.
jech la ti moletik la ˀune batik la saˀik ti ˀoˀe,
ch'abal la ti ˀoˀ tajmeke.

6 vaˀun batik ˀun chaˀe.
k'eltikik bu jtatik ti ˀoˀe xiik ti moletike.

7 vaˀun batik la tajmek ˀun,
ch'abal ˀo xa la ti ˀoˀ ˀune.

8 ta la xˀuch' la yaˀik tajmek ti ˀoˀ la ˀune.
te k'alal ˀun chaˀe.
jkuch'tik ti jk'abtike xiik la ˀun.

9 ta me xik'abin.
kaˀ voˀone xi la ti moletike.

TEXT 61

OF DROUGHT AND FLOOD

Marián López Calixto

Here is a story of long ago about travelling merchants. 1

It is about some old men who used to walk back and forth between 2
Chamula and Santa Catarina Pantelhó.[1]
These old men would put together bundles of things for sale.
Then they would go to peddle them in Santa Catarina.

Once they had purchased whatever they were going to take for sale, 3
They would set off on their journey.

They were accustomed to carrying drinking water with them. 4
Whenever they were thirsty, they would drink from their water supply.

Then, one day, the water supply ran out. 5
They searched and searched for water,
But there was simply none to be found.

With that, they said: "Let's be on our way. 6
Let's see if we can find water further on," said the old men.

They went a long way looking for water, 7
But there was simply none to be found.

They had become desperately thirsty. 8
"Well, what's to be done?
Let's drink our piss," they said.

"I'm going to pee. 9
I'll kneel down and bend over to catch it better," said one of the old men.

10 vaʔun k'abinik la ʔun.
jech la ti sk'abin la ʔune xch'amik la ta spixolik.
yuch'ik ti sk'abin la ʔune.
sbalin to la ti yoʔntonik la ʔune.

11 vaʔun k'otik la ta katarina la ʔun.
sk'anik la k'otel ti ʔoʔ la ʔune.

12 jech la ti ʔoʔ la ʔune.
toston la jun boch' ti ʔoʔ la ʔune.
k'ot la spuk'ik ti smatz'ik la ʔune.

13 ch'abal la ti ʔoʔ la ʔune.
jaʔ ʔo la k'epel ti banamil la ʔune.
yorail la korixma ti banamile.

14 vaʔun xchonik la komel la ti sbolomalik ti moletik la ʔune.
vaʔun k'alal cham la skotol ti sbolomalik la ʔune,
smanik la talel ti ʔixime ti chenek' la ʔune.

Then they peed. 10
  They collected their piss in their hats.
  Then they drank their piss.
  It helped to quench their thirst a little bit.

Soon they got to Santa Catarina. 11
  There they asked for water.

But there were problems with the water supply. 12
  A gourd cupful of water cost a *tostón*.[2]
  This bit of water they mixed with tortilla dough to make atole.[3]

There was simply no water anywhere. 13
  For it was the clear season of the year when there is seldom
    a cloud in the sky.
  It was the time of the annual dry season.[4]

Well, the old men sold their goods. 14
  Once they had gotten rid of their goods,
  They bought corn and beans.

FIGURE 88

Then they peed.
  They collected their piss in their hats.
  Then they drank their piss.
  It helped to quench their thirst a little bit.

15 ta yokik la ta xtalik ti moletik la ˀune.
k’alal la ta xtalik la ˀune ta la xˀuch’ la ˀep tajmek ti ˀoˀ la ˀune.

16 vaˀun k’alal la mi ta xk’abinik la yaˀi ˀune ta la xˀuch’ik ˀun.
jech la ti yan jxanobaletik lae te la schamuk la ta be.

17 ti povre kirsanoetike.
muˀyuk la bu la jutebuk ti ˀoˀe.

18 ˀulem la ti ˀuk’ume.
takin la tajmek ti banamile.

19 toj ˀabol sbaik toˀox ti ˀantivoetiok.
ch’abal toˀox la ti ch’ivit liˀ ta chamulaˀe.
jaˀ yuˀun la ˀun ti nom la ta xbatik ti kirsanoe la ˀune.

20 vaˀun k’un to la tal ti ˀoˀ la ˀune.
jech la ti ˀoˀ la ˀune.
chanib la k’ak’al yak’ ti ˀoˀ la ˀune.

21 jech la ti kirsano la ˀune noj la ta ˀoˀ la ˀun.
jech la ti povre kirsano la ˀune.

22 ˀoy la yuni sna.
ta slomlej ti yane.
noj la kom ta ˀoˀ.
ˀi t’uxi la ti spak’bal ti snaike.

23 vaˀun ˀoy la yuni ˀolik:
vayem la kom la ta tem ti ˀolole.

24 vaˀun jech la ti stot ti smeˀ ti ˀolol la ˀune:
lok’ jatavuk ta ˀora ti stot ti smeˀ ti ˀolol lae.

25 jech la ti ˀolol la ˀune:
te la cham ta ˀoˀ ti yolike.

Then they started the long walk home. 15
But before they departed, they drank a lot of water.

Whenever they wanted to pee, they drank their piss. 16
Other travelers who did not resort to this measure died right there on the road.

Poor people! 17
They didn't have even a drop of water!

The streams dried up. 18
The land was incredibly dry.

The truth of the matter is that our ancestors had a hard time of it. 19
For there was still no market in Chamula.
That's why the people had to go so far away to buy and sell.

Well, in time, the rains came. 20
And how it rained!
It rained for four days without stopping.

This deluge brought awful floods to the community. 21
This is what happened to the poor people.

They had their small houses. 22
And some of these caved in on their inhabitants.
The houses filled up with floodwater.
And the mud walls, soaked and weakened with the water, collapsed.

As for their small children: 23
There was a child who was left sleeping on the bed during the flood.

As for the child's father and mother: 24
The parents were fleeing for their lives.

But as for this child: 25
Their child died in the sodden mass of the collapsed house.

26 vaˀun k'alal la paj ti ˀoˀ la ˀune bat la sk'elik ti yolike.
vaˀun jech ti smeˀ stot la ti ˀolol la ˀune ˀoch la sk'el ti yolik la ˀune.

27 jech la ti yolik la ˀune:
te la puch'ul la ta stem ti ˀolole.

28 vaˀun jech la ti ˀolol la ˀune k'aˀel xa la ˀun.
vaˀun ti smeˀ la ˀune tzotz la ba stzak la ti yol la ˀune.

29 jech la ti yol la ˀune k'oˀ xa la ˀun.
jech la ti yol.
noj la lukum ta sbek'tal la ti ˀolol la ˀune.

30 jech la ti smeˀ ti ˀolol la ˀune k'alal la spet tzotz la ti yol.
jech la ti smeˀ la ti ˀolol ˀune:
toj ˀochel la sk'ob ta sbek'tal la ti yol la ˀune.

31 noj la lukum.
noj la ˀoˀ ta xch'ut ti ˀolol la ˀune.

32 jech la ti yol la ˀune,
jun la stuˀil tajmek ti yol lae.

33 jech la ti smeˀ la ˀune muˀyuk bu la smuk.
sjip la ˀech'el ta ˀoˀ la ti yole.

34 vaˀun jech ti ˀoˀ la ˀune.
lok'anan la stuk ta banamil la ti ˀoˀ la ˀune.
ˀi muˀyuk xa la bu ˀulanuk xa la ti ˀoˀ ˀune.

35 ˀi muˀyuk xa la bu mas la k'ep la ti banamil la ˀune.
ˀi ta xa la xˀak'olan lek li ˀoˀ la ˀune.
vaˀun ˀoy xa la lek ti ˀoˀ xkuch'tik la ˀune.

36 jaˀ jech la ti ˀantivoetike lae.
xi la jyalbun jun mol ta paraje tzajal ch'en.

37 yuˀun te li bat ta ˀabtel ta tzajal ch'en.
ˀi jaˀ te lik ˀo ti kuento ˀune.

When it stopped raining, they went to see about their baby. 26
The parents of the child went back in the house to check on their baby.

But this is what had become of their baby: 27
The child was lying facedown on the bed.

The child's body had already begun to decompose. 28
Then the mother grabbed up her baby in her arms.

The child's body had already begun to rot; 29
Her baby was in bad shape.
The baby's body was crawling with maggots.

The child's mother then pressed her baby to her breast. 30
And this is what happened to the mother of the child:
Her hand broke into the rotten flesh of her baby.

It was full of worms. 31
And the child's stomach was full of fluid.

And what's more, 32
The body of the child gave off an awful stench.

The mother did not bury her child. 33
She simply tossed the child in the water.

Such was the flood. 34
The water seemed to ooze forth from the very pores of the earth.
It seemed that it might never dry up again.

Nowadays, there are no longer such periods of severe drought. 35
Now it seems to rain just enough.
There is now water to drink in abundance.

This is an account of the ancestors. 36
An old man in Tzahal Ch'en hamlet told it to me.

I had gone there to work in Tzahal Ch'en hamlet. 37
It was there that the story came up in our talk.

38 k'alal lik ˀo ti kuentoe yuˀun k'epel tajmek.
jech ti mole:
ta xijchamotik xi ti mole.

39 laj ˀo.

When the subject of the story came up, it was because the weather 38
was getting very, very dry.
The old man said this to me:
"We are surely going to die," he said.

That is the end. 39

1 ˀoy jun kuento ta voˀnee.
xi ti juntote ˀo la viˀnal ˀech' ta mas voˀnee.
la jyalbun ti juntote.

2 jech la ti kirsanoetike laj la skuchik toˀox ˀixim.
ti moletike ˀixaˀik to la ˀo la jech skuchik toˀox ti ˀixim ˀune.

3 laj to la spokik ti spatik ti povre kirsanoetike.
toj ˀabol sbaik totil meˀiletike.
te xa la xˀok'lajetik smal sakub ti kirsanoetike ti viˀnal ti voˀnee.

4 ˀo la jlom ti kirsanoetike laj la saˀik sjol ti tzibe.
ˀaˀ xa la ti k'usi sk'uxiik ˀoe.

5 ˀo to la bu xaˀik ti kirsanoetike bu ˀo to la ˀoy ti ˀiximike.
bat to la saˀik ti ˀixime.
te to staik jun teˀ.

6 ti yanee buch'u staike ˀaˀ xa la te kuxul.
buch'u xa la ch'abal ti yiximike chamanuk la.

7 ˀaˀ xa la ti k'usi staanike:
mi pat loˀbol.
mi pat valeˀ.
mi pat naranja.
naka la smatz'el ti k'usi xa la staik ti sveˀelike ti voˀnee.

TEXT 62

About the Great Famine

Marián López Calixto

This is a story of times past.[1] 1
My uncle said that there was once a famine a long time ago.
My uncle told this to me.

This was in the time when people still worked as cargo bearers, carrying corn on their backs.[2] 2
The old men still have memories of those times when they worked as cargo bearers of bags of corn.

These poor people had to resort to washing their backs to extract the essence of the corn.[3] 3
The ancestors were, indeed, this miserable and poor.
There, each afternoon and morning long ago, people would cry from hunger.

There were some people who went out to gather the corms of ferns. 4
That is what they were reduced to eating.

There were some people who would go out to look for corn where it had once grown in the fields. 5
They would go out, hoping to find corn.
But they would find nothing there but dried up cornstalks.

There were others who found a bit of corn, and it was these people who survived. 6
Those who had no corn were likely to die.

There might be something lying around: 7
Maybe a banana peel.
Maybe a peeling of sugarcane.
Maybe an orange peel.
They would just pick up anything they found and suck on it for sustenance in times past.

8 k'alal la ˀoy ti viˀnale muˀyuk xa la bu ta xanavik ta be mi ta paxyal.
yuˀun xa la ch'abal junuk ti kirsanoetike ta bee.

9 solel xa la naka ˀaˀ puch'ajtik ta stemik.
ˀaˀ xa la ti yoˀontonike k'ux la tajmek.
solel xa la bak'ik ta viˀnal tajmek.

10 mi napuxuk xa la k'usi xa stam.
solel la ch'abal tajmek la loˀel.
toj chopol la ti viˀnal ti ˀech' ti voˀnee.

11 solel toj k'epel tajmek.
puru la taˀiv tajmek jujun k'ak'al tajmek.

12 jech' ti jkaxlanetike,
solel xa la ta xˀok'ik tajmek.

13 jech ti yane buch'u xa la ˀoy syentaˀike.
ˀaˀ xa la sk'uxik ti kayetaetike.

14 laj la kayeta stok.
solel xa ta xilajotik xi la ti jkaxlanetike.

15 pero muˀyuk chijchamotik ˀo yuˀun ti viˀnale.
kuch ta persa kuˀuntik.
pere ˀep li jchamotik ˀo noˀox kastiko yak' ti jtotike tajmeke.

16 k'uchaˀal.
yuˀun toyol la jiptik ti ˀixime.

17 jech'o ˀal la jyak' ti kastikoe.
jech ti kirsanoetik ˀune muˀyuk xa ta sjipik ti ˀixime.

18 yich'oj xa ta k'ux ti yiximike.
toj chopol yaˀik.

During these times of famine, no one was to be seen walking along the road for any reason, not even for pleasure. 8
There was not a single soul to be seen on the road.

They would just lie there in their beds. 9
Their hearts grieved.
Their bodies shrank to skin and bones from the famine.

There were no longer even radishes to be found. 10
There was simply nothing to eat.
This famine that happened long ago was really terrible.

The sky was clear day in and day out. 11
To make matters worse, the heaviest of frosts fell each and every day.

As for the Ladinos, 12
They, too, were reduced to simply weeping.

Even those who had stores, 13
They were reduced to eating crackers.

Then even the crackers ran out. 14
"Now, we are simply going to die," said the Ladinos.

"But we will endure this famine," said the Chamulas. 15
"We've got to survive."
But many of us did indeed die of the great punishment sent by Our Father Sun.

Why did all of this happen? 16
It was because we wasted a lot of corn.

That was the reason that Our Father Sun sent the punishment. 17
And that is why people no longer waste corn.

They now respect their corn. 18
And they realize that they once behaved badly.

1 jun kuento sventa moletik.

2 k'alal ch'i?ik tal ti moletike ti vo?ne lae:
toj lek to?ox la xch'i ti xchobike.
toj lek to?ox la xch'i ti sjavaxe.
toj lek to?ox la xch'i ti botil chenek'e.
toj lek to?ox la xch'i ti ?ibeschenek'.
toj lek to?ox la xch'i ti ranjero ?isak'e.
toj lek to?ox la xch'i ti smaile.

3 k'alal la ta x?ech' ti k'in san juane,
?oy xa la siyal ti xchobike.

4 k'alal la ta x?ech' ti k'in ta santa roxae,
ta xa la sk'anub ti xchobike.

5 toj lek to?ox ti banamil ti vo?nee.
xi ti anima jyayae ti vo?nee.

6 jech to?ox skotol ti kirsano ti vo?nee.
ti k'alal lek to?ox ti banamile.

7 ta muk' ta sak ta xlik ya?luk ti ?o?e.
jech ?o xal ti yo? ta ?ora ta xch'i ti chobtike.

8 yu?un sob ta xyal ?o,
ta k'in rosario ?oy xa?ox ?ach' ?ixim.

9 ti mas vo?ne tajmeke toj lek to?ox ti banamile.
xi ti ?anima jyaya?e.

TEXT 63

On How the Old-Timers Became Impoverished, Just Like Their Land

Manuel López Calixto

This is an account of how things were in the youth of those who 1
are now old men.

When those who are now old men were young children long ago:[1] 2
Cornfields still prospered and flourished.
Fava beans still prospered and flourished.
Scarlet runner beans still prospered and flourished.
Kidney beans still prospered and flourished.
White potatoes still prospered and flourished.
Squash still prospered and flourished.

At the time of the festival of San Juan,[2] 3
There would already be tender green beans growing amid the cornfields.

At the time of the festival of Santa Rosa,[3] 4
The tender ears of corn would already be turning yellow in the fields.

The earth was good and fertile long ago. 5
So said my late grandmother long ago.

That was what all people could still enjoy long ago, 6
When the earth was still good and fertile.

In the month of Muk'ta Sak, the rainy season would begin. 7
That is how the cornfields would get off to a good start.[4]

Since the rainy season began earlier then than now, 8
It was common to have new corn by the time of the festival
of the Virgen del Rosario.[5]

Long, long ago the land was still good and fertile. 9
So said my late grandmother.

10 ta k'unk'untik me ˀun.
mu xa bu ta xlok' yaluk ˀoˀ ta muk' ta sak.

11 ta xtal ti ˀoˀe.
pere jutuk ˀoˀ ta xak' ti ˀoˀe.

12 jech ˀo xal ti yoˀ lik sokik ti banamile.
ta k'unk'untik me lik ch'aiyuk stz'unobal ti javaxe.
ti ˀibeschenek'.
ti botil chenek'e.
ti ranjero ˀisak'e.

13 skotol lik la me ch'ayuk stz'unobal.
ti k'usi ˀoye.

14 ˀoy toˀox la ˀep xchijik ti moletike.
jech ˀo xal ti yoˀ la lek toˀox la xch'iˀe.

15 yuˀun ta la xak'bik jutuk sk'aˀal.
ti k'alal ˀoy toˀox la ti xchijike.

16 ta la xak'anbik jujutiˀ sk'aˀal,
juju petz ti xchobike.

17 pere yuˀun sob ta la xyal ti ˀoˀe.
jech ˀo la xal ti jlikel la ta xch'i ti xchobik toˀoxe.

18 pere yuˀun lek toˀox la ti banamile.
lek toˀox la xch'i k'usi jtz'untik ti voˀne laˀe.

19 jech la ti moletike,
mu la snaˀ xk'otik ta pinka.

20 jaˀ noˀox la ta xbatik ta kich' ˀikatzil,
k'alal ta tuxta.
k'alal ta soktom.

Slowly, very slowly, things changed. 10
The rainy season no longer began regularly in the month of *Muk'ta Sak.*

The rains would come. 11
But not many, and it would not rain very much.

The quality of the soil began to decline. 12
Slowly, very slowly, people's plantings of fava beans started to fail.
The same thing happened to their plantings of kidney beans.
So, also, with their plantings of scarlet runner beans.
So, also, with their plantings of white potatoes.

All types of crops started to fail. 13
Everything that they were accustomed to planting.

The old-timers still had lots of sheep. 14
That is why crops still prospered in those days.

The reason was that the sheep produced a good bit of manure. 15
That was when the old-timers still had sheep.[6]

They would put a little manure on each one, 16
On each hill of corn in the cornfield.

But recall that the rains typically came early in the growing season. 17
That is why the cornfields still grew so well back then.

Yet it was also because the soil was more fertile in those times. 18
Anything we planted would grow well back in those days.

As for the old-timers, 19
They weren't accustomed to going to work in the coffee plantations
in the lowlands as day laborers.

The only wage labor they did was to work as porters and bearers, 20
To Tuxtla Gutiérrez.
To Chiapa de Corzo.

21 jaˀ noˀox la yabtelik ti voˀne laˀe.
ta la xlik yalel ta joˀbel.
ˀoy la yikatz ta xyal ˀel ta tuxta.
ˀoy la ˀikatz ta sut talel.

22 ti k'alal la ta ˀabtejike,
jaˀ noˀox ta staik ˀo ti stak'inike.
jaˀ la jech ta xveˀik ˀo ti moletik voˀnee.

23 k'alal la mi lik li ˀabtelike,
ta la xˀabtejik stukik ti buch'un la ˀep xchijike ti moletike.

24 ta la stz'un ˀep yitaj.
ta la stz'un stuixik.

25 puro la tzoˀchij.
ta xak'be sk'aˀal ti yitaje,
ti stuixe.

26 k'alal la mi yijub ti stuixe ta la skuch ˀel xchon.
k'alal ta xbat ta ˀabtel ta xanobale.

27 ˀentonse ta la xˀech' ta joˀbel,
ta la xˀech' skuchbe yikatz yajval ti moletik la ti voˀne laˀe.

28 jaˀ noˀox la yabtelik ti xanobale.
xchiˀuk la ti ˀabtel ta joˀbele.

29 ˀentonse k'alal la lek toˀox xch'iˀ ti xchobik lae.
ˀak'o la mi juteb ti yosilike pere ta la xlok' ˀep yiximik.
ti k'alal ta toˀox la xak' ti ˀoˀe.
jech ˀo la xal ti yoˀ ta toˀox la xch'iˀe ti xchobike.

30 ˀentonse ta jujun la me ˀavil lik ta sokuk ti banamile.
mu la me xyal likel ti ˀoˀe ta muk' ta sake.
mu xa la me bu ta xyal ti ˀoˀe.

That was really the only wage labor they did back then. 21
They would depart from San Cristóbal.
They would carry loads of goods on their backs down to
Tuxtla Gutiérrez.
Then they would carry loads of goods back up to the highlands.

When they did wage labor of this sort, 22
It was the only way they could obtain money.
This was how the old-timers made enough money to eat in the old days.

When day labor of this sort began, 23
About the only people who did it were those old-timers who had
lots of sheep.

They were able to grow lots of cabbage. 24
They would also plant onions.

As fertilizer, they used just sheep manure. 25
They would put it on their cabbage,
And on their onions.

When the onions were mature they would take them to sell. 26
It was at this time that they would also get work as haulers of goods.

As they passed through San Cristóbal, 27
These old-timers would get jobs as haulers of goods for
Ladino traders.[7]

This was about the only kind of wage labor the travelers did. 28
This and the jobs they found in San Cristóbal.[8]

So it was when cornfields still did well and prospered. 29
Even those who had small landholdings were able to get abundant
harvests of corn.
This was when it still rained enough to nurture the crops.
That was why cornfields yielded well.

Then, with each passing year, the productive strength of the soil declined. 30
The rains would no longer come on schedule in the month of *Muk'ta Sak*.
Sometimes there would be no rain at all.

31 lik la me k'epuk,
k'alal la ta stz'un ti xchobike.

32 jaʔo la me ta xlik k'epuk,
ti yoʔ la me mu xa xch'i ne.

33 jech la ti xchijike,
lik la lajuk ta jtiʔval ch'iʔ.
lik me lok'uk tal ti mu jtiʔval ch'iʔe.

34 ʔentonse jaʔ la me jech lik pasikuk ta povre ʔun ti moletik ʔeke ʔune.
laj to la yilik jlom ti moletike,
k'alal ch'ay ti stz'unobalike.

35 ʔentonse k'alal lik saʔ yajnilik ti snich'nabike,
lik la yak'anbe yosil xnich'nab ti moletike.
lik la stuch'anbe yosil ti snich'nabe.

36 buch'un la ʔep yosil ti stot smeʔe,
jaʔ la jamal yosil yich' yuʔun ti snich'nabe.

37 jech ʔo la xal ti yoʔ la ʔoy ʔep yosilik li kirsanoetik.
yuʔun jaʔ la ʔep yosil ti stot smeʔe.

38 yan la lik bu jutuk noʔox yosil ti stot smeʔe.
jech ʔo la xal ti yoʔo jujutiʔ ti yosilik lae.

39 ʔentonse jech ʔo la me xal ti yoʔ pura la ta pinka ta xʔabtejik li kirsano,
ti yuʔun puro la ta k'ixin ʔosil ta xʔabtejike.

40 yuʔun mu la xch'i lek.
xchiʔuk jujutiʔ xa la ti yosilike.

Clear skies came to be the pattern, 31
Even at the time of the accustomed planting season.

It was because of this, the extended dry season, 32
That the cornfields no longer did well.

As for the sheep, 33
They were increasingly plagued by coyotes.
Coyotes appeared in growing numbers.

So it was, in this manner, that the old-timers became impoverished, just like their land. 34
There are still some of these old-timers alive today,
Those who witnessed the decline in the productivity of the land.

Furthermore, when their sons sought wives and homes of their own, 35
The old-timers would divide up their land among their children.
They would cut up the land, giving a portion to each child.[9]

As for those who had parents with lots of property, 36
These children would be the lucky inheritors of large parcels.

That is why, to this day, there are people who own a lot of land. 37
The reason is simply that their parents had a lot of land.

Those people whose parents own but a little bit of land get quite a different start in life. 38
This explains why these people, like their parents, have just small parcels of land.

This also explains why there are some people who must work almost full-time as day laborers on the coffee plantations, 39
Why they must go to work almost all year in Hot Country.

It all started because things did not grow well any longer. 40
It was also because of the increasing scarcity of land.

41 ˀentonse k'alal la mi batik ta pinkae.
ta la staik talel jutuk stak'inik.
ta la xvul smanik ˀep ti yiximike.
jech ˀo xal ti yoˀ pura ta nom ta xˀabtejik ti kirsanoe.

42 ˀentonse ˀa ti buch'un puru pas chobtik ta xˀabtejik.
k'alal mi lok' lek ti xchobike ˀentonse ta xchon yiximike.
ta staik lek stak'inik li jpaschobtike.

43 ˀentonse li kirsanoetike koˀol ta smalk'in sbaik.
ˀentonse li jpinkajele jaˀ la puru ˀixim ta smanik,
ˀentonse li jpaschobtiketike jaˀ la puru ˀixim ta xchonik ˀeke ne.

44 jech ˀo la xal jlom jpaschobtik;
jlom jsaˀ tak'in;
ti yuˀun ta spasik jutuk kanale.

45 ˀentonse buch'un ch'abal xchobe jaˀ ta sman ˀixim.
ˀak'o mi ch'abal xchob jaˀ ˀep ta sman ti yiximike.

46 jech ˀo xal mu xaˀik viˀnal li kirsanoetike.
yuˀun puru tak'in ta spas kanal ti kirsanoe.

47 jaˀ jech skotol kirsano,
ˀak'o mi jpetejetik.

So it was when people would go to work on the coffee plantations. 41
They found they could earn a bit of money for themselves.
They could then buy plenty of corn when they got home.
That is why, to this day, so many people go so far away to work.

Now, there are some people who just do corn farming. 42
Whenever they get a good crop they can sell their surplus corn.
The corn farmers make good money this way.

In this manner, people support each other. 43
Just as coffee plantation workers are obliged to buy corn,
So the corn producers are able to make a living by selling corn.

So it is that some people are corn farmers; 44
Some are wage laborers;
This is how they earn a living.

So it is that those who have no cornfields have to buy corn. 45
But although they have no cornfields, they are able to buy
substantial quantities of corn.

For this reason people are not hungry. 46
For these people are able to earn wages.

This opportunity is available to everyone. 47
Even the people from Petej.[10]

1 kuento ˀok'il ta voˀne.
veno li ˀok'ile kirsano toˀox ti voˀne.

2 bat la ta pinka ti kirsanoetik xchiˀuk yajnilik.
ti k'alal ˀech' ti viˀnal ti voˀnee.

3 ti k'alal batik ta pinka ti kirsanoetike ˀoy toˀox la stak'inik ta la sman yotik.
ta be ˀoy la ta kolonya ti bu ta sman ti yotik.

4 komo ti voˀne muˀyuk toˀox la karo puru la ta yokik ta xanavik ti kirsanoetik ti k'alal ta xbatik ta pinkae.
vaxakib la k'ak'al ta xanavik ta yokik ti voˀnee.

5 veno k'otik la ta pinka ti kirsanoetik xchiˀuk ti yajnilike.
k'ot la sk'oponik ti ˀajvalile.

6 li talkutik patron.
mu jnaˀ mi mu xavak'bunkutik kabtelkutik.
yuˀun li talkutik jsaˀkutik ˀabtel xchiˀuk kajnilkutik xi la ti kirsanoetike.

7 ˀaaa . . . liˀe muˀyuk ˀabtel.
batan ta na.
ba vayan xchiˀuk ˀavajnilik.

8 k'uchaˀal lavik' talel ˀavajnil.
mi yuˀun snaˀ xˀabtej ˀaˀ lek.

9 sutanik ta naik.
liˀe muˀyuk ˀabtel xi la ti ˀajvalil ta pinka.

TEXT 64

About How Coyotes Came to Chamula

Xalik López Castellanos

This is a story of coyotes in times past. 1
Indeed, coyotes were people long ago.

Some men had gone with their wives to the coffee plantation. 2
This was during a time of famine long ago.

At the time when they went to the coffee plantation, they still had 3
a little money with which to buy tortillas.
There was a place on the road to the settlement of Belisario
Domínguez where they could buy tortillas.[1]

Since these were the times when trucks still did not exist, people 4
simply walked when they went to the coffee plantations.
It took them eight days to get there on foot from Chamula
in times past.

Well, these men and their wives got to the coffee plantation. 5
They found the owner of the coffee plantation and spoke to him.

"We have come, sir. 6
I wonder if you might give us work.
For we have come with our wives seeking work," said the men.

"I see . . . but there are no jobs available. 7
Go on home.
Go sleep with your wives.

Why did you bother to bring your wives? 8
If they were good workers, it might make sense.[2]

Go home. 9
There's no work here," said the owner of the coffee plantation.

10 veno ˀentonse ti kirsanoetik bat la saˀik yan ˀabtel ta yan pinka.
komo ˀoy ˀep pinkaetik.

11 k'otik la ta jun ˀo pinka.
sjak'ik la yabtelik.

12 sk'oponik la ti yajval pinka:
mi ˀoy ˀabtel liˀe patron xiik ti kirsanoetike.

13 liˀe muˀyuk ˀabtel.
ˀoy ˀep viniketik ta xˀabtejik ˀech xtok.

14 muˀyuk ˀixim xa.
veˀik ch'abal xi la ti yajval pinka.

15 veno tekeˀ chaˀe ta xibat xiik ti kirsanoetike.
batan xi la ti yajval pinkae.

16 bat la ti kirsanoetike.
sutik la talel ta snaik xchiˀuk ti yajnilike ti ˀantzetike.

17 ˀoy la yalabik.
ta la xˀok'ik ta viˀnal tajmek ti ˀololetike.

18 mu xaˀok'ik mu xaˀok'ik.
ta xajman kotik xi la stotik ti ˀololetike.

19 ˀentonse bat la sman ti yotik ta kolonya velisaryo rominko.
te la bat sman ti yotike.

20 k'alal k'otik ta kolonya muˀyuk vaj.
mu la snaˀik xchonik ti kirsanoetik ta kolonya.

21 chonbikun jutebuk tajmek ti vaje yuˀun chichamkutik ta viˀnal tajmek xi la ti viniketike xchiˀuk ti yajnilike.
muˀyuk vaj ch'abal liˀe.

22 skotol kirsano ta xchamik ta viˀnal.
muˀyuk xa yiximik.
ˀech'a ˀal muˀyuk ta xchonik vaj xi la ti yajval kolonya.

Well, with that, the people went to seek work on another coffee plantation. 10
For in the same region, there were lots of coffee plantations.

They came to another coffee plantation. 11
They asked for work.

They spoke to the owner of the coffee plantation: 12
"Do you have work, sir?" the people asked.

"There is no work here. 13
We've got plenty of men working here, indeed, too many.

There's no more corn. 14
There's nothing to feed them," said the owner.

"Very well then, we'll be on our way," said the people. 15
"Go then," said the owner of the coffee plantation.

So the people departed. 16
They set off for home with their wives, their womenfolk.

The women had their children with them. 17
The children were crying from hunger.

"Don't cry, don't cry. 18
We'll buy you some tortillas," said the children's parents.

Then they went to buy tortillas at the Colonia Belisario Domínguez. 19
It was there that they tried to buy tortillas.

When they got to the Colonia there were no tortillas at all. 20
The people in the Colonia were not willing to sell tortillas.

"Please, please, sell us a few tortillas, for we are really dying of hunger," 21
said the men and their wives.
"There are no tortillas. None at all.

Everyone is dying of hunger. 22
No one has any corn left.
That's why no one is selling tortillas," said the boss of the Colonia.

23 ʔentonse ti viniketik xchiʔuk ti yajnilike batik la.
jutuk la mu junuk k'ak'al xanavik ta yokik' xchiʔuk ti yajnilike.

24 pero ʔaʔ la ti snich'nab ti viniketike ta la xʔok'ik tajmek.
ʔentonse ti viniketik xchiʔuk ti yajnilike k'unibik la ta be.

25 te la skuxik.
te la chotiʔik.
pero ta la xviʔnajik tajmek xchiʔuk ti yajnilike ti snich'nabike.

26 veno te la chotiʔik ta be.
te la tal jun jkaxlan ti bu ʔoy chotolik ta be.

With that, the men and their wives departed. 23
For almost a day they continued on foot, these men and their wives.

The children of these men wept bitterly. 24
Then the men and their wives themselves began to feel faint as
they walked along in the road.

There they rested. 25
There they sat down.
For they were very hungry, these men, their wives, and their children.

Well, there they were, sitting in the road. 26
And along came a Ladino there where they were sitting in the road.

FIGURE 89

There they rested.
There they sat down.
For they were very hungry, these men, their wives, and their
children.

27 bu chabatik xi la ti jkaxlane.
chibat ta jnakutik.
yuˀun ˀa jsaˀkutik ˀabtel ta pinka.
pere muˀyuk bu xak' abtel ti ˀajvalil ta pinkae.

28 liˀe ta xichamkutik ta viˀnal tajmek.
mu jnaˀ mi chik'otkutik ta jnakutik.

29 ta ˀox jman kotkutik ta kolonya pero mu xchonik.
ˀech xtok ch'abal xa ˀep jtak'in.
liˀe yik'al xichamkutik ta be xchiˀuk jnich'nabkutik xi la ti viniketik ti voˀnee.

30 veno mi yuˀun chachamik ta viˀnale ˀaˀ lek batanik leˀ ta vitze.
ˀoy ˀep veˀlil tey.
ˀaˀ lek batanik ta ˀora leˀ ta vitz,
xchiˀuk ˀanich'nabik ˀavajnilike.
xˀutatik la ti kirsanoetike.

31 veno batik la ti viniketik xchiˀuk ti yajnilike.
laj la xch'unik la.
batik la.

32 te la tuk' batik ta vitz.
ti bu lajyal ti jkaxlane.

33 k'alal k'otik ta vitze te la ta xvay staik teˀtikal chij t'uletik maˀilchonetik.
lik la ta ˀora ti teˀtikal chije ti t'ule ti maˀilchone.

34 ˀentonse ti viniketike bat la stzakik ta ˀora.
jlikel ˀa la smilik ta machita ti teˀtikal chije ti t'ule ti maˀilchone.
la smilik.

35 veno k'alal laj smilik ti teˀtikal chije ti t'ule ti maˀilchone lik la stiˀik xchiˀuk ti snich'nabike xchiˀuk ti yajnilike.
veno k'alal syak'el xa ta stiˀik ti teˀtikal chije ti t'ule ti maˀilchone jlikel la lok' sneik ta ˀora xchiˀuk ti yajnilike xchiˀuk ti snich'nabike.

"Where are you going?" inquired the Ladino. 27
"We're going home.
For we were looking for work on the coffee plantations.
But the boss would not give us work.

Here we are, dying of hunger. 28
We wonder if we will even make it home.

We tried to buy tortillas in the Colonia, but they wouldn't sell us any. 29
What's more, we haven't got much money left.
Here on the road we will soon die of hunger, children and all,"
said these men of long ago.

"Well, since you're dying of hunger you'd better head for the hills. 30
There's lots of food there.
You'd best be off for the hills right away,
You and your wives and children."
So it was said to these people.

With that, these men and their wives set off for the hills. 31
They took the Ladino's suggestion seriously.
And off they went.

They headed straight for the hills, 32
To the place that the Ladino had told them about.[3]

When they reached the wooded slopes of Motozintla Mountain, 33
They found deer, rabbits, and armadillos living there.
Suddenly, the deer, the rabbits and the armadillos got up and ran off.

The men went at once to hunt them down. 34
In no time at all, they killed deer, rabbits, and armadillos with their
machetes.
They killed them dead.

Once they had bagged the deer, the rabbits, and the armadillos, the men 35
and their wives and children began to eat their meal.
Once they were well started on their meal of deer, rabbit, and armadillo,
the men and their wives and children sprouted tails.

36 veno skotolik lok' sneik.
ta ˀora joybijik la ta ˀok'il skotolik ti kirsanoetik xchiˀuk yajnilik xchiˀuk snich'nabik.

37 te kom ˀo ta xchanul teˀtik.
pas ta ˀok'il ti kirsanoetike.

38 te kom ta svitzal motosinta.
muˀyuk xa bu sutalel ta snaik.

39 ˀech'a ˀal ˀoy xa ˀep ˀok'iletik tajmek.
ˀoy xa skotol banumil.

40 pero k'alal tal ti ˀok'il ta chamoˀe ˀoy la chaˀvoˀ viniketik.
tey la ˀech' talel ta svitzal motosinta.

41 lik la talel ta tapachula.
ˀoy la saˀik ˀabtel.

42 ˀentonse sutik tal ta snaik.
tey ˀech'ik talel ta svitzal motosinta ti chaˀvoˀ viniketike.

43 veno k'alal ˀech'ik talel tey ta svitzal motosinta te ˀoy staik neneˀ tz'iˀetike ta bee.
koˀol la xchiˀuk tz'iˀ yilel.
xˀok'ik ti neneˀ tz'iˀetike ta bee.

44 entonse ti viniketike jlikel ta spetik ta ˀora ti neneˀ tz'iˀetike.
bat la ta snaik k'alal ta sparaje.

45 kontentoik xa la ti viniketike bat ta snaike,
ˀaˀ la ti ˀoy xa stz'iˀike.

46 laj la xkuchik batel.
k'alal k'otik ta snaik ti viniketike k'ot la yak' veˀuk ti neneˀ tz'iˀe.
lek la veˀ ti neneˀ tz'iˀe.

Sure enough! All of them grew tails! 36
And at once, those people changed into coyotes, the men, their wives, and their children, all of them.

There they remained as beasts of the forest! 37
These people had become coyotes!

There they stayed on Motozintla Mountain. 38
And they never went home again.

That's why there are lots and lots of coyotes around nowadays. 39
They are now found everywhere.

Now, there were two other men who were responsible for taking coyotes to Chamula. 40
They were passing by Motozintla Mountain on their way up into the highlands.

They had begun their journey in Tapachula. 41
They had gone to look for work there.

Then, they set off for home. 42
These two men were passing by Motozintla Mountain.

Well, as they were passing by Motozintla Mountain they found some puppies in the road. 43
They looked just like dogs.
These little puppies were whining and whimpering in the road.

The men lost no time at all in picking up the puppies to cuddle them. 44
Then they proceeded to head home for their hamlets in Chamula.

These men headed for home in a very happy mood, 45
For now they had dogs of their own.[4]

They carried these dogs along with them. 46
And once these men got home, they fed the puppies.
The puppies ate eagerly.

47 ˀentonse ti neneˀ tz'iˀe ch'i muk'ib.
veno k'alal ch'i ti nene tz'iˀe jatav ˀel ta teˀtik.

48 muˀyuk bu xˀil ti yajvale.
ta ˀak'obaltik jatav,
ti vinike ta xvay.

49 k'alal lik ta yok'omale muˀyuk xa ti stz'iˀ.
bat to la saˀ pero muˀyuk xa la bu sta ti sneneˀ tz'iˀe.

50 bat ˀo la ta jyalel.
mu xa la bu sta.

51 ˀech'a ˀal ˀoy xa ˀep ˀok'il tajmek ta chamoˀ.
bol xa ˀep tajmek.

52 pero ta belel pinka tal ti voˀnee.
ˀech xtok kirsano toˀox ti voˀnee.

Soon the puppies grew up. 47
Once the puppies had grown up they ran away into the woods.

Their masters did not see this happen. 48
They ran away during the night,
While the men were sleeping.

When the day dawned, their dogs were already gone. 49
They went out to look for them, but they were unable to find their puppies.

They had run away for good. 50
The men never succeeded in finding them.

That is why there are now so many coyotes in Chamula. 51
They multiplied rapidly in no time at all.

They came originally from the road to the coffee plantations. 52
What's more, they were once human.

1 jun kuento ta voˀnee.
jun vinik ta sloˀilajik ti voˀnee.

2 ta xˀal sloˀil sventa k'usi ta xvul ti jchon mantaetike.
ti k'alal ch'abal toˀox ti karoetike.

3 ˀentonse ti k'alal lik sloˀil ti vinike yuˀun la sman sk'uˀ.
jech ti sk'uˀe toj toyol la stojol la stoj.

4 ˀa ti voˀne la xˀal ti ˀanima jtote:
ti k'usi la jmantike lek toˀox la ˀutzik.
ti k'usi jmantike yalel toˀox la stojol ti voˀne la tajmek xi ti vinike.

5 ta sloˀilaj ta k'ixin ˀosil ti voˀnee.
ˀa ti moletik lae lek toˀox la ˀutzik stojol ti sk'uˀik lae xi ti vinike.

6 pere mu la yuˀunuk ta karouk ta xtal ti mantaetike ˀa ti voˀne lae.
puru la ta karita vakax ta xtal yuˀunik la ti smantaike ti jkaxlanetike lae.

7 jech la ti jkaxlanetike,
toj ˀabol toˀox la sbaik ti voˀne lae,
ti k'alal ch'abal toˀox la ti skaroike.
k'alal la ta xtal ti ˀikatziletike puru la vakax ta skuch talel.

8 jech la ti kaxlanetike,
ta la xbatik k'alal ta tuxta.
ta xbat yich' talel.
ta vakax la ta xmuy talel la yuˀunik.

TEXT 65

Memories of Times Past

EVERYTHING WE BOUGHT WAS A LOT LESS EXPENSIVE AND COFFEE PLANTATION WAGES WERE BETTER BACK THEN . . .

Manuel López Calixto

This story comes from long ago. 1
A certain man was recounting things of time past.

He was telling of how traveling cloth peddlers used to come by. 2
This was when there were still no trucks.

The man's comments came up when he was buying clothing. 3
It seemed to him that the clothing that was for sale cost far too much.[1]

He spoke: "My late father used to tell this: 4
'In times past, whatever we bought was cheaper.
Things we purchased cost a great deal less long ago,'" said the man.

He told this some time ago in Hot Country. 5
"The old-timers could buy clothing for much less back then,"
said the man.

"But in times past, manufactured cotton cloth did not arrive in trucks. 6
Ladinos still transported their cotton cloth in oxcarts.

As for the Ladinos, 7
Even they were still poor long ago,
At that time they still had no trucks.
In those days, they would bring their bundles of goods by oxcart.

As for the Ladinos, 8
They would travel to Tuxtla Gutiérrez.
They would go to bring their merchandise.
They would bring it back up to the highlands by oxcart.

9 jech la ti vakaxike,
ta la spasbik xonob ti yoˀ la mu xlaj yok ta xanobale.

10 jech la ti vakaxe,
mu la bu ta skux yuˀunik.
k'alal la ta ˀak'obaltik ta xanavik ti vakaxe.

11 jech ˀo la xal ti yoˀ ˀoy spasojbik xonobe ti svakaxtike.
yuˀun ta la xanav k'ak'al ˀak'obal.

12 k'alal ta xbatik ta paxyal ta tuxta li jkaxlanetike,
kojatik la ta vakax ta xbatik k'alal ta tuxta.

13 jech la ti skaritaike,
ˀoy la snaik spasojbil.
puru la xan slamojbik ti snaile skaritaike.

As for the oxen, 9
Their owners would make leather shoes for them so they would not injure their feet on the road.

As for the oxen, 10
They were not allowed to rest.
They were forced to walk even at night.

That is why they made leather shoes for their oxen. 11
So they could travel by day and night.

Whenever Ladinos would take a trip to Tuxtla Gutiérrez, 12
They would go all the way to Tuxtla by oxcart.

As for the oxcarts themselves, 13
They had them fixed up with little carriage compartments.
These compartments mounted on the oxcarts were covered with canopies of palm leaves like small houses.

FIGURE 90

As for the oxcarts themselves,
They had them fixed up with little carriage compartments.
These compartments mounted on the oxcarts were covered with canopies of palm leaves like small houses.

14 ja? li?e li talel ta ta tuxta.
ta xtal k'alal jo?bel ti jxanobaletike.

15 puru la ta karita vakax ta xlik tal ti jkaxlanetik lae.
sventa la skaro?ik ?ek ti vo?ne lae.

16 jech la ti jkaxlanetike:
k'alal ta xbatik ta yutil jo?bele ja? puru la karita ka? ?une.
xi ti vinike.

17 k'alal mi ta xbatik ta paxyale,
kajajtik la ta karita ka? ta xbatik ti jkaxlanetike.

18 jech la ti parke:
le kotajtik no?ox la ti karita ka?e.
chukajtik la ta yok' te?.

19 jech la ti parketike:
puru to?ox la te?etik tz'unbikil yu?unik ti jkaxlanetik lae.
ta yamak'il ti skavilto?ik lae.
xi ti vinike.

20 jech la ti vo?nee.
k'alal yalel to?ox la stojol ti k'usi jmantike.

21 pere k'alal la ta xbatik ta ?abtel ta jo?bele,
chib tak'in jun k'ak'al ti stojolik lae.

22 k'alal mi jmantik ti jk'u?tike,
vakib ta tak'in ta xchaplej la ti k'u?ile.

23 k'alal mi smanik ti bek'ete,
?oxib la toston ta kilo stojol ti bek'ete.

They would come all the way from Tuxtla riding in these carriage compartments. 14
This was the way the traveling peddlers made their way to San Cristóbal de Las Casas.

The Ladinos would come and go in just like this, by oxcart. 15
They used this means of transportation instead of trucks long ago.

Something else about the Ladinos: 16
When they traveled about within San Cristóbal, they used only horse-drawn buggies."
So spoke the man.

"When they would go about town, 17
The Ladinos would ride in these horse-drawn buggies.

As for the main plaza, the park, it was like this: 18
This was the central place where the horses and buggies were available for hire.
They were tied up to the trunks of the trees.

As for this park and others in San Cristóbal: 19
The Ladinos had planted trees in them that grew to a great size.
The central plaza in front of City Hall was like this, like a small forest."
So the man spoke.

"This is how things were long ago. 20
Whatever we purchased was still inexpensive.

But bear in mind that when people worked for wages in San Cristóbal back then, 21
They were paid only two *reales*.[2]

When we bought clothing, 22
A set of cotton shirt and pants would cost six *reales*.

When they bought fresh meat, 23
It would cost three *tostones* a kilo.

24 jech la ti sesinae,
lajuneb la sentavo jchuk stojol ti sesinae.
xi ti vinike.

25 ˀa ti voˀne lae toj yalel ta stojol ti k'usi la jmantike.
ˀutzik la tajmek toˀox mi jmantik la ˀora.
chanib la pexu stojol jun ti ˀorae.
ˀa pere toj toyol stojol xi la ti kirsanoetike.

26 k'alal la ta smanik spixolike,
chaˀvinik la sentavo stojol jun ti spixolik lae.

27 skotol la k'usi jmantik yalelik la stojol tajmek toˀox ti voˀne lae
xi ti ˀanima jtote.
xi ti vinike.

28 jech la ti ˀixime.
pexu la stojol jun ˀalmul ti ˀixim lae.

29 k'alal ta mi batik ta ˀabtel ta pinkae,
jaˀ la toston stojolik jun k'ak'al ne.
yuˀun jaˀ la lek toyol tojolil ta pinka lae.

30 jech ˀo la xal ti yoˀ la ta xbatik ta ˀabtel ta nome,
k'alal la yalel ti tojolile.

31 yalel stojol k'usi jmantik.
jech ˀo la xal ti yoˀ la yalel ti tojolile xi ti vinike.

32 yuˀun yalel la stojol k'usi jmantik ti voˀnee xi ti vinike.
ˀa pere jaˀ la ti mas la voˀnee tajmek.
xi ti vinike.

As for the dried meat jerky, 24
A tied bundle of salted, dried meat strips would cost ten centavos."
This is what the man said.

"Long ago, whatever we bought was very inexpensive. 25
Even if we bought a watch, it was still very inexpensive back then.
A watch would cost but four pesos.
Imagine how funny it sounds: 'Ah, this is very expensive,'
the people would say.

Long ago, when they bought hats, 26
These hats would cost only forty centavos.

'Everything we bought was a lot less expensive back then,' 27
my late father told me."
That is what the man said.

"It was the same with corn. 28
An *almud* of corn cost just one peso.[3]

When people back then went to the coffee plantations to work, 29
Their wages were but a *tostón* a day.
But plantation wages were really *high* wages back then.

That is why they were willing to go so far away to work, 30
Even when, from the perspective of today, the wages seemed low.

For indeed, what we had to buy was also inexpensive. 31
That is why wages were correspondingly low," the man said.

"Yes, everything we had to buy was cheaper back then," said the man. 32
"But this was long, long ago."
So the man spoke.

1 loˀil yuˀun ti moletik voˀnee.

2 vaˀiˀun ti jˀabteletik ta kavilto ti voˀnee mu la sk'an saˀik peserente
mi snaˀ vune,
mi snaˀ stz'ibaje,
mi snaˀ lek kastiyae.
mu la sk'anik xˀoch ta peserente.

3 ˀaˀ la ta saˀik ti bu mas mol tajmeke.
mu la snaˀ vun.
mu la snaˀ kastiya.
ˀaˀ noˀox snaˀ jutuk ta smeltzan ti kirsanoe.

4 ˀaˀ ta saˀik ti bu mas mol tajmeke.
ti bu mas boˀlate.

5 ˀech la la snopik skotol jˀabteletik,
skotol pasaroetik.

6 ti mi yuˀun la jsaˀtik peserente snaˀ vune mu xtun.
moˀoje stuk ta xich' smoton tak'in li voˀotikne.

7 ch'abal ˀun.
ˀaˀ lek ˀaˀ ta jsaˀtik ti bu mu snaˀ vune,
mu snaˀ stz'ibaje.

8 jaˀ ˀun bi koˀol ta xkich'tik jmoton tak'intik xchiˀuk peserente.
koˀol chijk'opojotik xchiˀuk peserente.
koˀol ta xkich'tik jmoton poxtik.

TEXT 66

Accounts from Old Men about Olden Times

Xalik López Castellanos

Accounts from old men about olden times.[1] 1

Now, the cargo holders of long ago did not want to name as *presidente* anyone who could read, 2
Anyone who could write,
Anyone who knew Spanish.
If he had these skills, they wouldn't have him as *presidente.*

They simply sought out the eldest man. 3
Even if he couldn't read.
Even if he didn't know Spanish.
He simply had to have some skill in solving problems and grievances according to customary practice.

They sought out whoever was oldest. 4
Whoever was most senile.

All of the cargo holders were of this opinion, 5
As well as all the past cargo holders.

They would say: "If we were to name as *presidente* someone who was literate, it would not be a good thing. 6
Imagine what it would be like! He would get all the bribe money and courtesy gifts that should really belong to all of us.[2]

That won't do. 7
Far better for us to find someone who can't read,
Who can't write.

That's right. We should all receive gifts of money the same as the *presidente.* 8
We speak out and participate in hearing grievances the same as the *presidente.*
We receive the same gifts of rum liquor.

9 ti mi yuˀun la jsaˀtik ti snaˀ vune muˀyuk xa bu ta xkich'tik jmoton
tak'intik,
jmoton poxtik.

10 ˀechotik ˀek mu xa xuˀ jmeltzantik kirsano.
mu xa xuˀ xijk'opojotik mas.

11 ˀaˀ xa noˀos ti peserente ta spasotik ta mantale.
xiik la ti jˀabteletike.

12 ˀech'o xal ta saˀtik ti peserente mas mole,
mas boˀlat tajmek.

13 mu xaˀi kastiya.
mu snaˀ vun.

14 ˀech'o xal ˀaˀ ˀech ta sk'anik ti jˀabteletike:
koˀol ta xich' smoton poxik.
koˀol ta xich' smoton tak'inik.
yuˀun mu snaˀ kastiya ti peserentee.

15 ˀech xtok muˀyuk toˀox mayoletik.
ta k'un to lik saˀik ˀalperesetik martomaetik.
ta k'un to lik saˀik meˀ jchabejsakromento,
ˀalvajanto syalel kurusil.
ta k'un to lik saˀik peserente bu snaˀ lek vune.
bu xaˀik lek kastiyae.

16 mas bij xa.
mas kerem to.

17 pero ta mas tz'akal xa.
muˀyuk xa bu la jkil.
muˀyuk toˀox vok'emun.

If we were to name someone above us who could read, we would 9
lose out on our courtesy gifts of money,
Our gifts of rum liquor.

If that were the case, he could no longer hear and resolve people's 10
problems.
We could no longer speak out with authority.

The *presidente* would simply order us around, 11
So said the cargo holders in their self-interested wisdom.

And that is why they supported the old custom of naming as *presidente* 12
whoever was the oldest man,
One who was good and senile.

He should not know Spanish. 13
Nor should he be literate.

That was why the old-time cargo holders wanted to keep the old 14
customs:
They would all receive the same gifts of liquor.
They would all receive the same gifts of money.
For the *presidente* did not know Spanish.[3]

At the time of which I speak, there were still no constables. 15
Later, they started recruiting standard bearers and stewards.
Later they started recruiting the ritual servants known as caretakers
of the sacrament,
Raisers of the holy image, and lowerers of the holy image from
the cross.
Later, they began recruiting for *presidente* someone who was literate.
Someone who understood Spanish.[4]

People such as these would presumably be smarter. 16
They would also be younger.

But all of this was to come later. 17
I myself did not see the older customs.
I was not yet born.

18 ˀaˀ noˀox ti ˀech liyalbe ti jtote,
yuˀun la ˀech la jyil.
ˀech'o xal ˀech liyalbe ti k'alal kusul toˀoxe.

☩ ☩ ☩

19 ˀech xtok muˀyuk toˀox jmuskero ta jujun k'in,
muˀyuk toˀox vakax k'ok' ta smanik ta joˀbel.

20 ˀoy vakax k'ok' pero svakax ˀinyo ta camulaˀ.
te noˀox ta spasik.

21 muˀyuk toˀox vompa.
ˀoy ˀaˀ noˀox yolon k'ok'e.
pero martoma ta smanik ta joˀbel.

22 ˀech xtok ta k'unk'un lik sk'elik lek ti jtotik ta ch'ulnae.
lik sbonik lek ti santoetike.

23 ˀech'o xal ˀoy xa ˀep martoma,
ˀoy xa ˀep ˀalperez.

24 ˀech xtok ti moletik muˀyuk toˀox skotonik manta.
puru tzotz skotonik.

25 ˀaˀ noˀox svex ˀoy manta.
ta sman ta jobel pero te ta stz'is stuk.
ˀaˀ noˀox ta sman li mantae.

26 ˀech li skapaike puru xan (ˀaxibal xan sbi).
te ta sjalik ta chamulaˀ ta yan parajel.

This is just what my father told me, 18
For that is what he saw.
So this is what he told me when he was still alive.

Likewise, in the old days, there were still no Ladino musicians at all the fiestas, 19
Nor were there *toritos* of the type that the people now buy in San Cristóbal.[5]

There were *toritos*, but they were *toritos* made by the Chamulas themselves. 20
They made them there in Chamula.

Likewise, in the old days there were still no hand cannons.[6] 21
There were just skyrockets.
The stewards would buy them in San Cristóbal.

Likewise, at about that time, they began to take better care of the images of the saints. 22
They began to paint the images of the saints.[7]

For this reason there are now many stewards, 23
There are now many standard bearers.

So also in the old days the old men did not wear shirts of manufactured cotton. 24
Their shirts were made of handloomed wool.

Only their pants were made of manufactured cotton cloth. 25
They would buy the cloth in San Cristóbal but would sew the pants themselves there in their homes.
The only part they bought was the manufactured cotton cloth.

As for their rain capes, these were made of palm leaves [of a type called "rain-cape palm"].[8] 26
They would weave them right there in Chamula Center and in other hamlets.

27 ˀech xtok lek toˀox xch’i javax,
batz’i ˀisak’,
ˀisak’ ranjero,
ˀibes,
xchiˀuk chobtik.

28 pero ta ˀora tana mu xa xch’i javax.
mu xa xch’i ˀibes.
mu xa xch’i batz’i ˀisak’.
mu xa xch’i ranjero ˀisak’.
mu xa xch’i chobtik.

29 ti voˀnee lek xch’i batz’i ˀisak’.
lek xch’i javax.
lek xch’i ˀibes.
lek xch’i chobtik.

30 pero ta ˀora tana mu xa xch’i skotol.
ˀaˀ noˀox ta xch’i jutuk chobtik,
xchiˀuk ˀitaj,
xchiˀuk jutuk ranjero ˀisak’.

31 ˀech xtok jutuk xa ta xak’ ˀoˀ.
mechuk toˀox ti voˀnee.

32 ta xak’ ˀep ˀoˀ tajmek.
ta xak’ ˀep ˀoˀ ta junyotik.
ta ˀakosto ta spaj li ˀoˀe.
ta setyempre ta xak’ mas ˀoˀ.
ˀaˀ to ta xˀech’ jutuk ta ˀoktuvre.

33 pero tana jutuk xa ta xak’ li ˀoˀe.
yuˀun ta xak’ kastiko jtotik ta vinajel.
yuˀun li kirsanoe toj toyol ta xk’opojik.
toj toyol ta smil sbaik.
toj toyol ta stzaˀanik.

So also in the old days, the fava beans still grew very well, 27
As did native red potatoes,
Foreign white potatoes,
Kidney beans,
Even the cornfields themselves.

Now, it is really the case that fava beans no longer grow well. 28
Kidney beans no longer grow well.
Native red potatoes no longer grow well.
Foreign white potatoes no longer grow well.
Nor do the cornfields do well any longer.

Back then, the native red potato grew well. 29
Fava beans grew well.
Kidney beans grew well.
Cornfields grew well.

But in our time no crops at all seem to do well any longer. 30
Perhaps a bit of a cornfield,
Some cabbage,
A few foreign white potatoes.

It is also the case that it no longer rains very much. 31
Back then, this was not so.

It rained a lot in the old times. 32
It rained a lot in June.
Then in August it would let up.
Then again in September it would rain again.
Then towards October it would start to clear off a bit.

But it is really the case that it now rains less. 33
Perhaps Our Father Sun in Heaven has sent a punishment:
Perhaps people spend too much time arguing,
Too much time killing one another,
Too much time shitting.

34 ˀech'o xal mu xa sk'an xak' ˀoˀ li jtotik ta vinajele:
yuˀun li jkaxlanetik ta joˀbele toj toyol ta sjipik ˀixim.
toj toyol ta sjipik vaj.
toj toyol ta sjipik ˀisak' chenek'.

35 ˀech'o xal mu sk'an li jtotik ta vinajele.
mu xa sk'an xak' ˀoˀ.
mu xa sk'an xak' ˀixim ˀisak' chenek'.

36 ˀech la ti voˀnee.
ti k'alal ta spasik ti snaik ti moletike puru joˀbel ta xak'ik.

37 ˀech li yak'ile,
ta xbat smanik talel ta ch'enal ˀoˀ.

38 tzahal ak' sbi pat teˀe.
ta k'ixin ˀosil xch'i.

39 muˀyuk toˀox laˀux xchonik ta joˀbel.
ˀech'o xal puru ˀak' ta xchukik ˀo li snaike.

40 ˀech li jkaxlanetike puru nukul ta xchukik ˀo li snaike.
muˀyuk toˀox laˀux.

41 ˀoy li laˀuxe pero yuˀun toj toyol stojol.
ˀech'o xal mu sk'an smanik to jkaxlanetike ti chamulaˀetike.

42 ˀech'o xal puru nukul ta xchukik ˀo ti snaike li chamulaˀetike.
puru tzajal ˀak' ta xchukik ˀo snaik.

43 ˀaˀ noˀox jkaxlanetik ta nukul ta xchukik ˀo ti snaike.
ta ˀora tanae muˀyuk xa ta xchukik ta nukul snaik li kaxlanetike.
puru xa la laˀux ta smanik.

There may be other reasons why Our Father Sun in Heaven no longer wishes to send rain: 34
For the Ladinos in San Cristóbal throw away a lot of corn.
They waste a lot of tortillas.
They waste a lot of potatoes and beans.

Consequently, Our Father Sun in Heaven does not like this. 35
He no longer wishes to send rain.
He no longer wants to provide corn, potatoes, and beans.

There is something else from long ago. 36
When the old-timers built their houses, they would build them of thatch grass.

As for the vine bindings, 37
These they would buy in San Pedro Chenalhó.

"Red vine" was what they called this tree-bark fiber. 38
It grows in Hot Country.

At that time, they still did not sell nails in San Cristóbal. 39
For this reason they bound their houses together with red-vine fiber.

As for the Ladinos, they bound their houses together with cowhide strips. 40
They still did not have nails either.

There *were* nails, but they were very expensive. 41
For that reason neither the Ladinos nor the Indians wanted to buy them.

For this reason, the Chamulas sometimes bound their houses together with just cowhide strips. 42
But they sometimes used just red-vine fiber bindings to bind their houses together.

The Ladinos used only cowhide strips to bind their houses together. 43
Nowadays, to be sure, they no longer use cowhide strips to bind together their houses.
They just buy nails.

44 ˀech xtok muˀyuk xa ta spasik mas xamit snaik.
puru xa sminto.
puru xa latariˀo.
puru xa tak'in ta xak'bik yoyal.

45 muˀyuk xa ta xak'bik xamit spak'bal.
yuˀun ta svos ta ˀoˀ.

46 ˀech'o xal puru xa latariˀo.
puru xa siminto tak'in ta xak'bik.
mu xa sk'an smanik xamit.

47 ˀech li ˀinyoetik ta chamulaˀe,
mu xa sk'an smanik tzajal ˀak',
yuˀun toj nom tajmek xchonik.

48 la snopik ta smanik laˀux.
ˀech xtok mu xa sk'an smeltzan snaik joˀbel.
yuˀun li joˀbele mu xa sk'an xch'i lek.

49 ta xa xch'ay.
mu xa sk'an xch'i lek.

50 ˀech xtok li kirsano buch'u ˀoy sjobele toj toyol ta xchon ta jbok'.
ta sk'an ˀoˀlajuneb pexu ta sien.
ˀech'o xal mu xa sk'an smanik li joˀbele.

51 ˀech xtok li joˀbele.
toj toyol ta sk'ux ch'o.
toj toyol ta spas sna ch'o te ta jol na.

52 ˀaˀ ta ˀora ta sk'aˀ.
mu skuch yuˀun jal.

53 ˀech'o xal mu xa sk'an smanik lek li joˀbele.
yuˀun li joˀbele koˀol xa stojol xchiˀuk texa ta jobele.
ˀech'o xal la snopik ta smanik texa yuˀun koˀol stojol.

For that matter, they no longer use adobe bricks, either. 44
They now use concrete.
They now use bricks.
They now use metal girdings for the framework.

They no longer use mud-brick construction. 45
For it is easily weakened by rain.

That's why bricks are most common now. 46
They now use reinforced concrete.
They no longer use adobe-brick construction.

As for the Indians in Chamula, 47
They no longer use red-vine fiber construction,
For the places where they still sell the raw materials for it
are very far away.

They are inclined to buy nails. 48
Furthermore, they no longer make their houses of thatch grass.
The reason is that thatch grass no longer grows well.

It is now becoming very scarce. 49
It no longer grows well.

Another problem is that people who do have stands of thatch grass sell 50
units of four hundred bundles at very high prices.
They charge thirteen pesos per hundred bunches.
For that reason, people don't want to buy thatch grass.

There is another problem with thatch grass. 51
Mice chew it up a lot.
Mice are very fond of making their nests there in the thatched-grass roofs.

It rots in no time. 52
It doesn't last long.

That is why they no longer buy thatch grass very much. 53
For the thatch grass now costs as much as roof tiles cost in
San Cristóbal.
That is why people are inclined to buy roof tiles, for they cost the same.

54 muˀyuk xa mas ta smanik tzajal ˀak'.
puru xa laˀux ta smanik.

55 ˀech li tzajal ˀak'e muˀyuk xa bu ta xchonik.
yuˀun mu xa sk'an smanik li kirsanoetik ta chamoˀe.

56 ˀaˀ noˀox ti moletik voˀnee puru tzajal ˀak' ta smanik sventa snaik.
mu snaˀik mi ˀoy laˀux.
ˀech'o xal muˀyuk bu smanik.
mu xojtikinik laˀux.
jaˀ noˀox xojtikinik tzajal ˀak'.

57 pero ta ˀora tanae xojtikinik xa laˀux.
xojtikinik xa texa.
xojtikinik xa latariˀo.
xojtikinik xamit.
snaˀik xa spasik xamit.

58 laj xa xchanik ˀabtel ˀalvanil.
laj xa xchanik spasik latariˀo ta joˀbel.
laj xa xchanik spasik pox.

59 ti moletike mu snaˀik spasik pox.
mu snaˀik spasik xamit.
mu snaˀik xˀabtejik ta ˀalvanil.
mu snaˀik spasik latariˀo texa.
mu snaˀik vun.

60 ta k'un to lik xchanik jutuk vun li kirsanoetik ta chamulaˀe.
yuˀun ti voˀnee mu snaˀik vun skotolik.
mu snaˀik kastiya.

61 pero tana snaˀik xa jutuk vun.
snaˀik xa jutuk kastiya pero jutuk.

62 ˀech la ti voˀnee:
jutuk ˀox la jˀiloletik.
ju toˀox chamel.
ju toˀox jˀak' chamel.

They no longer buy red-vine binding very much. 54
They just buy nails.

So red-vine fiber binding is no longer sold at all, 55
For the people of Chamula no longer want to buy it.

The old men of long ago bought only red-vine bindings for their houses. 56
They didn't even know about nails.
That's why they didn't buy them.
They were not even acquainted with nails.
They knew only about red-vine fiber binding.

But now they certainly know about nails. 57
They now know about roof tiles.
They now know about kiln-dried clay bricks.
They now know about adobe bricks.
They even know how to make adobe bricks.

They have learned the skills of masonry. 58
They have now learned how to make kiln-dried clay bricks in
San Cristóbal.
They have now learned from the Ladinos how to make rum liquor.

The old men did not know how to make rum liquor. 59
They didn't know how to make adobe bricks.
They didn't know the skills of masonry.
They didn't know how to make clay bricks or roof tiles.
They didn't know how to read or write.

Slowly the people of Chamula learned something of reading and writing. 60
For it was the case that long ago no one knew how to read and write.
Nor did they know Spanish.

But now they *do* know something of reading and writing. 61
They now know a bit, but only a bit, of Spanish.

There is something else about the past: 62
There were still relatively few curers.
There was still not much sickness.
There were still not many witches.[9]

63 pero ta ˀora tana ˀoy xa ˀep jˀilol.
ˀoy xa ˀep jˀak' chamel.
ˀoy xa ˀep chamel.
skotol xa ˀoy ˀep.

64 ti voˀnee muˀyuk toˀox k'asemal.
muˀyuk toˀox potz'lom.
muˀyuk toˀox yan k'op.
muˀyuk toˀox ch'ulelal.
muˀyuk toˀox k'ak'al k'asemal.
muˀyuk toˀox sikil k'asemal.

65 ˀaˀ noˀox ˀoy komel.
ˀoy sk'ak'al ˀontonal.
ˀaˀ noˀox la.
pero ta ˀora tanae ˀoy xa skotol chamel.

✠ ✠ ✠

66 ˀech to voˀne te ta paraje peteje ta la spasik xonobil.
javal nukul sbi.

67 k'alal mi meltzajem xa ti xonobile ta xbat xchonik ta soktom,
ta tuxta,
ta ˀutzokojta, pero ti sbi leke koita.

68 nom ta xbat xchonik to sonobile,
batz'i toj ˀabol sbaik tajmek ti moletike.

69 k'alal mi sutik talel ta tuxtae ta xbat smanik nukul ta joˀbel.
veno ta tz'akal ta xbat saˀik talel pat teˀ ta teˀtik.
sventa ta sk'aˀesik ˀo ti nukule.
yuˀun te ta sk'aˀesik ti nukule.

70 k'alal mi k'aˀ ti nukule ta xbat sjosbik stzotzil ta nab.
te ta xbat sjosbik lek ti stzotzil.
ta spokik lek.

But in our time, there are now many curers. 63
There are now many witches.
There is now much sickness.
There is now all manner of sickness.

In times past, there was not yet much "soul-breaking illness." 64
There was not yet much Potzlom illness.[10]
There were not yet other types of serious complaints.
There was still not much "soul illness."
There was not yet much "hot soul-breaking illness."
Nor yet much "cold soul-breaking illness."

There was just minor "soul-loss." 65
There was "heat of the heart illness."
But just these in the old days.
But today, there is all manner of sickness.[11]

✠ ✠ ✠

In the past, they still made sandals in Petej hamlet. 66
These were of a type that was called "open thongs."[12]

When the sandals were all finished, they would go to sell them in Chiapa de Corzo, 67
In Tuxtla Gutiérrez,
In Ocosocuautla (or as it is known in Tzotzil, Koyta).

They would travel great distances to sell their sandals, 68
For the old-timers were truly very, very poor.

When they got back from Tuxtla Gutiérrez, they would go to buy cowhide in San Cristóbal. 69
Well, after that, they would go to the woods to fetch tree bark.
This was for curing the cowhide.
They would cure the cowhide right there in Chamula.

When the hide was cured, they went to the pond to scrape off the hair. 70
There they scraped off the hair.
They washed it well.

71 veno ta sk'iˀik ta k'ak'al ta xtakij.
k'alal mi takije ta slik spasik xonobil.

72 pero muˀyuk bu ˀep ta spasik kanal.
jutuk noˀox.

73 ˀech xtok ti stak'inike puru vun.
muˀyuk toˀox batz'i tak'in.

74 ta k'un to tal batz'i tak'in.
sepel mejikano sbi yuˀunik ti moletike.

75 ˀentonse k'alal cham ti moletike
ch'ay ti jpas xonobiletike.
ch'ay ti jk'aˀesej nukule.
ch'ay skotol.
ch'ay batz'i ˀisak'.
ch'ay javax.
ch'ay ˀibes.

76 mu xa sk'an xch'i yuˀun li kirsanoetik li tz'akal la jch'iikuke.
mu sk'an stam ˀisak' javax ˀibes ˀixim.
ta sk'eloj noˀox.

77 mu sk'an stam.
te ta stek'.
te ta xbat ta k'aˀep.

78 ˀentonse li jtotik ta vinajele mu sk'an.
yuˀun ˀaˀ sbek'tal.
skotol yuˀun.
ˀaˀ la jyak' sventa sveˀel ti kirsanoetike.

79 ˀech'o xal ti jtotik ta vinajele ˀilin ˀep tajmek,
yuˀun la jyil ti bat ta k'aˀep ti ˀisak'e ti javaxe ti ˀixime ti chenek'e.
ˀech'o xal li ˀisak'e li javaxe li ˀixime mu xa xch'i lek te ta chamulaˀ.

Then they spread it out in the sun to dry. 71
When it was dry they started making sandals.

But they didn't really make much money at this. 72
It was but a little bit.

As for their money, it was just made of paper. 73
There were not yet true metal coins.

Later, true metal coins came into circulation. 74
The old men called these "Mexican disks."

So, with the passing of the old-timers, 75
Gone were the sandal makers.
Gone were the tanners of leather.
Gone was nearly everything.
Gone was the native red potato.
Gone was the fava bean.
Gone was the navy bean.

These things no longer want to grow for those of us who came along later. 76
People no longer want to take good care of potatoes, fava beans,
navy beans, and corn.
They merely look at them.

They don't care about nurturing them. 77
They do the same as step on them.
So these plants are destined for the rubbish heap.

Now, Our Father in Heaven does not approve of this. 78
For these things are his body.
All are of his making.
These things he gave as food for the people.

That is why Our Father Sun in Heaven got angry, 79
For he saw that potatoes, fava beans, corn, and boiling beans were
being cast into the rubbish heap.
That is why potatoes, fava beans, and corn no longer grow well
in Chamula.[13]

80 ˀech xtok ti moletike muˀyuk bu mas xk'otik ta pinka.
jutuk noˀox.

81 te noˀox ta spas xchobik ta snaik.
mu snaˀik xbat spas xchobik ta k'ixin ˀosil.

82 pero ta ˀora tana ˀoy xa ˀep kirsano ta spas xchobik ta k'ixin ˀosil.
ˀoy xa ˀep kirsano ta xbatik ta pinka.
ˀoy xa ta saˀ yajnilik te ta pinka.
ta xik' sbaik xchiˀuk xinlan.

83 mu xa sk'an spas xchobik ta snaik.
ˀaˀ ta sk'an te ta xˀabtejik ˀo ta pinkae.

84 yuˀun te ta pinkae ˀaˀ ˀoy ˀep tak'in.
te ˀoy tak'in jujun savaro.

85 pero k'alal te ta sna li kirsano ta chamoˀe ch'abal stak'in jujun savaro.
ch'abal stak'in.
ch'abal skajvel.
ch'abal sbek'et.

86 pero k'alal te ta pinkae ˀoy sbek'et.
ˀoy stak'in.
ˀoy skajvel.

87 muˀyuk ta xˀabtej ta rominko.
ˀaˀ noˀox ta xbat ˀatinuk ta ˀuk'um.
ta xbat sk'el ˀantz ta be.

88 ˀech'o xal mu xa sk'an xˀabtej ta snaik.
te ˀoy ˀo ta pinka.

89 ˀoy yan ta sut talel ta sna.
ˀoy yan muˀyuk xa ta sut talel ta sna.
te sa nop xaˀi ˀabtel ta pinka.

So, also, the old-timers did not often go to work on the coffee plantations. 80
Not very much at all.

Right there, close to their houses, they would plant their cornfields. 81
They were not accustomed to going to the lowlands to plant their
cornfields.[14]

But now, in our time, there are really lots of people who go to plant 82
their cornfields in the lowlands.
There are now lots of people who go to the coffee plantations.
There are even those who seek wives there on the coffee plantations.
They marry Ladino women.

They no longer want to plant their cornfields at home. 83
They want to work there on the coffee plantations.

There on the coffee plantations there is lots of money to be had. 84
There one gets paid in cash every Saturday.

But back there at the people's homes in Chamula they don't get paid 85
every Saturday.
They have no money.
They have no coffee.
They have no meat.

But, there on the coffee plantations, people have meat. 86
They have money.
They have coffee.

They don't work on Sundays. 87
They just go to bathe in the river.
They go to watch the women on the road.

That is why they no longer want to work at home. 88
There they are, at the coffee plantations.

There are some who go home. 89
There are others who no longer feel like going home.
They get used to working there on the coffee plantations.

90 pero ti voˀnee mu sk'an xbatik ta pinka.
veno ta xbatik ta pinka pero ta sutik talel.

91 ˀaˀ noˀox ta xbat voˀob xemuna vaxakib xemuna.
ˀaˀ noˀox.
te sut talel ta snaik.

92 ˀech xtok ti moletik muˀyuk yoraik.
mu snaˀik sk'elik.
mu xojtikinik lumero.
mu snaˀik mi ˀora.

93 mu snaˀik sman spisolik ta joˀbel.
te noˀox ta smanik ta chamoˀ.

94 ˀentonse ta tz'akal lik smanik yoraik.
lik sman sraryoik.
lik sman spixolik ta jobel.
lik sman lek skotonik.
lik sman stuk'ik.
lik sman spoxtolaˀik.
lik sman smakinaˀik sventa ta slok'ik ˀo jolal.
lik smanik spoxil sjolik.
lik sman skaroik.
lik sman skaik.
lik spasik syentaik.
lik spasik lek.
lik smanik ch'ojon tak'in smokik.
lik smanik skoryonik.
lik smanik yarpaik.
lik yak'bik tak'in yeˀik.
lik sman spantalonik.
lik sman snenal satik sventa ta spasik ˀo k'in ta k'in tajimoltik.
lik sman sjokoik.
lik sman slampara kasolina.
lik smanik sˀinteronoˀik.
lik sman sapotoˀik ˀo skaxlan xonobik.
lik sman smulinoˀik.
lik sman sprensaˀik sventa ta spak'anik ˀo vaj.

In times past they didn't want any part of staying on the coffee plantations. 90
They would go to the coffee plantations but would always return.

They would spend five weeks, eight weeks. 91
Just that.
And then they would go home.

So, also, the old-timers did not have watches. 92
They couldn't tell time.
They couldn't recognize written numbers.
They didn't even know what a watch was.

They didn't have the custom of buying their hats in San Cristóbal. 93
They bought them right there in Chamula.

Then, with the passing of time, they began to buy watches. 94
They began to buy radios.
They began to buy their hats in San Cristóbal.
They began to buy shirts.
They began to buy shotguns.
They began to buy pistols.
They began to buy hair clippers.
They began to buy hair oil.
They began to buy trucks.
They began to buy horses.
They began to set up stores.
They began to fix things up.
They began to buy metal fence wire.
They began to buy accordions.
They began to buy harps.
They began to get fillings and ornamentations for their teeth.
They began to buy manufactured trousers.
They began to buy dark glasses for The Festival of Games.[15]
They began to buy flashlights.
They began to buy kerosene lamps.
They began to buy oil lamps.
They began to buy Ladino shoes and sandals.
They began to buy factory-made hand corn grinders.[16]
They began to buy tortilla presses.[17]

lik sman sbin tak'inik.
lik sman svalteˀik.

95 pero ta tz'akal xa lik smanik.
ti voˀnee mu xojtikinik.

96 ˀech xtok ta k'un to lik spasik talel ti jkaxlanetike.
porke ti voˀnee mu snaˀik spasik.

97 ˀech'o xal mu xojtikinik ti moletike.
mu xojtikinik skotol.

They began to buy metal pots.
They began to buy metal buckets.

It is only recently that they have begun to buy these things. 95
Long ago they did not know about these things.

So, also, it is only recently that they have started to adopt Ladino customs, 96
For long ago they didn't have these customs.

The reason was that the old men were not acquainted with these customs. 97
They were not acquainted with them at all.

1 loˀil yuˀun soltaro chaketa leva.
vaˀi ˀun ti kirsano ta chamoˀe la spasik leto xchiˀuk soltaroetik ta jobel.

2 pero ti soltaroetike sbiik chaketa leva.
ti jchamoˀetike sbiik jkuxkatetik la.

3 pero ti jchamoˀetike baˀyel la spasik k'in te ta sparajeik.
ta tzajal jemel.

4 yuˀun la ˀoy te jun jtotik ta snaik.
ˀech'o la xal ta spasik k'in ta sparajeik.

5 k'alal la ta spasik ti k'in jujutene,
ta la xbatik ta ˀuk'um xchiˀuk svobik xchiˀuk syolon k'ok'ik.

6 te la ta xbat ˀak'otajikuk ta ˀoˀlol ˀuk'um xchiˀuk ti jtotik xchiˀuk svobike.
ta ˀak'obaltik la ta xbat spasik ti k'in ta ˀoˀlol ˀuk'ume.

7 ti jtotike ta la xkuchik ˀel ta pek' ta spatik.
k'alal ta xˀak'otajike ta xkuchojik ta spatik ti jtotike.

8 te ta xˀak'otajik ta ˀoˀlol ˀuk'um ta ˀak'obaltik.
ˀech ti jtivobetike te chotolik ta ˀukum ta stijik ti svobike.
ti yolon k'ok'e te ta st'omesik ta tiˀ ˀuk'um.

SECTION 5

A Brief Chronicle of the Fourth Creation

TEXT 67

On Cuscat's War with the Frock-Coat Soldiers of San Cristóbal

Mateo Méndez Tzotzek

This is an account of the conscripted soldiers. 1
So. The Chamulas were carrying on a war with the soldiers
from San Cristóbal.[1]

The conscripted Mexican soldiers were called "frock coats."[2] 2
The Chamulas were called "Cuscateros."

The Chamulas began to celebrate their fiestas in their hamlet. 3
There in Tsajalhemel hamlet.

For there was a holy image that resided in one of their houses. 4
That is why they celebrated fiestas in their hamlet.

Every time they celebrated the fiesta, 5
They went to the river with their guitars and their skyrockets.

They went there to dance in the river with the holy image and 6
their guitars.
At night, they went to celebrate the fiesta in the middle of the river.

They carried the holy image on their backs with a tumpline. 7
When they danced, they carried the holy image on their backs.

They danced there in the river during the night.[3] 8
The musicians sat there by the river playing their guitars.
Others set off fireworks at the edge of the river.

9 k'alal ta xˀak'otajike ta xˀalik:
samataloma samataluˀixa,
xalataperes xalatakomes.
xiik la ti k'alal ta xˀak'otajik ta ˀoˀlol ˀuk'ume.
ˀech ta xk'ejinik jujuten ti k'alal ta xˀak'otajike.

10 ˀentonse ta tz'akal li pale ta joˀbele la jyaˀi ti ˀoy jun jtotik te ta paraje tzajal jemele.
bat sk'el yuˀun ta sk'an ta xˀojtikin yaˀi ti jtotike.

11 pero ti kirsanoetik ta chamoˀe la jyaˀik ti ta xbat ti pale ta tzajal jemele,
ti ta sk'an ta xˀojtikin yaˀi ti jtotike.

12 pero ti jchamoˀetik la jyaˀik ti ta xbat ti palee.
ˀentonse bat smakik ta be nichtojtik ta nopol paraje jol pajalton.

13 ta la smalaˀik ti palee.
pero ti kirsanoetike bat smalaˀik ta be xchiˀuk stuk'ik xchiˀuk smachitaˀik.

While they were dancing, they sang: 9
"*Samataloma, Samataluʔisha,*
Xalataperez, Xalatagomez."
So they spoke when they danced in the river.
So they sang when they danced in the river.[4]

Then, afterward, the priest in San Cristóbal found out that there was a holy image in Tsajaljemel hamlet. 10
He went to see, because he wanted to investigate the nature of the holy image.

But the people of Chamula found out that the priest was going to Tsajaljemel, 11
That he wanted to find out about the holy image.

Well, the Chamulas knew that the priest was going there. 12
So they went to block his way by Nichtojtik, close to Jolpajalton hamlet.

They planned to ambush the priest there. 13
The people were waiting by the road with their guns and their machetes.

FIGURE 91

They planned to ambush the priest there.
The people were waiting by the road with their guns and their machetes.

14 ta la smalaˀik ta be ti plae xchiˀuk skaˀe.
porke ti palee kajal ta kaˀ ti k'alal bat sk'el ti jtotik ta tzajal jemel.

15 pero mu snaˀ mi ˀoy buch'u ta nak'al ta be.
yuˀun kontento bat sk'el jtotike.

16 ˀentonse ti kirsanoetike te nak'alik tayak'ol be xchiˀuk stuk'ik xchiˀuk smachitaˀik.
vaˀi ˀun ti k'alal k'ot ti pale ti bu nak'alik ti kirsanoetike,
jlikel la jyak'bik tuk'e ti k'alal la jyilik ti k'ot ti pale xchiˀuk skaˀ ta be.

17 koˀol la xchiˀuk skaˀ ta be ta nichtojtik ta nopol jol pajalton.
te ˀicham ti pale xchiˀuk skaˀe.

18 muˀyu bu xk'ot sk'el ti jtotik ti bu ˀoy nak'al xchiˀuk ti kirsanoe.
ta be ˀicham xchiˀuk skaˀe.

19 ˀentonse ti jchamoˀetik ti k'alal yilik ti cham ti pale xchiˀuk skaˀe sutik ˀel ta snaik xchiˀuk stuk'ik.
ti palee ta puch'ul kom ta be xchiˀuk skaˀ.

They were waiting there by the road for the priest and his horse to pass by. 14
For the priest went on horseback when he went to investigate the holy image at Tsajaljemel.

But he didn't realize that there was someone hidden there by the road. 15
For he was happy that he was going to see the holy image.

Now, the people were hidden there above the road with their guns and their machetes. 16
So, when the priest came to the place where the people were hidden,
They quickly fired their guns when they saw the priest come along the road mounted on his horse.

He perished with his horse there in the road at Nichtojtik, close to Jolpajalton. 17
The priest died there with his horse.

He didn't ever get to see the holy image where the people had it hidden away. 18
He and his horse just died there on the road.

Then the Chamulas, when they saw the priest and his horse die there, returned to their homes with their guns. 19
The priest and his horse remained there lying dead on the road.

20 pero li soltaroetik ta joˀbel la jyaˀik ti cham ti pale ta be xchiˀuk skaˀe.
bat sk'elik.

21 bat staik talel la jyich'ik ˀel k'alal ta joˀbel.
te la smukik ta joˀbel ti palee.

22 ˀentonse ti k'alal la smukik ti palee bat smilik ti jchamoˀetike.
pero li jchamoˀetike la jyaˀik ti ta xbat ti soltaroetike.

23 bat smalaˀik ta be te ta tzajal ch'en, ta sbelel chamoˀ.
pero ˀaˀ baˀyel k'ot ti soltaroetike te ta tzajal ch'ene.
ti jchamoˀetike ˀaˀ tz'akal k'otik.

24 ˀentonse ti soltaroetik ti k'alal k'otik ta tzajal ch'en lik veˀikuk te ta tiˀ ˀuk'um.
te chotolik ta xveˀik.
muˀyuk bu ta stuk'ulanik mi ˀoy buch'u ta xk'otik.

But the soldiers of San Cristóbal found out that the priest had died there 20
on the road with his horse.
They went to investigate.

They went to find him and to bring him back to San Cristóbal. 21
They buried the priest there in San Cristóbal.

Then, after they had buried the priest, they set off to kill the Chamulas 22
to avenge his murder.
However, the Chamulas found out what the soldiers were up to.

They went to wait for them by the road to Tsajalchen hamlet, just off 23
the road to Chamula.
But it happened that the soldiers had gotten to Tsajalchen first.
The Chamulas arrived later.

When the soldiers arrived at Tsajalchen, they started to eat there at the 24
edge of the river.
They were sitting there eating.
They didn't realize that anyone was coming.

FIGURE 92

But the soldiers of San Cristóbal found out that the priest had
died there on the road with his horse.
They went to investigate.

25 vaˀi ˀun k'alal k'ot ti jchamoˀetike te ta tzajal ch'ene.
la jyilik ti te chotolik ti soltaroetike.
ta xveˀik te ta uk'ume.

26 likel la jyak'bik tuk' ti soltaroetike porke ti soltaroetike ch'ayem yoˀntonik
ta xveˀik.
k'alal ˀochik ta veˀele la syalesik ti stuk'ike.
la jyak'ik ta lumtik xchiˀuk skanyonik.

27 k'alal t'omesbatik ti tuk'e likik ta ˀora jatavik ˀel.
skotolik ti stuk'ik te kom ta tiˀ uk'um xchiˀuk skanyonik ti yotike
ti smoralike.
te kom ta tiˀ ˀuk'um ta tzajal ch'en ta nopol chamoˀ.

28 ˀaˀ te la spasik leto ti jchamoˀetik xchiˀuk ti soltaroetike.
jatavik skotolik ti soltaroetike.

29 batik k'alal ta joˀbel.
batz'i xiˀik tajmek.

30 ˀentonse ti soltaroetike batik noˀox ˀotro jten.
bat spasik leto xchiˀuk ti jchamoˀetike.

Well, the Chamulas got to Tsajalchen. 25
They saw the soldiers sitting there.
They were eating there by the river.

They seized the opportunity and quickly opened fire because the soldiers were busy eating. 26
As they began to eat, they put their guns down beside them on the ground.
They put them down beside their cannon.

When the Cuscateros' guns fired at them, the soldiers fled at once. 27
They left all their gear there at the edge of the river: guns, even their tortillas and shoulder bags.
They left all this stuff there at the edge of the river at Tsajalchen, close to Chamula Center.

That's where the Chamulas fought with the frock-coat soldiers soldiers. 28
All of the soldiers fled.

They retreated to San Cristóbal. 29
They were truly scared to death.

Then the soldiers returned for another engagement. 30
They went to fight the Chamulas once again.

31 pero ti jchamoˀetike la jyaˀik ti ta xbat ˀotro jten ti soltaroetike.
bat smalaˀik ˀotro jten te ta tzajal ch'en.

32 bat la xchiˀuk ˀantzetik.
ti ˀantzetik ta la skolta sba.

33 ta la sikubtas tuk' ti yoˀ la mu xt'om stuk' ti soltaroetike,
ˀaˀ la li sbe tzoˀe toj chopol la sat.

34 toj sik la.
ˀech'o la xal ta sikubtas ti tuk'e.

35 pero k'alal k'otik ti soltaroetik xchiˀuk ti stuk'ike ti tuk'ike muˀyuk xa bu sikub.
jlikel ˀit'om muˀyuk xa bu xiˀ yuˀun sbe tzoˀe.

36 ˀecheˀ k'ot ti ˀantzetike.
te lajik ta tuk' skotolik ti ˀantzetike.

But the Chamulas found out that the soldiers were coming again. 31
Once again, they went to wait for them at Tsajalchen.

This time, they went with their wives. 32
The women went to help them.

They went to chill the guns so that the soldiers' guns wouldn't fire, 33
For indeed, they had ugly and powerful assholes.[5]

They were very cold. 34
That is the way they were going to chill the guns.

But when the soldiers arrived with their guns, their guns didn't get cold. 35
Their guns fired at once and were not made powerless by the womens' assholes.

So the women had come in vain. 36
All the women died there from the bullets.

FIGURE 93

But the Chamulas found out that the soldiers were coming again.
Once again, they went to wait for them at Tsajalchen.

This time, they went with their wives.
The women went to help them.

37 ˀoch bek' tuk' ta schakik
lok' ta yeik ti viniketike.

38 laj to la yak'ik tuk pero jutuk xa la.
muˀyuk xa bu spasik kanal.

39 ti baˀyele la spasik kanal,
pero ta xchibal velta muˀyuk xa bu spasik kanal.
ˀaˀ ˀispasik kanal ti soltaroetike.

40 pero ti baˀyele muˀyuk bu spasik kanal.
pero ta xchibal velta la pasik kanal.
muˀyuk xa bu xiˀik.

41 muˀyuk xa bu xjatavik ti povre jchamoˀetike.
ˀep chamik tajmek.

42 cham viniketik;
cham ˀantzetik.
koˀol chamik.

43 ti soltaroetike muˀyuk bu xchamik.
ˀaˀ ˀispasik kanal.

44 ti povre jchamoˀetike muˀyuk xa bu stuk ˀel ta snaik.
te ˀicham skotolik ta tzajal ch'en.
ti soltaroetik sutik ˀel ta snaik ta joˀbel.

The bullets ripped into their asses 37
With such force that they tore through their bodies and ended up
in the men's mouths as they stood behind them.

They were still trying to fire, but not so much now. 38
It was clear that they were no longer winning.

Their first battle had been a victory, 39
Their second battle brought defeat.
So it was clear that the frock-coat soldiers were winning.

The soldier's own first battle had brought defeat, 40
But the second time they did win.
So they were no longer scared.

The poor Chamulas couldn't even run away. 41
Many of them died.

Men died; 42
Women died.
They all died in like manner.

The soldiers did not die. 43
They prevailed.

As for the poor Chamulas, they could no longer return to their homes. 44
They all died there, close to Tsajalchen.
The soldiers returned safely to their homes in San Cristóbal.

1 ʔoy jun kuento sventa jresaletik la ti mas voʔnee.

2 vaʔun k'alal la lik ʔo ti resal lae yuʔun ta la xtal la soltaroetik.
ti ta xʔalik la ti kirsano la ʔune.

3 vaʔun jech ti peserente ta chamula la ʔune ta la xʔal la smantal ti mas lek
ti taluk la ta pas resal la ʔune.
vaʔun ʔi ta la xtal ta naetik la yal ti mantal la ʔune.

4 vaʔun k'alal la ta xtal ti mayoletik la ʔune:
liʔ ta xkal jbel mantale:
batanik la.
ba ʔaʔik mantal.
mu jnaʔ k'usi ta xʔal ti peserentee.
xi la ta xʔal ti mayol la ʔune.

5 vaʔun mi mu la xch'un la ʔune vaʔun ta la xmilvan ʔun.
ʔa ti mi la ch'unbe la ʔune batan la ta chamula ʔun ta la xʔal komel.

6 ʔich'o la ʔech'el ʔamachita,
ʔo mi anamteʔ,
ʔo mi ʔajalamteʔ.
ʔich'o la ʔech'el ʔun.

7 mi muʔyuk la k'usi ʔoy la ʔavuʔun la ʔune ʔak'o kuchiluuk ta xavich'
ʔech'el la ʔun.
ʔo mi moʔoj lae ʔich'o la ʔech'el ʔatuk'.
jaʔ ti k'usi ʔoy ʔavuʔun la ʔune.

TEXT 68
About the Prayer Makers of Long Ago

Marián López Calixto

This is a story about the prayer makers of long ago.[1] 1

Well, when the prayer-making cult began, it was threatened by an 2
opposing force of soldiers who were making their way
to Chamula.
That is what people say about those times.

It was for this reason that the presidente of Chamula gave the order 3
that it would be best for all to come and show support
for the new cult.
Indeed, he even sent this order out into the hamlets, to people's homes.

So it was that the policemen from Chamula Center came and said this: 4
"We are here to give you a command:
Be on your way to the Center.
Go find out what you are supposed to do.
We don't know what the presidente has to say."
That is what they say that he commanded.

Indeed, if they had not obeyed these orders, then they would have 5
killed them.[2]
"Those who have heard and intend to obey, be off to Chamula Center,"
he ordered.

"Take with you your machetes, 6
Even your walking sticks,
Even the bobbin sticks from your looms,
Take these things with you.

If you have nothing to take as a weapon, even a knife will do. 7
If not that, then get your gun!
Whatever you've got!"

8 jaˀ la sventa la ti soltaro mi tal la ˀune.
ˀi ta la xˀak'bik ˀun.

9 vaˀun bu ˀoy la yajnil mastaroe jaˀ la ta sbisik ta jmeˀtik.
jaˀ xa jmeˀtik li tal xa.
ˀi jaˀ xa jmeˀtik santa roxa,
xiik xa la ti puta kirsanoetik la ˀune,
ti buch'u ˀochem ta pas resal la ˀune.

10 ta la spasbik la resal ti mu ˀantze.
la ti jmeˀtik santa roxa la yalojik la ˀune.
ˀu ta la xk'ejinik tajmek la ti ˀantzetik ti viniketike.

The weapons were intended to fend off the soldiers when they came. 8
They would be used against them.

As for the wife of the schoolteacher, she was being revered as a saint 9
right there in her home.[3]
"This, now, is Our Holy Mother who has come to be here with us!
This, now, is Our Holy Mother Santa Rosa!"
This is what these fucking people were saying,
Those who were devoted to the prayer-making cult.

Indeed, they prayed and paid homage to this fraud of a woman. 10
They really thought that she was Santa Rosa.
Imagine! Both women and men sang and carried on enthusiastically
in her honor.

FIGURE 94

Indeed, they prayed and paid homage to this fraud of a woman.
They really thought that she was Santa Rosa.
Imagine! Both men and women sang and carried on enthusi-
astically in her honor.

11 vaˀun ti jmeˀtik santa roxa la ˀune ta la xk'opoj la tajmek:
chanik me ti resal ˀune.
jaˀ me lek mu me xijchajmotik xi la ti mu ˀantz la ˀune.

12 vaˀun jech la ti povre kirsano la ˀune ta la xchan yokik ˀun ˀi ta la xˀanilajik tajmek.
ti povre kirsano la ˀune.

13 jech la ti smachitaik la ˀune, ti skuchiluik la ˀune ti snamteˀik la ˀune ti sjalamteˀik la ˀune jaˀ la ta sbechik ˀun.
jech la ti ta xchol sbaik la ta stz'el kavilto la ˀune.
ˀanil la ta xbatik la ta ˀanil.

14 pere mu la me xak'opoj.
tzinlan la ˀun.
mu la xak'opoj.

15 mi la k'opoj la ˀune:
buch'u ta xk'opoj taje xi la ti totil la ˀune.

16 ˀa ti mi yilotik la ˀune ta la xmilvan yuˀun mu la sk'an ti totile.
yuˀun xa la chanoj ti resal la ˀune mu xa la xtun xak'opoj.

17 vaˀun mi laj xchol la sbaik la ˀune ta la xˀal ti mu la xtun xa k'opoj la ˀune.
jech la ti totile xchuk'inoj la spistol jujot xokon ti totil la ˀune.

18 vaˀun mi la k'opoj lae ta la xavich' milel.
jaˀ la ta xˀak' ti spistol la ˀune.

19 vaˀun jech la ti chololik la ˀune ˀox vok' la spasoj la sbaik ˀun.
ti jvok' la ˀune te la ta stz'el kavilto.
ti yan jvok' la ˀune te la ta stz'el sna jˀoktov.
jech la ti yan jvok' la ˀune te la ta tiˀ ch'ulna.

Furthermore, Our Holy Mother Santa Rosa made pronouncements to 11
encourage her followers:
"Learn the new prayers!
If you learn them well, we shall not die," exclaimed that impostor
of a woman.

And on account of all of this provocation, the poor people had to march 12
and run about feverishly.
Such was the lot of these poor people.

They would thrust their machetes, their knives, their walking sticks, 13
their loom bobbin sticks, into the air.
They would do this as they marched by the cabildo.
They would march by in great haste, as though obsessed.

"You are not to speak. 14
Be silent.
Hush," was the command.

If you spoke, this would be the response: 15
"Who was that who spoke?" the leader would demand.[4]

And if they saw who it was among us who spoke, they would kill us, 16
for the leader didn't want any talking.
It was argued that if you had joined the prayer-making cult, it was not
fitting for you to speak informally.

So it was that when the marching formations took place, they said you 17
could not talk at all.
As for the leader, he had two pistols slung by a gun belt on either
side of his body.

So, if you spoke at all, you would get killed. 18
He would let you have it with his pistols.

Now, as for the military formations, these were made up of three divisions. 19
One division was there close to the cabildo.
Another division was over by what is now the clinic.
The other division was over there by the entrance to the atrium
of the church.

20 vaˀun ta la xˀal ti totil lae:
k'alal mi kal tana ˀune vol ˀabaik.
mi xichi tana ˀune ˀi ta xavol ˀabaik la ˀolol ch'ivit ˀun.

21 ta xajelav ta ˀora ˀun.
k'alal mi la jelav ˀune ˀi ta chak'ot ta yav ˀachiˀil ti bu lok' talel ˀun.
xi la ti totile.

22 vaˀun ta la xbat ta ˀora xvol la sbaik ˀun.
k'alal mi k'ot la xvol la sbaik la ˀune jech la ti snamteˀike la ˀune ta la sbechik ˀun.

23 vaˀun k'alal mi laj la sbechik la ˀune.
ta la xlajik ˀun jaˀ la ti ta sbechik la ˀun.
komo li yan la ˀune ˀoy la ye ti spuyaˀik la ˀune.
jaˀ la ta xˀak'ik la ˀun.

24 vaˀun k'alal ta la xtani sbaik la ˀune.
jech la ti yane lek la balal la ta ch'ich' ti sk'uˀ la ˀune.
jech la ti yane ˀoy la ta xk'ot ta sniˀ ti ˀavonteˀe ti spuyaˀik la ˀune.

25 mi la laj lae ˀi te la laj ˀun.
muˀyuk la ta ˀalel mi xalaj.

26 ˀa ti mi k'opoj lae ˀay li laj xa ˀun jaˀ yak' leˀe . . .
mi xachi lae yuˀun ta la xˀak' yan la ˀun yuˀun mu la bu k'ux ˀavaˀi.

27 vaˀun te:
la tz'inlan.
mu k'usi xaval.
ˀan la ch'an ˀun.

28 vaˀun jujun k'ak'al jech la ta spasik ˀun.
pes mi la laj la ˀin jip xi la ˀech'el ta spat kavilto.

Then the leader came forward and commanded: 20
"When I give the order, march towards one another.
When I say so, you are to move at once into the middle of the plaza.

You are to pass by the center of the plaza in double time. 21
Once you have made this maneuver, you are to march directly to the
position from which your opposing comrades set out."
Those were the leader's orders.

With that, they got quickly into the spirit of the assembly drill.[5] 22
As they met one another in the center of the plaza, they would
brandish their walking canes in threatening gestures.

Soon the exercise of thrusting and jousting with the weapons 23
came to an end.
This happened because there were many who got wounded in this
military drill.
The reason was that some of them carried lances with sharp edges.
They actually used them against their comrades.

Soon the formation broke apart in chaos. 24
Some people found that their clothing was washed with blood.
Still others had been struck by the sharp points of canes and lances.

If you got injured, you simply got injured. 25
No one cared if you got hurt.

And if you were to complain, "Oh, I just got wounded; that guy 26
stabbed me . . ."
If you said that, they would just land another blow, for one was not
supposed to be sensitive to pain.

Then, in such a moment, the leader would say this: 27
"Come on, shut up!
Don't say a word!
Keep quiet!"

Well, that is what happened every day. 28
If you were killed in these drills for conscripts, they ordered your body
to be thrown behind the cabildo.

29 vaˀun jech la ti jmuk'tot la ˀun jutuk xa la mu laj ta puyaˀ.
ti povre jmuk'tot la ˀune.

30 vaˀun jech la ti jmuk'tot la ˀune yil la ti tal la ti puyaˀ lae.
bat la ba stzak ta ˀora ti puyaˀe.

31 vaˀun jech la ti yajval ti puyaˀ la ˀune mu la bu yil k'uxi la bat ti spuyaˀ lae.
ˀay k'uxi bat ti jpuyaˀe ˀune xi la ti mu kirsano lae.
ch'ay xa kavron xi la ti mu kirsano lae.

32 vaˀun jech la ti jmuk'tot la ˀune bat la ba stzak ta ˀora la ti puyaˀ la ˀune.
likel la snak' ta xch'ut ta ˀora ti jpovre jmuk'tote.

33 vaˀun bat la ba xchol la sbaik ta ˀora.
vaˀun k'alal la xchol la sbaik la ˀune jech la ti jmuk'tote:
ta xibat k'abin kuˀun yuˀun ta xa xlok' ti jk'abe xi la ti jpovre jmuk'tote.

34 vaˀun bat la ba snak' ta be la ti sniˀ ti ˀavonteˀ la ˀune.
vaˀun sut la talel ta ˀora la ˀun.

35 vaˀun jech la ti yan la ˀune yak' xa la ta xlajik ta milel.
ti yan la ˀune jaˀ ta xlaj ta milel.
ti mu la xch'un ti mantal yuˀun sventa la ta xchol la sbaik la ˀun,
ˀi chukbil la ta xtal ˀun.

36 bat ba ˀaˀiˀo mantal yuˀun peserente.
mu jnaˀ k'uxi ta xal.
xi la ta xˀal ti mayol la ˀune.

37 vaˀun mi bat la ti povre kirsano la ˀune:
batan ta mejiko.
bat ˀak'o karta sventa peserente.
batanik ba chiˀino ta yak'el li kartae xi la ti peserentee.

In fact my own grandfather almost died from a lance wound. 29
Such was the fate of my poor grandfather.

It happened that my grandfather saw that a lance was coming his way. 30
He moved quickly to intercept it and grab it before it hit him.

As for the one who threw the lance, he did not realize what had become of his weapon. 31
"Oh, what's become of my lance?" this bastard cried.
"What's become of it? God dammit!" ranted this bastard.

Now, it happened that my grandfather had grabbed the lance as fast as he could. 32
My poor grandfather lost no time in slipping it into his own waistband as though it belonged to him.

Then he rushed to line up in march formation. 33
Then, as he went to get into place in the formation, my grandfather said this:
"I've got to take a piss, for it's about to run down my leg," said my poor grandfather.

With this trick, he was able to go and hide his own club, and the metal tip that was attached to it, there by the road. 34
Then he returned quickly to the march formation.[6]

Well, the others were already engaged in a frenzy of fighting with one another, even to the point of killing one another. 35
Others were also doomed to die.
Those who would not obey the marching orders,
They were bound as captives and forced to come forward.

"Go get your orders from the presidente. 36
Who knows what he will say."
That is what they said the policeman said.

Then, when the poor captives went to hear their fate, this is what they heard: 37
"Be off to Mexico City.
Go deliver this letter to the presidente of Mexico.
Go, help to deliver this letter," ordered the presidente of Chamula.[7]

38 vaˀun jech la ti povre kirsano la ˀun ta la xch'un ˀun.
veno ta xibat xi la ti povre viniketike.

39 vaˀun k'alal mi li jk'ototik la ˀune te la smilotik la ˀune.
ˀoy la lek la meltzajem la ˀek'el sventa la jmilobiltik la ˀun.
ˀi ˀoy la spajoj la jun la teˀ ˀi te la jipil la ti ˀek'el la ˀune.

40 vaˀun jech la ti ta lum la ˀune te la ˀoy jun chumanteˀ.
jaˀ la sventa la skajleb la ti joltike.

41 vaˀun ta la spech'otik la ˀun.
xchuk la ti jk'obtike.
ta la xchuk ti koktike.

42 vaˀun ta la xbat smeltzan la ti joltike.
vaˀun jech la ti ˀek'el la ˀune ta la skol ta la yalel la talel ˀun.

43 jech ti ˀek'el la ˀune toj ˀol la tajmek.
ˀoxvinik kilo yalel ti ˀek'el la ˀune.

44 k'alal mi yal la tale la ˀune toj setel la ti joltike.
jech la ti yane ta to la ta xˀavan la jutuk.
jech la ti yane muˀyuk xa la bu ta xijˀavan.

45 vaˀun k'alal mi li jlajotik la ˀun ta la smukotik ta lum.
ˀo mi moˀoj lae ta la sjipotik la ta nab.

46 vaˀun jech la ti xuleme jech la ti tz'iˀe ta la xbat ta yut ˀo.
ba stiˀotik la ˀun.

47 jech la ti ˀoˀe,
toj xin la tajmek ti ˀoˀe.
ˀi toj tzoj la tajmek.

With that, the unfortunate people had no choice but to obey. 38
"Well, I'll be going," said the poor victims.

Then, once we got to that place, they would kill us then and there.[8] 39
They had a great blade rigged up there for the use of the executioners.
They had this great axe blade suspended from a framework that was made of posts.

And there on the ground beneath it was a large, flat tree stump. 40
This was the block for our heads.

Then they would tie us up. 41
They would bind our hands.
They would bind our feet.

Then they would put our heads in the proper place. 42
With that done, they would let the blade fall.

As for the blade, it was very heavy. 43
It weighed sixty kilos.

When it fell, it severed our heads quite easily. 44
There were some people who still had the strength to cry out a little bit.
Still others of us could no longer scream at all.

Well, once we were dead they would bury us. 45
Or if they did not do this they would simply throw us in the lake.

As for the buzzards and the dogs, they did not hesitate to go out into the water. 46
They would go there to eat up our remains.

As for the water in the lake, 47
It gave off an awful stench.
And it had an intense color of red.

48 vaʔun jech la ti povre kirsanoe:
mi ʔoy smaj kirsano la voʔne,
ʔo mi ʔutvan la,
ʔo mi ʔelk'aj la,
ʔo mi li jʔilin,
jaʔ la jmultik ʔun.

49 veno tzak'ik tal leʔe yuʔun ʔoy smul xi la ti peserentee.
tzak xijyutotik la ʔun.
chuk xi la jnuktike ti jk'obtike ti koktike.
yoʔ mu la xijatavotike.

50 vaʔun mi chukul xa la skotol ti kok jk'obtik ta spetotik la ʔech'el ta ʔora ta sjol chumanteʔ.
jech la ti ʔek'el la ʔune ta la skolta la ʔun ʔi te la li jlajotik ʔun.
vaʔun jech la ti te ta spat kavilto la ʔune.

51 puru la kirsano te busul ta ʔo,
ti povre kirsanoe ti chamemik xa la ʔune.

52 pere ti ch'ich' la ʔun.
toj tzoj la te ʔoy ti ta ʔoʔe.

53 vaʔun jech ti yabtejebik la ʔune jaʔ la yak'be la sbaik ʔun.
jech la ti k'uyepal la ʔochem ta pas resal la ʔune,
laj la skotol yuʔun maʔuk la sk'an jtotik la ta xchanik ʔi lajik la ta milel ʔun.

54 vaʔun jecheʔ la ta xʔal ti ta xtal ti soltaro la ʔune.
vaʔun laj la smil la sbaik la stukik ʔun.

Now, as for the fate of the ordinary people of Chamula, things went badly: 48
If one had some prior accusation of assault,
Of having been involved in some quarrel,
Of alleged theft,
Of just having lost one's temper and gotten angry,
All of these became punishable offenses under the new regime.

"Well, bring him in, for he has a criminal offense to answer for," declared the presidente. 49
They would come and capture us.
They would bind our necks, hands, and feet.
All of this to keep us from running away.

Then, with everything—feet, hands, and all—tied up, they would carry us away to the surface of the stump. 50
Soon they would let loose the blade and there we would be done for.
That was what happened there behind the cabildo.[9]

There in the lake behind the cabildo there were piles of human corpses, 51
The bodies of poor people who had already died.

But just imagine what the bloodbath was like! 52
It lent an intense red color to the water of the lake.

So it was that these people actually used their tools and weapons to attack one another. 53
However many people who joined the prayer-making cult,
These people ended up getting killed themselves because Our Father Sun/Christ did not want them to join the prayer-making cult and engage in wanton killing.

In fact, they deceived people in telling them that soldiers were coming to destroy the cult. 54
The truth was that they were engaged in killing one another all by themselves.

55 ta k'un to la tal ti soltaroetik ˀune.
vaˀun jatavik la ta ˀora.
jech la ti yane bat la ba smilik ti soltaroetike.
vaˀun jech la ti soltaro lae ta smaj la sbaik xchiˀuk la chamula.

56 pere mu bu la kuch yuˀun ti kirsanoetike.
jech la ti yane ta la smilan la sbaik ti chamulae.
snaˀik mi ˀoy la sk'opon la ˀantz ti xchiˀiltak la ˀune.
jaˀ la ta smilik.
ˀi parte te la ta lum ta smaj la sbaik la ˀun.

57 toj chopol la tajmek ti mu kirsanoe.

In the end soldiers did come to intervene.[10] 55
Then some people fled at once.[11]
Others stayed to confront and kill the soldiers.
Thus, it is true that the soldiers finally came to engage in open combat with Chamula.

But the Chamula people did not prevail. 56
There were even some of the prayer-makers who killed one another.
They did this when they found out that some of their own comrades had been making illicit sexual propositions to their wives.
So they just killed the offenders.
There were still others who clubbed and injured one another in the military drills.

Indeed, these people were thoroughly misguided and evil.[12] 57

1 loʔil yuʔun jpajaroetik.

2 veno ti moletik voʔnee lik la xchanik resal.
pero mu ta sjolikuk stukik.
ta smantal pale xchiʔuk peserente xchiʔuk jves xchiʔuk ʔalkalteetik ta chamoʔ.

3 ʔentonse ti peserente ta chamoʔe k'alal yaʔi ti mantal yuʔun ti palee lik stzob ti kirsanoetike.
veno k'alal yaʔik ti kirsanoetike lek xa xaʔik.
pero mu skotolikuk ti kirsanoetik ti lek xaʔike.

4 jlom lek xaʔik.
jlom muʔyuk lek xaʔik yuʔun toj chopol ta chanel ti resale.

5 ʔech'o xal mu skotolikuk lek xaʔik.
ʔentonse ti buch'u kontentoike lek la xchanik ti resale.

6 jujun la k'ak'al ta xbatik ta jteklum xchiʔuk yajnilik.
te la ta xbat xchanik ta yut ch'ulna ta chamoʔe.

7 pero kontentoik la ta xchanik ti resale.
pero jujun la k'ak'al ta xbat xchanik ti resal xchiʔuk ti yajnilike.

TEXT 69

AN ACCOUNT OF THOSE WHO FOLLOWED PAJARITO

Mateo Méndez Tzotzek

This is an account of those who followed Pajarito.[1] 1

Well, long ago the elders got themselves involved with the 2
prayer-making cult.
However, it was not exactly their own idea.
It came as an order from the priest, the presidente, the *juez*, and the
alcaldes there in Chamula Center.[2]

Now, when the presidente of Chamula heard of the priest's wishes, 3
he began assembling people to do the the priest's bidding.
When some of the people heard this request for assistance,
they heeded it willingly.
Mind you, though, not all the people heard and responded eagerly.

To some, it seemed like a good idea. 4
Others thought that the proposal that they join this new cult and
learn new prayers was disgusting.

Therefore, not everyone heeded the call to join the new cult. 5
But, then, those who *did* like the idea set about eagerly to learn the
prayers and tenets of the new cult.

Every day they would go with their wives to the Ceremonial Center of 6
Chamula to learn the new prayers.
They would go to receive indoctrination right there in the
Chamula church.

They received the indoctrination very eagerly. 7
Every day they would go with their wives to learn the new faith.

8 pero k'alal xchanik ti resale lik sva?anik ?ajvalil sventa jtzobvanej yu?un ?a? ta stzob skotol ti kirsanoe.
?oy la kapitan.
?oy la jlisensyaro.
?oy la jves.

9 ?entonses ?a? ?ajvalil ti jvese ti jlisensyaroe ti kapitane.
?a? la x?al mantal.

10 yu?un ?a? stotik ti jresaletike.
ko?ol xa ta xkopojik xchi?uk peserente ?alkalteetik.

11 ko?ol xa ta x?alik mantal.
yu?un toj tzotz yabtel ti kapitane ti jlisensyaroe ti jvese.

12 ?entonse ti buch'u mu sk'an xbat xchan ti resale ta stik'ik ta chukel.
ba?yel ta stik'ik ta chukel.

13 veno ta tz'akal ta slok'esik chukel ta ?ak'obaltik.
ta la xbat yak' vun ta tuxta? ti buch'u mu xchan ti resale.
pere ma?uk la.

14 jresal jpajaro la sbi.
?ech ti kapitan ti jlisensyaroe ti jvese ?ajvalil yu?un jpajaro.

15 ?entonse ti jresaletik mi ?oy skrontoike ta xbat xchukik talel ta stik'ik ta chukel.
?entonse ta ?ak'obaltik ta slok'esik ta chukel ta xbat yak' vun ta tuxta?.

16 pero ?eche? la ta x?alik ti ta xbat yak' vun ta tuxta?e.
yu?un la ta xbat smilik ta kuchulumtik.

Now, in the midst of the indoctrination sessions, they set about 8
organizing themselves, and named recruiters to enlist
followers for the cult.
One of these was called the "captain."[3]
One was called the "lawyer."
And one was called the "judge."

The captain, the lawyer, and the judge were the bosses. 9
They gave the orders.

This was because they were the chief officers of the prayer makers. 10
They spoke with the same authority as the presidente and the alcaldes.

They now took to giving orders with the same authority as the traditional 11
officials.
This was because the captain, the lawyer, and the judge had become
very powerful.

It got to the point that they put those who did not want to join the 12
new cult in jail.
But putting them in jail was but the first step.

Afterwards, they would go at night to take them out of jail. 13
They would give transferral papers labeled "Tuxtla" to those who
refused to join the cult.
But this was really a grim joke.[4]

"Pajarito Prayer Makers" was what the cult members were called. 14
And the captain, the lawyer, and the judge were the commanding
officers of Pajarito's cult.

Now, this gave Pajarito's commanding officers the pretext to capture 15
anyone they didn't like and put them in jail.
And then they would go at night to take them out of jail and give them
their transferral papers labelled "Tuxtla."

But, in reality, it was a lie that they were given transferral papers for Tuxtla. 16
In truth they sent them to be executed in the hamlet of Kuchulumtik.[5]

17 ˀech'o xal ta xˀalik ta xbat yak' vun ta tuxtaˀ.
jujun la ˀak'obal ta smilik ti kirsano ta kuchulumtike.

18 baˀyel spasik kanal ti jresaletike.
ˀentonse ta tz'akalpat lajik ta milel ti jresaletik.

19 muˀyuk bu spasik kanal.
ˀaˀ la spasik kanal ti buch'u muˀyuk bu xchanik ti resale.

20 baˀyel lajik ta milel ti buch'u muˀyuk bu xchanik ti resale.
pero ta tz'akalpat ˀaˀ ˀispasik kanal ti buch'u muˀyuk bu xchanik ti resale.
la smilik ti buch'u la xchanik ti resale.

21 jlom ˀicham ti jresaletike,
yuˀun muˀyuk bu xaˀik mi la xlajik ta milel.
mu snaˀik ta smilatik.
muˀyuk bu xaˀik k'uxi chamik.

22 ti buch'u muˀyuk bu xchamike yuˀun la jyaˀik ta xlajik ta milel.
k'alal la jyaˀik ta xlajik ta milele jatavik ta ˀora.
muˀyuk xa bu te xvayik ta snaik.

23 jatavik xchiˀuk yajnilik.
batik k'alal ta rinkon.
batik nom xchiˀuk yajnilik.

24 pero baˀyel la jyutilanik ti buch'u muˀyuk bu xchanik ti resale.
k'alal ta xbat xchukik talel skrontoik ti jresaletike ta smajik ta be ti vinike.
porke ti skrontoik ti jresaletike ta xchukik talel xchiˀuk ti yajnilik.

That is why they said they were being sent to Tuxtla to deliver their documents. 17
In truth this meant that they sent people every night to be executed in Kuchulumtik.

Now, at first the prayer makers seemed to be winning. 18
But right in the wake of their victories came a succession of casualties for the prayer makers themselves.

They were not destined to win. 19
The winners in the conflict were going to be those who refused to join in with the prayer makers.

At first those who refused to join the cult of the prayer makers suffered casualties. 20
But in rapid succession thereafter those who refused to join the cult of the prayer makers started to prevail.
They killed the prayer makers.

Some of the prayer-makers died, 21
For they did not realize that they were vulnerable to death.
They did not realize that they could even be killed.
They did not imagine how they could possibly die.

Those who managed to survive were the ones who realized that they were, indeed, vulnerable to death. 22
When they became aware of the threat to their own lives, they fled immediately.
They refused to sleep in their own houses any longer.

They fled with their wives. 23
They went off to Rincón Chamula.[6]
They took their wives with them and went far away.

However, these people deserved this hardship, for they were the ones who had first tormented and fought with those who did not want to join the prayer-making cult. 24
For example, the prayer makers would accost and tie up their enemies, forcing them to come along with them, beating them on the way.
The prayer makers arrested the men along with their wives.

25 ˀech'o xal ti vinik ta smajik ta be.
ti ˀantze muˀyuk bu ta smilik.

26 ˀaˀ noˀox ta xˀak'bik ˀep ˀat tajmek ta bee.
ta xˀik'ik ˀel k'alal ta jteklum ti ˀantze.

27 pere muˀyuk bu ta smilik.
ˀaˀ noˀox ta xˀak'bik ˀep ˀat ta bee.

28 pero ti vinike ta smilik ta jyalel.
muˀyuk xa bu ta xk'ot ta jteklum.

29 te noˀox ta xcham ta be.
muˀyuk xa bu ta xbat yak' vun ta tuxtaˀ.

30 pero ti povre ˀantzetik situb la tajmek ti sbek'talike.
mu xa la xuˀ xanavik.

31 ˀaˀ la ti ˀoy toj nat ti ˀat tajmeke.
ˀoy la toj nat pero jich'il la.
ˀoy la toj muk' pero komkom la.
ˀech'o la xal situb tajmek sbek'tal ti ˀantzetike.

32 pero ta tz'akal muˀyuk bu spasik kanal ti jresaletike.
ˀaˀ noˀox spasik kanal ti buch'u muˀyuk bu xchanik ti resale.

33 ti buch'u la xchanik ti resale la spasik reva ˀek ti k'usi la spasike.
ˀech la spas reva ˀek ti k'usi la spasike.

34 ta la smilik ˀep ti kirsanoe.
la jyak'bik ˀep ˀat ti ˀantzetik ta bee.

35 ˀech'o xal ˀech la spasik reva ˀek.
ti yajnilik ti jresaletike la jyich'ik ˀep ˀat ta be ta snaik bu nakalike.

As for the man, they would beat him up brutally as they dragged him along. 25
But they would not kill the woman who was with him.

They would simply rape her, violently, right there on the path. 26
Then they would take the woman to the Ceremonial Center.

They would not kill her. 27
They would simply rape her continuously as they went along the road.

But, as for the man, they would murder him in cold blood. 28
He would never reach the Ceremonial Center.

He would meet his death right there on the path. 29
He would not even be sent to deliver his documents to Tuxtla to be summarily executed.

But the poor women suffered horribly from having their bodies swell up with cramps. 30
They could scarcely walk!

Some of the prayer makers had great long dicks. 31
Others had them long and slim and slender.
Still others had them big around but short.
That's why the women's bodies were swollen with irritation.

But, later on, the prayer makers stopped imposing their will. 32
It was those who refused to join the cult of the prayer makers who won out in the end.

As for the prayer makers, they got a taste of their own medicine. 33
They got a sample of what they themselves had done to others.

They had been involved in the murder of many people. 34
And many women had been raped by them along the road.

However, the victors engaged in some of the same behavior as those who were defeated. 35
The victors themselves were responsible for frequent rapes of women along the road and in their own homes.

36 ˀech ti vinike la jyich'ik milel ta be.
ta teˀtik bat yak'ik vun ta tuxtaˀ ˀek.

37 yuˀun ˀaˀ ta stojik ti k'usi la spasbik ti xchiˀiltake.
ˀentonse ti jvese ti jlisensyaroe batik k'alal ta rinkon chamula.
te jatavik ˀel xchiˀuk yajnilik.
muˀyuk bu xchamik.

38 ti kapitane jatav ˀel ta jobel.
te la bat snak' sba ta ch'el ch'ulna ta san mikolax ta nopol parke ta jobel.

39 ˀentonse ti kirsano ti buch'u muˀyuk bu xchanik ti resale la jyaˀik ti bu nak'al ti kapitane.
bat saˀik k'alal ta jobel.

40 k'alal k'otik ta jobel ti jmilvanejetike la sk'oponik soltaroetik ta jobel.
ˀabolajanik ba jmiltik ti kapitane.
yuˀun toj lek liyutilanunkutik ta jlumalkutik.

41 ˀijatav.
liˀ ˀitale.

42 leˀ nak'al ta tz'el ch'ulna ta san mikolaxe.
ˀech'o xal ˀabolajanik ba jmiltik xiik la ti jchamoˀetik muˀyuk bu xchanik ti resale.

43 veno lek ˀoy ba jsaˀtik.
k'uchaˀal ˀech spas xi la ti soltaroetik ta jobele.

44 ˀentonse bat la saˀik ti kapitane.
bat la ˀep soltaroetik xchiˀuk stuk'ik xchiˀuk ti jchamoˀetike.

Many prayer makers met their end along the road. 36
They, too, were sent to the woods to "deliver the documents to Tuxtla."

In this manner, the prayer makers were having to pay dearly for what they 37
had done to their own countrymen.
This is why the judge and lawyer had to go to take refuge in
Rincón Chamula.
They fled with their wives.
And so they did not die.

The Captain himself fled to San Cristóbal. 38
He went to hide out near the church of San Nicolás, which is close to
the park in San Cristóbal.[7]

Soon, the people who had opposed the prayer-making cult found out 39
where the captain was hiding.
They went to search for him in San Cristóbal.

When the people who were intent on killing him got to San Cristóbal, 40
they went to talk to the soldiers who were stationed
in San Cristóbal.
"Please, let's be off to kill the captain.
He's been stirring up no end of fighting and trouble for us in our town.

He ran away! 41
He's come here!

He's there in hiding near the San Nicholás church. 42
Therefore, please, let's be off to kill him," insisted the Chamulas who
had not joined the prayer-making cult.

"All right. Let's do it. Let's go find him. 43
Why would he do such things?" replied the soldiers.

So off they went to search for the captain. 44
Lots and lots of soldiers armed with guns accompanied the Chamulas.

45 vaˀi ˀun te la nak'al staik ti kapitan ta nopol ch'ulna ta san mikolax.
veno k'alal la staike ti kapitane la xchukbik sk'ob.
la snitik ˀel k'alal ta kamposano ta jobel.
te snitojikbat ta ch'ojon.

46 k'alal la k'otik ta kamposanoe laj la svaˀanik ta kurus ti kapitane.
laj la slich'bik sk'ob ta kurus te ta kamposano.
laj la schukik ta ch'ojon ta kurus.
laj la smakbik sat ta ˀik'al pok'il.

47 ˀentonse ti soltaroetike laj la yak'bik tuk' ti kapitane.
te la vaˀal ta kurus ta kamposano.

48 pero baˀyel to mu toˀox ta schame la laj yal ti kapitane.
k'alal mi li chame nujul me xamukikun.
ˀa li voˀone mu xicham ta jyalel.
ta jkuch muyel ti banumile.
ˀech'o xal nujul me xamukikun xi la ti kapitane.

49 veno lek ˀoy xi la ti soltaroetik xchiˀuk ti jchamoˀetike.
ˀentonse laj la yak'bik ti tuk'e.

50 ta baˀyel tuk'e muˀyuk la bu xaˀi jelav ti bek' tuk'e.
lek la ta vaˀal.

51 veno ta xchaˀ mojal tuk' ˀaˀ to yaˀi jelav ti bek' tuk'e.
toj majk'ujel la sjol ˀicham ˀo ta jyalel.

52 pero ˀaˀ noˀox sjol ˀimajk'uj.
ti sbek'tale te vaˀal ta kurus.

53 ˀentonse k'alal ˀichame la sjitunik ta xbat smukik.
pero baˀyel la sjok'bik xch'enal.

Sure enough, they found the captain hiding there near the San Nicolás church. 45
So, when they had flushed the captain out, they bound his hands.
They marched him straight to the San Cristóbal cemetery.
They force marched him there, pulling him along, his body bound up in a rope.

When they got to the cemetery, they stood the captain up in front of a cross. 46
They stretched out his arms on the cross there in the cemetery.
They bound him to the cross with a rope.
They placed a black scarf over his eyes as a blindfold.

Then they opened fire on the captain. 47
But he remained there, standing erect against the cross.

And, with life still in him before he died, the captain spoke: 48
"When I die, you should take care to bury me face down.
As for me, I shall not die in humiliation.
I shall rise from the grave.
Therefore, you should be sure to bury me face down," declared the captain.[8]

"Very well, that should be no problem," replied the soldiers and the Chamulas. 49
And with that, they let him have it with their guns.

He did not even seem to feel the lead pass through his body from the first shot of gunfire. 50
He remained standing erect.

Well, when the second shot was fired, it was then that he felt the lead smash through him. 51
It crushed his head and he seemed to die then and there.

But it was only his head that was smashed. 52
His body remained erect there on the cross.

Now, when he died, they untied his body and proceeded to bury him. 53
But first they dug the grave.

54 k'alal la sjok'bik ti xch'enale la smukik ti kapitane.
pero ti soltaroetik xchiˀuk ti jchamoˀetike muˀyuk bu xch'unik ti nujul ta smukike.

55 javal la la smukik.
muˀyuk bu xch'unik ti nujul ta smukike.

56 pero ti soltaroetike laj la xch'unik ti mu xcham ta tuk' ti kapitane ta skuch muyel ti lume.
jujun la k'ak'al ta xk'ot sk'elik ti soltaroetike ti bu mukule.
ta la sk'elik mi ta skuch muyel ti lume.
tz'akil la ti ˀoxib k'ak'al leˀ te la mukul.
muˀyuk la bu xlok'.
te ˀicham ta kamposano ta jobel ti kapitan yuˀun jpajaroetike.
muˀyuk xa bu xchaˀkux.

57 pero la spas reva ˀek ti k'usi la spase,
ti k'usi la smil ti xchiˀiltake.
ˀech ˀicham ˀek.

58 ˀentonse ti jchamoˀetik ti muˀyuk bu xchanik ti resale bat saˀik ti yan jresaletik ti jatavemike.
ta persa la saˀik ti jresaletike.
la smilik skotol.

59 baˀyel la jyich'ik tzakel ti buch'u muˀyuk bu xchanik ti resal ti ˀantzetike.
pero ta tz'akal li ˀantzetik li buch'u la xchanik ti resale la jyich'ik tzakel ti ˀantzetike.

60 ti viniketike la jyich'ik milel jujun k'ak'al.
la saˀik ta teˀtik ta naˀil ch'en mi ˀoy te nak'al.
mi ta nak'al staike ta smilik.

61 ta xˀak'ik ˀat ti ˀantzetike.
pero ˀaˀ ta xˀak'ik ti buch'u muˀyuk bu xchanik ti resale.

Once they had dug the grave, they buried the captain. 54
But the soldiers and the Chamulas did not heed his request to
bury him face down.

They buried him face up. 55
They did not heed his request that they bury him face down.

To tell the truth, the soldiers really believed that the captain would not 56
die from the gunshot and that he would rise up from the grave.
Every day the soldiers would go to check the place where he was buried.
They were checking to see if he would rise from the dead.[9]
But after three days he remained there, buried.
He did not escape death.
The captain of the Pajarito prayer makers died right there in the
San Cristóbal cemetery.
He did not come back to life.

He got just what he had coming, just what he had done to others, 57
Just as he had gone about killing his own people.
So it was now his turn to die, also.

The Chamulas who were opposed to the prayer-making cult went off in 58
pursuit of the prayer makers who had fled.
They were determined to find the prayer makers.
They wanted to kill them all.

In the beginning, it was the women who did not believe in the 59
prayer-making cult who were raped.
Afterward, it was the women who were devoted to the prayer-making
cult who were raped.

Men were killed every day. 60
They were flushed out from the woods and caves where
they were hiding.
If they found them in hiding, they would kill them.

And they would rape the women. 61
But this time those who raped and plundered were the opponents
of the prayer-making cult.

62 ˀech'o xal ti jresaletike jlom ˀichamik.
jlom muˀyuk bu xchamik.

63 ti buch'u muˀyuk bu xchamik batik k'alal ta rinkon.
ˀech'o xal te nakalik ta ˀora ta rinkon ti jresaletik ti voˀnee.
la jyich'ik ˀel nutzel ˀaˀ ti toj pukujik tajmeke.

64 ta smilvalnik.
ta xˀak'ik ˀat.

65 ˀech'o xal la jyich'ik nutzele.
ˀaˀ ˀinutzvanik ˀel ti buch'u muˀyuk bu xchanik ti resale.

66 pero k'alal kuxul toˀox ti kapitane ti k'alal tzobolik toˀox xchiˀuk ti jvese ti jlisensyaroe bat stzakik talel ti jkaxlanetik,
ti buch'u nakajtik ta yosil ˀinyoetike.

67 porke li jkaxlanetike ˀoy yan nakalik ta yosil jyan lum.
ˀech'o xal bat slok'esik.

68 mu sk'anik te nakal ta yosil ˀinyo.
ta persa ta xbat nakluk ta yosil stuk ti bu vok'e.

69 bat snutz lok'el ti jkaxlanetik ta ch'enal ˀoˀ,
ta sananterexe,
ta san pabloe,
ta malalenae,
ta mololе,
ta k'ixin ˀosile.

70 mu la sk'an te nakal ta yosil ˀinyoetik.
ˀaˀ la ta sk'an ti ta sbat nakiuk ta yosil stukike.

So it turned out that some of the prayer makers died in this conflict. 62
Some of the prayer makers survived.

Those who survived found their way to Rincón Chamula as refugees. 63
For that reason, those people who now live in Rincón Chamula are descendants of the prayer makers.
They were forced into exile, for they were very evil and wicked.

They killed. 64
They raped.

That is why they were forced into exile. 65
Those who drove them out were those who did not believe in the prayer-making cult.

But when the captain was still alive and when he was still in league with the judge and the lawyer, they extended their campaign by seizing Ladinos, 66
Those Ladinos who lived in Indian communities.[10]

For there were, indeed, some Ladinos who lived right in the municipal territory of other Indian communities. 67
That is why they went to force them to leave.

They didn't want them living in Indian communities. 68
They wanted to force them to go back and live in their own towns, where they had come from in the first place.

They went to drive the Ladinos out of San Pedro Chenalhó, 69
Out of San Andrés Larrainzár,
Out of San Pablo Chachihuitán,
Out of Magdalena,
Out of Tenejapa,
Out of Hot Country.

They didn't want any Ladinos living there in Indian communities. 70
They wanted them to go and live in their own communities.

71 la snutz ˀel skotolik li jkaxlanetik li buch'u nakalik ta yosil ˀinyoetike.
ˀentonse ti jkaxlanetike batik la k'alal ta jobel.
te la bat naklikuk ta jobel xchiˀuk yajnilik.

72 vaˀi ˀun k'alal la jyaˀik cham ti ˀajvalil yuˀun ti jpajaroe ˀi chaˀsutik ta snaik ti jkaxlanetike,
ti bu toˀox nakalik ta baˀyele.
ˀaˀ te sutik ˀo noˀox.

73 ˀech'o xal li jkaxlanetike ˀoy nakalik ta yosil ˀinyo.
nakalik ta ch'enal ˀoˀ.
nakalik ta sananterex.
nakalik ta molol.
nakalik ta sotz'leb.

74 pero ˀaˀ to ti k'alal cham ti ˀajvalil yuˀun jpajaroe.
ˀaˀ to ti k'alal cham ti kapitane,
ti k'alal jatav ti jvese ti jlisensyaroe.

75 ˀech xtok ti kapitane ti jvese ti jlisensyaroe ta ˀox xbat sk'anik talel ti svaxton san juan ta tuxtaˀe.
porke li svaxton san juane te ˀoy ta tuxtaˀ.

76 la jyelk'anik ti jkaxlanetik ti voˀnee.
laj la yelk'anik ti svaxton san juan ti jkaxlanetik ta tuxtaˀe.

77 ˀech'o xal ti jpajaroetike ta ˀox xbat sk'anik talel ti svaxton san juan ta tuxtaˀe.
bat xchiˀuk stuk'ik xchiˀuk smachitaik xchiˀuk snamteˀik ti jpajaroetike.
xˀak' tuk'uk ta saˀbatik ti svaxton san juane.

78 puru chamulaˀetik bat sk'anik talel ti vaxton.
pero muˀyuk bu spasik kanal ti jpajaroetike.

They succeeded in driving out all the Ladinos who lived in Indian communities. 71
The Ladinos took refuge in San Cristóbal.
They went with their wives to live there.

Then, when they found out that the leader of the Pajarito prayer makers was dead, the Ladinos returned to their former homes, 72
To where they had lived before.
They returned for good.

That is why, to this day, there are Ladinos who live in Indian communities. 73
They live in San Pedro Chenalhó.
They live in San Andrés Larrainzár.
They live in Tenejapa.
And they live in San Lorenzo Zinacantán.[11]

But this return of the Ladinos did not happen until the leader of the Pajarito prayer makers died. 74
Not until the captain himself died,
And the judge and the lawyer had fled.

While they were still pursuing their cause, the captain, the judge, and the lawyer were determined to go to Tuxtla Gutiérrez to demand the return of San Juan's staff. 75
This was because the staff was there in Tuxtla.[12]

The Ladinos had stolen it long ago. 76
In particular, it was the Ladinos in Tuxtla Gutiérrez who had stolen San Juan's staff.

That is why the Pajarito prayer makers were intent on going to Tuxtla Gutiérrez to demand that San Juan's staff be returned. 77
The followers of Pajarito went on this campaign armed with guns, machetes and walking sticks.
They were determined to reclaim San Juan's staff at gunpoint.

It was, indeed, Chamulas who sought to reclaim San Juan's staff. 78
But since they were also Pajarito's followers, they did not succeed in this mission.

79 ˀentonse ti soltaroetik ta tuxtaˀe la jyaˀik ti ta xbat xpojik talel vaxton to jpajaroetike.
toj lek xkaˀi ti mi tal xpojik ti vaxtone.
liˀ ta jmalatik xiikla ti soltaroetike.

80 pero ˀaˀ lek te ta xbat jmalatik ta jompana ti jpajaroetike.
k'alal mi talike ta xkak'betik sveˀelike te ta be.
muˀyuk ta xtal liˀ.

81 k'alal leˀ jaˀ lek te ta xkak'tik veˀikuk ta jompana.
sventa yoˀ xch'ay ˀo yoˀntonik ti jpajaroetike.

82 ta jsaˀtik ˀantzetik ta xbat yak'ik veˀlil ta jompana.
te ta xveˀik skotolik ti jpajaroetike xiik la ti soltaroetik ta tuxtaˀe.

83 ˀentonse ti soltaroetike laj la saˀik ti ˀantzetike xinlanetik te ta tuxtaˀe.
ˀaˀ la bat yak'ik ti veˀlil ta jompanae.
puru ˀantzetik bat yak'ik ti veˀlil ta jompanae.

84 k'alal mi la vak'ik ti veˀlile xajatavik me ta ˀora xˀutatik la ti ˀantzetike.
xiik la ti soltaroetik ta tuxtaˀe.

85 vaˀi ˀun k'alal k'otik ta jompana ti jpajaroetike te k'ot staik ti ˀantzetik xchiˀuk ti sveˀelike.
tekeˀ kuxik jlikeluk liˀe.
pero yoˀ to chakuxike xavuch'ik jujutiˀuk ˀakajvelik.
ˀech xtok chaveˀik jutukuk sventa yoˀ mu xalubik ˀo ta bee xiik la ti xinlanetike.

86 ˀamotonik muˀyuk chamanik xiik la ti xinlanetike.
xuˀuk chaˀe kolaval tajmek xiik la ti jpajaroetike.

Now, the soldiers who were stationed in Tuxtla Gutiérrez found out about 79
the Pajarito prayer makers' plans to reclaim San Juan's staff.
"We are well informed of their plans to steal back the staff.
We shall be waiting for them right here," said the soldiers.

"Or, even better, we will go to wait for Pajarito's troops over there at 80
Copainalá.[13]
When they show up, we will offer them something to eat right by
the road.
They won't make it this far [that is, to Tuxtla].

When they get to Copainalá, we will offer them something to eat. 81
This will help to distract Pajarito's people.

We will enlist some women to go and offer them free food there at 82
Copainalá.
That is where all of Pajarito's troops will enjoy their noon meal,"
plotted the soldiers from Tuxtla cynically.

With this, the soldiers went to enlist some Ladino women from Tuxtla 83
to stage the ambush.
They were supposed to offer a free meal at Copainalá.
It was to be just women, women alone, who would innocently offer the
free meal at Copainala.

"Once you have given them their food, you should get out of the place 84
as fast as you can," they said to the women.
So said the soldiers from Tuxtla.

So it was that when Pajarito's troops reached Copainalá, they found these 85
women there with food all prepared.
"Come now, rest here a little while.
And perhaps a bit of coffee to drink will help you relax.
Maybe you'd even like a little bit to eat so you won't get so tired
on the road," said the Ladino women.

"Don't worry about paying for it," coaxed the Ladino women warmly. 86
"Fine, then, thanks very much," agreed Pajarito's men.

87 laj la xch'unik.
laj la yuch'ik ti kajvele ˀi veˀik la,
laj la skuxik te ta jompana.

88 pero li povre jpajaroetike mu snaˀike mi ta xa smilatik.
muˀyuk bu stuk'ulanik mi ˀoy buch'u snak'oj sba ti vitz yuˀun jompana.

89 k'alal syakel ta xveˀik ti povre jpajaroetike ˀak'batik tuk'.
syakel ta sveˀik ta xˀuch'ik skajvelik ti k'alal ak'batik ti tuk'e.

90 muˀyuk bu xaˀik k'uxi chamik ti povre jpajaroetike.
te ˀicham skotolik ta jompana ti jpajaroetike.

91 ti soltaroetike te la nak'alik ta teˀtik ta vitz ta nopol jompana.
ˀech'o xal ti povre jpajaroetike muˀyuk bu xˀilik bu tal ti tuk'e.

92 ˀech ti ˀantzetik ti k'alal la jyak'bik sveˀel ti jpajaroetike jatavik ta ˀora.
jatavik skotolik.

93 ˀa ti yalojik xa ti soltaroetik ti ta xjatav ti ˀantzetik ti k'alal la jyak'ik ti veˀlile.
ˀijatavik ta ˀora skotolik.

94 vaˀi ˀun ti soltaroetik ti k'alal yilik jatav skotol ti ˀantzetike jlikel laj yak'ik ti tuk'e.
te la chamik skotol ti jpajaro ta jompanae.

95 muˀyuk bu xk'otik ta tuxtaˀ.
muˀyuk bu spasik kanal.
soltaroetik ta tuxtaˀ spasik kanal.

96 muˀyuk bu xuˀ yuˀunik spojel ti svaxton san juane.
te kom ˀo ta tuxtaˀ ti svaxton san juane.

With that, they accepted the invitation. 87
They drank coffee and had something to eat,
There at Copainalá where they stopped to rest.

Little did Pajarito's unfortunate troops realize that they were about to be ambushed. 88
They had no idea that there was anyone hiding there on the hillside by Copainalá.

And while Pajarito's poor men were still eating, the guns opened fire on them. 89
They were right in the midst of their meal and drinking their coffee when they were fired upon.

Pajarito's poor troops didn't even know what hit them. 90
There they died at Copainalá, every one of them.

The soldiers were hiding there in the forest on the hillside. 91
Therefore Pajarito's poor men didn't even see where the gunfire was coming from.

As for the women, as soon as they had served the meal to Pajarito's troops, they got out of there in no time. 92
They fled as fast as they could.

Indeed, the soldiers had told the women to leave as soon as they had served the meal. 93
So all of them fled and got away safely.

As for the soldiers, as soon as they saw that all of the women had gotten away from the place, they immediately opened fire. 94
Right there at Copainalá all of Pajarito's men died.

They never made it to Tuxtla Gutiérrez. 95
They did not succeed.
It was the soldiers from Tuxtla who won.

They did not succeed in reclaiming San Juan's staff. 96
San Juan's staff remained right there in Tuxtla Gutiérrez.

97 ˀech'o la xal li jkaxlanetike toj k'ulejik tajmek,
yuˀun te ti svaxton san juan ta tuxtaˀe.

98 yuˀun ti svaxton san juane ta la xˀak' ˀep tak'in tajmek.
yuˀun ˀaˀ smeˀ ti tak'ine.

99 ˀech'o xal toj k'ulej li jkaxlanetike,
li povre ˀinyoetike toj povreik tajmek.

That is why the Ladinos are very rich, 97
For San Juan's staff is there in Tuxtla Gutiérrez.

You see, San Juan's staff magically produces loads of money. 98
For it is the "mother of money."[14]

That is why Ladinos are very rich, 99
And why the poor Indians are very poor indeed.

1 ˀoy la jun kuento sventa leto ti voˀnee.
la jyalbun kaˀi jtot voˀnee.

2 ˀoy la leto.
ˀoy la leto sventa la chamulaˀ ti voˀnee.

3 baˀyi la tal ti karansae.
ˀispas la leto.

✠ ✠ ✠

TEXT 70

About How the Carranza Soldiers Came to Live with Us Forever as Rats

Marián López Calixto

There is a story about a war that happened long ago. 1
  My father told it to me long ago.

There was a war. 2
  There was a war that involved Chamula long ago.

First came Carranza. 3
  He was the one who stirred up the war.

FIGURE 95

First came Carranza.
  He was the one who stirred up the war.

4 ˀoy jun jkaxlan mu la sk'an la xlaj ti yalabtake.
bat la sk'an parte ta mejiko.
k'ot la ta mejiko sk'opon ti komierno ne.

5 mi xak'an xapojbun ti kalab nich'nabe,
xi la k'otel ti jkaxlane ta mejikoe.

6 k'uchaˀal xi la ti peserentee ti komiernoe.
yuˀun chuvajot xi la ti ˀajvaliletike.
melel xi la ti jkaxlane.

7 veno ˀak'o batuk ˀabtejuk yuˀun chuvajel leˀe xi la ti ˀajvalile.
veno xi la ti soltaroetike.

8 jech la ti jkaxlane bat la ˀabtejuk.
yich' la ˀech'el spiko.
k'ot la ta kampo.
mu la sk'an xˀabtej ti jkaxlane.

9 mi chapojbun ti jviniktake xi la ti jkaxlane.
moˀoj jecheˀ chaval xi la ti ˀajvalile.

10 ta me jyales ti jpiko ˀun chaˀe xi la ti jkaxlane.
yalesoˀ xutuk la ˀun.
veno xi la ti jkaxlane.

11 ˀisyales la ti spiko ˀune ˀa ti banamile.
toj lomel la ti banamile.

12 vaˀun bat la ta jun lum xtok.
k'ot la ta jun lum xtok.

There was once a Ladino who wanted to do something about the plight of his children.[1] 4
He traveled to Mexico City to seek justice.
He arrived in Mexico City and spoke directly to the government.

"Wouldn't you like to do something to defend and bring justice to my children, my offspring?" 5
This he asked upon arriving in Mexico City.

"Why should I?" replied the president of the government. 6
"We think you're a lunatic," said the various high officials of the government.
"That may be," replied the Ladino.

"Well, off to hard labor with him, for he is obviously crazy," declared the great leader. 7
"That's right," added the soldiers.

With that the Ladino departed to do forced labor. 8
He took his pickaxe with him.
He reached the countryside.
But this Ladino had no intention of doing ordinary labor.[2]

"Would you join me in defending and bringing justice for my people?" asked the Ladino. 9
"Not at all, for you are spreading lies," said the foreman of the work crew.

"So help me, I will strike a blow with my pickaxe," threatened the Ladino. 10
"Strike your blow, then," was the reply to him.
"Very well," said the Ladino.

And he proceeded to land a blow on the earth with his pickaxe. 11
And with that, the earth itself caved in.[3]

Then he proceeded to go to other communities also. 12
He reached these other communities in due course.

13 mi xak'an xapojun xut la k'otel ti karansae.
veno batik xi la ti karansae.

14 tal la ta mejiko.
k'ot la svok'ik ti ti? nae.
?ixchik'ik la ti nae.
yak'bik la kas.

15 yelk'anik la manta.
yelk'anik la k'u?il.

16 k'otik la ta sna peserente.
svok'bik la sna ti peserentee.

"Will you be willing to defend my cause?" he proposed to the Carrancistas when he arrived. 13
"Yes, let's be off," said the Carrancistas.[4]

They came to Mexico City. 14
They broke down doors.
They burned houses.
They started the fires by pouring fuel oil around.

They stole cloth. 15
They stole clothing.

They reached the presidential palace. 16
They broke down the doors of the presidential palace.

FIGURE 96

They reached the presidential palace.
They broke down the doors of the presidential palace.

17 ˀoy la ˀep la tajmek soltaro la ta sna ti peserentee.
ˀoy la jun soltaro, ta xak' tuk'.

18 spojbik la ti stuk'e.
ˀisjipik la ta kaˀ.
ˀismilik la ti soltaroe.

19 jelav la talel ta mejiko.
vul la talel ta joˀbel.
liˀ la nakie.

20 jech la ti soltaroe laj la yelk'an la ˀep la kaˀ.
sventa xkajiik ta xak' leto ta chamulaˀ.
ˀa ti kaˀ lae toj toyol la tajmek.
ti skaˀike mu la xkoˀolaj k'uchaˀal chak skaˀ liˀ ta ta jobele.

21 ˀispas la snaik ta xokon be.
ˀa ti soltaroe noj la ta be.
te la tzvayik la ta be.

22 slekoj te ˀoy la ta parke.
ti soltaroetike ˀa ti voˀnee te la ta parkee.

23 toj toyol la tzoˀ kaˀ.
jech la ti povre kirsanoetike ta la smesik ti parkee.

24 ch'abal la smes sventa ta smesike.
mi ch'abal la ˀames:
batan la ta teˀtik.
bat la saˀo tal ta ˀamese.

25 ta taryal la ta jmestik.
mi laj ˀames:
batan la ta ch'ivit.

26 mi mu la xak'an xames:
batan la ta chukel.

There were a great many soldiers involved in these events. 17
There was one soldier who fired a shot.

Then the Carrancistas stole the guns. 18
They loaded them onto horses.
They killed the soldiers.

Then they passed through Mexico City and headed this way. 19
They set off for San Cristóbal.
Here they settled in to live.[5]

Well, the soldiers stole lots of horses. 20
They did this so they could go mounted on horseback to take the warfare to Chamula.
These horses were veritable giants.
Their horses were not at all like the horses that people have around San Cristóbal today.

They would make shelters beside the roads. 21
The roads were filled to overflowing with soldiers.
They would sleep in the roads.

Still others were camped in the central park of San Cristóbal. 22
The soldiers of long ago were living right there in the central park.

There was horse manure everywhere. 23
So the poor local people had to sweep the park.

They had no brooms. 24
And if you didn't have a broom, they would command:
"Go to the woods.
Go and make a broom for yourself."

We were made to sweep horse manure by assigned amounts. 25
When you had finished, they would command:
"Off with you to the market."

If you didn't want to sweep, they would command: 26
"Off with you to jail."

27 ˀa ti soltaroetike muˀyuk la stilib spixolike.
puru la pixolal slapojik.
ˀa ti sbi ti soltaroetike karansa.

28 ˀa ti povre kirsanoetike sob la xtalik ta joˀbel.
k'alal la mi jutuk xa la sk'an xk'otik la ta joˀbele ta la snak' la sbaik
ta teˀtik.

29 ˀoy la yan ti povre kirsanoetike mu la snaˀik mi ˀoy la soltaro ta be.
ti povre kirsanoetike skuchoj la ˀech'el siˀik.

30 jech la ti viniketike ˀi la schepan la siˀik la komel ta be.
bat la ˀabtejuk ta kampo.
puru la kuch momol sventa la sveˀel la skaˀ ti soltaroe.
mi laj la ˀataryal xuˀ la xabat ta ch'ivit.

31 jech la ti yan ti povre kirsanoetike te la chotajtik ta teˀtik.
ti ˀantzetike ti viniketike jaˀ la la xˀochik ta chanib ˀora mal jtotik.
xuˀ xa la xˀochik ti kirsanoetike.

The soldiers did not have helmets. 27
They just wore big cowboy hats.
These soldiers were called Carrancistas.

Sometimes this would happen to the poor Indian people who were coming early to San Cristóbal to go to the market. 28
When they had just reached the outskirts of San Cristóbal, they would have to go hide in the woods.

There were other poor Indian people who did not know there were soldiers camped by the road. 29
These poor people were innocently carrying along their loads of firewood.

It turned out that these men who were carrying firewood would have to unload their bundles on the road. 30
They were forced by the soldiers to go to work in the fields.
They had to cut and carry lots of grass that the soldiers used to feed their horses.
Once you had finished your job, the soldiers would say, "Now, you can be on your way to the market."

Now, as for the other poor souls, they remained sitting there, hidden in the woods. 31
The women and men would not dare to proceed until four in the afternoon.
Then these people could be on their way into San Cristóbal.

32 jech ti ˀantzetike k'alal ta xˀochik ta yutil joˀbele ta sbon sjolik ta lortano.
mi mu la sbon ti sjolike ˀa ti soltaroe ta xak' ˀat.

33 laj yoˀntonik spasik leto ta joˀbel.
tal ta chamulaˀ.

34 ˀital xa me ti soltaroe.
tal xa smilotik.
mu yora, k'usi chijbatotik xiik la ti kirsanoetike.

35 ˀa ti povre kirsanoetike ˀixˀok'lajetik xa la.
ti povre kirsanoetike.

36 ˀa ti soltaroe ti stuk'ik xlilet xa la tajmek.
tal la ta naetik ta skotol parajeetik.

As for the women who had to go into San Cristóbal, these would dust 32
their hair with DDT powder.
If they did not change the color of their hair this way, the soldiers
would rape them.[6]

They finished their warfare in San Cristóbal. 33
They proceeded to Chamula.

"Now the soldiers have come! 34
Now they've come to kill us!
We're done for! What's to become of us?" exclaimed the people.

The poor people were weeping now. 35
Pity those poor people!

Then came the terrible shattering sounds of the soldiers' gunfire. 36
They were coming into the house compounds of all of the hamlets!

FIGURE 97

As for the women who had to go into San Cristóbal, these would
dust their hair with DDT powder.
If they did not change the color of their hair this way, the
soldiers would rape them.

37 ˀoy la yalak'ik ti kirsanoetike.
yelk'an la ti soltaroe.

38 ta la xˀelk'an bin.
ta la xˀelk'an vaj.
ta la xˀelk'an ˀixim.
ta la xˀelk'an tak'in.
puru la jˀelek' la ti karansae.

39 ˀa ti karansae ta la xch'ayik patan sventa la muˀyuk ti multae.
ˀak'o mi xamajvan,
muˀyuk multa,
ˀi muˀyuk la chukel.

40 ˀoy la yan ti kirsanoetike bu la smajoj la sbaik ta voˀnee.
te to la snaˀojik la la smilik ti xchiˀiltake ti kirsanoetike.

41 jech la ti karansae ta la stiˀ chij.
ta la stiˀ ˀalak'.
toj chopol it karansae.

42 jech la ti karansae pas la ta ch'o.
kom ti xch'ulel.

43 tal la yan soltaroetik.
ˀa ti sbi ti soltaroetike pajarito.
toj muk'tik la spixolik tajmek.

44 puru la pas leto jujun la k'ak'al tajmek.
ˀa ti tuk'e jaˀ la spasik to letoe.

45 vaˀun tal jun la jkaxlan liˀ ta joˀbele.
laj la spas jun k'op ta mejiko.
meltzaj la jun ˀaviyon ta mejiko.

46 tal la ti aviyone.
vul la ta joˀbel.
bat la sibtas la ti soltaroe.

Some of the people had chickens. 37
The soldiers stole them.

They stole cooking pots. 38
They stole tortillas.
They stole corn.
They stole money.
The Carrancistas were nothing but thieves.

The Carrancistas, indeed, did away with tributes and fines. 39
Even though you assaulted someone else,
No fine,
No jail.[7]

But, even long ago, there were people who assaulted one another. 40
There have always been people who would sometimes kill one another.[8]

Indeed, the Carrancistas ate stolen sheep. 41
They ate stolen chickens.
The Carrancistas were common criminals.

For this reason the Carrancistas became rats. 42
Rats became fixed in their very being as their soul companions.[9]

Then there came another kind of soldiers. 43
These were called the soldiers of Pajarito.[10]
They had hats that were truly enormous.

These people were feverishly involved in making war every day. 44
With their guns, they made war every day.

Then there appeared on the scene a Ladino, right here in San Cristóbal. 45
He communicated with Mexico City.
He arranged for an airplane to come from Mexico City.

The airplane arrived. 46
It swept into San Cristóbal.
It set out to frighten the soldiers.[11]

47 jech la ti jkaxlane laj la yich' la ʔech'el ʔep tan ta ʔaviyon.
bat la sk'el buy la ʔoy ti letoe.

48 jech la ti soltaroe yil la tal ti aviyone.
k'uxi tal leʔe xi la ti soltaroe.

49 yak'bik la tuk'.
k'alal la yak'bik la ti tuk'e,
jech la ti jchojeroe yak'be la yal tal ta tanil k'ok'.

It happened that the Ladino who arranged for the plane to come had it 47
well loaded with wood ash.
He went on board the plane to guide the pilot to where the battle
was going on.

It happened that the soldiers saw the plane coming into sight. 48
"What is that thing coming at us from up there?" asked the soldiers.

They fired shots at it. 49
Once they had fired their shots,
It happened that the pilot released a load of wood ash.[12]

FIGURE 98

They fired shots at it.
Once they had fired their shots,
It happened that the pilot released a load of wood ash.

50 ˀa ti soltaroetik jatavik la skotolik.
bat la ta kaˀ ta ˀora.
sutik la ta slumik ti soltaroetike.

51 jech la ti jkaxlane laj la stak la ta k'anel ti soltaro sventa mejikoe.
tal la ti soltaroetike.
ˀismakik la ta be ti kirsanoetike.

52 ˀa ti stuk'ike slomet xa la ta ventana liˀ ta bechijtik.
jaˀ ti soltaroetike.

53 tal la ti kirsanoetike sventa chamulaˀ.
ˀi ba la bat spasik leto xchiˀuk soltaroetike ti kirsanoetike.

54 jech la ti soltaroe ˀoch la talel ta parajetik.
tal la ta petej.

55 ˀispas la snaik ta jolvitz jaˀ ti bu la lek mas tzelej.
ˀi te la spas la snaik ˀa ti soltaroetike.

56 laj la yelk'an ˀalak'.
laj la yelk'an chij.
ˀi laj la yelk'an bin.
ˀa ti povre kirsanoetike ch'ay la skotol ti k'uxi la ˀoy ta snaik.

57 jech la ti soltaroetike puru la mil chij spas ta naetik.
tzkoban ti ˀantzetike.
jech la ti ˀantzetike laj la yak'bik la ˀich' ti smisike.

58 tal la jun soltaro:
mi xak'an ˀat xi la ti soltaroe.
tana sinyor xi la ti ˀantze.

59 veno xi la ti soltaroe.
ˀay ˀay ˀay chilaj xa.
k'ux tajmek ti kate xi la ti soltaroe.

The soldiers fled, all of them. 50
They dispersed at once, fleeing on horseback.
They all returned to their home communities.

It happened that the Ladino who brought the airplane was able to request troop reinforcements from Mexico City. 51
These soldiers arrived.
They went to head off the enemy by blocking the road.

The guns roared now with full force there in Ventana and Be Chijtik hamlets. 52
This was the sound of the soldiers.

The people from Chamula came forth to face them. 53
They went forward to make war with the soldiers.[13]

The soldiers even entered the hinterland of Chamula. 54
They came to Petej hamlet.

They made their encampments at the top of a mountain there where the site was high and the view was good. 55
There the soldiers made their encampments.

They stole chickens. 56
They stole sheep.
They stole cooking pots.
The poor people lost every little thing they had in their homes.

The soldiers would just kill lots of sheep in people's house compounds. 57
They would rape the women.
And the women, to defend themselves would put chile on their cunts.

A soldier would come up and say: 58
"Would you like to fuck?" the soldier would ask.
"Of course, mister," the woman would say.

"Fine, then," the soldier would say. 59
"Ay, ay, ay, it's all over.
My dick hurts like crazy," the soldier would say.

60 jech la ti soltaroe:
mu xa la sk’an xak’ ˀat ti soltaroe.
toj chopol tajmek ti ˀantzetike xi la ti soltaroe.

61 jech la ti povre kirsanoetike bat la ta teˀtik jatavuk.
ˀa ti puta soltaroetike bat la saˀvanuk ta teˀtik.
mi ta la sta ta teˀtik ta smil ta tuk’.

62 k’usi chanopik xi la ti kirsanoetike.
jaˀ lek batik ta joˀbel k’antik parte xiik la ti kirsanoetike.

63 vaˀun la lik la ta joˀbel.
sk’anik la parte.
ˀerasto la sbi ti jkaslan.

64 povre chamula.
mi te k’ot ti soltaroe xi la ti jkaxlane.
te k’to xi la ti kirsanoetike.

65 mu k’u xal ˀavoˀontonik li ˀay xa ta mejiko xi la ti jkaxlane.
veno lek ˀoy ˀun chaˀe xi la ti viniketike.

66 ˀak’o k’usi spas xi la ti jkaxlane,
mu xaxiˀik xi la ti jkaxlane.
veno xutik la ti jkaxlane.

67 jech la ti jkaxlane laj la stak ta k’anel jun ˀaviyon.
lok’ la jun semuna.
tal la ti ˀaviyone.
ˀivul la talel ta jobel ti ˀaviyone.

68 jech la ti jkaxlane:
batan ˀavokoluk ba sibteso.
ˀich’o ˀech’el tan xi la ti jkaxlane.
veno xuˀuk xi la ti jchojeroe.

69 tal la ta chamulaˀ.
jech la ti soltaroetike:
k’usi xa tal leˀe xi la ti soltaroetike.

So the soldiers decided this: 60
They were no longer interested in raping the women.
"My God, they're awful, these women!" the soldiers would say.

So it was that the poor people had to flee to the woods. 61
And the fucking soldiers would go to pursue them into the woods.
If they found them, they would kill them with their guns.

"What shall we do?" wondered the people. 62
"Let's go to seek justice in San Cristóbal," the people decided.

So it was that they arrived in San Cristóbal. 63
They sought justice.
Erasto was the name of the Ladino whom they sought out.[14]

"Poor Chamulas! 64
Have the soldiers gotten there?" asked the Ladino.
"They've arrived there," declared the Chamulas.

"Don't worry on that account, for I have already been to Mexico City 65
to resolve these problems," said the Ladino.
"Very well, then," said the Chamula men.

"Whatever happens," said the Ladino, 66
"Don't be afraid," said the Ladino.
"Very well," was their reply to the Ladino.

So it was that the Ladino was able to commission an airplane. 67
A week went by.
The airplane came.
The airplane flew right into San Cristóbal.

So, the Ladino gave orders to the pilot: 68
"Go, please, scare the soldiers away.
Carry wood ash with you," said the Ladino.
"Very well," said the pilot.

The pilot swept over Chamula. 69
And the soldiers exclaimed:
"What's that coming at us from up there?" they asked.

70 k'alal la tal yil ti aviyone li soltaroetike.
ˀi jatavik la.

71 ˀoy la skaˀik.
muyik la ta kaˀ ta ˀora.
jlikel la bat ta ˀora skotol la ti soltaroetike.

72 jech la ti yan ti kirsanoetike xˀok'ik xa la tajmeke.
k'usi xa tal leˀ ne xi ti yane.

73 jech la ti soltaroetike bat la ta slumal,
ti bu la likem talel.

74 ˀoy la xch'ulelik ti karansaetike.
puru la ch'oˀ.

75 jech la ti xch'ulelik ti karansaetike komanuk la ta naetik.
jaˀ yuˀun jech la kom xch'ulelik ti soltaroetike.

76 jech la ti voˀne muˀyuk la karo,
ˀi muˀyuk ˀaviyon,
muˀyuk la visikleta.

77 puru la ta kaˀ xanavik ti jkaxlanetike.
puru la kaˀ ta xanavik ti ˀajvalileteike.

78 jaˀ jech ti leto ti ˀech' ti voˀnee.
toj ˀabol la sbaik tajmek ti povre kirsanoe.

79 jaˀ jech laj ˀo ti kuentoetike sventa letoik.

When it got there, the soldiers saw the airplane. 70
They fled.

They had their horses. 71
They mounted their horses in no time.
At once, all the soldiers took flight.

It happened that some of the people wept desperately. 72
Others asked, "What's coming next?"

And so these Carrancista soldiers fled to their home communities, 73
Back to where they had come from.

But the animal-soul companions of the Carrancistas are still with us. 74
They are nothing other than common rats.

So it was that the animal-soul companions of the Carrancistas were made 75
to remain forever in our houses.
So it was that the soul companions of the soldiers remained with us.

So it was, long ago when there were no trucks, 76
No airplanes,
No bicycles.

People went about only on horseback. 77
The rich Ladinos would travel only on horseback.

So it was that the war happened long ago. 78
Pity those poor people!

And that is the end of these accounts of the time of war. 79

1 ˀoy jun kuento sventa jun ˀolol.
pero mol la k'alal la vok'e.

2 jech ti smeˀ ti ˀolole,
mu la bu k'ux la yaˀi k'alal la vok'e.

3 ˀi jech la ti mu ˀolol la ˀune,
mu la bu ˀok' k'alal la vok' talel.

4 jech la ti smeˀ ti ˀolol la ˀune sk'el la ti yole.
jaˀ to la yil mu mol la te chotol ti yole.

5 ˀay k'uxi la chotol ˀune.
pere k'uxi la jpas xi la ti mu ˀantze.

6 ˀuy ˀa ti yol la ˀune toj mol la tajmek.
jech la ti yisime sak xa la tajmek.
k'alal la ta sjol jun la snatikil la sjol ti mole.

7 jech la ti mol ˀolol la ˀune yal la sloˀil ˀun:
tekeˀ ˀun mu xa me jal ta xachiˀinik ˀun.
jaˀ ta jak' buchu k'uxi ta xak'anik ta chamelik ˀun.

8 xi la ti mol ˀolol.
ˀi xiˀ la tajmek ti stot smeˀ ti mol ˀolole la ˀune.

TEXT 71

About How the Old Child and the Mother of Sickness Brought the Fever Epidemic to Chamula

Marián López Calixto

This is the story of a child. 1
However, he was already old when he was born.

As for the child's mother, 2
She felt no pain at the time of his birth.

As for the strange child himself, 3
He didn't even cry when he was born.

So, then. The mother of the child stared at her son. 4
Soon she realized that the old man sitting there was her son.

"Ay, what is that sitting there? 5
What has happened to me?" exclaimed the poor woman.

Indeed, her son was very, very old. 6
His beard was already very white.
As for his hair, it was as long as that of an old man.

As for the old child, this is what he had to say: 7
"Well, you don't seem eager to keep me company for long.
So I will ask anyone who is interested: What kind of sickness do you desire?"[1]

So spoke the old child. 8
And the old child's parents were terrified.

9 vaˀun yal la ti mol ˀolol la ˀune:
ˀalikun,
mi xalampia.
ˀo mi ronxa.
ˀo mi viˀnal.
ˀo mi tan xi la ti mol ˀolole.

10 jech la ti stot smeˀ ti mol ˀolol la ˀune,
k'ak'al chamel ta jk'an xiik la ti stot smeˀ ti mol ˀolol la ˀune.

11 veno lek ˀoy ˀun chaˀe xi la ti mol ˀolole.
moˀoj jaˀ ta jk'an xi la ti kirsano la ˀune.

12 vaˀun laj la yal la komel ti sloˀil la ˀune.
ˀi te la ch'ay te ta yut la snaik ti kirsano la ˀune.
k'alal laj la yal komel la ˀune.

13 ˀuy jech la ti kirsanoetik la ˀune yal la sloˀilik la ˀune:
ˀoy vok' jkot ˀolol.
pere toj chopol tajmek la jyalbunkutik.

14 ta la xijchamotik k'ak'al chamel la ta xtal.
mu la me yora.
ta la me xtal ti chamele.
xi la jyal jun mol ˀolol xi la kirsanoetike.

15 vaˀun ti kirsanoe la ˀun k'unk'untik me la tal ti k'ak'al chamel la ˀune.
jech la ti kirsanoe laj la skotolik tajmek.
pere puru la k'ok' ta xˀak'batik la tajmek ti kirsanoetik lae.

16 vaˀun jech la ti yan la ˀune.
mi ta la xabat ta be ta xanobal ta ˀak'obaltik la ˀune te la jnuptik ta be smeˀ ti chamel lae.

17 vaˀun ˀoy la jun vinik yuˀun ta la xbat ta joˀbel ti vinik lae.
vaˀun jech la ti vinik la ˀune ˀoy la skuchoj la yikatz.

Then the old child spoke again: 9
"Tell me what you wish.
Measles?
Skin rash?
Famine?
Volcanic ash fall?" inquired the old child.[2]

Then the parents replied, hoping to receive a lesser affliction. 10
"We want the fever," said the parents of the old child.

"Very well, then, if that's what you want," said the old child. 11
"Yes, that's what we want," said the people.

And that was what the old child had to say. 12
And with that he disappeared to retire and repose in the homes
of the people.
That is, after he had left his strange message.

Alas! Soon the people began spreading the news: 13
"I gave birth to an animal child![3]
And I tell you what he came to tell us was just awful.

We shall all die of a fever that is on its way. 14
Indeed, our time is up.
The plague is already on its way.
That's what the old child told us," said the people.

Indeed, slowly but surely, the fever came upon the people. 15
Well, all of the people perished.
The fever was given to the people with great intensity.

Still another event happened at that time.[4] 16
If you went walking at night, you met the Mother of Sickness there
on the road.

Well, there was this man who was walking to San Cristóbal. 17
It happened that the man was carrying a load.

18 vaˀun skux la ta be ˀun.
k'uxi ta xtal tana taj ˀune xi la ti vinike.
ˀi te la yaˀbinoj tajmek ti vinike.

19 jech la ti smeˀ ti chamel la ˀune.
yantik la xnopoj la talel ˀun.

20 ˀoy la stampolik.
ˀoy la svobik.
ˀoy la yorkinaik.

21 ˀu ta xk'ejik la ta be ti pukuje.
tal xa me jk'ojtik.
tal xa me jk'intik xi la ti smeˀ ti chamele.
ˀi ta la xuxabajik tajmek.

22 vaˀun jech la ti vinik la ˀune te la smalaˀoj la ˀun.
ˀi yil la ti vinike.
ˀay kirsano xkil ˀune xi la ti vinike.

23 mi liˀote bankil.
mi ta xijbatotik.
tal xa me ti jk'ojtike.
tal xa me ti jk'intike.
ˀora k'ejinkutik ˀun.
mu me xavat ˀavoˀnton xi la ti smeˀ ti chamele.

24 ˀa moˀoj.
bu k'alal ta xabatik ta xibat ˀek xi la ti mu vinike.

25 vaˀun jech la ti mu vinike naˀbal la bat ˀek.
ˀi ta la skuchoj la ˀech'el ti yikatze.

26 vaˀun jech la ti pukuj smeˀ ti k'ak'al chamel ˀune ˀoy la yan max.
ˀoy la svanteraik.
ˀoy la svobik.
ˀu ta la xˀak'otajik tajmek.

Soon, he found himself resting a bit there by the road. 18
"What's that coming?" exclaimed the man.
There the man was listening intently to what seemed to be approaching.

It was none other than the Mother of Sickness. 19
She drew close to the man.

She had her drums. 20
She had her guitars.
She had her accordion.[5]

My God! How these diabolical creatures were singing there by the road! 21
"Our masquerade is upon us![6]
Our festival has come!" exclaimed the Mother of Sickness.
And they all whistled with abandon.[7]

The man had been waiting there. 22
Indeed, the man saw all of this.
"Why, it seems to be people I see coming," observed the man incredulously.

"Are you there, older brother? 23
Shall we go along together?
Our masquerade is upon us!
Our festival has come!
Now it's time for us to sing!
Don't let your heart be sad!" said the Mother of Sickness.[8]

"I wouldn't think of it! 24
Wherever you're going, I'm going there, too!" exclaimed the foolish man.

And, so convinced, the foolish man joined them on their journey. 25
He even picked up his load and carried it along.

Well, this demon, this Mother of Sickness, had monkey impersonators as companions. 26
They had their banners.
They had their guitars.
My God! They were also dancing around like dervishes!

27 vaˀun staik la ˀolol be la ti smeˀ ti chamel la ˀune.
mi ta xijkuxotik.
chepano me ˀakajon xˀutat la ti vinike.
vaˀun xchepan la ˀek ˀun.

28 vaˀun jech la ti pukuj la ˀune pas la ta tz'iˀ ˀun.
ˀi te noˀox la ch'ay ˀun.

29 ˀa ti vinik la ˀune majbat la sjol ˀun.
mu xa la snaˀ ti sbe la ˀune.

30 k'alal sk'el la ti vinike te la chotol ta naˀil ch'en.
ˀi ch'ay la ta yikatz ˀune.

31 vaˀun jech la ti vinik la ˀune jaˀ la ti ˀak'obaltik la ˀune.
mu la snaˀ k'uxi ta xbat.

32 vaˀun ti vinike la ˀune vaˀi la ˀun.
ˀi mu la xvaˀi la tajmek.

33 ˀi jaˀ la ti yok te xukul la ta ˀak' la ˀune.
xiˀ la tajmek ti vinike.

34 vaˀun jech la sbek'tal ti vinik la ˀune jun la stuˀil tajmek.
k'uxi la jpas taj ˀune xi la ti vinike.

35 vaˀun k'alal sakub la ˀune solel la lok' talel la ˀun.
ˀi vul la ta sna ˀun.
yal la ti sloˀil la ˀune.

36 mu jnaˀ k'uxi la jta ta be.
koˀoltik kirsano yilel.

37 vaˀun batik xiyutun.
vaˀun la jch'un ˀek ˀun.

38 solel li bat tajmek ˀi muˀyuk bu la jkaˀi k'uxi li bat ta jyalel.
jaˀ xa noˀox te ˀoy xa chotolun ta naˀil ch'ene xi la ti vinike.

In a little while, when they had traveled some distance, the Mother of Sickness spoke: 27
"Shall we rest?
Why not put down your load?" she suggested to the man.
And with that he put it down.

Then it happened that the demon, the Mother of Sickness, turned into a dog. 28
Right then and there, she disappeared.

The man felt that his head had been hit. 29
He no longer knew which way he was going.

When the man came to, he was sitting in a cave. 30
He had lost his pack of goods that he had been carrying.

The man found that it was the middle of the night. 31
He had no idea where he was going.

The man stood up. 32
But he wasn't able to stand up properly.

His feet had been hobbled with vines! 33
The man was terrified!

What's more, his body gave off a terrible stench. 34
"What's happened to me, anyway?" exclaimed the man.

Well, when it grew light, he simply set off on his way. 35
He found his way home.
He told his story.

"I don't know *what* I met on the road. 36
These creatures looked like people.

'Come along. Let's go!' they said to me. 37
Well—I obeyed.

I simply went along without really knowing where I was going. 38
Then I just found myself sitting in a cave," said the man.

39 k'u s?elan avilbe sat ti pukuj ?une xi la ti xchi?iltake.
mu stak' ?ilel.
ko?oltik makal li sate.
chop ?o smu sat.
toj tzoj tajmek.

40 va?un li bat ?un.
mu yora.
ta xa xicham ma? li?e.
mu xa xi?ech' ju?un xi la ti vinike.

41 va?un jech la ti vinik la ?une ?u likel la cham ?un.
puru la k'ok' ta x?ak'bat la tajmek ?un.

42 pero cham la ti kirsanoetik la ?une.
jech la yan ti povre kirsanoetik la ?un.

43 mu?yuk xa la buch'u ta xmukat ti vinike.
te la ta xlajanuk ta tz'i? ti kirsanoetike.

44 va?un jech la ti yan la ?une jatavik la ?ech'el ?un.
pere mu?yuk la me sk'u?ik k'alal la xjatavik la ?une.
t'ant'an la ta xbatik ta ?ora.

45 ?a ti mi ?a lapoj ?ak'u? la ta xabate ta la jkuchintik la ti chamele.
va?un mi t'ant'an la ta xijbatotik la ?un lek la ?un.
ja? la ta xk'exav ti k'ak'al chamele.

46 laj ?o.

"What did the demons' faces look like?" asked the man's relatives. 39
"They couldn't be seen very well.
It was as though their faces were covered with masks.
Their wretched faces were very strange.
They were of an intense reddish color.

So, I'm afraid I'm as good as dead. 40
My time is up.
I think I am going to die here and now.
I will not survive this."

Uuh! It was just awful! The man died in no time. 41
He was stricken with a very high fever.

Then, more people died. 42
And still others, poor souls, had the same fate.

There was not even anyone left to bury the man. 43
The people were simply finished off by the dogs.

It happened that some were able to flee. 44
But when they fled, they had no clothing.
They were naked as they rushed to run away.

If you had clothing on when you fled you would carry the sickness with you. 45
If you were naked, you might come out all right.
For nudity causes shame to the fever sickness.[9]

The account is finished. 46

1 loˀil yuˀun jvanjelista la xchik' jtotik.

2 vaˀi ˀun ti jvanjelistaetike la xchik'ik ta k'ok' ti jtotik ta ch'ulnae.
yuˀun mu sk'anik ti ˀoy ti jtotik ta ch'ulnae.

3 maˀuk la jtotik.
jepel teˀ la.
mu la snaˀ xk'opoj.

4 ˀoy la jtotik pero jun noˀox la.
li jtotik ta vinajele maˀuk la jtotik.
lus la.

5 mu la xuˀ jk'opontik.
pukuj la.

6 ˀoy la jun jtotik nakal ta ch'en.
snaˀ la sk'opon.
ˀaˀ la mero jtotik.

7 yan li ta ch'ulnae.
maˀuk la jtotik.
pukuj la.

8 ˀech'o la xal la xchik'ik ta k'ok' ti jtotik ta ch'ulnae.
pero skotol jtotik la xchik'ik ta k'ok'.

9 ˀa li ch'ulnae la smakik.
muˀyuk xa bu ta xˀochik li kirsanoetike.

TEXT 72

Of the Time of the Burning of the Saints

Mateo Méndez Tzotzek

This is an account of how the Protestants burned the images of the saints.[1] 1

Well, the Protestants burned up the images of the saints in the church 2
in a live flame.
The reason for this was that they didn't want there to be any saints
in the church.

According to them, these images were not gods. 3
They were nothing but carved wood.
They did not know how to speak.

They believed that there indeed *was* a god, but only one god. 4
Our Father Sun in Heaven, whom we revere, was not the true god.
He was, according to them, nothing but light.

They said that we should not pray to Our Father Sun in Heaven. 5
They said that he was a demon.

There *was* a god who lived in a cave. 6
The Protestants would pray to this god.
He was the true god.[2]

According to them, those in the church were different. 7
They were not like gods.
They were like demons.

That is why they burned up the saints in the church. 8
Truly, they burned up all of the images of the saints.

The church itself was closed. 9
People could no longer even go in.

10 la spak'bil vun ti tiˀ ch'ulnae ti yoˀ mu xa xˀochik ti kirsanoetike.
skotol ch'ulna mak.

11 ˀentonse ti jtotik san juan ta chamoˀe la slok'esik ˀel xchiˀuk jtotik machyo.
skotol jtotik la slok'esik.
bat snak'ik ta na ti yoˀ mu xˀilik ˀo ti jvanjelistae.

12 pero k'alal la slok'esik ti jtotik san juane la jyak'ik jun mol santo ti bu lok' ti jtotik san juane.
ti bu lek ti jtotike la slok'esik skotol.
bat snak'ik ta na.

13 ˀentonse ti bu chopol ti jtotike ˀaˀ te kom ta ch'ulna.
ˀaˀ te kom ti bu yav ti jtotik san juane.

14 k'alal k'ot ti jvanjelista ta ch'ulna la stzak ta ˀora ti jtotik san juane.
pero la xi'un yuˀun ta ˀaˀ ti jtotik san juane ti te chotole.

15 la stzak ˀel.
bat xchik' ta k'ok'.

16 pero mol santo xa.
maˀuk jtotik san juane.

17 skotol jtotik te ta yut ch'ulna.
pero maˀuk xa jtotik.

18 ˀaˀ noˀox ta sloˀlaik ti jvanjelistae.
puro xa mol santo.

19 vaˀi ˀun ti jvanjelistae la xchik' ta k'ok' ti skotol ti mol santoe.
ˀech'o xal la sbajik ti tiˀ ch'ulnae.

The door of the church was covered over with cardboard so that the people could no longer go in. 10
All the churches were closed.

Then they took away the images of Our Lord San Juan and Our Lord San Mateo. 11
They removed the images of all the saints.
They went to hide them in people's homes so that the Protestants couldn't see them.

But when they removed the image of Our Lord San Juan, they put an old image in Our Lord San Juan's place. 12
They removed all of the true images of the saints.
They hid them in the peoples homes.

As for the old, worn-out saints' images, these were left in the church. 13
They were left in the very place of the real images of Our Lord San Juan and others.

When the Protestants got to the church, they immediately seized the image of Our Lord San Juan. 14
They thought that it was the true image of Our Lord San Juan sitting there.

They took it out. 15
They went and burned it up.

But it was really only an old, worn-out image. 16
It was not the true image of Our Lord San Juan.

It seemed as though all the saints were right there inside the church. 17
But those were actually not the true images of the saints.

The Protestants had been taken in and deceived. 18
Those were nothing but old, worn-out images of the saints.

So it was that the Protestants burned up all of the old images of the saints. 19
With that, they boarded up the church door.

20 yuˀun muˀyuk xa te junuk jtotik ta ch'ulna.
yuˀun laj xa xchik'ik ta k'ok' skotol ti jtotike.

21 ˀentonse ti jvanjelistae la xch'unik ti cham ti jtotik san juane,
cham skotol ti jtotik.

22 pero muˀyuk chamem ti jtotik san juan xchiˀuk xchiˀiltake.
te ˀoy nak'alik ta na.
muˀyuk chamem.

23 ˀentonse ta tz'akal li jˀerasto ˀurvina ˀaˀ la smeltzan k'op.
ta snutz lok'el skotol ti jvanjelistae.

24 porke k'alal la xchik'ik ti jtotik muˀyuk xa bu ta spasik mixa pale;
jkaxlanetik ch'abal yuˀun bajal ti tiˀ ch'ulna.

25 ˀentonse k'alal la smeltzan k'op li jˀerastoe la sjamik ti tiˀ ch'ulnae.
ˀech ti jtotike ˀoch ta yut ch'ulna,
skotol jtotik.

26 ˀech ti pale ˀeke ˀoch spas mixa ta ch'ulna xchiˀuk jkaxlanetik.
ˀech ti jchamoˀetike ˀoch sk'oponik ti jtotike.

27 la sjamik ti tiˀ ch'ulnae.
ti jtotik san juane chaˀsut ta ch'ulna xchiˀuk xchiˀiltake.

28 ti kirsanoetik ta chamoˀe xmuyubajik xa la ti jam ti tiˀ ch'ulnae.
lik la sk'oponik ti jtotike.

29 la sjamik skotol ti ch'ulnae.
jam skotol ch'ulna ta joˀbel ta tuxta.

Not one saint's image remained in the church. 20
For they thought they had burned up all of the saints' images.

With this, the Protestants believed that Our Lord San Juan was dead, 21
That all of the saints were dead.

But Our Lord San Juan and his companions were not dead. 22
There they were, hidden in a house.
They were not dead.

Later on, after all this had happened, Erasto Urbina resolved the problem. 23
He drove out all of the Protestants.[3]

Why, when they burned the images of the saints, the priest couldn't even say the mass; 24
Not even for the Ladinos, for the door of the church was boarded up.[4]

Then, when Don Erasto finally resolved the problem, they opened the doors of the church. 25
So it was that the images of the saints went back to take their places inside the church,
All of the saints.

So it was that the priest once again could go in the church to say mass for the Ladinos. 26
So it was that the Chamulas could go in once again to speak to the saints.[5]

They opened the doors of the church. 27
And Our Lord San Juan returned once again with his companion saints.

The people of Chamula rejoiced, now that at last the doors of the church were opened once again. 28
They began speaking to their saints once again.

They opened all the churches. 29
They opened all the churches in San Cristóbal de las Casas and in Tuxtla Gutiérrez.

30 veno, skotol ch'ulna jam,
pero ˀaˀ la smeltzan k'op ti jˀerastoe.

31 ˀech xtok lik spasik ti k'ine.
ta spasik xa k'in jujun k'in.

Indeed, all the churches opened, 30
For Don Erasto had solved the problem.

Once again they began to have festivals. 31
Now they could have festivals on each and every feast day.

1 loˀil yuˀun be karo ta tuxta.

2 veno k'alal la spolik li be karo ta tuxtae toj ˀep chamik ti kirsanoetike.
cham jkaxlanetik.
cham chamulaetik.
cham jsotz'lebetik jsoktometik.
cham jvisteko.
cham jkomitan.
toj cham tajmek ti kirsanoetike.

3 vaˀiˀun te ta jokotaltik ˀaˀ te toj ˀep tajmek ti kirsanoetike.
yuˀun baˀyel ta st'omesik li tone.

4 k'alal mi t'om ti tone ta xbat ˀabtejikuk li kirsanoetike.
te ta xbat ˀabtejikuk ti bu t'om ti tone.

5 pero li tone yochol xa ta sbaj yalel.
ti k'alal te ta ˀabtejik ti kirsanoetike.

6 ta sjin yalel ti tonetik.
ˀentonse te ta xchamik li kirsanoe.

7 te ta stenujik ta ton xchiˀuk spalaik spikoik.
ˀoy yane k'alal ta st'om li tone te ta xˀabtej ta sba li tone.

TEXT 73

An Account of the Construction of the Highway to Tuxtla Gutiérrez

Mateo Méndez Tzotzek

This is an account of the construction of the highway to Tuxtla.[1] 1

Well, when they opened the way for the automobile road to Tuxtla, 2
many, many people died.
Ladinos died.
Chamulas died.
Zinacantecos and people from Chiapa de Corzo died.
Huixtecos died.
Comitecos died.
How the people died in great numbers!

Now, there by Jocotal, many people had assembled to work. 3
First, they proceeded to blow up the rock.

Once the rock had been blown apart, people were sent to work. 4
People were sent to work there where the rock had been blown apart.

But now the rock had fallen down in little bits. 5
This was the clean-up task of the workers.

Rock had collapsed in great heaps. 6
It was there that so many people died.

Some labored at loosening the collapsed rock with shovels and pickaxes. 7
Others worked there on top of the stone heaps once the rock
had been detonated.

8 k'alal t'om li tone.
muy ta vinajel xchiˀuk ton xchiˀuk spala spiko ti jpolbeetike.
muy ta vinajel xchiˀuk ton.

9 ta k'un to yal ta lumtik.
batik ta jemeltik.

10 te ˀichamik ˀaˀ li voˀne,
ti k'alal la sjamik ti be karo ta tuxtae.

11 ta lus ta svok'ik li tone.
baˀyel ta sjomik ˀep ti tone.
ta tz'akal ta xak'bik ti sk'ak'ale.

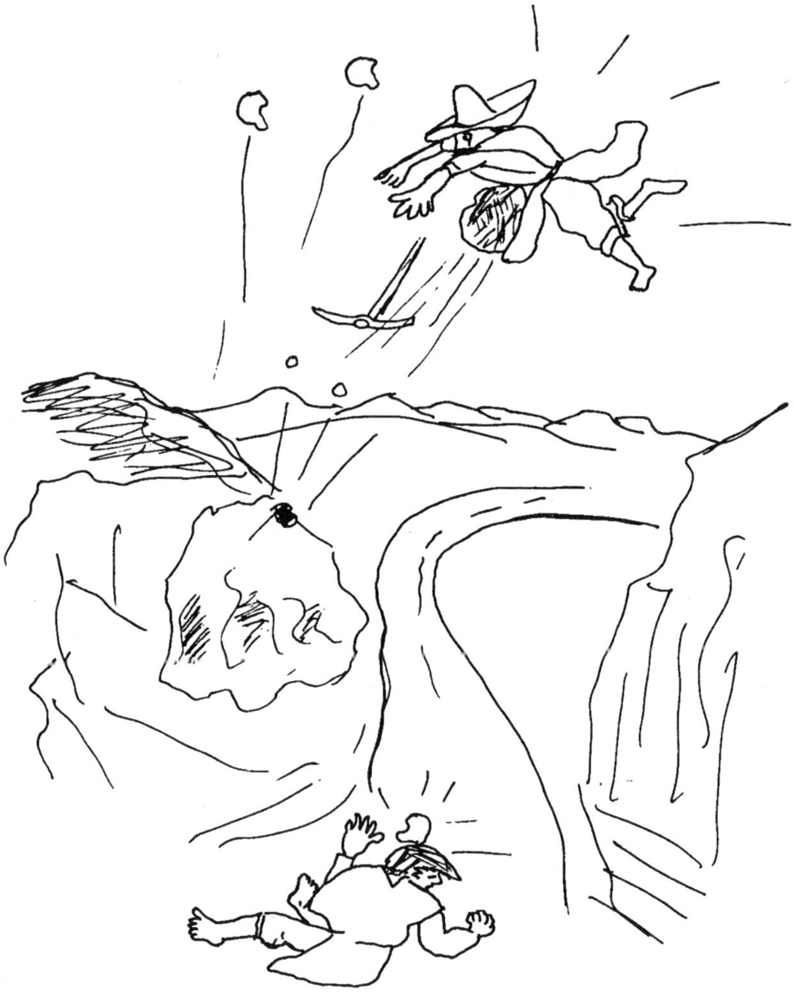

Then another blast of exploding rock would come. 8
Blown sky-high went the road workers, along with the rocks,
their shovels, and their pickaxes!
Flung up into the sky they went, along with the rocks!

Eventually, they came down. 9
They came to rest in the crevices.

There they died long ago, 10
At the time when they opened the Tuxtla road.

It was with a great light that they broke the stone apart.[2] 11
First they would dig a hole in the stone.
Then they would ignite the charge.

FIGURE 99

Then another blast of exploding rock would come.
Blown sky-high went the road workers, along with the rocks,
their shovels, and their pickaxes!
Flung up into the sky they went, along with the rocks!

12 pero ta lus laj xa ˀox yak'bik li smechae li yan tone.
    li yan tone muˀyuk to ta xak'bik smecha.
    te to ˀoy ta xak'bik li smechae.

13 pero naˀtik buch'u la jyak' k'ok'.
    ta ˀora jlikel ˀit'om ta ˀora li tonetike.

14 ˀech'o xal k'alal t'om li tone,
    te ˀicham li jpolbeetike.
    koˀol muy ta vinajel xchiˀuk tonetik.
    te ˀichamik ti jpolbeetik ta jokotaltike.

15 veno ta raraniˀe muˀyuk bu xchamik.
    mas te ˀaˀ noˀox ch'abal ˀoˀ sventa xˀuch'ik.

16 ch'abal ˀoˀ.
    nom to ta xbat saˀik to ˀoˀ ti k'alal ta xˀuch'ike.

17 ˀentonse ta k'un k'un muy talel ti be karoˀe.

18 vaˀiˀun te ta vaˀal ton te ˀicham jun jkaxlan.
    kerem to ti jkaxlane.

19 te muy tal ta skarosal li laktore.
    vaˀiˀun li laktore sut ta valopat.
    te ˀicham ti jkaxlan ta skarosal laktore.

20 ˀentonse ta joyijele te ˀichamik ˀep tajmek ti kirsanoetike.
    k'alal t'om la tone bat sk'elik ta ˀora.

21 yuˀun ta sk'anik ta x'ixlanik ti be luse sventa vok'omton.
    sventa ta xˀak' k'ok' ti be luse.

22 pero puro k'on ta be luse jich'ilik.
    ˀech'o xal ta sk'an,
    ta xˀixlan yaˀik ti be luse.

But they always placed the fuse for the dynamite on another rock, 12
away from the charge.
It was on those rocks where no fuse had yet been placed.
It would be on those stationary rocks where they would place the fuse.

No one told anybody about who was going to ignite the charge, or where. 13
In a moment, the stone would explode.

So it was that the stones exploded, 14
That the road workers would die there.
They flew to the heavens along with the rocks.
So the road workers died there by Jocotal.

Now, in the hamlet of Granadilla, they did not die in this manner.[3] 15
There it was simply a matter of there being no water to drink.

There was no water. 16
They had to go great distances for water to drink.

Then, ever so slowly, the road climbed up into the highlands. 17

Then it was in the hamlet of Vaʔalton that a Ladino died. 18
This Ladino was but a young man.

He had just climbed into the cab of the bulldozer. 19
At that moment, the bulldozer lurched backwards.
So the young Ladino died right in the cab of the bulldozer.

Then, again, there in Joyijel, many, many people died. 20
This was when they rushed over to see things just when the
rocks exploded.

The reason was that they hoped to strip some of the wrapping from the 21
cable that was used as a fuse for the charge.
This wrapping was used as fuel for the fuse.

This material on the fuse came in bright yellow strips. 22
That was why they wanted it,
That's why they wanted to strip away the wrapping from the fuse.

23 ta xtun yuˀunik ta yak'il spixolik.
ˀech'o xal bat sk'elik ta ˀora k'alal t'om ti tone.

24 pero komo muˀyuk to t'omem skotol ti tone k'alal k'otik ti viniketik ti bu t'om ti tone.
lik saˀik ti be luse.
muˀyuk bu ta stuk'ulanik mi ˀoy muˀyuk t'omem ti tone.

25 k'alal syakel ta saˀik ti sbe luse ˀit'om ti sbe ti luse.
muˀyuk bu ta stuk'ulanik.
te ˀichamik ti jsaˀbelusetike.

26 k'alal t'om ti tone muy ta vinajel xchiˀuk ton ˀi yal ta banumil.
te ˀichamik ti povre jpolbeetike.

27 pero ˀaˀ ta smul stukik.
maˀuk ta smul ti tone.
ˀaˀ ta smul ti kirsanoe.

28 ˀentonse ta tz'akal ˀicham ˀotro jten xtok te ta joyijele.
yuˀun laj xaˀox jyak'ik ti be lus ta tone.

29 pero li ˀanjel jlikel ˀavan ta ˀora.
jlikel ˀitzak ti be luse.

30 muˀyuk toˀox ta xjulavik ti kirsanoetike.
muˀyuk bu la jyilik k'usi tal ti ˀanjele.
vaˀiˀun ti tone jlikel ˀit'om.
pero ˀanjel la jyak' k'ok'.
te ˀichamik skotol ti kirsanoetike.

31 jipatik ˀel ta jemeltik xchiˀuk ton.
te komik ta yolon ton ti jpolbeetike.
Chib velta te chamik ta joyijel ti jpolbeetike.

They thought they could use this material as fastening cords for their hats.[4] 23
That's why they rushed over to look once the charge had blown the rocks apart.

But it turned out that the rock was still not fully detonated when the men came up to where rocks had been blasted. 24
They started in to search for strips of the fuse wrapping.
But they didn't realize that there was some of the rock that had not yet exploded.

When they were in the midst of searching for the fuse wrapping, the fuse itself blew up. 25
They hardly realized what had happened.
Then and there the people who were searching for the fuse died.

When the rock exploded, they were cast up into the sky and fell back to earth. 26
Then and there these poor road workers died.

But, in truth, this was their own fault. 27
It was hardly the fault of the stone.
It was the people's own fault.

Then, somewhat later, still others died in Joyijel. 28
This happened when they had just connected the charge to the rock.

Suddenly, the Earth Lord shouted.[5] 29
Just as suddenly the charge ignited!

The people were not fully aware of what was going on. 30
Indeed, they did not see how the Earth Lord had come.
Suddenly, the stones just blew up.
But the Earth Lord was the one who touched off the blast.
Then and there all of those people died.

They were cast away into the gullies. 31
There the road workers ended up, under the stones.
So it was on two separate occasions, road workers were killed there in Joyijel.

32 ˀentonse ta kampana ch'en te ˀichamik ˀep tok.
k'alal ta xbat xch'ay ti stonik xchiˀuk ti skaritaˀike.
te koˀol ta xbat xchiˀuk skaritaˀik.
ta xbat ta yolon be xchiˀuk stonik.

33 pero ˀanjel mu sk'an xˀech' be te ta kampana ch'en.
yuˀun te nakal ti ˀanjele.

34 vaˀiˀun te ta nachije ˀoch ˀel ti ˀijinyero ta yut ch'ene.
bat sk'opon sbaik xchiˀuk ˀanjel.

35 ti ˀanjele ˀoy sbi jtoch la sbi.
pero batz'i toj pukuj la tajmek ti ˀanjele.

36 vaˀiˀun ti jˀijinyero ˀoch ta sjak'be mi xuˀ xjelav ti be karo ta tiˀ ch'ene.
ˀech'o xal ˀoch ˀel sk'opon ti ˀanjele.

37 pero ti ˀanjele la jyal ti mu xuˀ xˀech' ti be karo te ta stiˀ snae.
ˀentonse k'alal lok' talel ti jˀijinyero ta yut ch'ene jyalbe ti yaj ˀabteltake:

38 liˀe mu la xuˀ xjelav li be karo.
xuˀ la xjelav pero liˀ chakomik jˀoˀlole.

39 jˀoˀlol ta xbatik ta snaik.
jˀoˀlol muˀyuk ta xbatik ta snaik xi la ti jˀijinyero.

40 xˀutatik la ti kirsanoetik ta nachij,
ti buch'u te ta xˀabtejik ta polbee yuˀun tuxtaˀe.

Then, near Campana Ch'en, there was yet another incident in which people died. 32
It happened when they went to dump the rocks that were loaded in their carts.
They also came to rest there forever, along with their carts.
They ended up being cast away at the lower edge of the road, along with their rocks.

The fact was that the Earth Lord did not want the road to pass by Campana Ch'en. 33
The reason that he objected was that this cave was the Earth Lord's home.

It happened that the road engineer went into this cave, there by Na Chij.[6] 34
He was going to talk to the Earth Lord.

The Earth Lord's name was Toch.[7] 35
This Earth Lord was terrible and ill tempered beyond words.

Now, it happened that the highway engineer went into his cave to ask him if it was all right for the highway to pass by the mouth of his cave. 36
That was why he went into the cave to talk to the Earth Lord.

But the Earth Lord declared that the highway was not to pass by the door of his home. 37
Whereupon the engineer, when he emerged from the cave, spoke to his work crew:

"The big highway cannot pass by this route. 38
It can be built here, but at great cost: half of you will have to stay here forever.

Half will return to their homes. 39
Half will never return to their homes," said the highway engineer.

This is what the people of Na Chij were told, 40
Those who were employed there as road workers on the Tuxtla highway.

41 ˀentonse ti kirsanoetik ta nachije mu la sk'anik ti te ta skomik jˀoˀlol ta stz'unub ˀanjel,
ti te ta xkomik ta yut ch'ene.
mu la sk'anik.

42 veno mi mu xak'anik liˀ chakomik jˀolole ˀaˀ lek ta xelav li be liˀ ta ˀolol naetike.
moˀoje chijchamotik jkotoltik xi la ti jˀijinyeroe.

43 ˀentonse muˀyuk la bu xˀech' talel ti be karo te ta stz'el sna ti ˀanjele.
ti bu sna jtoch' ˀanjele muˀyuk bu xˀech' te.

44 la saˀik yan ti bu xuˀ xjelav ti be karoe.
muˀyuk bu xˀech' be ta sna ti ˀanjele.

45 ˀentonse k'alal meltzaj ti be karoe bat ti karoe.
ˀaktovus sbi ti karoe.

46 bat ti karo xchiˀuk kirsanoe.
ta xbat k'alal tuxta.
skuchoj ˀel ˀep kirsano.

47 vaˀiˀun k'alal ta xa xk'ot ta kampana ch'ene te la ˀich'ay sat ti jchojer yuˀun ti karoe.
k'alal ti k'ot te ta kampana ch'ene te la sta xolombe laj la yil ti ˀaˀ be karoe.
lek la meltzanbil.

48 te la tuk' bat ti karo xchiˀuk ti kirsanoe.
te la tuk' ˀochik ˀel ta yut ch'en.

49 pero laj la yil ti chojero ti koˀol la xchiˀuk be karoe.
ˀech'o la xal te ˀibat xchiˀuk skaro ti jchojeroe.

50 te ˀibat skotol ti kirsano ta yut ch'ene.
muˀyuk xa bu xlok'ik talel.

Well, the people of Na Chij were not willing to sacrifice half of their number to remain there as slaves of the Earth Lord, 41
To remain there forever inside the cave.
They didn't want this at all.

"Well, if you don't want half of you to remain forever as the Earth Lord's servants, it would be best if the road were to pass through the middle of the settled area. 42
Otherwise, we'll die—all of us," declared the highway engineer.[8]

With that, the highway construction did not proceed by the route that would have taken it close to the Earth Lord's home. 43
Not there, no way! It did not come close to the home of Toch, the Earth Lord!

They sought another route where the highway could be built. 44
But this route for the road did not pass by the home of the Earth Lord.

Now, once the highway was finished, there was a vehicle that had a misfortune. 45
This vehicle was a bus.

This bus was loaded with passengers. 46
It was going to Tuxtla.
It carried lots and lots of passengers.

Now, just as it was approaching Campana Ch'en, the driver of the bus had trouble seeing things right. 47
Just as he got to Campana Ch'en, he came upon an intersection that looked for all the world like a regular highway junction.
It was well constructed.

And the bus headed straight at this point, along with its load of passengers. 48
And they all ended up going straight into a cave!

But, in truth, the bus driver thought it looked just like a highway. 49
That is why the bus driver took his bus by this route.

All the passengers ended up there inside the cave. 50
And now they could not escape.

51 te ˀibat xchiˀuk karo.
te ˀikomik ˀo ta yajval banumil.
te ˀikomik ˀo ta smosov ˀanjel.

52 yuˀun kuxul ti ˀanjele.
ˀech'o xal te ˀoch ˀel ti karo xchiˀuk ti kirsanoetike.

53 yuˀun ti ˀanjele ta sk'an smosov.
ˀech xtok ˀaˀ sventa ti be karo te ˀech'e.

54 ˀech'o xal ta smil ti kirsanoe.
yuˀun mu sk'an ti te ta xˀech' ti karo ta nopol stz'el snae.

That is where they ended up, along with the bus. 51
There they stayed with the Earth Lord.
There they remained as the Earth Lord's servants.

The truth of the matter is that the Earth Lord was alive and well. 52
That is why the bus loaded with people was forced to enter his domain there.

The truth of the matter is that the Earth Lord always has a pressing need for servants. 53
What's more, there was the provocation of the road that might have passed right by his home.

That is why he chose to kill people. 54
It was because he could not tolerate vehicles passing close to his home.

1 loˀil yuˀun jresaletik k'ak' ta k'ok'.

2 vaˀi ˀun ti vinike la xchanik resal xchiˀuk svixtak.
pero k'alal la xchanik lek ti resale la snopik ˀochik la ˀelek' ta sna slak'natak
ti bu nakalike.
pero ta ˀak'obaltik la ta xbatik ta ˀelek'.

3 ˀech xtok ta la xalbe ti xchiˀiltake:
ˀak'o mi xismilik pero mu xichamkutik.
naˀojkutik xa k'usi ta jpoj jbakutik xi la ti vinik xchiˀuk svixtake.

4 ˀentonse ˀochik ta ˀelek' ti bu nakalike.
pero ta k'ak'altik la ta xbatik ta ˀelek'.

5 k'alal la mi k'otik ta tiˀ nae ta la sjuchtaik ti yaviteˀe.
ta la sjam ti tiˀ nae.
ta xˀochik yelk'anik tak'in ˀixim k'uˀiletik.

6 ˀentonse ti slak'natake mu sk'anik ti ˀoy jˀelek'e.
ˀentonse komo yabinojik xa ti mu xcham ta milele:
batikik jpastikik reva mi melel ti mu xcham ta milele,
ti ta xal ta sjoibij ta tone,
ta sjoibij ta teˀe.
jk'eltik mi ˀech xal ti mu xchame xiik la ti slak'natake.

TEXT 74

An Account of the Protestant Prayer Makers Who Perished by Fire

Xalik López Castellanos

This is an account of the Protestant prayer makers who perished by fire. 1

It happened that some men and their older sisters were converted to the cult of prayer.[1] 2
But once they had learned well this cult of prayer, they began robbing the homes of their neighbors.[2]
By night they went thieving.

Furthermore, they would brag to their friends and relatives: 3
"Even if they kill us, we will not die.
Now we know how to defend ourselves," said the man and his older sisters.[3]

With this confidence in their personal safety, they became thieves in the neighborhood where they lived. 4
Even by day, they would go out and steal things.

Whenever they would come up to the door of a house with no one at home, they would break the lock bar. 5
They would open the door.
They would go right in to steal money, corn, and clothing.

The neighbors, of course, didn't want to be plagued by this thievery. 6
So, since they had previously heard that these people could not be killed, they came up with a plan:
"Let's find out if it's true that they cannot be killed,
These people who are said to dance around rocks,
These people who are said to dance around trees.
Let's see if it is true that they are immune to death," said their neighbors.

7 ˀentonse bat la smilik ta sna.
ta ˀoˀlol ta ˀak'obal batik.

8 laj la yich'ik ˀel jun limite kas,
xchiˀuk stuk'ik,
xchiˀuk smachitaik.
vakib la viniketik batik xchiˀuk stuk'ik.

9 ˀentonse k'alal k'otik ta sna ti jresaletike baˀyel la jyak'bik kas jujot chikin na.
k'alal la yak'bik kase la yak'bik k'ok'.
jlikel la tzak ta ˀora ti jobelal nae.

10 ˀentonse k'alal yilik tzak ti jobelal nae batik ta tiˀ na smalabik ti yajvale.
ti vaˀalik ta tiˀ na xchiˀuk stuk'ik smachitaˀik.

11 vaˀiˀun ti yajval nae mu snaˀ lik mi ta xa xich'ik milel porke solel la vayemik tajmek.
bu ta xaˀik mi ˀochem xa sk'ak'al ti snaike.

12 ˀaˀ to la ta xaˀik ti ta sbaj yal talel ti k'ok' ta sbaike.
ˀaˀ to la julavik skotolik,
pero ta xa la slom ti snaike.

13 ˀentonse likik la ta ˀora.
ˀavanik la.
pero ti snaike solel xa la tzakem.

14 k'alal ta yut na:
ay . . . julavanik.
ta xa xijchamotik.
ta xa slom ti jnatike.
naˀtik xa buch'u tal yak' k'ok' ta jnatik.
ay . . . kajval . . . jesus . . . xi la ti jun ˀantze.

With that, they went to the home of the prayer makers with the intention 7
of killing them.
They set off at midnight.

They carried with them a bottle of fuel oil, 8
Their guns,
Their machetes.
Six men went armed with guns.

Then, when they reached the home of the Protestants, they poured 9
fuel oil at each corner of the house.
Once the fuel oil was in place, they ignited it.
In no time the thatch-roofed house had caught fire.

When they saw that the thatch-roofed house was in flames, they went 10
to wait at the doorway for the victims to be forced out.
There they stood at the doorway, guns and machetes in hand.

Now, the occupants had no idea that they were about to be killed, 11
for they were fast asleep.
They did not realize that flames had already engulfed their house.

They only realized what was happening when the flames and embers 12
fell down upon them.
Not until this time did they wake up,
When the house was already collapsing on them.

Then, in panic, they got up. 13
They cried out.
But their house was now totally in flames.

From within the house one could hear the screams: 14
"Oh! Wake up!
We are going to die!
Our house is collapsing on us!
Who could have set our house afire?
Oh, Lord Jesus!" said one woman.

15 t'ant'an la lik.
bat la sjam stiˀ sna.
ta ˀox la sjatav pero mu xa bu xuˀ yuˀun.

16 k'alal jam ti stiˀ snae jlikel la jisbat ti tuk'e,
porke ti mataroletike te la vaˀalik ta pat tiˀna.
te la laj ti ˀantz ta mero tiˀ nae.
laj la yich' tuk' machita.

17 veno ta ˀox la xlok' ti jun ˀantz xtoke pero muˀyuk xa bu xlok'.
te noˀox ˀicham ta tiˀ na.
la jyich' tuk' machita.

18 lok' la ˀel jun xtok pero muˀyuk xa bu xlok'.
te noˀox ˀicham ta tiˀ na.

19 ˀentonse ti slajeb xa lok' ˀele.
muˀyuk xa bu xcham.
siempre spas kanal.

20 bit la batel ta ˀora ti ˀantze.
laj la yak'bik ti riplee ti machitae pero mu xa la bu xk'ot.
ta banumil la k'ot ti machitae ti riplee.

21 laj to la snutzik ˀel tajmek pero mu xa la bu staik.
te la ch'ay ta teˀtik.

22 ˀentonse ti ˀantze tuk bat k'alal joˀbel.
pero stuktuk la bat.
bat la sk'anbe parte ti pale ta joˀbele.
pero ta ˀak'obaltik la bat.

23 ˀentonse ti yane te k'ak' ta k'ok' te ta yut snaik.
ˀaˀ noˀox ti jun ˀantz jatave.

She got up stark naked. 15
She ran to open the door.
She hoped to escape, but she could not.

When she opened the door, a gun was fired at her, 16
For the murderers were standing right there behind the door.
Right there in her own doorway the woman died.
She died of gunshots and machete blows.

Well, still another woman was about to come out, but she did not manage to get out the door. 17
She died right in her own doorway.
She died of gunshot wounds and machete blows.

Still another tried to escape but did not succeed. 18
There she died, right in the doorway.

Well, the last one tried to escape. 19
But this one did not die.
Instead, she escaped.

This woman jumped aside. 20
They tried to hit her with guns and machetes, but none of these attempts to strike her succeeded.
The rifle shots and machete blows missed and hit the ground.

They pursued her hard, but did not succeed in finding her. 21
She disappeared into the woods nearby.

She then went straight to San Cristóbal. 22
She was all alone in her flight.
She was going to seek justice with the help of the Presbyterian pastor in San Cristóbal.
She went on this mission in the darkness.

But as for the others, they had perished in the fire there in their house. 23
Only the one woman was able to flee.

24 ˀentonse k'alal k'ot ta joˀbele k'ot sk'oj ti tiˀ nae.
te la vaˀal ta tiˀ na.
muˀyuk la buch'u sjam.

25 ˀentonse laj la xchaˀ k'oj ti tiˀ nae pero muˀyuk la buch'u stak'av.
te la vaˀal ta pat tiˀ na.

26 lik noˀox la schaˀ k'oj ti tiˀ nae ˀaˀ to te tak'avik ˀun.
laj la sjamik ti tiˀ nae.
mu la sk'an sjamik ˀaˀ la ti toj sob to tajmeke.

27 buch'u ˀot xi la ti vinik ti te nakal ta sna ti palee.
voˀon . . . yuˀun lilajkutik xa ta milel xchiˀuk ti jchiˀiltake.

28 ˀay smilunkutik ta jnakutik.
k'elavil liˀe jutukuk xa ti mu li chame.

29 solel lisnutzik tajmek.
ti ˀiˀay . . . xi la ti ˀantze.
ˀoch la ta ˀok'el tajmek.

30 ˀi . . . povre xi la ti vinik ti te nakal ta sna ti palee.
tekeˀ ˀochan talel mu xaˀok'.
ta xkalbetik yaˀi ta ˀora ti palee.
kaˀtik k'usi ta xal xi la ti vinike.

31 xuˀuk chiˀoctalel xi la ti ˀantze.
ˀoch la ˀel ta yut na ti bu ti snaik ti jresaletike.

32 bu lakomes ta ˀak'uˀ ne xi la ti palee.
te kom ta jna pero taje k'ak' xa ta k'ok'.
ˀaˀ ti hnae lom sa me tahe xi la ti ˀance.

33 pero k'uchaˀal chasmilik ˀun xi la ti palee.
ˀa li kirsanoetik mu sk'anik li jnaˀkutik xa li resale.
ˀech'o xal ta ˀox xismilkutik xi la ti ˀantze.

Then when she finally got to San Cristóbal, she beat on the door of the missionary compound. 24
There she was, standing at the door.
But no one would open it.

Then she knocked sharply again but no one answered. 25
There she was, standing in front of the door.

She had scarcely started to knock still another time when they answered. 26
They finally opened the door.
They had not wanted to go to the door before, because it was so early in the morning.

"Who are you?" asked the man who lived in the pastor's compound. 27
"It's me . . . it's that my family and I have just been assaulted by murderers.

They came to our house to murder us. 28
Look, I came very near to getting killed myself.

They chased me and chased me. 29
Ay! Ay!" exclaimed the woman.
And with that she broke into sobs.

"Oh, poor thing," said the man who lived in the pastor's compound. 30
"Well, come on in, and don't cry.
We'll tell the pastor right away.
Let's see what he'll have to say," said the man.

"Okay, I'll come in," said the woman. 31
And she entered the compound of the Protestant prayer makers.[4]

"Where did you leave your clothes?" asked the pastor. 32
"They remained in my house, but they are now all burned up.
Now my house itself is destroyed," said the woman.

"But why did they want to kill you?" asked the pastor. 33
"People didn't like it that we had learned the new prayers.
That's why they almost killed us all," explained the woman.

34 ˀay . . . povre xi la ti palee.
tekeˀ jmalatik sakubuk.
ˀok’om sob chijbatotik ta chamoˀ.

35 ta xijbatotik hsaˀtik ti jmilvaneje.
kaˀtik k’usi ta xal ti peserentee xi la ti palee.

36 xuˀuk chaˀe halal tot xi la ti ˀantze.
pero solel la sniknun tajmek ti ˀantze.

37 ta la siˀ tajmek.
mu xa la xuˀ xk’opoh.

38 pero ti ˀantz ˀoy la yaloh baˀyel.
yalohbe schiˀiltak slak’natak.

39 ˀa li ta vinajele maˀuk jch’ultotik.
lus koˀol schiˀuk joko.
mu xuˀ jk’opontik porke maˀuk jch’ultotik.

40 ˀoy jch’ultotik pero ˀaˀ noˀox ti bu ˀoy hun muk’ta teˀe.
ˀaˀ jch’ultotik.
muˀyuk yan jch’ultotik.

41 ˀech ta ch’ulnae.
maˀuk jch’ultotik.
k’aˀ teˀ.

42 mu xuˀ jk’opontik porke li jch’ultotike mu snaˀ sveˀ.
ˀa li ta ch’ulna snaˀ sveˀ chak k’uchaˀiotik.
ta sveˀ pom.
ˀech’o xal maˀuk jch’ultotik.

43 ˀoy jch’ultotik pero nakal ta banumil.
hun noˀox jch’ultotik ˀoy.

"Oh, you poor thing!" said the pastor. 34
"Well, let's wait for it to get light.
Early in the morning we'll go to Chamula.

We'll go to look for the killers. 35
We'll see what the presidente has to say about this," said the pastor.

"Very well, then, holy reverend sir," said the woman. 36
But the woman was trembling a lot.

She was terrified now. 37
She could no longer speak.

However, the woman had been at no loss for words before. 38
She had previously spoken to her relatives and neighbors
at some length.[5]

"In heaven, there is none such as Our Holy Father Sun. 39
His nature is no more than the light of a flashlight.
We cannot pray to him, for there is no such thing as Our Holy
Father Sun.

There is such a being as Our Holy Father, but he is found only at the site 40
of the great tree.[6]
He is truly Our Holy Father.
There is no other Holy Father.

The same false doctrine applies to the case of the church in Chamula Center. 41
That building has nothing to do with the one who is truly Our
Holy Father.
The images there are nothing but rotten wood.[7]

We cannot pray to them, for the true Holy Father is a being who does not 42
have the custom of eating things.
The saints who are in the church eat things just like we do.
They consume incense.
Therefore, they cannot be like our Holy Father.[8]

These saints may exist, but they live here on the earth as mortal beings. 43
There is but one Holy Father.

44 li mero jch'ultotike chumanteˀ.
ti bu ˀoy muk'ta chumanteˀe.
ˀaˀ jch'ultotik.

45 ta ch'ulnae maˀuk.
ˀecheˀ te.
ˀech'o xal mu xuˀ jk'opontik.

46 ˀech ta vinajele maˀuk jch'ultotik.
lus haˀ schiˀil jokoe xi la ti ˀantze.

47 ˀech la yalohbe ti schiˀiltake ti slak'natake.
ˀech'o la xal kap sholik ti slak'natake ti schiˀiltake.

48 la smilik ti jresaletike.
ˀentonse ti mataroletike jatavik skotolik schiˀuk yajnilik.

49 vaˀi ˀun ti palee bat sk'opon ti peserente ta chamoˀe.
la hyalbe ti ˀoy ˀanimae.

50 ˀentonse ti peserentee la stak ˀel.
ˀep mayoletik bat saˀik ti mataroletike.
ˀech xtok bat sk'elik mi melel ti la schik'ik ti na schiˀuk ti yajvale.

51 k'alal k'otik ta sna ti mataroletike ch'abal la te.
bajal la ti snaike.

52 pero ti nae lah la svok'ik.
ˀochik la ta yut na sk'elik mi te ˀoy ti matarol ta svaye.
pero muˀyuk bu staik.

53 ˀentonse bat la sk'elik ti na la schik'ike schiˀuk ti yajvale.
k'alal k'otik ti bu la schik'ik ti nae,
ˀaˀ noˀox la te busul staik ti stanil ti steˀel ti nae.
ti yajval nae mu la xvinaj bu.

The true Holy Father is on the stump. 44
The one on the big stump.[9]
That is the true Holy Father.

He is not to be found in the church itself. 45
The images of him there are false.
That is why we cannot pray to them.

The one who is called the Sun/Christ in heaven is not the true Holy Father. 46
The radiance of that false god is nothing but light, like that of a
flashlight," said the woman righteously.

This is what she told to her relatives and neighbors. 47
That is why her non-Protestant neighbors and relatives became furious.

So they killed the prayer makers. 48
Then the assassins fled together with their wives.

Well, the pastor went to talk to the presidente in Chamula Center. 49
He told him about the dead bodies.

The presidente responded quickly. 50
Many policemen set off to find the killers.
Other policemen went to see if it was true that they had set fire to
the house and its inhabitants.

And when they got to the home of the alleged killers, they were not there. 51
Their house was locked up.

As for this house, they broke into it. 52
They went in to see if the killers might be there asleep.
But they didn't find them.

Then they went to check out the house that had been burned down 53
with its inhabitants in it.
When they got to the site of the house,
They found strewn about nothing but ashes from the beams
of the house.
As for the inhabitants of the house, there was no sign of them
anywhere.

54 ˀentonse ti mayoletike lik saˀik ta yut tantik.
laj la sjotz'ik ti tantike.

55 ˀentonse te la la staik butuk ti bak ta yut tantike.
laj la stzobik ti bake.
laj la yak'ik ta hun koxtal.

56 laj la stxobik skotol ti baketike.
pero solel xa la k'ak'em ti baketike.

57 veno ti mayoletike la skuchik ˀel ti baketik k'alal ta chamoˀe.
te la smukik ti baketik ta kamposanoe.

58 pero ti mataroletike muˀyuk bu staik.
ˀaˀ to ta tz'akal la staik.

59 ˀentonse ti matarole bat sk'el sk'in htotik.
schiˀuk yajnil.
schiˀuk snic'nab.
schiˀuk skoryon.

60 naˀ mu yuˀun ˀun xa snopoh muˀyuk bu ta xic' stzakel.
ˀech'o xal bat sk'el sk'in htotik.

61 ˀentonse ti peserentee ti ˀalkalteetike snopojik sa k'uxi xuˀ stzakik ti matarole.
k'alal k'ot ti matarol ta chamoˀe mu snaˀ mi ta xich' stzakel porke kontento schiˀuk skoryon schiˀuk yajnil.

62 k'alal k'ot te nopol ta postaˀem baˀile te vaˀi jlikel schiˀuk yajnil schiˀuk skoryon.
pero mu snaˀ mi ta xich' stzakel.

63 ˀentonse te k'ot hun vinik:
mi latal ta k'in ˀek xi la ti vinike.
lital jlikeluk xi la ti matarole.

Then the policemen began to go through the ashes. 54
They poked around in the ashes.

Then they came across what looked like bones there in the ashes. 55
They gathered the bones up.
They put them in a burlap bag.

They gathered up all of the bones. 56
And these bones were really charred from the fire.

The policemen carried those bones all the way to Chamula Center. 57
They buried them there in the graveyard.[10]

But, as for the murderers, they did not find them right away. 58
Afterward, they did find one of them.

One of the killers had gone to see the festival in honor of Our Lord 59
Sun/Christ.
He went with his wife.
He went with his children.
He went with his accordion.

It was probably because he thought he would no longer be subject to arrest. 60
That is why he went to see the festival in honor of Our Lord Sun/Christ.

Then, as it happened, the presidente and the alcaldes plotted how to 61
catch the killer.[11]
Even as he arrived in Chamula Center, it did not occur to the killer
that he would be caught, for he was very much at ease with
his accordion and wife and all.

When he came close to the water-pump platform there in the Center, 62
he paused briefly with his wife and his accordion.
Little did he know that he was about to be arrested!

Right then and there a man came up to him and said: 63
"Have you come to see the festival, too?" said the man.
"Yes. I've come for a while," said the killer.

64 ba jsaˀtik jutebuk yakil ˀoˀ xi la ti vinike.
mo ˀoj yuˀun mu jk'an skuch' xi la ti matarole.

65 batik muˀyuk ˀep ta jman.
ˀaˀ ta hman bu mas chiˀe xi la ti vinike.
batik chaˀe xi la ti matarole.

66 ˀentonse bat la ti matarol schiˀuk yajnile.
ta la stij ˀel ti skoryone.

67 ˀentonse te la nopol kotol skaro javyier.
te ti bu ta schone ti yakil ˀoˀe.

68 te la ˀoy tzobolik ti peserentee ti ˀalkalteetike.
te la nopol ˀech' ti matarole.

69 ˀentonse mu la xk'ot ti bu ta schonik ti yakil ˀoˀe.
te la yich' tzakal ti bu kotol skaro ti javyere.

"Let's go have a drink of cane beer," said the man. 64
"No, I don't feel like drinking," said the killer.

"Let's go. We won't buy much of it. 65
"I'll buy the sweetest kind," said the man.
"Fine, let's go," said the killer.

With that, the killer and his wife started to move. 66
He went off, playing his accordion.

At this point he was there close to where Javier's truck was parked. 67
It was there that they had corn beer for sale.

The president and the alcaldes were assembled there. 68
And right there the killer was passing by.

It turned out that he never made it to where they were selling beer. 69
They grabbed him right there where Javier's truck was parked.

70 tzakbat la sk'ob yok.
jipat la muyel ta ba karo schiˀuk skoryon.

71 te la chukbat sk'ob yok ta ba karo.
pero mu la bu xaˀi k'usi muy ta ba karo schiˀuk skoryon.
ˀaˀ noˀox la ti muy ta karoe.

72 jlikel la bat ti karo k'alal ta joˀbele.
ˀech la bat ti matarole.

73 ti yajnil matarole te la vaˀal kom ti bu muy ti smalale.
te la kom.
sˀok' xa la schiˀuk yalabtak.

He was grabbed by his hands and feet. 70
He was thrown up, accordion and all, onto the truck.

There, up on the truck, his hands and feet were tied. 71
It all happened so fast that he hardly knew how he and his accordion
had gotten up on the truck.
He just landed there, up on the truck.

The truck took off right away for San Cristóbal. 72
That was how the killer departed.

The killer's wife was left standing there, right where her husband 73
had been put up on the truck.
There she stayed.
Now she and her children wept.

FIGURE 100

He was grabbed by his hands and feet.
He was thrown up, accordion and all, onto the truck.

74 ti matarole bat k'alal ta jobel.
bat ta chukel ta jobel ti matarole.

75 ˀaˀ noˀox jun la stzakik.
ti yane jatavemik.
ˀaˀ noˀox un la stzakik.

76 ˀech ti vinik ta ˀox xak' yakil ˀoˀe ˀecheˀ ta xal.
ˀaˀ noˀox ta sloˀla ti matarol ti yoˀ snop jaˀo ˀel ti bu ˀoy ti karoe.
ˀecheˀ ta xal ti ta xak' yakil ˀoˀe.

The killer was headed for San Cristóbal. 74
And the killer's destination was the San Cristóbal jail.

So it was that just one of the killers was caught. 75
The others fled.
It was just the one that they caught.

It turned out this way, for the man who invited him for a drink of cane beer was actually planted. 76
He was just leading the killer on so as to get him as close as possible to the truck.
The business about offering the cane beer was just lies.

FIGURE 101

The expulsion of the Protestants: Chamula Center, circa 1978

Lo quemaron mi
casa
me golpearon,
me robaron mi dinero
me violaron en
mi
Comunidad

FIGURE 102

Chamula Protestants staging a demonstration in the streets of San Cristóbal de las Casas, circa 1978

Afterword

At the beginning of what might be called "tales from true life" in Chamula, there is often a phrase that reminds storyteller and listener alike that history is unpredictable, that the courses of our lives hinge on outside forces, and that we have no way of knowing when we might be sent off in a new direction. "Jech li povre kirsanoe mu'yuk bu tzna' mi . . ." the line goes, "Little did the poor soul know that . . ."

So it is with the men who in 1965 began telling Gary Gossen the stories in this book. Little did they know that just a few years later collapsing world commodity prices, a prolonged national depression, and political upheavals in Chamula itself would send their own lives and those of their neighbors veering off their expected paths. All had been born and come to maturity in a community of migrant agricultural workers whose primary residence throughout their lives was Chamula itself. As I write, however—barely twenty years after the last of the stories in this book were told in 1980—tens of thousands of people who still think of themselves very much as Chamulas have been forced to relocate to shantytowns on the edges of Chiapas's cities; thousands more now inhabit agricultural colonies in the state's Lacandón jungle and central Grijalva River basin; and thousands from these new places as well as the home community itself live and work all or part of the year in Cancún, Mexico City, and the United States. Without knowing it, Gossen and his storytellers were recording these tales at the last possible moment before Chamulas ceased being able to think of themselves as a compact, more or less unified community and started to become a dispersed, increasingly pluralistic ethnic group.

For a historian, an unanticipated pleasure of these stories is the chance to hear the way historical knowledge was communicated within a conservative Maya community in that recent, more settled past. Through the 1960s most adult men and virtually all women in Chamula were still monolingual; almost everyone got around on foot, because rough truck roads had only reached a few of the community's scattered mountain hamlets; and the beginning of electrification was almost a decade away, so light bulbs, radios, and electric blenders would remain unavailable for some time yet. The rhythm of life was slower and—lacking the omnipresent ranchero music that would come with tape decks and radios—much quieter. Talking, especially storytelling, was the single greatest entertainment in this Chamula, and by the end of childhood young people knew a repertoire of tales that extended from the mythical past, through specific accounts of events in the lives of their parents, grandparents, and grandparents' parents, right up to the most recent gossip. Despite all the limitations of translating oral literature to paper, Gossen and his companions have captured much of the flow and verbal play of this tradition of storytelling. Reading here, one can have the feeling of eavesdropping on Chamulas telling stories in the way they told them for themselves.

What finally makes oral texts like these useful to historians, however, is their content as historical documents: what they actually tell us about the "verifiable" past. We look for telling details that will help us understand the life experience of people who, like the Chamulas, are unlikely to have left written records.

As it happens, for the last 100 to 150 years, the stories here are rich in such details. Not only do they supply concrete accounts of incidents from the lives of the storytellers' own ancestors, but simply by existing they also provide alternative, "from the other side" interpretations of events that had previously been described only from the point of view of non-Indians. In portraying the frenzy at the start of the Mexican Revolution, for example, one storyteller describes how Chamula insurrectionaries who hoped to take part in overthrowing the unjust state government in 1911 were so inflamed that as they practiced hand-to-hand combat they bloodied and even killed each other with the digging sticks, machetes, and other hand tools that were their only weapons. Meanwhile, when we read several stories covering the revolutionary years 1910–20, we find that despite the Chamulas' eagerness to take part at the beginning, they were systematically excluded and were eventually mistreated and exploited by armies on both sides. When the national revolutionary army, the Carrancistas, finally reached the community in 1915, far from behaving as liberators the soldiers stole and ate chickens, sheep, and corn; forced men to carry loads of grass on their backs from one mountain valley to another to feed their horses; and demanded sexual favors from the women. By the time of the famine of 1918, brought on by the collapse of agriculture under the weight of the war, Chamula men—many of whom had wanted to join the fight to regain control of their land and to end debt labor—were finding work carrying emergency loads of corn on their backs between cities, scraping the grain's dust off their sweaty bodies at the end of the day so that they could eat it. Beyond providing a fascinating vision of the Chamulas' experience of the Revolution, all of this utterly contradicts the stereotype in older historiography that the Chamulas and their Tzotzil- and Tzeltal-speaking neighbors were so culturally isolated that they remained aloof from the Revolution—that, in fact, they barely knew it was occurring (a stereotype that justified excluding the Chamulas and other Indians from many of the benefits of the Revolution through most of the remainder of the twentieth century).[1]

Beyond the stories' explicit content, however (a content that clearly becomes less "historical" in our sense of the term as we move back beyond the second half of the nineteenth century), in presenting them as parts of a whole, arranging them as best he could according to the chronology Chamulas themselves assign to them, Gossen has forced us to see them not as random folktales but as the rounded, broadly coherent "folk history" that they are to Chamulas. By itself, the existence of this native history is an interesting ethnographic fact. The sense of themselves as a very old people (which in fact they are), with a special relationship to the God who made the four creations, lends ballast to the Chamulas' sense that they have a right to a place in the world and deserve consideration as a people. It is an important part of their identity, beyond the objective truth of the particular tales.

It seems to me, however, that even apart from its content, the very existence of the Chamula folk history that Gossen has presented to us is an important historical fact. On its own internal evidence, great swaths of this traditional history preserve and carry forward such Maya, Mesoamerican ideas and structures as multiple creations, cyclically recurring patterns of events, and a layered universe in which spiritual beings—some with saints' names, others with names predating the arrival of Europeans—conduct a parallel existence and affect the lives of human beings. This is not by any means to say that the body of lore is unchanged by its sojourn through colonialism. On the contrary, it is heavily infused with Catholicism, Mexican national history, and the borrowings of half a millennium of immersion in the "West." But too many of its basic ideas and structures appear non-European in origin for one not to conclude that its fundamental form has persisted through the centuries since the conquest.

All of this suggests that at Chamula's core there is a body of knowledge and beliefs, an intellectual tradition, that—despite the obliteration of Precolumbian society and all the centuries of domination and exploitation that followed—has managed to persist. Beyond its specific content, is it not possible that this tradition's very existence, and the fact that it has been recreated generation after generation across almost half a millennium, can in some way inform our own histories of the Chamulas?

✠ ✠ ✠

The modern community of Chamula was established just over the hill from San Cristóbal, the Spanish capital of Chiapas, in the 1540s, approximately twenty years after the conquest. Made up of the survivors of three pre-European Tzotzil towns—Chamula, Analco, and Momostenango—its purpose from the first was to provide men and women to work for the Spanish colonists. With the exception of a couple of decades immediately after the conquest, then, when the future Chamulas were dispersed in small settlements on the lands of Spanish *encomenderos*, they lived most of the four and a half centuries between the Europeans' arrival and the late twentieth century in what was essentially a closely guarded labor camp.

Over the first 220 of those years, from the 1540s until the 1760s, Chamula was a *reducción*, a new town tightly settled around a mission church and overseen by resident Dominican friars. Every aspect of community life through these long centuries was managed by the missionaries: they supervised agricultural production, much of which was collective; they had final say over the selection of civil and religious authorities; they even took it upon themselves to make sure their "flock" increased by seeing to it that boys and girls had appropriate mates and were married soon after puberty. Moreover, all children attended catechism classes, men and women were made to confess regularly, and daily life—from the time people left their houses in the morning to the time they returned to them at end of day—was organized by the church's bell. Despite the intrusiveness of the friars' rule, however, the Chamulas seem for the most part to have gone along without incident. Undoubtedly they realized that, among other things, the powerful Dominican order protected them from predatory demands for tribute by Spanish civil authorities and managed the obligatory levies of laborers by San Cristóbal merchants and farmers, so that at least they did not threaten the community's existence.

When much less conscientious diocesan clergy assumed control of the Chamula mission in the 1760s, they attempted to continue—and benefit from—the strict mission-village regime established by the Dominicans. Well into the nineteenth century, there was a resident priest in the pueblo and more than one hundred masses a year were still celebrated in its church. Unlike their predecessors, however, from the first the secular priests attempted to use the community's land and labor for personal benefit. A recurrent complaint to civil authorities—whenever the Chamulas thought one of them might listen—was that the priests forced them to work on their families' haciendas, often a great distance from the highlands, and used their ecclesiastical authority to fine and beat them when they objected.

Eventually, in the mid-nineteenth century, control of day-to-day affairs passed from the clergy to representatives of the state government, in the process becoming less intrusive into intimate, private life—although no less effective at collecting taxes, expropriating workers, and dominating the town center. Only in the last decades of the twentieth century did Chamulas themselves finally assume most of the state and federal jobs within their territory and become directly responsible for representing higher levels of government to the local people.

There is nothing in the Spanish-language documents from all these centuries that even suggests the coherent intellectual order Gossen has opened for us. Nevertheless—despite the close, hostile, almost unceasing surveillance to which they were subjected—we do every now and then catch a glimpse that proves the Chamulas and their neighbors managed all along to maintain separate, secret religious traditions right under their colonizers' noses:

Item: In 1778 the priest in San Andrés, Chamula's neighbor to the north, reported that Andreseros and perhaps some Chamulas had been worshiping in a cave in the forest between the two communities. Entering the cave, he had found a thick stone table crossed by an arch of fresh green boughs and evidence that candles, amber, and incense had recently been burned. After confiscating or destroying everything he could and forcing the culprits to "empty the contents of their bowels" on the altar, he reported the matter to his superiors. They ordered the cave sealed "with black powder, picks and shovels" and the elders involved subjected to long penance.[2]

✠ ✠ ✠

Item: Seventy years later, in 1846, a new rancher who was planting sugarcane on land expropriated from Chamula and its neighbors to the north and east described with alarm a gathering of large numbers of people from adjoining communities at a small lake "which they hold to be sacred" near the peak of Tzontevitz, Chamula's highest mountain. Someone should investigate, he suggested, lest a rebellion be brewing.[3]

In these instances and others through the years, those reporting the heterodoxy always wrote as if they were surprised, as though they had never had any clue that such practices existed. Indeed, the very fact that these and other cases of "dealings with the devil" and "superstition" were only reported every so many years was interpreted by investigating priests to mean not that these were on-going traditions that whites and mestizos had only tripped over by accident. Rather, it was thought that in each case they had suddenly arisen anew, almost spontaneously, out of some deep, unchristianized place in the Indians' pagan souls. In part, this was surely a self-defensive interpretation on the priests' part; to admit that their charges regularly celebrated non-Christian rituals would be to confess their own ineffectiveness. In order to prevent such activities from arising again, the remedy prescribed was always a more rigorous monitoring of the comings and goings from native villages and redoubled religious instruction for those whose "primitive simplicity" had led them astray.

How do we know such non-Christian practices were continuous? Aside from being the only logical explanation for their repeated occurrence every few decades, we know the same practices that caused such alarm two hundred years ago still exist today. Praying and supplicating spirits in caves occur daily in Chamula and other highland communities. Similarly, every generation or so—the last two times in 1974 and 1994—the people of five neighboring Tzotzil and Tzeltal *municipios* on the northern slopes of Tzontevitz (Chamula, Chenalhó, Mitontic, Tenejapa, and Cancuc) have danced and thrown specially embroidered clothing into the miraculous lake that suddenly appears when rising groundwater rushes in to fill a cavity in the limestone geology. These are not sporadic occurrences with no connections among them. They are the expressions of a single, continuous non-Western religious tradition.

Through their long history as a closely watched mission village, in other words, the Chamulas—like their neighbors—somehow managed to preserve a separate religious and intellectual life that they knew they had to keep secret from their colonizers. Conceptually, they may have blended Catholicism and pre-European beliefs into one system at a fairly early date. (The incorporation of some Christian imagery into "old" religious practices suggests that this may be so.) But they knew which parts of their theology and history would not meet with the approval of their priests and Spanish speakers in general, and through almost half a millennium they effectively kept these parts to themselves. The language barrier and the lack of any real curiosity on the part of Spanish speakers regarding what indigenous people thought or believed undoubtedly eased the task. But to have preserved proscribed ideas and practices over such an extended period, in such close proximity to those opposed to them, also argues for an extraordinary solidarity among the people of Chamula and other indigenous communities with respect to non-Indians.

Finally, lest we think the secrecy of the indigenous community's parallel intellectual tradition ended in the nineteenth century—that somehow the barrier between indigenous thought and Western thought has disappeared in our own time—consider the following:

> Item: In the 1960s, when anthropologists working in Zinacantán, the community closest to Chamula, began publishing detailed accounts of animal-soul companions, native seers who solved health complaints by divining their spiritual causes, and rituals on mountaintops and at cave entrances, San Cristóbal's new bishop, Samuel Ruiz, asked the parish priest—a man who spoke some Tzotzil and had lived in Zinacantán off and on since his youth—what he knew of such things. The priest emphatically denied that they existed. At most, he claimed, the anthropologists might have picked up some vague notion of them from the oldest, most ignorant people. Ten days later, however, he retracted his words, having discovered on direct questioning that devout members of Catholic Action, men with whom he had worked closely for many years, in fact had a private, or maybe better, "hidden" ceremonial life of which he had known nothing.[4]

✠ ✠ ✠

For purposes of writing Chamula's history, does it matter that for centuries the community appears to have kept alive a separate, largely hidden intellectual and religious tradition? It seems to me that the answer is "yes," but to understand why this is so, let us look first at the way histories of the Chamulas and their neighbors are currently constructed.

As it happens, thousands of surviving documents from the sixteenth through the early twentieth centuries mention Chamula. Working through them methodically, historians can piece together the ways the community was administered from period to period, the ways its labor was used, how its people were disciplined, what saints they celebrated, and occasionally even such intimate details as how they courted and married.

Although rich in details, however, this kind of inventory taking leaves us with a rather static view of the past, still far from understanding the Chamulas as historical subjects. The next step, then, is to try to put them in motion, to see how they reacted to their surroundings through time. It is important to remember, however, that in the highlands of Chiapas we are forced to perform this task indirectly, through Spanish-language documents largely produced by civil and religious administrators. This introduces problems on both sides of the cultural divide. First, as I have said, indigenous people kept important parts of their lives secret from non-Indians—even those who, like priests, lived among them. And second, most Spanish speakers were not much interested in the Indians' side of the colonial encounter anyway. Their interactions with indigenous people tended to be superficial, and so their reporting also tended to stick to the surface. Unfortunately, in Highland Chiapas there is little chance to correct this unbalanced reporting with accounts from the Indians' side. Rarely (never that I can think of for Chamula) do we find a document in which indigenous people spontaneously explain their understanding of events and their intentions in their own terms. Indeed, for all the centuries from the conquest until the 1940s there does not appear to be a single extant document in Tzotzil produced by a native speaker.

In the absence of indigenous testimony, when historians are reconstructing transactions between Indians and the colonial world, the working hypothesis is that the Indians' actions should be construed as motivated by resistance. Trying to read the one-sided record of Indian-Spanish (criollo, mestizo, Ladino) interactions objectively, we presume that those with authority over people such as the Chamulas were generally trying to dominate and take advantage of them and that they in turn, from a position of relatively less power, were generally attempting to preserve or increase their control over their lives and goods. It is a minimalist assumption. Nevertheless, for purposes of describing the political economy and sketching indigenous people's navigation through it, it works.

By an ironic turn, however, this attempt to restore indigenous people's subjectivity, or "agency," by calling on resistance makes it seem that the initiative was always on the colonialists' side—that Spanish speakers were the active, positive side of the colonial dyad and that Indians were reactive and negative. In a version of the old puzzle about the sound of one hand clapping, historians are left with indigenous people whose existence we would not be able to detect at all if it were not for their being the target of blows aimed at them by the colonial regime. This is not such a problem if we propose to reconstruct the political economies of the past and explain indigenous people's place in them. Indeed, working along these lines, historians over the last twenty-five years have begun to fill in a "real" history for the people of Highland Chiapas, replacing the earlier speculative histories that leapt over all the centuries since the conquest to connect the modern Mayas directly to their Precolumbian ancestors.

For those who study—or live—in indigenous communities in the present, however, the kind of history we have been able to produce using the resistance/political economy model intuitively feels incomplete. Part of the problem, as I have said, is that colonial documents can only "see" people like the Chamulas at those times and places where they are in contact with the colonial society itself. In a sense indigenous history is only possible at those points where Indians brushed up against a colonial and elicited a document. Obviously, however, indigenous people existed—and exist—beyond their clinch with colonialism. In fact, elements of their collective life that could not easily be seen from the colonialists' vantage point—elements that Indians may even have tried to hide, such as native religious practices—may actually be essential to a full understanding of their resistance. In everyday social life, sharing a world of beliefs and knowledge—like speaking a common language—provides a source of solidarity and identification. In more extraordinary circumstances, sharing a world of meanings can raise "resistance" from an ad hoc, tactical maneuver ("protecting my fields from invasion by outsiders today") to a long-term strategic commitment ("saving the lands our ancestors received at the beginning of the Fourth Creation for our descendants through all time").

Gary Gossen has provided us with a rare treasure—a record of the Chamula intellectual tradition in our time. Although we cannot simply project the tradition he has presented onto the past, claiming it was the same in 1850 or 1750 and using it to analyze the mentality of the people we find there, we cannot deny that it exists. On internal and external evidence there is good reason to believe that it has existed continuously over a long period of time. Gossen's work sensitizes us to the centrality of the Chamulas' intellectual tradition and opens us to the role it undoubtedly played in forging solidarity and a sense of continuity through the crushing experience of centuries of colonial domination. In so doing he forces us to leave a space in our interpretation of history—or, for that matter, of present indigenous communities—for views of reality very different from our own.

Jan Rus

Notes

INTRODUCTION

1. See Gossen 1974b, 1985, 1999; Ricardo Pozas Arciniega 1954 for further ethnographic and historical background.

2. See Vogt 1994 for a discussion of the history of this endeavor; see Gossen 1985 for a history and general synthesis of Tzotzil literature, with a complete bibliography; see Gossen 1996 for a placement of Tzotzil literature in the context of greater Mesoamerica.

3. See, for example, his *Fairy and Folktales of the Irish Peasantry* (1888) and *The Secret Rose* (1897).

TEXT 1

1. Tzotzil belief does not recognize the Christian distinction among the parts of the Trinity. The multiple aspects of the supreme deities are represented in the Chamula church in the form of various images of the Sun/Christ and the Moon/Virgin Mary. The issue addressed in this passage is not the Trinity, for the Sun/Christ is the supreme deity; it is what we see as the physical manifestation of the Sun/Christ. The narrator is calling attention to the apparent manifestation—the sun—as distinct from the deity, whose whole body is represented in diverse images and known by many names.

2. This passage (verses 9–12) contains extremely complex cosmological referents to the structure of the heavens (see map 3). The sky consists of three layers, shaped like giant concentric vaults over the earth. The first layer is the sky that is visible to us and also closest to us. Here we see the reflected images of celestial phenomena that are actually occurring on the upper two levels of the sky. On the second level live the moon (Our Holy Mother in Heaven), the stars, and most of the recognized constellations and planets. The distinction between ordinary stars on the one hand and planets and constellations on the other is that the latter are perceived to move. Ordinary stars are believed to be stationary. "They don't know how to walk," is the customary explanation. On the third layer of the sky lives the sun himself, Our Holy Father in Heaven, and the sun's path of travel lies here. This path goes over and under the earth, delimiting the outermost extent of the Chamula universe. This path circumscribes the heavens, intersects the earth at the eastern and western cardinal points, and moves through the underworld in a path that is more or less the mirror opposite of the path through the sky (see Gossen 1974). Also found in the third layer of the heavens are a few major "stars" such as the Candle of Our Father (Venus at morning). Only the partial image of the sun, moon, constellations, and major stars (in the case of deities, their heads in particular) are perceived by people who look up at the sky. We see only the first level. Because the light of the head and face of the sun is greater than that of the moon, it is capable of penetrating two levels and is thus perceived as the "face of Our Father in Heaven." The moon, minor stars, and constellations, all of which live on the second level, have to penetrate only one level of the sky in order to be visible to human observers as phenomena occurring on the first level (see map 3 and figure 2).

1. This consultation was necessary because the Sun-Creator did not then, nor does he now, control the affairs of the Earth Lords, whose domain is the whole region under the surface of the earth, including caves, water holes, sinkholes, and crevices, which give access to the "inner earth" and the underworld. The inner earth is also associated with the Mexican mestizo cultural sphere, which is expressed by the fact that Indians usually produce a fat Mexican dressed as a cowboy when asked to draw an Earth Lord. All of this must also be a symbolic way of acknowledging Ladino economic and political dominance in the world beyond their municipal boundaries, for indeed the very goods (manufactured items made of metal, money, books, calendars, and so forth) that come from the Mexican mestizo national society as trade items are also believed to arrive in the Chiapas Highland trade zone via demons. The demons are thought to bring them to mestizos from the western horizon, where the Sun/Christ leaves them but where Indians cannot go. The routes that the demons follow to bring these trade goods are believed by many Chamulas to be the underground passages and tunnels that are the domain of the Earth Lords. Even the highways, visibly the routes by which many trade goods travel to the Chiapas Highlands, in all directions come from the Lowlands. The Lowlands are also known by Indians to be almost entirely in Ladino hands. Thus, in a sense, the Sun/Christ's consultation with the Earth Lords amounts to a dialogue with the Mexican/mestizo world, on which Indians depend to a great extent for their trade goods and wages (see Gossen 1999, 183–84).

2. "At the foot of your houses" means at the base of the hills and mountains, that is to say, in the valleys, for hills and mountains are the dwelling places of the Earth Lords.

3. This passage (verse 18) and the several verses that follow have complex cosmological referents (see maps 3 and 4). The basic assumption is that the sun's vertical orbit goes through the eastern sea in the morning (coming from the underworld). As the sun comes up, it causes the eastern sea (Tz. Sea of the Rising Sun) to boil and evaporate, leaving a giant, empty basin. Similarly, the sun causes the western sea (Tz. Sea of the Setting Sun) to boil and evaporate as it passes through that body of water on its way to the underworld. In the meantime a great Chiapas river, the Grijalva (Tz. Great River), which drains the Central Highlands, according to Chamula belief replenishes the eastern sea by day, running west to east, and the western sea by night, running east to west, thus changing its direction of flow twice each day. In this way fresh water reaches the empty basins of eastern and western seas, making the Great River something like a connecting canal between the two seas. (According to Western reckoning, the Grijalva River has its source in the Cuchumatán Mountains near the Guatemalan border and flows generally west to east, emptying into the Gulf of Mexico near the city of Villahermosa.) Other Chamulas—sounding like Western empiricists—say that, because of the prevailing topography, the Great River could not possibly reverse its flow from west-east to east-west. According to the traditional explanation, however, the western basin would fill up from the overflow of the eastern basin, finding a path via the northern and southern seas. Thus, at dusk, as the sun evaporates the western sea, overflow would reach the empty basin from the north and south, its ultimate origin being the flow of the Great River from west to east into the eastern sea. Whichever of the two explanations Chamulas offer, the arrival of the fresh water in the two basins causes a gradual rise of water level in the empty basin, which is the Chamula explanation for tides. It is interesting to note that few Chamulas have seen either of the oceans that surround Mexico, yet they have an explanation for tides, which are associated with the movement of the sun. I find this explanation of tides no more mysterious than our own, which ties them to the gravitational force of the moon.

4. This refers to the many subterranean streams draining the Chiapas Highlands, which are visible only where the limestone crust has collapsed, forming sinkholes or water holes. Many of these water sources have a swift current, which testifies to the fact that they are formed by underground streams.

5. "Where the earth ceases to be" literally means "where the earth ends," for the eastern and western cardinal points (as well as those of north and south) are found at the physical limits of the square earth island (see map 4). For this reason "the end of the earth" and "the foot of the sky" are sometimes used to refer to the location of the cardinal points.

TEXT 3

1. This line and, in fact, the entire passage assume the listener or reader knows that Our Father's body is corn, and the "place for his body" is the cornfield. While there is general agreement among all Chamulas that corn came originally from Our Father's body, there is no general agreement about which part of his body it came from. The most common explanation is that corn came originally from his inner thigh, maize silk thereby coming from Our Father's pubic hair. Other explanations identify the biceps of Our Father's arm as the part of his body that provided the first corn, in which case his underarm hair is given as the origin of corn silk. The extraordinary attention paid to the origin of corn in this and other Tzotzil narratives reflects the central place of corn in the diet. Tortillas and other corn-based foods are eaten three times a day all year. Corn, supplemented by beans, cabbage, chili, and tomatoes, is the staple without which life as Tzotzils know it would be inconceivable.

2. The reference to light is a metaphor for Our Father Sun's light, heat, blessing, and good will. To follow any evil inclination is to invite destruction, which is—even in modern times—associated with the death of the Sun/Christ. Solar eclipses occasionally remind people of this threat, for these events are explained as demons who come from the edges of the earth seeking to bite the sun to death.

3. This entire passage refers to knowledge of sex.

4. In Chamula the custom of seeking godparents to help a couple baptize their child is typically the father's responsibility. For the mother to take the initiative in the search for compadres invites the accusation that she is interested in her compadre for other than the accepted reasons of ritual solidarity, economic security, and friendship (that is, an extramarital affair). As in Mexican national society, compadrazgo in Chamula establishes a special relationship between the godchild and godparents as well as between the parents and the godparents. While it is common in Mexican society to seek compadres for several ritual events in one's child's life (baptism, first communion, and marriage), Chamula gives importance to the compadrazgo tie only for baptism. In Chamula it is a bond of special friendship and is usually accompanied by formal gestures of respect and consideration, not only upon establishment of the bond but throughout the lives of the participants.

5. In addition to the general notion that sex is evil, for it was first taught by the demon, in Chamula there is a general acceptance of the belief that women are accompanied by Our Father Sun from midnight to noon—the time of his rising aspect—and, potentially, by demons from noon to midnight—the time of the falling aspect of the sun, when he moves from the zenith of the sky to the nadir of the underworld. Thus, women are believed to be virtuous from midnight to noon and vulnerable to sin and evil from noon to midnight. This is one of the reasons Chamula men give for their preference that women carry water and wood—tasks that take them away from home—in the morning. Women who wander about in the afternoon are believed to be more prone to commit adultery than

those who remain at home during that time. The explanation is a clear legacy from the first creation, when the first woman learned about sex from the demon—probably, some Chamulas say, in the afternoon.

6. "Successor" comes from the Tzotzil *k'exol,* which is a ritual term also meaning "substitute." It is typically used in change-of-office rituals, the new officeholder being called the *k'exol,* or "replacement," for the past officeholder. In this passage the moon (Our Holy Mother) refers to the first woman as her "successor," the bearer of feminine tasks and responsibilities for humankind.

7. It is interesting to note that contemporary Chamula outer garments are made of wool, which was introduced only after the Spanish conquest. The earlier, First Creation, time dimension of this narrative is indicated by Our Holy Mother's teaching of weaving with cotton, which was native to the New World and was no doubt used by the Precolumbian Mayas. Chamula women continue to be expert weavers, using the backstrap, portable type of loom, but they now weave almost exclusively in wool, producing women's skirts, outer blouses, shawls, and headpieces and men's outer tunics. Women's inner blouses and men's shirts and pants are now made from machine-loomed cotton or bought ready made. It is important to mention, however, that several neighboring Indian communities continue to produce high-quality cotton textiles on backstrap looms. The thread for this cloth is machine produced and sold in skeins in Mexican trade centers such as San Cristobal de las Casas. For comparative purposes it is important to note that in the community of El Bosque, which was settled by emigrant Chamulas in the nineteenth century, hand-spun cotton is still used in weaving. Chamula women themselves use a large ceremonial blouse that is woven from cotton, but this type of blouse is no longer made in Chamula. Cotton blouses are made in all the neighboring communities, and hand-spun cotton is still made in Pantelhó and Venustiano Carranza.

8. Atole (Tz. *ˀul*) is a thick maize-starch gruel that is used as a stiffening and adhesive agent for both wool and cotton thread. Recently spun thread is soaked with atole to make it less fuzzy and easier to handle and to keep it from breaking easily.

9. The stiffened thread is attached to pieces of the loom for the original vertical threads (warp) of the cloth. These must be stronger and stiffer than the horizontal threads (weft).

10. There is a discrepancy between the information in the text and actual modern practice, in which the threads are separated while they are still wet with atole.

11. This apparently means no other duties besides weaving, cooking, wood carrying, and water carrying. The latter duties had already been assigned to her earlier in the narrative.

12. In Chamula there is a complex body of beliefs about animal-soul companions which, in its totality, amounts to a kind of philosophy of individual being (see Gossen 1975, 1999). Of Precolumbian origin, the concept involves the association of an individual—not of a group, as in the concept of totemism—with a soul companion, given at birth, who, for a lifetime, shares every stroke of fate of its human counterpart. Several animals enter into this classification scheme, ranging from jaguars and coyotes for the rich and powerful to rabbits and weasels for the poor and humble. Much of individual fate and fortune, as well as personality differences, is explained in this way. In this text it is interesting to note that Our Father created the large and powerful animals first, perhaps thinking that the task of populating the earth required strong people. Hence, it was necessary to create the strong animal-soul companions first and the weaker ones later.

13. This line is a fairly direct commentary on human inequality in the Chamula worldview. The fact that jaguar souls are not the soul companions of all people explains why

some people are richer and others poorer; why some are more powerful and others weaker; why some die as respected elders and others die early in life without accomplishing much at all.

14. It is not clear which sequence of days is referred to here. I believe, however, that the reference is to the four-day cycle that led to the victory of the Sun/Christ (Our Father) over the forces of evil (see texts 1 and 2, map 3). At the beginning of this cycle, Our Father is killed by the monkeys, demons, and Jews, for they fear his power to give light and heat to the world. He comes back to life, however, and on the first day after his burial and resuscitation he goes to the western edge of the earth. On the second day he goes from the western edge of the earth down to the nadir of the underworld. On the third day he begins his upward swing toward the eastern horizon, where he emerges at dawn of the fourth day. By noon of the fourth day he reaches the zenith of the sky, thus giving the earth the full benefit of Our Father's light and heat for the first time. At this time he also burns to death most of his enemies—the monkeys, demons, and Jews—and frightens the survivors into retreat outside the moral universe of the sun. Henceforth, the sun's path delimits the spatial limits of the universe and maintains the elementary units of time—day and night. Therefore, the third day referred to in this narrative seems to be the turning of the tide to cosmic optimism, as the sun on the third day emerges upward from the depths of the underworld to begin his trip to the eastern horizon. Ultimately, on the fourth day, he completes the cycle by emerging from the eastern sea in a ball of heat and light, causing the primeval oceans of the earth to evaporate. Hence (as described in the text), the third and fourth days of the sun's emergence cycle would have been the first time when plants could have survived on the earth. This is corroborated in text 8, verse 78 and text 9, verse 6.

15. This passage refers to the emergence of typical features of the karst-type limestone topography of the Chiapas Highlands, which is an area of heavy rainfall but without many surface drainage features such as creeks and rivers. The area is very mountainous but for the most part internally drained, typical features including subterranean streams, sinkholes, springs, deep water holes (cenotes), shallow water holes, seasonal swamps, and ponds. The relatively heavy rainfall, combined with the limestone substructure, has caused a pattern of weathered limestone surface features such as steep cliffs, landslides, and numerous large and small basins that have been formed by the collapse of the limestone substructure. There are thousands of cave openings and rockshelters, large and small, including some that lead to immense limestone caverns.

The cracks in rocks, referred to as the "door to the demon's house" in this passage, are often, in fact, small cave openings that lead to great cave networks inside the earth. These doors sometimes appear to be mere vertical cracks, but Chamulas note that they are meant to deceive, being just large enough for a curious person to enter and explore—sometimes, Chamulas say, never to return.

16. Earth Lords (*yajval banamil*) and their external manifestation as *ʔanjeletik* (from Sp. *ángel*) live in medium to large caves, often those with prominent rock-shelters. They are intimately associated with rain, thunder, and lightning. The tie between caves and rain is explained in part by the internal drainage system of the Chiapas Highlands as well as by the fact that rain-bearing clouds appear to emerge from the mouths of caves (see also text 2, note 1).

TEXT 4

1. Hot Country refers to the Pacific Lowlands, where Chamulas go frequently to work as day laborers (see map 4 and text 7, note 1).

2. This line is a standard Tzotzil salutation used when once arrives as a visitor.

3. This demon (Tz. *pukuj*) is the most common of all Chamula negative supernatural beings. It is hairy and black and is believed still to inhabit the passages of the underworld. Demons of this kind were among those who killed the young Sun/Christ child. They continue to be the most frequently mentioned of all the malevolent supernaturals in the Chamula cosmos.

4. This alludes to the narrator's opinion regarding the crimes and related domestic problems in Chamula today. Apparently, wasting maize—a sacred food—is comparable to sexual crimes, for the two seemingly unrelated themes are given equal weight in the narrator's discussion.

TEXT 5

1. Upon pursuing details of this text, I found that the narrator thought the "self-working tools" of the contemporary era (that is to say, machinery) had been left to Ladinos. This interpretation moves the significance of the text from commentary about magical events of time past to explicit analysis of economic and social inequality in time present. The narrator's allegation suggests collusion between the Sun/Christ and the demon to underwrite current Ladino economic supremacy under the guise of religious authority. The demon apparently convinced the Sun/Christ that Indians would not pray to him for help if they possessed "self-working tools." The original performance setting reflects this interpretation. The narrator was working with his father as they hoed the maize field. The father commented: "I'm very tired, but it's the demon's fault. It's his fault alone, for long ago Our Lord Sun/Christ did not have to work as we do. He would whip his tools and they would work by themselves. But the demon said to him: 'Don't leave them to your children. If you do, they will not pray to you.' That's why they did not receive them."

TEXT 6

1. This line contains a rather elegant pun in Tzotzil: *k'alal la ta xbat ti jtotike.* It could mean (1) "when Our Father departed (left)," or (2) "when the sun was departing," that is to say, "in the afternoon." In this passage the meaning is probably the first one. However, it is still an appropriate pun for the respectful frame of mind that is expected when one is telling and hearing about Our Father's activities.

2. Although the text does not report this explicitly, the narrator explained to me that Our Father molded the pine pitch into the form of a seated person. Figure 4 denotes that these resin images were placed at the four corners of the field. As elsewhere in the book, native drawings have served as in invaluable critical aid for me in preparation of the translations. Following this cue, the first part of the verse says literally "corner, corner, corner," which I have translated as "each and every little corner."

3. It is worth noting here and elsewhere in this text that exact repetition of words and phrases is characteristic of emotional or angry speech. The repetition behaves as an emphatic that intensifies the emotional content of the utterance.

4. This describes the origin of corn. See text 3, note 1.

5. It is noteworthy that the Tzotzil root word for children (*ˀol*) in this passage is the form used for a female speaker or actor. Since Our Father is the actor, this is a linguistic cue that Our Father is in his "nurturing mode" and is classified as a female. This is resonant with the androgynous or even bisexual identity of both deities and ancestors (*totilmeˀil* fathers/mothers) in the Tzotzil system of social classification.

TEXT 7

1. Hot Country refers to the Grijalva River Basin and the area known as the Soconusco, which is located on the Pacific coastal strip of Chiapas and includes the foothills of the Central Highlands (see map 4). The area ranges from sea level to about four thousand feet in elevation. One of the major coffee-growing regions of the state is found at the upper limit of this zone. The area is also an important corn-growing region. During late 1970s, when the text was set down, as many as half of adult male Chamulas worked seasonally as day laborers on the coffee plantations in this and several other coffee regions of the state. This source of seasonal income for Highland Indians had vanished by 1989, due to conditions in global markets and changes in Mexican government policy on subsidies and price support for export commodities. However, Chamulas still work as sharecroppers and day laborers in this corn-producing region. The narrator first heard the story when he was working as a field hand in the corn fields.

2. The tobacco gourd comes from the plant *Lagenaria sinceriana*. Its shape is peculiar, rather like a large teardrop. It varies in length from three to eight inches and has a maximum width, in the center, of about three inches. Its opening is small, so it is necessary to use a sharp, poking instrument to release the caked substance inside. The tobacco (*moy*) referred to, *Nicotiana tabacum*, is not smoked. Rather, it is used as snuff, mixed in a one-to-one combination with lime, the latter of the same type that is used for soaking and softening corn for preparation of tortilla dough. The snuff, taken principally on ritual occasions, is placed between the lip and gums. The narcotic effect is mild in itself, but in combination with rum—which is almost always consumed on the same occasions—the result is a multicolored, dizzy high. In the context of this story it is important to note that snuff is a sacred substance. It is not, to my knowledge, consumed as a recreational pastime. Snuff of the type discussed here is used by individuals who anticipate being in dangerous situations. It is said to protect the user against demons and also to give him or her courage.

3. The soul (*ch'ulel*) referred to is the part of the human soul configuration that is most central. It is the first part of the soul given to people (and to their corresponding animal-soul companions) at conception and is the last part of the life of the body to depart at the time of death. The soul is said to be located on the tip of the tongue. To say, then, that the hummingbird has a soul is to anthropomorphize it and, in this context, to render it sacred.

4. The only species of hummingbird known to live in the Central Chiapas Highlands is the White-eared Hummingbird, *Hylocharis leucotis*. Tzotzils, however, insist that there are two species of *tz'unun* (Laughlin 1975, 105). This distinction is of more than passing interest, for Eva Hunt has demonstrated in *The Transformation of the Hummingbird* (1978) that the hummingbird, as it is regarded in nearby Zinacantán, has two aspects: a large, white summer manifestation associated with the summer solstice and strong sun, and a smaller manifestation associated with the spring stubble-burning and planting time. She regards these as two transformations of the Nahuatl god Huitzilopochtli (Hummingbird on the Left), which survives from preconquest times in Zinacantán. During the Post-Classic period much of southern Mesoamerica had come under cultural influences from the Central Valley of Mexico. Relevant to the present text is the fact that both Chamulas and Zinacantecos believe that two species of hummingbird live in the area. Both communities regard them as sacred, being associated with the sun god and tobacco. Furthermore, it is clear that hummingbirds have carried a singular significance as a symbol and marker of natural and agricultural cycles among both ancient and modern Mesoamerican people.

1. Our Father of Nazareth derives from the Spanish Nuestro Señor de Nazarena, Jesus of Nazareth. His image, Christ with the cross on his shoulder, is in the Chamula church. However, as this deity has come into the Chamula pantheon, he is not the same as Jesus. He is a minor saint (*ˀitzˀinal jtotik*), vaguely related by lineage to *jtotik ta vinajel*, Our Father Sun in Heaven. Our Father of Nazareth does not have a permanent cult in Chamula to honor him. He appears in the processions on Easter Sunday, but as a vague relative of—not the same as—the Sun/Christ. He is the patron saint of dogs in Chamula.

2. Through the Dominican missionization of Chamula, the Biblical Jews (*jurioetik*, from Sp. *judío*) and Judases (*juraxetik*, from Sp. *Judás*) are linked conceptually with the Precolumbian monkeys (*maxetik*) and demons (*pukujetik*) as negative forces hostile to the social order created by and presided over by the Sun/Christ deity.

3. The halo of this passage refers to the rays of light and heat that shone around the young Sun/Christ's head. The forces of evil (Jews, monkeys, and demons) realized that this radiant heat and light would ultimately kill them; hence their interest in killing Our Father before he killed them. It is also relevant at this point to reiterate that Christ and the sun deity are one and the same being, Our Father (*jtotik*), in traditional Chamula belief. It is believed that what we see each day as the sun in the sky is really the radiant light and heat of Our Father's head. Since he travels in the third, outermost layer of the heavens, we do not see his body, only the reflection of his radiant head, which is so powerful that it shines through the inner layers of the sky. This belief system is supported by popular Mexican Catholic religious art and sculpture, in which Christ and the saints are typically represented with spectacular halos (see text 1, note 2).

4. There is some confusion (at least in my own mind) about the relationship of San Salvador (Jesus the Savior) to Our Father in Heaven (*jtotik*). It seems that they are two different aspects of the same deity. Our Father in Heaven travels in the third, outermost, layer of the heavens. Apparently, the radiance of his head—the light of the sun itself—which we perceive on the first, innermost layer of the heavens, is revered as San Salvador (see text 1, note 2).

5. This passage means that the Jews were struck by a thunderstorm. The angels (*ˀanjeletik*) are familiars and companions of the Earth Lords (*yajval banamil*), and the terms are often used interchangeably. Living in caves high on the mountainsides, they are seen in the form of rain clouds and lightning and are heard in the form of thunder. They would have been able to intercept the Jews in the climb up to heaven through their celestial mobility, thus punishing them with a great storm. (See text 2, note 1, and text 11, note 4, for discussion of these concepts.)

6. This is said to be the origin of the custom of eating fish on Ash Wednesday (Tz. *melculix tiˀ choy*, "fish-eating Wednesday") Jan Rus (personal communication, May 2001) states that traditional cargo holders still observe the custom by serving a soup of salted fish on this day.

7. It is important to note that this very method is used to raise a huge fifteen-foot cross for the annual ritual observance of the crucifixion on Good Friday. As in the text, the scene of this ritual observance is inside the Chamula church. The image of Christ is literally nailed to the cross in an almost exact repetition of the events recorded in the text.

8. Seventh Friday (*vukubal yernex*) is the Tzotzil way of saying Good Friday. The Lenten cycle in Chamula ritual is divided by Fridays—First Friday through Seventh Friday—followed by *savaro kuxel*, Holy Saturday, and *rominko kuxel*, Easter Sunday.

9. Each year on Good Friday, after Our Father is nailed to the cross, a straw-stuffed image of Judas, dressed as a Mexican mestizo, is burned. The charred remains are strung up by a rope and left to hang from the center of the main facade of the Chamula church until Easter Sunday.

TEXT 9

1. The phrase "she saw the face of her son" means that, from her vantage point on earth, his face was all she could see. To anyone on earth this is all that is visible of the Sun/Christ's totality, which is a whole anthropomorphic body according to Tzotzil belief.

2. This means not only that the sun and the moon are conceived as moving bodies but also that they follow similar circuits about the earth (see map 3). The sun is believed to move in the third level of the sky; the moon, in the second level. In both cases the route is over the earth, into the underworld, and up again from the eastern horizon. In both cases it is the faces of the deities that we perceive as radiant reflection penetrating through to the first level of the sky. The first level is the layer of phenomena that we can see from the surface of the earth. The circuits are organized in such a way that when the sun is in the center of the sky, the moon is near the nadir of her circuit in the underworld. Similarly, at the time when the moon is visible in the center of the sky at night, the sun is in the underworld near the nadir of his circuit. In this manner, either the sun or the moon deity is always watching over the affairs of humankind. (See text 1, note 2, and text 8, note 3.)

3. Traditional Chamulas believe that all the dead go to live forever in the underworld. This follows, as the text explains, from the basic solar orientation of human life: we go to the underworld because Our Lord Sun/Christ did so when he died. Unlike him, however, humans never return to earth as living beings. Their souls do return to earth on the eve of the Festival of the Dead (November 1, All Souls Day). On this occasion they go at around midnight to receive the food and drink offered to them by their relatives still living on earth. In actual practice the only ancestors so honored are those who have left land and property to the living.

4. This is a cryptic line concerning secret wisdom. It is of interest that the initiative in creating the cosmic division of labor for presiding over night and day is attributed to the moon. It is she, not the sun, who makes the first move (that is to say, giving birth to him) in establishing the cosmos. She makes a second instrumental move in going to see him to make arrangements for day and night. Her secret wisdom can thus be read as latent female authority, lending a kind of egalitarian balance to a social order that on the surface appears to be dominated by male authority. Throughout the text, including the final verse (15), the narrator emphasizes joint responsibility for the maintenance of cosmic order between the moon and her son. Also suggested in the "secret wisdom" passage is the menstrual cycle, which is associated by Chamulas with the lunar cycle. "To menstruate" is "to see the month" (*ʔilʔu*). Thus, Chamula women share Our Holy Mother Moon's cyclical nature, just as Chamula men share in the divine solar cycles through public ritual observance. Together, men and women work to maintain the integrity of this cyclically patterned universe, with different yet complementary powers.

TEXT 10

1. Marián, from the Spanish Mariano, is the older brother of Our Father Sun.

2. Xalik, from the Spanish Salvador, is a given name that means "Savior." It refers to Christ and hence, also, to Our Father Sun.

3. This refers to the traditional dome-shaped adobe or stone sweat-bath house that is found throughout Indian Mesoamerica. It is generally known in Spanish by the Nahuatl-derived term *temescal.* The steam is produced by tossing hot water on very hot stones that have been covered with aromatic and/or medicinal herbs. Some models, such as the one referred to in this narrative, require building the fire over and around the stones in the raised hearth at one end of the rectangular structure. The bath proceeds when the fire is reduced to coals. The coals are then removed, the hot water is brought and tossed on the hot stones, the door is closed, and the bathers lie down on a wooden platform and beat themselves with aromatic branches (see Gossen 1999: 15–18).

4. This and the following couplets (49 and 50) refer to the sun's travels over (day) and under (night) the earth. The sides referred to are the eastern and western horizons, believed to be the edges (that is to say, sides) of the earth.

5. Incense and other essences (tobacco, smoke, odor of aromatic plants and flowers) are typically present in Chamula ritual events. Ritual language also refers to incense as the food of Our Father Sun.

TEXT 11

1. Sinkholes are a common feature in this limestone area.

2. Mother of Earthquakes (*meʔ nikel*) is a supernatural being who lives under the earth and apparently looks something like a mermaid. Her tail movements are believed to cause earthquakes. Xalik later pointed out to me a small image in San Cristóbal de las Casas inlaid in the cornerstone of a seventeenth-century Spanish building known as the Palacio de Diego de Mazariegos. The image is known by the Indian community as Mother of Earthquakes, and frequently one sees flower offerings and candle wax near its base. It appears to be an image of Neptune, complete with flowing beard, fish body, and trident. However, the image is perceived as feminine by the Indian community. The non-Indian Mexican residents of the town appear to take little notice of the image.

3. The local alcoholic drink (*pox*) is a clear rum distilled by Chamulas from unrefined cane sugar. It comes in several grades, from weak ("cold") to strong ("hot") to very strong ("the flower of rum"), according to the Chamula Tzotzil classification system (see Gossen 1974b, 36–38). Several hamlets in Chamula specialize in the distilling of rum, and the location of the stills is extremely sensitive information, since none of the stills are licensed or pay state or federal taxes. This rum accompanies nearly all secular and religious transactions in Chamula today. The volume of rum that is consumed is extraordinary, although soft drinks—Coca Cola, Fanta (orange soda) and Pepsi Cola—have recently become acceptable substitutes for rum in many contexts. Rus reports (personal communication, May 2001) that the customs relating to drinking have radically changed in the period 1980–2000, with a great decrease in public use and abuse of alcohol.

4. The Earth Lord is known by two names: *yajval banamil* (owner of the earth) and *ʔanjel* (angel). The *ʔanjels* are familiars of the Earth Lord and sometimes actually represent him. These supernatural beings are part of a complex set of beliefs concerning the origin of rain and of metallic objects, including money and manufactured goods made of metal. The *ʔanjels* are also part of this complex of beliefs. In Chamula drawings they look like small, fat Ladinos (see figure 40), but they have great powers in connection with the fact that they supply rain. Thunder is their bellowing and crying as they send forth clouds from their mountain caves and crevices, and from these clouds comes rain. (It is perhaps the association of Christian angels with clouds in Catholic religious pictures that has encouraged the Maya link between Christian angels and Precolumbian rain gods.) Through the

link of clouds with caves and the Earth Lords' and *ʔanjels* realm, rain—by Chamula reckoning—is ultimately of subterranean origin. This may be partly explained by the fact that most water supplies in this limestone area do in fact come from water holes and springs, not from surface sources. Thus, in the text, the people's ability to see the Earth Lord's money inside the mountain makes them able to penetrate a great complex of knowledge and power associated with both economic and supernatural order. It would not be fitting for ordinary people to possess all of this knowledge; hence Our Father Sun's concern, which is recorded in this text.

5. The second part of verse 99 was added by the narrator, by way of clarification, in an interview that came after the original text was dictated. The Tzotzil in brackets is my own rendering of our conversation. The point is that clothes made of tree bark also leaked, just like the houses made of leaves.

6. San Juan (John the Baptist), the patron saint of Chamula, is believed to be a younger sibling of the Sun/Christ deity. According to other narratives, he did not come directly to Chamula but migrated from the Lowlands because his sheep did not like the hot lowland climate. Chamulas explain his association with sheep as coming from popular Roman Catholic pictures some Chamulas have in their homes that depict him as a shepherd with a small flock. Furthermore, the image of him in the Chamula church includes a lamb at his feet. Thus, he is associated with the whole complex of wool production, which to this day is a Chamula specialty in the Chiapas Highlands. Nearly all Chamula families keep a small flock of sheep. Chamula women are expert weavers, who not only make their families' clothing (see texts 26 and 27) but also have a small surplus of wool that they sell to other Indians as raw wool and as finished items of clothing.

7. This long sequence (verse 104) refers to San Juan's arrival in Chamula Ceremonial Center. San Juan caused a hill to collapse with an earth tremor, creating a depression that came to be a lake so that his sheep would have a place to drink. This lake can still be seen in the Ceremonial Center. San Juan's house in the passage refers to the Chamula church. The bell motif refers to an event that happened during the construction of the church: when the building was nearly completed, a bell appeared in a nearby tree and began ringing all by itself. It was later placed in the tower of the Chamula church, where it hung for many years. It is now cracked and non-functional but is kept as a sacred relic on the floor of the Chamula church (see texts 26 and 27).

TEXT 12

1. This passage (indeed, the whole first part of the text, verses 1–18) has both ancient Maya links and other expressions in contemporary Chamula ethnography. The concept of five days of darkness is related to the five-day month of *ch'ay k'in* (lost heat, lost festival) in the Chamula traditional solar calendar of nineteen months (eighteen months of twenty days plus the five-day odd month). The odd month is associated with the winter solstice and year renewal rituals in the annual cycle. This solar calendar is of great antiquity in the Maya area, dating from perhaps 1000 B.C., and survives today in many Maya communities (see Gossen 1974a). The month of *ch'ay k'in* now moves with the Christian liturgical calendar to fall in the five-day period of pre-Lenten Carnival (four days) plus Ash Wednesday. Chamula's annual solar renewal festival, called The Festival of Games, is celebrated during this five-day period each year and carries, among other themes, the theme of destruction and reconstitution of the social and cosmic order, to which the present text refers (see Gossen 1999). It is also relevant to note that the Christian liturgical calendar always places Carnival and Ash Wednesday in the dark of the moon and the first phase of

the new moon, allowing Easter to fall on the first Sunday after the first full moon following the spring equinox. The traditional Maya concern with "lost heat" at the time of the winter solstice merges conveniently with the lunar calendar that regulates the Passion cycle of Christian tradition.

2. People at this time were made of clay and could not move properly. The narrator explained to me that the people were being punished for their inability to move about and that this was why they were worried about how to get away from the impending disaster.

3. They broke their pots so as to release their souls. (Compare *Popul Vuh* reference, Tedlock 1996, 71–73). Broken potsherds are also offered during The Festival of Games (see text 12, note 1) as ritual tribute to the Earth Lords.

4. Feeling the wrist's pulse is the means of diagnosis in Chamula curing practice. The pulse is the "blood speaking" and enables the curer to determine the inner state of the patient.

5. The reference to Our Father's body in this passage is to corn, the most important and sacred of all foods in Chamula. Please refer to note 1., text 3, for comparison.

6. In other words, the reason for all sexual irregularities is that the demon taught the people about sex.

TEXT 13

1. Although it is not stated early in the text, the anonymous man referred to turns out to be a demon (see verse 55, line 1).

2. This is a conventional salutation upon arriving for a visit.

3. The term *krisano* (people, person, from Sp. *cristiano*) appears in other native text transcriptions as *kirsano.* This discrepancy represents a dialect variation that prevails among Chamula Tzotzil speakers. In this text, in fact, both forms are used. Therefore, I have not attempted to standardize the Tzotzil rendering of the word.

TEXT 14

1. This is an interesting reading of the evolution of Chamula religious history. One god is not enough, in the narrator's view, to take care of the complex division of labor represented by more than twenty saints who are honored and maintained in the Chamula church at the present time. All of these saints have sponsors, cargo holders, who serve for one year. Their task is to honor the saints with festivals and with daily prayers and candles. The idea of a single god on heaven and earth—a notion recently encouraged by both orthodox Catholic doctrine and by Protestant mission workers in the community—is alien to the plural authority system of the saints. This explains in part why traditional Chamulas view both orthodox Catholicism and Protestantism with such hostility. The idea of one god is viewed as primitive, according to the premises discussed in this text.

2. This verse is interesting as a commentary on spatial categories of the earth. The common contemporary view is that the earth consists of three types of space: woods (Tz. *teˀtik*), open, cleared land (Tz. *jamalaltik*), and houses (Tz. *naetik*). There is also a fairly consistent view that woods came first in the order of creation; then cleared land (presumably with the advent of farming, horticulture, and animal husbandry); and, finally, houses, which refers to structures specifically designed for human habitation and human subsistence activities. The latter category includes not only dwellings, but also churches, shrines, sheep sheds, and fowl sheds. There is also fairly broad consensus in the community that "woods" is a dangerous, threatening spatial category, whereas "fields" and "houses," through the greater presence of human control and occupancy, are safer and "better."

3. Accounts differ as to whether the destructive rain of boiling water was of earth or sky origin. Accounts also differ regarding whether the deluge was boiling water or ordinary rain. In this text it seems clear that the narrator believes the boiling water came from the hills and mountains in the form of clouds, just as most Chamulas view ordinary rain to do. Other texts in Part 1 clearly state that the boiling water rain came from the sky. It is important to note here and in the related texts (texts 17, 18, 19, and 20) that the geological and seismic history of Chiapas is full of records of actual rains of scalding hot water, the most recent of which occurred in April 1982, at the time of the eruption of El Chichonal volcano near Pichucalco, at the edge of the Chiapas Highlands. Apparently, the intense heat of volcanic eruptions superheats the atmosphere for miles above the earth, causing rain to fall as "boiling water." (See Duffield 2001 for a scientific account of this phenomenon.)

TEXT 15

1. *Seed* here refers to the newly created stock of people. *Seed* is broadly utilized in modern spoken Tzotzil and in the narrative tradition to mean a stock or race of animals, people, or plants. The noun *tz'unob* (seed) and verb *tz'un* (to sow) both have a horticultural context as the primary reference. It is worth noting that human and animal populations are treated as metaphorical equivalents of seed stocks of plants.

2. The giver of instructions is Our Father in Heaven himself.

TEXT 16

1. This text has a breathless, stream-of-consciousness quality that makes it seem somewhat rambling, in contrast to the more conventional plot lines that characterize other narratives in this section. This disjointed quality expresses both the exuberant personality of the narrator and the rather playful approach to the creative process on the part of the actors in the story. This text adds a touch of whimsy and improvisation to the rather staid behavior of Our Father Sun/Christ that is recorded elsewhere in the texts. As I have chosen to do throughout, I have not added any transitional lines to "help" the coherence of the plot. Clarification is added only in the form of notes.

2. Santo Tomás's (Saint Thomas's) older brother is Our Father in Heaven (the sun), who has already been introduced in the text. Our Father is the older brother of all the deities in the Chamula pantheon except Our Mother in Heaven (the moon), who is Our Father's mother. She is thus in an ambiguous class by herself, temporally and logically prior to Our Father but at the same time junior to him because she is female. This junior-senior ranking principle is related to the classification of siblings in Chamula kinship terminology. In Chamula terminology there is no general term for *sibling*, but there are four ranked sibling classifications (older brother, younger brother, older sister, younger sister) for a male speaker and four analogous terms for a female speaker. The deities in the Chamula pantheon, particularly the saints, are also arranged in rank order. Generally, elder saints are *bankilal* (senior) to less important or younger saints. The lesser ones are *ˀitz'inal* (junior) to the higher ranking ones. Generally, male saints are senior to female saints, except on the occasion of major festivals held in honor of female saints. Male saints and female saints are also ranked within their sex-specific groups. The relationship of deities to one another in the text should be understood in this context.

3. A tumpline is a fiber or leather head harness used by people to carry loads on their backs. It consists of a simple rope with a broad, sometimes padded, section that fits on the forehead. The two ends of the tumpline are attached to the load or to a bag, jug, basket,

or net that contains the load. The tumpline is a remarkably efficient system for carrying loads of incredible bulk (as many as ten or fifteen medium-sized wooden chairs) and weight (as much as one hundred kilos). It is a typical Indian artifact, which is very seldom seen in use by a mestizo Mexican.

4. Santo Tomás is calling to them as though they were small children or domestic animals.

5. It seems that some of the sprouted corn was moving along and was in the process of turning into something else.

6. Although this is not entirely clear, it seems that these pieces of corn were in the process of being converted into people.

7. There were two kinds of doves. This line of the text tells the origin of the wild dove or gray dove, which is well known as a corn thief. The bird is said to be particularly fond of newly sprouted corn plants. The other type, the tame or white dove, did not fly away but remained to become the tame dove.

8. The white dove is, of course, a pervasive symbol in Christian art. In this text, which involves Santo Tomás (Saint Thomas the Apostle), the dove is an attribute that appears in paintings and images of the saint that Chamulas see in their own church and in other churches in the Chiapas Highlands. It symbolizes the importance of the Holy Spirit in his life. Also pertinent to this text is the importance of the dove as a symbol of the human soul. The dove is often seen in Christian art as the soul leaving the body at death. In Christian art and metaphor, doves also represent the soul nourished by the Eucharist. Thus, the wild dove's eating early sacramental corn in this text appears to represent the human soul's tampering with its own being and potential. The dove here seems to be a Christian symbol overlaid, in complex fashion, upon a Precolumbian idea of predestination, or prefiguring of human creation, in the form of corn. The domestic dove respects Santo Tomás's and Our Father's will, while the wild dove does not, the remainder of the narrative describing the consequences.

9. The expression "each side of heaven" refers to the directions north and south. North is known in Tzotzil as "the side of heaven on the right hand" (*xokon vinajel ta batz'i k'ob*). South is known as "the side of heaven on the left hand" (*xokon vinajel ta tz'et k'ob*).

10. In the translation, I have reversed the order of *lived* and *died* in the Tzotzil original text because it sounds better to my ear.

11. The buzzard (presumably many of them) emerged from the little pieces of cowhide that Santo Tomás had prepared.

TEXT 17

1. The theme of baby tamales that appears in this text occurs in another context of Chamula life. So-called "baby tamales" are an important ritual food item that is prepared for the annual Carnival in February and exchanged as gifts between religious officials' wives at the event, known as The Festival of Games. The context is fitting, for this is the annual festival of reversals, the principal theme of which is the recapitulation of the birth of moral order from chaos. Ritual consumption of the "baby tamales" occurs early in the ritual sequence, denoting the barbarous habits of the ancient inhabitants of the earth (see Gossen 1999, 105–58).

2. The logic of this and the previous passage seems to be that they were determined to eat the child but felt that the chances of being caught were greater the longer they waited for Our Father to return. Since he had promised to return when the child had grown

up somewhat, they reasoned that if they ate the child at three months it would be easier to explain his death. They would also run less risk of being caught in the act of eating him.

TEXT 18

1. This verse begins an extraordinary series of couplets and triplets that are all introduced by a question. The highly formal question-and-response framework is like a catechism. The best parallel to this style that is known to me in the Maya ethnohistoric literature occurs in the *Chilam Balam of Chumayel* (Roys 1967: 88–89), in the section known as "The Interrogation of the Chiefs." There is at least some reason to speculate that the question-response framework is a very ancient narrative style, suitable for teaching and also for liturgical uses. This is suggested by the clear ritual-induction question-and-answer framework of the interrogation section of the *Chilam Balam of Chumayel.*

2. Corn is still sometimes processed in this way by simply putting dry kernels on a hot tortilla griddle until the corn darkens and often appears to be charred. It is a highly unusual form of corn preparation today, however. It is prepared and consumed in this way only as a ritual substance for funerals, the charred kernels being crumbled to form a black powder that is then added to rum to form a kind of suspension. This charred corn mixed with rum is drunk for three days by mourners to simulate the food of the dead. The drink is accompanied by tortillas made of blue/black corn, together with the usual beans. The antistructural characteristics of this funeral-ritual food are replicated in part by the monkey people's eating habits, as reported in this text. A further parallel is found in the fact that funerals require that the house fire be extinguished, to be rekindled in an outside hearth for use during the funeral. The outside fire that the monkey people kindled after the flood shares some of the attributes of the outside fire used today for funerals. Both are clearly inversions of the normative order that happen in times of chaos.

3. It is useful to note that the events of this text are partially recapitulated in the great annual ritual of reversal, The Festival of Games. During its celebration in February, monkey impersonators dressed in real howler monkey caps and nineteenth-century French military costumes (remnants of the Maximilian period of the French intervention) appear by the hundreds. The festival's major themes are militarism and ritual return to the primeval chaos of the time before the Sun/Christ imposed his order on the universe. Monkeys are principal characters in this festival, and much is made of their tendency to barbaric behavior (for example, use of the Spanish language, conspicuous consumption of greasy food, whistling, raucous behavior, and so forth). Another event of this immensely complex festival that recapitulates themes in this text is the ritual exchange of "baby tamales" between wives of the Passions, who are the major militaristic characters in the festival. The "baby tamales" are ritually prepared as giant (two-foot-long) bean-filled tamales. They are wrapped in canna-lily leaves and steamed like ordinary bean tamales; however, their great size (baby size), ritual exchange, and subsequent consumption make specific ritual allusion to the barbaric custom of the ancients: the consumption of one's own children. This explains the curious name "baby tamales" (Tz. *tamaliˀ jˀolol*), which is a conspicuously non-Maya lexeme (*tamaliˀ* is from common Mexican Spanish usage *tamal,* and derives ultimately from the Nahuatl) and is different from the name of ordinary bean tamales, which are known as "beany tortillas" (Tz. *chenek'ul vaj*). (For further details on The Festival of Games see Gossen 1999: 105–58.).

TEXT 19

1. Hot Country refers to the Pacific Lowlands of Chiapas. See text 7, note 1.

2. The visitor was Our Father himself.

3. *Guineos* are small, finger-sized bananas. Zapotes are large, round tropical fruits with orange-brown sweet flesh.

4. This passage refers to the fact that monkeys realize they are safer from predators and closer to a dependable food supply in the rain forest than in the temperate-zone forest.

5. From the point of view of the Chiapas Highlands, monkeys live very far away. The howler monkey, to which the narrative refers, prefers the deep lowland rain forest as its habitat. It is worth noting that a time-space principle of good/closer versus bad/more distant operates in evaluation of both animals and human communities (see Gossen 1974b, 29–30; text 52 in this book).

TEXT 20

1. This text provides a bizarre twist to the usual accounts, in which the destruction of the earth is ordered by the Sun/Christ deity as punishment for human failings, crimes, and other imperfections. Here it is clear that the destruction is ordered by San José (Saint Joseph) in a fit of ill humor. The people did not, insofar as the text tells us, deserve it. It is this injustice that the Sun/Christ deity proposes to remedy as he takes away from San José any responsibility for making the earth habitable. It is worth noting that this text reiterates a common theme in Part 1 (First Creation) accounts of human history: the relentless campaign of the sun deity to eliminate political competition, first against his mother, then against his older brother, and finally, against the other saints, including his "false father," San José.

2. This timing suggests that the destruction occurred in April and early May, which is sowing time in the Chiapas Highlands. The timing is of interest, for it coincides with the approaching summer solstice. It was at this very time, in the account of the Sun/Christ's first ascent into the sky at the beginning of the First Creation, that the monkeys, demons, and Jews were destroyed by the Sun/Christ's heat and light. It is also at this time in the annual agricultural cycle (May 3, the day of the Santa Cruz) that all Chamulas pay homage to the Earth Lords in the form of rituals of petition for rain. This ritual action takes place at water holes and caves and is thus thematically resonant with the place the ancestors went, in this text, in their attempt to escape the boiling rain. The rainy season generally begins in the first two weeks of May. This life-giving, cold rain of earthly origin contrasts sharply with the destructive, hot rain of celestial origin that is described in the text.

3. This passage means that it did not thunder (literally, "the angels did not shout")—that cosmological order was not yet established, for normal rain is believed to be the work of the Earth Lords. Thunder—"shouting" or "crying" of angels (Earth Lords)—accompanies normal, cold, life-giving rain, which, according to Chamula belief, is of earthly origin. Specifically, thunder comes from caves. This verse is also poetically interesting, for "crying" refers both to thunder and to human crying. The two senses of the word are set in contrast in the second and third lines of the verse.

4. Though the topic shifts from the flood to the stability and topography of the earth, this verse is nevertheless related to the first part. One of the reasons for the total devastation brought by the boiling water rain was that the earth had no relief. Because of the lack of varied topography, the cave to which the ancestors fled was not high enough to afford them much protection. The flatness of the earth seems to have contributed to a more complete destruction than even San José had in mind when he sent it as a punishment. Consequently, the conflict ensues later on as the Sun/Christ deity assumes responsibility for preparing the earth, a task in which San José has failed.

Missionary accounts of José as the earthly father of Christ seem to have entered Chamula tradition in a bizarre fashion. Being a generation above the Sun/Christ, José is a senior to him in the junior/senior Tzotzil ranking system. José must also be somehow logically prior to the Sun/Christ. He is therefore interpreted as a kind of adversary, a rival for power with whom the Sun/Christ must deal in a fashion that allows him to gain the upper hand in the struggle for authority. The remaining section of the text reports part of that struggle, at the end of which José remains prior but is rendered passive through the Sun/Christ's efforts. This can be seen in cosmological drawings (see fig. 2 in this book) in which San José is represented as a passive (nonmoving) celestial being who simply sits on a throne at the center of the sky on the third level, which is the Sun/Christ's level. In other texts in this book, Our Lord Sun/Christ feels obliged to do away with competition from his own mother (text 10) and his older brother (texts 21 and 22).

5. The people had apparently expressed displeasure to San José at the flatness of the earth, as the lack of relief caused frequent floods. Although this was part of his job, he was apparently unable to do anything about their complaints and thus became frustrated and angry with the people. This ill humor seems to be related to his own ineptitude.

6. Our Lord San Salvador (Tz. *jtotile jxalik*) is a junior aspect of Our Lord Sun/Christ in Heaven (Tz. *jtotik la vinajel*). Our Lord San Salvador is the aspect of the sun deity that is visible on earth. (See text 1, note 2, and figure 2.) Both aspects are involved in the following conversation, in which San José is spoken to but does not reply. This passage records one more episode in the full passing of male political power from the erstwhile "father" to the ambitious son.

7. In this passage, the two aspects (junior and senior) of Our Lord Sun/Christ are speaking to each other.

TEXT 21

1. Chamula Tzotzil greeting etiquette usually includes all countrymen as kinsmen, even though real kinship is not implied; hence, the uncle-nephew exchange in verses 4 and 5.

2. This curing session was simply one of diagnosis. The curer usually determines the problem by feeling the pulse of the patient's left wrist. He then tells the patient what candles, herbs, flowers, and food will be needed for the curing ceremony. The date of the ceremony is also set at such diagnosis sessions. The rum mentioned in the text is the customary gift that the patient offers to the curer in asking him to cure him. Once the curer has agreed to attend to the narrator's ailment and the diagnosis is made, the rum is drunk to seal the transaction.

3. For the sake of understanding the rest of the story it is important to know at this point that the younger brother is Our Father Sun himself. His older brother's name is Marián.

4. *Memela* tortillas (still made today) are small, thick tortillas that often have one or two holes in them. They are typically given to very young children as a snack food, for the holes make them easy to handle. They are also thought to encourage toddlers to learn to speak.

5. The size of a *memela* tortilla is approximately that of the end of a pig's snout. The two holes resemble the nostrils of a pig snout. The younger brother's (that is to say, Our Father Sun's) magical powers made a reality of the analogy.

6. The older/senior-first principle in Chamula walking order on the path is preserved here, adding to the humorous scene.

7. Pigs are often called "Marián" in joking speech. This story is also given as a semi-serious explanation of why Chamulas prefer not to eat pork. "After all, Marián is our uncle," they say. "Who ever heard of eating one's own uncle?" (The relationship is established by recognizing that all people are ultimately children of Our Father Sun.) Other Chamulas explain their preference for not eating pork in economic terms. They claim that pigs eat too much corn and that they do not have corn to spare. Others claim that pigs have repulsive habits, so who would want to eat them? Still others use ethnic criteria: pork is Ladino food, full of grease, and it makes one smell of grease. Why whould one want to smell like a Ladino?

TEXT 22

1. As described in Part 1 (The First Creation), Our Father Sun became the older brother of all the deities. Text 22 explains how his former older brother blundered into non-participation in the pantheon of deities through his own selfishness. Our Father Sun's cleverness also played a part in doing his older brother in. In this way Our Father Sun eliminated all sibling competition for supremacy in his family.

2. These beehives are the source of both grubs and honey, both of which are highly prized delicacies. However, getting the honey from one of the beehives is a considerable task, for they are typically found very high in trees. Sometimes honey-and-grub-getting expeditions involve not only a tree climb but also the danger of attack by angry bees. This explains Our Father's hesitation about getting the honey.

3. Gophers' incisors are indeed similar to sticks in appearance, for they are not tapered but rather, almost cylindrical in shape. That the folk etiology of gopher teeth should be sticks is thus morphologically plausible.

4. That is, he hung a gourd in the tree where his older brother had been. Our Father Sun made this substitution as an effort to deceive his mother into believing that his older brother was still alive. Although his trick may seem implausible, it nonetheless makes cultural sense in the sense that gourds are associated with magical food production, the reunification of the soul configuration of the body, and the capacity to speak. For example, gourd whistles are used to call the souls of the dead on All Saints Eve. They are also used to summon lost parts of souls during curing rituals. Gourds vaguely resemble human heads, thus aiding in the deception. (See texts 7 and 8 for further description of the cultural context of gourds. See also the *Popol Vuh* for a cognate case of a gourds being used as a substitute for a human head [Tedlock 1996, 97–98].)

5. The tortillas that Our Father Sun asked his mother to make are called *memela.* (See text 21, notes 4 and 5.)

6. This passage explains the origin of domestic and wild pigs. The two that Our Father Sun caught are the original stock, male and female, of domestic pigs; those that escaped into the woods became wild pigs.

7. The theme of the pig as "our uncle" is a joking theme that occurs with some frequency in Chamula. It is sometimes offered as an explanation for the fact that Chamulas do not generally like pork, for it is like "eating one's uncle." They also think it is too greasy and causes diarrhea. Furthermore, they know that pigs eat human excrement. Pork is far from being a food taboo, however. Pork sausage is sold in Chamula stores and is sometimes bought to supplement the basic bean and tortilla diet, but in general, pork is not prized as an everyday or ritual food. Chicken, beef, and dried fish are considered far superior if one has money to buy meat of any kind.

TEXT 23

1. The narrator gave the name of this type of wood as *ch'u te'* (belly tree), which is probably derived from *ch'ul te'* (holy tree). Also known as Spanish cedar (*Cedrela odorata*), it is a much-prized lowland hardwood used for benches, lamp stands, shelves, chairs, tables, doors, coffins, crosses, rifle stocks, and grain measures. Laughlin (1975) states that one variety of this tree is believed (in Zinacantán) to be a god because of its pungent incense-like aroma. Its wood is also used for saints and drums. Hence, Our Father chose a nonordinary wood for carving the second people.

2. When I asked the narrator more about this bow instrument, he said that in his youth (ca. 1900) mouth bows were still in existence in Chamula. He tried to find an old one (called *t'umparax*) for me to see but could not, so he made one for me that he claimed was like the ones he had seen and played as a boy. He described it to me as a "bow, just like the bows that you use with bows and arrows." This was indeed what it looked like. It was made from a slender stick, perhaps half an inch in diameter and about three feet long. He string the instrument with a low E-string (used) from a Mexican guitar, creating an arc that, at the center, made a distance of ten inches between the stick and the string. The instrument is played by holding the bow in the left hand and biting the bow about five inches below one end. The mouth, thus placed, forms a resonating chamber that can vary the quality but not the pitch of the sound. The string is plucked to mark the rhythm with the middle finger of the right hand.

3. Our Father Sun was still living on the earth at this time.

4. The narrator explained that the food mentioned here (*sibak*, literally "gunpowder") is actually powdered charred corn; the two substances look alike. It is worth noting that the eating of charred corn and charcoal is an inauspicious habit. Although charred food may have been carried in preference to other foods so that it would not rot from moisture, it nevertheless bodes ill (as do the buzzards that appear in the next couplet), because charcoal is the food of the Chamula dead in the underworld. It is consumed ritually (charred uncooked kernels of corn, powdered in aguardiente suspension) at funerals. There is also a feared supernatural being called the "charcoal cruncher," who has the form of a detached female human head and wanders about in the night seeking charcoal to crunch by people's hearths. She can be heard crunching on occasion and causes great fear in the household, for she is a sign of approaching death for someone in the house.

5. The narrator explained that the buzzards were already feeding on the floating human corpses. They expected that the man and his companion would soon die as well, so they were poised and ready, waiting for them to do so.

6. The Chiapas Highlands are characterized by an internal drainage pattern, so that most surface water is carried away not by rivers and streams but by sinkholes. These sinkholes lead to subterranean streams that empty into the Grijalva River valley at the edges of the Chiapas Highland mountain system. Thus, floods typically occur in the Highlands when the sinkholes get plugged up (which happened most recently in 1973 in the San Cristóbal valley). When floods subside, it is because the sinkholes begin to function properly once again. In this text an earthquake apparently came toward the end of the flood, creating the topographic features of the present (verse 28), which allow for proper drainage.

7. The reader will recall that caves are the dwellings of the demons.

8. The Tzotzil *be 'o* refers to a general class of topographic features that includes everything from valleys to ravines, ditches to river channels. The translation is an attempt to capture all of these possible meanings.

9. Monkeys are important "primitive" or precultural symbols in Chamula culture. Children are called monkeys (Tz. *max*) before they are baptized and receive names. Men dressed as monkeys (and also called *max*) appear by the hundreds as ambiguous and threatening ritual characters at the great annual festival of Carnival, which takes place in February and which is, among other things, a winter ritual of inversion of the social order (see Gossen 1999, 105–58).

TEXT 24

1. This setting is typical of the time and place in which Chamula stories are told. Although narrators seldom choose to mention where they heard a story that they tell in their own version of the narrative, this is an exception, revealing something of the social context of Chamula storytelling. Stories are always told in response to a stimulus, in this case the appearance of the dead raccoon in the hands of the hunters. Also, this text reveals that leisure time is a likely time in which to hear stories. Here the setting is a lowland cornfield, on a Sunday, when Chamulas are resting from the week's labor in the fields.

2. Our Father Sun was angry with these people because he had destroyed the First Creation in a flood and thought it unfitting that any people should survive. Besides their survival—which was bad enough in itself, as they were supposed to have died—they no longer ate corn, which was the food from his body that he had given the people of the First Creation. Thus, twice guilty, they had to be punished.

3. "Digging animal" (Tz. *jotzovil chon*) is another Tzotzil term for raccoon. According to the narrator's explanation, the raccoon has a kind of ancestral memory. The reason raccoons are so fond of corn today is that it was their food when they were still people. They have not lost their taste for it even though, for the most part, they are forced to forage for bulbs and plants in the forest.

TEXT 25

1. This custom of detasseling corn is widely practiced by Indians in Chiapas. By removing all but one tassel in a hill of four or five plants, all the strength of the detasseled plants goes to produce strong, heavily seeded ears. The one tassel remaining is sufficient to pollinate all the plants in the hill. Detasseling is done when the ears are formed but just beginning to show their silk. By this method approximately 75 to 80 percent of tassels in a field are removed.

2. It should be remembered that corn is Our Father Sun's body. Our Father Sun promises the weeds that, although it is unpleasant, they the weeds must allow themselves to be cut in order to allow Our Father Sun's body to survive on earth to provide food for people. However, as all know too well, the weeds and grass will also survive.

TEXT 26

1. Saint John the Baptist is the patron saint of San Juan Chamula, from whom the *municipio* (equivalent to the Anglo-American township) takes its name. The image of San Juan (junior aspect) has the place of honor in the Chamula church, just above the main altar, facing west. His festival, June 24, is one of the largest and best attended of all Chamula fiestas. All Chamula saints have a junior (Tz. *ˀitzˀinal*) and a senior (Tz. *bankilal*) aspect. Furthermore, the barrio of Chamula that is considered the most senior in rank (*bankilal*) is San Juan. It is of interest that San Juan has a close affinity with Our Father Sun, being one of his younger brothers. This special relationship to Our Father Sun is expressed not

only in his favored position in the Chamula church but also in the fact that Barrio San Juan lies generally east and north of the ceremonial center, thus giving it a favorable orientation in relation to the other barrios, which lie to the northwest (San Pedro) and to the west and south (San Sebastián) (see map 4). The highest point in Chamula (and, indeed, in the Central Chiapas Highlands) is Tzontevitz Mountain (Tree Moss Mountain, as it is translated in the text), which lies in Barrio San Juan. It is in this mountain that the senior aspect of San Juan lives. Thus, the seniority of San Juan in the rank of Chamula saints is only exceeded by that of Our Father Sun himself.

2. Xitalá refers to Sitalá, which is a Tzeltal-speaking *municipio* that shares a border with the *municipio* of Santa Catarina Pantelhó, which places it to the northeast of Chamula in an area that drops off quickly to Hot Country. The site of the old ceremonial center is said to have the remains of rock foundations and walls from an old church (or perhaps from a Precolumbian structure). The location stated in the text ("just above Xitalá") may also mean "east of," for the concepts of east/above are linked in Tzotzil cosmology (see Gossen 1974b, 35).

3. Both of these places lie within the present-day municipal boundaries of Chamula, thus placing them in the highlands in what is classified as Cold Country. Located about twenty kilometers due north of the present-day Chamula Ceremonial Center, they contain the remains (mounds and foundations) of some buildings at Jol Ch'umtik, probably of Precolumbian origin. Yaˀal Ichin is still an inhabited hamlet of Chamula.

4. See note 1 of this text for an explanation of junior and senior aspects of all Chamula saints. The senior aspect of San Juan lives in Tree Moss Mountain along with San Jerónimo (Saint Jerome), some other saints, and the animal soul companions. The junior aspect of San Juan lives in the Chamula church, and it is he who is represented in the image of that name.

5. This must have been a great spectacle to behold, for the narrator explained that the helpers were none other than San Pedro (St. Peter) and San Sebastián, the saints for whom the other two barrios of Chamula are named. With San Juan (the older) in the lead, San Pedro next, then San Sebastián, and the unnamed workers in the rear, they herded the great field of stones as though they were sheep.

6. The staff mentioned in this line is a common shepherd's staff, a typical accoutrement in religious icons and images as well as in the everyday life of Chamula households, both in the home community and in the diaspora communities. Sheep, along with chickens, turkeys, dogs, and cats, are the most commonly kept domestic animals.

7. There are dozens of places in Chamula today that bear the names of Bejel Ton (Sitting Stone) or Pajal Ton (Fixed Stone). Many of these places are named for wayward, uncooperative stones, still visible and conspicuous, which refused to be herded to San Juan's proposed church site in the ceremonial center. No ritual significance is attached to these places, although they serve as constant reminders of the past.

8. See note 5 in this text for a list of the saints involved in the stone-herding expedition. By this time Our Holy Father Sun had joined in to help.

9. In this and the previous verse (51), east (above) and west (below) are incorporated into the translation in their dual cosmological senses, which include both cardinal directions and relative locations (see map 4). This principle—east/up (or above) and west/down (or below)—is intended here, according to the narrator.

10. See note 1, in this text. It is important to call attention to an ambiguity regarding the residence of San Juan, stemming partly from the two aspects of the saint's beings, junior and senior. All Chamulas seem to agree that the main image in the Chamula church is of the junior aspect of the saint. However, the junior aspect also represents the senior aspect

for purposes of prayer and cult practice. Thus, the senior aspect is not visible but implicit. Although today the senior aspect of San Juan is believed to live in Tree Moss Mountain, he once apparently had a house there. Whether this was a shrine or chapel, no one seems to know. However, there is still a place-name on the mountain—San Juan's Window (Tz. Sventana San Juan). It is a small vertical cave opening near the top of the mountain with a cross shrine nearby that is often visited by curing parties. However, to my knowledge there is no remnant of a structure anywhere nearby.

TEXT 27

1. See text 26, note 1.

2. Ibid, note 2.

3. The narrator told me that he knows Chamulas who have heard this mysterious ringing from within a small body of water at Xitalá.

4. The town of Simojovel historically has been a Tzotzil-speaking *municipio*. It still exists and is located in a rich semitropical valley to the northeast of Chamula (see map 4).

5. See text 26, note 1.

6. See text 26, note 3.

7. Knowing that the younger aspect of San Juan lives in the Chamula church and that his older aspect lives in Tree Moss Mountain, I inquired how he could be both in Simojovel and in the Chamula church. The answer was that he has two younger brothers!

8. A fundamental premise in Chamula cosmology is the assumption that the Chamula Ceremonial Center lies at the very center of the earth. The "navel of the earth" (which is the exact center) is said to be marked by a stone that lies under the image of San Juan in the Chamula church. See figure 2 and map 4.

9. Hamlet Kuchulumtik lies right next to the present-day Ceremonial Center. It is not more than a fifteen-minute walk from this hamlet to the center.

10. This passage seems to mean simply that thorny bushes would make an unpleasant setting for people to live in.

11. Apparently the placing of his staff in the center of the lake began a magical process that caused the hill to collapse.

12. Owl Rock (Ichinton) is a place-name and also a hamlet of contemporary Chamula. Named for a prominent limestone outcropping that looks like a perched owl, it lies along the main San Cristóbal–Chamula road. There are numerous stories claiming that Owl Rock quarry also "resented" the construction of the road when it was originally built almost fifty years ago. Stories indicate that the spirit of Owl Rock quarry forced the engineers to reroute the road so as not to put it too close to Owl Rock. Thus, Owl Rock continues to be a sensitive area, as it was in the time of San Juan.

13. June 24 is the date of the traditional patronal festival of San Juan Chamula.

14. Several saints who had a life and existence separate from Christ in standard Christian doctrine are but aspects of Christ (Our Father Sun) in Chamula doctrine. The evangelist San Mateo (Saint Matthew) is one of these aspects of Our Father Sun. He represents the aspect of the dead Christ, recently removed from the cross but not yet entombed. This may mesh with Christian doctrine, as San Mateo was present at the Ascension of Christ and received Christ's blessing at the time of his final appearance on earth, after which Christ rose to heaven. San Mateo is often represented in religious art representing the Ascension of Christ.

TEXT 28

1. Zinacantán is a Tzotzil-speaking Indian community that borders on Chamula (see map 1). Zinacantecos have extensive corn-growing operations in the lowlands, and Chamulas often hire themselves out to Zinacantecos to work for them in their lowland cornfields. Hence, Chamulas have many business and trade relations with Zinacantecos. The rodent-trapping mentioned in this text is important not only as a pastime but as a source of food. The rodents customarily trapped for food, known as pig rats (*chitom ch'o, Sigmodon hispidis saturatus*), are the size of a large hamster. They taste rather like rabbit or squirrel and are customarily prepared by splitting them and roasting them over open coals.

2. See text 2, note 1 (First Creation). There is a large complex of beliefs about Earth Lords, who have snakes and the body of Ladinos as alternative forms. Earth Lords are responsible for rain, in which case they are known as *ʔanjeletik* (angels), as well as for all metal goods, including money and treasure, which are believed to come ultimately from the earth. They are associated with caves and often have snakes as familiars. Some Chamulas call snakes the "Earth Lords' chickens" for they roam about the Earth Lords' dwelling places much as chickens wander around human house compounds.

The image of the Earth Lord as Ladino is significant as a metaphor of political and economic domination of Indians by Ladinos. It is ironic that this deity, in Tzotzil called *yajval banamil* (owner, or lord, of the earth), has both the capacity to give or not give life-sustaining rain, and the control over trade goods and money. All of these powers symbolize economic and political domination of mestizo Mexicans (Ladinos) over Indians. The fact that the Indian who found the snake in the trap waited until it turned into a Ladino to obey its command is again indicative of the patron-client relationship of Ladinos and Indians in what is still essentially a caste system in Chiapas social life.

3. Another ironic twist of this tale is the snake's language. The alternate form of the snake is as a human Ladino, thus making Spanish the probable language that he would speak. This supposition is obviously wrong in the context of this tale, for the Good Samaritan Indian finds that the Ladino speaks Tzotzil—a pleasant surprise, since most Ladinos do not bother to learn any more than market Tzotzil. The explanation that makes sense to the Indian in the story is that the Ladino probably was no ordinary Ladino. This is soon clarified when the Indian discovers that the Ladino's home is a cave. The Earth-Lord identity of the Ladino is thus established, for only Earth Lords live in caves. It seems clear that the Earth Lord in this narrative is bilingual, perhaps the better to exploit Indian "clients," and it is true that Ladino merchants and landowners must usually know some Tzotzil in order to communicate with Indian workers and clients.

4. The expression *yahval ch'en* (owner of the cave) is related to *yahval na* (owner of the house), which is an honorific title given to a married woman. The expression is best translated as "mistress of the house," hence the assumption that the person who opened the door is female.

5. This is still another ethnic commentary. Chamula body aesthetics place high value on a fair complexion, particularly for women. Thus, in having a physical appearance like that of a Ladino woman (and also like that of the saints), she was a very desirable marriage partner to the Chamula man in the story. The contradictions are numerous, for while light skin is esteemed, it is also the sign of what they view as an amoral mestizo/Spanish culture that lies above Indians, economically and politically dominating the hierarchy of Chiapas social life. Yet, paradoxically, a light complexion is also a trait of gods and saints. Thus, the man received a woman whose potential for moral and immoral behavior, good and bad, were not really known. She was a "high-risk" spouse.

6. The man believed that she had harvested too much and that this would result in waste of food. The motif of the magically reproducing ears of corn is cognate with a similar passage in the *Popul Vuh* (Tedlock 1996, 102–104) in which the maiden Blood Moon is subjected to a test of identity by the grandmother of the hero twins, Hunahpu and Xbalanque. The grandmother sends her to the cornfield to harvest a netful of ripe ears of corn where there is but one clump. She succeeds in magically transforming little into plenty, thereby proving that she, Blood Moon, is truly the grandmother's daughter-in-law.

7. This is the standard origin story of red corn, but it is usually told in a much more fragmentary form than occurs here. The short version one usually hears is simply that the Earth Lord's daughter's husband hit her in the nose and that she wiped her nose on a nearby ear of white corn.

8. This passage constitutes the woman's rescue by her father, the Earth Lord. Rain, as I have noted, is fundamentally associated with the realm of the Earth Lords. The sudden storm that developed was not only a sign of the arrival of the woman's father but also of his wrath at the man's lack of appreciation of his wife's power to increase the volume and quantity of food.

9. In Indian households tortillas are typically served in somewhat squat gourd containers. They come in various sizes, the most popular being eight to twelve inches in diameter at the widest point, with a hole in the top that measures five to eight inches in diameter. These gourds are preferred tortilla containers because they keep the tortillas warm.

10. The bracketed phrase of this line in Tzotzil (*xi ti vinike*) is translated as "said the man." It refers to the long retelling of the tale as a quote from the original storyteller, which begins with verse 3. For stylistic reasons, I have ignored the phrase in the English translation.

TEXT 29

1. This text, though simple and direct in story line, proved to be a particular challenge to translate for two reasons. On a technical level the narrator uses the phrase *mu ʔantz* (bad woman) with unremitting frequency. The problem was how to capture this while avoiding a boring redundancy in English. Upon my discussing this with the narrator in both Spanish and Tzotzil, he laughed and gave me at least ten nuances of the "badness" of the protagonist; all of these contrasted with the opposite, *lekil* (good), which the woman might have been if she had not indulged in masturbation. This list, roughly translated, served as the composite word bank from which I drew the various renderings in English (disgusting, awful, terrible, wretched, depraved, evil, damned, poor, wicked, awful). I gathered from our conversation that Marián felt both pity and disgust, together with adolescent amusement, at the "poor woman's" plight and unfortunate demise. My translation attempts, at various moments, to capture the narrator's extremely mixed attitudes toward her.

In addition, the reader should know that the masturbation theme of the story was front and center in the narrator's personal concerns at the time of his recording of the story. In late adolescence and unmarried at the time, he talked incessantly and joyously about the subjects of sex and masturbation, leading me to believe that his enjoyment of the story reflected his own preoccupations. (See note 5, below; see also Gossen 1974b, 91–122, for examples of how sexual themes permeate other genres of informal, humorous speech.)

2. That is, she had to share one husband with lots of women and so did not get the attention she wanted.

3. The proportion suggested by the narrator was one man for every ten women.

4. The man was with another wife and noticed strange noises in the dark.

5. While the narrator is careful to place the bizarre events of the story safely back in the Second Creation, the themes are not far removed from Chamula life today. Masturbation is talked and joked about with great frequency among boys, unmarried men, and younger married men. Just what the verbal enthusiasm about the topic means in practice I do not know other than by hearsay, but masturbation is certainly practiced by many boys and men. Of girls and women, more apropos of the text, I do not know. Hearsay indicates that masturbation among girls and women is widely practiced, but my sources are mostly men talking about women, so who knows? At any rate Chamula public standards of inhibition and proscription regarding casual heterosexual affairs, premarital and extramarital alike, lie near the conservative end of the spectrum. Hence, most Chamula men acknowledge that mastrubation is sometimes "necessary," particularly during their long months of labor on the coffee plantations. Prostitutes are felt by most men to be too expensive and not worth the risk of disease. Masturbation is also felt to be necessary for young men who must wait to marry until they can afford the relatively high price of petitioning ceremonies and gifts to the parents of the bride.

Another theme of the text close to Chamula social life today is that of polygyny, or plural wives. Chamula custom allows a man to have as many wives as he can support. This, of course, is an alternative available only to the relatively rich. I would estimate that only 3 or 4 percent of Chamula men have two wives, while a handful of famous and wealthy old men have four or five wives. However, the plural-wife alternative seems to be stable only where each wife is housed separately and has her own supply of corn and beans. Even in these cases there are sometimes quarrels between wives over rivalry for the husband's attention and level of economic support. Hence, the picture given in the text (in which, apparently, the several wives shared a single house) is not far from accurate in terms of conflicts I have heard about regarding jealousy and dissastisfaction between cowives. The truth of this can occasionally be verified in divorce cases that come before the traditional tribunal in Chamula Ceremonial Center.

TEXT 30

1. Upon inquiring of the narrator, I learned that he stopped looking for curers because he ran out of money. This is consistent with present-day Chamula custom: curing usually stops when the money stops, not unlike what commonly occurs in modern American medical practice. (For more detail on Chamula curing practice and shamanism, see Gossen 1974b, 15–18, 209–15.)

2. The small beeswax candles mentioned in the text are important ritual symbols in connection with Chamula beliefs about death. Called "flashlights of the dead" (Tz. *sjoko anima*) that appear at wakes beside the corpse, in a casket with the corpse, at the annual Festival of the Dead (Tz. *k'in santo*) on November 1 and 2, and at curing ceremonies. These candles, which are also called *sera kantila* (from Spanish *cera*, wax) must be of beeswax and are believed to light the way of the dead as the tongue-soul (Tz. *ch'ulel*) goes to live in the underworld immediately after death. Hence, a small beeswax candle is anchored in the split end of a stick, which is stuck in the ground to the righthand side of the corpse (from its point of view) in the house where the funeral will take place. It is lighted as soon after death as possible, at the beginning of the three-day wake, its purpose being to light the way of the tongue-soul through the darkness of the underworld. An unlighted beeswax candle is also placed in the right inner elbow of the corpse, within the casket, and goes with the

body to the grave. This candle, which represents the husband or wife of the deceased (and is called "husband" or "wife"), serves to provide company for the soul of the dead as it travels to the underworld. It is at this point that the link between these beliefs and the text can be found. The man who mourns for his wife and wishes to go to see her in the underworld takes the symbol (the beeswax candle) of himself that has gone to the grave by his wife's elbow, using it and another like it to enter the underworld. He believes that the candles will light his way through the passages of the underworld. Usually such expeditions are made only by the souls of shamans, who do so for the purpose of curing the living. The man's adventure is bound to be extremely dangerous, to say the least.

3. The place of the underworld in Chamula cosmology is discussed in Gossen (1974b, 21–22). Mortuary customs are briefly discussed in Gossen (1974b, 168–71) and more extensively in Menget (1968). Chamulas generally believe that all of the dead go to the underworld in the form of their tongue-soul, which is the most essential of the three parts of the human soul. Only suicide victims, murder victims, and murderers go to another compartment of the underworld, where they are punished by being burned each night by Our Father Sun as he passes through the underworld part of his daily orbit. All other dead Chamulas live a quasi-ordinary life in the underworld, with these exceptions: (1) there is no sexual contact between men and women; (2) people eat charcoal and flies instead of tortillas, beans, and meat; and (3) earth day is underworld night and vice versa.

4. Each Chamula burial ground is near a small cave opening, called the "window of the underworld." These cave openings are different from ordinary cave entrances, which are believed to be outlets to the demons' great network of underground passages. The "windows" of the underworld are also distinct from the caves that are the domain of Earth Lords, the latter usually being associated with some source of water—a spring or the like. However, there is always the danger of getting lost in the inner passages of the earth, for there are believed to be places where the Earth Lords' caves, the demons' underground network, and the road to the underworld cross; hence, the need for candles so that one will not get lost.

5. The path of Our Father Sun is the route the sun takes through the underworld at night, thus creating day in the underworld during the earth's night. At the edge of this path, at the nadir of the sun's orbit in the underworld, sits San Pedro (Saint Peter), who is also known in Chamula as Our Father (Our Lord?) of the Underworld (Tz. *jtotik ta lajebal*). This is obviously the same San Pedro who in standard Christian belief sits in judgment in heaven. In Chamula belief he sits in the underworld at a small table and gives instructions to recent arrivals on how to get to the permanent dwelling place of the dead in the underworld.

6. San Pedro (in verses 16 and 19) is incredulous that a living man should have ventured so far into the realm of the dead. He believes at first that the man is dead and making his routine trek to the underworld. He is suspicious, however, and therefore asks in order to be sure. Finding that he is indeed still alive, he warns him that he is reaching the point of no return.

7. Included among the ways that the life of the dead in the underworld is much like life on earth is the sweat bath (Tz. *pus*), which is a routine part of ritual life and personal hygiene in Chamula today (see Gossen 1999, 15–19). The widowed husband in this passage does not realize that life in the underworld is different.

8. Flies, in lieu of beans and meat, are the routine food of the dead. The woman is apparently trying to recreate part of her life on earth by attempting to cook beans for her husband. He, however, attempts to heat up the fire by blowing on the coals, as one does on earth. This, of course, is a mistake.

9. Here as throughout the text, the narrator uses the adjective *mu* (bad, wretched) and the adjective *sonso* (foolish) to describe the man. This choice of words reflects the narrator's negative opinion of anyone who would be foolish enough to want to go to the underworld. In this text, as elsewhere in the book, characters become so attached to the narrator's descriptive valuejudgments that the whole noun phrase (adjective plus noun) becomes the name of the character, as in the case of the "wicked villain" of melodrama fame.

TEXT 31

1. The buzzard referred to is the "red-headed buzzard" (*Cathartes aura*), which is one of two species of buzzard that live in the Chiapas Highlands. The other is the "black-headed buzzard" (*Coragyps atratus*).

2. Cold Country refers to the home highlands, Hot Country to the lowlands in general (see map 4). The fact that the narrator equates outrageous human behavior with a distant time and unknown place is intelligible in terms of time-space principles that govern other Chamula appraisals of their moral community and its adversaries (see Gossen 1974b, 29–30).

TEXT 32

1. This text and text 31 are variants of the same story, told by two brothers who may have heard it originally from the same source in Hot Country, as both introductions suggest. Both are included here, in spite of the obvious redundancy, to show how two narrators relate the same story.

The red-headed buzzard (*Cathartes aura*) of this story is a bird of bad omen, for it symbolizes human laziness in its origins (as in this story) and its habits, consuming only what remains of dead animals without having made any effort to secure its own food.

TEXT 33

1. This is a key text that deals with a Chamula version of a heroic cycle found throughout Mesoamerica. In an important comparative study, Martin Pickands (1986) demonstrates that the narrative is cognate with several key passages in sixteenth-century Yucatec Maya texts, in the *Popol Vuh,* and with numerous contemporary Maya texts, including versions from Yucatán, Chiapas, and northeastern Guatemala. This suggests that the present account of the adventures of Juan López Nona (the name of all three brothers who are the protagonists of the story) is undoubtedly a significant remnant of Precolumbian Maya historical memory that is preserved in Chamula oral tradition. An appropriate comparative analysis of the text would be a book-length undertaking that is not possible within the scope of this book. The likely importance of the text is highlighted by the highly formal recitation—as if by rote memorization—of the terms of the peace treaty with the Guatemalans (verse 66). This passage and the subsequent, very beautiful passage (verses 72–75) describing the immortality of the heroes suggest that the text comes from the deepest substrata of Chamula historical memory. A possible key to unlocking this history may be found in the contemporary cult of Oshib Vinik (Three Men) that still exists in the pantheon of Chamula "saints" as an ostensible expression of the Holy Trinity (see note 12 of this text); I think the meaning of the Three Men goes beyond this.

2. The narrator clarified that these three men were brothers. The Tzotzil text itself does not state this fact.

3. For a discussion of the Chamula concept of the soul, see text 3, note 12. The Tzotzil word for soul that is used here (*ch'ulel*) indicates that it refers to the tongue-soul, the most

powerful and essential of the three souls that humans usually possess. However, the brothers in this text have supernatural powers, no doubt provided in part by the extraordinary "soul support" (for example, fire, whirlwind, and wasp) that they possess.

4. The staffs (Tz. *baxton*, from Sp. *bastón*) that they carried were of the type still used by Chamula constables. They are of a black hardwood, about a meter long and three centimeters in diameter. The staffs are the symbols of office for constables (Tz. *mayol*, from Sp. *alguacil mayor*) and also serve as weapons for defense.

5. The fact that the jaguar and coyote, very powerful animal-soul coessences for contemporary Chamulas, could not provide information about the demon's abductions suggests that their power was eclipsed by forces greater than their own. That they could not "speak" is interesting in light of Chamula beliefs regarding animal souls, suggesting that the forces of supernatural power of the three brothers and the demon were greater (or different) than the supernatural power that exists in the present era.

6. It is of some interest that the original Tzotzil text uses the Spanish loanword *muchachu* (from *muchacho*, Sp. for boy) to refer to the Guatemalan chief's son. This usage is characteristic of Chamula Tzotzil references to the offspring of non-Indians. *Muchachu* is also used to refer to the owners of "talking boxes," which are private oracles kept by many Highland Chiapas Indians. Thus, in using *muchachu*, the men are classifying the slain demon as not only foreign but also powerful.

7. The guitars had appeared magically from their staffs.

8. Upon my pursuing the logic of this event in a translation session, the narrator stated that the Guatemalans died because the three Chamulas threw ashes at them. The ashes quickly turned into weapons that killed the Guatemalans.

9. According to the narrator, this document is kept in the capital of Guatemala. The president of Guatemala takes care of it. A kind of peace treaty, it states that the Guatemalans have promised to let Chamulas alone forever and that they will never again attack Chamulas. It is worth noting that there are other aspects of Chamula life and thought that seem to restate some of the general information in this text. At the festival of Carnival in February, a document is read (in Spanish, a "foreign language") stating that soldiers once came from Guatemala to attack Chamulas. A mock war is staged at the same festival (using horse manure as ammunition) between Guatemalans and Mexicans. The war ends in a draw, suggesting a truce of some sort. Further, Chamulas generally dislike and distrust Guatemalans who work with them today on the coffee plantations in the lowlands. Chamulas argue that the Guatemalans will work for less and hence take jobs away from Mexicans (oddly echoing the same complaint of U.S. citizens who object to the use of cheap, illegal Mexican labor in American commercial agriculture).

10. Money was of no use to them, the narrator explained, for the three brothers had become like saints through their death by burning and resurrection. Since they were like saints, they no longer used money and did not charge for their services.

11. The "edge of heaven" is a place where the earth island ends and the great sea that surrounds the earth begins (see Gossen 1974b, 30–35). From there the path of Our Father Sun, which forms the dome of heaven and the limits of the cosmos, is visible (see map 3). The three men now live at a place in the cosmos that is close to the realm of Our Father Sun and also close to dangerous supernatural forces such as demons. Thus, the three brothers are defined as minor gods.

12. Each of the three brothers is called Juan López Nona, a name which, to my knowledge, is not invoked in any contemporary ritual or prayer but which is known as the name of a distinguished ancestor. The narrator explained that one of the three brothers had some

land in Chamula but was not married. He sold his land to the other two, so that they would have land to leave to their children before they went off to live at the edge of heaven.

In addition to the possible association of the three brothers with one name with the central Christian concept of the Trinity, it is also likely that the concept of a deity with several aspects has Precolumbian roots, for the multiple aspects of Precolumbian Maya deities are well known (see J. E. S. Thompson 1970, 198–200).

TEXT 34

1. The narrator explained that these events came at the end of the Second Creation, "about five thousand years ago." It should be borne in mind, however, that these are relative time periods. There is absolutely no consistency from one person to the next regarding the antiquity of the creations.

2. The invocation of Jesus is not really addressed to Jesus as a specific deity. In this context, it is an expletive.

3. This is the sound of a rooster's crow in Tzotzil. It may be related to the cock's crow at the time of the Passion of Christ.

4. The narrator explained that Indians and Ladinos still spoke the same language (Spanish) and were thus not clearly distinguishable from one another at the time of these events. They were being punished by the flood because they had eaten their own children.

5. The flood had isolated them on a mountain peak. This is how they had escaped the flood.

6. The reference here is to the "knot" that often occurs in a dog's penis during mounting, sometimes causing the dogs to get "hung up."

7. The origin of modern Ladinos, as described in this story, accounts for what Chamulas view as improper Ladino social behavior, particularly regarding male-female interaction in public. They view Ladinos' public displays of physical affection (for example, kissing, embracing, walking in close physical contact) as distasteful, reminiscent of their dog heritage. This appraisal of ethnic difference is, for Indians, a moral as well as a social commentary. They regard Ladinos' acquisitiveness, waste of food, irreverence for deities, and inclination to common crime (for example, theft and rape) to be linked both metaphorically and historically to the Ladinos' dog heritage.

8. Laughter, here and below in this text, (verse 70), is represented as a kind of presymbolic lingua franca for all human beings, the only mode of intercultural communication not based on language.

9. This reference is to corn, known in ritual speech as "the Sun/Christ's body." See text 3, note 1. Corn, the typical food of Indians, contrasts with wheat-based breads, which are associated with Ladinos.

10. This means that they were not procreating.

11. This passage is difficult to translate because the intent of the narrator is not to suggest that the sun ceases to make his daily orbit, but rather to state that once the habit of procreating was established in humankind, it was—in the deity's view—distasteful. That is why he chose to move through his daily cycle at a greater distance than had been his custom in the past.

12. Verses 54 through 56 are cryptic and strange. Upon seeking an explanation for them, I learned that the Sun/Christ deity felt ambivalent about his children's knowledge of sex. In line 54 he seems concerned that they did not have knowledge of procreation. In line 56 he seems to find that their knowledge of sex is distasteful. This ambivalence about

procreation stems from the fact that the demon taught the first people about sex. Specifically, he taught the first woman to have sexual intercourse; she then taught her husband. The narrator further explained that since knowlege of sex was taught by the Sun/Christ deity's chief adversary (the demon), sexual odors, being of evil origin, were offensive to the Sun/Christ. This is why he chose to draw progressively away from the mundane life of his children, to move into the sky. The present text reports this alienation, which explains in part the rule of sexual abstinence required of religious and civil officials at times when they are performing their ritual duties—on behalf of, and in the service of, the Sun/Christ and other deities.

13. This verse is a reference to the structure of the cosmos. The path of the sun deity marks the outermost limits of space in the universe. As the Sun/Christ travels at the third layer of the sky, it is only the radiance of his head and halo that we perceive as the sun. See text 1, note 2.

14. The reader will recall from a number of texts above that eating one another was the sin for which the people of the Second Creation were punished when the Sun/Christ sent the deluge.

15. This verse is a restrained, though negative, commentary reflecting Tzotzils' disapproval of the familiarity and freedom of Ladino male-female interaction in public places. The verb used for "speaking" in this passage (*k'oponvan*) does not refer to polite speech. It alludes to Ladinos' habitual use of the language of illicit sexual propositions in their everyday interaction. Such behavior within the Chamula community is punishable by fine and imprisonment according to Chamula common law. This passage is, therefore, to be read as a negative moral commentary on Ladinos.

16. The origin of the desirability of ethnic and linguistic separateness is considered at length in text 42.

TEXT 35

1. The translation of this verse derives from the verb *k'opon,* which in this context means "to speak to" or "to pray to." However, the meaning is broader, for praying to deities suggests a full range of respectful and appropriate behavior in relation to one's religious obligations.

2. This passage records a slightly different version of the teaching of procreation than that given in other texts, in which instruction in sex is attributed to the Demon Pukuj. In Chamula cosmology, there is a group of early supernaturals who have in common generally negative, amoral characteristics. These beings, freely mingling Precolumbian ideas and Christian indoctrination, include the Demon Pukuj, monkeys, generic demons, Jews, and, specifically, Judas. Judas presumably entered this select company through missionary teaching that it was he who betrayed Christ.

TEXT 36

1. The reader will find it interesting to compare this text with lines 2993–3064 of the *Popol Vuh* (Edmondson 1971, 96–98; Tedlock 1996, 109–10). Since the cognate K'iche' material so closely resembles that contained herein, this text serves as an excellent example of the Precolumbian roots of the Tzotzil narrative tradition as well as the pan-Maya occurrence of many of the motifs and tale types (see Gossen 1983).

2. The exact identification of the wasps and hornets is as follows: *chanul akov* (wasp, *Vespula sp*); *chak lakante'* (hornet, *Polistes sp.*); *sk'ak'al ya* (tarantula-killer wasp, *Pepsis sp.*). All are known to deliver fierce stings.

3. In a previous study of continuities between the *Popol Vuh* and the modern Chamula oral tradition, I have called particular attention to the uncanny similarity between the language and poetic structure of this magical formula as it occurs in the two traditions in exactly the same place in the same story (Gossen 1983, 321). This is Tedlock's rendering of the Quiché version of the formula:

> Arise, conjoin, you trees!
> Arise, conjoin, you bushes! (Tedlock 1996, 110)

Here is the present Tzotzil variant:

> Rise up, tree!
> Rise up, vine!

There is perhaps no point in my entire corpus of texts where the phylogenetic relationship of these two Maya traditions is more transparently evident.

4. I cannot resist calling attention to the clarity of the nature/culture conflict in this text. Rabbit and deer did everything possible to prevent Our Father from violating the woods, the realm of nature, for the purposes of making his cornfield. They failed, of course, but they resorted even to magic to prevent man and culture from moving into their territory. As I have noted, Chamulas fairly consistently recognize three general realms of social space: house areas (Tz. *naetik*), which are safe; cleared or open areas for field and pasture (Tz. *jamalaltik*), which are also safe; and woods (Tz. *te'tik*), which are ever threatening. They generally avoid the latter for fear, quite literally, of being subject to the power of spooks, demons, Earth Lords, and wild animals. In fact, much of their ritual action—from curing rituals to the great public drama of Carnival or The Festival of Games—emphasizes the somewhat precarious hold that humankind has on the safety of house areas and cleared areas—precarious because everyone knows that they were all "taken" from the woods. This human appropriation of the woods for areas of human habitation received the full blessing of Our Father, of course, but even he has trouble in getting his will to prevail, as this text demonstrates. It follows that people approach the task with some fear and trepidation. In fact people embark on the mission of wresting their space from the forest nearly every year, as they engage in the traditional Maya slash-and-burn style of agriculture. In its purest form this style of exploitation of the land is cyclical. A forest is felled and burned. The ash and organic matter remain to fertilize the cornfield for a period of several years. When fertility diminishes, the field is abandoned and the forest and brush are allowed to take over again for several years, after which it is once again slashed and burned to make a new cornfield, thus completing the cycle. In reality, however, population and land pressure in the Chiapas Highlands have made the practice of traditional slash-and-burn agriculture a system that is ideal but no longer economically feasible. In the vast majority of cases fields are seldom allowed to go back to brush and forest but rather are made to produce a crop every year with the help of organic and chemical fertilizers. In some cases abuse of the land is pushed too far and cornfields lose productive capacity altogether, becoming minimally productive sheep pasture or, at worst, eroded wastelands. This text, though an animal tale on one level, is also, on another level, a substantial commentary upon categories of social space as well as upon traditional Chamula agriculture.

5. This passage (verses 52–54) has complex cosmological referents. In assuming responsibility for deer and rabbit as their charges, the Earth Lords accept rabbit and deer as their familiars and helpers. It is said, in fact, that deer are the Earth Lords' mules or horses and that rabbits are the Earth Lords' burros. In both cases long ears are the key physical attribute that associates the wild animals (deer and rabbit) with the domestic animals (mules,

horses, and burros). Rabbit and deer are said to help the Earth Lords carry their large supply of silver money. Also included among the Earth Lords' familiars and helpers are the armadillo, known as the Earth Lords' stool because of its appearance (Tz. *tz'omol te'*, log stool, becomes *tz'omol chon,* stool animal); and the rattlesnake (Tz. *mokoch*), known as the Earth Lords' dog because it warns the Earth Lords of intruders in their domain and strikes and kills enemies of the Earth Lords. This group of animals, then, has a special relationship with the Earth Lords' domain (woods and caves) and affairs (most importantly, producing rain). It is also worth noting that the only one of these animals that serves as a human animal soul companion is the rabbit, who is a common soul companion of poor and humble people. The other animals (that is to say, deer) are excluded because they have cloven hooves. The soul-companion link of an animal species requires four limbs with five digits, making twenty, which is, indeed, the Tzotzil word for man (*vinik*) (see Gossen 1999, 225–45).

6. This discussion concerns deer and rabbit as species and as individuals. Chamulas believe that these animals enjoy a special protected status as a species, for they are the charges of the Earth Lords. In other words it is conceivable, according to Chamula premises, that certain kinds of animals—such as wasps and hornets, mentioned in this text—could simply disappear altogether, with neither Our Father nor the Earth Lords taking particular note. Deer and rabbit, in this sense, are privileged species. It is interesting to speculate why this should be so. I am convinced that it has something to do with the considerable importance they once had as game animals. This is no longer the case, for population density in most parts of Chamula means that game animals are rare. Domestic animals now supply almost all of the animal protein that Chamulas consume. Rabbit and deer remain highly desirable foods whenever they are available, however. To this day, whenever Chamulas do succeed in bagging a game animal (most commonly, armadillos, rabbits, deer, and several kinds of rodents), they pray to the Earth Lords, begging for forgiveness and understanding for taking a creature from their domain.

TEXT 37

1. While primarily a ruse to trick coyote and get away, this passage nevertheless reflects an inversion of a typical Chamula domestic problem, that of petitioning for permission to marry. Chamula courtship custom requires long and involved petitioning rituals in which the prospective groom's family offers substantial gifts to the father of the prospective bride. Accompanying these gifts is the request that the father allow his daughter to marry. The absurdity of the rabbit's explanation of why he was stuck in the beeswax image is total, for no Chamula father ever invites a man to marry his daughter. The thought of forcing a man to marry his daughter, to the extent of capturing him to do so, is utterly ridiculous. Thus, the rabbit seems to be cognizant of Tzotzil social rules, but the coyote is so stupid that he allows himself to be deceived by a totally implausible aberration of social custom.

2. The text does not explain how the trapping of the coyote released the rabbit. I asked the narrator about this, and he simply stated that part of the "deal" was that they would change places.

3. This explains the origin of the rabbit's short tail.

TEXT 38

1. "To turn one's tail inside out" is a Tzotzil idiom that might be more freely translated as "to kick up one's heels." I have translated this as "I'm going to party" because it goes better metrically with the rest of the verse.

2. In Tzotzil this little song is a nonsense rhyme. It is a form of taunt that ridicules a person's name. In this context, of course, the song is intended to deceive the coyote into thinking someone is coming, for its source, the rabbit's farting, suggests that a third party is present.

3. The problem is that coyote does not want to get his guitar wet while swimming across the river to catch the rabbit.

4. We are not told how the rabbit manages to escape. By leaving an unresolved question at the conclusion, the way is open for the narrator to launch into still another episode of the coyote and rabbit series. In this sense the coyote and the rabbit stories never really end. Coyote and rabbit always survive to encounter each other once again.

TEXT 39

1. Cancuc is a Tzeltal-speaking Indian *municipio* in the Chiapas Highlands (see map 1). Since it is a long day's walk from Chamula, the man presumably had to set out very early in order to get there before nightfall—hence, the early morning setting.

2. Rinsing corn is a step in the tortilla-making process. The corn for the next day's tortillas is cooked all night in the dying embers of the fire. It is typically cooked in a clay pot in a mild lime-water solution, the purpose of the lime being to soften the kernels and help them shed their outer layer. The cooked corn must be rinsed before grinding in order to remove the lime solution and to separate the kernels from the detached outer layer.

3. A sinkhole is a typical feature of Highland Chiapas limestone topography. It is a kind of cave that has the form of a pit in the ground whose botton cannot be seen. These openings are believed to be outlets in a vast network of underground passages that are the domain of the demons and Earth Lords. The suspicion voiced in the story that the demon carried the woman away makes the sinkhole a logical place to start the search.

4. Beginning with this passage, the narrator used the adjective *mu* with great frequency. In its most basic gloss, it means "bad," "repulsive," or "evil." Since its use in this text is almost a mechanical one that covers a vast range of the narrator's emotion with regard to the subject matter, from pity to condemnation to disgust, I have chosen to translate *mu* in the semantic context of each setting. The closest approximation of this usage is that of the repetitive use of "damned" or "fucking" as adjectives in English to serve almost as enclitics in such a line as, "Get the damned bread out of the fucking bag."

5. Garlic and tobacco (*Nicotiana tabacum*) are important traditional remedies, both preventive and curative, for dealing with problems of humans who come into contact with demons. Both substances are mixed with strong rum (*pox*) and applied as a kind of poultice to the face, genitals, and extremities as a means of warding off demons who might molest a night traveler. In this story the same substances are used in an attempt to cure the ills that the woman has suffered from her contact with the demon.

6. I inquired about the particular significance of this action. It appears to have none. The explanation offered was simply that the woman returned home naked, felt cold, and needed some makeshift covers; hence, the burlap bag. The foul smell of the woman's body was "proof" that the woman had been in contact with a demon.

7. Asked why the demon left so quickly, the narrator answered that it was thanks to the garlic and tobacco that they had applied earlier in the evening to the man's wife's body.

8. The wild blackberry roots are only a small part of a brew of many herbs and roots that is given today to cure illnesses associated with contact with demons. This group of illnesses is associated with swelling and infections that are believed to come from an intrusive

object or spirit. To illustrate the complexity lying beneath surface information that appears in texts, here is a complete recipe for *potzlom chamel* ("demon's illness") medicine. Thirteen pieces of each of the following are boiled for two hours in a potful of water with a half-liter of rum: wild blackberry root (root *Adenotrichus*); common dried red chiles (*Capsicum annuum*); garlic guinea-hen weed root (*Petiveria alliace*); hard brown sugar, pieces about one cm. square; cloves, individual pieces; yellow indigo bush leaves (*Dalea lutea*); Mexican coyote brush (broomweed) branch tips with leaves (*Baccharis vaccinoides*); wax myrtle, branch tips with leaves (*Myrica cerifera*); "gnats night" roots (*Stevia rhombifolia*); oak tree root (*Quercus segoviensis*); spiney nightshade root (*Solanum hispidum*).

9. The genitalia of demons are discussed at length in S. Blaffer (1972). The size and length described in this text are in agreement with general views of demons held by most Tzotzil people.

10. Dried, salted beef jerky, sold in the market in bunches of thin strips, is believed to be a favorite food of demons. It is also used in witchcraft rituals (in which case it is burned with fuel oil) and in cures of illnesses believed to be caused by witchcraft (in which case it is eaten, boiled, by the victim). Pinecones are widely believed to be the "demon's firewood" but are also used by very poor, aged and physically handicapped people who cannot cut "real" firewood. Thus, both pinecones and beef jerky have negative associations.

11. It is worth noting an odd parallel between the three-week gestation of the woman's child by the demon on the one hand and the same gestation period of Our Father Sun himself, according to some accounts, in the womb of Our Mother Moon in the First Creation.

12. The son had apparently inherited his father's wings.

13. The narrator explained that the baby demon was experimenting with the rock to see whether he would be able to bear the weight of his mother, whom he planned to take on an excursion. Other versions simply note that the rock was used to seal off the entrance of the cave so that the woman could not escape.

14. I asked the narrator to explain this passage. The response was that the demon-child's father had been so angry with him for helping his mother to escape that he bit him to death.

15. The details of the context in which this story was originally told are worth relating, for they show how closely a narrative situation is typically related to the content of the story told. In this case, as the text relates, the grandmother of the narrator believed that their house had been visited by a demon. It seems that the family dog had been injured during the night. The grandfather brought the dog into the house in the early morning. It was nearly dead, having been attacked from the rear, with a great gash running from below its anus to the dog's underside. Later that afternoon the dog died. In the early evening the grandmother heard a ripping sound, like that of a straw hat being torn. She asked her husband if he had left his hat outside, and as he had not, the grandmother believed that the ripping sound was actually the sound of the demon clawing at the side of the house. The injury and subsequent death of the dog led her to believe that a demon had been lurking about the house for several nights. The ripping noise they heard that night confirmed the belief that the dog had been a victim of the demon.

TEXT 40

1. The etymology and meaning of the word *ˀayin* are not altogether clear. Rus (personal communication, May 2001) states that it means "crocodile" or "alligator." The narrator, however, stated that the original telling of the story was inspired by his seeing a picture

of a whale in a magazine. This makes the Spanish *ballena* (whale) a plausible etymology for *ʔayin.* However, Chiapas Lowland river ecology and the narrator's drawing accompanying this text suggest that the aquatic monster actually looks more like a giant alligator. This would also explain the creature's amphibian capabilities (it seized the man on the riverbank and dragged him into the river). Such behavior is not unknown for large alligators, who occasionally steal calves from pastures near a riverbank and take them into the river for consumption. Because of my own uncertainty regarding this matter (and because an alligator cannot plausibly swallow a man whole), I have chosen to translate *ʔayin* as "water monster."

2. His companions had given him up for dead. In what follows (verses 25 and 26), the narrator assumes the companions knew that a water monster had consumed their friend.

3. The money-bag episode, although apparently a non sequitur, was explained by the narrator as a way of accounting for the reason the monster had attacked the man in the first place. He had been attracted by the colorful bag. That is why the man's hands had been chewed to pieces.

4. The narrator stated that there was a picture of a whale in the magazine.

TEXT 41

1. The text is a remarkably complete version of a classic European fairy tale (Tale Type 313, S. Thompson 1946, 87–93) that was introduced by contact with Spain. This tale seems to have had a singular appeal for Mesoamerican native people, for it is widespread throughout the region in the modern era (see S. Thompson, 1946, 90; J. E. S. Thompson 1930, 167–72; and Reid 1935, 110–12). The motifs concerning the king's daughters, their bathing scene, and the associated clothing as tokens of identity in relation to the destiny of the hero (see verses 52–110) bear striking resemblance to similar themes in the *Popol Vuh* (Tedlock 1993, 45–58; Tedlock 1996, 167–70).

2. The Dead Sea of Sine is a real place-name in Mexico. A large bay located on the Pacific Coast of the state of Chiapas, it is a place most Chamulas know about but very few have ever seen. By virtue of its being at the very edge of the western sea, it is not a place any Chamula would ever admit to wanting to visit, for it would expose one to the dangers of visiting the very edge of the universe. From here, according to Chamula cosmological principles, one could actually see the Sun/Christ deity, Our Father, plunge into the western sea at sundown, causing the water to boil and evaporate. This is said to be a fearsome spectacle. The only beings who go there regularly (besides the Ladino Mexicans who live there) are demons, who make the trek daily, via their underground passages, to reap the wealth of metal coins and manufactured goods (that is to say, machetes and axe blades) that Our Father leaves there each day as he completes his daily cycle and plunges into the western sea. From there, the demons deliver the goods to Ladinos who take them to the highlands to sell to the Indians at what the Indians consider to be unfair prices (see Gossen 1999, 22).

3. This passage apparently seeks only to emphasize that the journey took a long time, that is to say, several years.

4. The word *tostón,* as it is here, is archaic. It refers to a Mexican coin, with a value of fifty centavos or a half-peso, that has been in and out of use at least four times in the twentieth century. While Mexico's modern monetary system is a decimal system, common usage—particularly among older, traditional people at the time this text was transcribed—linked then-modern coins to older coins. A *tostón,* worth fifty centavos, is also worth four reales, a real being twelve and one-half cents. There are eight reales to a whole coin unit

(comparable to "bits" in English, in which two bits equals twenty-five cents). This explains the odd reference in time to the tale—"you have a *tostón* to go" means four years, suggesting that the whole journey took eight years.

5. This means two years, based on the explanation in note 4.

6. North is a direction of good omen. (See Gossen 1974b, 33, for a discussion of the cosmological associations of this directional symbolism.) The fact that the road leads north suggests that good things are ultimately to come.

7. The narrator later explained that the king's daughter was able to fly because she could turn herself into a dove at will.

8. Xun, the boy hero of the story, is a Chamula. One of the most fundamental Chamula premises about the cosmos is that Chamula is located in the center of the square island that is the earth (see Gossen 1974b). When Xun is asked where his home is, his response, like that of most Chamulas today, is "at the center of the earth." See maps 3 and 4.

9. It is not altogether clear how she found out about the trick. The narrator said, when he was asked about it, that she probably had seen all of this in a dream. Subsequent episodes in the text also contain mysterious prior knowledge that the narrator regards as being provided by information in dreams.

10. It is not clear why the king's daughter is called a queen rather than a princess. That, however, is how the text reads, so *queen* is retained here and below.

11. Although the text does not tell us, one may speculate that his wealth came from his association with the king's daughter, who has magical powers. To build a store in contemporary Chamula is a sign of having "made it." Having a store, usually a one-room house on a main road or path, is a sign of surplus wealth, for current estimates place the value of a small store and a modest stock of candles, soft drinks, flashlight batteries, and so forth, at about twenty thousand pesos—or about one thousand dollars (U.S., 1979 values), a figure far greater than an average Chamula's annual income.

12. Xun's interest in having servants is another sign of ostentatious prosperity. Almost no Chamulas today can afford either the cash or the negative gossip that go with the patron-servant relationship. Xun, therefore, is an exceptional Chamula—credible, no doubt only because his great adventure took place in the Third Creation, before the current era.

13. The reader should note the anomalous nature of this courtship transaction, for Tzotzil courtship rules allow no direct communication between the male suitor and his prospective bride. Furthermore, these transactions involve the male suitor's parents as petitioners. In this narrative the fact that the queen herself addresses the suitors directly and sends them away is the opposite of traditional bride-petitioning protocol. Perhaps her unusual instrumental behavior is due to her "foreignness" or merely to the fact that she is estranged from her parents and that they are not present to deal with the suitors on her behalf.

TEXT 42

1. "Stinking Ladino woman" is a derisive ethnic pun based on the similarity of the word *xinulan* (Sp. *señora*, lady) and *xin* (to smell, to stink). Any Ladino woman is referred to in colloquial Tzotzil by this term. The pun is funny because Ladinos are thought to have bad breath, which is explained by their affinity for dogs (as related in the present text), whose breath is also foul.

2. This verse, which appears to be a non sequitur, is intended to do two very different things: (1) to give an etymology of why San Cristóbal de las Casas, the old colonial town

and trade center of the highlands, is called *hobel* (grass); and (2) to provide a setting that is sufficiently wild to make plausible the exotic story that follows. The place is pertinent, for San Cristóbal is the major commercial, cultural, political, and ethnic center of the Mexican mestizo lifestyle in the area. It has had this role throughout the postcontact period into the present. *Ladino* (from old Sp. rendering of Latino) was used up to the period of the Reconquista in southern Spain to distinguish Spanish-speaking Christians from Moors and Jews. In the setting of the Jewish diaspora, it also refers to Spanish- and Portuguese-speaking Sephardic Jews, and specifically to the dialect that they speak. The term came to parts of the New World, particularly Chiapas and northern Central America, where it was and still is used to distinguish bearers of Hispanic culture from Indians. The Tzotzil word for Ladino is *kaxlan,* which derives from *castellano* (Sp.), the formal term designating the mainstream dialect of Spanish that was brought to the New World. The term also refers to chickens in Tzotzil, no doubt because they were introduced by the Spaniards. The pun "Ladino/chicken" suggested by the word *kaxlan* is not lost on the Tzotzils, who regard Ladinos as animal-like in their behavior. This ethnic commentary is developed in the text.

3. This brief list neatly sums up the Chamula opinion of Ladino male/female interactions—doglike. Chamulas never tire of commenting condescendingly on Ladino social behavior. They regard public flirtation as scandalous. Men simply should not speak to women to whom they are not related by real or ritual kinship. The proper exception to this rule is in business transactions in the marketplace. Married couples do not typically touch each other in public or engage in any public demonstration of affection. When walking, they proceed in single file, male first, female second. This not only is the custom but is practical as well, for most footpaths have room only for single file movement.

4. This no doubt suggests that Ladinos' dog heritage is reflected not only in their shameless public behavior but also in their habitually violent character.

TEXT 43

1. I choose "person" to translate *vinik* (man, twenty), for although it literally means "man" in contrast to "woman" (*antz*), in this case it is clearly meant to indicate the generic human condition, as in "humankind." Dennis Tedlock solved this translation problem another way in his book on the ancient and modern K'iche' (see Tedlock 1993) by translating the K'iche' cognate of this word as "vigesimal being," for the attribute of having twenty digits is a diagnostic feature of people in general as well as being the word for "man" and "twenty."

2. For a full discusion of the Tzotzil concept of the soul, see Gossen 1999, 225–46.

3. *Batz'i k'op,* "the true language," is the Tzotzil word for Tzotzil. The word *batz'i* also means "true," "right," "genuine." Thus, a measure of linguistic chauvinism is built into the very name of the language.

4. This series of emotional phrases (verses 17–20) serves to emphasize that all did indeed speak a single language and were thus capable of communicating and working together.

5. The logic of this arrangement—Ladinos first, Indians second, in order of language acquisition—is consonant with the Chamula view that saints, who are the common ancestors of all people, are Ladinos. Like saints, Ladinos have greater power than Indians in most spheres of contemporary life. Furthermore, nearly all Chamula images of the saints as well as of Our Father Sun and Our Mother Moon have fair skin and non-Indian features. Paradoxically, it is nevertheless true that Chamulas believe themselves to be morally superior to Ladinos and that it is Tzotzil, not Spanish, that is the "true language."

6. *Kaxlan* is the Tzotzil word meaning Ladino, or bearer of the Spanish-speaking Mexican cultural tradition. It comes from *castellano,* which refers to Castilian, or the standard Spanish language. Thus, ethnic and linguisitic identity are explicitly tied together in Chamula thinking.

7. For several decades it has been the goal of Mexican Indian primary education to teach Spanish to Indian children, thereby facilitating their participation in Mexican national culture. This policy, called *castellanización,* has generally used Indian language texts only for elementary teaching of the idea of sounds in relation to written symbols. After the first few years Spanish is "ideally" the language of instruction. Teaching of literacy in Indian languages has never been a specific goal of Indian education in modern Mexico.

8. Father Miguel Hidalgo is traditionally acknowledged by Mexican written history as being the father of Mexican Independence. He gave the famous "Grito de Dolores" proclamation ("Long live Our Lady of Guadalupe! Down with bad government! Death to the Spaniards!") on September 16, 1810, launching the Mexican independence movement against Spain. This date is celebrated as Mexico's Independence Day. It may be of some importance to Chamula historical reckoning (though it is not mentioned in this Chamula text) that Miguel Hidalgo was a parish priest who was close to poor village people. He felt a special affinity for mestizos and Indians, and in many ways, both theological and intellectual, distanced himself from the Spanish criollo establishment. Among other achievements he learned and used a number of Indian languages in his parish ministry. These aspects of his background, according to fact and legend as recorded in Mexican school textbooks and history books, contributed to his sensitivity to the problems of the poor and oppressed in colonial Mexico. Condemned to death as a subversive, he faced a firing squad on July 31, 1811.

TEXT 44

1. Here and elsewhere in these texts, the spoken form of the verb *kutz siʔ* (to fetch firewood), is retained in the Tzotzil text, although it is actually an elision of *kuch* (carry) and *siʔ* (firewood).

2. Other versions of this narrative use the same event to explain the origin of red corn (see text 28).

3. Other versions of the narrative elaborate the background of this paradox—namely, that the man's wife was the daughter of the Earth Lord and had the magical power to make humble food supplies multiply. Thus, the man's milpa had more potential than he realized (see text 28).

4. The theme of twin vessels that magically cause food to multiply is represented ritually at The Festival of Games, which is the annual year-renewal festival that is celebrated in Chamula at Carnival time in the annual fiesta cycle. Hereditary ritual specialists known as *jbajbinetik* (tappers of pots) have the responsibility for ritual maintenance of twin ceramic water drums. These drums are played by them as an accompaniment to the dance of the warriors that occurs as a major ritual sequence at The Festival of Games, which is a reenactment of the creation of (that is to say, the renewal of) the Chamula social order. The drums are explicitly associated with agricultural rogation ritual and with the plentious food supply that is provided by ritual sponsors of the festival in the form of great banquets. (See Gossen 1999, 123–26; Bricker 1973, 109–10 for the ethnographic context of the water drums and their link with ancient and contemporary Maya ritual symbolism.)

5. In verse 23 and many other verses in this text, the adjective *-uni* is attached to nouns. This adjective, which means "little," "dear" or "cherished," is comparable to the

diminutive *-ito* or *-ita* suffix in Spanish. Since the diminutive is hard to render in English with the ease and frequency that characterize its use in Tzotzil and Spanish, I have tried to capture the sense of it with adjective and noun phrases such as "good little meal." What is consistent about Tzotzil use of the *-uni* qualifier is its positive affective meaning. It is as much a sign of positive and sympathetic evaluation on the part of the narrator as *mu* (bad) is a sign of disapproval on the part of the narrator. These adjectives behave as evaluative markers for the narrator more than they serve the purpose of exact qualification of attributes of a noun.

6. This passage is peculiar, for Earth Lords are generally associated with caves, water holes, and the underworld (see text 2, note 1). In this case the sky habitat seems to be related to the phenomena of clouds, rain, and lightning, which—though believed to be of earthly origin (clouds and rain are said to come ultimately from caves)—nevertheless move above and around the surface of the earth when it rains. As for their permanent habitation, Earth Lords live in caves in the sides of mountains and valleys. The circumstances of the Earth Lord's original gift of his daughter to the man is explained in the cognate version of this text that appears in this book as text 28. The gift was given because the man had rescued an injured snake, a familiar of the Earth Lord, and returned it to its home.

TEXT 45

1. The theme of seeking money from the Earth Lord in a cave is very much alive today. It is a strategy I have often heard considered as people contemplate their poverty. It is also an explanation given for cases of people who seem to acquire a great deal of wealth "too quickly." Earth Lords have been discussed in notes to many of the texts. They are specifically associated with rain, clouds, and metallic goods of Ladino origin, the most important of which is metal coins. Dozens of anecdotes tell of illicit digging for the Earth Lords' treasure. Other accounts tell of bargaining for treasure directly with the Earth Lords. This text is definitely of the latter type. Invariably, dealing with Earth Lords is regarded as dangerous, not only becasue they inhabit the earth along with *pukujetik* (demons) but also because they are specifically represented in descriptions and drawings as ethnic Ladinos, who are typically regarded by all Indians as adversaries in the realm of everyday political and economic affairs.

2. The number thirteen is signficant in ancient Maya calendrics, divination, and astrology, for it is the series 1–13 that meshes with twenty named days to form the 260-day ritual calendar known as the Tzolkin. Thirteen is therefore an important numeral factor that underlies the great fifty-two-year Calendar Round, which marked the duration of cosmic eras in ancient Maya long count calendrics (73 x 260 days equals 52 x 365 days). The 260-day calendar does not survive as such in Chamula, although the ancient Maya solar calendar (eighteen months of twenty days plus a five-day special month) is very much alive in the community as an agricultural almanac. (See Gossen 1974a for a full description of contemporary Chamula calendrics; Coe 1966 for ancient Maya numeration and calendrics.)

3. The Earth Lord's furniture was made of stone; hence, the allusion to sticking to the stone if the man had sat down.

4. The chest in question was probably one of the locally made wooden boxes with hinged lids that are used for clothing storage in most Chamula homes. The approximate dimensions of these storage chests are one foot by two feet by eighteen inches deep. More elaborate, nicely finished versions of these chests are used by religious officials to store ritual paraphernalia such as costumes, ribbons, banners and necklaces when they are not in use for festivals. Such boxes are also used to store special pieces of ritual dress for the

saints. Another use of the boxes is as oracles—"talking saints." They continue to be an important source of divination and prophecy in San Juan Chamula. Typically, the chests contain religious objects that are said to have the power of speaking through their owners to paying clients who consult them regarding financial, amorous, and health-related problems. Thus, the chest where the man placed the old hoe that he had received from the Earth Lord was an appropriate place to put it. He apparently offered incense to the chest with the hoe as a gift of "food" for an object of supernatural power. Incense is used in most Chamula ritual settings, and, when ignited, is said to provide food, via the smoke, for religious objects and deities as well as for ritual officials.

5. The narrator explained that the hoe had turned into a snake. Snakes are believed to be familiars and also alternative forms of Earth Lords.

6. He apparently only realized at this point that the snake was actually one of the Earth Lord's alternate forms or his "representative" which had been sent to fulfill the Earth Lord's promise of help.

TEXT 46

1. Their business was a cooperative one; one made the leather soles, the other made the binding straps. Sandals are still widely used today, but soles are now made of used rubber-tire tread material. Straps are still made of leather.

2. The Tuxtla–San Cristóbal road is the ancient trade route that goes up the Ixtapa Valley. Still in existence as a rough road and path, it goes through territory that lies mostly in the modern *municipio* of Zinacantán. The Pan-American Highway, constructed in 1950, follows the rim of the valley (see map 1). For most traffic, it has supplanted the old ox road and footpath that was in use at the time of the events reported in this narrative.

3. This cave is located near the Zinacanteco hamlet of Nabenchauk (see map 4). It is worth noting that the cave lies in territory that is not the Chamulas' own. Perhaps this has something to do with the extraordinary threat it poses.

4. This custom clearly seems to be borrowed from Spanish Catholic tradition. However, it should be remembered that the cross symbolizes the presence of the Lord Sun/Christ, not merely the Christian sign of the cross.

5. The expletive *vuruto* (from Sp. *bruto*) is much stronger in Tzotzil than it is in Spanish. Furthermore, the English cognate "brute" hardly works as an equivalent to expletives proper to an angry monster. Therefore, "asshole" is an approximate—if imperfect—attempt to capture the intensity of the demon's wrath.

6. Narrative descriptions and drawings of demons typically represent them with wings, which would account for this demon's mobility.

7. This is a joke. The speaker (one of the heroes) suggests that his companion is not doing his fair share of wiping up the mess after the slaying. He says humorously that the demon is his companion's father.

8. The narrator explaines that the salt application has the function of negating the evil power that might remain within the heart and body of the demon. Otherwise the demon might regenerate itself and return to life.

9. "Governor" is a loose translation of the Tzotzil *ʔajvalil*. It actually means "person in highest authority." Here it is translated as "governor" because Tuxtla Gutiérrez, the destination of the heroes of the story, has been the capital of the state for about a century.

10. *Pox,* which is homemade sugarcane rum, is consumed on nearly all ritual occasions in Chamula.

TEXT 47

1. "These soldiers were among the number who would not die" behaves as a kind of refrain in verses 1 and 2. Upon pursuing the meaning of the line, I learned that the narrator's uncle told him there were twenty soldiers in the group in the mountain, of whom one, the captain, is the soldier who speaks in the text. The number twenty, the basic traditional Maya calendrical unit, suggests that the narrative may carry some vestige of the Precolumbian supernatural world. This interpretation is further suggested by the narrator's explanation that, in the event of warfare, the soldiers' guns would function as thunderbolts that might destroy "bombs and airplanes," if such weapons were used against the Chamulas. This text has some interesting points of stylistic and thematic similarity with text 33 ("Of War and Peace with the Chief of Guatemala"), which is by the same narrator.

2. As I have noted, caves are associated with Earth Lords and angels, who are responsible for rain and foreign goods, particularly those made of metal—that is to say, money. Chamulas go to caves to offer prayers and candles to the Earth Lords. These rituals usually have petitions for rain as their principal goal. However, shamans are also said to obtain special powers from encounters with Earth Lords. These powers may be good or evil in their application. In this text the transaction in the cave is clearly seen by the narrator to have a positive end, for the soldiers are "like Earth Lords," who will come to the defense of Chamula in time of peril. They also give power to shamans who seek them out, as is clearly seen later in the text.

3. Here the narrator explained to me again that the spokesman for the soldiers was like an *ʔanjel*, or Earth Lord. He suggested that the journey was a supernatural one of vigilance and help to all just warriors, not necessarily a particular battle mission, saying that these supernatural soldiers came out every Thursday to "take the sun" and clean their guns in the countryside near their cave home. He further explained that they, like saints and other supernaturals, neither eat nor urinate nor defecate.

4. San Juan, Chamula's patron saint—like all Chamula saints—has a junior and a senior aspect. His junior aspect is the image in the church in the Chamula Ceremonial Center. His senior aspect, according to most accounts, lives in Tzontevitz Mountain, the highest point in Chamula territory and in the Central Chiapas Highlands. This association suggests that the site of the events in the text is Tzontevitz, the most sacred mountain in Chamula.

5. The man referred to in the text is the narrator's uncle, Domingo Gómez Lunes. The uncle, who is the source of the text, told it to the narrator as a kind of testimonial anecdote describing the way in which he had received power as a shaman. Speaking with Earth Lords and their associates is as important a source of power as dreaming. Dreaming usually involves the shaman's animal soul companion as the principal actor, whereas communication with the Earth Lords is generally a one-on-one encounter between shaman and Earth Lord, usually taking place in caves.

TEXT 48

1. Demons are associated with the whole inner-earth complex of supernaturals, which includes Earth Lords and their familiars, snakes, and deer. Demons are couriers for the Earth Lords, believed to bring manufactured and metallic goods, including money, from the western limit of the universe. It is there that Our Lord Sun/Christ deposits them at a place called *yav calintario* (place of the calendar), which, on cosmological drawings, is located right where the sun plunges into the western sea at sundown (see Gossen 1999, 21–22). From there demons are said to bring the goods to Ladinos, who in turn sell them at great

profit to Indians. Demons, therefore, are believed to have a direct link with the source of money.

2. The expression "to become companions" is a formulaic means used in Tzotzil narrative for reporting the sealing of contracts between humans and negative supernaturals. The term does not signify literal companionship but rather the commitment of a human's loyalty, destiny, and productivity to the wishes of the supernatural.

3. They thought that the one-hundred-year term of the loan was a steal, for they did not expect to live that long. It seemed that they would be rich for life.

4. Verses 28 and 29 report a standard greeting formula that is used commonly whenever friends and relatives meet after a long or short separation. There is no English equivalent known to me that can render this formalism in any way other than the literal manner that has been used in the translation. The redundancy (that is to say, "Did you come"/"Yes, I came") is perhaps reminiscent of "How are you'/'I'm fine" and other such formulaic greetings that occur in many languages. As the conversation develops after the initial greetings, the text (verses 30–46) offers a remarkably faithful rendering of the verbal protocol of a formal drinking conversation. All the formal redundancy is retained in the translation.

5. A *cuarta* is a quarter-liter bottle.

6. Beginning with verse 49 and continuing through verse 57, the text becomes extremely difficult to translate because it involves three sets of quotations: (1) what the man said to the demon, (2) as he told it to his compadre, (3) as related in toto to his wife. This embedded quotation scheme is simple to handle in Tzotzil narrative style but very awkward to render in translation. I have resisted the temptation to edit out the section, hoping that the reader gets some sense of the glorious redundancy of Tzotzil narrative style.

7. The cure that the demon proposes to use is actually used by Chamulas to stop bleeding and prevent infection in severe cuts. A poultice made of beef tallow and powdered charcoal is applied directly to the wound.

8. The narrator explained that the woman was menstruating. Furthermore, she urinated a little bit whenever the demon peered at her "wound."

TEXT 49

1. The Demon Pukuj, discussed in the notes to other texts in this book, is the best-known and most frequently encountered of Chamula demons and spooks.

2. The Ladino is actually the demon himself, who is disguised in order to deceive his potential victim.

3. Santa Marta is a Tzotzil community within the *municipio* of San Pedro Chenalhó (see map 2). It is a traditional center for the brewing of *yakilvo?*, a beer that is made from fermented cane juice. Even today, vendors from Santa Marta appear in Chamula Center on fiesta days to sell this cane beer. In the time period discussed in this narrative, some Chamulas earned a living by walking to Santa Marta to bring jugs of this beer (carried by tumpline on their backs) for resale in Chamula. The term *yakilvo?* also refers to corn beer (*chicha* in Spanish), which is still used in some highland communities on riual occasions. The narrator did not state the type of beer.

4. From this line forward, the "man" in the dialogue is the narrator's friend.

5. The Demon Pukuj is believed to be black and hairy with red eyes and mouth. The narrator explained that the pubic hair, reddish-skinned penis shaft, and red foreskin made the demon think he had found his own image. The key similarities seem to be the black hair and red "mouth."

6. The club referred to is a heavy stick, approximately a meter long, made of a black hardwood (*'ak'te,'* heart of palm). It is rectangular in cross-section and has a hole in one end so that it can be carried on the shoulder, suspended by a thong or strap. Such clubs are used as aids for walking on slippery, muddy paths. They are also used for defense against attacks by animals and human adversaries. The only Chiapas Highland community known to me in which these clubs are still a part of men's everyday attire is Tzeltal-speaking Tenejapa.

7. Again, the logic seems to be that the demon is attracted by the blackness that makes him think he is encountering a fellow evil being.

8. It is of ethnographic interest that the red jug referred to in this passage is the traditional three-earred red clay water jug that is still in use as a water-carrying jar in many parts of the Chiapas Highlands. All of these jugs are manufactured in the Tzeltal-speaking village of Amatenango del Valle, which is located on the Pan-American Highway about fifty miles south of San Cristóbal (see map 1). These jugs have been an important item in regional trade for centuries and are only now being replaced by their plastic counterpart.

TEXT 50

1. This is a reference to the hat as an integral part of a man's clothing. It is a required part of a male's public persona. This is reinforced by the common pun that the "hat" of the penis is the foreskin. The "hat" of the penis is "taken off" only privately during an erection and sexual activity. The hat of this tale is, according to the narrator, at all times of both types. With this link the tale becomes a humorous commentary on competitive male sexuality between the larger, senior male (deer) and the smaller, junior male (rabbit). The competitor theme becomes even more complex when one remembers that deer are animal familars of Earth Lords (associated with Ladinos) and do not have twenty digits; thus, they are not animal-soul companions. Rabbits (who have twenty digits) are animal-soul companions of humble, poor Indians. The narrative is concerned not only with male sexuality in ranked Tzotzil society but also with ethnicity and sexuality in the larger Mexican national society.

TEXT 51

1. See figure 77, the narrator's drawing of this creature. The Backwards Wailing Man is one of a sizable group of monsters that inhabits the woods. It is known for the distinctive trait of having a face on both the front and back of its head. It also deceives people by having its feet attached backwards, so that an innocent person may find himself face-to-face with the creature while thinking that it is going the opposite direction. It is also said that because the creature has two complete faces, it is able to project its voice in order to deceive people about its whereabouts.

2. The narrator of this story is a master storyteller. The long sequence of lines that follows (verses 12–22) illustrates Marián's special skill at narration of fast-moving events. There is no time for leisurely narration, for major events are developing quickly. He uses an urgent narrative style to move things forward during the monster's attack: a subject line (first line of couplets), followed by an elaboration (second line of couplets). This urgent style does not subside until verse 23, in which a calmer narrative voice resumes. Then, in verse 26, the fast pace resumes, lasting to the end of the narrative. The style of the story is breathless, intended to shock in its immediacy and tragedy.

TEXT 52

1. The Lacandons are a remnant group of a few hundred Lowland Mayas who live in what remains of the rain forest of southeastern Chiapas. Their traditional lifestyle, based on hunting and small-scale horticulture, is seriously threatened in our time, because their rain-forest habitat is being destroyed to make way for an expanding timber and cattle industry. Traditional Lacandons, both men and women, wear long homespun cotton tunics, and both sexes wear their hair long. Although few in number, they come to San Cristóbal with some frequency. Since they are radically different in dress and appearance from Highland Indians, they typically provoke comment from the Tzotzil people when they see them in the streets. It is of interest in the broader ethnographic context that a ritual official who is called the Lacandon Chief plays an important role in Chamula's great annual ritual of solar renewal, The Festival of Games (Gossen 1999, 115–18).

2. Please see the discussion of Chamula classification of social space in text 2, note 1; and text 14, note 2.

3. This verse reports the popular Tzotzil etymology of the tribal name Lacandon, which is pronounced *lakanton* in Tzotzil. Its component parts are: *lakan* (to cook) and *ton* (stones); hence, the content of this passage.

4. Of all the Roman Catholic sacraments, baptism is the only one to which Chamulas attach significance in belief and in practice. Baptisms are usually performed on feast days in the church in the Chamula Ceremonial Center, for these are the only occasions for which priests are welcome in the Chamula Center. The context of the baptism is always highly social. Not only are baptisms performed for large numbers of children on a single occasion, but they also occur in the midst of festival activity that involves hundreds of casual observers. Furthermore, each family with a child to baptize is required by custom (as well as by church law) to enlist one or more sets of godparents (Sp. *padrinos*) to sponsor the child's spiritual and material upbringing and provide occasional gifts for the godchild. The godparents, according to Hispanic custom, also become compadres of the child's parents. This is an extremely important social bond in Chamula society, for it creates alliances between adults that go beyond consanguineal and affinal kinship ties. The nonkin-based bonds are important for political, personal, and economic well-being. The cooperation of compadres is crucial for coping with the demands of both private and public life in Chamula society; in fact, the compadre bond is more significant than the child-godparent relationship. All of this helps to explain why the narrator of the text emphasizes perceived irregularities in Lacandon baptismal customs.

TEXT 53

1. This text concerns Chamula views of their neighbors, the Tzeltal-speaking Tenejapanecos (see map 2). Although the two *municipios* share a long boundary and have similar customs, Chamulas and Tenejapanecos are suspicious of each other. The text relates a typical set of Chamula beliefs about the Tenejapanecos' propensity for the use of witchcraft against Chamulas. The traditional defense against witchcraft and its practitioners (*j?ak' chamel,* givers of sickness) is to engage a strong shaman or another witch to do supernatural battle with the malevolent soul of the offending person or that of his agent, that is to say, a witch who has been hired by the offending person. The complex logic of these supernatural encounters is described in Gossen (1999, 225–45).

2. Chamula women have traditionally done weaving and clothing production as cottage industries for several neighboring Indian communities. As the clothing designs in wool and cotton differ considerably from one community to the next, the clothing must be taken

to the appropriate community for sale, usually on fiesta days, when there is a large volume of market activity. Presumably, the trip of the Chamula couple to Tenejapa that is reported in this text was just such a marketing trip.

3. The bats referred to, vampire bats (*Desmodus rotundus*), are indeed a scourge to the everyday life of people in Chiapas who keep livestock, both small and large. These nocturnal bats bite sheep, pigs, cattle, and even horses behind the ear, a location where mammals cannot easily disengage the attackers with their feet or their mouths. The bats inject an anticoagulant substance that prevents the wound from healing. Thus, the bats are able to return, night after night, to feast on the blood. It is more often infection than blood loss that makes vampire bats a fairly common cause of death for domestic animals.

4. This passage reveals that the story is not just a chronicle of an event but an etiological narrative about the origin of worms and bats as livestock plagues in general. To this day Chamulas blame Tenejapaneco witchcraft for causing these problems. This belief is also reflected in the reluctance of Chamulas to purchase oranges from Tenejapaneco merchants (Tenejapa is a zone of significant orange production), as they believe that oranges from Tenejapa are usually prone to be wormy.

5. This passage and the one that follows (verses 34 and 35) relate a complex theory of causation in witchcraft and counterwitchcraft. The central concept is that of a rope or cord that ties the three parts of a person's soul together. The rope is a supernatural link that ties a person's tongue-soul (*ch'ulel*) to that of his two soul companions (Gossen 1999, 225–45) and to his candle of destiny in the sky. Since both the senior soul animal and the candle of destiny are found on the third (uppermost) layer of the sky, it is hard for ordinary individuals to gain access to them, much less to defend them from assault by witchcraft. The "rope" or "cord" of the text is a way of speaking of the integrity of the parts of the soul. When the cord is exposed, it can be cut or otherwise violated, causing illness or death to the victim. The form of witchcraft addressed in these passages is called "cutting the cord." The only means of defense against this form of witchcraft is to cut the cord of the assailant's soul, which is precisely what the defender from Venustiano Carranza does.

6. This narrative also has implicit etiological significance, as it explains not only why Tenejapanecos are viewed as traditional enemies of Chamula but also why Venustiano Carranza is viewed as a traditional ally. Venustiano Carranza (formerly known as San Bartolomé de los Llanos) is a Tzotzil-speaking *municipio* that lies to the southeast of the Central Highlands, as a much lower elevation than Chamula (see map 4). Perhaps its spatial removal, combined with its ethnic (Tzotzil-speaking) similarity, explains its unusual role as provider of strong supernatural specialists who are willing to help Chamulas in time of need. Jan Rus has suggested (personal communication, June 2001) that this town's singular importance as a center for curing specialists (along with Simojovel at the other side of the Tzotzil realm) may be related to the fact that both *municipios* lie at the edge of the highlands and thus have access to medicinal plants and herbs from three different ecological zones—highland to temperate to lowland. The fame of Venustiano Carranza shamans is vouched for by most Chamulas whom I have known well. Frequently, curers from this town are the last level of recourse when local Chamula specialists have not delivered the desired results.

TEXT 54

1. This evil spirit, a witch, is a minor personage in the contemporary Chamula supernatural world. It is variously rendered in several Tzotzil dialects as *potz'lom, potzlom, pots'lom,* and *poslom.* In this text the Potzlom turns out to be one of the soul companions of a witch.

2. The narrator explained to me that part of the Potzlom's strategy for tricking people is to sound like a human being, so that people are attracted to its humanlike crying.

3. It is of interest to note that the numeral classifier used for the Potzlom in the Tzotzil text is *kot*, which is appropriate in reference to animals. The human classifier *vo?* is conspicuously absent.

4. The Tzotzil text in verses 19–21 has plural verb forms, suggesting that the man is not alone but is making this petition together with someone else, perhaps with members of his family. Although I am uncertain about the identity of the actors, I have opted to use the plural form in the translation in an effort not to change the sense of the original Tzotzil.

5. Most Chamula homes have two cross shrines, one inside the house and one on the edge of the exterior patio, which is adjacent to the front door. These two shrines are the sites of periodic domestic rituals, curing rituals, and other forms of religious practice.

6. At this point it becomes clear that this particular manifestation of the Potzlom is, in fact, a witch that has transformed itself into one of its familiars in order to do harm to its victim (see Gossen 1999, 225–45). It is pertinent to know that the Potzlom is one of several soul companions of a witch who seeks to do harm to the man in the text. Witches typically have an ordinary soul-companion animal (usually a nocturnal carnivore such as a jaguar, ocelot, or coyote) and an anomalous soul companion. The latter class includes domestic animals, birds, monsters, and other creatures that do not conform to the class attributes of ordinary animal-soul companions, that is to say, wild mammals with twenty digits. Note in the accompanying drawing (figure 81) that the Potzlom is represented with four digits on its front feet and three digits on its hind feet and is anomalous in opting to dance on two feet.

7. The pig is, no doubt, another member of the witch's soul-companion configuration. It is also appropriate as a witch's familiar, because it is a domestic animal with cloven feet. The Potzlom has vanished, leaving the pig as its alternate form.

8. This passage makes sense only if one remembers (see verse 9) that there are originally three Potzloms. Only one has been killed. Furthermore, all of them presumably have multiple soul coessences; that is to say, a witch is hard to kill.

9. This passage (verses 39–41) is exceedingly difficult to translate, as it constitutes a dialogue among the several coessence/soul companions of the witch who had been contracted to do the bidding of a paying customer.

10. "Water" in this passage means blood. It is referred to in this way when Potzloms converse with one another as though they were in their human form. It is said the Ptozloms drink blood as naturally as humans drink water. According to the narrator, this makes their dialogue about "water" as kind of professional joke.

11. They turned around in a circle three times in order to turn themselves into people once again so that they could not be identified as witches.

TEXT 55

1. See text 3, note 12; text 54, note 6; text 56, note 1 for basic information about soul concepts. The term *ch'ulelal*, which introduces this account, is not the soul itself (*ch'ulel*) but rather an illness or affliction of the soul. The text illustrates how dreams reveal the identity and adventures of the soul and how these concepts explain human destiny. A discussion of this particular text appears in Gossen (1975) accompanying a straight prose (that is to say, noncouplet) translation.

2. It is necessary to know that the actor is actually both a jaguar (that is to say, the particular jaguar who was the godfather's animal-soul companion) and, via the animal-soul concept, the godfather himself.

3. This verse introduces a problem in translation for which there is no easy solution. Since the jaguar in the narrative is the coessence/animal-soul companion of the narrator's godfather, the choice of "hand" or "paw" as the extremity with which he deflects the gunshot is not an easy call. I have chosen "hand," because it is the jaguar's anthropomorphic tie to his human counterpart that informs the plot line of the narrative.

TEXT 56

1. This account is one of dozens I have heard about the intimate link between human destiny and animal souls. This key concept, which links self and body with community and cosmos, is known throughout Mesoamerica under various rubrics such as *tonalismo* and *nagualismo.* It is discussed in its Tzotzil and pan-Maya variants in Gossen (1975), Rachun Linn (1989), Vogt (1970), Villa Rojas (1947), and Watanabe (1989). See also Gossen 1999, 225–46.

This narrative appears to be without a conclusion, an anomaly that was the subject of discussion at the time that I translated it with the assistance of the narrator. In essence the narrative reports a domestic tragedy. It relates the circumstances that lead a woman inadvertently to killing her own animal soul companion. It is not reported explicitly at the end of the narrative that the woman who kills the weasel dies herself after she clubs the weasel to death. I have supplied a bracketed line that provides this additional information.

Weasels, like all primary animal-soul companions are mammals with twenty digits. These characteristics link them to human counterparts; indeed, the word for "man" is *vinik,* meaning "twenty," Weasels are average in power, lying midway between humble soul companions such as rabbits, and powerful soul companions such as jaguars.

2. In this line and in verse 8 the narrator moves briefly from third person to first person. I have retained this shift in person in the translation as it attests to the immediacy of the problem of the link of animal souls and human destiny in everyday life. It is the subject of frequent discussion, particularly as details of this problem become manifest in the content of dreams (see text 55, in which the whole plot line devolves around the link between dream, person, animal soul, and destiny).

3. The affinities of the soul animal—most typically a mammal—with its human counterpart are probably reinforced by the similarity in the nurturing behavior of mammalian mothers in relation to their relatively helpless offspring.

4. The gender of the weasel is here translated as female, as the narrator knows that the woman is dealing with her own animal soul companion. The soul companion is always of the same sex as its human "owner."

5. The final line in the English translation is my addition, for the woman's subsequent death was a fact that only emerged in a translation session and discussion of the text with the narrator. He explained that she died three days later, covered with bruises and burns on her skin, all of which proved that the woman, in her fit of wrath, had actually slain her own animal soul companion, and, hence, herself.

TEXT 57

1. Finca Victoria, where the present narrator heard the story, is a coffee plantation in the Pacific Lowlands.

2. The exchange recorded in verses 7–13 is a classic "flirtation on the road" banter. The reason that the woman is consistently described as "bad" in the text is that she has spoken openly to a strange man, taking a course that invites seduction. The man also errs, according to Chamula custom, by taking the bait.

3. This response is the rattle of a rattlesnake's tail. The woman was just then in the process of turning into a snake.

4. See figure 84, which was drawn by the narrator.

5. Although I attempted to do so, I could not find out why it took ten men to do this task. It may be a formulaic way of saying the task was difficult.

6. This man was apparently the owner of the field where the snake-woman had been buried. He was not the original victim.

TEXT 58

1. This narrative is a three-part variation on a single theme: men who change into women. As the three parts are related only thematically and in no way share a single story line, I have indicated the transitions with semantic breaks for greater clarity. The text demonstrates the strong tendency of Tzotzil storytelling to follow serial themes, one story evoking another in the same vein. It is also worth noting that the narrative reveals an interesting pattern of gender asymmetry in Chamula narrative motifs. That is to say, men have repeated encounters with strong natural, immoral, and supernatural women who take away their virility or power—who, indeed, change them into women. There are, to my knowledge, no narratives in all of Tzotzil literature that involve women becoming men. Women become supernaturals of various types and sometimes revert to their mythical position of power, which is superior to that of men (as in the mythical time when the moon deity still held power greater than her son, the sun). Women do not have to become men to gain power, however, for their power is primeval and initial, the source of the generative power of the human condition. Male power is ostensibly greater but is also more derivative, more fragile, and—ultimately—more ephemeral (see Gossen and Leventhal 1999).

2. The scene is set for social calamity; no decent Chamula woman should speak to a strange man, even when it is he who initiates the conversation. She should avoid the encounter altogether. In this case not only does the conversation take place, but it is she who inititiates it, revealing immediately that she is a witch, a prostitute, or a supernatural being masquerading as a human in order to get the man in trouble. Illicit "talking on the road" constitutes a frequent source of social friction and is among the more frequent types of criminal offense to be heard in the Chamula traditional courts. Typically, it is the man who initiates the encounter. The woman typically refuses to speak and reports the attempt to her family, which then takes the case to court, accusing the offender of *jk'oponvanej ta be* (being a person who is prone to speaking on the road). This usually leads to a conviction. The offender typically has to pay a fine, serve a jail sentence, or engage in some task of forced labor for the community. This narrative thus begins with a humorous parody of a common criminal offense.

3. The narrator explained that the curer lived in Venustiano Carranza. This Tzotzil-speaking community is well known today as the home of powerful curers. Frequently, Chamulas go there to seek cures when local practitioners cannot produce desired results. The events that follow in the narrative took place in Venustiano Carranza. See text 53, note 6; map 4.

4. The sexual encounter with the cow, the narrator explained, was the curer's strategy to make his patient's penis return.

5. It is the custom in Chamula domestic life for women to use food and food preparation as "chips" in social transactions and sexual relations. Failure to provide meals is a common gesture of female dissatisfaction with a husband's sexual performance or displeasure with other aspects of his behavior.

6. This is the "first man" noted in verse 32 of this text. The "wife" mentioned here is either a lover or a second wife, for she is obviously not a person to be taken home as a principal wife.

TEXT 59

1. Verse 7 has several implicit messages, which were clarified only in conversations with the narrator. First, the man suspected that his lack of success in hunting was being caused by his wife's infidelity. Also, in other versions of this story it is the man's dogs who inform him that she is, indeed, being unfaithful to him. In the end the dogs are deprived of speech forever as punishment for precipitating the tragedy that appears in the text. In this version the dogs are simply companions, and they are not permitted to accompany the man on his trip home because he knew they would bound ahead and give away his arrival.

2. The woman directs her lover to urinate through a crack in the wall of the house. Since traditional house walls are of the wattle-and-daub type, there are often openings in the adobe structure, particularly when the house is old and poorly maintained (see figure 86).

3. This is possible, for the floors of Chamula houses are simply hardened earth.

4. The narrator explained that the woman's husband had come home for breakfast and then gone off again to hunt, a strategy to make it seem to her that the daily routine was normal.

TEXT 60

1. Although the custom has declined somewhat in the last few decades, it is still the norm for the prospective groom's father and mother and specially designated petitioners to go on the groom's behalf to the prospective bride's home to request her hand for the would-be groom. Elaborate ritual speech and sometimes extravagant gifts accompany these petitioning rituals, the degree of complexity, repetition, and kind and quantity of gifts depending on the wealth of the young people's families. For nearby Zinacantán (whose customs are similar to those of Chamula) the ethnographic coverage and interpretation of these rituals is unusually thorough (J. Collier 1968; Vogt 1969). Elopement used to be the exception, causing a measure of disgrace for the new couple. Changing customs, in light of economic exigency, have made elopement–such as that humorously described in this text–more acceptable in the present time. However, this text represents not an objective representation of this custom but rather an ironic burlesque of what is really a subject of deep concern and anxiety for both parents and children. The tale is funny precisely because the subject is extremely serious. The story is told from a highly biased and brutal male point of view, the rape and subsequent "pleasure" of the woman in the experience being reported as a lighthearted incident. In reality the events related in this text would be legitimate grounds for murder or other severe sanctions.

2. The petitioning ceremony cannot proceed unless the prospective bride's parents receive the petitioners who come on behalf of the groom. In the case of this narrative, the locked door is a sign that there will be no discussion of the matter.

3. The bull-roarer is an eight-inch piece of beveled, polished wood that is attached to a string or cord. It makes a whistling noise as it is swung rapidly around in circles.

Although presently in use only as a children's toy, the narrator said that the "humming sticks" had once been used for divination and witchcraft.

4. The young man insouciantly addresses the father-in-law by the proper, respectful term *tata,* which I have here translated as "sir," for I know of no English equivalent. *Tata* is funnier in Tzotzil than "sir" is in English because its use presumes a normal petitioning and courtship history, which, of course, was far from the case in this narrative.

TEXT 61

1. Santa Catarina Pantelhó is a Tzotzil-speaking *municipio* that lies about thirty kilometers to the northeast of Chamula. Walking time from Chamula to Santa Catarina is about two days.

2. A *tostón* is a fifty-centavo coin worth half a peso. In the context of the time at which the events of this narrative are supposed to have taken place (the nineteenth or early twentieth century), the price of the water was extremely high. The volume of the gourd measure used depends on the size of the gourd, varying in volume from one to three cups. The measures are made from dry, round gourds approximately six inches in diameter, cut in half. They are still used today for drinking water, coffee, atole, and corn gruel (see text 41, note 4)

3. This drink, tortilla dough mixed with water, is the standard field and road subsistence food even today. It is often accompanied by dry tortillas.

4. The dry season in the Chiapas Highlands runs from early December to late April.

TEXT 62

1. It is not certain which famine is discussed in this text. In follow-up questions I discovered that the narrator's uncle was about sixty years old when he told him this account in the early 1960s. Thus, the uncle would have been a young man at the time of the great famine and influenza epidemic of 1918. That is my best judgment as to the placement of the events in our own historical reckoning.

2. This refers to the means of transporting goods in bundles or bags on people's backs using a tumpline. Of Precolumbian origin and still in common use, the tumpline is a simple strap that is attached to a bundle or bag. A strap runs across the bearer's shoulders and across his forehead, where the strap widens for a more comfortable fit. His head and neck thus keep the load in place on his back, the bearer's hands and arms remaining free from encumbrance.

3. The narrator explained that this line means the people had so little to eat that they would wash their backs and then drink the water with the corn dust—that which had sifted out to their backs through the burlap—suspended in it. The water, which tasted of corn, was considered to be slightly filling and made them feel better even if they could not consider eating the corn kernels themselves. The narrator assumed that the corn was not their property (that is to say, that they were hired to carry it for someone else) or that it was in such scarce supply that it was unthinkable to remove kernels to eat as they were walking.

TEXT 63

1. This narrative was collected in 1968. Assuming that those who were then "old men" were sixty to seventy years old, this would mean that the ethnographic present reported here comes approximately from the decade 1900 to 1910. The narrator heard this material from his grandmother, who told him what things were like in her own youth. The subject

of this narrative arose when the grandmother was commenting on the threat of a drought. She noted that in the old days things were better.

2. This festival takes place on June 24.

3. This festival takes place on August 30.

4. Muk'ta Sak, roughly meaning "great dawn" or "great whiteness," is a month in the old Maya solar calendar that is still used in Chamula (see Gossen 1974a). One of nineteen months (eighteen twenty-day months and one five-day month), it corresponds to the Gregorian calendar dates of March 1 to March 20.

5. This festival is October 7.

6. It is worth noting that the physical ecology of San Juan Chamula over the past few decades has, in fact, been a story of slow decline, owing in large part to the relatively great population density. The physical ecology, agricultural productivity, and demography of Chamula and nearby Zinacantán are discussed at length in Collier (1975).

7. I pursued some conversation on this subject with the narrator. He explained that then, as now, going to work as a laborer in the Ladino community was an option that those with substantial land for corn and wool production did not have to consider. It was apparently those with medium land resources—sufficient for truck gardening—who stood to benefit most from work as porters. They would receive a fee for hauling commissioned loads in addition to their own vegetables. There were other advantages to working as a hauler. If their own vegetables were taken as far away as Tuxtla for sale, they would bring more money, for cool-weather vegetables such as cabbage do not grow well in Hot Country. Thus, a round trip to Tuxtla could bring cash both from the sale of produce and from services as a hauler, making the trip doubly lucrative. The means of hauling was to secure or tie goods in a wooden pack frame (Tz. *karlote*), which was then supported and stabilized on the back by means of a tumpline.

Rus informed me (personal communication, May 2001) that only the wealthiest, most powerful nineteenth-century merchants (the Larraínzars, the Cuetos, and the Urbinas) engaged in large-scale employment of Indian porters. Thus, the economic activities that are reported in this text may have larger significance as a testimony to the importance of Indian laborers (as bearers) in facilitating the economic florescence of Chiapas in the late nineteenth and early twentieth centuries (see Rus n.d.).

8. Porters who had carried vegetables to San Cristóbal for truck farmers would then hire themselves out to carry other goods to Tuxtla Gutiérrez (see map 1). Thus, those who had to work as porters could find hauling jobs that would take them from their hamlets to the lowlands and back again.

9. Chamula inheritance custom gives equal portions of land to females and males.

10. The narrator concludes by referring to his own hamlet, Laguna Petej, which is among those that are most dependent on wage labor for survival. Landholdings are too small for subsistence and are held by many people. Petej is more typical than atypical in this respect.

TEXT 64

1. According to the narrator, Belisario Domínguez is a rural settlement on the old road to the Pacific Lowland region of Chiapas, known historically as the Soconusco. The people in the narrative were following the traditional walking route to the principal regions of coffee production in Chiapas. The coffee plantations of this region are located on the subtropical Pacific slopes of the Chiapas Highlands. The route they followed goes south

from the Central Highlands toward Guatemala, then west, down toward the coastal town of Tapachula.

Rus (personal communication, May 2001) suggests that a more plausible identification of the Belisario Domínguez locale mentioned in the text is the rural settlement of this name that lies just over the border from Chamula in the territory of the *municipio* of Chenalhó. Historically (dating from the nineteenth century), it has been occupied by the Chamula colonists, first as tenant farmers on the German-owned Finca San Francisco, and later—under post-Revolutionary land reform law—as *ejidatarios* (titled grantees of agrarian reform parcels). During both periods it would have been a hospitable place to stop en route to the coffee plantation zone to seek work.

2. This is a common sexual pun—work and sexual activity are synonymous. Usually lighthearted, it here assumes a dark class and racial connotation The coffee-plantation owner is callously asking if they simply brought their wives to service them sexually. He does not really believe that they would be good workers. The coffee-plantation owner is almost a parody of himself and his kind in this passage, for his malicious and condescending inquiry ignores the fact that the wives and children accompany the men because there is nothing to eat at home.

3. The hills referred to in this passage are actually a mountain known as Cerro de Motozintla. It is a prominent topographic feature found near the town of Motozintla de Mendoza, near the Guatemalan border. The narrator said that the people in the account went into the central part of what is today a *municipio* known as Motozintla de Mendoza, named for the mountain located in the municipal territory.

4. Believing the puppies to be dogs, the men thought they had found a real prize, for dogs are highly valued in Chamula homes as watchdogs and killers of vermin such as rats and mice. They are also believed to scare coyotes away. Good dogs command a fairly high price. However, mortality is high, for they are given only occasional scraps of tortilla dough to eat and are expected to fend for themselves for the most part.

TEXT 65

1. The setting is a coffee plantation. Traveling peddlers made rounds of the workers' quarters on the plantations on paydays. Since the plantations were far removed from trade centers, the peddlers were the workers' only source of manufactured goods. It may be of interest that the historical present of this narrative would have been the 1960s, when the items offered for sale were already manufactured clothing. Only one generation before—presumably the original narrator's historical reference point for comparing "then" and "now"—the chief item offered for sale was plain machine-made cloth (*manta,* the Sp. loanword that appears in the narrative).

Rus (personal communication, May 2001) read this text for clues about the time period to which it probably refers. His best judgment is that it refers to the early to mid-1930s. The real giveaway, he says, is the narrator's description of the trees in the central plaza of San Cristóbal de las Casas as a "small forest" (verse 19). These great trees were cut down around 1938.

2. A peso was divided into eight parts. A *real* was 12 1/2 centavos, two reales were 25 centavos, and so forth. This terminology was still used by both Ladinos and Indians in the 1960s and 1970s for units of 25, 50, and 75 cents. Four reales, 50 centavos, was also known as a *tostón.* (See text 41, note 4.)

3. An *almud* is 0.8 of a dry liter measure.

1. The ethnographic present referred to in this narrative is the period 1900–1930, corresponding to the youth and young adulthood of the narrator's father.

2. It was and still is the custom for plaintiffs to offer the municipal officials a gift of cash or rum liquor as a token of appreciation for adjudicating legal problems. In recent years bottled soft drinks have become acceptable gifts as well.

3. The narrator presents a darkly humorous parody of the self-interested logic of old-time Chamula politicians and elders. He also mocks the self-interest of the new generation of young, literate cargo holders, for they would almost certainly be no more honest than the elders had been. Because the narrator himself has been marginalized from both the old and the new systems, he speaks with the voice of a somewhat cynical outsider. I have attempted to capture the nuances of his point of view in the translation of the recital of the elders' point of view (verses 6–14). This passage uses the term "cargo holders" to refer to officials, civil and religious, who served and still serve the community as elected or appointed municipal leaders. Some of the traditional "cargos" (or offices) date from the Spanish colonial administrative structure. Other "cargos" are Constitutional, a term that designates required local administrative posts under post-1857 or 1917 Constitutional laws.

The traditional premodern cargo system as just described in the text was perceived as a problem by Mexican state and federal officials. In 1936 the Chiapas State Departamento de Protección Indigena forced all Indian communities in the state to accept a municipal government reform law that required municipal *presidentes* to know Spanish, ostensibly to facilitate communication between government agencies and Indian communities. As an adjunct to this legislation there was another requirement that Spanish-speaking scribes (*escribanos*) be appointed to serve the communication needs of the remaining monolingual and elderly cargo holders in their dealings with government agencies. Because most of the *escribanos* had learned Spanish in government schools, they were usually young men who had been exposed to Mexican national culture and language in a context designed by federal authorities. Thus, it was not just literacy that was sought as a qualification for the *escribanos*. Mexican officials were interested in creating a small nucleus of individuals who would be close to local communities but were also aware of Mexican national agencies' interests in modernizing Indian communities through the various programs of social change known collectively as *indigenismo*. The original *escribanos* and their families have received Mexican government support as they have moved successfully to form the oligarchy that has controlled Chamula politics since 1936. Only by the late 1980s did the oligarchy appear to be failing as the sole nexus of political and economic power in the community. (See Rus 1994 for details on the period in the change of Chamula municipal government.)

4. Verse 15 carries detailed ethnographic information that cannot be conveyed properly in translation. The narrator also appears to be exaggerating somewhat , as the structure of the cargo system has not changed, since 1936, as fundamentally as suggested here. What has occurred (and what seems to be the underlying theme) is that the cargo system has expanded in most types of positions to accommodate a steadily increasing population. Public-service positions, both civil and religious, have traditionally served as strategies for involving as many people as possible in centralized community activities, the goal being to achieve broad participation and, hence, commitment to the legitimacy of the central political authority. Public-service positions are also an acceptable, even honorable, means of translating surplus and borrowed wealth into honor and prestige in a cultural milieu in which conspicuous consumption by individuals is not viewed favorably. Hence, there are demographic, political, and economic reasons for an expanded cargo system.

Of the positions mentioned, *alféreces* (standard bearers) and *mayordomos* (stewards) are major religious cargo holders who are responsible for maintenance of the cults of the saints. The *mayoletik* (constables) are attached to specific civil cargo holders and have, in addition to their police duties, the roles of tax collectors, messengers, and runners for the central political system. The remaining positions mentioned in verse 15 are minor roles, but they have some interesting traits, notably their focus on the involvement of old people, women, and people charged with criminal behavior. The *alvajanto* job (probable Sp. etymology unknown; perhaps *alza santo,* "raising up the image of the saint") job is a cargo position for Good Friday. There are three *alvajantos,* one for each barrio, who must serve for three years and should ideally be followed by their sons. The *presidente* appoints *alvajantos* if no family successor is apparent. They are old men (over fifty years old) who have the job of tying the hands and feet of the image of Christ that is ritually crucified each year on Good Friday. They also drive in the nails. The *yalel skurusil* (Descent from the Cross) is also a cargo position for Good Friday. There are two of these, one for Barrio San Pedro and one for Barrio San Juan (see map 2). Their job is to buy, place, and do the ritual prerequisites for placing the baskets of white candles, camomile, and laurel on the steps of the tomb of the crucified Christ on Good Friday, just after the crucifixion. Later that day they must give a ritual meal (*kompiral*) for their helpers and standers-by. This cargo is *mulil;* that is, it is given as a punishment to those who have money but will not pay their debts, to men who beat their wives unjustly, to who leave their wives, and so forth. The *chabej sakramento* (caretaker of the sacrament) position is reserved exclusively for women. They are the permanent caretakers of the crucified Christ, and theirs is a lifetime job. There are six such caretakers for each barrio, chosen by the *presidente* and the *bankilal ˀ alkalte.* Not infrequently, this job is also *mulil,* or given as a punishment for public offenders. The eighteen women must forswear all future husbands. That is to say, they may never marry if they are maiden women; if they are widows (which is the most common case), they may not seek another husband. Hence, most are old ladies. The only time their work is done is during Holy Week, when they must buy candles and incense for the dead Christ and carry him around the plaza on a litter.

5. *Toritos* (Tz. *vakax k'ok'*) are large metal or cane frames in the shape of bulls that are charged with a timed series of explosives and fireworks. They are constructed in such a way that a person can place the frame over his head and shoulders, bend over, and simulate a bull's charging about as the charges go off in a series. The *torito* is a staple secular attraction at major Chamula festivals.

6. Hand cannons are receptacles made of heavy metal that are loaded with gunpowder and ignited, providing a thunderous explosion. A staple part of fiesta celebration today, they are fired off at the same time as skyrockets to mark major moments in sequences of ritual events.

7. This report is ironic and telling, as the period of change reported corresponds with the early and middle 1930s, a time at which strong anticlerical legislation at the national level, begun by President Calles in 1926, was being implemented at the grassroots level in Chiapas. The Chamula church was officially closed in the early 1930s by order of federal officials. Chamulas took the images of saints into hiding—some to caves, others to remote hamlets—for safekeeping. Far from translating into local anticlerical feeling, the closing of the church actually appears to have encouraged commitment to the maintenance of the saints' cults and to traditional religious practices. When the church finally reopened a few years later in 1937 by order of Chiapas governor Efraín Gutiérrez, the traditional religious organization, sponsored by the *alféreces* and *mayordomos,* was stronger than ever. (These historical details were provided by Rus, personal communication, May 2001.)

8. This is the sweet brahea palm (*Brahea dulcis*).

9. The Tzotzil word for "witch" is *j?ak' chamel* (thrower of sickness). Thus, the relationship between sickness (*chamel*) and witches is both linguistically and logically close for all illnesses. Both physiological and psychological symptoms are traditionally attributed to the work of witches. Traditional curers have as one of their most important functions the diagnosis and treatment of illnesses caused by witches. Thus, there are linguistic, semantic, and logical links in this verse (and in verses 63–66) that are difficult to capture in translation. See related discussion in texts 53, 54, 55, and 56 and related notes in these same texts.

10. "Potzlom illness" is caused by direct or indirect contact with a witch who transforms him- or herself into a hairy, black, red-eyed creature or Potzlom. This illness has both physical and mental symptoms.

11. The illnesses noted in verse 65 are minor, according to Chamula classification, in contrast with those listed in verse 64. The minor illnesses (those in verse 65), according to the text, have always been around and affect only one of the three sets of souls that each individual possesses. The major illnesses (those of verse 64) can affect all three sets of souls. They are more serious in that the symptoms are more complex, harder to diagnose, and harder to cure. See Gossen (1999, 225–45) for further discussion of Chamula theory of illness. It is not outside the native theory of illness—which places heavy emphasis on social well-being as related to physical wellbeing—to state that this passage reflects a palpable sense of social malaise in time present.

12. These sandals, no longer used, consisted of a leather or rubber sole with attached leather straps that were bound around the foot and ankle. Those currently in common use consist of a rubber sole, a woven leather superstructure with an open toe, and a heel strap.

13. The narrator of this text is an unusually gifted artist and social commentator, as can be seen in the parallelism between the verses concerning ecology (76–79) and those concerning illness (62–65). Both passages reflect a darkly pessimistic view of time present, perhaps reflecting his own life history and the extreme poverty and ecological desolation of his home hamlet of Petej.

14. This verse refers to the common custom among the Highland Tzotzils of renting lowland farmland to raise corn for domestic consumption and as a cash crop.

15. Dark sunglasses are a part of the *mas* (monkey) costume used by men at the February Carnival, The Festival of Games. In this context dark sunglasses are a parody of male Ladino Mexican dress. Ladinos, foreigners and precultural beings are a major theme of this festival of inversion (see Gossen 1999, 105–58).

16. This refers to a factory-made table-mounted grinder similar to a standard food chopper. Used to grind cooked corn, it partially replaces the old mano and metate. As of 1979, all Chamula homes still retained the manos and metates for various types of food preparation. However, as of this publication date, the mano and metate have virtually disappeared from Chamula households that have electricity.

17. Tortilla presses of both wood and metal construction have partially replaced hand molding of tortillas, which was the traditional method. However, tortilla presses, even in the mid-1980s, were far from commonly used throughout Chamula. Most households preferred the traditional-molding method—patting the dough on top of plastic sheeting that is placed on a low stool.

TEXT 67

1. This text refers to the so-called Cuscat Rebellion, or War of Santa Rosa, which was a Tzotzil political and religious movement that occurred in 1868-70. Centered in Chamula and eventually involving nine Tzotzil Maya towns in the Chiapas Highlands, this classic

revitalization movement sought freedom from Mexican (Ladino) domination and the restoration of an Indian community with an Indian religious and political organization, together with an Indian pantheon of gods. Although historians have objected to the interpretation of this dramatic set of events as an extension of the so-called Caste War of Yucatán (1848–50), the two movements came from the same period and shared some structural and thematic features. Both movements sought Maya ethnic affirmation and religious revitalization against the backdrop of the liberal political, economic, and social policies that characterized Mexican governments of the time. Stated simply, this meant that there was a window of opportunity for assertion of local, grass-roots interests.

State-mandated privatization of Indian communal lands had been taking place under both Liberal and Conservative governments since 1826, and the issue was an old and continuing grievance. In the period 1868–70 Chamulas sought to take advantage of the Liberal Reforma of those years to emancipate themselves from Conservative, Catholic taxes and emoluments, causing concern on the part of the local Ladino/Consevative establishment over the issues (discussed in this text) of decentralized, unauthorized cult celebrations and the murder of the local Catholic priests. All of the antiestablishment, anticentralist resistance carried with it a quasi-boycott of the Chamula central market, located in the municipal center, by Indian vendors and buyers themselves, depriving state and church authorities of this convenient central setting for levying and collecting taxes. The authorities felt so threatened by the potential Indian uprising that they sent government troops to put down the rebellion promptly. This text, therefore, expresses one of the many moments in colonial and modern history when Chamulas have mounted a studied and articulate resistance to oppressive church and state authority. (I am grateful to Jan Rus [personal communication, May 2001] for his documentary and interpretive assistance in the preparation of this note.)

Secondary literature on the movement abounds, excellent summaries appearing in Bricker (1981, 119–26) and Rus (1983, 1989). The larger historical context is presented, with a comprehensive current bibliography, in T. Benjamin (2000), which incorporates much of the material in Rus (1989). The general characteristics of the period are summarized in Carmack, Gasco, and Gossen (1996, 196–237). A detailed analysis of the present text appears in Gossen (1977). Köhler (1999) presents an exhaustive analysis of the movement that is based on thirty-eight oral historical accounts from both Tzotzil and Spanish speakers. Full Tzotzil and Spanish texts, in addition to German translations, are given.

2. The term *chaketa leva* comes from the Spanish *chaqueta leva* (frock coat), a type of dress uniform that included a tailed frock coat. This uniform was worn by French and Spanish soldiers in the nineteenth century, and the Mexican soldiers who carried out the massacre that is recorded in this text undoubtedly wore the same type of uniform; hence, the Tzotzil generic term "frock coats" for these soldiers. What appears to be a remnant model of this uniform is worn today by monkey impersonators/clowns at the annual carnival festival that is celebrated in Chamula. An alternative etymology for the term is suggested by Rus (personal communication, May 2001) who believes that it comes from a Mexican colloquial term (*chaqueta*) that refers to a "Spanish loyalist soldier from the War of Independence." In this sense the frock coat (*chaqueta*) would stand for, or symbolize, the wearer of the uniform. The word *leva* refers to conscription. Thus, in this reading, "conscripted soldier" becomes a more accurate translation than "frock-coat soldier." However, I like both translations and have used both of them in this translation.

3. In correspondence from Victoria R. Bricker regarding this text, she points out that river locations have some historical and symbolic significance as stages for reversals of the social order in other Indian communities in the Chiapas Highlands: "It is possible that here

the text is indirectly referring to the Tzeltal Revolt (1712), for a number of crucial events took place at riversides in Cancuc, Chenalhó, and Chilón (see map 1). In Chenalhó one ritual event of Carnival, called *ch'ayel ta ʔuk'um,* occurs at the riverside (see Bricker 1973, 140). When Cancuc was captured by the Spaniards in December 1712, four female witches were carried to the riverside, where they tried to unleash magical weapons (earthquakes, whirlwinds, lightning, thunderbolts) against the Spaniards. Also, according to Pineda (1888, 96, 99), one of the battles in the Cuscat Revolt took place on a hill behind the 'mills of Chamula,' which I assume means beside the river" (personal communication).

Rus, who has also read this passage regarding the location (by the river) of the ritual celebrations of the Santa Rosa/Cuscat cult, gives a very literal interpretation: ". . . the site of Cuscat's church in Tzajaljemel was right above the stream bed of the 'Taki ukum,' the little river that flows west-to-east behind the last row of hills in Chamula, and then down, out to the North through San Andrés. The riverbank is flat, and slopes up to the flat ledge where the church was, so it's perfectly possible that the description in line 8 [of this text] is just straight-forward geography. (Later in lines 24–25, there's a reference to San Andrés's 'Tzajalch'en,' which is also above the Taki ukum.)" (personal communication, May 2001).

4. Victoria R. Bricker has helped me to illuminate possible meanings of this enigmatic ritual language. She writes, with reference to the present text: "One of the three Indian sponsors of the cult was Manuela Pérez Jolcogtom (Pineda 1888, 77); she could be *shalataperes.* The boy who was crucified was Domingo Gómez Checheb; he could be *shalatakomez,* as could Agustina Gómez Checheb. *Samataluisha* could be either Agustina Gómez Checheb, who was known as Santa Luisa (Molina 1934, 368), or Luisa Quevedo, the wife of Ignacio Fernández de Galindo, who was an instrumental Ladino leader who was allied with the Indian cause. Galindo's pupil, Benigno Trejo, assumed the name San Bartolomé (Saint Bartholomew) (Molina 1934, 371); he could be *samataloma.* If *samataluisha* is Luisa Quevedo, then the first two refer to Ladinos, one male, one female. If *shalatakomez* refers to Domingo Gómez Checheb, then the second two refer to Indians, one female, one male. Thus you have Ladinos *versus* Indians and males *versus* females, which would enable you to scan this in terms of couplets" (personal communication).

A further note is required in order to clarify Bricker's reference to the crucifixion in the first paragraph of this note. It was widely avered in nineteenth-century historical and literary sources (cited by Bricker) that a young Chamula man named Domingo Gómez Checheb was crucified on Good Friday, 1868, in an effort to promote the legitimacy of an indigenous Christ who would lead a separatist, rebel Chamula church. This historical detail in relation to the War of Santa Rosa has been widely discredited by recent scholarship. Indeed, the theme of the crucifixion in the movement is totally absent from this and other indigenous texts that consider the subject. The crucifixion theme should perhaps be laid to rest as a racist myth that was promoted by Ladinos to justify their massacres and other abuses of native people, both then and now (see Rus 1983).

I would also like to note that in their poetic structure, the ritual formulas that (according to this text) were sung during the riverside rituals are not at all unlike the songs and ritual language that accompany Chamula ritual proceedings today.

5. This motif—the use of unarmed women as the front line of defense—appears in nearly all native and Mexican accounts of the battle. In particular, women lined up as the two opposing forces went to battle with their skirts raised and their bare buttocks exposed to the Ladino line of fire. The narrator of this text gave an explanation of this odd tactical strategy in the text itself (verses 33–34): their buttocks and genitalia are believed to be "cold," whereas enemy guns are "hot." It appears that the strategy was an effort to use sympathetic magic to render the Ladino guns cold and useless. It is also suggested in the text that this

Chamula battle strategy would surprise and frighten the Ladino soldiers; the method failed, however. The women were slaughtered, and—as the text states so poignantly—the attack was so swift and fierce that the bullets tore through the women's bodies and "ended up in the men's mouths," thus destroying both men and women in the Chamula line of defense. (See Gossen 1977, 271–72, and Gossen and Leventhal 1999, for further interpretation of this passage in relation to female roles in Chamula mythology and cosmology.)

TEXT 68

1. This text about the "prayer makers" appears to report a conflation of events from the so-called Pajarito Rebellion of 1910–11 (at which time the source of the story, the narrator's grandfather, who was a participant, would have been a young man) and the earlier War of Santa Rosa of 1868–69 (see text 67). This inference is based on a number of factors. First, the narrator's grandfather's role as an eyewitness and participant places these events in the early twentieth century. Second, the reference to the schoolteacher's wife's assuming the role of Santa Rosa (Saint Rose) (verses 9–11) is not corroborated by other reports of the Pajarito Rebellion. However, it is clearly recorded that Luisa Quevedo (wife of Ignacio Fernández de Galindo, a mestizo school teacher who participated as an advocate of the rebel cause in 1868) did assume the title of Santa Luisa. She became a part of the entourage of Agustina Gómez Chechev, the Chamula woman who had declared herself to be the Mother of God and also Santa Rosa. Thus, it seems clear that Santa Rosa enters the present text as a kind of "memory" of the role that women played in the Cuscat Rebellion (see Bricker 1981, 119–25, and note 3 of this text).

A third factor that suggests the conflation of the Cuscat and Pajarito rebellions in the present text is the use of the pejorative generic term "prayer makers" in reference to this movement and its followers. The term is applied today to Protestant evangelical converts and, indeed, to practitioners of any "new" religious movement. Those individuals in the Chamula traditional community who are opposed to "new religions" use this very language, often citing the trouble that was provoked by the Cuscat and Pajarito "prayer makers" as good reasons for avoiding any affiliation with "new" cults and religious practices. So—from the point of view of the traditional community that is represented by the narrators of this book—all new religions and their faithful converts are "bad." As recently as the first months of 1994, in the wake of the violent beginning of the Maya Zapatista Movement, Chamula civil and religious authorities mounted an outspoken public campaign against the movement, no doubt invoking the memory of more than a century of experience with such "new creeds," all of which brought civil conflict, violence, and humiliation to the community (see Peres Tzu 1996).

The present narrative concerns the so-called Pajarito Rebellion of 1910–11. This armed rebellion, which involved elements of religious conflict and local civil war, is extensively documented in Moscoso Pastraña (1972), and I have also relied on oral historical sources. The complex political and religious events of the Pajarito Rebellion took place against the backdrop of the final years of the Porfiriato (the long-lived regime of the dictator Porfirio Díaz) and the beginning of the Mexican Revolution. Rus has commented as follows on the historical content of this text:

> The Pajarito rebellion occurred in the context of President Francisco Madero, a very moderate, land-owning, spiritualist "revolutionary," having assumed office after Porfirio Díaz was forced to resign following a fraudulent election. No one knew which sides Madero would favor in all the regional struggles around Mexico, so both the San Cristóbal party (Conser-

vative and very Catholic) and the Tuxtla party (Liberal and secular, but not necessarily anti-Catholic) sent telegrams to President Madero making the pitch *they* were the true revolutionaries and democrats in Chiapas, that they had always doubted Porfirio Díaz (though neither said that to Díaz when it would have mattered), and that he should favor them. Both, that is, were "pro-Revolutionary," at least in word, in 1910–11 (personal communication, May 2001).

Against this backdrop, the Pajarito Rebellion took shape as an effort orchestrated by conservative San Cristóbal clergy—specifically, the famous bishop of Chiapas, Francisco Orozco y Jiménez—who sought to enlist Chamula Indians in the Ladino effort to oppose the political aspirations of Tuxtla Gutiérrez (see map 4). In this manner regional conflict beyond Chamula was perhaps *the* formative factor in launching the Pajarito Rebellion. Indeed, it was a continuation into Revolutionary era of conservative San Cristóbal against Tuxtla Guitiérrez over the decision to move the state capital of Chiapas from San Cristóbal to Tuxtla Gutiérrez in 1892.

While these regional and national contexts undoubtedly help to explain how and when events of the Pajarito Rebellion took place, there was the local scenario itself, led by Jacinto Pérez Chixtot (known as Pajarito, from the Tzotzil Chixtot, which is a species of bird). Pajarito, who came from the hamlet Saclamanton in San Juan Chamula, became the military leader of a conservative Catholic movement that was orchestrated by the conservative Ladino clergy for their own purposes. As understood by Pajarito's followers, the Chamula movement sought the realignment of local religious and political authority in the name of a revitalized "true Catholic faith." Bishop Orozco y Jiménez of San Cristóbal sent lay women missionaries to lobby on behalf of this orthodoxy; perhaps this explains the passages in the text that discuss the leadership role of a female prayer maker who declared herself to be the "mother of God." The text also reveals that Chamula followers of this movement came to believe (no doubt following some understanding of Orozco y Jiménez's ideological and religious campaign against liberal Tuxtla Guitérrez) that San Juan's staff had to be recaptured from Tuxtla Guitérrez. The staff was said to have been removed by Ladino officials, who stole it in the nineteenth century. The cult was thus conceived to serve the political and religious interests of San Cristóbal in its dispute with Tuxtla. Tragically, it became something more than this: a scenario of local civil war that pitted Chamulas against Chamulas. It is this local scenario of the conflict that is vividly depicted by the text's narrator.

Although the movement has a complex set of national, regional, and local contexts, a simplified chronology follows. Pajarito's army, allied with Conservative forces in San Cristóbal, was summarily defeated in several lowland battles by Liberal progovernment forces in September 1911. A peace treaty was signed on October 13, 1911, and a general amnesty was granted by the state government in a November 17, 1911 decree. This amnesty officially exonerated Pajarito and his followers from prosecution or punishment. However, Pajarito's followers and his proclerical allies in the Ladino community were suspicious and urged him to stay in hiding. Between 1912 and 1914 he remained out of sight in Chamula, but not without causing a bitter local civil war in which his contender for power, Mariano Mechij, organized Chamulas who supported him (Mechij) against the supposed constituents of Pajarito. Pajarito's sympathizers apparently lost in these encounters, and many of his followers escaped imprisonment and torture only by fleeing. The refugees fled to a settlement known as Rincón Chamula, in the *municipio* of Solistahuacán, which, to this day, retains a variant of Chamula traditional culture. It apparently had existed as a Chamula emigrant community since the 1880s.

When the tides of the ongoing Mexican Revolution shifted in 1914 with the effective occupation of San Cristóbal by revolutionary Carrancista forces, Pajarito was apparently convinced that he was exempt from prosecution under the guarantees of the November 1911 amnesty decree. He was also attracted by the rhetoric of the Revolution, as he understood it, with its special concern for equal rights of Indians and Ladinos, rich and poor. He planned to speak with the revolutionary occupation forces and so, in October 1914, he went to an old hacienda (San Nicolás, mentioned in the text) to hide out until the opportune moment came to speak with the authorities. He did not realize that his Chamula enemies had informed the revolutionary authorities of his past and more recent activities of sedition against the revolutionary state and of his crimes against fellow Chamulas. Unbeknownst to him, a warrant was issued for his arrest and execution as an enemy of the state. He was arrested at Rancho San Nicolás, imprisoned, apparently tortured for several days, and then shot by a firing squad on October 22, 1914, in the municipal cemetery of San Cristóbal de las Casas, where he was buried.

2. This line appears to be an aside directed to the listener.

3. Rus has studied this text and this passage at length. He agrees with me that the present narrator's description of the role of a Santa Rosa (Saint Rose) "impersonator" probably represents a conflation of particular events fo the 1868–69 War of Santa Rosa with the present account of the Pajarito movement. However, this detail about the leadership role of women in the initiation of the movement is, in essence, corroborated by documentary evidence. Rus writes, in relation to this text:

> The movement was actually started by groups of pious Catholic women from San Cristóbal de las Casas preaching in Saclamanton [a Chamula hamlet] beginning in 1903–4 at Bishop Orozco's behest. His intention seems to have been to set up an alternate power structure within Chamula to that installed by the labor contractors around the turn of the century. . . . Both the movement and Pajarito appear to have been Orozco's and the conservative Catholics' creatures all along. . . . that there were ladina rezadoras who came to Chamula and taught new prayers—and, along with everything else, pushed the cult of the Virgen de Guadalupe, one of Orozco's favorites—seems to be true. So maybe the essential, "intimate" details about what went on in these prayer meetings isn't wrong; it's only the interpretation of public events beyond the ken of the person who told the story to the narrator that's dubious (personal communication, May 2001).

4. The commander was Pajarito himself. Silence was required because Santa Rosa (Saint Rose), the symbolic focus of the cult, as a live saint had to be honored and respected with silence.

5. The narrator explained that the exercise was a practice drill to teach the Chamulas to use their domestic tools in battle. It was also an exercise in military discipline.

6. The narrator explained that this was the grandfather's trick to deceive everyone into believing that the intercepted lance was his own weapon.

7. The narrator's explanation was that the "letter" was actually an execution order that the victim was required to carry to the execution site. The victim did not know that "Mexico City" was in fact Kuchulumtik, a hamlet contiguous to Chamula Center that was apparently the mass execution and burial site for casualties of the conflict. The allusion to the "presidente" in this passage is also ironic. The *presidente* in Chamula Center sent the letter to his counterpart, the "president of Mexico," who was actually the execution officer at Kuchulumtik. The victims were led to believe that the letter contained an explanation of their cases, to be adjudicated at a higher level.

8. In this verse (line 39) and elsewhere in the text, the narrator moves from third-person narrative style to first-person plural as if in a gesture of empathy, that is to say, as though these events happened to "us." Second-person pronoun and verb forms are also used to involve the listeners in the events (verses 25, 26, and 28), as though the events happened to them.

Rus comments on this passage and the shift of narrative voice as follows: ". . . in switching from third to first person, the narrator is identifying with the 'loyalists' who were executed against the 'pajaritos' who did the killing. Since the latter were forced to leave the community when the rebellion failed, it makes sense that modern-day Chamulas would identify with the hunted victims, whose descendants they would be" (personal communication, May 2001).

9. There is a discrepancy of locations in this text, between the nearby hamlet of Kuchulumtik and the area of the cabildo, as the execution site. I have no basis for saying that either is correct but can only observe that the text itself claims that both sites were under the control of the *presidente,* who called them both "Mexico City."

Rus comments on this question as follows: "I've heard from others that 'the Pajaritos' carried out their executions behind where the cabildo presently sits—more or less off to the corner where the school is. It was called 'bik'it tuxta' (Little Tuxtla) . . . in fact, it is still called this today by old people . . . because those executed had supposedly been allies of the state governors and labor contractors against the Chamula masses" (personal communication, May 2001).

10. This passage suggests that Mexican troops intervened in what was actually an abortive and tragic civil conflict. There is no mention anywhere in the text of the original instigation of the cult, which is said to be attributed to conservative Ladino church leaders. Furthermore, no documentary sources suggest that state or federal troops intervened at this local time and place in the conflict. That was to come later. The text describes the local, violent incubation period of the movement—a moment in Chiapas history that is not documented elsewhere (Jan Rus, personal communication, May 2001). See text 69 for an account of the phases of the Pajarito movement that involved military confrontation with state and federal troops.

11. These and subsequent groups of refugees and exiles from the conflict fled to what is known as Rincón Chamula, in the *municipio* of Solistahuacán.

12. From this passage in the text proper and numerous comments by the narrator in my conversations with him about the prayer makers, it is clear that he regards the entire movement as a ruse designed by disreputable Chamulas to exploit and tyrannize honest members of their own community.

TEXT 69

1. See text 68, note 1, for historical background on the armed conflict of 1910–11 that was led by Jacinto Pérez Chixtot, known by the nickname of Pajarito. Text 69 carries unusually vivid details on the social organization of the rebellion. It also carries the account of the conflict forward in time from the account recorded in text 68, including details of the period of actual armed confrontation with Chiapas state-sponsored militias, at which time Pajarito's troops were decisively defeated. Text 69 also includes a vivid account of Pajarito's execution before a firing squad. Furthermore, the text is of particular interest because the narrator was a small child of four or five at the time of the Pajarito War. His parents were eyewitnesses of the events, and his mother, in fact, was the source of this text. She apparently told it to him after he asked why people were praying so fervently in the Chamula church.

2. *Presidente* (president or chief magistrate), *juez* (judge), and *síndico* (fiscal and legal officer) are "constitutional" offices, each held by a single individual. Together, they comprise civil authority under the state. These positions date from the post-Independence period. *Gobernadores* (governors), *alcades* (mayors), and *regidores* (regents) are "traditional" colonial offices that are held by several individuals. Together, they comprised civil authority under the Spanish Crown and still exist as a part of the modern civil hieraracy. The *alguaciles* (sp. constables) in Chamula are also known as *mayores* or *mayoletik*. In colonial documents there was one *alguacil mayor*, who was commander of the other *alguaciles*. Apparently, however, the Chamulas kept only the last part of the title and applied it to all individual police officers. At the period to which this text refers, as is the case today, civil authority was comprised of all of the above offices, making local government a kind of cumulative historical legacy that reflecting both the colonial and modern period. This is pertinent to an understanding of the present text, as the officers mentioned in verse 2 represented the highest authorities in the civil government, which meant that Pajarito's followers had, in fact, captured the local authority structure. It is the violent aftermath of this local coup that is recorded here and in text 68.

As for the kind of men who served in constitutional offices in Chamula circa 1892–1914, it is probable that in 1910 the *presidente* of Chamula was bilingual and possibly even literate. He and others mentioned in verse 2 of the text 69 were the quisling officials (that is to say, sold out to Tuxtla) against whom Pajarito rebelled. It is not clear how Pajarito and his men took over from them, but possibly when the Díaz government fell—taking with it the Chiapas government—municipal offices were also vacated (Rus, personal communication, May 2001).

Although the text's narrator had never heard of him, it is likely that the priest referred to in verse 2 is none other than the bishop of Chiapas, Francisco Orozco y Jiménez, or his representative, who is said to have used the Chamulas' religious zeal for his own political ends, thus precipitating Pajarito's armed rebellion against the anticlerical, liberal elements of Tuxtla Gutiérrez (see Moscoso 1972, 31–59).

3. The captain was Jacinto Pérez Chixtot, Pajarito himself.

4. The label of "Tuxtla" (the code name for the local execution site) is significant and ironic in the context of this rebellion, for the anticlerical, liberal forces of Tuxtla Gutiérrez, the state capital (see map 4), were precisely the forces that the Chamula movement opposed in its early stages. The labeling of the execution site as Tuxtla places the opponents of the rebellion precisely where the ideology of the supporters of the rebellion would have them: in Tuxtla and dead.

5. See text 68, notes 7 and 9, for a discussion of this place-name. It was an execution site near the Ceremonial Center.

6. Rincón Chamula is a community in the province of Solistahuacán that was established by Chamula emigrants in the 1880s. It was also the destination of preference for exiles and refugees from the Pajarito Rebellion. It is located in the Chiapas Highlands but is removed by two to three days' travel time by foot and about four hours (today) by truck or bus.

7. Other oral accounts identify the San Nicolás chapel where Pajarito hid as the chapel of the old Hacienda San Nicolás that is located in the eastern outskirts of San Cristóbal (Moscoso 1972, 95–96; map 4).

8. This final request was actually an act of defiance and challenge to his executioners. He was so sure that he would rise up alive from the grave that he challenged them to make it harder for him to do so. From what follows in the text, it is clear that several people actually believed that he would rise up from the dead.

9. The link with the resurrection of Christ is obvious here. It should also be noted that Our Lord Sun/Christ of the Chamula First Creation narratives spent three days in the underworld before emerging on the fourth day to create the cosmos. Obviously, Pajarito was a powerful, charismatic leader who provoked some to believe in his divinity.

10. This phase of Pajarito's rebellion came after the initial period, which was restricted to Chamula itself. It is in this phase that the Chamula civil conflict, which had been encouraged by proclerical Ladinos, was actually turned against the Ladinos, becoming a movement of ethnic separatism and revitalization directed specifically against Ladinos who lived in small ethnic enclaves in the Indian communities. Rus has commented on this passage in the present text as follows:

> After the Pajaritos took over in Chamula (with all of the *lujo de violencia* described elsewhere), they went around recruiting Indians in other municipios to join them in their war against the state government that had sold-off their ejidos and forced them into labor recruitment. This phase was very quick—a few weeks—and was marked by Pajarito lieutenants visiting the native *ayuntamientos* of San Andrés, Chenalhó, and so forth. Although San Cristóbal conservatives may have been sympathetic to the Ladinos in these towns, it was also the case that almost all of the small-town Ladinos were (1) poor and "lower class," and thus not the *coleto's* [nickname for upper-class Ladinos from San Cristóbal] "kind of people," and (2) somehow involved in labor contracting (as contractors, very small landowners, store-owners who created debt, or rural police), and thus allies to Tuxtla instead of San Cristóbal. It was *after* this period of recruiting other Indians that the Pajaritos went off to battle in the lowlands in company with the *gente decente* [gentry] of San Cristóbal who formed the "Batallón Las Casas." That is, the San Cristóbal gentry didn't seem to mind at all—until later—that Indians had rousted Ladinos out of the pueblos. Indeed, they may have encouraged them to recruit the Indians of other municipios in order to increase their own troop strength! (personal communication, May 2001).

11. It is worth noting that, even now, no Ladinos live in Chamula. Outside of priests, school teachers and their families, and *secretarios municipales, no* Ladinos have ever lived in Chamula Center or owned land or houses there. In this, the *municipio* is unique. All of the communities in the list given in verse 73, as of 1980, did have a small Ladino population in residence.

12. Upon my questioning the narrator about the staff, he stated that it had been stolen from Chamula long ago and is in the possession of the governor of Chiapas in Tuxtla Gutiérrez to this day. All civil officials, including the *presidente,* carry metal-tipped staffs like the one stolen as symbols of their offices and responsibilities. It is unclear whose staff was stolen, but it obviously is one of some importance. Whatever its identity, it appears to symbolize local political authority that has been taken from Indians and placed in the hands of Ladinos.

13. Jompana (see corresponding Tzotzil text above) is the standard modern place-name of Copainalá, which is located near Tuxtla Gutiérrez (see map 4). (My thanks go to Jan Rus for clarifying this place-name mystery.)

14. The concept of boxes and objects that are magical sources of wealth has many variants in Chamula tradition. These objects are usually said to originate with or be in the possession of Ladinos, demons, or Earth Lords or their surrogates. Personal testimony and many narratives report that Chamulas can occasionally obtain these magical objects and their power to produce wealth (see texts 45, 48), but such possession is never normal. It can derive from sheer luck, such as coming upon a buried chest while hoeing one's cornfield. More typically, objects that are "mothers of money" are obtained through shady deals

with Earth Lords, Ladinos, or demons. The ultimate cost to Chamulas is usually high. They must compromise themselves in some fashion or sell their souls—or even their lives—to Ladinos in order to obtain these objects.

Another interesting aspect of this complex of beliefs is that "mothers of money" are usually obtained through individual, not collective, transactions. Thus, the present narrative is unusual in several ways. First, it is a case in which the object (San Juan's staff) is said to be of Indian, not Ladino, origin. Second, it is said to be related to the collective wealth of all Indians (see verse 99), not just of individuals. Finally, this case is unusual because Pajarito's people collectively seek to reclaim the staff for the well-being of the whole Indian community. This is seen in the unusual ending of the narrative, which is an explanation of generic Indian poverty in relation to generic Ladino wealth. The text is noteworthy in the narrator's obvious disapproval of Pajarito and his cause throughout. Yet, in the end, the judgmental tone softens and Pajarito is cast almost as a martyr who tried to restore wealth and power to his people by trying, in vain, to reclaim San Juan's staff.

TEXT 70

1. This text, more than some others in the book, requires a fundamental suspension of the Western reader's sense of the outlines of twentieth-century Mexican history. The text is a mythological account of the Mexican Revolution (1910–17). The characters are mostly generic types—rather like those of classic French theatre—whose stereotypical characteristics and actions are more important than their specific identity. The Ladino who is mentioned first is of this type and is to be understood as a magical prophet/visionary whose skin is white but whose intentions and actions transcend his class and ethnic origins. This generic character is well known in Chamula historical reckoning, beginning with the saints themselves in accounts of the First and Second Creations and continuing into our time, embodied by such individuals as Erasto Urbina (who appears later in this text). The latter, mayor of San Cristóbal in the 1940s, implemented many policies that benefited the Indian communities of the Chiapas Highlands. Subcomandante Marcos, of post-1994 Zapatista fame, is a more recent character of the same generic type. The narrator of this text actually suggested, during our translation sessions, that the Ladino mentioned might have been either Father Miguel Hidalgo (the early nineteenth-century cleric who is credited with precipitating Mexico's independence movement from Spain) or Erasto Urbina, whose historical actions in Western reckoning belong to the 1930s–50s.

In addition to the difficulty presented by the ambiguity of historical actors who are both unspecified and imbued with magical power, one has the difficulty of understanding actors whose lives are telescoped both backward and forward in time. In a sense they are immortal heroes who live in cyclical time and become active in times of chaos and stress. The Mexican Revolution was, of course, such a period in the history of the Chiapas Highlands, and it is related in this text as a replay of events that Chamulas have experienced before and will undoubtedly experience again. The "good" Ladino mentioned here typically appears in Chamula historical reckoning, his role clearly that of an intermediary who takes the plight of the poor and humble to the attention of the authority system. Thus, the initital events in the Revolution, as related in this text, are seen as occurring in a time of heightened consciousness of social ills. The Ladino's actions in the passages that follow (verses 4–13) offer a chronicle of his perceptions of social malaise. Here, the Ladino's actions are those of a supernatural hero, with the vision and power of a prophet who seeks to raise the consciousness of all Mexicans to the plight of the poor. In this sense the narrator's understanding is not at radical variance with the romantic and heroic accounts of the Mexican Revolution that one finds in vehicles of Mexican popular culture, from textbooks to corridos.

It might be useful to compare the heroic plot of this text with similar stories from earlier time periods in the book. Of particular interest is text 43 ("Of the Great Stone Stairway to Heaven"), in which the narrator credibly attributes to the Mexican "white" hero Miguel Hidalgo a key role in the resolution of an earlier conflict involving asymmetrical Indian/Ladino relations in the Third Creation. There are two other narratives of heroes-in-waiting: text 33 ("Of War and Peace with the Chief of Guatemala") from the Second Creation and text 47 ("Of an Encounter with the Soldier on the Mountain") from the Fourth Creation. In all of these stories (perhaps reflecting a contemporary variant of Maya cyclical time reckoning), heroes emerge when they are needed to resolve conflicts and then disappear, sometimes leaving instructions to people to call on them again in a future time of need. Further commentary on this subject, with reference to the same texts, among others, appears in Gossen (1999, 1–30, 159-88).

2. This passage means that although he appeared, with pickaxe in hand, to be a common laborer, he was, in fact, interested in ideological labor. The following passages reveal that he also had supernatural powers of persuasion.

3. This supernatural action, intended to call attention to the seriousness of his mission, recalls the action of San Juan, who, when founding San Juan Chamula and preparing to build his church in the Second Creation, struck the earth and caused a great landslide that shaved away the side of a large hill standing behind the cabildo (town hall) in Chamula Center. His action also created the small pond that lies at the foot of this hill. Both the landslide area and the pond are visible today in Chamula Center. (See texts 26 and 27.)

4. Here the generic Ladino instigator finds Venustiano Carranza himself, who has apparently already assembled a group of followers predisposed to be sympathetic with the Ladino's call to arms. Carranza, who was president of Mexico (1915–20), appears, in the present account, to have been initially persuaded by the Ladino's stated cause. The irony, however, is that in this reading Carranza and his followers became quickly sidetracked from the noble calling of the Ladino, and sought only power and personal gain from their ensuing military activities. In this sense the text corroborates much of what documentary historians understand about the era. Carranza himself was a "very upper middle class man who was governor of Coahuila in Northern Mexico when Madero was assassinated and Revolution broke out. His efforts were all to have his government recognized by foreign countries, to put down the 'rebellions' of Zapata and Villa, and to restore 'institutionality'" (Rus, personal communication, May 2001).

5. The occupation of San Cristóbal by Carranza's troops, as recorded in this text, was a historical event that meshes with Mexican documentary accounts of the period. San Cristóbal (see map 4) was a key center of popular resistance to the revolutionary movement, for it had long been the center of Chiapas's wealthy Hispanic elite. In the regional political climate of the time, Carranza felt it necessary to occupy San Cristóbal because of the counterrevolutionary sentiment there. In a recent summary of this period, Rus comments as follows: ". . . the revolution of the 1910s . . . in the Chiapas highlands was little more than a civil war between an occupying army, the Carrancistas, and bands of local, counter-revolutionary landowners who fought them for control of the region between 1914 and 1920. Indians were excluded from this revolution. More than excluded, they were mistreated by both sides, which fought battles across their land, requisitioned their food and labor, and punished entire villages thought to have collaborated with 'the enemy'. . . . the 'time of Carranza' in the Maya languages of the highlands, is generally remembered with distaste" (1994, 265).

This counterrevolutionary movement survived in Chiapas long after the war was officially over in 1917. It is against this chaotic backdrop, spanning the period from 1910 to

1920, that the events in this text should be seen. The Indian communities of the area were never involved in the ideological issues of the Revolution but were exploited by all Ladino troops of both revolutionary and counterrevolutionary loyalties as a source of forced labor and commandeered provisions.

6. The narrator explained that the DDT powder (whatever its dire health consequences) made the women's hair look white, allowing them to pass as old women and apparently making them unattractive to the soldiers.

7. This is an interesting and ironic reading of popular mestizo Mexican ideology about the Revolution. The narrator has clearly understood what is publicly touted about the Revolution and has reinterpreted it in light of his own experience, recalling that the Carrancistas did not hold themselves accountable for their own offenses against justice, like those they set out to abolish.

8. The discussion of this passage with the narrator produced the interpretation that the social order required a punitive system. From what comes before and what follows, the narrator is saying, the Carrancistas were common criminals, flouting justice at the same time that they pretended to defend it.

9. The Tzotzil word for the common rat (*Rattus norvegicus*) is *karansa*. This is a rather rapid lexemic response to events that, at this writing, are only seventy years old. The rats, apparently of Asian origin (in spite of the species name that links them with Norway), came to Mexico only in the eighteenth century. At any rate the common rat is known by Chamulas to have been the animal soul companion of the Carrancistas. This explains their predatory behavior. Rus adds to this discussion another native explanation for the name of the common rat: that with a large number of unburied dead during the influenza epidemic of 1918, the rats fattened on the dead and wounded—not unlike the Carrancistas (personal communication, may 2001).

10. See note 13 of this text; also texts 68 and 69 for a discussion of Pajarito.

11. Chiapas history records that the first aircraft ever seen in Chiapas came during the Mexican Revolution. Just who sent the plane(s?)—and for what purpose—I have not been able to establish.

12. The bombs and gunfire from the airplane were apparently perceived as looking like ash. In this area ash occasionally falls from the sky following volcanic eruptions. The most recent case of a major volcanic ashfall was in April 1982, on the occasion of the eruption of El Chiconal volcano. Thus, it seems that the previously unknown sight of smoke and ammunition emitting from the airplane was understood according to the Chamulas' previous experience with volcanic ashfalls. It should also be recalled (see texts 14, 17, 20) that the First Creation ended with a rain of boiling water, a phenomenon that occurs in nature immediately following some volcanic eruptions. Thus, ash from the sky is a symbol of great threat and potential destruction.

13. It is necessary to realize that this passage forward is a replay of the battle that has previously been recounted, in which the soldiers were dispersed by gunfire (ash) from the airplane. The narrator clarified that the Chamulas who encountered the soldiers in battle were, in fact, supporters of Pajarito—the Chamula radical who had been enlisted by the bishop of San Cristóbal, Francisco Orozco y Jiménez, to enter the war as a countertevolutionary, proclergy force against the revolutionary forces of Carranza. Thus, at least some of the Chamulas who are involved in this passage are not just resisting the predations of the Carrancistas. They are fighting a cause that they came to believe in, namely that the Revolution was evil and anticlerical and would ultimately destroy their religion and their community. Whether right or wrong (and there were as many Chamulas who opposed Pajarito

as those who supported him), the Chamulas who were engaged in the battle that follows were probably of two convictions: those who were merely terrified by the Carrancistas' predations and those who were actually allied with Pajarito's counterrevolutionary forces. It is perhaps helpful to note, as this account moves forward, that the forces sent from Mexico City with the airplane helped both the forces of Pajarito and those of his native opposition. The result (though not reported here) was that Chamulas were left with their own civil conflict once Carranza's forces had been frightened away.

14. See note 1, this text, on Erasto Urbina as a generic "good Ladino." See also Rus 1994, 274–81, for details on this extraordinary individual and his key role in the implementation of government policy reforms that benefitted the Indian communities of the highlands in the 1930s and 1940s. Said to be of part-Indian heritage, he was a fluent speaker of Tzotzil and Tzeltal as well as Spanish. He ran the campaign in the highlands for President Cárdenas's candidate for governor of Chiapas in 1936 (Efrain Gutiérrez); in turn, he was made the head of the Departamento de Acción Social, Cultural y Protección Indígena (better known as the Departamento de Protección Indígena). While doing the job, he ran for and was elected to the state legislature for 1938–40. State legislators are known as *diputados locales,* and at that time—as is still the case to some extent—the *diputado local* was in a sense the *jefe político* of his region: the highest local "elected" official, and really, the boss. When the governor changed after the 1940 election, Erasto became municipal president of San Cristóbal, serving 1941–44. When he retired from politics, he continued to manage the family business (a hardware store), a setting in which Indian customers were always well treated and granted favorable terms for making purchases on credit.

TEXT 71

1. This text refers specifically to the great Mexican influenza epidemic of 1918, which the narrator's father remembered as occurring when he was about ten years old. It also refers generally to all cases of massive illness. Epidemics, by Chamula reckoning, are extraordinary in that they depart completely from the highly individual and specific theory of illness that is embodied in the concept of animal soul companions and other parts of the human soul configuration. All of these components are vulnerable to loss, injury, or other afflictions, usually due to the ill will of an enemy. The realm of traditional shamanism, from diagnosis to treatment and cure, is focused on specific afflictions of specific individuals. (See Gossen 1999, 225–45.) For this reason radically different explanations must be sought for *general* illnesses that strike the entire community. This text offers two accounts of the unseen background of the epidemic.

2. This list represents the class of major disasters, not just illnesses. The last major volcanic ashfall, in October 1902, resulted from the eruption of the volcano Tacaná, about 250 kilometers southwest of Chamula. Another major eruption occurred in the spring of 1982, near Pichucalco, north and east of Chamula. Some ash from this eruption fell in Chamula. Thus, all the alternatives offered on the list are real threats in the present era, the Fourth Creation. The parents *choose* an item not on the list (verse 9), hoping that the "fever" will be a lesser affliction than those presented as choices.

3. Here the Tzotzil reads: *ˀoy vok'jkot ˀolol.* It is noteworthy that the numeral classifier for animals, *kot,* is used to describe the child. The shift in classifier from human to animal is a potent evaluative dimension that I have tried to retain in translation.

4. Another aspect of the epidemic, which begins here, apparently deals with a man who escaped the main epidemic only to find another manifestation of it, just as lethal, in another setting.

5. This passage is noteworthy in that the Mother of Sickness has drawn from three categories of traditional instruments to make up her musical company. The combination is "unclean" to say the least. The drum is a most sacred instrument, associated with the flute, that accompanies the high points of ritual observance in Chamula. The guitar is part of the harp-and-guitar complex that accompanies all ritual events of any significance. The accordion is a secular instrument, associated with roving monkey-costumed musicians at the annual February ritual of reversal, The Festival of Games. This combination of instruments is odd, and thus appropriate, for an antistructural personage such as the Mother of Sickness.

6. Unlike some other Highland Chiapas communities, Chamula does not use many masks in its ritual observances. The only regular characters who use masks are marginal figures—clowns and bullfighters—who appear at major festivals not as principals but as fillers in the ritual round. This clown is called a *vakero* (cowboy, from Sp. *vaquero*). He is dressed in a clown suit of dotted pajamas and wears a commercial clown mask. He carries a bullfighter's cape and taunts the bull. The bull is a gunpowder-charged frame made of wire, complete with a bull's head, which is carried on the back of a man appointed to the task. He dances around as the charges go off, charging the three clowns. This event is associated with the eve of the festival—the night before, *yixperex* (from Sp. *víspera*, eve of an event). It takes place in the atrium, the walled compound of the church in the Ceremonial Center. For major festivals this activity is repeated on the morning of the festival day itself. On both occasions it is accompanied by a mestizo band and is regarded as entertainment, not religious activity. The only other use of masks in Chamula ritual observance involves not real masks, but modern sunglasses. These are used by the monkey impersonators at The Festival of Games, who appear both as ritual assistants to the principals and as free-lance lay merrymakers. Both masked figures contribute to this ritual of reversal its antistructural tone, a return to the barbarism of the early stages of man's experience on earth. The sunglasses, of course, place foreigners and Mexican mestizos—who habitually wear sunglasses—in a class with monkeys and precultural barbarians. Thus, the masked assistants of the Mother of Sickness in the text suggest threat and precultural chaos together with the presence of Ladino (mestizo) cultural symbols. The bizarre entourage of the Mother of Sickness alarms the man in the text precisely because he confronts something that is neither everyday nor sacred but is cluttered with images from several parts of his own and foreign experience.

7. Whistling is a significant part of the typical behavior of monkey impersonators at The Festival of Games, as is the ritual use of the Spanish language. Whistling is rather like Spanish, as both are viewed by Chamula cosmology as premodern. Through the Third Creation, everyone—including Chamulas—spoke Spanish. Hence, the entourage of the Mother of Sickness draws heavily on antistructural symbols, both from mestizo culture and from Chamulas' own accounts of antiquity—a time in which people could not speak but made whistling sounds like those of monkeys.

8. This long verse is the welcoming speech of the Mother of Sickness. It scans well into three separate couplets, but since the spirit of it is a full unit, I have placed all six lines together.

9. This cryptic line has other referents in Chamula narrative, belief, and practice. It is believed that human nudity is a kind of ultimate defense of supernatural power. Other narratives (see texts 49 and 54, verses 21–23) indicate that demons are frightened and embarrassed by the sight of human genitalia. Nudity is, indeed, a frequently used remedy for unexpected encounters with demons in Chamula everyday practice. It is also tempting to suggest that the present passage (line 44) is a statement of popular wisdom

about clothing and bedding carrying germs of contagious diseases; hence, the survival value of nudity.

TEXT 72

1. The events related in this narrative refer to the period between 1926 and 1936, the time—beginning with the regime of President Calles—of the most extreme anticlerical policies of the post-Revolutionary era. The period was a culmination of the disestablishment of Catholicism as the official state religion that had begun with the secular reforms of the Constitution of 1857. The churches of Chiapas were, indeed, closed for several years during this period, and there was a great deal of local vandalism directed against church property, including the churches' contents. The churches were reopened in 1936, reflecting the wishes of President Cárdenas, but with the proviso that the clergy could not wear religious garb. To this day there is no established church in Mexico, and there is virtually complete freedom of religious practice and affiliation, a policy that Chamulas have used to their advantage in sustaining a highly traditional form of Maya/Christian public religious practice. United States-based Protestant missionaries also took advantage of this window of opportunity. They began proselytizing in Chiapas in the 1940s, with the full blessing of Mexican state officials. Protestantism and reform Catholicism (post-Vatican II) have been summarily rejected by the Chamula central government, a sentiment that persists to this day. A nascent Protestant movement that began in 1965 was crushed in the early 1970s by the wholesale expulsion of hundreds of Protestant converts from the community. It is worthy of note that the narrator in this text classifies the anticlerical secular policies of the state and federal government in the 1930s as being of Protestant inspiration, which is not an unreasonable inference given the tone of those times. This interpretation also makes sense from the perspective of 1968, when this text was dictated—a time when Protestantism was a palpable threat to Chamula traditional belief and practice.

2. This interpretation of evangelical Protestant belief—that the "true god" dwells in a cave—was unclear to me. Upon my discussing the passage with the narrator, he stated that since the Protestant God was obviously, in his view, a false one, it made sense that he should dwell in a cave, for Chamula cosmology associates malevolent supernaturals (Tz. *pukujetik*) as well as Earth Lords and the practice of witchcraft with caves and subterranean passages. Needless to say, this is not a charitable reading of Protestant theology (see text 2, note 1; text 39; text 74, note 1).

3. Erasto Urbina, a quasi-mythic personality in recent Chamula oral history, was an extraordinary historic figure. Chamula oral history credits Don Erasto with many noble acts on behalf of Indian people, some of which cannot be verified from the written record of twentieth-century Chiapas history. Heroic deeds spanning the period from the Mexican Revolution (1910–17) to the 1950s are attributed to Erasto Urbina, making him a bigger-than-life culture hero. The description of him as playing a key role in resolving the anticlerical policies of the federal government in the 1930s, however, appears to be absolutely true (see text 70, notes 1 and 14, and Rus 1994).

4. Here we are given to understand that the anticlerical policies of the 1930s affected not only Indians but also Ladinos. This interpretation matches standard historical accounts of the period.

5. This passage is of theological interest, for it states the widely held Indian view that Indians and Ladinos use the churches for different purposes. Ladinos, it is said, go to mass;

Indians do not. Indians go to speak and pray to the saints, asking their intervention and favor. The mass and eucharist are of little interest to them.

TEXT 73

1. The segment of the Pan-American Highway that traverses the Chiapas Highlands was constructed between 1949 and 1952. It now connects the capital city of Tuxtla Gutiérrez with San Cristóbal and Comitán and reaches to the Guatemalan border (see map 1). Prior to construction of the highway, there was no access by modern roads to the area. An ox road, that is now located in the modern territory of Zinacantán connected Ixtapa and San Cristóbal, acting as the principal link of communication between the lowlands and the Chiapas Highlands.

It is interesting to note the sequential structure of this narrative, which moves systematically from episodes that take place in the lowland stretches of the highway to episodes that take place closer to home in the highland hamlets of Zinacantán. It is also noteworthy that the sources of death and misfortune for the road workers move from natural to supernatural ones as the sites shift from the lowlands to the highlands. Early misfortunes include accidents related to blasting, landslides, machinery failure, and death from dehydration. Later tragedies bring the increased involvement of Earth Lords, who are angry about the violation of their homes—mountains and caves—along the route of the highway as it moves closer to the highlands, where the Chamula and Zinacantán Ceremonial Centers are located.

2. The "great light" (Tz. *lus,* from Sp. *luz,* light) refers to dynamite.

3. Granadilla, a small hamlet that belongs administratively to Zinacantán, is one of many communities that depend on limited water holes during the dry season. The problem alluded to in this text no doubt refers to the greatly increased pressure on limited water supplies, which—even for the small community of Granadilla—are a problem in a normal dry season.

4. Although I do not have access to sources of information on the technology of blasting from this period, the narrator explained that the wrapping on the fuse cable was made of a coarse yellow fabric. Strips of this material were attractive as potential cords for use in the manufacture of traditional Indian hats. The cord would have been used as a chin strap and as a strap for hanging the hat up when it was not in use.

5. This means that a lightning bolt struck, followed by a clap of thunder. The lightning struck the charge cable and ignited it, causing the charge to explode.

6. Na Chij is a large hamlet in Zinacantán (see map 4). The Pan-American Highway passes through the middle of the residential area of the community, virtually cutting it in half. The narrator explained that the decision to route the highway through the center of the community was made in order to avoid offending the Earth Lord of Campana Ch'en. The original route chosen by the highway engineers, in consultation with the community, apparently skirted the hamlet but would have passed directly under the Earth Lord's cave, for which the place Campana Ch'en (Bell Cave) is named. The events of this narrative explain how the Earth Lord's wrath aroused such fear of retribution that all parties decided to do things his way. The people apparently agreed to the route that would take prime residential, horticultural, and milpa land in preference to the more marginal land that had originally been selected as the right-of-way in the hope of lessening damage to the community's land base.

7. It is extraordinary that this Earth Lord has a particular name: Toch. I have been unable to trace a plausible etymology for the name, but the task may prove a rewarding

one for some future Mayanist, for it is the only case of a named Earth Lord known to me in the Tzotzil literature. All other references to Earth Lords in Tzotzil narrative are either generic ones or references to place-name, as "the Earth Lord who lives in Tzontevitz."

8. It is difficult for me to resist speculating that this event was orchestrated by the engineers to persuade the Zinacantecos of Na Chij that it would be better for the road to go straight through their hamlet than around it. Since Na Chij is a very level valley, it was much more convenient for the engineers to run the highway directly through the center of the hamlet. Resistance to the center route (as opposed to the more difficult bypass route) was probably lessened in some way by the engineer's reference to the Earth Lord's threats if the road should pass too close to his house. I should note that the narrator expressed no interpretation of the events to prompt this note, which reflects my opinion alone.

TEXT 74

1. This narrative records some climactic events in the recent, volatile history of the Chamula Protestant movement. The movement began in 1964 when the brothers Domingo Gómez Hernández and Miguel Gómez Hernández (better known as Miguel Kashlan) converted to the Presbyterian sect and became involved in helping U.S. missionary Ken Jacobs translate the New Testament to the Chamula dialect of Tzotzil at the mission headquarters in San Cristóbal de las Casas. Between 1965 and 1969 the number of converts reached 120. Soon the traditional government of Chamula began to feel threatened by the refusal of Protestant converts to pay taxes to support the religious festivals in the Ceremonial Center. Furthermore, the Protestants were fervently opposed to the consumption of alcohol. This created a fiscal problem, because the sale of *pox* (locally distilled sugarcane rum) is an important revenue producer for religious and political officials. In hamlets where there were many Protestant converts, this source of revenue dried up, for there were no longer customers for this product. Furthermore, the ruling oligarchy who controlled the traditional government of Chamula had worked out a successful relationship of coexistence with state and national officials of the PRI (Partido Revolucionario Institucional), the official party of Mexico's one-party political system at the time. This informal arrangement carried guarantees of municipal autonomy regarding local matters in exchange for unilateral Chamula support of PRI's policies on state and national matters. The nascent Protestant movement represented a palpable threat to the community's successful central authority system and its related policies of ethnic separatism and intolerance of internal factionalism. With all of these important political factors figured into the formula, the municipal authorities in 1967 apparently—albeit unofficially—authorized harassment of Protestant converts in an effort to drive them out. The technique used was burning down their homes. It is these events of 1967 that are reported in text 74.

After that time Mexican officials vacillated in their policy regarding whom to support: the Protestants, whose constitutional rights to *ejido* land parcels and to freedom of religion were clearly violated by the oligarchy that drove them out; or the oligarchy itself, whose political loyalty to the PRI had been faithful for many decades. As of 1982 Mexican officials had apparently opted to continue supporting the traditionalists. The end result of what is known in Tzotzil as the War of the Evangelists was a mass exodus of Protestant converts from the community between 1965 and 1982. As of 1982 they numbered about two thousand. As of 1987 most of the Chamula Protestant exiles lived in slumlike settlements, subsidized by the church, around the edge of San Cristóbal. Other, more fortunate converts, have with church backing succeeded in purchasing plots of private land at some distance from Chamula. Some have, indeed, become prosperous.

The Protestant movement is a very significant force for social change in the Chiapas Highlands at the present time, and all the Indian communities in the area have had to cope with it. Some have done so through wholesale conversion to Protestant demonimations; others (such as Chamula), through purging and excluding Protestantism altogether; still others, through some form of coexistence with it. The events reported in text 74 are played out against this backdrop (see Gossen 1999, 209–24).

As this book goes to press, there are clear signs of reconciliation of Maya Christian traditionalists with Chamula Protestants. For example, as of August 2000, the Prince of Peace Evangelical Christian Church, the first Protestant church ever built in Chamula municipal territory, had just opened its doors to worshippers (*Houston Chronicle,* August 10, 2000, 24).

2. It should be noted that the narrator himself is a traditionalist whose circle of friends and associates in Chamula strongly opposed any concessions to the Protestant movement. Therefore, this text and the alleged Protestant actions must be understood to be highly biased interpretations of the events.

3. This is a reference to the new Protestants' understanding of the missionaries' teachings regarding eternal life.

4. The compound referred to in this passage is the extensive Presbyterian mission compound in San Cristóbal de las Casas. It contains the missionaries' living quarters and offices as well as assembly facilities for church meetings and services. Eventually, when the Protestant movement in Chamula gained both a greater number of converts and greater hostility from the traditionalists, the compound became a temporary housing facility for dozens of refugee families who had been run out of the community.

5. What follows (verses 39–46) is an eloquent paraphrase of what traditionalists believe to be Protestant theology.

6. The "great tree" is one of the Protestant terms for distinguishing their concept of the Christian cross from that of the Maya Christian traditionalists.

7. This passage refers scornfully to the main church in Chamula Center, which is the center of all traditional religious practice since it contains the "navel of the universe" as well as the living images of the deities, the saints, (which the Protestant woman derides as "nothing but rotten wood").

8. The passage assumes the listener knows that traditional saints "ingest" incense as food. This is explicitly stated in language that accompanies traditional rituals. It is apparently the similarity of saints to people that makes them seem to the Protestants to be impostors, unworthy of being regarded as gods. See text 10, verse 50 and note 5.

9. The Tzotzil word *chumante*ˀ (stump), in addition to *muk'ta te'* (great tree), seems to be a common term used by Protestants to convey the concept of the Protestant Christian cross, as distinct from the Tzotzil *kurus* (from Sp. *cruz,* cross), which is central to traditional Tzotzil ritual language and closely linked to Catholic theology and to the Maya Christian concept of the Sun/Christ deity.

10. The burial took place in the cemetery by the ruins of the San Sebastián church in Chamula Center. This cemetery is unique in the community as it is the only common burial ground. Most burials take place in local hamlet cemeteries. The San Sebastián graveyard is also important as a common facility for dealing with the burial of people who die from anomalous causes or who cause unnatural death of others. All murder victims, murderers, and suicide victims are customarily buried there. Also, within the confines of the roofless walls of the San Sebastián church, amid the rubbish and vegetation, autopsies are carried out by shamans on the eyeballs of people who are believed to have died from witchcraft.

These witchcraft victims may or may not be buried in the church ruins, but the autopsies for important or doubtful cases are always conducted there.

11. The alcaldes are high-ranking civil officials in the community. All legal and criminal matters are ultimately dealt with by the *presidente* in consultation with the alcaldes.

AFTERWORD

1. See texts 62 and 68–70.

2. "Sobre Ydolatrías, Pueblo de Chamula," investigation initiated by Father Josef Ordóñez y Aguiar, Chamula, Chiapas, March 13, 1778 (Archivo Histórico Diocesano de San Cristóbal).

3. Affidavits taken from Salvador Piñeyro and Andrés Trujillo by Father Mariano Laso, San Cristóbal, Chiapas, February 4, 1846 (Archivo Histórico Diocesano de San Cristóbal).

4. Bishop Samuel Ruiz, "La iglesia latinoamericana en las culturas, reto y esperanza para la pastoral" (Mexico City: Centro Nacional de Pastoral Indigenista, March 24, 1971, offset).

Bibliography

Anderson, Arabelle. 1957. Two Chol Texts. *Tlalocan* 3: 313–16.
Applebaum, Richard P. 1967. San Ildefonso Ixtahuacan, Guatemala. *Seminario de Integración Social Guatemalteca. Cuadernos.* Series 3, vol. 17: 82 pages. Guatemala City.
Barlow, R. H., and Valentín Ramírez. 1962. Tonatiw iwan meetstli. *Tlalocan* 4: 55–61.
Benjamin, Thomas. 2000. A Time of Re-Conquest: History, the Maya Revival, and the Zapatista Rebellion in Chiapas. *American Historical Review* 105 (2): 417–50.
Blaffer, Sarah C. 1972. *The Black-Man of Zinacantan: A Central American Legend.* Austin: University of Texas Press.
Boas, Franz. 1912. Notes on Mexican Folklore. *Journal of American Folklore* 25: 204–41.
Breslin, Patrick. 1992. Coping with Change: The Maya Discover the Play's the Thing. *Smithsonian* (August): 79–87.
Bricker, Victoria R. 1973. *Ritual Humor in Highland Chiapas.* Austin: University of Texas Press.
——. 1974. The Ethnographic Context of Some Traditional Mayan Speech Genres. In *Explorations in the Ethnography of Speaking,* edited by Richard Bauman and Joel Sherzer. Cambridge: Cambridge University Press.
——. 1981. *The Indian Christ, the Indian King: The Historical Substrate of Maya Myth and Ritual.* Austin: University of Texas Press, Austin.
Bruce, Roberto D. 1974. *El Libro de Chan K'in.* Mexico City: Instituto Nacional de Antropología e Historia.
Burns, Allan F. 1983. *An Epoch of Miracles: Oral Literature of the Yucatec Maya.* Austin: University of Texas Press.
Burstein, John, Amber Past, and Robert Wasserstrom. 1979. *En sus propias palabras: cuatro vidas tzotziles.* San Cristóbal de las Casas, Mexico: Editorial Fray Bartolomé de las Casas.
Cáceres, Carlos L. 1946. *Chiapas: síntesis geográfica e histórica.* Mexico City: Talleres linotipográficos de la editorial Forum.
Calnek, Edward E. 1988. *Highland Chiapas before the Spanish Conquest.* Papers of the New World Archaeological Foundation, no. 55. Provo, Utah: Brigham Young University.
Carmack, Robert M., Janine Gasco, and Gary H. Gossen, eds. 1996. *The Legacy of Mesoamerica: History and Culture of a Native American Civilization.* Upper Saddle River, N.J.: Prentice Hall.
Chambers, Erve, and Philip P. Young. 1979. Mesoamerican Community Studies: The Past Decade. *Annual Review of Anthropology* 8: 45–69.
Cicco, G. de, and Fernando Horcasitas. 1962. Los Cuates: un mito chatiño. *Tlalocan* 4: 75–76.
Cline, Howard. 1944. Lore and Deities of the Lacandon Indians. *Journal of American Folklore* 57: 108–10.
Coe, Michael. 1966. *The Maya.* New York and Washington, D.C.: Praeger.
Colby, Benjamin, and Lore Colby. 1981. *The Day Keeper: The Life and Discourse of an Ixil Diviner.* Cambridge: Harvard University Press.
Collier, George A. 1975. *Fields of the Tzotzil: The Ecological Bases of Tradition in Highland Chiapas.* Austin: University of Texas Press.

Collier, George A., with Elizabeth Lowery Quaratiello. 1994. *¡Basta! Land and the Zapatista Rebellion in Chiapas.* Oakland: Institute for Food and Development Policy.
Collier, Jane F. 1968. *Courtship and Marriage in Zinacantán, Mexico.* Middle American Research Institute, Publication 25. New Orleans: Tulane University Press.
Comaroff, John. 1966. Ethnicity, Nationalism, and the Politics of Difference in the Age of Revolution. In *The Politics of Difference: Ethnic Premises in a World of Power,* edited by Edwin Wilmsen and Patrick McAllister, 162–84. Chicago: University of Chicago Press.
Corzo, Angel M. 1943. *Historia de Chiapas: la leyenda de la patria.* Mexico City: Editorial Protos.
Craig, Sienna, and Macduff Everton. 1993. May Dreams: Pride and Resistance in the Highlands. *Summit* (Fall): 60–69.
DeLoria, Vine. 1969. *Custer Died for Your Sins: An Indian Manifesto.* New York: MacMillan.
Duffield, Wendell. 2001. At Least Noah Had Some Warning. *EOS* 82 (28), July 10, 2001: 305–309.
Dyk, Anne. 1959. Mixteco Texts. *Summer Institute of Linguistics,* Linguistic Series 3: 248 pages. Norman, Okla.
Edmonson, Munro S. 1971. *The Book of Counsel: The Popol Vuh of the Quiché Maya of Guatemala.* Middle American Research Institute Publication 35. New Orleans: Tulane University.
Foro Nacional Indígena. 1996. *Resolutivos de la Mesa 1. Autonomía.* Unpublished ms. of a document circulated January 3–8, San Cristóbal de las Casas, Mexico.
Foster, George M. 1945. Sierra Popoluca Folklore and Beliefs. *University of California Publication on American Archaeology and Ethnology* 42: 202–36.
Fought, John. 1972. *Chorti (Mayan) Texts.* Philadelphia: University of Pennsylvania Press.
Geertz, Clifford. 1963. The Impact of the Concept of Culture on the Concept of Man. In *The Interpretation of Cultures,* 3–54. New York: Basic Books.
Giddings, Ruth Warner. 1959. Yaqui Myths and Legends. *University of Arizona Anthropological Papers* 2: 73 pages. Tucson.
Goetz, Delia, and Sylvanus Morley. 1950. Popol Vuh: *The Sacred Book of the Ancient Quiché Maya.* From the Spanish translation by Adrián Recinos. Norman: University of Oklahoma Press.
Gosner, Keven. 1992. *Soldiers of the Virgin: The Moral Economy of a Maya Rebellion.* Tucson: University of Arizona Press.
Gossen, Gary H. 1972. Chamula Proverbs: Neither Fish nor Fowl . . . In *Meaning in Mayan Languages,* edited by M. S. Edmsonson, 205–33. The Hague, Netherlands: Mouton.
——. 1974a. A Chamula Calendar Board from Chiapas, Mexico. In *Mesoamerican Archaeology: New Approaches,* edited by Norman Hammond, 217–53. London: Gerald Duckworth.
——. 1974b. *Chamulas in the World of the Sun: Time and Space in a Maya Oral Tradition.* Cambridge: Harvard University Press.
——. 1974c. To Speak with a Heated Heart: Chamula Canons of Style and Good Performance. In *Explorations in the Ethnography of Speaking,* edited by Richard Bauman and Joel Sherzer, 389–413. London: Cambridge University Press.
——. 1975. Animal Souls and Human Destiny in Chamula. *Man* (Journal of the Royal Anthropological Institute) 10 (New Series): 448–61.
——. 1976. Language as Ritual Substance: Chamula Views of Formal Language. In *Language in Religious Practice,* edited by William Samarin, 40–60. Rowley, Mass.: Newbury House.
——. 1977. Translating Cuscat's War: Understanding Maya Oral History. *Journal of Latin American Lore* 3 (2): 249–78.

——. 1979. Cuento yuʔun ʔololetik (Children's Stories). Pamphlet published by INAREMAC, a privately funded foundation in San Cristóbal de las Casas, Mexico.
——. 1983. El *Popol Vuh* revisitado: una comparacíon con la tradición contemporánea de San Juan Chamula. In *Nuevas Perspectivas sobre el Popol Vuh,* edited by Robert Carmack and Francisco Morales, 305–30. Guatemala City: Piedra Santa.
——. 1985. Tzotzil Literature. In *Literatures. Supplement to the Handbook of Middle American Indians,* vol. 3, edited by Munro S. Edmonson and Victoria R. Bricker, 64–106. Austin: University of Texas Press.
——. 1993. The Other in Chamula Tzotzil Cosmology and History: Reflections of a Kansan in Chiapas. *Cultural Anthropology* 8 (4): 443–75.
——. 1996. The Indian Voice in Twentieth Century Mesoamerican Literature. In *The Legacy of Mesoamerica: History and Culture of a Native American Civilization,* edited by Robert M. Carmack, Janine Gasco, and Gary H. Gossen, 442–71. Upper Saddle River, N.J.: Prentice Hall.
——. 1999. *Telling Maya Tales: Tzotzil Identities in Modern Mexico.* New York: Routledge Press.
Gossen, Gary H., and Richard M. Leventhal. 1999. The Topography of Ancient Maya Religious Pluralism: A Dialogue with the Present. In *Telling Maya Tales: Tzotzil Identities in Modern Mexico,* edited by Gary Gossen, 159–87. New York: Routledge.
Grimm, Jacob, and Wilhelm Grimm. 1962. *Grimm's Fairy Tales: Complete Household Tales of Jakob and Wilhelm Grimm.* 2 vols. New York: Heritage Press.
——. 1999. *Teutonic Mythology.* 4 vols. London: Routledge.
Guiteras-Holmes, Calixta. 1961. *Perils of the Soul: The World View of a Tzotzil Indian.* Glencoe, Ill.: Free Press.
Hansen, Terrance L. 1957. *The Types of the Folktale in Cuba, Puerto Rico, the Domonican Republic, and Spanish South America.* Berkeley and Los Angeles: University of California Press.
Haviland, John. 1977. *Gossip, Reputation, and Knowledge in Zinacantan.* Chicago: University of Chicago Press.
Heaney, Seamus. 2000. *Beowulf: A New Verse Translation.* New York: Farrar, Straus and Giroux.
Holland, William. 1963. *Medicina maya en los altos de Chiapas: un estudio de cambio sociocultural.* Colección de Antropología Social 2. Mexico City: Instituto Nacional Indigenista.
Hunt, Eva. 1997. *The Transformation of the Hummingbird: Cultural Roots of a Maya Ritual Poem.* Ithaca: Cornell University Press.
Huntington, Samuel. 1996. *The Clash of Civilizations and the Remaking of the World Order.* New York: Simon and Schuster.
Hymes, Dell. 1981. *"In Vain I Tried to Tell You": Essays in Native American Ethnopoetics.* Philadelphia: University of Pennsylvania Press.
Johnson, Irmgard Weitlander de, and J. B. Johnson. 1939. Un cuento mazateco-popoluco. *Revista Mexicana de Estudios Antropológicos* 3: 217–26.
Karasik, Carol. 1988. *The People of the Bat: Mayan Tales and Dreams from Zinacantán,* translated by Robert M. Laughlin. Washington, D.C.: Smithsonian Institution.
Köhler, Ulrich. 1999. *Der Chamula-Aufstand in Chiapas, Mexiko: aus der Sicht heutiger Indianer und Ladinos.* Muenster, Germany: LIT.
Kramer, Fritz. 1971. Literature among the Cuna Indians. *Ethnologiska Studier* 30. Gothenberg, Sweden: Goteborgs Etnografiska Museum.
LaFarge, Oliver. 1947. *Santa Eulalia: The Religion of a Cuchumatán Indian Town.* Chicago: University of Chicago Press.
LaFarge, Oliver, and Douglas Byers. 1931. *The Yearbearers' People.* Middle American Research Series, Publication 3. New Orleans: Tulane University Press.

Laughlin, Robert M. 1975. *The Great Tzotzil Dictionary of Lorenzo Zinacantán.* Smithsonian Contributions to Anthropology 19. Washington, D.C.: Smithsonian Institution Press.
——. 1976. *Of Wonders Wild and New: Dreams from Zinacantán.* Smithsonian Contributions to Anthropology 22. Washington, D.C.: Smithsonian Insitution Press.
——. 1977a. *Of Cabbages and Kings: Tales from Zincantán.* Smithsonian Contributions to Anthropology 23. Washington, D.C.: Smithsonian Institution Press.
——. 1977b. *Of Shoes and Ships and Sealing Wax: Sundries from Zincantán.* Smithsonian Contibutions to Anthropology 25. Washington, D.C.: Smithsonian Institution Press.
——. 1994. The Mayan Renaissance: Sna Jzi'bajom, the House of the Writer. *Cultural Survival Quarterly* 18 (4): 13–15.
——. 1995. From All for All: A Tzotzil-Tzeltal Tragicomedy. *American Anthropologist* 97 (3): 328–42.
Lemley, H. C. 1949. Three Tlapaneco Stories from Tlacopan, Guerrero. *Tlalocan* 3 (1): 76–82.
León-Portilla, Miguel. 1962. *The Broken Spears: The Aztec Account of the Conquest of Mexico.* Boston: Beacon Press.
——. 1969. *Pre-Columbian Literatures of Mexico.* Norman: University of Oklahoma Press.
León-Portilla, Miguel, and Earl Shorris. 2001. *In the Language of Kings: An Anthology of Mesoamerican Literature–Pre-Columbian to the Present.* New York: W. W. Norton.
Lönnrot, Elias, comp. 1963. *The Kalevala, or Poems of the Kalevala District.* Translated by Francis P. Magoun, Jr. Cambridge: Harvard University Press.
Lord, Albert. 1958. *The Singer of Tales.* Cambridge: Harvard University Press.
Madsen, William. 1960. *The Virgin's Children.* Austin: University of Texas Press.
Mason, J. Alden. 1963. Folktales of the Tepecanos. *Journal of American Folklore* 27: 149–210.
Mason, J. Alden, and Aurelio M. Espinosa. 1924. Porto-Rican Folklore. *Journal of American Folklore* 37: 249–56.
Mechling, William H. 1912. Stories from Tuxtepec, Oaxaca. *Journal of American Folklore* 25: 199–203.
Méndez Guzmán, Diego. 1998. *Kajkanantik Jch'ulta Tiketik te Leke Sok te Chopole. (El Tajkanantik, los dioses del bien y el mal).* (Dual Tzeltal/Spanish Edition). Letras Mayas Contemporáneas, 3rd series, vol. 5. Mexico City: Instituto Nacional Indigenista.
Menéndez Pidal, Ramón. 1963. *Poema de mio Cid.* Madrid: Espasa-Calpe.
Menget, Patrick. 1968. Death in Chamula. *Natural History* 77: 48–57.
Miller, W. S. 1956. *Cuentos Mixes.* Mexico City: Instituto Nacional Indigenista.
Mitchell, Stephen. 1996. *Genesis: A New Translation of the Classic Biblical Stories.* New York: HarperCollins.
Modiano, Nancy, in collaboration with Nancy Dileanis, Gary H. Gossen and Robert Wasserstrom. 1977. *Los tzotziles y los tzeltales en el pasado. Folleto 1: Antes de la Conquista.* San Cristóbal de las Casas, Mexico: Escuela de Desarrollo Regional, Instituto Nacional Indigenista.
Molina, Cristóbal. 1934. *War of the Castes: Indian Uprisings in Chiapas, 1867–1870.* Translated by Ernest Noyes and Dolores Morgadanes. Middle American Research Series, Pamphlet 8, Publication 5. New Orleans: Tulane University Press.
Moscoso Pastraña, Prudencio. 1972. *Jacinto Pérez "Pajarito": el último Chamula.* Chiapas, Mexico: Editorial del Gobierno del Estado de Chiapas, Tuxtla Gutiérrez.
Nash, June. 1997. The Fiesta of the Word: The Zapatista Uprising and Radical Democracy in Mexico. *American Anthropologist* 99 (2): 261–71.
Orellana, Sandra. 1975. Folk Literature of the Tzutujil Maya. *Anthropos* 70: 5–6.
Parsons, E. C. 1936. *Mitla, Town of Souls.* Chicago: University of Chicago Press.

Peres Tzu, Marián. 1996. The First Two Months of the Zapatistas: A Tzotzil Chronicle. Introduced and translated by Jan Rus. In *Indigenous Revolts in Chiapas and the Andean Highlands,* edited by Kevin Gosner and Arij Ouweneel, 121–32. Amsterdam: Center for Latin American Research and Documentation (CEDLA).
Pickands, Martin. 1986. The Hero Myth is Maya Folklore. In *Symbol and Meaning beyond the Closed Community,* edited by Gary H. Gossen, 101–25. Albany: Institute for Mesoamerican Studies, State University of New York.
Pineda, Vicente. 1888. *Historia de las sublevaciones indigenas habidas en el estado de Chiapas.* San Cristóbal de las Casas, Mexico: Tipografía del Gobierno.
Pozas Arciniega, Ricardo. 1954. *Chamula: Un pueblo indio de los Altos de Chiapas.* Mexico City: Memorias del Instituto Nacional Indigenista, Vol. 8. Reprint, Mexico City: Colección de Clásicos de la Antropología Mexicana, no. 1 (2 vols.), Instituto Nacional Indigenista, 1977.
——. 1959. *Juan, the Chamula: An Ethnological Re-Creation of the Life of a Mexican Indian.* Berkeley and Los Angeles: University of California Press.
Rachun Linn, Priscilla. 1989. Souls and Selves in Chamula: A Thought on Individuals, Fatalism and Denial. In *Ethnographic Encounters in Southern Mesoamerica: Essays in Honor of Evon Zartman Vogt, Jr.,* edited by Victoria R. Bricker and Gary H. Gossen, 251–62. Albany, N.Y.: Institute for Mesoamerican Studies, State University of New York at Albany.
Recinos, Adrián. 1918. Cuentos populares de Guatemala. *Journal of American Folklore* 31: 472–73.
Recinos, Adrián, and Delia Goetz. 1953. *The Annals of the Cakchiquels.* Norman: University of Oklahoma Press.
Redfield, Robert, and Alfonso Villa Rojas. 1934. *Chan Kom: A Maya Village.* Chicago: University of Chicago Press. Abridged edition, 1962, Chicago: Phoenix Press.
Reid, John Turner. 1935. Seven Folktales from Mexico. *Journal of American Folklore* 48: 107–12.
Riding, Alan. 1989. *Distant Neighbors: A Portrait of the Mexicans.* New York: Vintage Books.
Rosenbaum, Brenda. 1993. *With Our Heads Bowed: The Dynamics of Gender in a Maya Community.* Albany: Institute for Mesoamerican Studies, State University of New York at Albany.
Roys, Ralph L. 1967. *The Book of Chilam Balam of Chumayel.* Norman: University of Oklahoma Press.
Rus, Jan. 1983. Whose Caste War? Indians, Ladinos, and the Chiapas "Caste Wars" of 1869. In *Spaniards and Indians in Southeastern Mesoamerica,* 127–68. Lincoln: University of Nebraska Press.
——. 1989. The "Caste War" of 1869 from the Indians' Perspective: A Challenge for Ethnohistory. *Memorias del Segundo Coloquio Internacional de Mayaistas,* Vol. 2: 1033–47. Mexico City: Universidad Nacional Autónoma de México.
——. 1994. The "Comunidad Revolucionaria Institucional": the Subversion of Native Government in Highland Chiapas, 1936–1968. In *Everyday Forms of State Formation: Revolution and the Negotiation of Rule in Modern Mexico,* edited by Gilbert M. Joseph and Daniel Nugent, 265–300. Durham, N.C.: Duke University Press.
——. n.d. Coffee and the Re-colonization of Highland Chiapas, Mexico/1892–1912. Unpublished manuscript in the author's collection.
Schoembs, Jakob. 1905. *Material zur Spache von Comalapa in Guatemala.* Dortmund, Germany: F. W. Ruhfus.
Shaw, Mary, ed. 1972. *Según nuestros antepasados: textos folklóricos de Guatemala y Honduras.* Guatemala City: Instituto Lingüístico de Verano.

Siegal, Morris. 1943. The Creation Myth and Acculturation in Acatán, Guatemala. *Journal of American Folklore* 56: 123–25.
Stross, Brian. 1977. *Love in the Armpit: Tzeltal Tales.* Museum Brief No. 23. Columbia: Museum of Anthropology, University of Missouri.
——. 1978. *Demons and Monsters: Tzeltal Tales.* Museum Brief No. 24. Columbia: Museum of Anthropology, University of Missouri.
Taggart, James M. 1983. *Nahuatl Myth and Social Structure.* Austin: University of Texas Press.
Taller Tzotzil [Tzotzil Workshop, anonymous]. 1986. *Abtel ta pinka.* Ba'yel livro, vo'ne lo'il ta Chamula [Working on the Coffee Plantation. First book in a series, Chamula Accounts of the Past]. San Cristóbal de las Casas, Mexico: INAREMAC.
Tambiah, Stanley. 1996. The Nation-State in Crisis and the Rise of Ethnonationalism. In *The Politics of Difference: Ethnic Premises in a World of Power,* edited by Patrick Wilmsen and Patrick McAllister, 124–43. Chicago and London: University of Chicago Press.
Tax, Sol. 1949. Folktales in Chichicastenango: An Unsolved Puzzle. *Journal of American Folklore* 62: 125–35.
Tedlock, Dennis, trans. 1983. *The Spoken Word and the Work of Interpretation.* Philadelphia: University of Pennsylvania Press.
——. [1985] 1996. *Popol Vuh. The Definitive Edition of the Mayan Book of the Dawn of Life and the Glories of Gods and Kings.* New York: Simon and Schuster.
——. 1993. *Breath on the Mirror: Mythic Voices and Visions of the Living Maya.* San Francisco: HarperCollins.
Thompson, J. E. S. 1930. Ethnography of the Mayas of Southern and and Central British Honduras. *Chicago Natural History Museum Anthropological Series* 17, no. 1: 120–72.
——. 1970. *Maya History and Religion.* Norman: University of Oklahoma Press.
Thompson, Stith. 1946. *The Folktale.* New York: Holt and Winston.
——. 1955–58. *Motif Index of Folk Literature.* 2nd ed., 6 vols. Bloomington: University of Indiana Press.
——. 1961. *The Types of the Folktale: A Classification and Bibliography.* 2nd revised translation and enlargement of Antti Aarne, *Verzeichnis der Marchen-typen.* Folklore Fellows Communications no. 184. Helsinki: Suomalainen Tiedeakatemia.
Tozzer, Alfred M. 1907. *A Comparative Study of the Mayas and Lacandones.* New York: Macmillan.
Trens, Manuel B. 1957. *Historia de Chiapas.* Vol. 1. Mexico City: Tallers gráficos de la Nación.
Valladares, L. A. 1957. *El hombre y el maíz.* Mexico City: B. Costa-Amic.
Villa Rojas, Alfonso. 1947. Kinship and Nahualism in a Tzeltal Community, Southeastern Mexico. *American Anthropologist* 49: 578–87.
Vogt, Evon Z. 1969. *Zinacantán: A Maya Community in the Highlands of Chiapas.* Cambridge: Belknap Press of Harvard University Press.
——. 1970. Human Souls and Animal Spirits in Zinacantán. In *Echanges et communication, mélanges offert à Claude Lévi-Strauss a la occasion de son 60eme Anniversaire,* edited by Pierre Maranda and Jean Pouillon, 1148–67. The Hague: Mouton.
——. 1994. *Fieldwork among the Maya: Reflections on the Harvard Chiapas Project.* Albuquerque: University of New Mexico Press.
Warren, Kay B. 1992. Transforming Memories and Histories: The Meaning of Ethnic Resurgence for Mayan Indians. In *Americas: New Interpretive Essays,* edited by Al Stepan, 189–210. New York and Oxford: Oxford University Press.
——. 1998. *Indigenous Movements and Their Critics: Pan-Maya Activism in Guatemala.* Princeton, N.J.: Princeton University Press.

Watanabe, John. 1989. Elusive Essences: Souls and Social Identities in Two Highland Communities. In *Ethnographic Encounters in Southern Mesoamerica: Essays in Honor of Evon Zartman Vogt*, edited by Victoria R. Bricker and Gary H. Gossen, 263–74. Albany, N.Y.: Institute for Mesoamerican Studies, State University of New York at Albany.
Wolf, Eric R. 1982. *Europe and the People without History*. Berkeley and Los Angeles: University of California Press.
Yeats, William Butler. 1888. *Fairy and Folktales of the Irish Peasantry*. London: W. Scott.
——. 1897. *The Secret Rose*. London: Lawrence and Bullen.
Zumwalt, Rosemary. 1988. *American Folklore Scholarship*. Indiana University Press, Bloomington.

Index

DATE

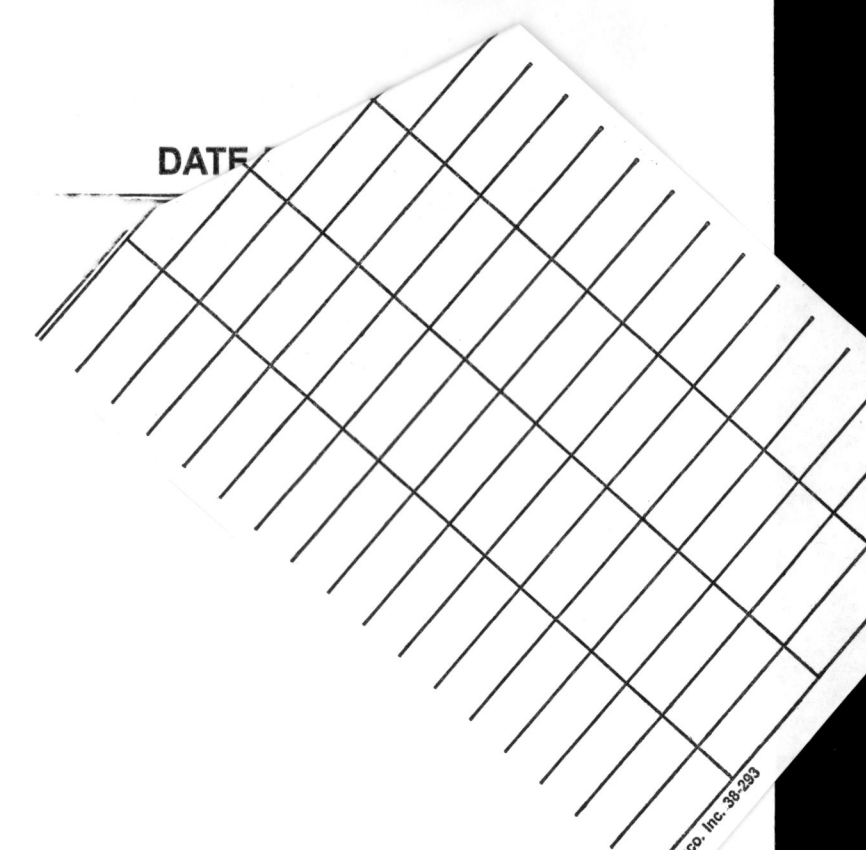